Therapeutic Recreation Leadership and Programming

Robin Kunstler, ReD, CTRS

Lehman College of the City University of New York

Frances Stavola Daly, EdD, CTRS

Kean University

Human Kinetics

Library of Congress Cataloging-in-Publication Data

Kunstler, Robin Ann, 1951-
  Therapeutic recreation leadership and programming / Robin Kunstler and Frances Stavola Daly.
     p. cm.
  Includes bibliographical references and index.
  ISBN-13: 978-0-7360-6855-0 (hard cover)
  ISBN-10: 0-7360-6855-4 (hard cover)
  1. Recreational therapy--Textbooks. I. Daly, Frances Stavola. II. Title.
   RM736.7.K86 2010
   615.8'5153--dc22

                            2010003699

ISBN-10: 0-7360-6855-4 (print)
ISBN-13: 978-0-7360-6855-0 (print)

The Web addresses cited in this text were current as of January 2010, unless otherwise noted.

Acquisitions Editor: Gayle Kassing, PhD; **Developmental Editor:** Jacqueline Eaton Blakley; **Assistant Editors:** Elizabeth Evans and Anne Rumery; **Copyeditor:** Joyce Sexton; **Indexer:** Andrea Hepner; **Permission Manager:** Dalene Reeder; **Graphic Designer:** Bob Reuther; **Graphic Artist:** Dawn Sills; **Cover Designer:** Keith Blomberg; **Photographer (cover):** Laurence Mouton/age fotostock; **Photographer (interior):** © Human Kinetics, unless otherwise noted; **Photo Asset Manager:** Laura Fitch; **Photo Production Manager:** Jason Allen; **Visual Production Assistant:** Joyce Brumfield; **Art Manager:** Kelly Hendren; **Associate Art Manager:** Alan L. Wilborn; **Illustrator:** Kelly Hendren; **Printer:** Sheridan Books

Printed in the United States of America   10 9 8 7 6 5 4 3 2 1

The paper in this book is certified under a sustainable forestry program.

Human Kinetics
Web site: www.HumanKinetics.com

United States: Human Kinetics
P.O. Box 5076
Champaign, IL 61825-5076
800-747-4457
e-mail: humank@hkusa.com

Canada: Human Kinetics
475 Devonshire Road Unit 100
Windsor, ON N8Y 2L5
800-465-7301 (in Canada only)
e-mail: info@hkcanada.com

Europe: Human Kinetics
107 Bradford Road
Stanningley
Leeds LS28 6AT, United Kingdom
+44 (0) 113 255 5665
e-mail: hk@hkeurope.com

Australia: Human Kinetics
57A Price Avenue
Lower Mitcham, South Australia 5062
08 8372 0999
e-mail: info@hkaustralia.com

New Zealand: Human Kinetics
P.O. Box 80
Torrens Park, South Australia 5062
0800 222 062
e-mail: info@hknewzealand.com

E4067

CONTENTS

PREFACE

Every day, therapeutic recreation (TR) professionals experience the rewards and challenges of providing quality services in complex and sometimes frustrating health care settings and community environments. The broad social changes, diverse demographics, shrinking resources, and competing interests affecting our work settings have major effects on our day-to-day practice. To provide high-quality services to clients, and maintain the integrity of the TR profession in the context of 21st-century developments and conditions, therapeutic recreation specialists (TRSs) must effectively communicate the purposes of TR. For the TRS, it is the day-to-day practice of TR that truly demonstrates what TR is and what it can accomplish for participants.

The purpose of this book is to provide a thorough and detailed understanding of "how to" carry out the responsibilities and tasks of the TRS on a daily basis, according to the highest ethical standards and the best practices of the profession. Ethical principles should be first and foremost in our interactions with our clients as we provide TR leadership. We believe that the information in this book will enable the TRS to develop TR experiences that are life affirming and that spring from the foundations, theories, and concepts that direct our actions.

This book is the only TR text that focuses primarily on TR leadership and highlights that the power of TR comes from the synergy created by the blending of the roles of recreation specialist and therapist. The heart of TR practice is the delivery of TR leadership, a concept and a role that have not been fully described in the literature of the field. We have developed a definition of TR leadership that combines the strategies and techniques used by therapists to promote growth with the abilities of the recreation specialist to create and facilitate leisure experiences. This "blended" role distinguishes TR practice from both recreation service and rehabilitation-oriented approaches, and reflects the term *therapeutic recreation* as we use it in this book. In all the TRS's daily interactions with clients, she delivers TR leadership, embodying ethical principles and applying professional knowledge, abilities, and skills.

People of all ages, demographic characteristics, and abilities, regardless of health status or level of functioning, may benefit from TR services. People may be served in any type of setting, including community-based programs, nonprofit organizations, schools, health care institutions such as hospitals, outpatient and adult day programs, long-term care, group homes, residential facilities, prisons, and private homes. Neither the setting nor the diagnosis or condition of the individual is what defines TR. Therapeutic recreation is characterized by the application of the TR process, which are the actions performed by the TRS to plan and deliver appropriate TR programs. In TR the focus is not only on the outcomes of participation, but also on the meaning of the experience to the individuals and on how this experience helps them to grow and change. In this book, the word *client* is used for the most part to describe the individual with whom the TRS works. *Client* denotes a recipient of services who willingly participates with the service provider. We also use the word *participants* at times, which conveys the active involvement of the clients.

There continues to be debate in the TR profession regarding the definition of the field and the scope of practice. The field is currently using several different terms to define itself. Therapeutic recreation, recreation therapy, and recreational therapy are the three names most commonly used. We have chosen to use *therapeutic recreation* throughout this book because we believe this term best conveys the range of services provided and the settings and clientele served by TRSs. Therefore, we use the term *therapeutic recreation specialist*, which parallels the profession's primary credential of Certified Therapeutic Recreation Specialist (CTRS).

This book is organized into three parts that take the reader through the process of developing a way of *thinking* about TR practice, to *creating* a framework for TR practice, to *applying* TR leadership. Part I, "Establishing a Foundation for Ethical Practice," sets the stage for the TRS to design and deliver TR programs. In chapter 1 the reader explores the core concepts of leisure and recreation and their relationship to a definition of TR. What it means to have a mindset for ethical practice is explained, along with an examination of bioethical principles and the TR codes of ethics. Chapter 2 discusses the core values and principles underlying TR practice and seven well-recognized TR practice models. In chapter 3, eight contemporary approaches to program planning are described along with implications for TR program planning. The four steps in the TR process—assessment, planning, implementation, and evaluation—are explained and illustrated. Chapter 4 goes into depth about the blended role of TR leadership and the knowledge, skills, and abilities of therapists and leaders that merge in the application of TR leadership.

Part II, "Creating the Structure of TR Practice," presents TR clients, programs, and methods. The TRS matches the needs of the clients with the appropriate programs and selects strategies to facilitate the achievement of predetermined client outcomes. Chapter 5 presents prevailing definitions of health and healthy behaviors along with the most frequent common concerns that may be shared by a range of TR clients, regardless of their primary diagnosis or the setting in which they are served. Case studies of clients with common concerns have been developed that identify a TR model, goals and objectives, and a TR plan. Chapter 6 introduces the TR toolkit, which contains specific recreation activities in five major program areas. Evidence of their effectiveness, benefits, implementation methods, and risk management concerns are covered. Chapter 7 describes specific strategies the TRS uses with the client during participation to promote growth and learning; these include identifying learning styles, communication, motivation, instructional techniques, feedback, and debriefing. Chapter 8 explains useful procedures for evaluation of the TRS, the TR programs, and the progress of clients. Regulatory agencies, performance improvement, and research processes are discussed.

Part III, "Applications of TR Leadership," covers organizing and delivering TR programs in detail.

Chapter 9 confronts the reality that we offer a weekly or monthly calendar of activities to meet the needs of many individuals. It provides direction for balanced unit-wide programming that includes scheduling, group size, and environmental considerations. In chapter 10, the dynamics of a TR group including roles, stages of development, and characteristics are explained. The entire process of planning and structuring TR groups and the actual leading of a TR group are illustrated step by step. Chapter 11 describes the settings for one-to-one TR programming, with activity suggestions, guidelines for TRS–client interactions, and ethical practices. Finally, chapter 12 presents a call to action for the emergence of TR as a mature profession in the 21st century.

Each chapter begins with a list of things you will learn from reading the chapter. Throughout the chapters, certain concepts are highlighted regularly. These include ethical principles, the benefits of TR participation, risk management concerns, the importance of keeping the focus on clients' needs and interests, cultural considerations, and the qualities of the TR environment. In addition, much of the information in the chapters is illustrated with concrete examples of real and imaginary clients, which bring to life the practice of TR as described in these pages. Sidebars provide additional resources, learning activities, TR stories, programming suggestions, checklists, and tools for everyday practice. Finally, each chapter concludes with a summary and a set of learning activities for personal reflection and small-group discussion.

Whether you are a student, a new practitioner, or a seasoned professional, we hope this book will affirm your belief in the power of TR. We believe that growing as a TRS is a professional obligation to ourselves, the individuals we serve, our colleagues, our profession, and society. Join us in this ongoing process of learning as we continually strive to practice ethically and from the heart.

ACKNOWLEDGMENTS

We would like to acknowledge the hundreds of TR students who have inspired, delighted, and taught us over the years, as well as our TR colleagues in both practice and teaching, who have shared with us the joys and challenges of this unique and meaningful profession. The many participants in our TR programs have motivated us by their joy in their experiences and their pride in their own accomplishments.

A deep and heartfelt thank-you to Gayle Kassing, acquisitions editor at Human Kinetics, for the impetus for the project and for her constant encouragement, excellent feedback, and limitless patience. To Jacqueline Blakley, developmental editor, a special thank-you for her finesse, skill, support, and gentle and effective prompting to bring this project to completion.

Special thanks and appreciation go to Magalys Ciccosanti, CTRS, for her careful, thorough, and honest reading of this text and her many valuable suggestions; to Janet Listokin, CTRS, for her indispensable contributions to many of the sidebars; to Noelle Moore, CTRS, for her willing and able research assistance; to Fred Greenblatt, CTRS; Dina Trunzo, CTRS; and Holly Pope, for providing key materials for specific chapters. To all our friends who said, "Aren't you done yet?" To Tasha, Max, Bart, and Emmett, our four-legged friends and companions, whose antics amused and diverted us as we worked. To our families: the Daly men (husband Bill, sons Ryan and Chris), once again, for their patience, love, support, and willingness to accept a part-time wife and mother while I devoted weekends, holidays, and hours of once family time to the creation of this book; and Anita Daly, mother-in-law, whose experiences are woven throughout these pages; and to Barton Kunstler, my brother, who has always led me by example and covered my bases, and to my husband Michael Carney for patience, pride in our efforts, space, love, and the freedom to create; and our parents, whose spirits permeate these pages.

Lastly, to a friendship that survived the ups and downs of weekends, Fran's health issues, and Robin's extra job responsibilities, without which this book would not have been written.

PART
I

Establishing a Foundation for Ethical Practice

In part I we examine the roots of the TR profession—the core values and core principles that represent what we believe and guide our work, as well as the bioethical principles that apply to TR practice. Exploring, analyzing, and reflecting on the foundations of the field are essential to professional practice. Reflection enriches our practice; we appreciate our own work more, which enhances its quality and meaning.

The foundations of our profession are brought to life in the models, processes, and methods we use in TR on a daily basis. As TR practitioners, we blend the knowledge, skills, and abilities of the recreation specialist and the therapist to deliver TR leadership and programming. Our purpose is to help individuals improve their health, well-being, and quality of life as they experience the benefits of recreation and leisure. You will come to understand that therapeutic recreation is a thoughtful and complex process of great value to clients when practiced by a self-aware and competent TRS.

A Mindset for Ethical Therapeutic Recreation Leadership

In this chapter you will learn about:

- A mindset for ethical practice
- Definitions of therapeutic recreation
- The concept of therapeutic recreation leadership
- Functional and existential outcomes
- Bioethical principles
- NTRS and ATRA Codes of Ethics
- Ethical issues that arise in therapeutic recreation practice
- Models for ethical decision making

Aspiring to the highest level of professionalism should be the goal of any practitioner working with people. A critical step in advancing the **therapeutic recreation** (TR) profession to a higher level of practice lies in developing a way of thinking, or a mindset, about TR. A mindset is a mental attitude that reflects one's values and beliefs and that influences how one interprets and responds to situations. It is difficult to act effectively—or indeed, do anything well—if professionals do not reflect on their actions and assess the thinking, feelings, and values behind those actions. By concentrating and focusing on the meaning and process of one's professional practice, the professional can provide a higher-quality and more effective service. The practice of TR, as addressed in this book, centers on the concept and actions of TR leadership to help clients achieve the goals of improving health, well-being, enjoyment, and quality of life as guided by the ethical standards of the TR profession. Understanding on a deeper level what TR is, its roots in leisure and recreation, and the potential impact of TR leadership enriches TR's contribution to society. Therapeutic recreation serves any person who could benefit from TR services.

Developing a **mindset** about one's profession is an ongoing process, shaped by both hands-on experience and critical reading, reflection and discussion of important principles, concepts, practices, and trends. An educated professional reads not only about his discipline but also about social issues, current events, research findings, and related topics that affect everyday practice. This process ultimately influences one's beliefs, strategies, and methods as a TR specialist (TRS). It is the TRS's personal and professional hallmark, which becomes a part of her approach to planning and leading TR programs and her reputation as a practitioner. When a profession is practiced according to a mindset that has been developed through a process of reading, thinking, discussing, and analyzing the values and principles supporting services, it can fulfill a more meaningful role in society. This chapter explores what it means to have a mindset for ethical practice and to be an ethical practitioner. It also addresses the meaning of TR, the concept of TR leadership, ethical principles and codes of ethics, and their relevance to TR practice.

DEFINING THERAPEUTIC RECREATION

The first step in developing an ethical mindset for TR practice is to understand the definition of TR and what a TRS does. Many definitions of TR have been written and refined over the years. These definitions often reflect the time period in which they were developed, the trends in health care and human services at that time, and the unique perspective of the author. Definitions of professions do evolve along with society. Nonetheless, "virtually every definition of TR includes the notion of involvement in activity that is oriented to treatment, education or recreation as a means for improving the health and well-being of people with disabilities" (Sylvester, Voelkl & Ellis, 2001, p. 16). Four common themes have been identified in most definitions of TR (Bullock & Mahon, 2000):

- Purposeful use of recreation activities
- Enhancement of functioning through recreation participation
- Focus on the whole person in the context of his or her environment
- Long-term improvements in health, well-being, and quality of life as core concerns

On the basis of these commonalities, the authors have put forth a composite definition of TR:

> engaging individuals in planned recreation and related experiences in order to improve functioning, health and well-being, and quality of life, while focusing on the whole person and the needed changes in the optimal living environment. (Stavola Daly & Kunstler, 2006, p. 179)

Additionally, an important component of an evolving definition of TR, according to Sylvester and colleagues (2001), is the concept of leisure. Their definition expands on the generally accepted meaning of TR to include the idea that "recognizing the potential of leisure for contributing to the quality of life of all people, therapeutic recreation facilitates leisure opportunities as an integral component of comprehensive care" (p. 17). A focus on leisure, in addition to recreation as described in the composite definition, can be considered the unique contribution of TR to the comprehensive services provided to clients. Let's take a brief look at leisure and recreation.

Leisure and Recreation

Leisure and *recreation* are words that are often used interchangeably and may have particular meanings to each individual. The general public considers leisure to be free time or a certain type of activity (Shank & Coyle, 2002) that is done for fun or relaxation. Various definitions, from many countries and cultures, imply that the meaning of leisure is closely linked to choices freely made in one's free time, or choices about how one spends free time. "Leisure" comes from the Latin word "licere," meaning freedom. The French word "loisir" means free time, and the English word "license" means permission to do something. The word "liberty" also comes from the Latin "licere." Leisure has a strong connection to education as well, as can be seen in the French word for school, "lycee." This reveals that leisure has been viewed over centuries as a period of time in which one is free to do something personally enriching or educational. However, we do not experience leisure every time we engage in a freely chosen activity; a state of mind is required also. A **leisure "state of mind"** is characterized by feelings of competence and mastery, accomplishment, self-satisfaction, freedom, and the meaning leisure holds for the individual. Freedom to make meaningful and personally rewarding choices has been a focus of TR service.

Recreation is generally viewed as an activity one chooses to do for fun or to share an experience with others, or for some specific benefit that is meaningful to the participant. "Recreation" comes from the Latin word "recreatio," meaning "that which refreshes or restores" (McLean, Hurd & Brittain Rogers, 2005, p. 38). Recreation can be defined as voluntary, nonwork activity engaged in for the attainment of personal and social **benefits** (Shank & Coyle, 2002). While recreation is usually done for fun or pleasure, it may also involve serious commitment to learning a new activity and improving a skill. Serious commitment can produce enjoyment or deep psychological absorption, as well as a sense of control and competence. Participating in recreation can restore, refresh, and renew the individual. In TR, the fun aspect of recreation can be motivating to people by helping them to "re-create themselves" through participation.

Recreation is the specific activity or program that an individual, professional, or agency organizes for participation. As TR professionals, we structure and conduct a wide range of recreation activities to appeal to our clients and help them to meet their goals. While we cannot "program" leisure, we plan recreation programs to enable individuals to experience leisure. Leisure is a personal experience an individual has that can occur through participation in meaningful recreation. Studying the concepts of leisure and recreation contributes to developing a mindset for TR practice that reflects key human values and enhances the TR profession's significance and meaning for clients. One characteristic of a profession is that practitioners establish professional organizations that provide leadership on a number of professional issues and concerns.

Realistic Reflections/Getty Images

Recreation is generally viewed as an activity chosen for fun or to share an experience with others.

Therapeutic Recreation as Defined by Professional Organizations

There are two national professional organizations in TR, the **American Therapeutic Recreation Association** (ATRA) and the **National Therapeutic Recreation Society** (NTRS). Both organizations have developed and adopted definitions of TR. These definitions serve to crystallize current perspectives regarding the practice of TR. In 2009, ATRA replaced its definition of TR with a definition of "recreational therapy."

The following is the NTRS definition of therapeutic recreation (2000):

> Therapeutic recreation uses treatment, education, and recreation services to help people with illnesses, disabilities, and other conditions to develop and use their leisure in ways that enhance their health, functional abilities, independence and quality of life.

The ATRA definition of therapeutic recreation (1993) is as follows:

> Therapeutic Recreation is the provision of Treatment Services and the provision of Recreation Services to persons with illnesses and disabling conditions. The primary purpose of Treatment Services, which is often referred to as Recreation Therapy, is to restore, remediate or rehabilitate in order to improve functioning and independence as well as reduce or eliminate the effects of illness or disability. The primary purpose of Recreation Services is to provide recreation resources

and opportunities in order to improve health and well being.

ATRA also offers the following definition of recreational therapy (2009):

> "Recreational Therapy" means a treatment service designed to restore, remediate and rehabilitate a person's level of functioning and independence in life activities, to promote health and wellness as well as reduce or eliminate the activity limitations and restrictions to participation in life situations caused by an illness or disabling condition.

In comparing the two definitions of TR, we can see a common feature: TR serves persons with illnesses and disabilities, or disabling conditions. In addition, NTRS includes service to people with "other conditions," which may be interpreted to refer to people who are homeless or youth at risk, for example, who do not fall into traditional categories of disability or illness. Both definitions of TR include treatment and recreation as the services TR provides, but NTRS also includes education as one of its services. ATRA's definition of recreational therapy is a substantial change from its previous definition of TR in that it identifies only *treatment* as the service provided by the profession. ATRA's new definition of recreational therapy (RT) represents a significant shift from its own definition of TR, which did include the provision of recreation services. It appears from its definition that NTRS covers a broader range of services and a wider range of clients than does ATRA.

Both the NTRS definition of TR and the ATRA definition of RT focus on health. ATRA uses the term "wellness" and NTRS uses the term "quality of life." The most significant distinction between ATRA's definitions of TR and RT is that ATRA has removed any reference to recreation; services are now limited exclusively to treatment and no longer include recreation service as a means of improving health and well-being. The definition of recreational therapy also differs significantly from the NTRS perspective, which places primary emphasis on the development and use of leisure. See table 1.1 for a comparison of the three definitions.

In developing a mindset for TR practice, examining and reflecting upon these definitions to determine which best expresses one's beliefs and views is a meaningful exercise. The struggle to define TR has been viewed by some as an impediment to the development of the profession. The premise of this book is that the purpose of TR cannot be limited to the provision of recreational therapy (as in the ATRA definition) or geared only to helping clients develop or use leisure (as in the NTRS definition), but should be inclusive of both as well as emphasizing the use of recreation as both a means and an end. An umbrella or combined approach may be more relevant in an increasingly multicultural and diverse world (Dieser, 2008). This approach holds that TR is used *simultaneously* as "a medium for therapeutic change" and "as an enjoyable outcome that is pursued for its own sake" (p. 26).

TABLE 1.1

Comparison of the NTRS and ATRA Definitions of TR and RT

	NTRS TR	ATRA TR	ATRA RT
Types of services	Treatment Education Recreation services	Treatment services Recreation services	Treatment services
Clients served	People with illnesses, disabilities, and other conditions	Persons with illnesses or disabling conditions	People with activity limitations and restrictions in life situations caused by an illness or disabling condition
Purpose	Develop and use leisure in ways that enhance health, functional abilities, independence, and quality of life	Restore, remediate, or rehabilitate in order to improve functioning and independence Reduce or eliminate the effects of illness or disability Provide recreation resources and opportunities in order to improve health and well-being	Restore, remediate, and rehabilitate a person's level of functioning and independence in life activities Promote health and wellness as well as reduce or eliminate activity limitations and restrictions to participation in life situations

CHARACTERISTICS OF THERAPEUTIC RECREATION

Similar to the practice of other therapies, TR participation is based on an individual assessment and plan designed to help the client achieve specific goals or outcomes. Outcomes represent the measurable changes in the client from his entry into the program to his departure. Other therapies may even use recreational activities to achieve outcomes. In particular, the differences between TR and occupational therapy (OT) have not always been clear because OT not only utilizes recreation-type activities such as cooking and arts and crafts in its services, but also addresses outcomes similar to those of TR. Physical therapists offer exercise programs, social workers offer group activities, and psychologists may use games; yet all focus on the outcome that will be achieved at the point of departure from services.

There are two important characteristics, however, that define TR as distinct from other therapies. The difference between TR and any other therapeutic service is that TR provides both purposeful intervention and a leisure context (Robertson & Long, 2008). While TR is providing a purposeful intervention directed toward achieving an outcome, TR also provides a leisure context. The leisure context means that the TRS creates conditions to enable the clients to successfully experience leisure *during* the TR program. This adds to the meaning and the quality of the therapeutic recreation program by offering both leisure opportunities and intervention services. Leisure experience, as described earlier, includes choice making, competence, and positive feelings during and after involvement. Services provided by other professionals, while outcome focused, do not occur in a leisure context. This context not only helps to define TR but is also the characteristic that distinguishes it from other therapies.

The leisure context characterizes both TR and recreation services, but it is the provision of purposeful intervention that differentiates the two. Recreation services are based on general group needs and interests, rather than designed for a particular individual as in TR. Broad goals are set for recreation groups and programs, and individual changes are not formally measured. Recreation specialists conduct programs that possess the qualities of recreation—they are fun and enjoyable, restorative and refreshing, and challenging to participants and provide opportunities to learn and use skills. The recreation specialist plans and organizes the physical, social, and natural environment by selecting the appropriate setting for a program, gathering the necessary equipment and supplies, and providing the leadership so that participants can experience the benefits of leisure (Edginton et al., 2004). As Paul Haun, the noted psychiatrist, wrote in his classic book *Recreation: A Medical Viewpoint* (1965), the essential skill

The Difference Between Recreation and TR

When you participate with your friends in a recreation activity, such as going to a movie, you expect to have a good time. You may look forward to the social interaction with your companions, being entertained by the movie, and going out to a new restaurant afterward and analyzing the film director's technique in a discussion over dinner. You can accomplish these desired outcomes of the experience on your own, as well as through interaction with your friends, without the assistance of a qualified professional. But what if you didn't like the movie? What if the restaurant wasn't accessible? You may still have had fun because you and your friends joked about the experience, you were able to find a different restaurant at the last minute, and had a great conversation over dinner. You were able to experience recreation and its benefits and did not require the services of a TR professional to help you learn specific skills in order to be successful.

But what if you don't have adequate conversation skills? Are you too shy to ask people to join you? Maybe you don't know how to find information about the times of the movies or the location of the restaurant because of a physical or cognitive limitation. Perhaps you can't pay attention for the full length of the movie. Perhaps you have poor budgeting skills and don't know how to put aside the money the outing will cost. If the outing did occur, maybe the restaurant turned out to be too crowded and you wanted to go someplace else. A TRS can help you learn the new skills and behaviors needed to have a successful outing, as well as help you to have fun during the therapeutic and educational process. For clients, therapeutic recreation is an opportunity to learn, practice, and utilize new skills and behaviors, as well as to experience the joys of recreation and leisure.

of the recreation worker is "his open invitation to another human being to come and play, to have fun, to experience the zest of emotional release limited by nothing but the rules of the game. His unique skill is getting the willing consent of another person to take the plunge into play . . ." (p. 82).

While the TRS also creates an environment with the intention of clients experiencing these benefits, the difference between recreation and TR is that TR is purposefully focused on achieving outcomes based on individual needs. In TR, outcomes include improving health, increasing functioning, changing behavior in a positive direction, or finding meaning and purpose in life. **Functional outcomes**, those that are instrumental for living, have long been the focus in health care; however, **existential outcomes**, those that provide meaning to life or enhance quality of life (Shank & Coyle, 2002), are becoming more valued (Ross & Ashton-Shaeffer, 2001). The TRS's unique skill as a recreation leader contributes to existential outcomes for the client. In fact, the TRS has been identified as the "existential therapist" (Richter & Kaschalk, 1996) on the medical treatment team, the professional "who is concerned with the clients identifying activities that are motivating and affirming of their abilities" (Sylvester et al., 2001, p. 57). Having a mindset for ethical TR practice includes understanding the significance of the leisure context to achieving the purposes of TR outcomes. Purposes are achieved through the provision of TR leadership by the TRS.

THERAPEUTIC RECREATION LEADERSHIP

This book takes the perspective that **therapeutic recreation leadership** is the core of the day-to-day practice of TR and deserving of much greater attention. The meaning and process of TR leadership have not been thoroughly explored in the TR literature (Austin, 2004), nor has TR leadership been discussed as a unique concept. An assumption of TR practice has been that TR leadership is characterized by the roles and responsibilities of both a therapist and a recreation specialist, with one or the other predominating based on any number of factors. These factors could include the TRS's personal philosophy, skills, and qualities; the nature of the setting; or the characteristics of the clients.

In the composite definition of TR, the word *engaging* is used, implying that a major task of the TRS is to attract the attention of potential participants and to draw them into involvement in TR programs. TR leadership "involves the ability to influence the

activities of clients toward accomplishing sought outcomes" (Austin, 2004, p. 324). The TRS makes the clients feel that they are being paid attention to, that they are understood, and that the TRS is aware of their unique needs. During a TR session, the client may find meaning in the doing of the activity itself (leisure context), may find meaning because the activity is a way to achieve a goal or behavioral change (functional intervention), or may experience a combination of both. At times the practice of TR has been focused on functional outcomes without attention to creating a leisure experience, which might be considered recreational therapy; or focused primarily on the recreational aspects of the activity to the exclusion of the individual client's desired outcomes, which has been viewed as "special" recreation. Therapeutic recreation may be considered the integration of therapy, education, and recreation to produce the conditions necessary for a client to experience leisure. The concept of TR leadership reflects this integration and provides a framework for what the TRS actually does on a day-to-day basis, grounded in the values and principles of the profession.

We have developed a definition of TR leadership that extends the umbrella definition by blending the simultaneous functions and practices of a recreation specialist with those of a therapist. This definition incorporates Robertson and Long's (2008) two criteria for TR, purposeful intervention and leisure context, into the practice of TR leadership to create a synergistic effect that heightens the TR profession's contribution to health and human services:

> Therapeutic recreation leadership is the unique blending of the therapist's purposeful application of therapeutic strategies and facilitation techniques with the recreation specialist's abilities to create and facilitate leisure experiences in order to deliver TR services according to the highest ethical standards.

This definition is the beginning of a fuller exploration of the unique role of the TRS and provides guidance and direction for *how* the TRS conducts programs and offers services on a daily basis. As with the definitions of TR itself, it invites comments and refinements as the field evolves in response to and reflects the changing world. One constant in practice, despite the inevitable changes in one's day-to-day responsibilities, is to behave ethically and thoughtfully in all we do.

ETHICAL PRACTICE

Ethical practice, simply put, refers to practice that conforms to established professional standards

(Kornblau & Starling, 2000). But it is more than just reading or hanging up a code of professional ethics on the office wall. Ethical practice involves understanding the meaning of one's work and carrying out daily responsibilities according to ethical theories and concepts, often embodied in a code of ethics. By understanding and valuing ethical principles, TRSs can carry out their jobs in a more meaningful fashion. Daily actions are rooted in professional values and beliefs. "Whether we realize it or not, we *do ethics* everyday" (Shank, 1996, p. 52). **Ethics** can be thought of as "moral rules" about what one should or "ought" to do, not what one "has" to do according to laws and regulations. Many believe that ethics are of concern only when one is dealing with critical issues, such as life and death, but that is far from the truth. Professional ethics are standards of conduct that guide daily practice and are concerned with the quality of the lives of the individuals served day to day. This is known as the "ethics of the ordinary," which suggests that the "small decisions about the content and order of one's daily life" (Caplan, 1990, p. 38) are ethically important.

Daily actions are rooted in professional values and beliefs.

Four Bioethical Principles

The area of ethics that is relevant to all professions providing health care services, programs, and treatment is known as **bioethics**. Bioethics is concerned with

- the rights of individuals receiving health care and services;
- safety of the services provided;
- equal and adequate access to health care resources and treatments; and
- the laws, standards, and regulations that govern health care services and their delivery.

The four major bioethical principles are well-being, autonomy, privacy, and justice. The next sections describe each, with implications for TR practice.

WELL-BEING

"Well-being pertains to protecting and promoting the welfare of clients," recognizing them as capable of growth (Sylvester et al., 2001, p. 54). The two main components of well-being are **beneficence**, which means doing good, and **nonmaleficence** (or nonmalfeasance), which means doing no harm. It is the ethical obligation of all health care professionals not to harm or hurt their clients, physically or psychologically. To support the well-being of clients, practitioners are ethically obligated to be competent to do their jobs. The professional's responsibility is always to have the clients' best interests foremost in the decisions made about their care and the actions taken to provide services. This may be characterized as "seeing the person in the patient." A person receiving services is a human being, with life experiences, values, and beliefs that may be overlooked in a service setting. There may well be times when professionals disagree among themselves about what is in the best interests of a client's well-being, or the client may disagree with the professionals. Perceptions of what may be good for the client, or harmful to the client, may differ according to any given individual's viewpoint. The "good" thing to do may not always be clear-cut, and determining what may be helpful or harmful to a client can become an ethical dilemma that is not easily resolved.

This principle requires that the interests of the client be paramount in decisions and services. For example, a TRS was assigned to take a group of six clients from an addictions treatment unit on a walk to a local store. She felt that several of the clients might try to purchase drugs and that she could not effectively supervise a group of six. Since she felt that she was not competent to supervise six clients by herself and wanted one additional staff member to accompany the group, she expressed her concerns to her supervisor. The supervisor told her that she had to take all six on the outing because it was in their best interests to go for the walk. What is the "good" thing to do in this situation? "Good" courses of action might include adding another staff member to help supervise, but what if no one is available? Another possibility might be splitting the group in half and taking two shorter outings, but there might not be enough time. To protect the clients' well-being, the TRS should not conduct an activity when she feels that the safety of the clients could be compromised.

AUTONOMY

The next major bioethical principle is autonomy. **Autonomy** refers to people's rights to make their own choices and to determine the course of their lives. This is also known as **self-determination**. Therapeutic recreation professionals have an ethical obligation to promote the autonomy of clients. Autonomy not only refers to the ability to make one's own choices and decisions, but also includes the ability to act upon those decisions. There is a distinction between **decisional autonomy** (having preferences and making decisions) and **executional autonomy** (being able to carry out one's decisions) (Collopy, 1988). Both decisional and executional autonomy are included in the six-step process of "being self-determined." This process, developed by the American Institute for Research, consists of the following steps:

1. Identify and express one's own needs, interests, and abilities.
2. Set expectations and goals to meet one's needs and interests.
3. Make choices and plans to meet goals and expectations.
4. Take action to complete plans.
5. Evaluate results of actions.
6. Adjust plans and actions, if necessary, to meet goals effectively.

Reprinted, by permission, from C. Bullock and M. Mahon, 2000, *Introduction to recreation services for people with disabilities: A person-centered approach*, 2nd ed. (Champaign, IL: Sagamore Publishers), 47.

The first three steps reflect decisional autonomy, and the last three refer to executional autonomy. The process of being self-determined reveals that ethical responsibility goes beyond helping a client make a decision. Professionals must also facilitate their clients' ability to act upon the choice, evaluate the outcomes, and change their actions accordingly.

Going through this process reinforces the client's autonomy.

Clients also have the right to refuse treatment and services, even when professionals believe these are the proper care for the client. Working with clients whose health and well-being is compromised due to illness, disability, or other limitations may put the TRS in the difficult position of wondering if she should assist a client in carrying out a decision that appears irrational. Some clients even may be incapable of expressing their wishes at all. At such times, professionals may follow the principle of **parentalism**, which acknowledges that while "people of all ages never stop growing and changing" (Sylvester, 2005, p. 12), some clients may truly be in a state of diminished capacity that affects their decision-making ability (Sylvester, 2005). According to this principle, professionals can act as caring, nurturing parents who at times need to intervene to protect the well-being and safety of clients. However, thinking that one always knows what is best for the client and acting accordingly is known as **paternalism**. Paternalism has been called a danger of professionalism (Hutchinson & Lord, 1979) in that professionals may tend to overlook the client's wishes. Professionals need to reflect on their decisions and actions to ensure that they are not falling into a pattern of paternalism.

Parentalism may be necessary when clients are deemed incompetent to make their own decisions. At this point, the principle of **substituted judgment** can be followed. Substituted judgment requires professionals to make decisions on the basis of what *clients* would decide they want for themselves if they were competent to do so, and not what the *professional* would decide. However, professionals may disagree among themselves about when that point is reached. Family members and legal guardians also may have an opinion. Nonetheless, TR has an important contribution to make to clients' autonomy, because it may be the one service area in which clients are capable of making, or are allowed to make, meaningful personal choices. Therapeutic recreation can provide a range of choices to preserve autonomy within a safe environment. The examples presented earlier demonstrate the conflict that sometimes occurs between the clients' exercise of their autonomy and the need to protect the clients' well being.

PRIVACY

The third bioethical principle is **privacy**, which includes **confidentiality**. Privacy can be defined as the right to control access to one's person and to information about oneself. In the course of the workday, a TR professional learns personal information about clients at team meetings, from clients' records, and from the clients themselves. It is a privilege to have access to client's personal information. Therapeutic recreation specialists must honor the privacy of this information at all times, sharing it appropriately and in the best interests of the client's care and treatment.

Confidentiality means that personal information about clients can be accessed only by those who have a right to this information as part of their work with the client. In the relaxed and natural environment of a TR program, clients also may confide information about themselves that they wish the TRS to keep secret. This may place the TRS in the position of hearing something that could be harmful to the client or others. The professional can never promise the client to keep this type of secret if it represents a threat to anyone's safety. For example, if a client tells a TRS he wants to kill himself, or that he knows his roommate wants to hurt someone else, the TRS must report this information.

Confidentiality also means never gossiping or telling stories about clients to others. Care must be taken not to use clients' full names or other identifying characteristics in conversation or in correspondence that is not confidential. Confidentiality is related to trust. The nature of the leader-therapist relationship with clients is based on trust. When trust is damaged, this may affect the progress of services (McLean & Yoder, 2005). Privacy is central to the dignity of the individual and his potential to benefit from services. For example, a client may share with the TRS private information regarding her sexual feelings, which does not involve a threat or harm to anyone. The TRS knows from attending **team** meetings that there has been some speculation about the client's sexuality. Based on her training in the bioethical principle of confidentiality, the TRS decides not to divulge this information to the team. Do you think she did the right thing?

The importance of the privacy of clients' health information was recognized by the U.S. government in 1996 with the passage of the **Health Insurance Portability and Accountability Act (HIPAA)**. The privacy rule of this law set standards for the use and disclosure of "individually identifiable" information related to a person's physical or

The HIPAA Privacy Rule

The Health Insurance Portability and Accountability Act (HIPAA) was enacted by the U.S. Congress in 1996 to streamline the transmission of health care information and to reduce costs. However, because electronic transmission poses threats to patient privacy and confidentiality, the privacy rule was developed by the Department of Health and Human Services and went into effect in 2001.

The privacy rule covers the following patient information:

- Name
- Address
- Date of birth
- Telephone and fax numbers
- E-mail address
- Occupation
- Employer
- Social security number
- Relatives' names
- Medical record numbers
- Member or account numbers
- Certificate numbers
- Voiceprints
- Fingerprints
- Photographs
- Codes

Health care personnel cannot release patient information for anything other than "permissible purposes" or outside of the work environment. If health information needs to be disclosed for business-related purposes, authorization by the patient or legal guardian is required.

Confidentiality is emphasized: "Providers must make a reasonable effort to disclose or use only the minimum necessary amount of protected health information in order to do their jobs."

Employers who sponsor health plans also have to comply with the privacy rule to protect their employees.

For more information, see www.dhhs.gov/ocr/hipaa.

mental condition or the provision of health care to an individual. Under this rule, only the minimum amount of information necessary for treatment and business operations is to be disclosed. The patient has the right to decide if he wishes to disclose this information for any other purpose. All staff in health care facilities receive training on HIPAA regulations. The TRS needs to be informed of and adhere to these regulations in order to protect clients' privacy and maintain confidentiality of sensitive information related to their health status and care.

JUSTICE

The fourth bioethical principle is **justice**. "The principle of justice encourages equitable treatment to the least-likable client" (Jacobson & James, 2001, p. 240). Justice means that everyone is treated fairly, and that resources and services are allocated in a fair and equitable manner. In TR, justice also means that everyone has the right to recreation and leisure. Justice is often discussed in terms of **distributive justice** and **comparative justice**. Distributive justice ensures that persons are not excluded from an equitable share of society's benefits and obligations (Hemingway, 1987). In TR, all clients should have equal opportunities for participation in a variety of activities of their choosing. Therapeutic recreation specialists must be careful not to practice favoritism by giving special consideration to a well-liked client. Examples of this are: giving a client a personal gift, putting a client at the top of a sign-up sheet for an out trip that is limited in the number who can participate, or changing a program schedule to accommodate one person. In addition, in a diverse society, discrimination and bias may affect the allocation of resources. When there are clients who speak a language other than English or any other dominant language, they may be excluded or limited in their programming options. This is contrary to the principle of justice, as well as the laws of a just society.

Comparative justice means balancing the needs of the individual with the needs of others when there is competition for scarce resources. Advocating for fair access to resources is a professional obligation of the TRS. Yet TRSs are often in the position of providing services disproportionately when staff shortages exist and clients cannot receive the amount of time and assistance they may need. In this era of shrinking fiscal resources and limited access to services, and perhaps also due to discrimination and bias, justice takes on even greater significance. A group home for people with developmental disabilities plans a trip to an amusement park, which requires a payment that not all residents can afford. Should the trip be denied to all, in the interests of justice? Or is there another solution?

A Mindset for Ethical Practice

The "right" course of action to take is not always obvious or clear-cut. Many ethical issues become front-page news. Patients on life support, abortion, access to health care, rights of minors to self-determination, assisted suicide, and research on inmates are examples of how critical it is to ponder and reflect upon the implications of ethical principles for the everyday lives of our clients and ourselves. Ethical practitioners seek to increase their understanding of ethical principles and refer to them for guidance in their daily work in the field. The four major bioethical principles—well-being, autonomy, privacy, and justice—are embedded in the codes of ethics of all professions serving human beings. Having a mindset for ethical practice includes

- adhering to the TR codes of ethics;
- knowing and complying with the rules, regulations, laws, and standards that govern TR practice;
- reading about and discussing ethical issues;
- attending conferences and workshops on ethics;
- implementing a process of ethical decision making;
- organizing or participating in an agency's ethics committee; and
- conducting and participating in regular in-service trainings on ethical principles and issues.

Codes of Ethics

As members of a profession, TRSs can refer to a professional **code of ethics**, which represents a public declaration of a profession's values, duties, and intentions to protect clients. A code of ethics states what ethical professionals *should* do in their daily practice. Codes contain the standards of behavior of the profession, which describe how professionals ought to act, what their responsibilities and commitments to society are, and what is considered right or wrong to do in practice. The code "articulates the moral obligations and commitments" (Sylvester et al., 2001, p. 53) of the profession. A profession's contract with society is to provide services in a morally acceptable manner (Henderson et al., 2001). Both NTRS and ATRA have developed and published codes of ethics. These are included in appendixes A and B.

The ATRA Code of Ethics begins by describing the use of the code, identifying the TR personnel who should follow the code, and stating that membership in ATRA implies a commitment to follow the code. ATRA's code is composed of 10 principles with a description of the meaning of each one.

The NTRS Code begins with a preamble that presents a philosophical framework and purpose for TR and a statement about the mission of NTRS and the obligation of its members to follow the code. The NTRS Code consists of six obligations of the professional to self, others, and society. Each obligation includes specific ethical behaviors. In addition, NTRS has published a significant document, the Interpretive Guidelines (1994) of the Code of Ethics that expands upon the meaning and application of the ethical principles embodied in the obligations. NTRS includes the profession's obligation to *society* as a significant component of professional practice. This obligation includes advocacy as an ethical responsibility of the profession to the people it serves, "advocating for their inalienable right to leisure, recreation, and play in clinical and community settings," and is based on the belief that "play, leisure and recreation are the primary focus of the profession" and are of value to society. The responsibility of the TR profession is to articulate this value to society and to contribute to social policy by linking leisure, play, and recreation to the quality of individual and community life. The *NTRS Code of Ethics* and *Interpretive Guidelines* have been called "two of the most important documents ever to emerge in this profession" (Shank, 1996, p. 32) because they help *all* TR professionals to put professional values and beliefs into ethical practice.

The key principles or obligations common to both codes can be summarized as follows:

● The TRS has the duty and responsibility to be a professional with integrity. This means being honest with self, clients, colleagues, and society. The TRS is fair in dealings with all others and strives to be competent in his work, while always seeking to improve his knowledge and skills (NTRS Obligations 1, 3, and 5; ATRA Principles 5, 6, and 9).

● TRSs have the highest obligation to the clients they serve. They seek always to do what is in clients' best interests, to respect their individuality and rights to make their own decisions and choices, and to respect and safeguard their privacy, always in accordance with prevailing standards, regulations, and legal mandates (NTRS Obligations 2, 4, and 5; ATRA Principles 1, 2, 3, 7, 8, and 10).

● To be an ethical professional also means having a duty to treat other people with whom one works, other members of society, and the TR profession with respect, honesty, and fairness to the best of one's ability. The TRS also has a responsibility to society as a whole, to serve the health and well-being of clients and to advocate for the rights to leisure and recreation for all people (NTRS Obligations 1, 2, 3, 4, 5, and 6; ATRA Principles 1, 2, 4, and 6).

Adhering to these codes of ethics creates an environment of respect, caring, sincerity, commitment, and dedication. The codes help the TRS understand how to practice according to ethical standards. The language and format differ, but the two codes outline the same standards and types of behavior for TR professionals. Choosing one code over the other as a guide may be based on personal preference for language or style or on one's own judgment about which gives more effective guidance, but in either case the TRS can be confident that he is following an appropriate code of ethics for the TR profession. Although the TR profession has two codes, ethical principles are ethical principles, similar in many professions. However, a code of ethics is not "an absolute guide to behavior or decision-making" as much as a starting point (Kornblau & Starling, 2000, p. 15) for ethical practice. Table 1.2 on page 14 provides a comparison of the two codes.

UNETHICAL PRACTICE

What actually constitutes *unethical* practice? While unethical practice can be actions that are illegal or obviously harmful, it can also be activity that is unreasonable, unjustified, ineffective, unfair, or immoral. Unfortunately, many situations are not black and white, and judgments often reflect personal beliefs and values (Kornblau & Starling, 2000). Issues such as abortion, assisted suicide, life support, birth control, and even the rights of residents in a health care facility to smoke cigarettes trigger emotional reactions based on personal beliefs that may affect the professional's decisions and actions. Some practitioners may choose to change jobs rather than stay in a situation requiring them to do things that do not reflect their values. However, one's ethical obligation to act in the interests of clients always outweighs one's personal needs and self-interests (Shank & Coyle, 2002). Differing perspectives between staff and clients may be due to differences in culture that affect beliefs and values. While it is not necessary to agree with one's clients, the TRS should endeavor to understand their points of view

TABLE 1.2

Comparison of NTRS and ATRA Codes of Ethics

NTRS Code	ATRA Code
Obligation 1. The obligation of professional virtue: integrity, honesty, fairness, competence, diligence, and self-discipline	Principle 4. Justice Principle 5. Fidelity Principle 9. Competence
Obligation 2. The obligation of the profession to the individual: well-being, loyalty, respect, and professional practice	Principle 1. Beneficence Principle 2. Nonmaleficence Principle 3. Autonomy Principle 6. Veracity Principle 7. Informed consent Principle 8. Confidentiality and privacy Principle 10. Compliance with laws and regulations
Obligation 3. The obligation of the profession to other individuals and society: general welfare and fairness	Principle 1. Beneficence Principle 4. Justice
Obligation 4. The obligation of the professional to colleagues: respect, cooperation, and support	Principle 5. Fidelity
Obligation 5. The obligation of the professional to the profession: knowledge, respect, and reform	Principle 9. Competence
Obligation 6. The obligation of the profession to society: service, equality, and advocacy	Principle 3. Autonomy Principle 4. Justice Principle 10. Compliance with laws and regulations

in order to provide the most appropriate and effective services (Getz, 2002). The health, welfare, and dignity of clients should always be the foremost consideration in guiding professional behaviors (Jacobson & James, 2001).

Ethical Issues

Ethical issues may arise when the TRS faces complex situations in professional practice. The following are three types of ethical issues that may pose challenges or ethical dilemmas in the professional's work with clients:

● *Foundational* issues, which relate to the meaning of the core concepts of leisure, autonomy, health, and quality of life

● *Systemic* issues, which refer to access to health care and societal resources

● *Clinical* issues, which result from the caregiving relationship of practitioners with clients (Collopy, 1996)

Table 1.3 presents the specific TR practice issues that fall under each category. Clinical issues most directly relate to the topics in this book because

they have to do with the face-to-face interactions between TRSs and their clients. However, these interactions are significantly influenced by the first two sets of issues.

FOUNDATIONAL ISSUES

Foundational issues represent areas of human experience that are very subjective. Everyone experiences leisure uniquely; the meaning of leisure varies for each individual. How one defines health and quality of life is also very personal. The exercise of autonomy varies by culture. Western culture places a very high value on individual freedom and responsibility. Native American and Asian cultures value the group's decisions and choices over those of the individual. Another situation in which an issue can arise regarding autonomy occurs when clients with diminished mental capacity are unable to make wise decisions. The TRS has a responsibility to safeguard clients' rights to autonomy and to leisure as components of health and quality of life. This role may bring the TRS into conflict with clients' families or other professionals who do not value leisure as highly, or who do not consider clients as competent enough to make all their own decisions just because

TABLE 1.3

Types of Ethical Issues

Foundational	Systemic	Clinical
Freedom and autonomy	Health care regulations	Rights of clients
Meaning of health and leisure	Allocation of resources	Boundary issues
Quality of life	Access to services for poor	Privacy and confidentiality
Biomedical technology	Prioritizing who gets services	Decision making for the incapacitated
Human suffering	Financial consideration in providing services	

they are in a health care setting. Therapeutic recreation specialists may find themselves facing ethical dilemmas over foundational issues.

SYSTEMIC ISSUES

Systemic issues also can be a concern of TR. Distributive justice is the principle that ensures equal access to resources and services for all. However, the reality is that not all people have the means to obtain the treatment and programs they need. Who gets served, and who decides? Will TR someday be denied to those whose health insurance does not cover services? Will the pressure to produce measurable outcomes result in denying participation to patients who are not able to make gains in specific areas of functioning? How will the TRS react in these situations? Referring to a code of ethics is of assistance when one is faced with these conflicts.

CLINICAL ISSUES

Clinical issues are the closest to the TRS's daily practice. They are the direct outgrowths of the foundational and systemic issues. They may occur in the context of the caregiving relationship and have the greatest impact on the client's daily life. This relationship "involves an inherent respect for every person as a unique human being" (Van Andel, 1998, p. 183) and for his ability to make informed choices. Clinical ethical issues include

- the rights of clients,
- decision making for those who are incapacitated,
- privacy and confidentiality, and
- boundary issues.

Clinical issues arise when clients' abilities to make informed choices and exercise their autonomy are compromised. The growing numbers of people with chronic illnesses whose decision-making capacity is impaired have focused attention on the concept known as ethic of care (Keller, 1996). According to the **ethic of care,** health professionals are encouraged to embrace caring as a manifestation of seeing "the client as a growing person rather than as a diagnostic label hung on a disease" (O'Keefe, 2005, p. 73). A caring professional is attentive and compassionate, communicates, and performs caring actions. Asking the client what she needs and how she wishes her needs to be addressed demonstrates respect for the client as an autonomous individual. Sylvester posed the question, "What kind of person should I be to practice therapeutic recreation?" (2002, p. 330). A TR practitioner is one who cares about and for his clients, gives care, and evaluates the client's response to the care given (Sylvester, 2002). The TRS must realize that there is no single right course of action that applies to every client (Keller, 1996). This confusion about what to do in a given situation can lead to an ethical dilemma.

Ethical Dilemmas

One of the demands professionals face is to know the ethical thing to do in a situation that may not present clear-cut choices about the ethical course of action to take. A code of ethics can be a guide, but it cannot cover all the possible circumstances that one may confront. The codes present ethical principles to be integrated into everyday practice. A defining characteristic of ethical practice is having a method of resolving ethical dilemmas. These dilemmas may challenge one's personal beliefs and values.

Aristotle, the Greek philosopher, wrote that it's not enough to know the right thing to do in a given situation; we also must act upon that knowledge and engage in ethical action (McLean & Yoder, 2005). It may be an automatic assumption that

The Ethics Audit

These are five questions you should ask yourself if your supervisor wants you to do something that doesn't seem quite right:

1. Would you be ashamed to tell your spouse or children you did it?
2. Would you mind if the local newspaper reported that you had done it?
3. Would you be upset if someone else did it to you?
4. Is it legal?
5. Are you tempted to seize on rationalizations like "Everyone else is doing it" and "It won't hurt anyone"?

Reprinted, by permission, from N. DeMars, 1998, *You want me to do what? When, where and how to draw the line at work* (New York: Simon & Schuster, Inc.).

professionals behave ethically, yet the day-to-day realities of caregiving in a professional environment may interfere with ethical practice. For an elderly resident in a nursing home, the seemingly small, everyday decisions may include when to get up in the morning, what time to eat, what to wear, what activity to attend, and when and with whom to socialize. However, even well-meaning staff, due to overwork or lack of awareness of these issues, may make these daily decisions instinctively and without considering the resident's interests or preferences. Yes, it often seems much easier and quicker for the staff to make these decisions, but safeguarding the right of the *individual* to decide is the ethical thing to do. This situation raises the ethical issues of well-being and autonomy. There will be times when an individual seems to lack the mental competence or physical capacity to make choices and decisions such as these, or even more critical ones like the decision to refuse lifesaving treatment. How do we know, when that time comes, whether to respect a person's wishes or to rely on the intervention of professionals? In these situations, an ethical dilemma may arise.

An **ethical dilemma** is "a choice between two equally compelling alternatives . . . [that] requires a choice between equally compelling values" (Kornblau & Starling, 2000, p. 5). The complexity of a particular dilemma may not be apparent at first glance. Ethical dilemmas call into play personal values as well as professional values. At the time when a professional is trying to resolve an ethical dilemma she is most alone, because ultimately, the resolution of the dilemma falls solely on that person (Shank, 1996). Resolving dilemmas may seem like an overwhelming responsibility because we are

dealing with the needs and concerns of human beings. This is one reason why developing an ethical mindset for practice entails ongoing reflection and discussion with other practitioners about ethical issues. Making the decision includes following a process for determining ethical courses of action and resolving ethical dilemmas.

Ethical Decision Making

Three approaches are typically used in ethical decision making to help determine the ethical course of action. They are

● the consequence-based (teleological or utilitarian) approach,
● the rule-based (deontological) approach, and
● the virtue-based (consequentialist-contextual) approach.

CONSEQUENCE-BASED APPROACH

Taking a consequence-based approach to decision making means that an ethical decision should be based upon the consequences of that decision. In other words, the decision and subsequent course of actions should produce the greatest good and least harm, or the best overall consequences for the greatest number. Planning activities that appeal to the greatest number of people would seem to produce the greatest good. However, one problem with this approach is that it overlooks what is good for the smaller number of people to the advantage of the majority. In order to protect the interests of the minority, decision makers must carefully weigh the consequences of the decision to be implemented. If the desired consequence is to serve the greatest number of people, regardless of the needs and interests of the minority, the TRS will offer programs, perhaps bingo, a movie, a barbeque, or entertainment, that attract a large number of participants. This could interfere with providing meaningful activities to people whose preferences differ from those of the majority. Another example of an ethical dilemma could arise when participation in a TR group is restricted to people who meet certain criteria so that participants will get the maximum benefit from the activity. But other clients would like to attend. Should they be allowed to?

UNIVERSAL RIGHTS APPROACH

The second approach to ethical decision making holds that there are universal rights or rules that determine right and wrong behavior, regardless of the consequences. This approach also implies that there are certain obligations and responsibilities to others, as part of human and civil rights, that help protect the rights of the minority overlooked in the first approach. However, rules and rights may conflict when one is trying to resolve a particular issue; following the rules may have costly consequences. Deciding which rules and rights in the codes of ethics have priority in order to make ethical decisions is a focus of this approach, which may also require relying on one's own judgment (McLean & Yoder, 2005) about what is the right or ethical course of action. While honesty is an ethical obligation, aren't there times when telling someone a truth may not be in her best interest? Should an elderly person with dementia who keeps asking for his mother be told that she died 50 years ago? In the case of autonomy, should a client with lung disease, who is cognitively capable of making this decision, be allowed to smoke cigarettes in a residential facility? How should the TRS, who promotes healthy behaviors yet is assigned to distribute his cigarettes, balance this client's exercise of autonomy with her ethical obligation to do no harm?

VIRTUE-BASED APPROACH

The final approach to ethical decision making is based on considering the consequences of the decision to be made within the context of the given situation. This rational approach to resolving a dilemma is combined with the understanding, empathy, and compassion that the TRS has toward her clients, as well as her understanding of their lives. This reflects the ethic of care and the character of the TR

Developing an ethical mindset for practice entails ongoing reflection and discussion with other practitioners about ethical issues.

© Jon Feingersh/Blend Images/Corbis

professional. In this approach, we have to question ourselves and our own motives about the decisions we make (McLean & Yoder, 2005). Ethical decisions often reflect the character of the decision maker, the kind of person he is and wants to be, and how professionals are expected to behave. Yet different people have different opinions about what constitutes good or ethical character.

This approach requires professionals to ask themselves if they can live with their decisions and if they have a clear conscience once their decisions are made. Should the girlfriend of a client be told that he has AIDS? In a health care setting, a client's right to privacy is considered paramount; however, in this example, the client's actions may do serious harm to his girlfriend. In the team meeting, the discussion centers on the fact that the man is the actual client of the agency and that protecting his rights over hers is the agency's legal responsibility. However, the TRS feels, given the potential consequences of not telling the girlfriend, that her own ethical obligation to do no harm to other individuals is compromised by the team's viewpoint. The TRS should reflect on what personal experiences and values are influencing her decision. These could include personal experience with someone who has AIDS, attitudes toward men's behaviors in relationships, or beliefs about people who have AIDS. If the TRS tells the girlfriend, can she live with her decision, with a clear conscience, and accept the possible consequences given that she has violated the client's confidentiality and the agency decision?

One pitfall of the virtue-based approach is its assumption that the person or persons making the decision are persons of good character, have developed an ethical mindset, and will act with integrity.

Ethical Decision-Making Models

When you are faced with a problem or a situation that just doesn't "feel right" to you, you may be facing an ethical dilemma. Throughout this book, situations are presented that may have ethical implications. Several models have been developed for the TR field to help TRSs determine whether they are dealing with a real ethical dilemma, and if so, how to approach and resolve it.

A FRAMEWORK FOR ETHICAL REASONING

The first model is a framework for ethical reasoning that was based on important work done by TR ethicists and the ATRA Ethics Committee (Shank & Coyle, 2002). It includes six steps:

1. Gather the facts of the situation.
2. Determine if an ethical problem exists by referring to the code of ethics.
3. Identify alternatives for action.
4. Identify the consequences of each alternative course of action.
5. Choose a course of action.
6. Evaluate that choice.

To determine which alternative to select, the TRS should reflect on how the relevant ethical principles are upheld or violated by each course of action.

GUIDELINES FOR ETHICAL DECISION MAKING

The second ethical decision-making model was also developed from work done by TR ethicists (Jacobson & James, 2001). These guidelines for ethical decision making consist of eight steps:

1. Identify the behavior in question.
2. Determine the TRS's responsibility in the situation.
3. Separate out one's personal values from the professional issues.
4. Consider if there is a legal issue involved.
5. Identify if there is an ethical principle involved and, if so, which one.
6. Identify alternatives and consequences.
7. Select the best course of action.
8. Review the results of the decision.

Remember that not every difficult situation is truly an ethical dilemma. That is why it's important for professionals to have an ethical mindset—so that they are continually reflecting on the impact of their decisions and actions on their clients. An easy-to-remember six-step process designed by the authors, called FACE-IT, incorporates this critical point:

FACE-IT PROCESS

F: Gather the FACTS.

A: Weigh the ALTERNATIVES.

C: Evaluate the CONSEQUENCES.

E: Apply the ETHICAL principles.

I: IMPLEMENT the decision.

T: TRUST in people.

All three models cover the same major steps in the process. To determine which model you are most comfortable using, apply each one to the earlier example of the client with AIDS. Ethical dilemmas can create tension and unease for the practitioner and in the workplace. TR specialists should recognize that addressing ethical dilemmas is an essential aspect of professional practice. Ultimately, faith in human beings to be good and do good should guide the decision-making process.

● Summary ●

Becoming a TR professional is a response to a call to meet the needs of individuals to express their rights to health, well-being, recreation, and leisure through the provision of specialized services. To fulfill the role of the TRS, an individual should develop a mindset based on an understanding of the meaning of TR and of the ethical principles that govern daily practice. By blending the skills and qualities of the traditional roles of leader and therapist, the TRS delivers the professional service of TR leadership to help clients reach their personal goals. Providing TR leadership is a privilege and responsibility that adheres to the codes of ethics of the TR profession. However, ethical issues may arise that challenge the TRS's beliefs and values. Ongoing reflection and active engagement in behaviors that enhance the application of ethical principles are the mark of a true professional. Understanding the core values and principles that guide TR practice is essential to providing TR leadership. These will be discussed in chapter 2, which also explains TR practice models and their applications to a variety of TR settings.

● Learning Activities ●

1. In a small group of students or fellow professionals, compare the ATRA and NTRS definitions of TR and recreational therapy to the composite definition of TR. How do these differ? Which one best expresses your understanding of TR?

2. Review codes of ethics of other professions, such as those of the National Association of Social Workers, the American Occupational Therapy Association, the National Recreation and Park Association, the Child Life Council, or the American Physical Therapy Association. How are they similar to TR codes of ethics?

3. Based on the concept of TR leadership, what types of skills does a TRS need? Compare your list with that of a fellow classmate or coworker.

4. For each of the four bioethical principles, can you think of a situation in which you encountered an ethical issue? Pick one of the situations and apply the ethical decision-making models to determine if the course of action you chose was in accordance with ethical principles.

5. Watch the news on TV for several days. What types of unethical behaviors are reported?

6. Review what it means to have a mindset for ethical practice. Make a plan to engage in the activities that will help you develop your mindset. These activities could include engaging in self-awareness activities, keeping a journal of your experiences, self-monitoring your responses to challenging situations, books and journal articles you might read, or workshops on ethical issues you could attend.

7. In class or an in-service training session at work, engage in a discussion on the ethical principles common to the ATRA and NTRS Codes. Give examples of how each principle is applied in professional practice. For example, what does it mean to be competent on the job? Do you need certain technical skills to carry out various activities or specialized knowledge of particular diseases to work with your clients? How should you go about ensuring your own competence?

8. After reading the following case study, answer the questions as a way to learn how to reflect on and apply ethical principles to a real-life situation. You are working with an 11-year-old girl who was injured in a bicycle accident. During a TR session she reveals to you that she didn't fall off her bike but that her injuries were due to parental abuse. She begs you not to tell anyone because she is afraid her parents will get angry with her and she will be taken from her home. What would you do? Which ethical principles apply in this situation? This may be a "no-brainer" because you are legally bound to report this information. But what if the case does not involve a legal harm? What if the child asks to talk to you about her struggles with homosexuality? She asks you to promise not to tell anyone. What ethical principles apply? What if you yourself are gay, if you are conflicted about your sexuality, or if you believe homosexuality is wrong? How will this affect your actions?

Therapeutic Recreation Values, Principles, and Models

In this chapter you will learn about:

- Core TR values—the right to leisure, autonomy, optimal health, and quality of life
- Core TR principles—the humanistic perspective; the ecological perspective; inclusion; and fun, pleasure, and enjoyment
- The relationship of the core values and principles to TR philosophy
- Purposes of TR practice models
- Factors that influence the selection of models
- Common features of TR models
- Critiques of TR models
- Components and applications of seven TR models to different settings and client groups

A mindset for ethical TR practice embraces the values and beliefs of the profession that form the foundation of TR service. The values and principles of TR, which are the basis for practice, have been represented in a number of models that serve as frameworks for professional services. This chapter identifies and describes four core TR values and four core TR principles that represent the ideals and beliefs of the TR profession, followed by a discussion of seven TR practice, or service, models.

FOUR CORE TR VALUES

Values may be characterized as the established ideals of a profession and are reflected in professional ethics. Values identify what the profession considers to be worthy and useful as a guide for practice. They may even arouse an emotional response in us because of their meaning and importance. A profession's values should become part of the pattern of one's daily practice. The TRS not only cherishes these values, but articulates and expresses them in her work (Purtilo & Haddad, 2002). Values influence the types of services a profession provides and the methods it uses to deliver those services. As the TRS matures as a professional, her values may evolve as a result of her experiences and continued learning. Thus, the TRS develops a professional personality based on the values of the profession. The four core TR values are the right to leisure, autonomy, optimal health, and quality of life. The TR professional safeguards these values for clients, advocating for their rights to these values in their lives and providing the services to ensure them.

Right to Leisure

The right to leisure means that all individuals, regardless of their special needs, illnesses, disabilities, limitations, or other circumstances that may affect their full participation, have the right to pursue leisure as "a condition necessary for human dignity and well-being" (National Recreation and Park Association, 1999, p. 1) and are entitled to the assistance required to facilitate the leisure experience. Leisure is characterized by

- perceived freedom from barriers and constraints, and perceived freedom to choose one's actions without the interference or control of another;
- perceived competence that one has the skills and abilities necessary for successful participation in satisfying experiences;

- intrinsic motivation to engage in an activity for personal feelings of satisfaction and enjoyment rather than due to any extrinsic factors that influence the behavior; and
- feeling that one has the ability to have an influence or impact on an experience (Edginton, DeGraaf, Dieser & Edginton, 2006).

Particularly powerful leisure experiences are often characterized by a feeling of being connected to oneself and to the universe, and waking up to see "a glimmer of what is true" (Howe-Murphy & Charboneau, 1987, p. 45). This experience has the potential to be a turning point in the process of healing from either a physical or an emotional harm. Leisure, therefore, can contribute to a better quality of life and a higher level of well-being.

Understanding the meaning of leisure is essential to practicing TR. The focus on leisure experience is the unique contribution of TR to health care and human services. In a traditional medical model, or in a society that has negative attitudes toward the capabilities of people with disabilities and limiting conditions, access to leisure experiences has been restricted, to the detriment of those individuals. For them, leisure may be the one area of their lives in which they choose activities for the personal meaning and fulfillment those activities bring. They are intrinsically motivated to be involved in leisure experiences because the rewards and benefits are in the "doing" of the activity itself and not derived from an external source. Leisure is an opportunity for the individual to express and develop his talents and interests. It may be seen as an arena for the expression of one's unique identity, in which a person is free from constraints on that identity and free to express identity. "One of the potential joys of participating in therapeutic recreation is that individuals have an opportunity to explore their true selves in a challenging, accepting, supportive and conscious environment" (Howe-Murphy & Charboneau, 1987, p. 47). Therapeutic recreation is the only helping profession that has the right to leisure as one of its foundational principles and acts as an advocate for the rights of all individuals to leisure. The TR profession's responsibility to articulate the value of leisure to other health professionals is vital to meeting the needs of clients.

The concept of leisure also has been discussed in terms of **flow**. Flow is an optimal experience that may occur when the challenges of an activity are matched to the skill level of the individual. If an activity is too challenging and the participant does not perceive she has the skills to successfully engage in it, she may feel frustrated and give up. On the other hand, if the activity is not sufficiently demanding of the participant's skills and abilities, she may feel bored or apathetic. But when there is a satisfactory match between challenge and skill, flow results. Flow is characterized by feelings of perceived competence, loss of awareness of time, deep concentration, and feelings of intense involvement (Csikszentmihalyi, 1990). Recreation activities, the primary modality of TR, often result in flow (or leisure) because they involve challenge, excitement, rewards, choices, concentration, structure, and pure fun.

Most definitions of leisure emphasize individualistic values as opposed to the collective or communal values of groups such as Native Americans, Asians, and Latinos. A growing professional concern is that TR practice does not adequately acknowledge a cultural bias in favor of Western values based on individualism. A conceptualization of leisure that goes beyond intrinsic motivation to incorporate a social orientation has been recommended (Dieser, 2004). A social orientation recognizes the influence of our relationships (e.g., family, ethnic group) and the social roles that people fill (e.g., parent, child) as motivators for leisure and as sources of meaning. The social orientation is very much in keeping with the core principles of TR, as the profession acknowledges and incorporates others in planning clients' leisure opportunities. Whether or not one takes an individualistic or social orientation to leisure, expressing one's right to leisure is closely related to the value of autonomy.

Autonomy

Autonomy can be defined as the right to govern oneself, to make one's own decisions and choices, and to be self-determining. Autonomy, as discussed in chapter 1, is also a key bioethical principle. One very meaningful contribution that TR makes to the lives of its clients is helping them maintain some degree of autonomy by providing opportunities to make choices. Leisure may offer the most opportunity for clients to experience autonomy because leisure is characterized by freedom and self-determination (Lahey, 1987). Embracing autonomy as a value means basing services on what the individual defines as his needs and goals. However, in health care settings, people often find their self-determination and autonomy eroded by the nature of the institution, their compromised health status, and their placement (rightly or not) in a dependent role.

Ethical practice requires that the TRS not violate clients' autonomy by making decisions for them, justified as "the professional knows best." Without autonomy, TR loses the qualities that make it most meaningful to the client. While a certain amount of dependency may be needed as clients give their consent to be treated, they trust that the health care team is acting in their best interests (Austin, 2004). "If limits are to be placed on the client's autonomy, this needs to be discussed by the treatment team and communicated to the patient at the outset of treatment" (Jacobson & James, 2001, p. 242). The hope is that clients will then make the choice that is in their best interests. If the choice still poses a danger to the client, the team may choose to intervene to protect him. This is a course of action professionals should reflect upon carefully in their decision-making process. The TRS may help clients learn, if necessary, a process for making and acting upon decisions.

Another concern regarding autonomy is that it is seen as primarily a Western cultural value, which may cause conflict in individuals from cultures

A social orientation recognizes the value of relationships as motivators and sources of meaning.

that emphasize a more collective approach to decision making. For example, a person from a non-Western culture may value the needs and wishes of the whole group over his own, which affects his decisions about his leisure pursuits, health care choices, or both. While a cross-cultural perspective encourages TRSs to examine both their biases and their competence to effectively serve people from all cultures, autonomy can be upheld as an ethical principle (and a core TR value) as long as individuals can make their decisions and choices "according to their cultural world-view" (Sylvester, Voelkl & Ellis, 2001, p. 73). Research studies have shown that self-determination, the "perception of freedom to make choices and the ability to initiate choices," contributes to enjoyment (Devine & O'Brien, 2004, p. 210). Clients whose cultural values place a high priority on relational and role-determined leisure may benefit from the group participation and opportunities to fulfill meaningful roles and responsibilities that TR programs offer. This high regard for the individual's total being relates closely to the third value, optimal health.

Optimal Health

The commitment to the right of all individuals to strive for and experience optimal **health** is one of the fundamental values of the TR profession. "The mission and purpose of TR has always been anchored in a commitment to facilitating the achievement and maintenance of health" (Coyle & Shank, 2004, p. 112). Therapeutic recreation recognizes and provides services from the perspective that an individual's state of health is a result of the relationships among physical, social, spiritual, psychological, and emotional factors; lifestyle habits, environmental conditions, culture, family, and social supports are also acknowledged as significant influences on health. The World Health Organization (WHO) defines health as "a state of complete physical, social, and mental well-being, and not merely the absence of disease or infirmity" (Fazio, 2008, p. 113). **Well-being**, the "achievement of a good and satisfactory existence as defined by the individual" (Fazio, p. 363), is closely related to one's perception of health. People served by TR have impairments that may preclude them from achieving complete or optimal health. However, emphasizing a person's intact strengths, what the individual *can* do, is a foundation of TR practice. In fact, today, all health and human services emphasize looking at the whole person when providing services, taking into account that all parts of a person are interrelated and affect one another. The factors

that have the greatest influence on health, such as exercise, diet, safe behaviors, and recreation participation, are under the individual's control and can be seen as reflecting a person's beliefs and values regarding what is meaningful and important to life. Utilizing one's abilities and strengths reinforces a positive identity and can serve as a tool to engage in healthy behaviors. The TRS can encourage clients to take more responsibility for their own health as they learn about healthy behaviors.

This holistic approach to health is often referred to as **wellness**. Wellness emphasizes individual responsibility for health through the practice of a health-promoting lifestyle (Stumbo & Peterson, 2004). Recreation participation, as part of a healthy lifestyle, contributes to wellness. Wellness can be achieved within the limitations imposed by a disease or disability (Carter, Van Andel & Robb, 2003). Persons who are ill or at the end of life can experience wellness if they are responding to life's challenges according to their own life plan and achieving the potential they feel capable of achieving. The following is a definition of health perhaps more suited to the realities of the circumstances that can affect health status:

> a dynamic level of psychophysical well-functioning, suitable for adapting to one's circumstances and effective for choosing and acting on the private and public values that constitute one's plan for life. (Sylvester, 1987, p. 79)

This definition also acknowledges health as a significant value, worthy of the attention of the TR profession. As a vital component of health services, TR can incorporate the holistic approach by supporting **Healthy People 2010**, the national health agenda put forth by the U.S. Department of Health and Human Services. The first goal of Healthy People 2010 is to increase not just longevity, but also the quality of life (Fazio, 2008), which is one of the core TR values. Other nations, such as Canada and Australia, have launched similar initiatives. In Australia, the National Health Strategy was established in 1994 to promote better health and health practices. *Active Australia* serves this national agenda by encouraging people to participate in sport and physical activity. In Canada, the Health Act was passed in 1984 to ensure that all Canadians have access to essential health services and to promote their physical and mental well-being.

Quality of Life

Quality of life is a person's assessment of her position in life, taking into consideration her perception of her physical and psychological health, family and social relationships, level of independence, work, financial status, and living situation in the context of her environment and values. Quality of life involves both subjective measures, such as one's sense of well-being and availability of opportunities, and objective measures, including functional status and access to resources (Lehman, 1995). This assessment will vary from person to person even when the overall circumstances seem quite similar. A person who seems to have everything may not be happy, whereas a person who is quite ill and without apparent resources or family ties may feel very positive about life. Perceptions of quality of life vary with the passage of time, changes in relationships, and changes in circumstances, particularly after a life-altering event that requires professional services (Drench et al., 2007). Quality of life "touches the heart of what life is about, what it means to be human" (Carter et al., 2003, p. 19). It directs the TRS to treat a client as a whole person, with unique needs, desires, and interests that affect the selection of services. Therapeutic recreation can contribute to people's perception of their quality of life by "opening the fullness of leisure to all citizens" (Lahey, 1996, p. 27). Leisure experiences, which produce feelings of freedom, joy, and satisfaction, are essential to quality of life (Carter et al., 2003).

These four values of TR—the right to leisure, autonomy, optimal health, and quality of life—are closely related. Taken together, they express key beliefs about the value of TR as it offers the opportunity to experience leisure, to make choices within the context of one's cultural values and beliefs, to strive for health, and to enhance quality of life. A strong theme linking TR values is respect for the uniqueness of each human being, each with his own specific beliefs, viewpoints, needs, and desires that affect his attitudes and actions. Therapeutic recreation specialists treat all persons with dignity and respect for their individuality and the many contexts of their lives. Therapeutic recreation services focus on improving functioning in all domains to promote health and wellness, providing supports and resources and facilitating self-determined leisure experiences. Professional values are brought to life as principles that guide practice.

FOUR CORE TR PRINCIPLES

Principles are fundamental beliefs that guide professional practice. They represent our ethical obligation to serve TR clients and the TR profession according to the highest possible standards.

Principles are accepted as a basis for providing services and programs consistent with the values of the profession. Principles give direction for how to deliver services. The following are four principles essential to understanding what TR is and why it is a valuable service:

- TR services are provided from a humanistic perspective.
- TR takes an ecological approach to service provision.
- Inclusion is both a meaningful process and a goal of TR services.
- TR programs are fun and provide pleasure and enjoyment to the participant.

The Humanistic Perspective

The first key principle is that TR services are provided from a **humanistic perspective**. The humanistic perspective views individuals as capable of growth and change and having the desire to fulfill themselves as well as to demonstrate concern for others. This view derives from a school of psychology known as **humanistic** or **growth psychology**, among whose main proponents were Abraham Maslow, Carl Rogers, and Fritz Perls. Humanistic psychology takes an optimistic and positive view of human nature, holding that people are motivated to become more self-aware in order to better themselves. By understanding their motivations and expressing their feelings, individuals can more effectively meet their own needs. Humanistic psychology also recognizes that people are social beings and desire contact with others. Through interaction with caring professionals, clients feel nurtured, understood, and supported as they strive to meet their needs in healthy and satisfying ways. They may be trying to change negative behaviors and to learn new strategies for a happier, less stressful, more meaningful existence. Humanistic psychology focuses on "tapping previously unused creative talents and energies" (Austin, 2004, p. 35). It also assumes that people are autonomous and capable of self-direction.

TR professionals believe that people can discover and utilize their strengths and abilities in the context of the therapeutic relationship. Rogers believed that the nature of the relationship between the client and therapist, rather than the use of any specific therapeutic technique, was the most important element in helping the client (Okun, 2007). To be an effective therapist, according to the principles of humanistic psychology, requires compassion, caring, and empathy for the client's concerns and feelings. The therapist communicates this to the client by developing rapport and trust through the use of appropriate helping and listening skills. Once trust is built, the client will demonstrate greater willingness to work with the therapist. The client comes to believe the therapist can help guide him to a better situation in life. Even if a given technique or program doesn't work well with the client, the client is willing to continue with the therapist because he believes that the therapist has his best interests at heart and is sincerely trying to help. This relationship can be seen as growth promoting and is similar to the relationship the TRS forms with clients. This type of relationship is essential to what makes TR therapeutic. Through this relationship the individual can discover his abilities and talents and experience personal growth. People are considered capable of making choices and decisions about their behaviors and about how they respond to their environment. This relates to the second core principle, which is that TR operates from an **ecological perspective**.

The Ecological Perspective

The ecological perspective holds that people are interconnected with all the systems in their environment and that as a result of their interactions with these systems, growth and change occur. **Environment** does not mean just the physical world, but also the community, neighborhood, social institutions, family, friends, and other people that individuals come into contact with. In other words, all the interactions people have with elements in their environment can have an effect on them and have the potential to change them. In turn, people have the potential to influence the elements in the environment. This perspective acknowledges the interdependence of people and environments and reflects the holistic approach to health and well-being. An approach that recognizes the important role of the physical and social environment in contributing to health and quality of life is known as a **contextualized approach**, which takes into consideration the circumstances of a person's life in the planning of services.

An ecological perspective could serve as a guide to TR practice (Shank & Coyle, 2002). The ecological perspective has integrated two traditional approaches to TR services: the medical model, which focuses on the individual as possessing deficits that need intervention, and the community model, which perceives the environment as faulty and in need of change (Howe-Murphy & Charbon-

neau, 1987). Therefore, the ecological perspective directs the TRS to address three categories of goals:

- Goals directed toward individuals
- Goals focused on the environment
- Goals directed toward the interactive processes between people and their environments

The TRS must engage in a process of self-evaluation and ongoing professional growth because of her own potential impact on the client and the environment. The TRS provides support and assistance to create a safe and fun environment that promotes respect and friendship and facilitates maximum opportunities, participation, and leisure experiences. The ecological approach to TR includes working to change the environment by addressing physical, attitudinal, and behavioral barriers to participation in order to promote a better life for the client, the family, and the community. This idea of looking at the whole picture relates to the third key principle: inclusion.

Inclusion

Inclusion has recently been defined as empowering people who have disabilities to be valued and active members of their communities by making choices, being supported in daily life, and having opportunities to grow and develop to their fullest potential (Stavola Daly & Kunstler, 2006). Earlier efforts at promoting the participation of people with disabilities in their communities focused on their physical integration into settings with people who did not have disabilities. This did not necessarily promote social integration or interaction between the groups of people. Table 2.1 outlines some important factors in the historical process of moving toward inclusion.

However, according to the inclusion principle, it should not be necessary to *integrate* people with disabilities *into* the nondisabled community because this is *everyone's* community! Inclusion implies that everyone deserves to be part of her community from birth (Dattilo & Guerin, 2001). Truly inclusive communities value the diversity and differences of their members. Inclusive communities offer friendship, support, and resources to facilitate full participation in everyday life. In inclusive communities, the emphasis is on the quality of social relationships that are developed and maintained through participation in recreation and other community activities (Wachter & McGowan, 2002). These relationships are seen as beneficial to those without disabilities as well as people with disabilities.

TABLE 2.1

The Building Blocks of Inclusion

Building blocks	Definitions
Deinstitutionalization	The move away from large-scale, institution-based care to small-scale, community-based facilities, which began in the late 1960s
Accessibility	Equal entry into and participation in physical facilities and programs by all people; accomplished through the elimination of architectural, administrative, and attitudinal barriers in order to create a usable environment
Normalization	Making available to people with disabilities the patterns and conditions of everyday life that are as culturally normative as possible
Integration	Physical presence and social interaction of people with and without disabilities in the same setting
Mainstreaming	Movement of people into the activities and settings of the wider community
Least restrictive environment	The environment that imposes the fewest restrictions and barriers on a person's growth, development, and participation in a full life
Supports	Friendships, social networks, assistance, and resources that enable a person to participate in the full life of his or her community
Person-first language	Language that puts the word "person" or "people" first in the sequence of a phrase or sentence to emphasize a positive attitude toward the individual, as in "a person with a disability" rather than "a disabled person"
Inclusion	Empowering people who have disabilities to be valued and active members of their communities by making choices, being supported in daily life, and having opportunities to grow and develop to their fullest potential

Stavola Daly, F. & Kunstler, R. (2006). Therapeutic recreation. In Human Kinetics (Ed.). *Introduction to recreation and leisure*, pp. 177-196. Champaign, IL: Human Kinetics, Inc. p. 184.

Inclusion is increasingly being recognized as a goal for many recipients of TR services (Sylvester et al., 2001), particularly because quality of life can best be attained in the community. Therapeutic recreation has a vital role in developing and using strategies to educate and change community agencies to foster inclusion (Scholl, Dieser & Davison, 2005). TRSs can work with agencies, organizations, and communities to overcome the physical, social, and attitudinal barriers to recreation participation. While many efforts have been made to overcome physical barriers through accessible and barrier-free design, nonetheless attitudes are considered the major obstacle to inclusion. When attitudes change, social acceptance, interdependence, and support networks and services develop in the community and full inclusion happens (Devine & O'Brien, 2004). Inclusion has been called the most self-determining and person-centered service that TR can offer (Bullock & Mahon, 2000).

Full inclusion will be achieved when society affirms the right of all people to participate in all aspects of life and pursue recreation in the optimal environment of their choice (Devine & O'Brien, 2004).

Fun, Pleasure, and Enjoyment

The fourth principle that guides TR practice is that participation in recreation is fun, pleasurable, and enjoyable. Unfortunately, in recent years, TR has been described as "fun and games" with a negative connotation, because fun is characterized as lighthearted, nonserious, amusing, and playful. In fact, fun is a highly valued experience that gives meaning to life. Therapeutic recreation specialists should recognize, promote, and celebrate the importance of having fun (Hutchinson, LeBlanc, & Booth, 2006). Fun and pleasure have been viewed in TR as both the means to motivate clients to participate in beneficial programs and as worthy ends in themselves. Initially, "the primary motivation for the client lies in the pleasurable, satisfying experience gained from participation" (Austin, 2001, p. 53). **Pleasure** is a positive, desired, enjoyable experience, the opposite of pain. **Enjoyment** has to do with how deeply involved a person is in an intrinsically motivated activity and "is consistent with concentration, effort and a sense of control and competence" (Dattilo & Kleiber, 2002, p. 84). The value of TR is jeopardized if TR programs are not enjoyable (Mobily & Ostiguy,

2004). The aim in TR is for clients to have true recreation experiences, eventually enjoying their recreation pursuits so much that the activities become ends in themselves and are not done only to achieve a goal or outcome (Austin, 2004). Clients have the right to enjoy their lives even if they never reach the goals and outcomes set down in their treatment plans (Caplan, 1990; Sylvester, 2005). The debate in the profession continues over whether TR intervention is solely a tool to achieve outcomes or is the provision of opportunities for leisure experiences; but fun, pleasure, and enjoyment are fundamental to quality TR services.

The TRS is guided in her work by the principles of the humanistic perspective; the ecological perspective; inclusion; and fun, pleasure, and enjoyment. The four principles articulate the belief that people are capable of growth and change, are self-determining, and have the right to live in an environment that supports and enables full participation, with pleasure and joy, in activities of their choosing.

Any individual may benefit from learning how to have more fulfilling leisure experiences.

robert lerich - Fotolia

RELATIONSHIP OF VALUES AND PRINCIPLES TO PHILOSOPHY

Values and principles, the ideals and beliefs that contribute to the professional mindset, are expressed in a philosophy of practice. The four core values and four core principles merge to form a philosophy of TR, expressed as follows.

People can experience leisure, which is characterized by freedom, joy, perceived competence and control, and expression of their unique identity, through engaging in recreation. Leisure in and of itself, as experienced through recreation participation, may hold significant meaning and value for people as well as contribute to their health, well-being, and quality of life. Any individual may benefit from learning how to have more fulfilling leisure experiences. The TR profession recognizes that people are autonomous beings, capable of making choices, and affirms the right of all people to leisure, recreation, optimal health, well-being, and quality of life. The TR profession affirms its ethical responsibility to assist individuals, organizations, and communities to overcome barriers and create leisure opportunities and services, as well as to advocate for the purposeful use of recreation to improve health, well-being, and quality of life. Therapeutic recreation specialists develop strategies and programs, facilitate changes, provide supports and resources, and advocate for an inclusive society.

THERAPEUTIC RECREATION PRACTICE MODELS

The relationships among values, principles, and philosophy are often expressed in a service or **practice model**. A model serves as a guide for professional practice. It is a visual representation of the relationships among philosophy, theories, and the real world. Therapeutic recreation services should be based on a model of service that depicts the purposes of TR and the components of TR services. Using an appropriate TR service model is a component of ethical practice. Having a professional mindset includes knowing about, understanding, and selecting and applying appropriate models of services. Choosing a model depends on many factors including the agency's mission and goals, the needs of the clients, the regulations of accrediting bodies and governmental oversight agencies, and the professional philosophy of the practitioner. These are benefits of delivering services according to a model:

- Providing meaning and structure to programming
- Communicating to other disciplines the purposes of TR and the types of services provided
- Ensuring that clients receive the services and interventions best suited to their needs and goals
- Serving as a basis for research and evaluation

In TR, a number of models have been developed over the years. A model should be chosen that is closely aligned to the mission, goals, and needs of the particular agency. Each of the TR practice models described next reflects an interpretation of TR services that is based on the prevailing theories, concepts, and societal influences dominant at the time the model emerged. All the models are based on the assumptions that TR services produce positive change in clients and that TR services are "designed to maximize client control in recreation" (Sylvester et al., 2001, p. 108). Bullock and Mahon (2000) also have identified common themes in TR models that incorporate the core values and principles of TR practice. These are the common themes:

- Services are provided along a continuum of growth and intervention.
- Services are based on a strong belief in the abilities and strengths of the individual.
- The client's freedom and self-determination increase over the course of the services.
- The therapist's control decreases as the client progresses along the continuum.
- The client's involvement and participation in the natural community (environment) increase over time.

The common themes strongly reflect the core TR principles of the humanistic perspective, the ecological perspective, inclusion, and fun and enjoyment. One criticism of these models, as well as of definitions of leisure as mentioned earlier, is that they emphasize predominantly Western cultural values of independence and individualism. Non-Western cultures often value interdependence, family supports, and a nonlinear approach to health. To ensure that these cultural values are upheld, the optimal living environment for the individual should take into consideration the client's world view, values, and community. The core TR principle of the ecological perspective also reflects the importance of the people and systems in the client's life when one is providing services and assisting in planning and decision making. Practicing TR from the ecological view addresses this criticism.

Another critique of the models is that they seem to emphasize independence as a goal for all people. Independent functioning may not be realistic for some people served by TR, such as those with terminal illness, Alzheimer's disease, or a progressive neurological disorder. Neither does everyone view independence as a meaningful goal. Yet individuals in these groups can achieve meaningful experience through TR, and this idea should be incorporated in TR models. This criticism can be addressed if one adheres to the core TR value of optimal health, as well as the core TR principle of emphasizing the fun, pleasure, and enjoyment that come from participating in TR.

The models also have been criticized because they focus primarily on services targeting the individual as a person with a problem that needs to be corrected (Dieser, 2002). To guard against the negative effects of this focus, the TRS should uphold the core TR value of autonomy, which implies that people have the right to define their own needs and express their expectations of services. The core TR principles, as well, guide us to take a broader view. The humanistic perspective, with its holistic approach, recognizes the individual as a whole person with strengths that can be enhanced through TR, not just with problems to be "solved." In addition, the ecological perspective and inclusion emphasize that the community, defined broadly, also can be in need of change and benefit from TR intervention. Practicing TR from an ethical mindset with ongoing reflection on the core TR principles and values will contribute to developing future practice models that adhere strongly to the foundations and key beliefs of the profession. Future models should address the responsibility of the TR profession to work with communities and organizations to develop and implement strategies to foster interdependence, social supports, and an inclusive environment.

Some of the most well-known TR models are the **Leisure Ability Model**, the **Health Protection/Health Promotion Model**, the **Therapeutic Recreation Service** and **Therapeutic Recreation Outcome Models**, the Optimizing Lifelong Health through Therapeutic Recreation Model, the Self-Determination and Enjoyment Enhancement Model, and the Interaction Model. The following sections briefly describe the purposes and components of each of these and present examples of how they may be applied in TR practice.

Leisure Ability Model

The Leisure Ability Model is probably the best known of the models, as it was published in 1978 (see figure 2.1). It was based on earlier work in the field by Ball (1971) and Frye and Peters (1972), which described three components of TR services provided along a continuum. The three components have come to be known as **functional intervention**, **leisure education**, and **recreation participation**. In this model, the purpose of TR is to help clients develop an appropriate **leisure lifestyle**. On the basis of the TR assessment, clients are provided the appropriate services in the relevant components. A client who needs to develop or improve basic skills that are important to leisure functioning, such as gross motor skills, daily living skills, or attention span and concentration, receives services in the

functional intervention component. As the client's skills increase, she progresses along the continuum to the leisure education component, working on increasing leisure awareness, knowledge of leisure activities and resources, and social skills. Building on these newly acquired skills, the client moves into the recreation participation component of TR services. Here she participates as independently as possible in self-chosen recreation activities and programs, with as little assistance from the TRS as necessary. As the client moves along the continuum, she acquires increased control over behavior and decisions, and the TRS decreases his level of control and the amount of assistance provided. It is impor-

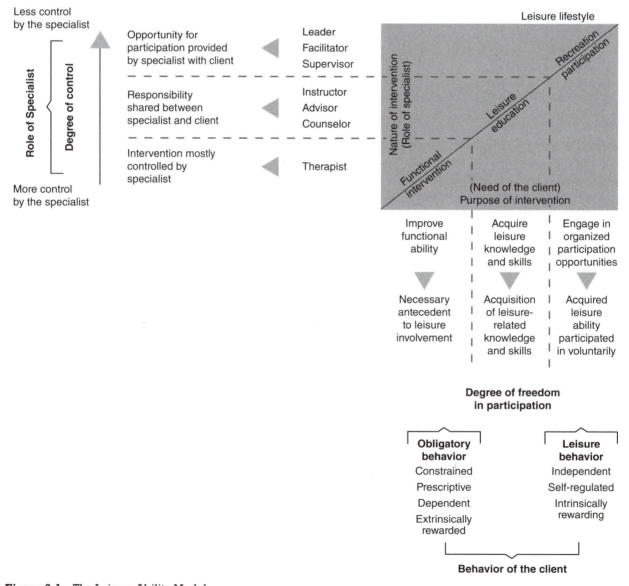

Figure 2.1 The Leisure Ability Model.

Fig. 2.2, p. 39 from THERAPEUTIC RECREATION PROGRAM DESIGN, 4ᵗʰ ed. by Norma J. Stumbo and Carol Ann Peterson. Copyright © 2004 by Pearson Education, Inc. Reprinted by permission.

tant to note that not all clients need to develop skills in all three components and that they may receive services in more than one component at the same time.

This model places the *primary* focus of TR services on "leisure ability." For example, this model could be followed in a day program for psychiatric patients who need to develop satisfying and healthy leisure interests to help them in their struggles with depression, stressful situations, and social isolation. In the functional intervention component, they may participate in building basic skills, such as taking turns or not shouting or cursing, in order to participate in a group activity. In the leisure education component, they may identify sources of stress and experiment with different kinds of recreation activities that reduce their stress and promote feelings of relaxation and control. In the recreation participation component, they may attend recreation activities of their choice in the community with others.

Another setting where this model could be applied successfully might be a group home for adults with developmental disabilities. They may need to improve physical fitness, social skills, and knowledge and utilization of leisure resources in the community in order to engage in satisfying leisure. Basic fitness skills could be improved through functional intervention; appropriate social behaviors to utilize in a community fitness center could be developed through leisure education; and joining and attending a local gym for exercise and socialization could be the focus of recreation participation.

In both these settings, TR places major emphasis on helping clients to improve their abilities and knowledge relative to their leisure behavior. Potentially, any individual who has barriers to satisfying leisure behavior could be a candidate for TR services, as that is the foremost contribution TR is making to the client's life. Benefits achieved from healthy recreation participation can have carryover value into other aspects of people's lives. It can be seen, then, that successful use of this model would be in a setting where the contribution of a leisure lifestyle to the health and well-being of the clients has been recognized by the administration and the other professional disciplines. Working within this model also opens up possibilities for collaboration and coleadership, for example conducting a stress management group with a psychologist in the day program, or running a healthy dining-out program with a nutritionist in the group home.

Health Protection/ Health Promotion Model

The Health Protection/Health Promotion Model (see figure 2.2) was developed by David Austin and initially presented in 1991 as a response to the rising costs of health care and the belief that it was necessary to position TR as an important, if not essential, service in the health care arena. Similar to the Leisure Ability Model, this model describes three components of TR service: *prescriptive activities, recreation,* and *leisure.* However, it differs in identifying the purpose of TR as helping the client to recover from a threat to health and to achieve optimal health. According to the model, the way to do this is through participation in the three components of

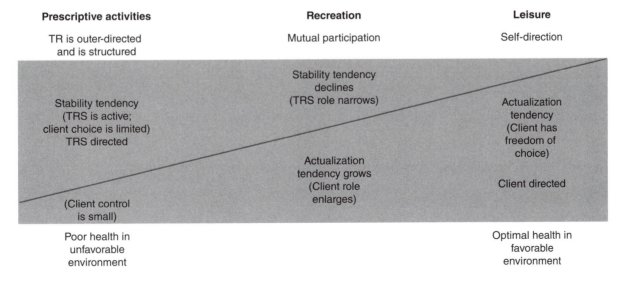

Figure 2.2 Health Protection/Health Promotion Model.

Reprinted, by permission, from D.R. Austin, 2004, *Therapeutic recreation: Processes and techniques,* 5th ed. (Champaign, IL: Sagamore Press), 176.

services. In the activities component, the TRS prescribes activities, based on an assessment, to help the client feel safe and secure, less depressed and anxious, and more motivated and in control. These activities could include simple, success-oriented activities such as listening to music or aromatherapy. As the client begins to stabilize his health, the TRS works with him to choose recreation activities that help to improve his health and develop skills. For example, doing arts and crafts could improve attention span, concentration, and fine motor skills. Participating in exercise could improve physical fitness and reduce stress. In the leisure component the client becomes independent in making and implementing choices that promote health on an ongoing basis, such as joining a health club, taking an art class, or participating in a book discussion group. As the client progresses through the three services, he becomes healthier, more independent, and more in control of his life.

This model could be applied in health care settings that focus on treating illness or alleviating the effects of disability, as it dovetails well with overall treatment and rehabilitation goals. For example, a short-term rehabilitation unit for clients who have had a stroke might be an appropriate setting in which to use this model. As a client begins to recover from the stroke, the TRS provides emotional support and may offer recreation experiences, such as exercise and arts and crafts, that address the physical and emotional impacts of the stroke. As the client begins to improve, the TRS can assist her with making new recreation choices as well as learning adaptations to former recreation interests. As the client nears discharge, the TRS can collaborate with her to develop a plan for leisure participation in the home and community, which could contribute to the client's ongoing improvements in and maintenance of health status. The TRS can work with rehabilitation team members such as the physical therapist, occupational therapist, and speech therapist to provide a holistic and well-integrated plan of care. Using this model puts the focus on the primary role of TR as contributing to improving health.

Therapeutic Recreation Service Delivery Model

The Therapeutic Recreation Service Delivery Model and its companion Therapeutic Recreation Outcome Model were first presented by Carter, Van Andel, and Robb (1996). The purpose of TR in these two models is to help the client attain his optimal level of health and well-being. The Therapeutic Recreation Service Delivery Model articulates a role for TR in four areas of service: diagnosis/needs assessment, treatment/rehabilitation, education, and prevention/health promotion (see figure 2.3). The focus of TR is on improving functioning, health status, and quality of life through participation in recreation activities. In this model, much as with the Leisure Ability Model and the Health Protection/Health Promotion Model, the client moves along a continuum of components of service; however, this model delineates four components rather than three. The TRS follows the model by conducting the assessment, prescribing appropriate recreation activities as interventions, educating the client about health and well-being, and helping to implement ongoing lifestyle changes that promote health after discharge. Recreation activities can serve as both a treatment intervention and a leisure experience.

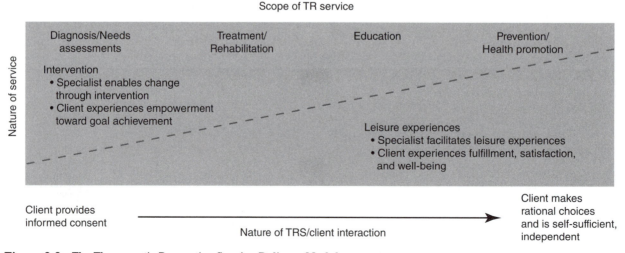

Figure 2.3 The Therapeutic Recreation Service Delivery Model.

Reprinted by permission of Waveland Press, Inc. from G. Van Andel, 1998, "TR service delivery and TR outcome models," *Therapeutic Recreation Journal* 32(3): 180-193.

This model, as with the Health Protection/Health Promotion Model, would be well suited to a health care setting that recognizes the importance of ongoing health promotion and client responsibility in achieving successful recovery from illness and increasing quality of life.

This model could be applied in a cardiac care unit, where a client who has suffered a heart attack could engage in exercise in the treatment phase, learn how manage stress and order healthy foods in restaurants in the education phase, dine out as an enjoyable leisure experience, and join a local fitness center as part of health promotion and prevention. This model might also be used in an early intervention setting where the goal is to ameliorate the effects of disability on a young child. Treatment could be provided in the form of group games to improve social interaction, attention span, and motor skills; education for the family about community recreation resources; and ongoing health promotion through participation in a weekly recreation program where the child can maintain the gains in functioning resulting from intervention. Such treatment also contributes to improving overall quality of life for the whole family through fun experiences.

Therapeutic Recreation Outcome Model

In the Therapeutic Recreation Outcome Model, the purpose of TR is to improve quality of life by increasing functional capacity and health status (see figure 2.4). Quality of life is related to functioning in six behavioral domains: cognitive, psychological, physical, spiritual, social, and leisure. According to the model, TR services can be provided to address deficits in all six domains. As the client's functioning improves, health also should improve. The client does not necessarily have to improve in *all* areas of functioning. Improvements in only some, or even one, of the domains could result in increased quality of life. For example, clients with progressive or terminal illnesses may not improve their physical health, yet they can experience increases in spiritual, leisure, or psychological health (or more than one of these) through TR services. In a hospice for people with cancer or AIDS, gains in spiritual health could provide quality of life at its most fleeting moments. Writing a letter to loved ones, listening to music, and reminiscence are among the TR programs that could improve quality of life.

This model also could be applied in a nontraditional setting such as a shelter for people who are homeless. Improvements in functioning could

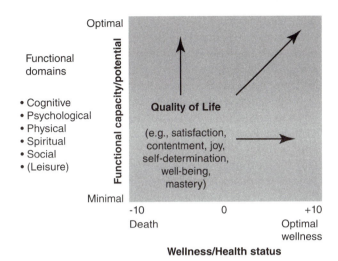

Figure 2.4 The Therapeutic Recreation Outcome Model.

Reprinted by permission of Waveland Press, Inc. from G. Van Andel, 1998, "TR service delivery and TR outcome models," *Therapeutic Recreation Journal* 32(3): 180-193.

address all the domains. For example, the TRS could help clients increase communication skills (social domain), learn how to appropriately express emotions (psychological), develop awareness of the value of recreation in their lives (leisure), learn a decision-making process (cognitive), increase physical fitness (physical), and explore what is meaningful in life (spiritual). By developing these skills and attitudes, the individuals may be able to improve their life situation and its quality. This model will be successfully applied in a setting where the other disciplines recognize the vital contribution that TR makes to improving functioning as a means of increasing quality of life.

Optimizing Lifelong Health Through Therapeutic Recreation Model

The Optimizing Lifelong Health Through Therapeutic Recreation (OLH-TR) Model was developed by Wilhite, Keller, and Caldwell in 1999 (see figure 2.5 on page 34). In this model, the purpose of TR is to enhance health and minimize the effects of illness and disability over the life course. This model reflects the growing emphasis on inclusion and lifelong recreation participation for people with disabilities as one means of maintaining and promoting health throughout the life span. People's health fluctuates over the course of their lives, so they may need different types of adaptations and assistance to cope with life changes at different points in time. Besides the services provided in a treatment or health care setting, TR also may be needed periodically to help clients adapt their recreation skills and needs as their health status varies. Unlike the models described previously, this model is more circular than linear. It takes into account that health status fluctuates and does not usually progress in a straight line from illness to health. This model is particularly well suited to people with chronic conditions such as AIDS or substance abuse because of their fluctuating health status and the nonlinear course of their illness (Kunstler, 2004a). The model consists of four processes: *selecting*, *optimizing*, *compensating*, and *evaluating*. The TRS helps the client to

● select appropriate activities suited to his interests, abilities and resources;

● optimize goal attainment through engaging in activities;

● compensate for impaired abilities by selecting alternative activities, adaptations, or both; and

● evaluate the effectiveness of these activities in contributing to a healthy leisure lifestyle.

In this model, leisure lifestyle is seen as a contributor to lifelong health.

The OLH-TR Model can be utilized in settings that provide a progression of services, such as facilities for long-term care where TR is provided to independent seniors who may move to an assisted living unit and then to a skilled nursing unit. As the older adult's health changes, so might the activities and needed adaptations and resources provided by the TRS. Also, a TRS in a community-based agency, such as an agency for people with AIDS or people with multiple sclerosis who have fluctuations in their health status, may see clients on and off as they utilize home care, day care, and support services according to their health needs. In these settings, the TRS can effectively apply this model with its focus on both health and leisure.

Self-Determination and Enjoyment Enhancement Model

The Self-Determination and Enjoyment Enhancement Model, developed and refined by Dattilo, Kleiber, and Williams (1998), is also circular rather than linear (see figure 2.6). In this model, the pur-

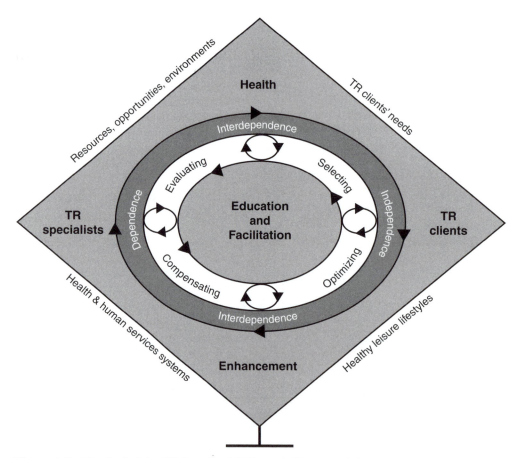

Figure 2.5 The Optimizing Lifelong Health Through Therapeutic Recreation Model.

Reprinted, by permission, from B. Wilhite, M.J. Keller and L. Caldwell, 1999, "Optimizing lifelong health and well-being: A health enhancing model of therapeutic recreation," *Therapeutic Recreation Journal* 33(2): 98-108.

pose of TR is to increase self-determination and enjoyment in order to achieve functional improvements in clients with illnesses and disabilities. This model reverses the more traditional direction of TR services, in which functional improvements lead to independent functioning and life satisfaction. Here, the expectation is that becoming more autonomous and experiencing enjoyment will lead to improvements in health status. As clients make choices about which activities they will engage in and as they experience the benefits of this participation, the expectation is that they will be more motivated toward and more capable of making improvements in their functioning. Much as in the other models, the TRS assesses skills, makes adaptations, provides a supportive environment, gives feedback, and helps the client through the processes. This model would work well in a setting where the TRS is able to plan and implement a wide range of recreation programs suited to clients' interests and goals. For example, in physical rehabilitation facilities, psychiatric hospitals, and substance abuse treatment centers with a long-term length of stay, there could be enough time for the clients to make progress in developing recreational interests and then advance to improving functioning.

Interaction Model

The Interaction Model is based on the ecological perspective as described by Howe-Murphy and Charboneau (1987) and is worthy of renewed attention (see figure 2.7 on page 36). The ecological perspective, as discussed earlier, recognizes that human beings are in dynamic interaction with, and influenced by, their environment. The Interaction Model emphasizes the importance of the environment to the individual's health and well-being. In this model, the purpose of TR is to maximize quality of life, enhance leisure functioning, and promote acceptance of persons with disabilities within the community. This seems to be the only model stating that a *primary* role of TR is to address the needed changes in the environment, in addition to addressing the needs of the individual. Both the environment and the individual may possess characteristics that can benefit from intervention. Applying this model, therefore, involves assessing the individual client and the environment. The environment includes the philosophy and professional practices of the agency; the TR professional's beliefs, values, and skills; the abilities and attitudes of the client; and the barriers and resources in the environment. Once this comprehensive assessment is completed, goals are set to address both the needs of the individual and those of the environment, plans are put in place and implemented, results are evaluated, and the participant is followed up in the home community. This model could be applied successfully in an agency where clients are returning to the community and the TRS has the opportunity to work within the community to create supportive networks and resources, such as

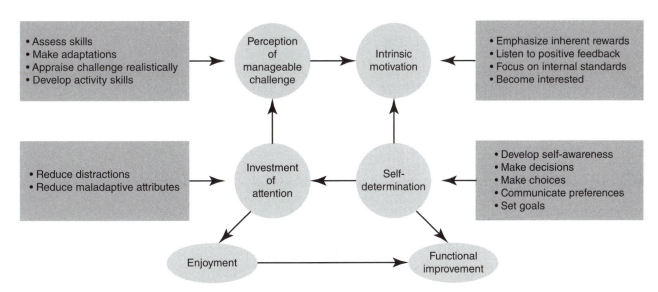

Figure 2.6 The Self-Determination and Enjoyment Enhancement Model.

Reprinted, by permission, from J. Dattilo, D. Kleiber and R. Williams, 1998, "Self-determination and enjoyment enhancement: A psychologically-based service delivery model for therapeutic recreation," *Therapeutic Recreation Journal* 32(4): 258-271.

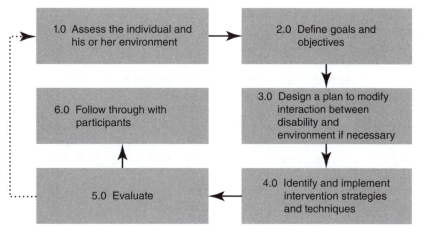

Figure 2.7 The Interaction Model.

HOWE-MURPHY, THERAPEUTIC RECREATION INTERVENTION: AN ECOLOGICAL PERSPECTIVE, 1st Edition, © 1987, p. 39. Reprinted by permission of Pearson Education, Inc. Upper Saddle River, NJ.

transition services for adults with developmental or physical disabilities.

The Interaction Model could also address behavior changes in others who support the individual. For example, in an after-school program for children with disabilities, one child may be the target of bullying. A goal for the child could be to develop strategies to cope with the bullying. A goal for the environment could be to develop positive group behavior among the children by helping them learn tolerance and participate together in a recreation activity in which the victimized child can have a successful role.

An in-home program is another setting in which the Interaction Model could be used. For example, when working in the home setting with a person who has dementia, a TRS would try to reduce any negative impacts that the environment may have on the client's ability to function at the highest level. The TRS would implement a comprehensive assessment to evaluate the abilities and needs of the person and also the conditions in the physical environment and the skills of the caregivers. The person who delivers Meals on Wheels may be a significant social contact for an elderly individual at home. Helping family members and the person

with the disability learn new ways to interact through recreation may alleviate stress on the caregivers. An example of a modification in the physical environment is increasing lighting in the home of someone with Alzheimer's disease, which has been shown to decrease confusion.

Summary of TR Practice Models

These TR practice models reflect the four TR values and four TR principles described earlier in the chapter. Using a practice model holds great benefits for TR professionals. It helps TR professionals to communicate the purposes and benefits of TR services and to provide the most suitable interventions and experiences for clients. A model can serve as a framework from which to develop specific programs best suited to the needs of the clients. The models do not provide details on the content and process of specific TR programs. Individual practitioners and the profession as a whole can present appropriate interventions to be used according to the models. Using a model contributes to the profession's knowledge of how TR works most effectively. Research should be conducted to see whether or not the models actually work in the manner described and produce the predicted results (Ross & Ashton-Shaeffer, 2001). In the future, more models are sure to emerge that will reflect the conditions and philosophies of the time in which they are developed. A good model "will be influenced by the past, reflect current realities, and provide a progressive dynamic direction for the future" (Voelkl, Carruthers & Hawkins, 1997, pp. 210-211). Contemporary concerns about cost-effective services, multicultural considerations, inclusion, and existential outcomes will certainly be factors in future models. The Leisure and Well-Being Model (Carruthers & Hood, 2007) and Together We Play (Scholl et al., 2005) are two of the more recently developed models that reflect some of these more recent trends.

● Summary ●

The values and principles of a profession are the basis for ethical practice. Values and principles are expressed in a professional philosophy that articulates the beliefs about the purpose of a profession. Professionals have a calling to serve the public trust by addressing needs in accordance with their training and standards for practice. The seven TR service models presented in this chapter embody the four core TR values (rights to leisure, autonomy, optimal health, and quality of life) and the four core TR principles (humanistic perspective; ecological perspective; inclusion; and fun, pleasure, and enjoyment). Therapeutic recreation service models, based on a philosophy of TR, provide valuable guidance and direction for the provision of TR services. All TR professionals should develop programs using the framework of a model. Therapeutic recreation specialists are encouraged to be flexible and creative in applying models in order to provide the most appropriate and respectful services to their clients. Further reading, reflection, discussion, and evaluation of the profession's foundations will help the TRS to develop a mindset for ethical practice.

● Learning Activities ●

1. Review the four core TR values. How important is each of them to your life? Can you think of a time when one or more of them was compromised? How did you feel? How did the situation improve?

2. Look through several days' worth of newspapers. How often do you see news stories that involve violations of the core TR values? In what types of situations do these violations occur? Discuss these news stories with a small group of classmates or fellow professionals to obtain a broad picture of the types of violations that can occur.

3. In a small group, design a TR program based on the four core principles for a setting of your choice. What types of services would you offer to ensure that the principles are followed?

4. In your own words, write a philosophy of TR based on the four values and principles that is personally meaningful to you. Read it to others in your group to compare how you expressed your ideas. What can you conclude from the different interpretations?

5. Based on your reading and understanding of the seven TR models, how valid are the criticisms of these models? How would you address these criticisms in one of the models you might select for use?

6. In small groups, discuss each of the models and their applications. For each one, select an additional setting or group of clients to which the model could apply.

7. Which model do you personally prefer? Write a short paper for class explaining how your choice reflects your TR philosophy. Divide into small groups with others who chose the same model and discuss what you have written.

8. Given the following case, select a TR model to apply. Why did you choose it? Explain how you will provide TR services to David according to the components or the steps of the model.

David is a 12-year-old boy on an inpatient pediatric unit who is receiving chemotherapy for bone cancer. His current recreation activities are limited due to the effects of chemotherapy and to the hospitalization. David's treatment has resulted in fine motor problems in addition to fatigue and pain episodes. David is socially isolated, spending many hours in his room watching TV. He has expressed interest in being able to play video games so that he can interact with his peers on the unit and with his friends and siblings when they come to visit.

Program Planning Approaches and the Therapeutic Recreation Process

In this chapter you will learn about:

- Eight contemporary approaches to programming and their implications for TR practice
- Therapeutic recreation standards for practice
- The four steps in the TR process
- The assessment toolkit, interview, observation, and homemade and standardized tools
- Assessing leisure, functional characteristics, readiness to change, and the environment
- Goal setting
- Discharge planning
- Scheduling and implementing TR programs
- Evaluating client progress
- The TRS's responsibilities as a member of the team
- The impact of the eight approaches to programming on the TR process

A primary responsibility of the TRS is to provide TR leadership of individual and group TR programs that are designed and developed for the clients served. Therapeutic recreation leadership is the unique blending of the therapist's purposeful application of therapeutic strategies and facilitation techniques with the recreation specialist's abilities to create and facilitate leisure experiences. In accordance with the highest ethical standards, the TRS plans programs that are relevant, meaningful, and valued. A significant factor that affects TR program design is the contemporary approaches to programming used in health care, human services, education, and other societal institutions. These approaches change over time, as different issues and concerns come to the forefront of the public consciousness, and are a reaction to social, political, and economic conditions. Program design also is influenced by the regulations of government agencies and accrediting bodies that oversee the organization's services and activities; the mission and goals of the organization and of the TR department; the standards of practice of the TR profession; the TR service model that the TR department follows; and the individual characteristics, needs, and goals of the clients. This chapter discusses the eight approaches to programming and their impacts on TR program planning, the guidelines provided by the standards of practice of the TR profession, and the implementation of the TR process.

First, a quick explanation of the TR process, which is implemented for each individual client with whom the TRS works and which provides direction for the design of TR programs. The TR process consists of a series of steps designed to fulfill the purposes of TR. These are the four basic steps:

1. **A**ssessment of the client and his world
2. **P**lanning the specific goals or outcomes, objectives, and TR interventions for the client
3. **I**mplementation of the TR plan
4. **E**valuation of the client's progress and revision of the plan, if needed

These four steps are also referred to as the **APIE** process. Each step has several components, so a presentation of the process may sometimes include more than four steps. The TR process is always carried out in the delivery of TR services, regardless of setting or population served. "The TR process can occur anywhere and is feasible in any setting" (Mobily & Ostiguy, 2004, p. 188). Depending on the setting, the individual client plan may be known as a treatment plan; a care plan; or a service, educa-

tion, or program plan. The implementation of the TR process and the design of the individual TR plan will be affected by the eight approaches to program planning because they reflect the current demand for increasingly relevant as well as cost-effective services.

EIGHT APPROACHES TO PROGRAMMING

The eight approaches to programming used in today's complex world of health and human services, which will have a bearing on TR planning for the foreseeable future, are evidence-based practice, active treatment, outcome-oriented programming, benefits-based programming, person-centered planning, the strengths-based approach, the continuity of lifestyle approach, and the inclusion approach (see table 3.1 for definitions of each). The approaches are grouped in two categories, the clinical approach and the personal growth approach. It is important to recognize that these approaches have distinctive features as well as overlaps and that the most successful program planning will be based on a combination of at least several approaches.

Clinical Approaches

The first three approaches, evidence-based practice, active treatment, and outcome-oriented programming, reflect TR clinical practice. Clinical practice is "a systematic and planned process intended to facilitate change in a client's health and well-being" (Shank & Coyle, 2002, p. 61). In TR clinical practice, recreation and other activities are used primarily as the *means* to reach "targets for change" (Shank & Coyle, 2002, p. 54). Targets or outcomes are precise statements of

- new knowledge or skills a client will learn;
- a cognitive, physical, or social adaptation to functional limitation; or
- growth in the client's realization of what can make her life more satisfying and meaningful.

EVIDENCE-BASED PRACTICE

Evidence-based practice (EBP) began in the 1990s as a result of the pressure on health service providers to demonstrate accountability for the costs and results of health care and treatment. As the costs of health care and medical services have grown astronomically, there has been a corresponding demand for all types of medical and health professions to utilize treatments and procedures proven to be effective at producing desired results. Evidence-based practice is "care that is based on the use of systematically acquired evidence to determine whether an intervention . . . produces better outcomes than alternatives . . ." (Institute of Medicine, 2001, p. 46). In other words, the intervention that can most successfully address a given health care condition or disease should be selected in accordance with the findings of well-designed and -executed research studies. Practitioners are responsible for weighing the evidence in light of the needs of the client and choosing the most effective course of action to produce the desired outcomes.

The type of research that investigates the outcomes of different interventions is known as **efficacy research**. By utilizing the results of efficacy research relevant to TR—research that investigates the outcomes of different TR interventions to determine their effectiveness—the TRS can select interventions for a particular client based on the best evidence available. Therapeutic recreation specialists have the obligation to read research articles published in professional journals in order to stay current with the latest findings and, if possible, engage in efficacy research studies, thereby contributing to the body of knowledge about the efficacy of TR services. The TRS's ethical responsibility is to be up-to-date in professional knowledge, to be competent in practice, and to do good for clients. Therefore, incorporating EBP into daily work would seem to be a sound ethical practice. This approach helps to close the "science-to-practice gap" (Drake, 2005, p.

TABLE 3.1

Eight Approaches to Programming

Clinical approaches	Personal growth approaches
Evidence-based practice: Practice based on research evidence combined with professional expertise and judgment to select the best method to treat a specific condition	**Benefits-based programming:** Motivating participation in programs by emphasizing the benefits of the activity, rather than the activity itself
Active treatment: Treatment considered medically necessary that specifies the intensity, frequency, and duration of service required to produce an outcome	**Person-centered planning:** Placing the individual at the center of designing services, with collaboration from family and others, focused on personally meaningful goals
Outcome-oriented programming: Programs based on what is meaningful, relevant, and realistic in a client's life in order to achieve desired outcomes	**Strengths-based approach:** Focusing on strengths, resources, and capabilities of the client, family, and community in order to increase feelings of control and the ability to achieve goals
	Continuity of lifestyle: Continuing activities, behaviors, and environmental features that existed prior to a major change in a client's life in order to maintain quality of life
	Inclusion: Individuals are entitled to self-determination regarding engaging in activities and living in the environment of their choice, with supports to both the client and the community to eliminate barriers

Selected Professional Journals Related to TR
- Therapeutic Recreation Journal
- Annual in Therapeutic Recreation
- American Journal of Recreation Therapy
- Adapted Physical Activity Quarterly
- Journal of Leisure Research
- Leisure Sciences
- Research Quarterly for Exercise and Sport
- Journal of Park and Recreation Administration
- Journal of the Canadian Association for Leisure Studies

45), the gap between what research findings tell us is effective and what we actually do with our clients.

There have been some concerns that EBP places too much emphasis on research findings without considering the expertise of the practitioner and the uniqueness of each client. Yet EBP is a reflective process (Lee & McCormick, 2002) that also encompasses the clinical expertise and judgment of the practitioner, or what has been termed **judgment-based practice of care** (or **clinical judgment**) (Polkinghorne, 2004). This refers to care that the practitioner provides based on her knowledge, skills, empathy, creativity, and experience. Each client is a unique human being who will respond in a singular way. To the extent that human behavior and reactions are predictable, it is in everyone's best interests to apply research findings. But insofar as every individual is also unique, the TRS, as with others engaged in therapeutic relationships, relies on her professional judgment of what is needed for a particular client. For example, it is well accepted, based on a number of research studies, that physical activity improves mood. In applying this research finding to TR programming, the TRS may recommend a walking program for one client and a workout in the gym for another.

The choice of which physical activity to include in a client's plan should be a judgment based on the professional's expertise applied to the specific situation of the particular client. Another example of applying EBP relates to the results of two separate research studies, which showed that participation in a water aerobics program reduced blood pressure, body fat, and body weight in elderly community residents (Shank, Kinney & Coyle, 1993). A TRS working with similar clients may conclude that water aerobics is the best choice of physical activity for her clients. Before she makes that decision, she must weigh this evidence in light of the unique characteristics of the individual residents. To cite one further example, an extensive analysis of research on people with developmental disabilities showed ample support for the effectiveness of community integration, friendship development, and lifelong leisure skill development programs (Crawford, 2001). In applying EBP, the TRS can cite this information to support providing these types of programs.

What are the implications of evidence-based practice for TR program planning? Because EBP involves making decisions about what is the best treatment or service for a particular client, the TRS should carefully document the reasons for her choices of interventions based on the research evidence. "Evidence-based practice is the process of applying the results of outcome research to improve day-to-day TR services to clients" (Stumbo, 2003, p. 18). The TRS should also observe and record the effects of TR program participation on clients in order to collect evidence for future decision making. In carrying out the TR process, the TRS includes interventions and programs in the TR plan that she has a reasonable expectation will be effective, based on a review of the evidence coupled with her own professional expertise. Therapeutic recreation specialists design treatment and program protocols that present a rationale for the use of a particular TR intervention. This rationale must be based on efficacy research. "A critical issue for therapeutic recreation remains the failure of practitioners to incorporate the TR research base into contemporary practice" (Crawford, 2001, p. 343). However, remember that EBP also relies on the professional's judgment of what is in the best interests of the client. In all our services, "caring" for the individual should be our guide (Fazio, 2008). Evidence-based practice and judgment-based practice of care signify that both research evidence and professional expertise should influence decisions about the plan of care or services. Utilizing EBP is very useful in providing active treatment, which is the next approach to program planning.

ACTIVE TREATMENT

Active treatment refers to services that are considered "medically necessary to treatment or rehabilitation of the individual and are instrumental in achieving outcomes that are efficient and effective" (Shank & Coyle, 2002). Active treatment is not prescribed to provide comfort and support, but is intended to ameliorate disease or to optimize independence and prevent loss of abilities. To be considered active treatment, any service must meet four criteria:

● Be prescribed, supervised, and monitored by a physician

● Be delivered according to an individual plan of care based on an assessment

● Specify the intensity, duration, and frequency of the intervention

● Be based on a reasonable expectation of improving the patient's condition, as well as reduce the need for continued medical care (Shank & Coyle, 2002)

One setting where active treatment can be implemented is long-term care. The **Minimum Data Set (MDS)**, the federal assessment used in long-term care facilities (Centers for Medicare and Medicaid Services, 2008), includes a section that can be filled out by a **Certified Therapeutic Recreation Specialist (CTRS)**. Under Section T1, "Special Treatments and Procedures," a CTRS can record the duration and frequency of a treatment she delivers, as long as that treatment meets the following specific criteria:

- Treatment must be provided in 15-minute increments.
- Treatment must be physician ordered, including indication of the frequency, duration, and scope of treatment.
- Treatment must go beyond the general activity program offered by the facility.

Therapeutic recreation does meet some of the criteria for either active treatment or special treatment according to the MDS. All TRSs develop individual treatment, care, or program plans for clients based on an assessment. These plans are written with the expectation that they will help the clients reach their goals. Many plans include a schedule specifying the intensity or length of each individual session (thirty minutes), the frequency of, or how often, the sessions are offered (three times per week), and the duration or time period the sessions will last (three weeks). Also, in many settings, physicians do refer clients for TR services. Despite these practices TR is still *not* accepted universally as active treatment, nor as a reimbursable service.

Active treatment requires an estimate of the *amount* of the intervention needed to produce improvement. This is a significant shift in thinking for TR. Just as a physician prescribes a course of medication for a disease (including the dosage, how often the patient takes the medication, and for how long a period), and just as a physical therapist specifies a number of visits per week for a certain number of weeks to rehabilitate a physical problem, the TRS must indicate the intensity, frequency, and duration of TR sessions in order for the treatment to be considered "active treatment." This "dosage" should be based on the expectation that it is a reasonable amount that can improve the patient's condition. The TRS might recommend TR for a client to address cardiovascular functioning and mobility in the form of a "group walking program 30 minutes per session, three times per week for 12 weeks." The TRS should have evidence on which to base this plan, for example an analysis of 21 studies in patients with restricted blood flow in their legs showing that those who exercised for 30 minutes at least three times a week over several

months had the best results (Davies, 2000). This type of evidence would help support the amount or dosage of TR to be specified in the individual plan. This process is a challenge for the TR profession that can be addressed through efficacy and effectiveness research studies, but that will require the wholehearted effort of all professionals.

Active treatment has positive implications for TR practice, but also raises some challenges that TR has not had to face that often. In most TR settings, clients are encouraged to attend as many TR programs as they wish for as long as they want. This supports the client's personal autonomy and right to make choices about participation, and reflects core TR values and principles of right to leisure, autonomy, quality of life, and fun, pleasure, and enjoyment. However, with active treatment it would be necessary to restrict participation in a program only to clients for whom the program has been "prescribed," and to offer other TR programming that is *not* active treatment so that there are options for participation for all clients. TRSs may be reluctant to tell a client she could not attend a program because it was not part of her active treatment.

A positive implication of active treatment for TR program planning, regardless of whether or not TR is reimbursable in a given setting, is that it encourages the TRS to consider what "dosage" of programming is effective at producing results for clients. Length of stay of clients in a particular setting will influence the type of programming provided. If a given TR intervention takes more time to produce an effect than the typical length of stay, alternative activities may be a better choice. In nonmedical settings, active treatment may not be an issue; however, active treatment has been adapted to the needs of people with developmental disabilities who are receiving nonmedical services. For this population, active treatment is seen as a method of promoting independence and maintaining an optimal level of functioning. Nevertheless, active treatment entails careful and thoughtful consideration of the choice and scheduling of TR activities, and this can be helpful in any type of setting. Ethically, TRSs are responsible to do no harm to clients, respect their autonomy, be fair in allocation of resources, and be knowledgeable and competent in providing services. Clients have the right to refuse treatment. The TRS should discuss with clients the options available and respect their choices. As professionals we are guided by our expert knowledge and by the therapeutic relationship we have developed with clients in determining appropriate outcomes for them, which leads to the next approach.

OUTCOME-ORIENTED PROGRAMMING

Outcomes are the "immediate, specific results of an intervention program" (Ross & Ashton-Shaeffer, 2003, p. 127). They are a major concern in health care, human services, education, government, business, and other social institutions. The main impetus for the outcomes movement has been the need to control costs of services, as well as to ensure that money is being spent wisely to yield tangible and meaningful results. Putting an emphasis on the outcomes of services should lead to improved programs, better decisions about resource allocation, and higher staff morale as they see more concrete and worthwhile results from their efforts. In TR programming, outcomes are the "measurable change in clients' health status or well-being after receiving TR intervention" (Riley, 1991, p. 59). Identification of the outcomes of a TR program should rest on evidence-based practice and judgment-based practice of care. It is the professional responsibility of TRSs to know which outcomes are valued in their agencies and by their clients, and to adopt a TR practice model that reflects these outcomes.

To design programs that will lead to desired outcomes for clients, TRSs can examine the **outcome-oriented programming (OOP)** approach. Outcome-oriented programming involves designing programs to produce measurable, relevant, and meaningful client outcomes (Stumbo, 1996).

It characterizes TR programs as either Type I or Type II.

Type I programs, also known as *cafeteria programs*, are typically for large groups; all clients receive the same program without a focus on individual goals. There is little expectation of a measurable behavior change. Type I programs, typically less structured, offer participants a diversional experience with the benefits of socialization, relaxation, and entertainment. They have a place in many long-term care settings, such as nursing homes, adult day care, and group homes, as part of the fabric of daily life. They are also found in short-term settings, such as a physical rehabilitation or psychiatric unit, as a relief from clinical interventions, a place to practice new skills, or a means to enjoy recreation. Activities such as movies, sing-alongs, parties, or large-group games such as bingo may fall into this category.

Type II programs, on the other hand, are therapeutic because they are based on an assessment, specify individual goals for the clients, and represent a meaningful and appropriate placement for a client that is designed to produce measurable outcomes. Type II programs are offered in small groups or on a one-to-one basis to help the client work toward achieving his goals. Type II programs can include arts and crafts, cooking, stress management, leisure education, physical fitness, games, or any of the myriad TR activities. For example, to increase attention span and concentration, appropriate choices could be arts and crafts, table games, or cooking based on the assessment of the client and the evidence reviewed by the TRS in developing the individual plan. The TRS provides TR leadership to guide the client toward the desired behavioral changes, which can include acquiring new information, learning new skills, or increasing the ability to function in a particular behavioral domain. It is *how* the TRS plans and conducts the activity that helps the client reach his goals.

There are seven characteristics of outcome-oriented, or Type II, programs (Stumbo, 1996). These programs

- are systematically designed prior to implementation,
- are part of a larger system of programming,
- are individualized based on client needs,

Group card games, which focus on diversion rather than behavior change, are an example of a Type I program.

Bananastock

- have relevance to the client (are crucial to his future),
- have importance to the client (relate to his lifestyle),
- have timeliness to the client (are scheduled for effective use of time available to produce the specified outcome), and
- are able to produce the desired results (the specified outcomes).

The seven characteristics of OOP embody principles of sound program planning. They direct the TRS to help the client achieve real results in the context of what is meaningful, significant, and realistic in his life. Emphasis should be placed particularly on TR programs that focus "on outcomes valuable to individuals with disabilities" (Wilhite, Hodges & Peebles, 2003, p. 87). This reflects the ethical principles of autonomy, competence, protecting the well-being of clients, and cooperating with other professionals to provide the most effective services. To produce meaningful outcomes necessitates an approach consistent with the work of other professionals who are helping the client. By identifying specific, concrete, and measurable goals or outcomes for the client, as part of a team effort when appropriate, we can select and implement TR programs that are expected to achieve these results. Although outcome-oriented programming is part of the larger context of services for the client, the TRS should keep in mind that there may be times when TR goals and team goals differ, even to the point of conflicting with each other.

Conflicting Goals

A TRS working in a group home, in collaboration with an adult client who has an intellectual disability, sets a goal for the client to become a member of a community softball league. The group home treatment team believes that the client should join Special Olympics. These differing goals reflect views on the client's abilities as well as differing philosophical perspectives. Which goal reflects the characteristics of OOP? How could the TRS and the team resolve the difference?

Length of stay represents a significant challenge in providing OOP. Diversional programming can easily become the norm in facilities with a very short length of stay, where it may seem that there is not enough time to achieve specific, measurable changes. On the other hand, in settings with long-term or even permanent placement, it may seem that the client is not in a treatment-oriented setting but rather a living environment. However, in both types of settings it is possible to work on meaningful goals. To achieve these goals, it is imperative for the TR profession, as for any health care profession, to ask, "What changes can my professional practice reasonably be expected to produce in a given period of time?"

To answer this question, the TRS relies on the evidence-based practice approach, structures services as active treatment, and delivers OOP. For example, in an acute psychiatric unit with a four-day length of stay, the TRS consulted the evidence on what TR interventions would best meet the assessed needs of clients. The clients typically suffered from depression, stress, and social isolation. The TRS determined that he could best meet their needs with a program in which each client would learn how to use one stress management technique such as alternate nostril breathing or meditation, engage in walking to improve mood, and identify one community resource for physical activity and socialization. At the end of their stay, all the clients were able to demonstrate how to manage their stress and state the resource and contact information for a community facility. The answer to the question about reasonable expectations influences what interventions are selected to address the specific problems and functional limitations of the clients in a given setting. In the example of the client who wished to join a community softball team, the length of time available to help her achieve her goal would certainly determine how realistic it would be to achieve the goal. The TRS would have to adjust the plan to help the client move closer to the goal, but the goal might not be fully realized within the amount of time available for services.

SUMMARY OF CLINICALLY ORIENTED MODELS

These first three models are clinical approaches in that they are reflective of TR clinical practice. In planning, these models are not mutually exclusive but interrelated. The TRS will apply the principles and methods of all three clinical models in designing services by using evidence to provide active treatment within outcome-oriented programs. The two types of outcomes addressed by TR are

Understanding Outcomes and Benefits

A client may be prescribed an outdoor group walking program to improve cardiovascular endurance, a functional outcome. Another client may work out in the gym to achieve the same outcome. Why have we chosen two different paths to the same outcome? For the first client, social support and being outdoors may be important benefits that he needs or desires and that may serve as motivating forces to encourage his participation. For the client in the gym, those benefits may be less crucial as she prefers to focus and concentrate on her workout. She may benefit from improved self-esteem or body image as she watches herself in the mirror. Even if the client in the walking program does not make a measurable improvement in cardiovascular functioning, he may experience the benefits of improved mood and increased motivation to continue his treatment due to the socialization, group support, and enjoyment of the natural environment. He may continue walking for the pleasure and enjoyment it gives him. The client in the gym may benefit from feeling better about herself and her ability to concentrate on something that matters to her. It's possible that an individual may not even recognize the benefits experienced until a later time.

We will use the case of Mrs. Green to illustrate the relationship between existential outcomes and benefits. Mrs. Green was diagnosed with multiple sclerosis at the age of 40. She continued in her job as a health professional until age 50, when the MS progressed to the point that she was unable to work. She uses a wheelchair for mobility and is able to use a computer with adaptive devices. Her goal, as expressed to the TRS, was to find purpose in her life, which is an existential outcome. In discussion with the TRS, she came up with the idea of starting and facilitating a support group for people with MS and their families. This fulfilled her goal as she was able to continue making a contribution to the lives of other people. She also obtained benefits from her participation in the support group, where she met families with children, like her own, and was able to expand her social network. Although these benefits weren't her primary motives in starting the support group, they were valued by Mrs. Green.

functional and existential. Functional outcomes are directed toward improving aspects of health and functional abilities; existential outcomes center on achieving meaning in one's life and developing or reinforcing one's identity. Therapeutic recreation also offers the potential for clients to experience the benefits of recreation that come from participating in TR programs. Whether or not a client is successful in attaining an outcome, he can experience the benefits of recreation and may choose to continue participating in a meaningful activity because of these benefits.

The essence of the TR leadership role is that the TRS engages clients in activities that can produce both the specific outcomes of a therapeutic intervention and the benefits of participating in recreation. The TRS creates individual TR plans that are both outcome oriented and benefits based. The TR professional needs to understand how participating in different recreation activities can produce various outcomes and to consider the potential benefits a person might derive from these activities. Thera-

peutic recreation also serves *all* clients, even those who do not have "rehabilitation potential," such as individuals with profound mental retardation, some forms of schizophrenia, advanced Alzheimer's disease, or terminal illness. These individuals may not be seen as candidates for outcome-oriented treatment, and spiritual or existential outcomes may represent their most realistic and meaningful goals. They may also be able to experience the benefits of recreation.

Personal Growth Approaches

The remaining five approaches emphasize the importance of personal growth and autonomy in client services. These approaches are benefits-based programming, person-centered planning, the strengths-based approach, continuity of lifestyle, and inclusion. These approaches are based on the existential value of emphasizing what is meaningful in life and contributes to a sense of one's identity. Understanding these concepts, which are at the heart of TR practice, is vital to carrying out the TR process.

BENEFITS-BASED PROGRAMMING

Benefits-based programming (BBP) was developed in the early 1990s to communicate to the public that recreation services could be a significant component of a community approach to addressing specific social problems and enhancing community life (Rossman & Schlatter, 2000). The professional leadership in the recreation field believed that the public was not aware of the valuable benefits that recreation services could provide to the overall community. Recreation departments were encouraged to specify the benefits of recreation participation in their mission statements and to emphasize the goals that recreation services are designed to achieve. The TR profession as well recognized the usefulness of the benefits-based approach for conveying what TR can contribute to client services. Therapeutic recreation can utilize the BBP approach to identify the benefits and outcomes of recreation experiences, as well as to link the outcomes of participation in a given activity to the outcomes the client is trying to attain. Several authors have identified categories of benefits that can result from TR program participation. These categories include physical health, cognitive functioning, life satisfaction, benefits to caregivers, prevention of a worsening condition, and growth and personal development (Ross & Ashton-Shaeffer, 2003). Essential to implementing BBP is maintaining a cross-cultural perspective. When the TRS is identifying the array of benefits of TR programs, it is important for her to consider that people's culture, religion, and ethnicity can influence which benefits they value (Dieser, Magnuson & Scholl, 2005) and to plan accordingly.

To incorporate the benefits approach in TR programming, TR agencies and departments in the United States can look to *Healthy People 2010*, the comprehensive, nationwide health promotion and disease prevention agenda, for direction in formulating missions and goals relevant to contemporary efforts to promote a healthier society. *Healthy People 2010* presents 28 focus areas related to different health conditions. Of these, four have been identified as of particular interest to TR: disability and secondary conditions, physical activity and fitness, educational and community-based programs, and substance abuse (Howard, Russoniello & Rodgers,

Photo courtesy of Isabella Geriatric Center.

Intergenerational programming can offer clients such benefits as natural interaction between the generations, as well as opportunities for older adults to nurture children and for children to learn from and appreciate the older generation.

2004). Specific objectives under disability and secondary conditions include reducing the number of people with disability who report being depressed and increasing the proportion of people with disabilities who participate in social activities, receive sufficient emotional support, and report life satisfaction (Sable & Bocarro, 2004). These objectives are identical to the benefits clients can obtain from participation in TR programs. Ethically, BBP reflects the principles of being knowledgeable about our clients and TR activities, doing good for clients, increasing the body of knowledge of the profession, and serving society.

When working within an agency, the TRS has a general understanding of the needs and problems of the population being served. She applies this information to the selection of a set of programs and interventions that can address the clients' issues. Knowledge of the benefits of recreation activities helps the TRS to select TR programs that have the potential to produce the desired outcome for the individual. Therefore, participation in a recreation activity can provide benefits to participants that can assist them in achieving their particular outcomes. Benefits of programs can also be used to motivate individuals to participate. Benefits-based programming teaches professionals to promote the benefits gained from participating in programs, rather than promoting the activity itself. Most clients have not participated in the range or variety of recreation activities they may be exposed to in a TR program. This lack of experience or familiarity may be a barrier to their involvement.

A specific activity may not sound appealing to a client, but if the TRS connects the activity to the benefits a client is seeking, this may motivate him to try the activity. For example, a middle-aged, single man admitted to the hospital for a heart attack is placed on the cardiac rehabilitation unit. He is willing and eager to participate in the exercise and physical fitness activities in the TR program because he believes they will help him recover from his heart attack and achieve his functional outcome of improving cardiovascular functioning. However, he does not see how the cooking group is relevant to his needs because he eats out every day with friends and is not interested in learning how to cook. The TRS explains the benefits of the cooking group—that he will learn how to make healthier choices in restaurants and request healthier meal preparation techniques from the chef in the company of the other patients. These are benefits that have meaning to him because they relate to his lifestyle. After he participates in the cooking group, he has learned how to cook and enjoys the social atmosphere of preparing a meal with others. This encourages him to plan to invite his friends over to his home for a monthly dinner that they will prepare together. He has gained more control over what he eats, which helps him feel more relaxed and promotes his health. Therefore, in addition to achieving his outcome related to cardiovascular health, he has derived additional benefits that support an overall healthier and more satisfying lifestyle. Understanding the lifestyle of the client is an essential component of the next approach.

PERSON-CENTERED PLANNING

Person-centered planning (PCP) is a process whereby persons with disabilities, with the support of families, direct the planning and allocation of resources to meet their own life visions and goals (Indiana Family and Social Services Administration, n.d.). Rather than designing services and programs based on "What services do we have to offer this client?" PCP shifts the focus to "What can we do, together, to help this individual achieve his goals?" Person-centered planning emphasizes collaboration among the individual, his family, friends, service providers, and other members of his support network. Collaboration requires that the family and professionals listen to the individual, encourage his desires, and identify and support what really matters to him. Ideally, the individual directs the

services and the allocation of resources to help meet his goals.

Therapeutic recreation has a tradition of placing the individual at the center of services; PCP goes further in that the individual is empowered by the network of supporters to be the prime motivator in determining his future, vision, goals, support and services (Indiana Family and Social Services Administration, n.d.). Person-centered planning is also grounded in quality of life, one of the four core TR values. Quality of life is the individual's subjective assessment of how he feels and what is important to him. Quality of life is dependent, in part, on self-determination or autonomy, another core TR value. Self-determination means that the individual has the degree of control he wants over the events and activities in his life and that he makes choices and decisions free from undue external influence or interference (Dattilo & Klieber, 2002). The ability to act on these decisions gives the individual a feeling of control over his environment, leading to psychological empowerment (Bullock & Mahon, 2000). The concept of self-determination has become very influential in services for people with developmental disabilities and chronic psychiatric conditions who are living with their disability long-term. For these individuals, self-determination and inclusion have become primary goals. Person-centered planning places self-determination and inclusion at the heart of its process.

In planning TR services, the PCP approach provides many guidelines for the TRS. Person-centered planning emphasizes getting to know a person and her needs, goals, and dreams from her own perspective (Garner & Dietz, 1996). During the assessment process, the TRS should take the time to listen and understand the individual. Her likes and dislikes, decision-making processes, and perception of her own strengths are vital to providing successful services. The client's autonomy and informed choices should influence the planning stage. However, "clients are not always clear about what they want, especially if they are not accustomed to envisioning possibilities due to a cycle of dependency; or if they are experiencing the shock of crisis" (Murray, 2003, p. 235). Therefore, the TRS should collaborate with the client in an exploration of her experiences, desire for change, and personal goals. As the client becomes more aware and more able to share her ideas, programs can be developed that build on her strengths, utilize and develop her network of community supports, and acknowledge and incorporate her cultural background. The TRS should also work with the support network and the individual to design programs based on her preferences that can help her achieve her own goals. Programming is an ongoing, dynamic process that requires continuous review and evaluation. If problems or obstacles arise, solutions need to be discussed with the client to ensure that they are consistent with her needs and desires. As people age, their circumstances, functioning, developmental needs, and personal interests often change and will require modifications and adjustments to the programs. Even as the individual staff members change jobs, the ethical commitment of the professional to the client is to carry on the PCP approach with respect for her autonomy, treating her fairly in cooperation with other professionals and advocating for her right to recreation and leisure opportunities.

The case of Bradley, a 55-year-old man with autism, demonstrates a successful application of PCP (Hodges, Luken & Hubbard, 2004). On the basis of Bradley's repeated statements of his desire to retire from a vocational workshop, he was referred to the TRS. He collaborated with the TRS to develop a transition plan to meet his retirement goal of "doing nothing." However, regulations governing his services and living arrangements required him to be out of his residence for 6 hours per day. The challenge to the TRS was to respect his wishes within the restrictions imposed by the regulatory agency. Once this was explained to Bradley, he agreed to learn more about opportunities to pursue in retirement, including volunteering and attending senior centers; he then selected several of these to explore. At every step of the process, the TRS and Bradley worked together. Bradley also participated in all team meetings that dealt with his services. Even a new friend that he made at a senior center was invited to participate in one of the team meetings. After one year, Bradley was able to set the agenda for and lead his own team meetings. At the end of three years, he expressed a change in his concept of retirement from "not working" to "starting something new."

STRENGTHS-BASED APPROACH

The **strengths-based approach** (SBA) represents a shift in service provision from focusing on the problems, deficits, or disorders of clients to emphasizing the strengths, resources, and capabilities of clients, their families, and communities. Viewing clients as competent participants in the planning process increases their feelings of control over their lives. Perceived control is a major factor in life satisfaction. As with PCP, in the SBA the capacities, competencies, and resources that exist within and outside the individual, the family, and the environment are foremost in planning. The professional helps clients identify abilities they possess that may not be obvious even to themselves or their families (Fast & Chapin, 2000). This approach has been used in mental health and in family services, as well as in work with children, older adults, and people with developmental disabilities to increase their capacity to achieve goals. Efforts are concentrated on assisting the client to identify, obtain, and sustain personal and environmental resources for successful living, working, and playing in the community (Fabry, 2002). In TR, the TRS can create situations in which clients can use their abilities and strengths to achieve personal goals, because change occurs when the TRS collaborates with the individual. The SBA also has a connection to **positive psychology**, which is based on helping individuals, families, and societies not merely cope, but thrive. Magnifying strengths rather than fixating on weaknesses can alleviate anxiety and depression and promote physical health. In positive psychology, as in SBA, treatment focuses on developing constructive and life-enhancing feelings and behaviors (Carruthers & Hood, 2004).

The SBA, along with positive psychology, has powerful implications for TR programming. The implications of positive psychology for TR practice were described in an article in the *Therapeutic Recreation Journal* (Carruthers & Hood, 2004). According to the authors, positive psychology strategies—avoidance of habituation, active engagement, increasing the number of pleasant events in daily life, and focusing attention on the pleasurable aspects of experience—are relevant to TR services. Clients improve their health and well-being when they

1. break patterns of behavior that are not satisfying or productive,
2. actively participate in social and physical activities to enhance positive mood,
3. maximize positive experiences in daily life that bring pleasure, and
4. reflect on the positive and pleasurable aspects of an experience.

Therapeutic recreation programs can maximize clients' health and well-being by including opportunities to try a large variety of recreation activities; socialize with others; engage in physical activity; experience relaxation; and discuss, reminisce about, and journal about the experience and effects of participation. Individuals also deserve the chance

TABLE 3.2

Therapeutic Recreation Applications of Positive Psychology Strategies

Positive psychology strategies	TR applications
Break patterns of behavior that are not satisfying or productive.	Provide opportunities to try a large variety of recreation activities.
Actively participate in social and physical activities to enhance mood.	Schedule activities that promote social interaction and physical movement.
Maximize experiences in daily life that bring pleasure.	Support efforts to engage in preferred recreation activities that are fun, enjoyable, and relaxing. Establish volunteer and mentoring programs. Assist in creating daily plans that have opportunities for positive engagement.
Reflect on the positive and pleasurable aspects of an experience.	Provide opportunities to reflect, reminisce, and journal about the effects of participating in different activities. Encourage identification of personal benefits derived from recreation participation.

to lead a meaningful life by making a contribution to others, the community, or the world through volunteerism, mentoring, and creative activities (Carruthers & Hood, 2004). See table 3.2 for TR applications of positive psychology strategies.

An example of applying the SBA involves a 15-year-old Latino teenager referred to the TRS because of disruptive behavior in school and truancy (Sklar & Autry, 2008). The CTRS identified the teen's strengths as enjoying sports, being outdoors, working with his hands, and helping others. She helped him enroll in the Latino Teen Corps, whose members engaged in community service projects; and he became an Environmental Ambassador, volunteering with agencies on conservation projects. This demonstrates a TR plan based on the client's preferences that the TRS helped him to identify; it incorporated local community resources and resulted in the client changing negative patterns of behavior through becoming engaged in positive and satisfying activities. This example shows that a client can use his strengths to accomplish an activity or task and then build on those strengths to add on a new task that requires additional learning. The SBA encourages the TRS to create situations in which clients can use their abilities to achieve personal goals.

The person-centered and strengths-based approaches and positive psychology all emphasize the value of striving to attain personally meaningful goals. In the assessment and planning phases of the TR process, the TRS should help the client identify her strengths, what she desires to change, and what successful experiences she has had at making change in her life (Murray, 2003). In addition the TRS

should involve the family and significant others, look at the whole person, and focus on participation in inclusive lifelong leisure as a goal (Anderson & Heyne, 2007). The SBA embodies the ethical principles of autonomy, nonmaleficence, cooperation with others, service, and advocacy.

CONTINUITY OF LIFESTYLE

Another approach that emphasizes the lifestyle of the client incorporates the concept known as **continuity of lifestyle** (COL). Continuity of lifestyle can be defined as "sameness within change" (Bergland & Narum, 2007, p. 39), and refers to helping individuals maintain consistency in their lives by continuing activities and behaviors they engaged in prior to a major change in their life. This concept has been applied to long-term care, assisted living, children of divorce, and persons with autism. (For the latter, COL is not necessarily advocated because of major changes in a person's life, but with the idea of minimizing the disruptions caused by even a minor change.) Continuity of lifestyle reflects the shift in health care settings from a medical to a more social model of care, based on measures of well-being, belonging, comfort, and satisfaction with daily life.

These characteristics of quality of life are highly valued by older adults in transition from one living situation to another. In long-term care, there is a mandate to "see the person in the patient" by recognizing that each resident had a personal identity and a history prior to entering long-term care and has one beyond the medical diagnosis. This affects program planning because activities must be person appropriate rather than age appropriate, as well as relevant to the resident's culture and religion, particularly as the long-term care population has diversified. For community-dwelling elderly moving from their own home to assisted living, for individuals with developmental disabilities moving away from their parents into a group home, and for a woman and her children relocating after a stressful divorce, COL guides service providers to help integrate these clients into their new neighborhoods. This strengthens a diverse community, fosters independence, and eases challenging transitions. Continuation of familiar leisure interests and participation in desired activities can help maintain a COL, strengthen one's identity, and enhance quality of life.

In carrying out the TR process, the TRS needs to thoroughly understand the client's prior lifestyle and interests and design a plan that incorporates these activities and the client's values as much as possible. Connecting clients to others who share interests and similar experiences can promote feelings of comfort and well-being. Creating an environment that includes familiar characteristics, decor, and objects promotes a sense of continuity. In long-term care, the emphasis on culture change reinforces the COL concept by empowering residents to make decisions regarding what to wear, when to get out of bed, when and what to eat, and what they want to do, which makes the facility more like a home. A resident in long-term care who throughout her adulthood read the daily newspaper over a cup or two of coffee was invited by the TRS to attend a current events group. Although the resident enjoyed *reading* the news, she did not enjoy discussing it with others. The TRS respected her choice of not attending the group, as this was consistent with her preferred lifestyle. In the same nursing home, a number of residents were retired entertainers who were used to working until after midnight and then having a late-night meal. To continue their lifestyle, the TRS programmed activities from 9 to 11 p.m.

For individuals who experience a catastrophic change, such as a traumatic brain injury, stroke, spinal cord injury, or loss of limb, the principles of the COL approach guide TRSs to provide the following as needed:

- Adaptations in the home environment
- Adaptive equipment
- Information on accessibility to desired activities including transportation
- Support and guidance to family members so they can maintain the integrity and normalcy of the family unit

These services can provide comfort and promote satisfaction with aspects of daily life. Ethically, COL reflects beneficence, competence, respect for persons, and cooperation with other professionals in the planning of services.

INCLUSION APPROACH

The final approach to program planning is the **inclusion approach**. Inclusion has been viewed as a philosophy, a goal, and a process. It also can be applied as an approach to program planning. For clients with physical and developmental disabilities, inclusion has been viewed as essential to their attaining quality of life. In addition, inclusion has been discussed as having benefits for *all* members of a community. The National Recreation and Park Association (NRPA) position statement on inclusion (1999) emphasizes the potential of inclusion to enhance the quality of life for all people, to promote their growth and development, to foster relationships, and to develop a supportive community. The four inclusion concepts (NRPA, 1999) are as follows:

- Right to leisure for all individuals
- Quality of life enhanced through leisure experiences
- Support, assistance, and accommodation
- Removal of barriers to participation in all recreation and leisure services

The implications of the inclusion concept are that the client exercises his self-determination to live in the environment of his choice, according to its norms and standards of behavior, and to participate in the activities he desires. For the TRS, the implications are that the client's goal is to live in the most inclusive environment possible and that all TR programs are geared toward helping the client achieve that goal. Inclusion as a goal has typically been discussed in relation to individuals with developmental and physical disabilities; however, recognition is increasing that it is applicable to those with chronic mental illness (Hebblethwaite & Pedlar, 2005), people who are homeless (Klitzing, 2004), or people who are returning to their community from a period of incarceration (Pedlar, Yuen & Fortune, 2008), as well as anyone else who may be a recipient of TR services. Inclusive communities give rise to feelings of safety, familiarity, acceptance, and identity among their members (Dattilo & Guerin, 2001). Inclusion implies interdependence among community members, who share responsibilities and help one another. Inclusion can be seen as the final point along a **continuum** of services and settings. The continuum moves from complete segregation of people with disabilities, to physical integration of people with disabilities into settings with people who do not have disabilities, to social integration and interaction among people with and without disabilities, to the recognition that all are members of the same community and can offer friendship and support to one another.

More and more, inclusion is becoming a goal of TR programming in almost any setting. However, barriers to inclusion exist; the TRS's role is to assist in minimizing and removing the barriers. Barriers are both internal, related to the individual's functioning, and external, related to the environment (Sylvester et al., 2001). Internal barriers include skill limitations, dependence, health and fitness limitations, and lack of knowledge. External barriers include financial constraints, lack of qualified staff, lack of transportation, inaccessible facilities, poor communication supports, ineffective service systems, and—the most powerful—negative attitudes. Practices that overcome barriers and promote inclusion have been identified as both administrative and programmatic (Carter et al., 2004). Administrative practices that the TRS can cultivate to facilitate inclusion include the following:

- Having inclusive agency mission and goal statements
- Hiring qualified professionals
- Collaborative planning
- Advocacy
- Marketing to reach all people
- Staff and instructor training
- Transportation assistance
- Relocation to accessible facilities
- Documentation of outcomes

Helping community agencies and organizations implement these administrative practices reflects the core TR principle of ecological perspective by targeting the environment for needed changes. Communities can become more inclusive as a result of the intervention of the TRS.

Programmatic practices to address the internal barriers to inclusion include using equipment adaptations, assistive devices, task analysis, peer partners, behavioral techniques, and skill-level programming. Social contact that is deep, genuine, and intimate also can influence inclusion efforts positively (Devine & O'Brien, 2007). One way to foster quality social contact is to ask individuals with disabilities to explain their conditions to others who are encouraged to ask questions so they can learn more. Visit the Web site www.justcallmegeri .com to get to know one individual who is happy to share her personal experiences with others to promote understanding and inclusion. Keep in mind, however, that not all individuals with disabilities are willing or able to explain their conditions to others, nor are they obligated to do so. The TRS can structure recreation situations so that all participants interact and get to know one another, have the opportunity to contribute their strengths and skills and assist one another, and are on a "level playing field" in which universal design features ensure that facilities and environments are usable by all.

As has been mentioned, inclusion is a process as well as a goal. It may be appropriate for individuals with severe disabilities to begin certain activities in a segregated environment. This may pose an ethical dilemma, as there are varying philosophical positions on the need for separate programming. One view is that some individuals could more successfully learn the skills needed for participation in preferred environments in segregated settings. However, according to the inclusion approach, this should occur only to the minimal extent needed for the client to develop the skills and obtain the supports to achieve the goal of full inclusion. An example of this approach is *Project FreshenUp: Fitness and Recreation Enrich Student Health, Education and Nutrition Using Play. FreshenUp* was based on a theory that youth with disabilities who developed healthy fitness and recreation skills for ongoing participation would more successfully transition from high school to success in the workplace. As designed and implemented by one of the authors, *FreshenUp* engaged high school students with disabilities in a therapeutic recreation, sports, and fitness program in a university fitness and athletic complex open to the public. One of the goals of *FreshenUp* was for the students to improve their social behaviors in order to be able to successfully participate in typical community recreation environments. To reach this goal, college student buddies conducted an assessment of and designed a plan for their teenage buddies, under the supervision of a CTRS. They also provided quality social contact; used task analysis, and appropriate activity and equipment adaptations and teaching strategies as needed; and participated together in fitness, group recreation, and sports programming.

FreshenUp offered physical integration in a community setting, skill instruction in preferred activities, formal or structured social integration with trained buddies, and informal or unstructured social integration including casual interaction with members of the public. Feedback from participants and their parents indicated that the teens increased their self-confidence and expanded their knowledge of recreation activities for continued participation, of fitness practices, and of healthy snacks. Staff reported observations that the teens learned how to successfully manage the social and behavioral demands of participating in a community facility. If the teens subsequently choose to become members of this or another community facility on their own and actively participate with peers, they will have achieved full inclusion. Clients' preferred environments and activities may change over time as their needs, interests, and abilities change. The inclusion approach reflects the cyclic TR practice models, which recognize that as clients change over time, so will their goals and services.

SUMMARY OF PERSONAL GROWTH APPROACHES

These last five approaches, BBP, PCP, SBA, COL, and inclusion, with their emphasis on personal growth and autonomy, may lead to ethical dilemmas. Clients' choices may conflict with the TRS's professional and personal values. Clients may choose to continue unhealthy behaviors such as ignoring dietary restrictions, smoking cigarettes, and maintaining a sedentary lifestyle. The TRS may try to help the client change, but if the client is not willing, this raises ethical issues of client self-determination, who judges what is best for the client, and how to promote clients' well-being. Clients may view pornography, use ethnic slurs, or gamble. These behaviors may conflict with the TRS's personal beliefs about what is moral behavior. Should she share her views with the client or report these behaviors to the staff? This raises issues related to the ethical principles of privacy, autonomy, and honesty. A client's family may prefer to keep him in segregated programming, fearing that he could not succeed or would be rejected in an inclusive environment. Whose wishes prevail? In placing the client at the center of services, the TRS must continually use the codes of ethics as her guide.

Summary of the Eight Approaches to Programming

The eight approaches to programming have relevance for the planning and delivery of TR services.

Each approach influences at least several of the steps in the TR process. The TRS can apply

- evidence-based practice to select interventions based on research findings combined with professional expertise;

Photo courtesy of Helen R. Muller.

Nettie found that ceramics programming encouraged her personal growth and autonomy.

- active treatment to plan the duration, frequency, and intensity of the intervention;
- outcome-oriented programming to designate outcomes for the client that are meaningful, relevant, and realistic;
- benefits-based programming to understand the benefits that clients seek from activities and to explain to clients the benefits of the activities included in the plan;
- person-centered planning to position the individual at the center of the planning process;
- the strengths-based approach to build on and reinforce the client's strengths;
- the continuity of lifestyle concept to understand who the client was before the TRS met him and his interests, habits, and patterns, as well as to plan activities that reinforce his lifestyle; and
- inclusion as a process and a goal in order to promote the client's abilities and opportunities to live in the environment and engage in the activities of his choice and in order to assist the community in overcoming barriers to inclusion.

No matter what TR practice model is followed, these eight approaches guide the development of the TR plan and place TR services firmly in the arena of current practice.

STANDARDS OF PRACTICE

The TRS follows the laws and regulations that govern TR services, the codes of ethics of the profession, and the TR standards of practice. Internal **standards of practice** are established by a profession to describe its scope of services, a minimum acceptable level for delivery of the services, and specific procedures of the profession. The standards include a mandate for a written plan of operations with policies and procedures for the operation of a department, a description of personnel qualifications, and a commitment to conducting research and adhering to a code of ethics. Both ATRA and NTRS have developed standards of practice for TR. ATRA has established 12 standards, and NTRS has established eight. Both ATRA and NTRS have standards that relate to the TR process: ATRA has six, and NTRS has three. Much as with the codes of ethics, a TRS may follow one or the other set of standards, but both cover the essential aspects of TR services and serve as a benchmark for what constitutes a quality TR department. Both sets have standards for planning TR services that include developing a plan for the client based on an assessment of the client's behaviors. The plan should

- include the client's past interests and functioning;
- be developed with the client and his family or significant others (or both);
- contain measurable goals, objectives, and interventions; and
- be consistent with the overall agency plan for the client.

According to the standards, the client is to be provided with a schedule of available TR services. The TRS is responsible for evaluating the client's progress and revising the plan if needed. The TRS documents the client's progress and reactions to TR participation and is a member of the team of professionals in the agency. The TRS also develops a discharge or transition plan. As we examine the TR process, you will see how it reflects the standards for practice.

THE TR PROCESS

The **therapeutic recreation process** is dynamic; it reflects the contemporary issues and approaches that affect all disciplines at any point in time. The four steps in the TR process are assessment, planning, implementation, and evaluation. This four-step planning process is not unique to TR. It is carried out in similar fashion by most health care and human services professionals who provide individualized services. To effectively carry out the TR process, the TRS builds a therapeutic relationship with the client; possesses self-awareness and genuineness, empathy, and respect for the client; concentrates on the client's strengths; and allows the client as much control as possible (Austin, 2001).

Assessment

Assessment can be defined as "a systematic process of gathering and synthesizing information about the client and his or her environment using a variety of methods, including interviews, observation, standardized tests, and input from other disciplines and significant others, in order to devise an individualized treatment or service plan" (Stavola Daly & Kunstler, 2006, p. 188). This information forms the foundation of the individual TR plan and provides a baseline of the client's functioning and status prior to intervention, which can be used to measure progress toward the desired outcomes.

There are guidelines and regulations that require assessments to be done in a specific period of time and to cover particular topics, which vary from agency to agency, depending on the oversight authority. In long-term care, an initial assessment must be conducted within 14 days of admission. In a psychiatric unit, the assessment must be completed within 48 hours of admission. This information should be part of every TRS's orientation and included in the policy and procedure manual of the TR department. The TRS will obtain the specific regulations that affect TR services from her agency administrator or department head.

Regardless of the setting or specific components of the assessment, TR assessment should adhere to the following guidelines, which reflect person-centeredness, inclusion, and self-determination (Bullock & Mahon, 2000):

- Seek as much input as possible from the individual.
- Assess strengths, abilities, and desires as well as deficits and needs.
- Assess the physical and human environment as well as the individual's skills and needs.
- Remain focused upon the individual's goals and how he would like them to function in his life.

To conduct a meaningful assessment, the TR department should develop an **assessment proto-**

col, which indicates the type of assessment methods to be used, such as standardized tests, questionnaires, and interview questions; areas for observation and general guidelines for carrying out the assessment procedures; and the assessment toolkit. The assessment protocol should reflect the mission and purposes of the agency and the TR practice model followed by the department. In selecting the assessment procedures, the TR staff must

consider the amount of time needed to administer them and determine if a procedure is realistic and reasonable in the context of the work setting. The TRS should not collect information that duplicates what is readily available in the client's record or from other disciplines. It is essential that the TRS have the skills to conduct the assessment, which fall within the scope of TR practice. Assessments are conducted on clients at times of change in their

Assessment Toolkit

The TRS should assemble an assessment toolkit of items and objects with which the client can interact in order to obtain an accurate understanding of the client's capabilities and functional limitations.

Assessing Skills Using Toolkit Items

- **Fine motor skills:** Use pens, crayons, scissors, paper, books or magazines, dice, deck of cards, small balls, toys (for children), pictures or photographs, cell phone.

    Can the client pick up the objects from the tabletop, take them and pass them to the TRS, hold them in a usable manner, handle and use them correctly?

- **Gross motor skills:** Use balls, light hand weights, Ping-Pong paddle.

    Can the client pick up the objects, demonstrate range of motion in the arms to reach and swing, pass the objects to the TRS?

- **Cognitive skills:** Use reading material, paper-and-pencil games, puzzles, pictures.

    What level of reading material can the client read, comprehend, explain, and discuss?

    Can the client solve puzzles and games and follow directions?

    Can the client make a choice when given a set of options?

    Can the client identify objects or people in pictures or photos?

- **Social skills:** Use silverware and napkins, snack food, beverage, cell phone.

    Does the client demonstrate proper use of utensils and good manners?

    Does the client know how to open food and drink packages and dispose of them properly?

    Are eating habits socially acceptable?

    Can the client use a cell phone to make and receive a call?

- **Affective skills:** Use cartoons, joke books, pictures of people.

    Does the client respond appropriately to humor?

    Can the client accurately identify emotions expressed by people in the pictures?

- **Leisure skills:** Lists and pictures of recreation activities, portable media player, CD player, laptop, age-appropriate games.

    Can the client identify the activities in words or pictures?

    Can the client indicate past and present likes and dislikes and potential future interests?

    Does the client demonstrate a broad range of knowledge and interests in activities?

    Can the client use electronic equipment?

    Does client have knowledge of games?

life, whether due to illness, injury, loss, trauma, or relocation. Recognizing what the client is experiencing emotionally reflects the ethic of care. The TRS is obligated to use his skill to put the client at ease and foster an environment that encourages the client to engage in the assessment process. The client may benefit from participating in the assessment insofar as she has a chance to express herself and discuss topics of importance that have not been addressed in other interviews. The client has the right to refuse to answer any questions or to participate in any form of testing.

In order to conduct the assessment, the TRS reviews the sources of assessment information. These include the client herself, her family and significant others, the TRS's observations, observations and input from members of the team, results of standardized tests, and the client's record. The TRS may be required, in accordance with agency policy, to contact the client's family by phone or letter, introducing herself and asking if there is any information they would like to provide regarding the client and his needs, interests, and strengths. The client's record includes demographic information that is valuable in planning the TR program. Factors such as medical and social history, level of education, employment history, family structure, religious observances, voting practices, and area of residence may influence a client's participation in TR. If this information is in the client's record, it is not necessary to ask about it again unless clarification or amplification is needed. In the initial meeting with the client to conduct the assessment, the TRS can utilize more than one method.

The TRS can also bring along an **assessment toolkit**. The assessment toolkit contains simple, everyday objects that the TRS can use during the assessment interview to determine a client's level of ability in different skill areas. While many skills can be assessed by the TRS through conversation and observation, she may find it helpful to use the toolkit to more actively and purposefully engage the client. The TRS asks the client to interact with the objects as necessary to obtain accurate and useful assessment information. The TRS's manner should be respectful, and it is important to put the client at ease. The TRS may want to explain that the purpose of interacting with the objects is to help in determining the client's level of ability and need for assistance or support during TR programs and in setting meaningful goals. Using the full combination of assessment methods helps to provide a comprehensive portrait of who the client is.

THE INTERVIEW

The interview involves face-to-face contact with the client. In conducting the interview, the TRS engages the client in conversation, asking both structured and unstructured questions. Remember, an interview is a conversation, not an interrogation! It can be carried out by "listening to the client's story" (O'Keefe, 2005, p. 78). This does not necessarily mean that the client will talk for a long time, telling her life story; it does mean that she has the right to reveal her perceptions of her health, strengths, needs, and desires and to have these recognized as valid by the professionals caring for her. This truly places the client at the center of her care as she expresses what outcomes and benefits are meaningful to her, and embodies our ethical principles to respect the client's autonomy and to do what is good for the client.

The interview has three purposes (Austin, 2004). First, the interview is the opportunity for the TRS to begin to develop a rapport and therapeutic relationship with the client that will influence the client's participation in TR services. Second, it provides the essential information about the client on which to base the TR plan. Third, the TRS can use the assessment interview to give the client an orientation to what TR is and to the TR services that will be available to her. The TRS should have a guide for what information to gather in a logical order.

A study conducted of TRSs in Canada (Pedlar, Hornibrook & Haasen, 2001) led to the development of an approach to assessment based on the humanistic perspective, one of the core TR principles. The approach includes these elements:

● Listening to the client, empathizing, and "attending," rather than trying to collect as much information as quickly as possible. This demonstrates respect for the client and increases her sense of control.

● Using understandable and straightforward language.

● Being clear about the purpose of your visit and explaining what TR is.

● Using self-disclosure appropriately.

● Taking time to develop a rapport, which may mean not using assessment instruments and tools on the first visit but instead discovering who this person is.

These guidelines will help the TRS conduct the interview in an ethical manner, with respect for the client's dignity and integrity. Ethical practice includes having an interpreter for clients who speak or use a language other than that of the TRS. Children should not be used as interpreters, if at all possible, because this places an undue burden on the child by reversing the roles of parent and child.

The TRS decides on the appropriate place to conduct the interview, either the client's room, the TRS's office, a quiet area used for this purpose, a corner of a day room, or another suitable location that is private, free of interruptions, nonthreatening, and conducive to interaction. The TRS opens the interview by introducing himself, his role, and the purpose of the meeting and makes small talk to put the client at ease. He explains that the interview process protects the client's confidentiality and privacy and that the information will only be shared with other members of the team as appropriate. The TRS may ask the client how she would like to be addressed (e.g., as Mrs. Garcia or Inez). He can then ask if this is a convenient time or if the client would like him to return at another time, state an approximate time for the length of the interview, and make sure the client is comfortable and ready to engage in the interview. If the client does not wish to comply with the interview and the TRS is unable to complete the assessment, he must record this to meet the deadline for completion of the assessment. When a client does not have the language or cognitive skills to either understand the process or provide sufficient information, the TRS uses other methods such as showing the client pictures or objects or interviewing the family to gather their input. Families have extensive information on the client that may not be available from any other source. Yet they also are emotionally involved with their family member, which may color their perspective regarding the client.

Carrying out the interview draws on the skills of the TR leadership role. The TRS uses his communication skills to make the client feel comfortable, facilitates her engagement in the interview, and utilizes a variety of techniques to elicit relevant responses. It is critical that the TRS use language that the client understands. For example, if the TRS asks a client to describe her "leisure lifestyle," she probably does not have an adequate understanding of the concept to give a relevant response. Even the words "recreation" and "leisure" have very different meanings to different people. People's age, experience, and demographic characteristics affect their perceptions of concepts that we take for granted. The TRS should use language that has meaning to the client. For example, we would ask a child about his play, but would not use the word "play" with an

Conducting a client interview calls on the TRS's communication skills.

Human Kinetics/Kelly Huff

elderly person. If a person has a cognitive impairment, we would use simpler language than with an adult who has normal intellectual functioning. The conversational approach makes finding common ground easier. During the interview, the TRS also is making observations of the client's nonverbal behaviors, which may be indicators of her level of comfort or responses to questions.

If the TRS is also giving the client an orientation to the TR program, he may give the client a calendar or schedule of programs that are available, or even a tour. The TRS should also give the client a "two-minute warning" that the interview will soon be over, summarize what has occurred, and ask the client if she has any questions or anything to add or if there is anything else the TRS can help with. The TRS should thank the client and indicate when and where the next TR service will occur.

OBSERVATION

Observation is a method of assessment whereby the TRS views the client and gathers relevant information. Observation for the purpose of assessment is a systematic and structured process that focuses on specific information about the client. This may include physical, cognitive, social, and emotional behaviors; activity skills; and participation patterns. Observations may be done with or without the knowledge of the client; the TRS's ethical responsibility to do no harm and protect the client's rights is of utmost importance. **Formal observations** require the TRS to develop a procedure for the observation that is consistent and is based on accurate identification of what is to be assessed. Developing the ability to accurately observe and record what one is observing is a skill that is vital for reducing the influence of biases that any of us may have. Discussing observations with other staff helps the TRS be sure he has correctly described what he has seen. When the TRS is reporting on observations, whether orally or in writing, his role is to describe what he has observed, not to interpret by suggesting possible reasons for the client's behavior.

During the assessment interview, as well as at all the other times the TRS sees the client prior to writing up the assessment, he is making **casual observations**. These are simply the things we happen to notice and remember from our interactions with a client. However, while casual observation can yield important information, it can be very subjective. For example, a younger TRS may describe a young male client dressed in baggy jeans and an oversized T-shirt as dressed appropriately for his age. An older staff member may call this style of dress "sloppy." Casual observation does not always reveal the context in which the behavior occurs. The TRS should verify information obtained through casual observation with other sources prior to including it in the assessment.

The TRS's observations also can be influenced by other staffpersons' assessments of a client. If we read a client's chart, record, or history prior to meeting her, we may form preconceived notions about that person's abilities and who that person is. If we meet a client without obtaining this background, we may overlook some critical information that will affect our interactions. Each professional has to find the approach that gives him the best foundation on which to build a therapeutic relationship and a viable, worthwhile plan for the client. Professional practice often involves trying different methods and evaluating their effectiveness. The TRS has the ethical responsibility to be competent in his professional practices, treat clients with respect for their autonomy and privacy, and cooperate with other professionals to complete an accurate and honest assessment.

IN-HOUSE AND STANDARDIZED ASSESSMENT TOOLS

Agencies may have their own in-house, multidisciplinary assessment form with sections to be completed by each discipline. The TR section may cover client's interests, activity patterns and skills,

barriers to recreation participation, perceived needs, adaptations, and functional skills in a checklist or an open-ended format. Many TR departments also create their own forms to help them gather information particularly relevant to their own setting. In addition to the areas already mentioned, forms could include relevant demographic information, checklists of activity interests, and skill levels relevant to participation in TR and community activities.

"Homemade" forms are very useful, but may be subjective or yield inaccurate or inconsistent information and should be supplemented by use of valid and reliable **standardized assessment tools** or **instruments**. These tools have been developed and repeatedly tested to ensure that the results are accurate. "The use of tested and standardized instruments is much more likely to provide the kind of valid and reliable client information necessary in today's environment" (Zabriskie, 2003, p. 331). Standardized tools are available that measure functional skills, cognitive status, physical fitness, recreation interests, leisure attitudes, values and behaviors, motivation, self-esteem, and depression. These tools can have various formats—questionnaire, checklist, survey, and open-ended questions. In choosing a standardized instrument, the TRS should determine that it will be helpful in obtaining the type of information that is relevant, and that it is practical to administer given the nature of the setting, the characteristics of the client, and the time available to conduct the assessment.

If the TRS is going to administer or ask the client to fill out an assessment tool, he should explain the purpose and give clear instructions. While use of standardized tools is highly recommended in TR practice, the TRS has the responsibility to ensure that the tools are culturally sensitive. The TR profession is committed to fair and equitable services to all people and advocates for their rights. A culturally sensitive assessment protocol helps to fulfill these ethical obligations. Are the items on the assessment form relevant to the client's background and life experience? Could the questions be interpreted as offensive to someone's beliefs and values? Are the language and format of the assessment battery comprehensible to the client? In addition, clients may be illiterate, or unable to read or write in their own language, and may need the TRS to read the form to them and write down their answers. The TRS also should consider how the client's attitudes toward health, illness, disability, and receiving health and treatment, based on their cultural influences, affect their responses.

AREAS TO ASSESS

In conducting the assessment, the TRS is obtaining information that is useful in planning the TR services for the client. Based on the influence of the programming approaches discussed earlier in the chapter, this information includes the outcomes and benefits the client desires and her strengths, needs, and lifestyle. The TRS's most significant contribution to the overall assessment of the client is the leisure assessment.

Leisure Assessment

The TRS's unique contribution to the team is his knowledge of the significance of leisure and recreation to health and quality of life. A leisure assessment gathers information about the following:

- Attitudes and beliefs about leisure and its meaning, value, and significance in one's life
- Needs that can be met through recreation participation, such as needs for socialization, physical activity, intellectual stimulation, fun, accomplishment, community involvement, development of new interests, and challenge
- Participation in recreation activities, both current and hoped-for future participation, and reactions to and feelings about these activities
- Recreation participation patterns (when, where, with whom, with how many, how often) and what has influenced the formation of these patterns (such as family, social networks, cost, availability)
- Recreation activity skills and skills in developing, utilizing, and evaluating recreation resources, including financial resources, transportation, accessibility, and social skills
- Barriers to satisfying leisure experiences

Closely related to the leisure assessment is gaining a fuller understanding of the client's lifestyle. Many open-ended questions can be asked to add to our understanding of who a client really is and what might be helpful to her. What is a typical day like? What causes and relieves stress? What are things the client particularly enjoys? Nurses and occupational therapists may ask questions regarding time use and hobbies. However, the TRS may be the only member of the team who has assessed what gives meaning and value to the client's life (Richter & Kaschalk, 1996, p. 87). Our perspective is vital to the full depiction of the client as a whole person. It is our ethical responsibility to competently fulfill the role we have prepared

for, according to our professional standards and in cooperation with the team.

A standardized tool that has been rigorously developed for use as a leisure assessment is the *Leisure Diagnostic Battery* (LDB) (Witt & Ellis, 1989). There are both long and short versions that measure perceived freedom in leisure and that can be used with anyone over the age of 9, including persons with moderate intellectual disability. The LDB short form is easy to use. The LDB can be used in conjunction with the LDB Barriers Scale to obtain a good indication of people's perceptions of their barriers to participation in leisure. Barriers include lack of time, money, social opportunities, motivation, communication skills, information, and accessibility.

Another tool that can suggest what motivates an individual to participate in leisure is the *Leisure Motivation Scale* (LMS) (Beard & Ragheb, 1983). The LMS is appropriate for clients with the cognitive ability to understand the questions, although it is acceptable for the TRS to assist a client in completing the scale. Four factors are considered motivators: intellectual, social, competence-mastery, and stimulus-avoidance. Results give a good indicator of what types of experiences the client would respond to. To determine leisure interests, the TRS can use a checklist or pictures of activities, such as *LeisureScope Plus* (Burlingame & Blaschko, 2002). Therapeutic recreation specialists are encouraged to select appropriate standardized instruments to incorporate into their assessment procedure.

Functional Assessment

The TRS also conducts a **functional assessment** in order to develop a fuller understanding of the client's skills and needs. This is an assessment of the client's functioning, which includes physical, cognitive, social, and emotional behaviors and abilities. See table 3.3 on page 60 for functional behaviors assessed in TR. The TRS wants to know how the client's level of skill will affect participation and whether or not TR interventions can help improve skills or mitigate the negative impact of lack of a particular skill. **Functional skills** such as vision, hearing, speaking ability, fine and gross motor skills, mobility, social interaction, ability to follow directions, comprehension, emotional expression, and control all have an impact on the client's daily activities. A handy assessment tool that addresses these skills and can be used with most populations is the *Functional Assessment of Characteristics for Therapeutic Recreation-Revised* or FACTR-R (Burlingame & Blaschko, 2002). The FACTR-R is designed to assess the functional skills needed for leisure participation.

TABLE 3.3

Functional Behaviors Assessed in TR

Physical behaviors	Cognitive behaviors	Affective or emotional behaviors	Social behaviors
Mobility	Attention span	Anger control	Conversation skills
Fitness	Memory	Frustration tolerance	Assertiveness
Endurance	Judgment	Mood	Cooperativeness
Strength	Sense of direction	Ability to feel joy	Response to competition
Coordination	Orientation	Self-esteem	Group skills
Fine motor skills	Decision making	Anxiety	Conflict resolution
Gross motor skills	Following instructions		Degree of interaction
Balance	Ability to follow rules		
Flexibility	Abstract thinking		
Range of motion	Learning ability		
	Comprehension		

This information can be substantiated through consultation with the other professionals on the team, such as the physical therapist, the nurse, or the social worker, either in discussion, at team meetings, or through review of their documentation on the client.

Readiness Assessment

How ready is the client to participate in services that will lead to positive changes in her life? **Readiness assessment** is a common practice in psychiatric rehabilitation programs, but it has usefulness in other types of settings as well. An important principle of TR leadership is to "start where the client is at." One way to assess how ready the client is for treatment, or how receptive she will be to participating in TR, is to consider the **stage of change** the client is in (Austin, 2004; Shank & Coyle, 2002). The stages of change refer to how ready a person is to make changes in her life. The stages are (1) precontemplation, (2) contemplation, (3) preparation or determination, (4) action, (5) maintenance and possibly relapse, and 6) termination (Prochaska & DiClemente, 1982).

The following are the characteristics of persons at each stage:

● Stage 1. **Precontemplation:** Clients are not ready to think about changing their behavior because they are (1) reluctant due to lack of knowledge, (2) rebellious and do not want others to make decisions for them, (3) resigned to their situation and hopeless that change is even possible, or (4) rationalizing, or giving reasons they do not need to change.

● Stage 2. **Contemplation:** Clients admit that they could benefit from change but are not yet ready to do anything about it; this stage can continue for a long period of time.

● Stage 3. **Preparation or determination:** Clients are ready to take action to make changes, but may lack coping skills to help them through the change process and may need assistance in identifying and overcoming barriers to change.

● Stage 4. **Action:** Clients have formulated and implemented the plan to make changes.

● Stage 5. **Maintenance:** Change has been made and new behaviors are established. The danger of relapse into old behaviors exists because clients may become less vigilant about supporting their new behaviors with positive actions.

● Stage 6. **Termination:** The new behavior has become engrained in the client's lifestyle.

The TRS will undoubtedly encounter clients at each of these stages, as well as in danger of relapse. The TRS can use the stages of change to determine the client's readiness to engage in TR and for direction on how to interact with and motivate the client. It may take the TRS more than one session to determine the client's stage of change, but this information can be very useful in tailoring the TR approach to the needs of the client. Chapter 7 describes specific techniques the TRS uses at each stage in order to help the client.

Environmental Assessment

More and more, TRSs are providing services in the community or in clients' homes, or helping to prepare clients for their eventual return to their personal living situations. In these cases, an **environmental assessment** of the home and community is an essential practice based on ecological and inclusion principles. The environmental assessment covers the equipment, supplies, space, furnishings, and resources available to the client in her home for recreation participation; the other people and support networks that are or can be part of her life; and the resources of the neighborhood and surrounding community. An excellent leisure education activity

Environmental Modifications

Consider these examples of environmental modifications for clients with different needs.

In-Home Modifications for a Woman With Dementia

Mrs. L. is an 80-year-old widow with dementia who has lived in her own apartment with a full-time caregiver since her husband's death two years prior to this assessment. A geriatric care manager was called in by the family to oversee Mrs. L.'s needs. The manager determined that the caregiver was providing excellent physical care and careful supervision of Mrs. L. but that her quality of life could be improved. A CTRS was contacted to complete an assessment of Mrs. L.

During the TR assessment, Mrs. L. responded to her name, made eye contact for up to 2 minutes, had unclear speech, and poor attention span. She could not follow directions or respond to verbal or auditory cues and required complete assistance to ambulate short distances when she was not using her wheelchair.

The CTRS obtained information from the family regarding Mrs. L.'s past interests, lifestyle, and favorite foods, colors, scents, music, and television shows. Due to Mrs. L.'s limited functional capabilities, the CTRS determined that the majority of TR interventions should be directed at modifying the environment to provide increased sensory stimulation to Mrs. L. and maximize her potential to interact with her surroundings and caregiver. The TRS then conducted an environmental assessment.

The following modifications were recommended and implemented:

- Display family photographs from earlier years at Mrs. L.'s eye level (when she is seated in her wheelchair) to reinforce her long-term memory, as current photos have little meaning to her.
- Place within her visual field photo albums and colorful magazines on cooking, travel, and nature, which were her prior interests.
- Open curtains and blinds to let in daylight.
- Place live plants and fresh flowers on surfaces close to her wheelchair.
- Hang a large clock and a large calendar, as well as seasonal decorations as appropriate, on the wall opposite her usual position in the living room.
- Be sure TV is at her eye level. Show old TV shows and home movies.
- Obtain age-appropriate toys and games for grandchildren when they visit.
- During mealtime, have Mrs. L. sit at the kitchen table and handle nonbreakable food preparation items such as dish towels, potholders, and wooden spoons.
- Prepare favorite family recipes.
- Set the table with colorful tablecloths and napkins that contrast with the dishes.
- Put makeup, jewelry, and perfume on Mrs. L. daily, as this was typical of her lifestyle.
- When she is going out, provide her with a handbag that contains tissues, lipstick, coins, keys, and gloves.

is to have clients compile a personal leisure resource inventory, which can include anything from a telephone to a computer to photo albums, art supplies, and sporting equipment, to a front porch or backyard, close neighbors, a bus stop on the corner, nearby park, public library, movie theatre, or a senior center. A delivery person for meals on wheels, a neighbor walking a dog, or a mail carrier can be a significant social contact for an isolated older adult or person with a disability. Building a network of support is essential for successful inclusion and for improving and maintaining quality of life. The environmental assessment reflects the holistic practice of TR. Therapeutic recreation is not just about leading activities; it is about enhancing a person's life through meaningful engagement in the world.

A TRS doing an environmental assessment in the client's home assesses physical and social factors by answering the following questions:

- Is there adequate space, lighting, ventilation, comfortable seating; easy access to equipment and supplies; and a table or other surface for recreation participation?
- Is there adequate soundproofing from distracting noise?
- Is the space clean, free of clutter and hazards that could cause falls, and free of distracting odors?
- Does the client have media equipment, music, books, art objects, pictures, or a collection (dolls, stamps, and so on)?
- Are there personal objects, family photos, clocks, and calendars in view?

- Is there a pet?
- Who is available to participate with the client in recreation—friends, neighbors, family members, volunteers?
- How accessible are the home and the surrounding community for ease of movement, reliable transportation, and recreation opportunities? Is there a porch, yard, or garden; a nearby mall with a mall walkers' program; a public library with a book discussion group; an adult education program or a youth center?

Health care settings have recognized the significant impact the environment can have on a person's functioning and quality of life. Facility-wide initiatives such as **culture change** and the **Eden Alternative** in long-term care are aimed at humanizing the environment by giving more control to clients, bringing in plants and animals, and making the setting more home-like and less institutional.

IMPACT OF THE EIGHT APPROACHES TO PROGRAMMING ON ASSESSMENT

Assessment is affected by the benefits-based, person-centered, strengths-based, and continuity of lifestyle approaches because they emphasize looking at the whole person in the context of her physical and social environments, identifying her strengths, and determining which benefits she values and which aspects of her lifestyle she wishes to continue. During the assessment the TRS should actively obtain this information, not just focus on needs and limitations. These approaches also direct the TRS to gather information on the client's environments,

Modifications of a Day Room for a Girl with Developmental Disabilities

In a day program for individuals with developmental disabilities, Rosa became unmanageable during the TR program held in a large day room. She would run back and forth across the room shouting and jumping up and down. The TRS had difficulty calming her down. When the TRS asked her to sit down and complete the arts and crafts activity, Rosa refused. Yet Rosa was normally quiet and attentive in classroom sessions. After a consultation with the team, it was concluded that the large, open space of the day room affected Rosa's ability to concentrate in a calm manner. The team decided that the room size had to be adapted to promote Rosa's positive behaviors. A set of dividers was placed across the room to create a separate, smaller space in which she completed her project. The dividers were then removed, and she was invited to join the structured large-group activities. Rosa was able to achieve her individual goals in the group because of the space adaptations made. This demonstrates the value of the ecological perspective in examining the factors that contribute to successful goal achievement. In this case it was the physical environment that became the target of the TRS's intervention to enable Rosa's accomplishments.

according to the inclusion approach, and identify the optimal living environment for the client.

Ethically, in conducting the assessment, the TRS is fair, honest, respectful, and competent in accordance with the standards of the TR profession. The TRS's adherence to ethical principles is fundamental to the integrity of the assessment process. After the TRS has completed the assessment procedures, he is responsible for writing up the assessment according to agency and department guidelines. This report generally includes a summary of what the TRS has learned about the client as a result of the assessment process, including strengths, limitations and functional status, and recommendations for (a) intervention, (b) referral, or (c) no services (Carter et al., 2003). The summary leads directly into the second step of the TR process, planning.

Planning

The second step in the TR process is planning. Planning involves several tasks:

1. Setting goals
2. Writing statements that indicate how we will know the goal is achieved
3. Planning discharge
4. Scheduling TR interventions

The first task is to indicate the goals for the client.

GOAL SETTING

A **goal** is typically considered to be a broad, general statement of intent or direction of services. Goal setting is influenced by the person-centered approach to planning, which places the client at the center of her services; the strengths-based approach, which emphasizes planning to help clients meet the goals they desire; and continuity of lifestyle, in which goals are set that will help a client maintain the qualities and activities in her life that are personally meaningful and relevant. The goals should be developed in collaboration with the client. With reference to our discussion of existential outcomes, if we ask our client, Paulette, what is important to her to accomplish, she will be more personally committed to the goal than if a team of professionals has decided what is "good" or "right" for Paulette to achieve. People are much more likely to be successful when they are working on something that is personally meaningful and of their own choosing. In some facilities, the team works together to identify goals for the client. Then each discipline specifies the interventions that will be used to meet the team's

goals for the client and identifies the discipline-specific goals. For instance, if a goal for Paulette is to lose weight, the doctor may adjust her medication, the dietitian will come up with an eating plan, and the TRS will develop an exercise program. In addition, the TRS may set a goal with Paulette for her to identify community resources she can utilize for ongoing physical activity participation.

The person-centered planning approach also influences goal setting in stating that the client and perhaps her family should be present at the team meeting when her individual plan is developed or finalized. Even though the practice is not always carried out or feasible for the client and family, it is our ethical obligation and vital to the planning process to obtain clients' input. It is also the TRS's leadership responsibility to advocate for what the client sees as making her life worth living. With the focus today on measurable outcomes, it is crucial to keep what matters to the client at the forefront of planning. In planning, we should ask the clients to "create a vision" (O'Keefe, 2005, p. 80) of what they want their life to be, and then keep that vision in front of them as a guide, a motivator, and a source of the hope to be able to realize their strengths.

Making Goals Measurable

As mentioned earlier, terminology is not always consistent from one setting to another. What one agency may call goals, another may call **measurable goals**; a third may use the word "outcomes." Regardless of the word, the basic principle is the same: to specify a direction for the client. This direction may be expressed in somewhat general terms, such as "improve physical fitness," "improve social interaction skills," or "increase attention span"; or it may be more specific as in "increase mobility" or "improve ability to engage in a one-to-one conversation." Specifying the exact amount and quality of behavior that will show us that the goal has been met is the second task in planning. A *measurable* goal is one that is modified by a specific performance measure or measurable outcome, as in "improve physical fitness *as demonstrated by the ability to walk a mile in 30 minutes three times per week on the indoor track.*" Adding the modifier means that if the client can perform the behavior, she has reached her goal of improving physical fitness, because at the point of beginning the walking program she could walk only one-quarter of a mile in 30 minutes. Ability to walk farther in the same period of time is an indicator of fitness. We know this from reviewing the evidence, as guided by the evidence-based practice approach.

In settings that use a general goal rather than a measurable goal, the TRS writes **behavioral objectives** that include a specific behavior the client is to demonstrate, the criterion or standard for how well the behavior is to be performed (the quality and quantity of behavior), and the conditions under which the behavior will take place (where, when, and under what circumstances). In the measurable goal just discussed, "walk a mile" is the behavior; "30 minutes three times a week" is the criterion because it specifies the quantity of walking necessary to demonstrate fitness; and "on the indoor track" is the condition because it tells where the behavior will take place. The behavior is always expressed as an action that the client is to perform. Behaviors can be physical, social, cognitive, or emotional. But they must be observable. To say that Paulette *"knows* where she can go to exercise" is not adequate. How can we tell that Paulette knows? She has to indicate knowledge by writing down the information, stating it verbally, or pointing out places when given a list. This is behavior we can observe. So we must also indicate how the client will demonstrate that she has achieved the goal. If we want to know how much weight Paulette has lost, we can ask her. But if she is weighed on a scale and the weight is recorded, we have obtained an observable, measurable indicator of her progress toward her goal. Whether an agency uses the term measurable goals, outcomes, performance indicator or measure, or behavioral objective, the principle is the same: The statement is a specific description of a measurable, observable behavior that represents progress toward or achievement of a goal or outcome.

Goal Setting as an Ongoing Process

Goal setting is a process. In addition to walking and adhering to a proper diet, Paulette may also need to learn new cooking techniques and develop assertiveness skills in order to politely but firmly refuse offers of desserts. As she increases her walking distance and learns new recipes, she may become confident about being more assertive regarding her dietary needs. As she progresses, new goals may be set. Paulette may need to shop for new clothes and learn what stores to go to, what types of clothes to buy, even how to budget. Achieving even one goal, such as losing weight, has many components and also can involve many different types of recreation participation for a client. This relates closely to our earlier discussion of functional and existential outcomes. Paulette's functional outcomes relate to walking, proper eating habits, and assertiveness.

An existential outcome for Paulette, linked to what gives meaning and purpose to her life, is to join her brothers and sisters on their annual hiking vacation. Achieving the functional outcomes will improve her abilities to achieve her existential outcome, and wanting to accomplish the existential outcome may motivate her to work toward attaining her functional outcomes.

DISCHARGE PLANNING

Discharge planning involves making a plan to help the client become ready for discharge from an institutional setting or from the services of an agency. The increased cost of health care, coupled with the mandate that people have the right to live in their optimal environment, has focused attention on preparing clients for their life after discharge. It is expected that, as a result of the treatment and services received, the client eventually will be ready to move on to a less costly setting and require fewer professional services. This involves preparing a client for a return to his own home or a move to a more residential or long-term care setting. In either case this move is in the best interests of the individual because it generally means living with fewer restrictions and more control over one's life. "The eventual goal of all rehabilitation efforts is the return of the client to as normal a living circumstance as possible under the best quality of life conditions possible" (Mobily & Ostiguy, 2004, p. 218). Discharge planning starts on the day the client is admitted to your facility or begins to receive your services.

Discharge planning encompasses transitional planning, which "involves assisting clients to find the services they need to make a successful return to their lives in the community" (Sylvester et al., 2001, p. 330). The transitional plan includes recommendations to programs and services in the community, as well as a follow-up plan to track the client's progress. Without follow-up we cannot be sure that the client is able to stay with the plan or needs assistance. Many TRSs are not allowed by their agency to continue contact with their clients after discharge; however, this contact may be essential to the success the client has in returning to her community or in her next service setting. Some TR agencies have developed transitional services to help smooth the move from one setting to the next. This is a welcome trend in TR and reflects person-centered and continuity of lifestyle approaches.

In developing the discharge plan, the TRS must keep in mind the principles of the person-centered, strengths-based, and continuity of lifestyle approaches. The TRS maintains a focus on what will contribute to the client's quality of life and what will be meaningful and significant to the client in the future. The TRS helps the client prepare for discharge, identifying the specific skills and behaviors that will facilitate the next placement, and then helps the client to acquire or improve these skills and behaviors. The TRS and the client consider what activities and resources will be important and useful to the client after she is discharged. Once she is ready for discharge, the TRS also provides written information on her leisure interests, recreation patterns, and needs for adaptations for the professionals who will work with the client in the future. The TRS may contact the TR or recreation professionals to whom the client has been referred in order to help ease her transition. Many people are hesitant or fearful about going to a new place, and any support during this change can be critical to success. If the TRS does not consider what the client's life will be like after discharge and work on what will help her in the future, the TRS is doing a disservice to the client. We want our time with our clients to have significance in their lives. We have characterized TR as a thoughtful process. When we plan and implement TR services, we should always be thinking and reflecting about the meaning and value of our work to our clients, how we can enhance our efforts, and how we can best serve the needs and interests of the human beings with whom we are privileged to work.

SCHEDULING

The third task in planning is **scheduling,** which involves developing a schedule of TR programs and interventions for the client. The TRS is guided by all eight approaches to program planning in designing the client's schedule. Selecting appealing TR activities for the client reflects the person-centered, strengths-based, and continuity of lifestyle approaches. The TRS suggests and selects interventions that incorporate the client's strengths, interests, and needs, in collaboration with the client to the extent possible. Benefits-based programming also affects the TR plan because certain desired benefits associated with a recreation activity may serve to motivate the client to begin and sustain participation. Knowing that Paulette enjoys socializing helps

the TRS develop a plan of TR programs that have this as a benefit. For Paulette, social interaction is not a goal because it is not an issue for her, but the social benefits of group walking and cooking may stimulate her to adhere to her plan.

In addition to selecting TR programs in accordance with the individual's needs and preferences, the TRS uses the evidence-based practice approach to select interventions that have proven to be effective in meeting a particular goal. Once the interventions have been chosen, the TRS schedules them according to the components of active treatment (frequency, duration, and intensity), as in "group walking on the indoor track for 30 minutes, 3 times per week, for 3 months." If we check our plan for Paulette against the characteristics of outcome-oriented programming, we see that the plan is meaningful and relevant to her, is realistic, can be accomplished in a timely manner, can reasonably be expected to be successful, and is part of the overall approach to Paulette's services. Consistent with our emphasis that what *happens* to the client in TR rather than what the client *does* in TR is paramount to successful TR service, we might consider using the term *recreation experience* rather than the word *intervention* (O'Keefe, 2005) in describing what we provide in our programs. The value of TR is that it is a total experience involving a recreation activity, TR leadership, and the client's goal or vision.

As well as delineating the schedule of TR programs, TR planning includes describing the nature

Social benefits of group programming can help a client adhere to a plan.

of the interaction between the TRS and the client, known as the **facilitation techniques**. Facilitation techniques are the methods the TRS uses to help the client attain her outcomes. These techniques, discussed in chapter 7, include motivation processes, reinforcement strategies, leadership styles, and teaching methods that are best suited to the client's particular needs and characteristics. The TRS motivates the client to begin participation, uses reinforcers to encourage ongoing involvement, gives feedback to inform the client how she is doing, and varies leadership styles as needed to facilitate progress. Facilitation techniques are a component of TR leadership, and their effective use cannot be overemphasized as the key to opening our clients to change and new possibilities in their lives. The TRS should specify the particular techniques to use in the client's TR plan.

The TRS ensures that appropriate space, facilities, equipment, and staff are available as required for programming, taking into account the other activities and services being provided. Availability even affects the choice of what programs can realistically be offered. This all takes place in the context of the overall TR schedule, which has been developed within the framework of the other activities and services being delivered in the setting. Therapeutic recreation staff may collaborate with other disciplines by coleading programs, which also requires coordination of scheduling.

IMPACT OF THE EIGHT APPROACHES TO PROGRAMMING ON PLANNING

Planning is influenced by evidence-based practice, active treatment, and outcome-oriented programming with their emphasis on developing meaningful and relevant goals and outcomes that can be achieved in a timely manner. These approaches also direct the TRS to base the selection of TR interventions and programs on evidence from research studies, and to designate the frequency, duration, and intensity of programming. Goal setting and selecting the programming are influenced as well by the benefits to be obtained from participation, the client's strengths, the prior lifestyle of the client, and the barriers to inclusion the client faces. The TRS writes up the plan, shares the plan with the client, to the extent possible depending on the client's capabilities, in language that is comprehensible to the client, places it in the client's chart or record and shares it with the team. Depending on the setting, the TRS may provide a copy of the plan to the client's family in person or via e-mail or letter.

This completes the planning step of the TR process. Carrying out planning relies on a set of ethical

principles: to be competent at what we do; to use procedures and methods in which we are trained; to do what is in the best interests of our clients; to make sure that clients know the benefits, risks, and time involved in TR programs; to inform them of what they might expect from participation; and to ensure that our plan complies with the laws and regulations governing the TR profession. We are diligent in designing programs that use resources efficiently, and we collaborate with other professionals to provide the highest-quality services. The client's choice and autonomy regarding participation are to be respected at all times.

Implementation

The third step in the TR process is implementation, which is carrying out the TR plan. Nowhere is TR leadership more in evidence than in the implementation of programs, when the client is engaged in purposeful intervention in the leisure context. It is at this point that TR leadership is most clearly displayed. The TRS creates the TR environment, in which she nurtures a person's willingness to change. The TRS motivates the client to engage in TR, conducts one-to-one and group programs, and facilitates the client's participation during TR. Too often, TRSs think that scheduling a client to attend a program will lead not only to participation but also to personal growth and change for the client. Merely attending a program does not guarantee that a client will strive for or achieve outcomes. This is why TR is a planned and thoughtful process. To facilitate the client's progress, the TRS observes the client's behaviors and reactions, provides feedback, and processes and debriefs the TR experience with the client in language that is appropriate to the client's level of understanding and lifestyle. Implementation is also affected by the health and functional status of clients, which can fluctuate. People may be unable to participate as scheduled because of unexpected visitors or a rescheduled appointment, for example. Implementation of the TR plan requires flexibility, adapting quickly to changes, and creativity in making adjustments to the schedule that still fulfill the purposes of TR.

IMPACT OF THE EIGHT APPROACHES TO PROGRAMMING ON IMPLEMENTATION

Implementation draws from all eight approaches to program planning. We implement programs based on the evidence; we facilitate clients' attainment of outcomes and benefits; we offer both Type I and Type II programs as appropriate and make clear what our purposes are; we keep the person at the center of the services, utilize and reinforce their strengths, and emphasize the continuity of valued parts of their lifestyle. We implement programs in the natural environment and assist clients in achieving their goals to live in as inclusive an environment as they choose. Parts II and III of this book cover much more on implementation. From an ethical standpoint, implementation obligates us to respect our clients' choices regarding participation, obtain their informed consent to participate, be competent in the programs we offer, provide services fairly, use resources efficiently, be aware of how our personal preferences may affect our programming, and protect the well-being of our clients during participation.

Evaluation

The fourth and final step in the TR process is **evaluation**. Evaluation of the individual TR plan involves determining how successful the plan was at helping the client achieve her goals. The client's status at the time of evaluation is compared to her status at the time of assessment. This is an indicator of the progress the client has made as a result of participating in TR services. Progress is *measured* both quantitatively and qualitatively. **Quantitative measures** involve numbers; the TRS measures the amount of change that has taken place. **Qualitative measures** pertain to the benefits, quality, and meaning of the experience for the client and is expressed by the client. Evaluation is also categorized as formative or summative. The TRS should be observing and evaluating the client during and after every interaction to ensure that the TR plan remains appropriate. This is **formative evaluation**, occurring during the program and leading to immediate changes in the program if necessary. It may be that Paulette is scheduled for the afternoon walking program but after a couple of days the TRS observes that Paulette is lethargic during the activity. The TRS has noticed that Paulette is more motivated in the mornings. She asks Paulette if she would prefer to attend the morning walking session because she seems more energetic at that time. Paulette agrees. Changing the time she attends is an example of applying the results of formative evaluation. **Summative evaluation** occurs at the end of the program and leads to revisions for the next time the program is offered. It may result in changing the time, location, format, leadership style, or content of a program. An example of this is that at the end of the walking program, the TRS determines that the clients attending the morning sessions have been more successful at reaching their goals than the clients

in the afternoon session. She uses the results of this summative evaluation to reschedule the afternoon session to a morning time slot.

It is as critical to *document* the client's progress as to evaluate it. It's often said that "if it isn't written, it didn't happen." **Documentation** is a key responsibility of TRSs. Documenting a client's progress involves being honest, accurate, and objective while protecting the client's privacy and confidentiality. Frequency of evaluation is determined by the regulations governing the facility's programming and the agency's and TR department's policies. The TRS may document on a daily, weekly, biweekly, monthly, or quarterly basis as specified by the policies on documentation. Specific quantitative measures can be taken at predetermined intervals as indicated in the plan. Paulette may weigh herself daily or weekly. Her walking distance may be measured at each session, at every third session, or at the end of every month. Her verbal reactions to her progress can be recorded whenever they occur or on a regular basis. At the end of the three months, Paulette's progress is summarized (summative evaluation). The summary would include the time and distance she has walked, her weight loss, and other behaviors indicative of her ability to maintain a healthy weight.

In addition to the walking program, Paulette attended assertiveness training, attended cooking sessions, and went on shopping trips as part of her goal-directed weight loss program to support her new lifestyle and promote ongoing healthy weight control. Paulette may now demonstrate her functional outcomes: She refuses foods she does not want to eat; she can cook according to a set of healthy eating guidelines; and she has purchased new clothing within her budget. These results are recorded on a form designed for the purpose, written as a progress note, or otherwise documented according to the policies. In addition, Paulette may describe the progress she has made toward achieving her existential outcome of going on the hiking vacation with her siblings. The TRS may ask Paulette about other benefits she has obtained from the program. These could include learning new leisure activities, discovering that cooking is a creative and relaxing outlet for her, and finding that the walking program has motivated her to try other fitness activities. She may express feelings of self-confidence and pride in her accomplishments. These statements are examples of qualitative measures and should be recorded for evaluation purposes. It's valuable to quote the client's exact words as a true indicator of what is meant and of her experience. "An essential element of efficacy is the client's affirmation that the experience was helpful in achieving the vision" (O'Keefe, 2005, p. 81).

REPORTING TO THE TEAM

In just about every setting, the TRS works as a member of a team of professionals with a common purpose. In health care this may be called the treatment team, the interdisciplinary team, or the care planning team. There are also teams in education and human service settings. The team meets regularly to develop and review the plan of care or services for the client. The TRS's professional responsibility as a member of the team is to provide an accurate report on the results of the TR assessment as well as on the client's participation and progress in TR. The TRS has a significant contribution to make to the team's understanding of the client. The client may behave more naturally in the relaxed setting of the TR environment and display strengths and behaviors that other team members have not observed in their own treatment milieus. Most other disciplines focus primarily on the client's problems or deficits. In TR we focus on the whole person, what he can do as well as what he cannot. We utilize the client's strengths to overcome his limitations. This allows us to see clients multidimensionally and report accordingly to the team. Therapeutic recreation is also the environment most like "real life"; the client can try out new behaviors and skills, with the support and understanding of the TR staff, in the setting that most closely approximates everyday living. This perspective gives a fuller picture of the client than other staff may see.

As TR is often the profession whose contribution to the therapeutic process is least understood by other disciplines, it is the ethical obligation of all TR professionals to convey to the team the serious intent and significance of TR. By utilizing the evidence-based practice, active treatment, outcome-oriented, and benefits-based approaches, TRSs can convey that TR services are on a par with the other services represented on the team. Therapeutic recreation specialists have a duty to be well informed regarding the TR profession and their clients, up-to-date and well versed in their practices, and articulate in their participation on the team. The TRS should not describe a client's participation in terms of what TR activities the client has attended; her responsibility is to explain the progress the client has made toward outcomes. For example, the TRS states that the client "has learned healthy cooking techniques as demonstrated by planning a week's menu according to the American Heart Association's guidelines for a heart healthy diet," not that the client "came to cooking group." The point is to show that the client has achieved a functional outcome valued by the team. The TRS can also report the existential outcome, for example by saying, "The client has stated that cooking relaxes her and she finds it a satisfying new hobby." This provides the team with a more comprehensive understanding of what the client has accomplished. Further, the TRS can report that the client has benefited from socializing with other participants in the group and that they have served as a support to each other to reinforce their newfound health-promoting behaviors.

Recognition and acceptance of TR's contribution to the team is in the hands of each TRS, in his display of professional behavior and expertise. The TRS also shows respect for the input of other team members and answers their questions thoughtfully and courteously. There may be times when members of the team disagree with the TR approach or with an issue that concerns the well-being of the client. "Turf" issues may arise when one team member feels that another is doing work outside of his professional scope of practice. At times, it is useful to acknowledge that overlap does occur. Disagreements are normal and should be handled maturely and professionally and could be seen as opportunities to maximize services to the client. Therapeutic recreation specialists often are the advocates for the client's existential needs and should be aware of their ethical obligation to do their best for clients, in their best interests. We are also obligated to respect clients' privacy and respect and cooperate with our colleagues and their professions. Successful teamwork is a result of effective communication among knowledgeable, well-informed, mature professionals for the good of the clients.

REVISING THE PLAN

Evaluation is useful because it provides a measure of how much and what type of progress has been made. Just as importantly, evaluation also increases our understanding of which TR programs, approaches, and techniques work and which don't, offering direction for revising or modifying the plan. We may actually name the fourth step in the TR process "evaluation and revision." If the results of an evaluation are not used to revise the services as needed, we are doing a disservice to our client. The client will not always make progress that can be observed and measured. Lack of progress should be documented in the client's record, and the plan should be revised as necessary. There may be several reasons the plan did not work, as discussed in chapter 8. These reasons involve factors related to the client, the TRS, the family and significant others, or other staff members. We can look at these factors to determine what may have caused the lack of progress so we can rectify or address the situation. For example, if the team is not consistent in its approach to the client, this should be discussed at a team meeting. If family members are interfering with the client's participation, meeting with the family and discussing the program, the client's goals, and the family's role can help. If the client is not responding to the particular activity or program, a different one may be introduced. If the TRS is not using the appropriate facilitation techniques, more suitable ones should be used. It is unethical to continue to pursue a course of action that we know is not in the best interests of our clients or not meeting their needs.

IMPACT OF THE EIGHT APPROACHES TO PROGRAMMING ON EVALUATION

Evaluation is affected by evidence-based practice as we determine if in fact the programming and services produced the desired outcomes. Were the frequency, duration, and intensity of service adequate to achieve the outcomes? What benefits were obtained from participation? Was the client able to utilize his strengths to overcome his limitations? Did he make progress toward attaining his preferred lifestyle, environments of choice, and a more inclusive life? Through evaluation the TRS determines if the eight approaches have been followed to best serve the client. As discussed earlier, in reporting to the team, the TRS refers to the eight

approaches in order to most clearly express TR's contribution to the client's services and progress.

Evaluation has become a critical concern in many arenas because it is the indicator that services are producing results. Because of the vast investment of human, physical, and financial resources in health care, human services, and education, society is demanding proof of tangible, measurable, and meaningful outcomes. Concrete evidence is necessary to ensure that services will continue to be provided as needed. However, these services must be efficacious—capable of producing the results desired by clients, organizations, regulatory bodies, government oversight agencies, and society in general. What is valued at one point in time may not be of consequence at another point. Our ethical responsibility is always to do good for our clients and to view their welfare as the guiding principle in delivering our services. This can create ethical dilemmas, when the demands to produce valued results conflict with what is best and right for an individual. In some settings there is a push to have as many clients as possible attend a TR program. This turns a small, outcome-oriented Type II program into a Type I or cafeteria program, which is less likely to produce desired outcomes because the TRS is unable to provide TR leadership to so many clients at once. Relying on our codes of ethics, discussing these issues with other professionals, and continually reflecting on our professional practice can aid us in addressing these dilemmas.

● Summary ●

Therapeutic recreation program planning is one of the major responsibilities in the provision of TR leadership. Fulfilling this responsibility professionally and ethically requires knowledge of the current trends and issues in society that affect the delivery of services. Hallmarks of a profession that is up-to-date with the latest developments and practices are utilizing research findings; being systematic and precise; striving to provide meaningful and effective services that produce valued outcomes; and keeping the client at the center of services by recognizing her strengths, unique characteristics, and vital role in planning. Applying these approaches ensures that the TR process is dynamic and relevant to the changing world and the evolving needs of human beings. New approaches will surely emerge as the conditions that affect TR and other professions change. The four steps in the TR process will remain constant, but the techniques and methods we use will continue to be adjusted and modified as we strive to meet the highest standards in accordance with our ethical principles.

To take on the responsibility of facilitating change in another human being, TRSs are ethically obligated to strive to be caring, competent, creative, and consciously aware professionals. The TRS is a catalyst for the change and growth of clients and is a facilitator of meaningful human experience. The professional TRS understands and embodies the values and principles of TR and demonstrates, through everyday actions, commitment to the highest standards of practice. The qualities essential to providing TR leadership are described in chapter 4.

● Learning Activities ●

1. In the case of Paulette in the chapter, which of the eight approaches to programming were used to deliver her TR services? How could you apply the remaining approaches to programming for Paulette?

2. In a small group, brainstorm how you would apply the strengths-based approach in a nursing home, the benefits-based approach in a program for youth at risk, outcome-oriented programming in a group home for adults with developmental disabilities, and inclusion as a process in a day program for those with chronic mental illness.

3. Obtain copies of the LDB short form and Barriers Scale and complete the forms with a small group. Discuss your scores. Do your results seem to give an accurate picture of your perceived freedom and barriers to leisure participation? According to the stages of change, how ready are you to make a change to overcome your barriers?

4. Conduct an environmental assessment of your own home or that of someone you know. What changes could you make to improve the environment to overcome barriers to recreation participation and/or to facilitate more satisfying leisure?

5. Assemble an assessment toolkit. Demonstrate to classmates or other TR staff how you would use the items in your toolkit to conduct an assessment of a client. Carry out an actual assessment using your toolkit on a client or classmate.

6. Think of someone you know who has a health or behavior problem in need of change. According to the guidelines given in the chapter, conduct the interview portion of the assessment with this person. How comfortable did you feel conducting the interview? What aspects were easy for you? Which ones were more challenging? Share these personal reflections in a small group.

7. Review current events as reported in the newspapers, on TV, or online. What examples do you see of applications of the eight approaches to program planning?

The Blended Role of Therapeutic Recreation Leadership

In this chapter you will learn about:

- The components of the blended role of TR leadership
- The knowledge and skills of the therapist and the leader
- Cross-cultural competence and diversity
- Maintaining appropriate professional relationships through an understanding of boundary issues, transference and countertransference, and self-disclosure
- Interpersonal skills of the TRS
- Nonverbal and verbal communication
- Types and uses of power
- Motivation theories
- The environmental context of TR leadership

The best TR practice derives from the synergy created when the knowledge and skills of a therapist and a recreation specialist combine. **Synergy** means the working together of two or more components to lead to a result greater than the sum of their individual results. When combined effectively, the roles of therapist and recreation specialist become indistinguishable, and the TRS emerges as a gifted and effective practitioner. The degree to which a TRS can express this vital view of the field and its objectives, and translate them into practice, in large part determines the extent to which the TRS can influence clients to participate meaningfully in TR services. It also contributes to other professionals' understanding of the meaning and purposes of TR. Therapeutic recreation leadership is most clearly observed in the implementation phase of the TR process as the TRS strives to maximize the quality and meaning of the TR experience for clients.

This chapter focuses on the qualities of TR leadership and the knowledge, skills, abilities, and personal resources needed to be an effective TRS. A full understanding of and ability to deliver TR leadership requires understanding the roles of both the therapist and the recreation specialist. The effective integration of the two roles results in skilled professional practice in accordance with ethical principles.

THE COMPONENTS OF THE BLENDED ROLE

Therapeutic recreation leadership was defined in chapter 1 as *the unique blending of the therapist's pur-*

The blended role of TR leadership combines the helping techniques of the therapist with the skills of creating a recreation experience.

Photo Library c/o A. Grapes/Custom Medical Stock Photo

poseful application of therapeutic strategies and facilitation techniques with the recreation specialist's abilities to create and facilitate leisure experiences in order to deliver TR services according to the highest ethical standards. Carrying out this blended role requires maturity, self-awareness, and continual reflection on ethical principles, as well as the TRS's

● professional beliefs about the value and power of recreation participation in bringing about change and being meaningful to the individual and the group;

● cross-cultural competence and interpersonal and motivational skills, and

● ability to plan and organize creative programs within the professional environment.

The TRS, in fulfilling the blended role, draws upon the sensitivity, self-awareness, and interpersonal communication skills of a therapist or helper, as well as the program planning skills, motivational abilities, and creativity of a recreation specialist. In TR, the dynamic potential of leadership often has been unrealized. Practitioners may focus too much on achieving the clinical or functional outcomes, thereby sacrificing the recreation experience, or tend to emphasize the recreational nature of the experience rather than the purposefulness of the TR intervention, or conduct activities with little regard for either the valued benefits or outcomes.

In other words, the TRS may emphasize the product resulting from participation more than the process, which also can be described as focusing on the task the client is engaged in to the detriment of the experience the client has during the program. Conversely, at other times the TRS may be conducting an activity for its fun qualities without enough emphasis on achieving outcomes. Finally, the TRS may be conducting an activity without emphasizing its meaning or benefits, just to fill the time. The TRS's ethical responsibility is to actively engage with clients to facilitate their development of skills and competencies that will help them achieve greater quality of life and well-being. Understanding and applying the components of the blended role contribute to realizing the potential of TR.

Knowledge and Skills of the Therapist

Therapeutic recreation leadership incorporates the perspective of a therapist or helping professional. Therapists address clients' problems with the expectation of a change in their status or behavior. The therapist is often viewed as a "helper" whose goal is to assist clients in reaching their maximum potential in a way that is meaningful and self-fulfilling. Effective helpers are individuals who, through education and training, have developed a set of beliefs and behaviors that provide a depth and intensity to their interactions with others. Therapists act with purpose and are able to communicate the value of what they do to peers and clients. They believe that people are not only capable of change, but are also capable of helping themselves and using their strengths to make change occur. This reflects the humanistic perspective, a core TR principle.

Through the relationship with the TRS, clients can gain insight into their personal experiences and demonstrate new behaviors that are more satisfying and productive. The TRS uses himself as a catalyst or instrument of change in the client's life. This therapeutic use of self implies that the TRS is capable of forming a therapeutic relationship or alliance with clients that leads to the clients' attaining a better quality of life (Shank & Coyle, 2002). To be this instrument of change, the TRS has an obligation to explore his personal ideas about illness, disability, and other defining client characteristics. The TRS must be aware of his values and of how those values influence his daily practice. This is the foundation of what it means to be a therapist. While this is important for any professional working with people, in work with people who have illnesses, disabilities, or other conditions it becomes critical to be aware of any personal attitudes or beliefs that could affect the professional's interactions. Therapists are expected to uphold the highest ethical standards because of the sensitive nature of their work with clients. Integrity, honesty, competence, and respect are ethical principles with great relevance to the therapeutic relationship.

In order to develop an effective therapeutic relationship, the therapist needs specific knowledge, skills, and abilities. These include knowledge of assessment, facilitation techniques, and therapeutic strategies; cross-cultural competence; knowledge of environmental influences; understanding of the risks and benefits inherent in therapeutic relationships; and skill in therapeutic communication and motivational strategies. The personal interactions between therapist and client, based on the knowledge, skills, and abilities of the therapist, are significant factors in helping a client achieve goals. What distinguishes TR from other therapies is the blending of the therapist's foundational knowledge and skills with those of the recreation specialist in the provision of TR leadership.

Knowledge and Skills of the Recreation Specialist

Therapeutic recreation leadership incorporates the abilities of the recreation specialist to create and facilitate leisure experiences, and to motivate individuals to participate in activities and to experience the benefits of recreation participation. This reflects the core TR value of the right to leisure. Recreation specialists believe in the value of leisure experiences, the power of leisure to be a transforming influence on people's lives, and the significance of leisure in contributing to quality of life. These beliefs infuse the work of the recreation specialist as she emphasizes choice, perceived competence and control, intrinsic motivation, and the benefits derived from participation. Planning programs and leading groups are skills at which the recreation specialist should excel.

A competent recreation specialist is first and foremost a successful leader who knows a wide range of recreation activities, designs creative and stimulating programs, develops resources, applies risk management strategies to ensure a safe environment, is flexible, energetic and enthusiastic, understands group dynamics, communicates effectively, and successfully engages participants in satisfying recreation opportunities. The knowledge and skills used to plan and lead recreation experiences are at the core of the recreation specialist's contribution to TR leadership. It is important to examine how recreation leadership has been defined, in order to fully understand the concept of TR leadership.

Several authors have offered definitions of leadership. Leadership has been defined as "a process designed to produce changes in others' behaviors through the use of interpersonal influence" (Niepoth, 1983, p. 129). Another definition emphasizes communication as the key to successful leadership: "the interpersonal influence exercised by a person or persons through the process of communication" (Russell, 2005, p. 16) toward goal attainment in a given situation. A more comprehensive definition of leadership is a "process employed by the leader to assist individuals and groups in identifying and achieving their goals. Leadership may involve listening, persuading, suggesting, doing and otherwise exerting influence on others" (Edginton, Hudson, Dieser & Edginton, 2004, p. 68). To provide leadership, recreation specialists should be trustworthy, understand human nature, and have a positive attitude about what can be accomplished and experienced. Most definitions of recreation leadership, similar to these three, emphasize

Emotional Intelligence

Being emotionally intelligent is a factor common to successful leaders and successful therapists. Research in the field of leadership has explored the link between leadership effectiveness and emotional intelligence (Ruderman et al., 2001). **Emotional intelligence (EI)** is defined as "the ability to perceive emotions; to access and generate emotions so as to assist thought; to understand emotions and emotional knowledge; and to reflectively regulate emotions so as to promote emotional and intellectual growth" (Mayer, 1999). An emotionally intelligent person manages his emotions and demonstrates emotions that are appropriate to a given situation. For example, a TRS who possesses emotional intelligence does not lose her temper with clients or peers even though she had a difficult time at home before coming to work. Goleman (1995), who popularized the concept of emotional intelligence, identified four associated competencies: self-awareness, social awareness, self-management, and social skills. Emotionally intelligent leaders possess self-awareness and strong social skills and are motivated, courteous, respectful, and empathic. As already discussed, effective TR leadership blends the qualities of therapists and recreation leaders. The sets of knowledge, skills, and abilities of both professional roles are enhanced by this synergy. As we explore the skills and abilities required to practice TR leadership, we will consider these competencies in more detail.

establishing a vision and influencing the behavior of others. These actions facilitate the clients' vision of what they wish to accomplish and motivate them to be actively engaged in the TR process. Fairness, competence, diligence, well-being and autonomy are the ethical principles with particular significance for the leader-participant relationship.

THERAPEUTIC RECREATION LEADERSHIP

Understanding TR leadership as a blend of the roles of therapist and recreation specialist helps to answer the question, "What kind of person should I be to practice therapeutic recreation?" (Sylvester, 2002, p. 330). The person who provides TR services is a person who is self-aware; possesses the ability to communicate, motivate, and influence; expresses empathy; respects their diverse backgrounds and beliefs; and values the potential impact of recreation experiences.

Self-Awareness

Self-awareness is a fundamental aspect of being a professional. It is the TRS's ethical responsibility to develop self-awareness in order to influence others in a healthy and constructive manner. Developing self-awareness is an ongoing process involving reflecting on one's own attitudes, feelings, and values and monitoring their effects on behavior. This

process promotes the TRS's growth and development. Self-awareness enables the TRS to

- understand clients more quickly because she understands herself and how people behave;
- avoid imposing her values on clients, which can result in judgments that may negatively affect practice; and
- recognize any limitations in her ability to help clients with behaviors that she feels uncomfortable about or disapproves of (Austin, 2004).

Knowing yourself and how you feel about helping and working with others is the first step in becoming an ethical practitioner. Who we are relates to our individual value system, which we develop throughout our lifetime and which generally reflects the values and beliefs that have been imparted to us from family, religion, culture, or society. A self-aware person understands his value system and acts accordingly. Values are beliefs that influence behaviors. Personal and professional values merge in everyday practice. As a self-aware professional it is important that your actions be value based. **Value-based behavior** results from reflecting upon one's beliefs and attitudes and making a conscious effort to assess, clarify, and embrace those values that are important for professional practice (Davis, 2006). As a TR professional you are expected to make a commitment to reflecting on and clarifying your values so that they do not interfere with your practice.

As TRSs we have an ethical responsibility to treat all clients in a fair, honest, respectful, and helpful manner. Understanding any prejudices or negative opinions we may have about people, based on their ethnicity or disability, is one aspect of self-awareness. Another aspect is our obligation to know ourselves so that we do not seek to meet personal needs in relationships with our clients. Personal needs such as the need to be liked or the need for attention, power, or control can negatively affect interactions with clients. This can pose a difficulty for the beginning TRS who, because of age and life experience, may not be fully aware of unmet personal needs. The only needs you should satisfy in your professional relationships with clients are the needs to feel of service and to have a sense of accomplishment and pride in helping another.

A professional who lacks self-awareness is in danger of allowing stereotypical beliefs to affect her attitudes toward clients. Stereotyped views may include negative attitudes and beliefs about people with disabilities, prejudices toward people of a different culture or ethnicity, and value judgments of others' behaviors. If these stereotypes are allowed to dictate the TRS's behaviors, she not only is less effective but is behaving unethically. Examples of stereotypical thinking are the belief that people with Alzheimer's disease don't need to go to programs because they'll forget what they did anyway, the belief that a person in a wheelchair can't participate in sports, and the belief that a person who abuses alcohol or other drugs will never be able to change. These attitudes limit our potential to assist our clients because they lower our expectations about what they can achieve.

Becoming self-aware is a thoughtful process that entails reflection, experience, and a conscious commitment to professional practice; but just being self-aware is not enough. Self-awareness, values, and understanding ethical practice affect the professional therapeutic relationship or alliance that the TRS forms with the client. Understanding the code of ethics and the four core TR values and four core TR principles (discussed in chapter 2) helps form a

Suggestions for Developing Self-Awareness

- Practice mindfulness: Be aware of the moment you are experiencing.
- Evaluate your behaviors and interactions with others. How are you perceived? How do others react to you? Are you comfortable with how you behave and what you say?
- Keep a journal: Record your experiences each day.
- Make a list of your talents and strengths.
- Carry on a conversation looking in a mirror. What is your reaction to your own body language? Are you aware of how others see you?
- Audiotape a conversation you are having. Is your speech clear, and is your tone of voice appropriate? Does your language express what you want to convey about yourself?
- Make a list of things about yourself that you'd like to improve. Set goals for how you can address these.
- Write a personal philosophy statement identifying your values and beliefs. Do your behaviors actually match your values and beliefs? Are these your beliefs or ones you have carried over from your family and other influences without thinking about what they mean to you and how they influence your actions?
- Take a formal personality test. Numerous such tests are available that may afford you some insight into how you interact and view the world. Some of the best known are the Meyers-Briggs Type Indicator, the Minnesota Multiphasic Inventory (MMPI), the Keirsey Temperament Sorter, and the Sixteen Personality Factor Questionnaire.
- Find a mentor or someone you trust to give you honest and balanced feedback.
- Read, read, read.

foundation for practice and provides a framework for developing cross-cultural competence.

Cross-Cultural Competence

A TR professional must understand and respect the individual differences of each client and demonstrate this in her behaviors, attitudes, and beliefs on a daily basis (Shank & Coyle, 2002) in order to help "people from all cultures to meet their needs" (Sylvester et al., 2001). This concept is known as **cross-cultural competence**, which is the ability of a "professional to work effectively in cross-cultural situations" (Davis, 2006, p. 152). Cross-cultural competence is developed through "the lifelong pursuit of increasing personal awareness of other cultures" (Getz, 2002) and is the TRS's ethical responsibility as expressed in the codes of ethics. Being culturally competent is an evolving process, and people often go through various stages in that process. Professionals gradually incorporate cultural awareness into their daily interactions with the goal of instinctively being able to provide culturally competent care. These are the four stages of cultural competence:

Unconscious incompetence: not being aware that one is lacking knowledge about another culture

Conscious incompetence: being aware that one is lacking knowledge about another culture

Conscious competence: learning about a client's culture and providing culturally specific interventions

Unconscious competence: automatically providing culturally congruent care to clients of diverse cultures

From Purnell and Paulanka 2003.

In order to work in TR with clients from cultures that differ from one's own, the TRS should first learn about her clients' cultures, beliefs, values, and attitudes and how these influence behaviors. Culture influences the meaning people attach to experiences and what is considered either appropriate or inappropriate behavior. Preferences for recreation activities, health practices, responses to illness and stress, and communication may all be influenced by culture. Understanding culture then takes place on two levels: above the surface and below the surface. Above the surface are the things that we can see, hear, touch, or taste such as dress, speech, gestures, eye contact, food, music, ceremonies, and celebrations. Below the surface are the deeper beliefs, values, and traditions of a culture. The TRS cannot fully understand a culture by its surface behaviors alone. Identity from a cultural perspective incorporates both levels. A TRS must be able to cross cultural borders in order to practice effectively. A comprehensive knowledge of other cultures that goes beyond the typical special event activities is necessary in order to develop meaningful and realistic outcomes and facilitate effective treatment. A TRS may not believe that a certain behavior is appropriate for herself but should acknowledge that this behavior is valid and appropriate for another individual when understood in the context of that person's culture (Gollnick & Chinn, 2008).

All of us have attitudes that we may or may not be able to change, but how those attitudes affect our behavior is under our control. Being aware of the influence of attitudes on behaviors will help the TRS monitor her conduct for ethical practice. The TRS needs to be wary of **ethnocentrism**, which is the belief that one's own culture is superior to others. See table 4.1 to determine your attitude toward cultures different from yours; the higher the score, the more ethnocentric you are in your views of other cultures. While to a certain extent it is natural to value one's own culture, these beliefs should not be a barrier to understanding and valuing other cultures. When the TRS refuses to view a client's behavior in the context of his cultural beliefs and practices, she is behaving unethically. This closed attitude is detrimental to the therapeutic relationship. Increasing one's self-awareness by reflecting on one's attitudes or stereotypes about a specific culture is the beginning of the process of becoming culturally competent. When cultural awareness, sensitivity, and knowledge are incorporated into the application of the TR process, the TRS ensures that she is acting in an ethical and competent manner.

How we communicate with our clients and the way they communicate with us are directly influenced by culture. Effective communication cannot occur without cross-cultural competence. The types and meanings of gestures and facial expressions, style of clothing, and even the use of time and space vary from culture to culture. In Western cultures people say "no" by moving the head from side to side, but in some other cultures they move the head up and down. People may smile not to signify understanding but to be agreeable. Revealing clothing may be viewed as a fashion choice in one culture but sexually provocative in another. Taking off a hat or head covering is expected in certain situations as a sign of respect; if a TRS does

TABLE 4.1

Ethnocentricity Scale

	Strongly agree	Agree	Disagree	Strongly disagree
1. I am against buying foreign imports.	4	3	2	1
2. I find it frustrating when someone from another country doesn't understand what I say.	4	3	2	1
3. I would have a hard time living in another country.	4	3	2	1
4. I feel uncomfortable when I'm around people from another country.	4	3	2	1
5. I do not care for ethnic food.	4	3	2	1

From R. Kunstler and F. Stavola Daly, 2010, *Therapeutic recreation leadership and programming* (Champaign, IL: Human Kinetics). Reprinted, by permission, from R. Russell, 2005, *Pastimes: The context of contemporary culture*, 3rd ed. (Chicago, IL: Sagamore Press), 162.

not know that people may wear a head covering in accordance with religious beliefs, misunderstandings may result. In Western cultures, arriving late for a program or appointment is seen as disrespectful. However, punctuality is not a universal value; other cultures are more flexible about schedules and appointments. Another important issue in the health care setting is discussing a patient's health status or illness. In some cultures this is considered disrespectful and is discouraged. This topic is discussed further in chapter 5.

Developing cross-cultural competence applies to cultural groups based not only on ethnicity or national origin, but also on age, disability, gender, religion, economic status, race, sexual orientation, shared interests, or living environment. Examples include deaf culture; Hells Angels; age-segregated communities; and gay, lesbian, bisexual, and transgendered groups.

Subcultures, present in all societies, share some of the beliefs and attitudes of the primary culture but also have their own patterns of behaviors and beliefs. **Diversity** refers to the variety of people and groups that exist within any society. Most settings where TRSs work are becoming increasingly diverse as societies become more multicultural. Along with understanding cultural differences, beliefs, and practices based on ethnic background, the TRS should acquire knowledge of and demonstrate respect for people of all groups.

Professional Relationships

The nature of the TR environment is such that clients often develop close relationships with the TRS, attributable to the friendly and relaxed atmosphere that recreation experiences create. Clients may feel more comfortable expressing themselves in the TR setting, which is perceived as "nonclinical." Having fun can sometimes lead to confusion about where the professional relationship ends and friendship begins. It is not difficult to understand that clients may mistake the relaxed and empathetic atmosphere of TR as something other than therapeutic. Therapeutic relationships are powerful in helping to change people's lives, but maintaining appropriate relationships that promote healing and growth requires thought and effort. Respecting the boundaries between the personal and professional, understanding transference and countertransference, and appropriate use of self-disclosure are concerns that may arise in the provision of TR leadership.

PROFESSIONAL BOUNDARIES

Boundary refers to the invisible line that defines the limits between professional and personal behavior. Boundary issues arise when the TRS's conversations and actions in the presence of the client cross the line demarcating appropriate professional behaviors. Boundary issues can present real ethical concerns. For example, acts such as hugging clients when they do well or are in need of comfort may not be considered appropriate in certain settings, such as treatment centers for mental health and substance abuse. These behaviors may send mixed messages to clients about the nature of the TRS's relationship with them. In other settings, such as long-term care for residents who are elderly, touch is more acceptable. Even here, however, residents who are confused may misunderstand the meaning of a gesture like this. In settings with children and individuals who have developmental disabilities, issues of sexual abuse are of grave concern and physical contact is often discouraged. Unfortunately, the TRS's best intentions may be misinterpreted. The TRS must always monitor her feelings and actions to ensure that appropriate boundaries are maintained.

Keep in mind that clients may have been struggling with boundary issues before they even began receiving services. Serious ethical concerns arise when the TRS fails to recognize that his relationship with his clients has crossed the line from professional to something more personal. **Boundary intelligence** means being able to apply interpersonal skills in a professional manner and understanding that establishing a therapeutic relationship requires not just self-awareness, but also vigilance regarding how clients are responding to us (Adams, 2005). There is a difference between a therapeutic relationship and a social relationship. "In therapeutic relationships it is the role of the therapist to give help and the role of the client to receive help" (Austin, 2002b, p. 118). While the connection between the TRS and client exists, its sole purpose is to fulfill the purposes of TR. This relationship is not intended to be reciprocal. As discussed earlier, the TRS should not seek to meet personal needs within the client–therapist relationship. The reward for the TRS in her professional practice is in the satisfaction gained from helping another person. The TRS should work with the team to help clients understand the meaning of boundaries in their personal lives and to determine if boundary issues have hindered their abilities to achieve their goals.

Boundary issues that may arise relate to accepting gifts from clients; giving out home addresses, phone numbers, and e-mail addresses; and having contact with clients after their discharge. If the TRS has a page on a social networking site, she should consider the appropriateness of its content in the event that her client views it and how it might affect the professional relationship. Therapeutic recreation specialists should encourage their agencies and organizations to have discussions on boundary issues and to set reasonable and fair policies regard-

ing touch as well as these other concerns. As always, professional knowledge and competence, as well as the code of ethics and agency policies, serve as guidelines for acceptable interactions.

TRANSFERENCE AND COUNTERTRANSFERENCE

Another set of issues that may arise in therapeutic relationships is transference and countertransference. **Transference** occurs when clients project or redirect issues and feelings onto the TRS that are really an outgrowth of prior experiences and relationships. These feelings may take the form of anger, attraction, mistrust, dependency, or idolization. The client is unaware of what he is doing. Working out these problems is beneficial to the client, but dealing with transference issues requires the skills and training of mental health professionals. Most TRSs typically have not developed this level of skill and should present concerns that transference is occurring to the team or an appropriate professional in the work setting. The team can provide the TRS with guidelines and suggestions for how to respond to the client in this situation.

On the other hand, **countertransference** can occur when the TRS begins to treat the client as if he were a person from her past. The TRS transfers to the client feelings related to her past experiences or previous relationships as a result of unresolved issues that she may have. A client may remind her of a grandmother, her own child, or even a former best friend or boyfriend. If the TRS finds that this is occurring, she should discuss the matter with the appropriate staff member, who can provide guidance as to the proper course of action. A skilled mental health professional can use countertransference to gain insight into her own and the client's behaviors and motives. Again, self-awareness and self-monitoring are essential to ensuring that countertransference does not negatively affect the professional relationship between the TRS and the client.

SELF-DISCLOSURE

Self-disclosure is the careful and thoughtful sharing of personal information, by the TRS, in the context of the therapeutic relationship for the purpose of increasing the client's self-understanding. This is information that would normally not be known or available to the client. The TRS uses self-disclosure as a means of demonstrating empathy in order to build trust, to help clients understand that what they are feeling or experiencing is not so unusual, and to help them develop insight. Self-disclosure is used to benefit only the client, and not the TRS. The TRS must be careful about what she chooses to disclose

A Case of Countertransference

Ann is a TRS at a rehabilitation and long-term care center. Most of the residents are the traditional geriatric nursing home population; however, in the last year, a younger group of clients have been admitted with a primary diagnosis of multiple sclerosis. Ann has recently been reprimanded by staff for becoming too close to a new client, Mary. Ann spends all her extra time with Mary and often stays late after work to visit with her. Ann explains to the supervisor that she and Mary are the same age and that Mary reminds her of a friend she had in college who died in a car accident. Ann says, "Spending time with Mary is like having my friend back." She has told her supervisor that she sees nothing wrong with the situation because she is not neglecting her duties, but some of the other clients have complained that Mary is receiving special treatment. Ann insists that this is not the case and that in fact Mary is benefiting from their relationship. The supervisor tells Ann that she must limit her contact with Mary and maintain professional boundaries. Do you think the supervisor is justified in telling Ann to change her behavior with Mary?

and when. Self-disclosure may backfire if clients pass judgment on the information provided by the therapist. It should not lead to the client's feeling concern for the TRS or being burdened by the information the TRS has shared. For example, a young woman who is depressed because of a divorce may feel that no one has ever suffered as she is suffering. The TRS may share that she too has had an unsuccessful relationship that left her heartbroken, but found ways to cope and go on. If the TRS instead had shared that she was fearful about how she might behave toward her ex-husband if she saw him again, and the client becomes worried about how the TRS is feeling, the TRS has overburdened the client. The TRS should carefully monitor whether she is disclosing personal information appropriately.

Self-disclosure may occur unintentionally when a client googles the TRS. Much information is posted online that we have no control over. Clients may learn personal information about the TRS that affects the professional relationship. The TRS should be aware of this possibility and be alert to any signs that a client has obtained or is using information inappropriately. The TRS should discuss these concerns with the team, as ethical issues may arise when our self-disclosure is misinterpreted by a client. To maintain a professional, therapeutic relationship with clients also requires interpersonal skills including communication and the ability to use power and influence.

Interpersonal Skills

Interpersonal skills are an essential component of effective treatment (Hebert, 1997) and central to TR leadership. **Interpersonal skills** are skills used in face-to-face contact with our clients and coworkers; they "include the ability to read and manage the emotions, motivations, and behaviors of oneself and others during social interactions or in a social-interactive context" (West Virginia Department of Education, 2008, p. 7). Critical to professional practice and to developing and furthering the relationships among TRSs, clients, and other professionals are knowledge and understanding of how human beings communicate; demonstration of sensitivity and empathy; and appropriate uses of patience, silence, power, and influence.

Interpersonal skills are often confused with personality traits. Personality refers to the unique qualities that reflect who a person is. Therapeutic recreation specialists have been viewed as having or being expected to have certain specific traits that make up the "TR personality," such as good at communicating, enthusiastic, positive, optimistic, outgoing, high energy, creative, fun loving, patient, genuine, and well organized. Due to the upbeat, enjoyable environment these traits help to create, however, TR is not always seen as "serious" work and success is often attributed primarily to the "personality" of the TRS and not to a set of professional skills. These personality traits do indeed contribute to successful TR leadership, but have led other professionals to misinterpret TR as just the provision of activities that are fun, designed to pass the time without focusing on goals and outcomes. This view diminishes the value and credibility of TR programs, causing TR to be seen as "therapy lite," and the TRS as the "play lady" or "party person." TR is

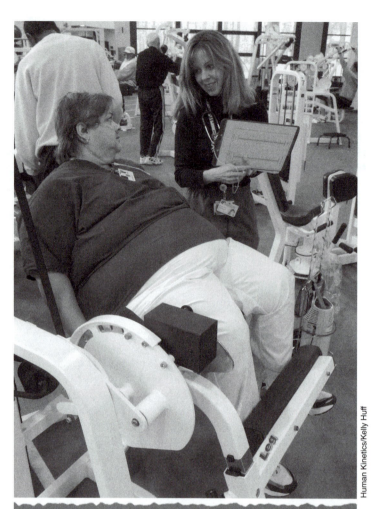

The TRS is responsible to develop interpersonal skills, regardless of her own personality traits.

Human Kinetics/Kelly Huff

seen as "soft," and its clinical or therapeutic value is not recognized. On the contrary, when combined with the TRS's professional knowledge and skills, these traits are vital to successfully fulfilling the purposes of TR. A qualified TRS will demonstrate these traits in the context of delivering effective TR programs. If a well-prepared TRS with the requisite knowledge and skills does not feel she possesses some of these essential personality traits, she should not be discouraged. One theory of leadership, known as the **Great Man Theory**, addresses just this concept (Russell, 2004). When initially formulated, the theory explained that a successful leader is a person who was born with inherent traits or abilities, and thus it was believed that leaders were "born, not made." Yet as the theory evolved, it was reinterpreted to support the belief that potential leaders indeed could be developed through appropriate training, education, and mentoring. Thinking of these traits as skills that can be developed, rather than personality characteristics with which we are born, facilitates developing and applying them as a function of TR leadership. Cultivating the interpersonal skills that are crucial to working with people is a core competency for TR practice and advances the development of the profession.

COMMUNICATION

Good communication skills are a hallmark of an effective TRS. The TRS uses communication skills and techniques to develop, nurture, and maintain the therapeutic relationship. **Communication** involves both verbal and nonverbal exchanges

Tommy's Story: The Meanings of Words

Tommy is a 13-year-old boy who is in a physical rehabilitation unit for a sport-related injury. Tommy plays on a highly competitive Little League baseball team in his community. Tommy's father is a coach and an avid baseball fan. He and Tommy have expressed concerns about when Tommy will be able to return to Little League. The TRS, when asked by Tommy and his father about his progress, states, "Tommy is doing well in therapeutic recreation and making good progress. He has increased his ability to stand independently by 25 percent." Since Tommy has been brought up by his father to believe that "good" isn't good enough and that 100 percent is the only acceptable grade, Tommy, as well as his father, misinterprets the TRS's comments. Instead of feeling good about his progress, he feels as if he has let himself, his father, and the TRS down. Tommy's father expresses anger that Tommy is not making greater and faster progress. As a competitive child with an equally competitive father, Tommy has a frame of reference for success that places little value on the word "good." Tommy and his father appear to value success only in terms of words like "best," "excellent," and "outstanding." In this situation, the TRS must work on communicating to the parent and Tommy the exact nature of his progress in terms that are meaningful to them.

between individuals. It is composed of expressing ideas and thoughts verbally through words and nonverbally through body language, as well as receiving what others are expressing both verbally and nonverbally.

Verbal Communication

Verbal communication focuses on "language," that is, the specific words used and their meanings. Words express the cognitive content of what a person is communicating, such as content referring to people, places, events, and things. Each of us attaches specific meanings to words, beyond the dictionary definitions, based on background and life experience. Therefore our clients may interpret the words we say differently from the way we intended, and what they mean when they speak to us may be misinterpreted as well (Engleberg & Wynn, 2000). This impedes the therapeutic relationship and can seriously hinder a client's progress.

The TRS needs to check that the client understands what she is saying and that she understands what the client is saying. It is not uncommon for TRSs to be uncomfortable with clients' statements about their feelings, as in "I want to die" or "Nobody cares about me." When a client shares personal feelings, the TRS may feel uncomfortable because these issues are sensitive and she may not know how to respond. She may say, "Things will get better" or "*I* care about you." But this has the effect of denying the client's feelings rather than demonstrating empathy and understanding. Taking in and comprehending the verbal and nonverbal content of the client's communication can help the TRS gain a more complete understanding of the client. Truly listening means that the TRS understands the meaning behind the words. In this case the client may be feeling extreme loneliness or helplessness. The TRS could say "You feel very lonely" or "You feel as if you don't have enough control over your life." Allowing the client to express his true feelings, or reflecting back to the client the feelings behind his words, may enable him to develop greater insight and self-awareness. The TRS should try to identify which emotions she has difficulty dealing with as part of her own ongoing process of self-awareness and should learn and practice useful communication techniques and responses. This demonstrates

Choosing the Best Words

Which Is the Best Response?

Johnny states to the TR specialist, "My doggie got run over today."

Which response should the TRS give?

1. Well, that's one less mouth to feed.
2. Well, it's just an animal. Cheer up! It could be worse.
3. I'm sorry to hear that, Johnny.
4. You're feeling awfully sad about losing your little dog, aren't you?
5. It's very sad to lose such a close friend.

If you chose 1: This is an irrelevant or harmful response as it shows no sensitivity to what has occurred or understanding of what Johnny is experiencing.

If you chose 2: This denies Johnny's feelings.

If you chose 3: This is essentially neutral, neither hurtful nor helpful.

If you chose 4: You are acknowledging Johnny's unexpressed feelings of sadness and adding to his ability to understand the situation.

If you chose 5: You express total understanding of what he is feeling, which enables him to feel comfort because the depth of his loss is recognized and acknowledged.

Adapted from *Reflective Listening* handout using modified Carkhuff Scale of responses, n.d.

that the TRS has respect for the client, has a true desire to help, and sees the client as an individual.

Nonverbal Communication

Nonverbal communication is conveyed through body language and expresses the feelings behind the words. Body language includes body posture and position, tone of voice, facial expressions, and gestures. Body language may be a truer indication of people's real feelings than the words they use, because most people tend to be more comfortable talking about concrete, tangible events, people, and activities, known as **cognitive content**, than about their emotions. It also is easier to respond to words than to the feelings behind the words, as we have already seen. Feelings, whether unspoken or verbally expressed, are known as the **affective content** of communication. When we express our feelings, we may be revealing our hopes, fears, doubts, and insecurities, leaving us vulnerable to rejection and disappointment. Many of our clients have met with failure during their lives and may be hesitant to share their feelings openly. The TRS should be alert to the unspoken messages clients may be communicating through their body language.

The TRS also should become aware of what her own body language is expressing. If our body language and verbal language are not congruent, that is, if they do not convey the same meaning, this can lead to confusion, distrust, and a breakdown in the communication process. Saying "I really want to help you" in a monotone while turning away from the client conveys "I don't care" more powerfully than if those words had been spoken. Nodding and smiling can offer encouragement without any spoken words at all. Both patience and listening are communicated through body language.

Patience

Working with people who have faced the challenges of illness, disability, or other conditions requires **patience**, which is often viewed as a personality trait of helping professionals. Yet patience is a skill that can be acquired as well as further developed. Patience deserves particular attention, both as a quality of the TRS and as a skill we can help our clients develop. To be patient is to have the ability to postpone gratification or wait for something rather than expecting something to happen immediately. This also includes being patient with yourself and the client, paying attention to the client, not rushing him, listening, and using silence when appropriate. Therapeutic recreation specialists must be patient in their interactions with clients, allowing them the time they need to make their own decisions

and to accomplish their goals. Change takes time. The foundation for change is built from hard and deliberate work. The TRS can also teach clients the art of being patient so that they do not become frustrated with their progress and abandon all they have achieved. Our responsibility can also be to help our clients look at situations in a new way and accept that it takes time to accomplish change and meet goals.

Lack of patience can harm the therapeutic relationship. If the TRS displays impatience (or frustration or loses her temper) with clients, interrupts when clients are speaking slowly, or does something for clients rather then giving them time to do it themselves, he is behaving in an unethical manner. Having a bad day is not an acceptable excuse for a TRS. The issue is not whether or not a TRS has the right to *feel* impatient with the client; it is that the TRS cannot *act* impatiently with the client.

Patience does not mean *not* setting appropriate limits for a client who needs them. A pleasant, talk-

Suggestions for Developing Patience

Hesitate before responding. Count to 5 before saying something you'll regret.

Focus on the now. Stop thinking about what is going to happen next while you are in the middle of doing something. If you are doing arts and crafts with a group, don't think about activities scheduled for later in the day.

Procrastination is not patience. Don't put off things you have to do. Putting things off only creates anxiety and interferes with completing tasks on schedule.

Reflect on impulses. If you see something expensive that you want to buy or if you are upset with someone over something that was said, wait 24 hours. Give yourself time to weigh all your options.

Don't interrupt when others are talking. Listen.

Relax if you have to wait your turn. Use the time to make observations of your surroundings or think about a project you are working on or a new undertaking.

ative patient in a psychiatric unit may use conversation as a distraction from dealing with her issues. Or she may use it to manipulate the TRS to allow her not to participate or not complete a project when that is one of her goals. Patience involves being alert to a client's negative behaviors, delaying tactics, or motivational problems that affect her progress. It is the TRS's role to help the client identify obstacles to her progress and to determine what is necessary for the client to move forward. The TRS may need to "lose patience" with a client by no longer accepting certain behaviors and redirecting her to the task at hand. The TRS may determine, in consultation with the team, when this is appropriate.

Listening

Listening helps the TRS learn the client's "story." Listening is the process by which the brain absorbs the meaning of what the client is saying in order to understand the facts and ideas being expressed. Listening requires attention and concentration and can encourage the client to communicate more fully and openly. Listening has three components:

- Being attentive to the client
- Receiving and comprehending the cognitive and affective content of the client's communication
- Reflecting one's understanding back to the client

By attending carefully to what the client says, the TRS demonstrates support for and acceptance of the client. Attending includes making eye contact, focusing on the client, not being distracted, and not interrupting, as well as nodding, saying things like "Um-hmm" or "I see," and being patient. Listening contributes to the therapeutic relationship by demonstrating the TRS's empathy. **Empathy** is "a kind of holistic listening that can unite the therapist with the patient" (Davis, 2006, p. 85). It means "knowing what it must feel like to be this client" (Shank & Coyle, 2002, p. 197). Part of expressing empathy is acceptance (Carter et al., 2003), as the TRS acknowledges the client in the moment of communication without judgment. Empathy is reflected in the TRS's ability to clearly relate to the client's experience, to understand the meaning of the experience, and to reflect that back to the client to promote growth and healing. Empathy is not **sympathy**, which is feeling compassion for the client and the circumstances of his life and current situation, but is an acknowledgement of and respect for the client's experience from his own perspective. As TRSs emphasize the meaning of the TR experience and how this experience helps the client to grow and change, empathy is one of the keys to the client's success in TR.

To be effective, the TRS must listen carefully rather than rush in with responses and comments. Often the TRS wants to be reassuring and offers suggestions and advice rather than allowing the client to express his feelings and come up with his own solutions. Instead of making a quick remark that doesn't truly respond to the client's needs and feelings, the TRS can acknowledge these feelings with empathy. This builds trust between the TRS and the client and can lead the client to develop more insight into and acceptance of his situation. Ironically, silence is a technique that can be used to enhance communication.

Silence ●

Silence is an underused and misunderstood communication technique; however, it is vital to creating a therapeutic relationship. Many people are uncomfortable with silence, expecting that there should be conversation whenever people are together even if it's just "small talk." It is considered polite to converse so as not to be seen as rude or even hostile. Sometimes silence is used as a punishment to hurt another human being, or is an indication of resistance to cooperation, participation, or exploration of uncomfortable feelings. But silence also can be used to enhance communication between the TRS and the client. Silence used in this context can allow individuals to take their own time to think and can lead to deeper reflection and more meaningful responses. By being silent, the TRS demonstrates respect, empathy, patience, and thoughtfulness about what the client is trying to communicate. Silence can also give clients time to follow directions, figure out how to do something on their own, and organize their thoughts, especially if they have a neurological or learning disorder. Clients can be taught about the use of silence and practice this during TR programs in order to learn how to cope with external and internal stressors that are difficult or overwhelming. If a client lashes out verbally at people when she feels hurt or threatened, the TRS may help the others understand that they have the right be silent as an effective response to such behaviors. Clients can use silence to help them maintain their self-control and take the time to express their feelings more appropriately and accurately.

The TRS may find that severely disturbed clients perceive silence as threatening. On the other hand, people from some cultures may not be comfortable with sharing their feelings and may stay silent, or may feel it is disrespectful to share without having been invited to. The TRS is encouraged to be patient and understand when clients need the time to reflect and respond, or when silence may be too uncomfortable for a client and cause undue stress, or when silence goes against cultural practices. Although patience, listening, and the use of silence can help us gain insight into the client's feelings and promote the development of the therapeutic relationship, these ways of responding also show that the TRS feels sensitivity and caring even for a client who is at a loss for words. The TRS may need to learn how to be silent, as it may not come naturally or easily. It is valuable to learn to be comfortable with silence and not to interject a comment when the client may need more time to formulate a response.

COMMUNICATION STYLES

While communication skills are a powerful TR tool, it is equally important to develop an understanding of the client's communication style. Each person has his own typical mode of self-expression. People can tend to be loud and expressive, or be quiet and thoughtful, or use a lot of gestures; they can be seen as aggressive or passive, or indirect or very forthright. Communication style can be based on factors such as culture, upbringing, health condition, prior experience, and learned responses. A single behavior can be due to any one or a combination of factors:

- A client who makes poor eye contact may either have low-self esteem, suffer from social anxiety disorder, or simply come from a culture in which looking directly at another person can be considered disrespectful, as in Asian cultures.

- A client who is loud and argumentative may simply be reflecting his family's communication

style and not meaning to be aggressive or hostile.

- Clients who are quiet, are not very verbal, and have a flat affect are often misjudged as being uninterested or bored. In fact, they may be shy or may lack confidence.

- Older adults may not be comfortable sharing personal information with a young TRS who uses contemporary language or who is the age of their grandchild.

Men and women also may differ in their communication styles and in the meanings they attach to words and body language. Men tend to be more focused on cognitive content, women on affective content. Women are often interested in talking about and furthering the growth of their relationships and want to discuss or process their feelings. Men tend to be more concrete and comfortable discussing actions that could be taken. Men may initially see things as black or white and may not always be interested in the details. In a hospice setting, the TRS might be trying to comfort a married couple whose adult son has just died from AIDS. The father may be unable to express his anger verbally and retreat into silence. The mother may be crying and talking about her beautiful son and how heartbroken she is. The TRS may offer comfort to the mother by listening to her, reflecting her feelings, and touching her arm in a caring way. With the father, it may be helpful for the TRS to focus on what needs to be done to prepare for the funeral as a way of helping the father regain some feeling of control over the situation.

Misreading a client's communication style can lead to wrong assumptions about what matters to the client; for example, a TRS might perceive that a client does not care about getting well or that he is hostile or resentful about being in the program. Sensitivity to the many variables that influence how a person communicates is necessary for effective TR leadership. Communication is complex primarily because people are complex. The TRS should keep in mind that a client's behavior makes sense in the context of the client's world. It is the TRS's responsibility to understand the basis of a client's behavior and help him understand how this behavior may be affecting his everyday life. Clients also may misinterpret the TRS's communication style and verbal and nonverbal expressions. Understanding clients in the context of their total life experience is necessary for communication to be successful. In order to maximize TR's potential contribution to improving clients' well-being, the TRS also has to be aware of the amount of **power** and influence she has on their behaviors and feelings.

Photo courtesy of Fran Stavola Daly.

Nonverbal communication can be just as powerful as verbal communication.

POWER

Power is not a dirty word! Many people are frightened by the idea that they may possess the power to influence the actions or outcomes of others. But understanding power, its sources, and its usefulness in achieving goals in TR is a valuable skill that the TRS can use in his work with clients. Power represents the degree of influence one has over people's behaviors and the environment, or the ability to control the environment and the behaviors of others in a given situation. An individual's power varies depending on the circumstances. You may feel you have a lot of control or influence over your work situation but feel powerless in your personal relationships. You may feel able to influence your friends to do certain things but not effective in persuading other members of the team of the value of a course of action you suggest.

The most common types of power are legitimate, expert, referent, reward, and coercive (Austin, 2009; Jordan, 2007; Russell, 2004). **Legitimate power** derives from an appointed position and the authority that is placed in a position according to the organizational structure. The professional's job title in and of itself implies responsibility, power, and decision-making authority. In TR, job titles have not been standardized, leading to confusion over the scope of practice and even the legitimacy of the TRS's role as a professional, particularly in health care settings. One school of thought is that the title "recreation therapist" or "recreational therapist" more closely aligns TR with other rehabilitative therapies regardless of whether this is as an appropriate description of the TRS's responsibilities. Credentialing, in the form of professional **certification** or licensure, lends legitimacy to the practice of TR. It provides standardization despite the varying job titles and brings TR into line with all professions that endorse a specified set of qualifications for practice.

Expert power is based on the professional's knowledge in his specific area of professional preparation. When clients feel that the TRS "knows" what he is doing as it relates to their medical situation, health condition, or specific assessed needs, they put their trust in the TRS. Being a professional implies that you possess expertise, and that is why others trust you to provide services with their best interests at heart, even if you are a stranger. The clients' trust in our knowledge and ability to enhance their well-being motivates them to participate in our activities and programs. Expert power also is crucial in our role as team members since knowledge is an essential component when it comes to gaining and maintaining the respect and collaboration of our peers. Over time, legitimate power is less influential without the expertise to support it. A person in a designated authority position loses respect and the ability to influence others if he lacks the knowledge and skill to bring about results.

The success of TRSs at helping people to achieve outcomes is to a large extent due to **referent power,** the "personal character" (Russell, 2004) of the individual TRS. While this may sound like a trait in the

Therapeutic Recreation Certification

The **National Council for Therapeutic Recreation Certification (NCTRC)** is the internationally recognized credentialing organization dedicated to the professional certification of TR specialists.

NCTRC reviews and processes over 1,000 applications each year from candidates for the Certified Therapeutic Recreation Specialist (CTRS) examination. Applicants qualify for the exam based on a combination of education and experience. The computer-based, multiple-choice examination is offered three times a year at hundreds of sites and is administered by a nationwide educational testing service.

NCTRC maintains the registry of CTRSs, processes annual maintenance of certification, renews certifications every five years based on evidence of continuing professional development, and engages in ongoing review of certification standards. NCTRC also handles disciplinary and misrepresentation complaints.

NCTRC actively markets the value of the CTRS credential, educating the public and the profession and advocating for consumer protection.

Visit the NCTRC Web site at www.nctrc.org for complete information on TR certification.

"TR personality," it really reflects the ability of the TRS to develop rapport and establish a therapeutic relationship with the client. People come to TR programs because of the TRS's "appeal" or personal connection to the individual, not only because of the TRS's position of authority or expertise. *Charisma* is tied to the concept of referent power. The word "charisma" comes from a Greek word meaning "gift" or "divine favor" and refers to a certain "magnetic attraction" that a person may possess. Charisma is viewed as the leader's innate ability to both attract people to TR programs and exercise exceptional influence and persuasion over them. However, as with other leadership abilities, it appears that some aspects of a charismatic personality can be developed. Behaviors such as speaking clearly and directly, letting people know you care about them, being genuine, and using relaxed and open body language are all skills of the charismatic leader that also are required of effective therapists. The TRS may use his innate charisma to connect with, attract, and persuade clients; but unless he has expertise to support this innate quality, clients may lose their trust in him and their interest in participating in TR programs.

Reward and *coercive power* can be a source of controversy in TR practice. **Reward power** is based on the ability to control a person's receiving recreation as a reward or benefit. The intrinsic reward of participating in TR programs is the "fun" and positive experience that the client has. Therapeutic recreation often provides experiences that people desire and enjoy very much: opportunities to feel control, feel competence, make progress, socialize, engage in self-expression, be creative, obtain food, or take a trip. In some facilities, non-TR staff may consider attending recreation and special events rewards for good behavior. They may even view TR, when prescribed as a form of treatment or intervention, as a reward rather than as a service to which the client is entitled. Using recreation as a reward or punishment may pose an ethical dilemma because the right to leisure and recreation is a core TR value.

Coercive power, the power to take away recreation opportunities, may have an effect on client's autonomy and dignity because it influences behavior via threat or punishment. The application of coercive power can include expressing open disapproval of a client's behavior or threatening or applying punishment as a way to influence his behavior. Coercive power should not be confused with the TRS's setting standards of appropriate behavior for a program prior to implementation. Meeting these standards could become a goal for the client. If a client cannot meet these standards initially, he cannot participate in this particular program but should have other recreation options available whose standards or criteria he does meet.

In some settings, such as those using a token economy, the TRS may not have control over whether or not recreation is used as a privilege to be earned. The TRS should reflect upon and discuss the ethical issues in this situation. Regardless of personal feelings or prior experiences with the use of power, the TRS must recognize that consciously or not, he is influencing the actions and reactions of his clients. It is our ethical responsibility to be aware of how we may influence others and to use this power according to the ethical standards of integrity, respect, fairness, honesty, and competence. Understanding the types of power and their impacts will enable the TRS to more effectively and successfully interact with other professionals as well as motivate clients to participate in TR to achieve their goals.

Motivation

Motivation is the cause or stimulus of action, the driving force that initiates and directs behavior. It's the answer to *why* you want what you want and do what you do. The TRS may find that much of her energy is spent trying to motivate clients to participate in TR. Due to their physical capabilities, mood, or personal circumstances, they may not respond to the TRS's efforts. To successfully motivate other people, you first and foremost have to be motivated yourself. Therapeutic recreation leadership is most effective when the TRS herself is intrinsically motivated to help her clients through the provision of TR programs. A self-motivated person is goal directed, is enthusiastic, takes chances, and is eager to learn new things. Many self-motivated TRSs have high energy levels and are health conscious. They practice what they preach by balancing the demands and responsibilities of their work and their personal life, and have a positive attitude that they convey in their everyday dealings with others. The TRS who is self-motivated understands and values the core principles and values of TR and knows that recreation participation is inherently motivating, which is demonstrated by his satisfying and fulfilling leisure lifestyle. The traits and behaviors of a highly motivated person can be learned and nurtured through education, training, and self-reflection. The TRS's reflection on her own degree of self-motivation can give her keen insight into the wants and needs that motivate clients. Motivation theories attempt to identify those things that drive a person's motivation and give guidelines for motivational strategies, which will be discussed in more detail in chapter 7.

In the following sections we address several motivation theories: transformational leadership, intrinsic and extrinsic motivation, needs theory, choice theory, self-efficacy, and consequences.

TRANSFORMATIONAL LEADERSHIP

The theory of **transformational leadership** suggests that leaders achieve success by inspiring others to believe that they can achieve great things (Kouzes & Posner, 2008). The success that clients have in reaching their goals is in part due to the inspirational leadership provided by the TRS. The trust established in the therapeutic relationship is essential to enabling the clients to transform their situations by achieving their goals. The TRS is often viewed by clients as a role model because she possesses the qualities of a transformational leader. These qualities include passion, enthusiasm, charisma, an inclusive yet individually focused orientation, honesty, loyalty, and fairness. These qualities reflect the ethical mindset of TR practitioners to provide services in the best interests of clients and to be competent and knowledgeable about what clients need and desire to accomplish. Transformational leaders enable people to achieve above and beyond what they might expect, given their own abilities.

INTRINSIC AND EXTRINSIC MOTIVATION

Individuals experience both intrinsic and extrinsic motivation. **Intrinsic motivation** is the motivation that comes from within the individual and is derived from the satisfaction or positive feelings resulting from doing an activity or task. The *doing* of the activity or behavior is rewarding and motivating in and of itself. When a person is intrinsically motivated, the behavior that results is more satisfying and longer lasting than with other sources of motivation. Intrinsic motivation, along with freedom of choice and perceived competence, is one of the defining characteristics of leisure. The leisure experience may provide both intrinsic motivation, in which the doing of something is personally satisfying, and extrinsic motivation, in which something is done with the hope or expectation of a reward. Feeling good about oneself, feeling fulfilled, and having a sense of accomplishment are all benefits of intrinsic motivation. Although many TRSs complain that their clients are not motivated, the wise TRS recognizes that all people are motivated—they just may not be motivated to do what she wants them to do. The TRS's role is to help clients find their "inner motivator."

Transformational leaders inspire others to believe that they can achieve great things.

AP Photo

When a person appears to lack internal motivation, incentives or rewards may be needed to engage him in TR programs. This is known as **extrinsic motivation**, or motivation through the use of factors or incentives external to the individual. Most people are familiar with external motivators in everyday life: prizes, a desired item, food, money, recognition, praise, attention, affection, a promotion, or even a smiley-face sticker. People may engage in an activity or behavior because they want the external reward as much as or rather than because they obtain internal satisfaction from doing the task. For example, while many TRSs are intrinsically motivated to do their jobs, the delivery of a paycheck every two weeks may also be a powerful extrinsic motivator. Extrinsic motivation can initiate behavior but does not guarantee continuation of the behavior or satisfaction from engaging in the behavior. In the absence of intrinsic rewards from one's job, a substantial paycheck may keep one working but will not bring job satisfaction. In the absence of extrinsic rewards, negative behaviors may result as an effort to elicit an external response or recognition. A child who is abused by his father may still want to stay with him because he receives some attention from his father, even if it's in the form of harm. Acting-out behaviors are often bids for attention. The desire for attention is one of the most powerful human motivators. The

TRS should be sure to give appropriate and ample attention to her clients.

With clients, as with TR professionals, there is also often a point where the external motivator loses its effectiveness because the person has become oversaturated or bored with the reward. If the amount of the reward is not increased, the motivation may start to lag. If the external motivator is removed, the person may go back to the original behavior or habits if he has not developed the intrinsic motivation to support the new behavior or activity. Most importantly, while external motivators can be helpful, the role of the TRS is to facilitate the movement of people from extrinsic motivation to intrinsic motivation. Too much reliance on extrinsic motivators can hinder development of internal motivation due to overemphasis on the external rewards and not the internal benefits. Involvement in TR activities can enhance a person's internal motivation when the activities are challenging, offer meaningful choices and recognition of accomplishments, and provide positive interpersonal contacts and group experiences.

Ethically, TRSs should do no harm through the use of extrinsic motivators. They should guard against "bribing" as opposed to providing meaningful incentives for and outcomes of participation that demonstrate respect for the client's dignity and well-being. Incentives should be appropriate to the person's age, interests, cultural values, health status, and personal situation. The TRS must be competent in use of motivational techniques, honest with clients, and fair and just in her allocation of rewards. She must monitor her own behaviors so she is not misusing motivators to improve her own status or to misrepresent the true success of TR services—for example, using refreshments to "lure" participants in order to increase attendance when participation is inappropriate, irrelevant to the program, or harmful to the clients.

MOTIVATION BY NEEDS

Many theories of motivation are based on the belief that human needs are the driving force behind behavior. A need can be viewed as a psychological or physiological condition that causes a person to act in such a way as to satisfy that condition. Needs can be met in positive, healthy, and constructive ways or in negative, unhealthy, and destructive ways. The drive to meet our needs is so powerful that clients will misuse alcohol, drugs, or food or engage in criminal behavior to deal with unmet needs. The role of the TRS is to help clients meet their needs through the more affirmative experience of recreation.

Maslow's Hierarchy of Needs

Maslow's (1971) hierarchy of needs is one theory often used to explain what motivates behavior. Maslow described motivation as the process of meeting human needs that exist on five levels in a hierarchical order:

1. Basic physiological needs such as food, water, clothing, shelter, rest, and exercise
2. Needs for security, safety from physical and emotional harm, and social stability
3. Needs for friendship and family, need to love and be loved, and need for belonging
4. Need for self-esteem, recognition, status, and respect of others and need to be a unique individual
5. Self-actualization or realizing one's full potential, culminating in altruism or doing for the good of others—includes need for meaning and purpose in life, creativity, and autonomy

According to Maslow, people are motivated to fulfill their lowest-level need first, and as that is fulfilled they move on to meet the next highest level of need. If the TRS is attempting to engage a resident in a group activity (level 3) and the client is fearful that someone will steal his things from his room (level 2), that may be the reason he refuses to participate. His lower-level need for security has not been met, so he is not motivated to fulfill a higher-level need to belong to a group. However, people also can seek to meet their needs in any order or may have many needs that they seek to meet at one time (Jordan, 2007). For example, the TRS often interacts with people who have not met all their physiological needs, such as individuals who are homeless. Nevertheless, they may be willing to engage in group activities in which they can utilize their skills and abilities and address their higher-level needs for safety, love, and belongingness, as well as self-esteem. One of the strengths of TR programming is that TR experiences are provided primarily in a group format which helps to meet many human needs. If a person feels welcome and accepted in a group, this may help satisfy her need for belonging, while praise from group members may promote her self-esteem (Engleberg & Wynn, 2000). An example of an activity that can meet multiple needs is exercise. An exercise group can meet a physiological need for physical movement, a need for emotional safety through stress reduction, a need to be social and belong to a group, the need to develop self-esteem through performing the movements successfully, and the need for self-actualization through fulfillment of one's potential to be a fit and healthy person. Understanding the needs that a given activity can meet can help the TRS motivate clients to participate by emphasizing what matters to each individual.

The TRS can apply the principles of Maslow's hierarchy of needs by

- identifying what need the client is seeking to meet,
- recognizing that recreation participation can meet almost all needs, and
- understanding that leisure is a means by which an individual can ultimately achieve self-actualization (Cordes & Ibrahim, 2002).

Glasser's Choice Theory

Another approach to understanding how needs motivate behavior has been developed by Glasser (1998) and is known as Choice Theory. Glasser identified five needs or wants that drive people to action:

- Survival and security
- Belonging and being loved
- Power and respect
- To be free
- To have fun

These needs are seen as universal and exist in all people. Fundamental to meeting these needs is the ability to exercise power or control in ways that have a positive impact on daily life. Behavior, then, is the action taken to satisfy one or more of the basic needs. According to Choice Theory, all needs, including fun, are viewed as innate, and learning how to meet these needs is its own reward.

This view is congruent with TR philosophy. The best way to learn is to have fun while learning. Fun is also an important component in developing relationships with other people. This approach to motivation provides a unique affirmation for the use of recreation and play as a therapeutic intervention for someone experiencing a health crisis. Application of this theory to the practice of TR means that the role of the TRS is to help clients develop better coping skills and recognize that there is always an opportunity to have some control over their actions and choices. Therapeutic recreation provides clients with opportunities to make choices and have control, as well as to create new ways to satisfy their needs that are not self-destructive or do not lead to unhappiness. When clients laugh and have fun while interacting with others during TR programs, they have truly opened themselves up for a learning, and possibly life-changing, experience. Table 4.2 shows the relationship between Maslow's and Glasser's theories with TR applications.

One application of Choice Theory to TR is to encourage people to take photos, known as learning pictures, of a situation in which they are satisfying their needs, such as a photo of the client participating in an activity of his choice. The TRS can facilitate a group in which clients create personal picture

TABLE 4.2

Comparison of Needs Theories With TR Leadership Implications

Maslow's hierarchy of human needs	Glasser's Choice Theory of needs	TR applications to meeting human needs
Physiological	Survival	Offer emotional support; meet basic needs through activities of daily living skills, grooming, snacks, and comforting environment; provide TR programs that are familiar and soothing, including cooking, fitness, and relaxation.
Security	Security	Offer reassurance and adequate information, TR programs that are familiar and success oriented, and a safe environment.
Love and belonging	Belonging and being loved	Encourage involvement and contribution in group activities, peer support, buddy programs; offer TR that fosters feelings of being needed such as animal-assisted therapy, horticulture, and volunteering.
Self-esteem	Power and respect	Provide feedback on clients' accomplishments, assist them in self-evaluation; offer TR programs with opportunities for recognition, responsibility, and leadership.
Self-actualization	Freedom and fun	Encourage choice and the expression of one's identity through development of talents and skills in recreation activities; assist with resources to realize one's potential; use humor.

albums. These albums can be used as a reminder and as a tool to support the clients' abilities to meet their needs by utilizing their strengths in positive ways. Therapeutic recreation leadership involves identifying and reinforcing clients' strengths so they can increase their perceptions of their capabilities, thereby increasing their motivation. This is related to self-efficacy.

SELF-EFFICACY

Self-efficacy is defined as one's perception of being able to meet one's goals and satisfy personal needs in a positive way, or as the judgment of one's own capability to accomplish a task or a particular level of performance (Bandura, 1997). This judgment is based on a person's belief about his ability to control events that affect his life and his capability to organize, as well as execute, a course of action. The development of self-efficacy begins in infancy when a baby first realizes that his actions can cause the actions of others to occur. While the child's relationships with parents, siblings, and peers are powerful agents in the development of self-efficacy, culture and physiological responses to stress also influence one's perceptions of self-efficacy. Efficacy perceptions influence choices that a person makes in all aspects of her daily life, particularly her ability to cope with stress.

Understanding the concept of self-efficacy is useful for TRSs in their efforts to motivate clients. A person's perceptions of self-efficacy may affect his achievement of goals—goals that the team knows are attainable—when his negative perceptions of his capacity to succeed decrease his motivation to act. This perception is not static; it can be influenced and enhanced under certain circumstances, but many people have entrenched views that are not easily changed. Through TR participation, a client may begin to change his perceptions of his self-efficacy as he interacts with the TRS, receives feedback on his efforts, and accomplishes successful outcomes. Some clients achieve outcomes in TR even when they have not been successful in other therapies because of the motivating qualities of the recreation experience provided by the TRS (Kunstler & Sokoloff, 1993). In TR we often utilize the recreation experience to help clients transcend their limitations and as a result transform their outlook on life and their current circumstances. What the TRS does is *intentional*. It does not just happen. It is planned and thought out, resulting in a change of direction and perception for those involved.

Therapeutic recreation leadership that motivates clients involves striking the right balance between those aspects that facilitate the recreation experience and the application of therapeutic techniques that focus on achieving outcomes. Motivation will continue to be a daily challenge for the TRS as she addresses the circumstances of her clients' lives. However, understanding how needs, wants, intrinsic and extrinsic factors, and self-efficacy influence motivation enables the TRS to successfully engage clients in TR programs, with the hope that this will result in long-term benefits. What motivates any individual is a result of a combination of factors, such as personal demographic characteristics and personal experiences.

TR LEADERSHIP FROM AN ENVIRONMENTAL PERSPECTIVE

More and more, the environment is being recognized as a significant influence on clients' success and well-being. We define the **TR environment** as "the distinctive atmosphere that exists in a TR room or space, surrounds a TR program, or is present in the structured or unstructured contact between a TRS and a client or group of clients." From this definition, we can see that the TR environment is an invisible quality or mood that supports the delivery of TR leadership and that is external to individuals. However, therapeutic recreation leadership is directed not only toward individual clients. It is also a process directed toward the environment in which the client lives or will live. According to the core TR principle of the ecological perspective, the TRS's responsibilities include addressing environmental factors that influence the client's life and are in need of change. The TR goal is to create an environment that is a healthier, more supportive, and inclusive community for all people. This may mean working with families, other agencies, and community groups that affect the client's life. Activities of the TRS could include advocating for clients' rights, teaching a family recreation skills and adaptations, developing support networks, training an organization's staff on inclusion, and working to eliminate barriers to accessibility and inclusion. The TRS's behaviors, values, and attitudes interact with the needs and personal characteristics of the clients, the organization, and the social, economic, and political atmosphere (Howe-Murphy & Charboneau, 1987) to form a dynamic and highly interactive relationship to create change. The TRS's knowledge and skills used to create both a supportive TR environment and a supportive community environment are strengths of TR leadership.

● **Summary** ●

This chapter has explored the qualities and functions of the recreation leader and the therapist and how these roles blend to create TR leadership. "Leadership isn't dependent upon the qualities of the leader alone, but rather is a complex mix of variables that interact with each other" (Howe-Murphy & Charboneau, 1987, p. 285). This mix produces a synergistic effect that expands the range of outcomes clients can achieve from TR participation. Therapeutic recreation leadership uses both therapeutic techniques and leadership strategies to facilitate clients' positive growth and ability to derive meaning and benefits from the TR experience. The components of the blended role of TR leadership include the TRS's self-awareness, cross-cultural competence, ability to maintain appropriate relationships, interpersonal skills, knowledge and application of motivation principles, and an environmental perspective. The TRS also possesses creativity, flexibility, and skills in planning and organizing that are used to deliver quality TR programs. This is the kind of person a TRS should be to practice TR. In the next section of the book, we will build on the conceptual foundation of TR philosophy and ethical principles, the programming approaches and processes, and the qualities and skills of the TRS to apply TR leadership in the delivery of programs and services. Chapter 5 presents the common concerns of clients served by TR, along with a description of how to apply TR leadership in carrying out the TR process according to the TR models.

● **Learning Activities** ●

1. Review "Suggestions for Developing Self-Awareness" on page 75. Select three of the activities to carry out. Share your experiences in a small group.

2. Have you heard colleagues or classmates talk about clients, staff, or fellow students in language that demonstrates a lack of understanding of their cultural or ethnic background? Have you observed that these attitudes negatively influenced their behaviors and interactions? In a small group of classmates or fellow professionals, discuss which ethical principles apply in this situation. How should this situation be handled?

3. You are a TRS in a day care program for older adults. You have become friendly with the family of one of the participants in the program. They invite you to "Mama's" birthday party at a restaurant on the weekend. Your agency does not have a policy on this. What are the ethical issues that may arise if you accept this invitation? If you wanted to turn down the invitation, what would you say to the family? Compare your course of action to that of other members of your group.

4. In a small group, discuss the theories of motivation. Which theory best explains what motivates you? Identify one aspect of your life in which you would like to be more motivated. How can you use motivation theories to increase your own motivation?

5. With a partner, practice being silent. Sit facing one another and make eye contact, but do not speak. See how long you can remain silent. Reflect on how not speaking affected you. How could silence be used to help clients?

6. In a small group, analyze the definition of TR leadership and the components of the blended role. Discuss how these concepts serve to distinguish TR from other professional fields of practice. You might also write a short paper on this topic.

7. Reflect on leaders you have known. What types of power did they hold? How effectively did they use their power? Which types of power do you feel you possess? How can you make more effective use of your own power to influence others to make positive changes in their lives? Which public figures do you admire for their effective and fair use of power?

II

Creating the Structure of TR Practice

Who are our clients? How do we help them? There are common concerns many of our clients share. Understanding the common concerns and the circumstances that affect our clients' lives is critical to designing and delivering meaningful services. A multitude of recreation experiences are available that can engage them in meaningful and productive steps toward their personal goals. TRSs use the strategies and techniques of both therapists and recreation specialists to motivate, guide, teach, and facilitate our clients' growth and learning. To ensure the quality of our services we evaluate ourselves, our programs, and our clients' progress; apply sound risk management procedures; and demonstrate sensitivity to cultural variations, all with an ethical mindset.

Common Concerns of Therapeutic Recreation Practice

In this chapter you will learn about:

- Common client concerns according to behavioral domains: leisure, physical, cognitive, affective, and social
- Good health and healthy behaviors
- Six dimensions of wellness
- Environmental influences on health and wellness
- Therapeutic recreation approaches and programs that address the common concerns
- Applications of TR models and the TR process to common concerns
- How TR can collaborate with other disciplines
- Risk management and cultural, ecological, and ethical considerations in addressing common concerns

The TR process requires an assessment of the total person, including both the strengths and the limitations or problems that affect healthy functioning. Although the TR process is applied to clients individually, many clients share **common concerns** or problems, despite their particular diagnosis, health condition, disease, or disability. These common concerns can be grouped according to functional domains. In the various domains, the TRS will most likely address the following concerns, regardless of setting:

- **Leisure domain**. "Leisure lack," boredom, workaholic behaviors, substance abuse, and other antisocial behaviors. (Leisure is presented here as a functional domain not only because TR is the profession within health and human services that places distinct emphasis on leisure but also because its significant contribution to well-being is too often overlooked.)

- **Physical domain**. Low levels of physical fitness, limited mobility, overweight, chronic pain.

- **Cognitive or intellectual domain**. Limited attention span and concentration, forgetfulness and memory loss, poor executive functioning skills such as decision making and judgment, difficulty following instructions, poor or limited comprehension.

- **Affective or emotional domain**. Difficulty managing stress, low self-esteem, inappropriate expression of emotions, depression, anxiety.

- **Social domain**. Social isolation, lack of social skills, inappropriate social behaviors.

In addition to the specific characteristics of the clients with whom the TRS works, the TRS can address the clients' common concerns, rather than diagnoses or "labels," to plan comprehensive and effective TR services. Table 5.1 presents the common concerns according to domains.

This chapter discusses the common concerns within each domain, as well as guidelines for TR practice addressing those concerns. A case study of two clients who share a common concern follows the discussion of each domain in the context of one of the TR models presented in chapter 2. Each case has a slightly different format to illustrate a variety of practice approaches. These case studies demonstrate how the TRS implements TR with her clients to assist them in their efforts to attain optimal health. The TRS has a pivotal role in helping clients overcome their limitations and maximize their strengths in order to achieve health and well-being. Therapeutic recreation services are planned and delivered in the context of the client's unique abilities, functional status, and life experiences. The TRS should choose an appropriate TR service model to help set relevant goals and select meaningful TR programs for clients. In addition to the leisure, physical, cognitive, affective, and social domains, the physical and social environments can present particular challenges for a client attempting to achieve optimal health.

UNDERSTANDING HEALTH AND WELLNESS

In order to understand and address clients' common concerns, the TRS must have an understanding of health, a core TR value (see chapter 2), and what it means to be healthy. The definition of health has evolved over the years from the mere absence of

TABLE 5.1

Common Concerns by Behavioral Domains

Leisure	Physical	Cognitive	Affective or emotional	Social
Leisure lack	Low levels of physical fitness	Limited attention span and concentration	Inability to handle stress	Social isolation
Boredom	Limited mobility	Forgetfulness and memory loss	Low self-esteem	Poor social skills
Workaholism	Overweight	Poor executive functioning	Inappropriate expression of emotion	Inappropriate social behaviors
Substance abuse and other antisocial behaviors	Chronic pain	Difficulty following instructions	Depression	
		Poor or limited comprehension	Anxiety	

disease to "a dynamic process aimed at achieving a sense of balance and integration between body, mind and spirit" (Shank & Coyle, 2002, p. 17). There are many similar contemporary definitions of health; this particular one is relevant to TR practice because of its emphasis on balance. This "striving for balance" applies to all individuals regardless of health status or the presence of an illness or disability. Health is affected by conditions that a person has no control over as well as personal lifestyle choices. In addition, cultural background, ethnicity, and religion affect an individual's beliefs about health and the causes and treatment of health conditions and illnesses.

For persons with chronic illness or disability, health must be defined "within the context of their current life situations, not in the context of their pre-illness/disability conditions" (Lee & McCormick, 2002, p. 237). From this perspective, two people with the same disease or disability may have different levels of functioning (Stumbo & Peterson, 2009) and quality of life. This is one reason the TRS should consider common concerns, despite diagnosis, when planning TR programs. A person with a disability may achieve good health by attempting to live a balanced life that maximizes his strengths and minimizes his limitations. Making healthy lifestyle choices is a major component of living as healthy a lifestyle as possible, regardless of individual circumstances.

Health conditions may be (1) **congenital**, present at birth, or (2) **adventitious**, acquired after birth. Some congenital conditions, such as spina bifida and cerebral palsy, are nonprogressive; others, such as muscular dystrophy, are progressive in that the individual's functioning worsens over time. Adventitious conditions may be due to heredity or the effects of lifestyle choices, or may occur by accident or for unknown reasons, and can be either progressive or nonprogressive.

Whether a person is born with a medical condition or acquires it, throughout his life span he is continually presented with choices regarding his health. Healthy lifestyle choices can help to minimize the negative impacts of health conditions. Therapeutic recreation has a pivotal role in helping clients make healthy lifestyle choices, and "if successful at it, therapeutic recreation will empower people for healthier and more rewarding behaviors and lifestyles" (Mobily, 2000, p. 304). Making healthy choices is known as wellness, defined as "adopting healthy lifestyle habits that will enhance well-being

Cultural Perspectives on Health and Treatment

White European cultures believe in the standard Western medical model, according to which the physician is powerful and all-knowing and can diagnose and cure what ails the patient by using modern medical technology and treatment. More recently, great interest has developed in Eastern medicine and complementary and alternative methods.

Black cultures adhere to many traditional beliefs and practices, including spiritual healing and natural medicines. They believe in the power of positive change and the power of prayer and may seek alternative health care. Health results when mind, body, and spirit are in harmony. Persons from these cultures may distrust the health care system and practitioners.

Asian cultures believe that the balance of forces and energy affects health, and believe in the use of herbs. They respect authority and may not feel the need to discuss treatment options. People tend to be reserved and may not express emotions openly or speak up if they are in pain.

Latino/Hispanic cultures are similar to the Asian culture and believe that health is a gift from God. Disease or disability may be seen as punishment for sins or a result of the "evil eye." People in these groups expect to be treated with respect, with a handshake, eye contact, and a warm greeting. Families expect to be involved in the client's care.

Native American cultures also follow traditional folk wisdom and believe that illness is caused by disharmony of physical and spiritual forces. The mind, body, and spirit must all be treated for healing to occur.

Data from Noonan, Sharby, and Ventura 2007.

while decreasing the risk of disease" (Floyd, Mimms & Yelding, 2008, p. 2). Another definition of wellness is "an active process of becoming aware and making choices to create a healthier lifestyle, in all of life's dimensions" (Donatelle, Snow & Wilcox, 1999, p. 7). According to these definitions, an individual makes the choice to engage in wellness activities, which leads to a perception or sense of well-being. Well-being includes having access to and being able to successfully utilize psychological, social, cognitive, physical, and environmental resources (Carruthers & Hood, 2007). Well-being is all-encompassing, incorporating a person's own assessment of her status in all aspects of life. We cannot tell another person what her level of well-being is, because it is her subjective assessment of her level of happiness.

The core TR value of autonomy, which involves self-determination with regard to making one's own choices, is generally accepted as essential to ongoing involvement in wellness activities to promote health and well-being. Five basic behaviors are associated with a healthy lifestyle and are behaviors over which an individual has some degree of control:

● Eating a balanced diet
● Maintaining healthy weight
● Not smoking
● Engaging in regular **exercise**
● Practicing safe behaviors such as wearing seat belts in a car, not drinking and driving, and safe sex

Other behaviors that promote health include managing stress, helping others, striving for balance among the roles in one's life, and pursuing activities that are meaningful and personally rewarding.

Six Dimensions of Wellness

Wellness has been described as having six dimensions. To be considered in a state of health, a person must be able to successfully balance the following six dimensions by engaging in the specific wellness activities of each dimension (Spangler & O'Sullivan, 2006; Floyd et al., 2008):

● Physical wellness: The optimal physical condition of the body, attained through physical activity and good nutritional choices, which helps prevent disease.
● Intellectual wellness: The state of having an active and healthy mind, which is promoted through lifelong learning, mentally stimulating activities, and acquisition of critical thinking skills.

● Emotional wellness: Being able to enjoy life, adapt to change, and cope with challenges, which results in increased self-efficacy, self-esteem, feeling in control, and motivation.
● Social wellness: The ability to interact with others and be comfortable in group settings so that one can experience intimacy and a sense of belonging; having a social network or support system that offers friendship and meaningful relationships.
● Spiritual wellness: Finding meaning, purpose, and value in life.
● Environmental wellness: Creating an environment that supports health and well-being and appreciating and preserving the natural environment.

Therapeutic recreation programming can incorporate wellness activities that are instrumental for attaining well-being. The TRS can support the client's efforts toward attaining balance in the six dimensions by working with her to reinforce her strengths in order to maximize what she can accomplish, use these strengths to minimize the impacts of her illness or disability, and reinforce her efforts to overcome limitations. All clients share common concerns as they struggle toward optimal wellness and well-being. Working with these common concerns requires careful attention to TR guidelines for daily ethical practice.

Health, Well-Being, and Ethical Practice

Well-being includes not only people's health but also their values, which contribute to a life of worth and dignity (Sylvester et al., 2001). It is the ethical obligation of the TRS to have concern for the well-being of the persons they serve. The TRS's ethical responsibilities are to treat clients fairly and equitably and to be nonjudgmental about their behaviors while respectful of their potential for growth and change. First and foremost, as a professional, the TRS must make sure that his own behaviors toward clients do not reflect any negative judgment about their health condition or the behaviors that may have led to that condition. The TRS may encounter clients whose behaviors he personally disapproves or whose behaviors conflict with his own value system. A professional maintains objectivity about his clients so he can accept the client's view of reality that motivates her behavior. The TRS validates clients' feelings and concerns by confirming or acknowledging that their beliefs or attitudes are legitimate. By validating a client's behaviors and beliefs, the TRS is helping the client begin the process of change. As already noted, achieving better health is about making good choices. Often clients have had little or no experience with choice making. Incorporating opportunities for making choices allows a client to feel a degree of control and can be highly motivating with regard to trying new behaviors. The TRS has an ethical responsibility to support the client's autonomy by providing the client with only the amount of assistance that is needed, thereby reducing the risk of a client's becoming overly dependent on the TRS.

Ecological Considerations

One point that is stressed in this book is that the individual's home and community environment may be a significant contributing factor to his optimal functioning, health, and well-being. From an ecological perspective, not only the client, but also the client's community and environment, should be assessed for needed changes. Common concerns related to the ecological perspective include

- location of leisure opportunities,
- availability of transportation,
- accessibility of facilities,
- attitudes of staff and community members,
- availability of adaptive equipment and devices,
- availability of support groups,
- service providers' philosophy of inclusion, and
- family awareness and understanding of the person's health (Howe-Murphy & Charbonneau, 1987).

The concept of **environmental press** (Lawton & Nahemow, 1973) suggests that environments can influence a person's ability to accomplish tasks. When an illness strikes, what might normally have been a comfortable environment may begin to "press" on the individual due to the changes in health status. For example, Mrs. Kelly, an older adult who has lived alone for many years, has a stroke that leaves her with some weakness on her right side. Her once-comfortable house and neighborhood now present many challenges to her. Although she can walk with the use of a walker, she has difficulty going up and down stairs, fatigues easily, and is afraid of falling. Prior to the stroke she had walked to a senior center three days a week and attended church activities once a week. Mrs. Kelly no longer feels that she is able to walk to these programs alone. An environment that had included adequate recreation resources has begun to "press" on her because

of the lack of transportation, accessibility issues, and the need for physical assistance and emotional support. As a component of TR services, the TRS can offer information and resources to Mrs. Kelly and her family, to the professionals involved in her care, and to community members and organizations. Other responsibilities of the TRS following the ecological approach are to

- help clients engage in self-advocacy activities,
- acquire and offer training in the use of adaptive equipment,
- organize support groups and develop networks, and
- serve as an advocate for enhanced leisure opportunities for all people.

No program plan is complete without consideration of the ecological factors that affect a client's life.

LEISURE DOMAIN

Leisure experiences can significantly contribute to overall health and well-being. Examining leisure as a functional domain reveals that being able to engage in specific leisure-related behaviors is an indicator of health, can promote health, and contributes to the well-being and quality of life of the individual. "Leisure involvement is an important aspect of health, wellness and quality of life" (Stumbo & Peterson, 2009, p. 13). Leisure involvement or behavior includes

- awareness of the meaning and value of leisure;
- knowledge of a range of leisure activities;
- skills to engage in leisure experiences including activity, social, transportation utilization, budgeting, time management, and grooming, and
- knowledge of the availability and use of leisure resources.

Ideally, this set of behaviors contributes to a satisfying leisure lifestyle. Leisure lifestyle was defined by Peterson as "the day-to-day behavioral expression of one's leisure-related attitudes, awareness, and activities revealed within the context and composite of the total life experience" (Stumbo & Peterson, 2009, p. 14). The quality of one's leisure lifestyle is a significant factor in overall quality of life. As the TRS helps clients improve their leisure lifestyle by helping them make positive leisure choices based on authentic motivation (Dixon, 2008), their overall lifestyle improves. This is the

Leisure is a vital human need that contributes to better health.

Photodisc/Getty Images

foundation of the Leisure and Well-Being Model (Carruthers & Hood, 2007), which aims to assist the TR profession in effectively communicating the importance of TR in health and human services.

Common Leisure Concerns

Common concerns related to leisure lifestyle include leisure lack, boredom, workaholism, substance abuse, and other antisocial behaviors.

LEISURE LACK

Leisure lack, a term coined by Neulinger (1978) refers to the chronic or temporary absence of the experience of leisure resulting from personal or societal factors and sometimes their interaction. Personal factors may include

- lack of awareness—the individual has never developed a sense that leisure is important or could be meaningful in life or lead to positive outcomes;
- lack of self-confidence or belief in one's ability to be successful at or enjoy leisure experiences;
- lack of knowledge of what's available, what might be satisfying or enjoyable, and how to go about marshalling resources to engage in leisure;
- lack of skills to plan and carry out activities and to determine if they are choices one wants to pursue; and
- lack of social contacts and friends to do things with or knowledge of how to make friends.

Societal factors include

- lack of networks,
- lack of opportunities,
- poor dissemination of information about what is available,
- unqualified staff at recreation programs, and
- limited opportunities for people with financial or other barriers.

Leisure lack contributes to boredom and may also lead to workaholic behaviors or engagement in other destructive or unfulfilling behaviors. The following factors may be involved:

- The individual hasn't been able to discover and take part in leisure experiences.
- Life activities have been seriously curtailed due to an acquired severe disability such as head injury, spinal cord injury, or stroke.
- Progressive disorders such as Parkinson's, ALS (amyotrophic lateral sclerosis), Alzheimer's disease, multiple sclerosis, or AIDS affect a person's participation.
- A developmental disability or multiple disabilities have impeded opportunities to develop leisure experiences.
- Life circumstances, family upbringing, or social deprivation prevented the person from experiencing and building leisure opportunities.

Families with a child who has a disability may experience leisure lack because of the time and energy they must devote to meeting the child's needs. Their circumstances impede the development of healthy family recreation that would actually help reduce the stress of caregiving and the impact of the disability on the family, and that could emphasize the child's strengths. Siblings often suffer from feelings of guilt, responsibility, and neglect that can be counterbalanced by overcoming leisure lack in the family.

BOREDOM

Boredom can be considered a lack of interest in or difficulty concentrating on the current activity (Fisher, 1993). It can be due to too little or too much stimulation (Mundy, 1998). When individuals perceive that an action or task is too difficult for them, they may become frustrated, give up, and consequently not engage, thus becoming bored. Conversely, if things seem too easy and routine, they may choose not to get involved, which also can lead to boredom. If a person has not developed a repertoire of healthy leisure choices, this quest for the "right" balance between challenge and skill (which produces flow) can lead to engaging in activities that may be unsatisfying, nonproductive, or even destructive (Csikszentmihalyi, 1990). From a leisure perspective, this means that individuals have not connected with an activity or experience that truly engages them. They may be aware of a need they wish to satsify but unable to identify what they could do to meet that need. On the other hand, perhaps they can't identify the need and therefore don't know how to fulfill it, don't know what options are available, or aren't interested in the options they are aware of (Mundy, 1998).

Boredom is associated with depression, substance abuse, antisocial behaviors, disabilities, and social isolation. The TRS may confront boredom in clients who have been institutionalized for long periods of time, who have never developed a leisure lifestyle or the personal resources to create interest for themselves in any situation, or who have been overprotected and sheltered due to illness or disability and have developed **learned helplessness**. In learned helplessness, the person has developed feelings of being helpless due to a perceived lack of control over events and therefore doesn't make an effort. Learned helplessness can lead to a decreased perception of well-being and alienation from one's community (Howe-Murphy & Charbonneau, 1987).

WORKAHOLISM

In **workaholism**, people are "addicted" to work, spending excessively long hours and large amounts of energy on their jobs. This may be due to internal or external pressures to produce and perform, as well as the use of work as an excuse not to go home and face other issues in one's life. While some people may truly enjoy their jobs and are able to maintain their health with an extreme work schedule, others may develop health issues such as stress-related disorders, heart conditions, or stroke. In fact, in Japan the term for this condition is "karoshi," which means "death from overwork." "Type A personality" is a popular term for a person who may display workaholic behaviors. Workaholism can affect relationships as individuals neglect other aspects of their lives. They also may cite lack of time as a reason for not engaging in leisure activities. The TRS may encounter workaholic behaviors in clients who have suffered stroke, heart attack, **addiction** to prescription drugs, depression, anxiety, and other health conditions related to neglect of basic fitness and nutrition.

SUBSTANCE ABUSE AND OTHER ANTISOCIAL BEHAVIORS

Substance abuse has been called a "leisure disease" because it occurs during free time. Rather than engage in positive leisure pursuits, individuals initially choose to take drugs out of curiosity, peer pressure, lack of other options, a desire to escape or self-medicate, or as an act of rebellion. Over time, this experimentation or casual use can develop into a dependence or addiction, which has a destructive effect on their everyday life. This is the nature of addiction, which implies a compulsion over which the individual has little control. In addition to alcohol and other drugs, both legal and illegal, people may become addicted to behaviors such as exercise, shopping, sex, gambling, overeating, or undereating. People with substance abuse problems may present other health problems due to wear and tear on the body, neglect, head injuries from falling or accidents, asthma, diabetes, gum disease, oral cancer, pneumonia, liver disease, and AIDS. Clients may suffer from disorientation, exhaustion, anxiety, confusion, memory loss, and depression. They may be facing family, legal, housing, and job-related issues. Some may be suicidal. People with substance abuse and addiction problems may have leisure interests but either neglect them or no longer enjoy participating in them. To overcome an addiction, the TRS can help clients see that the addiction is hurting them, that they possess the self-efficacy to overcome it, and that there are rewarding alternative experiences available to make life without addiction worthwhile (Kunstler, 2001).

Other antisocial behaviors may also be seen as leisure-related concerns. Teenagers may engage in delinquent or criminal acts. Vandalism may result because "there's nothing to do"; harassment of others or graffiti may be a means to assert people's identity and existence; gang membership offers safety and security as well as participation in a social group; and violent behaviors can be means to achieve status or assert dominance and obtain feelings of control. Lack of challenging leisure opportunities, role models of leisure engagement, and safe and stimulating environments contributes to antisocial behaviors. However, it is not only young people who engage in these behaviors. The TRS works with these leisure concerns in programs for youth at risk, for youth and adults who are incarcerated, and for sex offenders, as well as in halfway houses providing reentry assistance for parolees.

The TR Approach to Leisure Health

The TRS's approach to those with leisure concerns includes sensitivity to what may be the cause of an issue. The TRS must treat clients with respect, recognizing that they may not understand the meaning and value of leisure. She should be skilled in the professional practices of leisure education, and possibly leisure counseling, in order to address leisure concerns. As clients begin to overcome these concerns, she should be a role model of positive and healthy leisure attitudes and behaviors. The TRS offers a range of leisure experiences for clients to try, assists them in making new choices, and encourages their autonomy. She gives feedback on how they are responding to various activities. She assists clients with developing a balanced leisure lifestyle. One way to facilitate a balanced lifestyle is to help clients develop a repertoire of leisure interests that draw on activities from the various wellness domains. Another approach is for the client to identify one primary leisure interest that incorporates all of the domains. Sailing requires physical activity; cognitive skills for selecting strategies and for the study of

winds, weather, and tides; emotional skills to handle stress and pressure; and social skills appropriate for working with the crew. It is important that the TRS have a comprehensive resource file or guide and established linkages with community organizations for leisure participation during treatment and after discharge. The TRS should also address family needs in order to help the client overcome leisure concerns.

THERAPEUTIC RECREATION PROGRAMS FOR LEISURE HEALTH

Leisure education is the central approach to working with people with leisure concerns. Leisure education includes developing awareness of the value of leisure, identifying potential leisure interests, learning new leisure skills, and acquiring knowledge of leisure resources and how to use them. Making choices and weighing alternatives are essential components of leisure education. Leisure education can be provided in a one-to-one, group, or family format. Family recreation should be a goal of TR and leisure education. Many families can benefit from identifying and learning new leisure pursuits that can promote enjoyment and family unity and minimize the effects of illness or disability. Many families have not developed positive and healthy leisure behaviors, let alone acquired an understanding of how leisure can benefit the client as well as the family as a whole. Family recreation programs should be offered in early intervention programs for families with a young child who has a disability; youth at risk; adults with workaholism, substance abuse, or other antisocial behaviors; and caregivers of older adults. Reducing stress, sharing positive experiences, seeing the client as a competent person who can take pleasure in life, and learning new skills can reduce the effects of leisure concerns on the entire family. Social skills training, values clarification, assertiveness training, and time and stress management are incorporated into leisure education. Relaxation, yoga, and tai chi can help clients lower stress and develop a more balanced lifestyle. Discussion groups, expressive arts, and outdoor recreation activities are appropriate approaches to reducing the impact of leisure concerns.

Sailing is an example of a leisure option that incorporates all of the behavioral domains.

Photo courtesy of William Clausen.

CULTURAL COMPETENCE

Leisure choices may be dictated by cultural background and practices. These should be respected. When working with children, the TRS is obligated to respect the parents' wishes and beliefs as well. Cultural preferences may also influence activities such as dancing, cooking, and eating; rules for male–female contact; and appropriate clothing for participation in leisure activities. Some participants may not be allowed to wear slacks, bathing suits, or other revealing clothing. The TRS must understand cultural differences and preferences and work with the client, parents, and other family members to make adaptations when necessary. Leisure education should be provided within the context of the individual's own cultural practices and beliefs. Membership in groups based on families, ethnicity, or significant others is an influence on the meaning that participants attach to leisure experiences. For example, members of cultures that have collectivistic values, such as Native Americans, are more affected by social factors that influence leisure behavior (Dieser, 2004). Leisure education can follow a psychosocial-educational model in which leisure involvement is viewed as the result of interaction between social variables of group relationships, political influences, and environmental patterns, as well as the individual's own needs, values, and attitudes (Dieser, 2004). This incorporates an ecological perspective from which the TRS can help leisure organizations develop multicultural and anti-discriminatory practices and policies.

TEAM COLLABORATION

Therapeutic recreation is probably the least-understood discipline on the team. The TRS may have to work hard in order to educate the team about the meaning and value of the leisure domain and the idea that a satisfying leisure lifestyle may be considered an indicator of overall health and well-being. The TRS must articulate to the team, the families, and the clients the importance of leisure to health, well-being, and quality of life. He must educate the team about how their collaboration can help reinforce healthy leisure choices, as well as explain how participation in TR supports the work other disciplines do with clients. Depending on the setting, the TRS works with the team to support their efforts and in return obtain the team's support of TR goals. Given the range of leisure options, the TRS may draw on every member of the team for assistance, information, and support to plan the most effective programs and provide needed adaptations. The TRS could colead a family leisure education or leisure counseling group with a social worker or psychologist.

RISK MANAGEMENT

Risk management involves anticipating what might go wrong in a program, planning ways to avoid problems, and developing procedures to respond appropriately when something does go wrong. Risk in the leisure domain relates to factors that are inherent to the client, the activity, and the environment. Clients who are in treatment for substance abuse and other addictions, or incarcerated for criminal behavior are at high risk of continuing these activities. The TRS must be very observant of possible indicators. Most treatment settings will discharge clients who are caught in these activities. Some programs practice harm reduction, in which it is accepted that clients may be using drugs; however, the TRS should ensure that these individuals are not pressuring others to use. The TRS should follow the established procedures of the agency in reporting this behavior. Program protocols may need to indicate that clients under the influence cannot participate, for safety reasons. Also, clients may act out or become aggressive or violent. The TRS should be sure to be included in agency training on behavior management and crisis intervention techniques. SCIP is an example of a training program that teaches "strategies for crisis intervention and prevention." If clients are permitted to go on community outings, careful supervision is required so that clients do not engage in negative behaviors such as taking drugs, gambling, or making contacts with former acquaintances. The TRS should be alert for signs of relapse, a danger with clients who are in recovery.

Clients may have negative associations with recreation activities or environments that they previously engaged in under the influence. A basic 12-step strategy is to avoid the persons, places, and things associated with an individual's addictive behavior. The TRS must carefully assess the client's triggers in these three categories. For example, many games have betting components, which may be a risk for a person with a gambling addiction. Sports and bowling are often associated with alcohol use. Because it may be very difficult to avoid such triggers in the client's daily life after discharge, such as family members who engage in the risky behaviors, the TRS can help the client learn strategies to decrease risk using assertiveness training, role playing, and stress management, and offering alternative choices. Also, the client's new choices may cause conflict with the family and others who have not yet recognized or understood what constitutes healthy leisure. Families themselves may be dysfunctional and engage in destructive behavior, or they may be overprotective and fearful of allowing the client to participate. It is true that some leisure activities present physical risks. In adventure activities such as high ropes courses or rock climbing, the risk factors may be obvious. But other recreation activities such as arts and crafts, games, food activities, and outdoor recreation also involve risk. It is imperative that the TRS consider all risk factors when implementing activities and take appropriate precautions. See chapter 6 for risk management for specific recreation activities.

ETHICAL PRACTICE

The TRS, in addressing leisure concerns, should be on guard against promoting his personal leisure interests rather than presenting the broad range of choices that a client might find appealing. As already mentioned, clients with leisure concerns may have engaged in behaviors the TRS disapproves of, but the TRS cannot allow his personal values to interfere with the services he provides. People also find it hard to understand why those who engage in self-destructive or dangerous behaviors can't "just stop." Not being able to stop is the nature of the condition; and in order to best meet clients' needs, the TRS should not fall victim to that kind of thinking. Failure to provide a client with appropriate professional support diminishes the benefits the client achieves from TR programs and can reflect professional incompetence and unethical professional behavior. If a client engages in illegal behavior, the TRS is responsible for complying with agency regulations on reporting.

In the relaxed environment of the TR program, the fun element of recreation may interfere with accomplishing goals. The TRS and the client may lose sight of the purpose of the activity, which can compromise progress. The fun atmosphere can also cause clients to misconstrue the nature of their relationship with staff. Clients may also be similar in age to the TRS, and this similarity may compromise professional boundaries. The TRS must be conscious of this issue and maintain an appropriate relationship with clients at all times. If the TRS himself gets drunk and comes to work with a hangover or talking about his drinking experiences, this is unethical and unprofessional behavior.

Case Study

This case has to do with two adolescents on a pediatric rehabilitation unit where the TR department follows the Leisure Ability Model (Stumbo & Peterson, 2004). The purpose of TR in this model is to help clients develop an appropriate leisure lifestyle. The Leisure Ability Model has three components that exist along a continuum of services from functional intervention to leisure education to recreation participation. In this case, goals and objectives are presented for each of the three components.

BACKGROUND

David is a 12-year-old boy on an inpatient pediatric unit receiving chemotherapy for bone cancer. David was diagnosed with the condition two years ago. He lives at home with his family (parents, older sister, and younger brother). Prior to diagnosis, David was actively engaged in a number of school activities—the science club and basketball, and after-school activities including soccer, swimming, and playing video games. Because of his treatment schedule, David has been forced to miss school and reside in the hospital for extended periods of time. His current recreation activities are limited due to the effects of chemotherapy and hospitalization. In addition to fatigue and pain episodes, David's treatment has resulted in fine motor control problems. He can no longer play video games because he has lost the ability to use the controls and keyboard. These limitations have caused leisure lack. David has expressed interest in being able to play video games so that he can interact with his peers on the unit and with his friends and siblings when they come to visit.

Tommy, a 13-year-old patient on the pediatric rehabilitation unit, has a sport-related spinal cord injury at the T-9 level, resulting in partial paralysis of the lower limbs. His parents have been informed that although he has made progress, after discharge Tommy will require use of assistive devices to walk, including a wheelchair as needed. Prior to his injury Tommy played in a baseball league and also enjoyed playing basketball with his friends. He has expressed concern that he will no longer be able to participate in his favorite sports. On the unit, Tommy complains of boredom and frustration and refuses to participate in the regular unit activities.

The TR assessment indicates that both clients need to adapt to the changes in their physical conditions and their abilities to participate in their favorite recreation activities. David enjoys the social interaction with peers and the challenges of video

Common Concerns of Therapeutic Recreation Practice ● **105**

games. Tommy enjoys the challenges and competitiveness of sports. Goals are developed for David and Tommy for each phase of the leisure ability model in order to maximize their ability to increase their leisure opportunities, experience the benefits of participation, and engage in these activities as independently as possible.

GOALS AND OBJECTIVES

Goal for David and Tommy: Improve leisure lifestyle

Objectives for David

Functional intervention objective: David will correctly use adapted devices, as judged by the TRS, to play video games three times a week.

Leisure education objective: After one week, David will play three newly learned games, according to the rules, with peers.

Recreation participation objective: David will participate in open recreation sessions on the unit three days a week for 30 minutes each session.

Objectives for Tommy

Functional intervention objective: After participating in the mobility training obstacle course three days a week for two weeks, Tommy will independently maneuver a wheelchair.

Leisure education objective: Tommy will acquire skills to play wheelchair basketball after two weeks of attending the skills development program, three days a week for 30 minutes.

Recreation participation objective: Tommy will play a game of wheelchair basketball according to the rules, in the hospital gym, after three weeks of TR.

THERAPEUTIC RECREATION LEADERSHIP

According to the Leisurability Model, the level of TRS involvement exists along a continuum: The TRS applies maximum control as therapist, then modifies this degree of control and assumes the role of educator, and finally functions as a facilitator as the client assumes the maximum control possible over his leisure experiences. The TRS conducts an activity analysis of the activities that the client identified as his recreation interests. Activity analysis helps the TRS determine how the activities of choice can address the client's needs, as well as the adaptations needed to facilitate successful participation. The TRS also uses task analysis to identify a series of small steps necessary to carry out the activity. The

TRS collaborates with the occupational therapist to identify and obtain adapted devices to support David's fine motor skills, and with the physical therapist to address Tommy's mobility skills.

David's Progress and Discharge Plan

After three weeks of TR, David has learned three new video games of choice and has successfully utilized adaptive devices. During open recreation, he invites other clients to play with him according to the rules. The TRS has discussed with him the opportunities available in the community, and he is willing to explore available options.

Upon discharge, David will join the Parks and Recreation Center youth recreation program. The TRS will work with the family to achieve this goal.

Tommy's Progress and Discharge Plan

After three weeks of TR, Tommy has learned to play wheelchair basketball according to the rules and is able to maneuver his wheelchair independently for the course of the game. He has stated, "I really like this, I didn't think it could be so much fun."

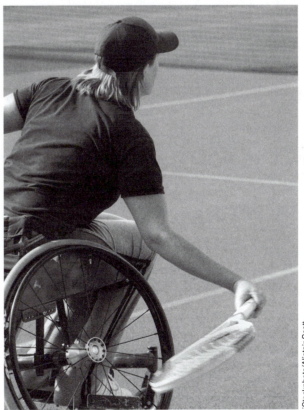

TR can play an important role in making recreation opportunities available to people of all abilities.

Upon discharge, Tommy will register for the adapted basketball program at the Parks and Recreation Center and will identify one other sport he would like to engage in. The TRS will work with the family to achieve these goals.

ECOLOGICAL PERSPECTIVE

The TRS works with the family and siblings to involve them in activities so that they can continue to support David's and Tommy's leisure involvement after discharge. In preparation for discharge, the TRS also collaborates with Tommy's and David's parents and siblings to identify community supports and possible opportunities for inclusion. The TRS also assists the families in locating resources and learning how to use adapted equipment, as well as appreciating the importance of recreation in the lives of the family and the client. As advocate, the TRS contacts the local parks and recreation agencies and other community services to ascertain available programs, procedures for registration, and requirements for participation. The TRS works with the clients and families to ensure follow-up and successful community reintegration.

The TRS has the unique role of educating the community on the benefits and importance of a wide range of community-based and supported leisure opportunities in order to reduce the problems caused by leisure concerns. The TRS works with local agencies and organizations to develop barrier-free and accessible programs and facilities that support inclusion. The TRS can offer training to other organizations' staffs on a variety of topics, including leisure education, how to use adapted equipment, and how clients' disabilities might affect their recreation participation. The TRS should also consider public speaking and lobbying to improve community services to clients.

PHYSICAL DOMAIN

The **physical domain** includes the condition of the human body, the behaviors involved in maintaining a healthy body, and the ability to use the physical capabilities of the body to perform daily activities. As mentioned earlier, the behaviors that support a person's achievement of physical health and wellness include regular exercise; eating properly and maintaining a healthy weight; stress management; nonsmoking; and practicing safe behaviors such as using seat belts and not drinking and driving. Actively engaging in activities and behaviors that protect and promote good physical health influ-

ences a person's ability to control the body in a purposeful and skillful way. The many benefits of good physical health include psychological health and well-being; falls prevention; weight control; reduction in symptoms of chronic conditions including high blood pressure, heart disease, and diabetes and in the risk of colon and other cancers; and psychological conditions including depression and anxiety disorders (United States Department of Health and Human Services, 2000).

In trying to identify what it means for any given client to be physically fit, it is necessary to consider both her age and her lifestyle. Fitness for a person who does not work may include the ability to perform daily tasks from cleaning the house to climbing stairs, while fitness for a working person should include being able to work a full day as well as perform household and leisure activities. In either case, having enough energy "left over in order to engage in leisure is the common element for defining fitness" (Rimmer, 1998, p. 2).

Physical fitness has four components (Teague, Mackenzie & Rosenthal, 2006):

- **Cardiovascular endurance:** The ability to sustain moderate whole-body activity for a prolonged period of time.
- **Flexibility:** The range of motion at a joint or a series of joints.
- **Muscular strength and endurance:** Strength is the ability of a muscle to exert force, and endurance is the ability of a muscle to sustain effort over time to complete activities of daily living and perform activities such as carrying or lifting objects and climbing stairs without relying on one's arms.
- **Body composition:** Total body mass index and body fat distribution. The more body fat a person has, the lower the level of fitness. Body composition is the relationship of several different components of a person's weight, that is, body fat, muscle, and bone (Quinn, 2008). While genetics is a factor in body composition, it is lifestyle that appears to be the most important influence on body composition. Body composition concerns can range from too little weight to excessive weight (Quinn, 2008).

Common Physical Concerns

Common concerns in the physical domain include low levels of physical fitness, limited mobility, overweight, and chronic pain.

LOW LEVELS OF PHYSICAL FITNESS

Low levels of physical fitness can be due to illnesses, health conditions, or disabilities or to lifestyle behaviors.

- Impaired cardiovascular endurance is associated with conditions such as ALS, asthma, chronic obstructive pulmonary disease, cystic fibrosis, emphysema, heart disease, lung cancer, and Down syndrome. Lifestyle factors that negatively affect cardiovascular endurance include poor diet, sedentary lifestyle, smoking, and exposure to environmental conditions (e.g., pollution, secondhand smoke, and poor ventilation).

- Poor flexibility may be due to arthritis, cerebral palsy, orthopedic impairments, paralysis, Parkinson's disease, stroke, and a sedentary lifestyle.

- Lack of muscular strength and endurance can be due to cerebral palsy, Down syndrome, Guillain-Barre syndrome, multiple sclerosis, muscular dystrophy, myasthenia gravis, and stroke, as well as a lack of exercise and physical activity.

- Poor body composition can be due to a physical disability that has prevented exercising, such as arthritis or spinal cord injury, sometimes coupled with a poor diet; side effects of medications; limited physical activity; Prader-Willi syndrome; eating disorders; metabolic disorders; diabetes; poor nutrition; and excessive consumption of food. These conditions can lead to additional concerns such as anxiety, cognitive distortions, depression, fatigue, reduced cardiovascular functioning, osteoporosis, stunted growth, and other endocrine disorders.

Obviously many conditions are related to the common physical concern of low level of physical fitness. Apart from the primary impacts of the particular diagnosis, those with poor physical fitness face challenges with one or more of the following common physical health concerns.

LIMITED MOBILITY

Limited mobility refers to a diminished capacity to move the body independently, which reduces a person's ability to attend to daily needs, participate easily in everyday activities, and access leisure experiences. Limited range of motion (ROM) in the lower limbs impedes one's capacity for moving around independently, and limited ROM in the upper limbs impedes the ability to carry out tasks independently. A component of mobility is **agility**, that is, the ability to change body position, which depends on balance, coordination, and speed. Poor mobility causes increased heart rate and oxygen consumption, slower walking speeds and gait timing problems, and balance disorders that contribute to poor muscular development and decreased flexibility (Durstine et al., 2000).

A variety of disorders and diagnoses can cause ambulation and other mobility problems. These include developmental disabilities, such as cerebral palsy and spina bifida; muscular dystrophy; cancer; cardiovascular disease; arthritis; spinal cord injury; traumatic brain injury; and visual impairments. Behaviors that contribute to poor mobility include physical inactivity; lack of exercise; and not using assistive mobility devices such as wheelchairs, walkers, crutches, and canes due to lack of availability, lack of information or knowledge, or simply unwillingness.

OVERWEIGHT

Overweight refers to excess weight in proportion to one's height. Weight concerns are often related to the relationship between the amount of activity engaged in and the type and amount of food consumed. In addition, people may have a genetic predisposition to overweight or may be taking medications that have weight gain as a side effect. One can determine whether a person is overweight using weight-for-height charts or a **body mass index (BMI)** calculator. Although BMI is a popular measure, it is based on height and weight and does not take into account body composition, amount of muscle mass, or frame; therefore it may not by itself be a good indicator of overall fitness (Donatelle, 2004). A BMI of 30 or above is considered an indicator of **obesity**. About 90 percent of people with obesity are considered mildly obese, which is 20 to 40 percent over their ideal body weight. Another 7 to 8 percent are considered moderately obese, which is 40 to 99 percent over their ideal body weight. The

---

Calculate Your Body Mass Index

To calculate your BMI go to www.nhlbisupport.com/bmi or www.cdc.gov/healthyweight/assessing/bmi

remaining 2 to 3 percent are considered morbidly, severely, or grossly obese at 100 percent or more over their ideal body weight. Obesity affects health because it is a strong contributing factor to the development of poor mobility, back pain, arthritis, high blood pressure, diabetes, cancer, depression, and social isolation and can exacerbate preexisting conditions.

CHRONIC PAIN

Many medical conditions are accompanied by acute pain that subsides or disappears when the condition is treated, as with a broken leg. In many instances, however, pain does not go away. This is known as **chronic pain**, which can be defined as pain that persists longer than the expected time frame for healing, or pain associated with a condition or

---

U.S. Government Guidelines for Physical Activity

Children and Adolescents

Recommendation

One hour or more of moderate or vigorous aerobic physical activity a day, including vigorous-intensity activity at least three days a week.

Suggestions

- Examples of moderate-intensity activities: hiking, skateboarding, bicycle riding, brisk walking
- Examples of vigorous-intensity activities: bicycle riding, jumping rope, running, soccer, basketball, ice and field hockey
- Muscle-strengthening activities three days a week, for example, rope climbing, sit-ups, tug of war
- Bone-strengthening activities three days a week, for example, jumping rope, running, skipping

Adults

Recommendation

- Two and a half hours a week of moderate-intensity activity, or one and a quarter hours of vigorous activity (in bouts of at least 10 minutes).
- For greater benefits: 5 hours a week of moderate intensity or two and one-half hours of vigorous intensity.

Suggestions

- Moderate: walking briskly, water aerobics, ballroom dancing, gardening
- Vigorous: race walking, jogging or running, swimming laps, jumping rope, hiking uphill
- Muscle-strengthening at least two days a week: weight training, push-ups, sit-ups, carrying heavy loads, heavy gardening (six to eight different exercises for 8 to 12 repetitions each)

Older adults: Follow guidelines for adults when possible. If at risk for falling, add exercises to maintain or improve balance. For flexibility try yoga, tai chi, and stretching.

Adults with disabilities: Follow guidelines for adults when possible; avoid inactivity.

People with chronic medical conditions: Engage in physical activity as much as possible, with guidance of health care provider.

www.hhs.gov or www.healthfinder.gov/prevention or www.cdc.gov

disease that cannot usually be eradicated or cured (Kunstler, Greenblatt & Moreno, 2004). Chronic pain is categorized into three types:

1. Pain that lasts after the normal recovery from a disease or an injury
2. Pain associated with a chronic medical condition
3. Pain that develops and persists in the absence of identifiable organic problems (Lesser & Pope, 2007, p. 388)

Pain can occur in any part of the body and may range from mild to intense (Jeffrey & Morof Lubkin, 2002). Since sources of pain can be diverse and complex, determining both cause and course of treatment may take time. Professionals may misunderstand what a person with chronic pain is experiencing, resulting in poor or inappropriate treatment. Conditions that can cause chronic pain are arthritis, back injuries, carpal tunnel syndrome, fibromyalgia, muscle weakness and musculoskeletal disorders, burns, cancer, AIDS, and neuropathy. People who experience chronic pain may also be prone to addiction (as a result of treatment with pain medication or self-medication with alcohol or illegal drugs), depression, anxiety, social isolation, frustration, fatigue, sleep disturbance, low levels of fitness, and reduced mobility.

The TR Approach to Physical Concerns

The TRS has a vital role in addressing two of the most significant factors that negatively affect physical health, which are lack of physical activity and poor dietary habits. In order to do this, the TRS needs knowledge of

- the factors influencing physical health;
- the benefits of physical activity;
- the spectrum of opportunities for physical activity;
- nutrition standards; and
- government guidelines for physical activity for adults, children, and people with disabilities.

The creative TRS will design programs to motivate clients to try a variety of physical activities in a range of formats. The TRS's choices of TR programs, leadership approaches, and motivational strategies to address common physical concerns are based on the client's assessments and the resources available within the service setting as well as the client's long-term social and physical environments. Available space and facilities, specialized skills, and budgetary support influence the choice of TR physical activity programs. To select the most feasible and appropriate TR programs, these are questions the TRS should consider:

- What type of space is available for physical activity?
- Are facilities such as a gym, tennis court, swimming pool, or outdoor activity area available?
- Does the program leadership require specialized skills in activities such as tai chi, yoga, adapted aquatics, or aerobics?
- Is there access to a therapeutic riding program, adapted golf, or Wii game system?
- Can the TRS collaborate with other staff, including dietitians, physical therapists, or exercise specialists, to develop and implement relevant programming?

Improving physical health depends on a person's willingness to take action, as well as on the development of his abilities. The TRS should recognize the barriers that prevent a person from becoming physically fit and should develop strategies to help clients overcome the barriers. Barriers could include lack of time, energy, willpower, skill, resources, and social support or fear of injury and family obligations (Teague et al., 2006). Motivation can be a major challenge for anyone with a physical concern. The TRS should keep in mind that people may be sensitive or embarrassed about their inabilities to perform physical activities or about their weight. They may have a long history of experiencing failure or negative reactions from others due to their physical condition. They may have tried to exercise or lose weight in the past but were unsuccessful in achieving or maintaining results. The TRS can approach this issue with clients by setting realistic short-term goals, using reinforcements, offering praise and rewards for efforts, and building in achievable successes.

A short-term goal could be walking for 10 minutes rather than going to the gym for half an hour; the amount of time can be gradually increased as the client accomplishes each smaller goal. Providing reinforcement, praise, and rewards includes giving positive feedback for every effort the client makes; the TRS might say, for example, "You can be proud of the effort you've made by walking every day. I'm impressed by your commitment to your health. You'll be able to go on that walkathon." The TRS should identify the basic skills essential for participation in any fitness-related activity (Long-muir, 2003). Skills development may be required before a person can participate in sport or fitness programs. Specific activities may have particular fitness requirements for successful participation. For example, coordination is required for table tennis, and endurance is required for walking. The TRS may work with the client on a one-to-one basis or in a regular group session to improve his basic skills before he engages in a specific activity. The TRS also can vary the pace of an activity, starting with a slower, less demanding routine or a less physically challenging activity and progressing to a more demanding routine or more challenging level when the client is able (Longmuir, 2003).

In addition to establishing short-term goals, providing positive reinforcement, and developing basic skills, several other approaches have been shown to be successful (Durstine et al., 2000) in sustaining participation in physical activity. Recreation is fun and can attract people to participate in and adhere to exercise. Making activities enjoyable is what TRSs do. When a person experiences an activity as enjoyable or fun, he is more motivated to participate. The TRS can enhance the fun aspects of physical fitness activities by offering variety to keep the sessions interesting and by limiting competition,

which is often frustrating to participants. Tracking clients' progress and providing opportunities for them to demonstrate progress through simple tests or challenges can also be highly motivating. If possible, engage the client's caregivers or friends in the experience so that when he leaves your facility or program he has a social support network outside (Durstine et al., 2000), ready to encourage and participate with him. Research has shown that support of family increases adherence to exercise programs (Kunstler, 2000). The TRS should plan to help clients maintain new behaviors after discharge or apart from their TR involvement. Encouraging a client to participate in a water exercise class in the facility may be highly motivating; but if the client returns to the community and swimming facilities are not available, it will be difficult for him remain active if this has been his only option. When implementing a client's individual plan, the TRS should select activities that are meaningful and relevant to the individual and feasible for his lifestyle.

THERAPEUTIC RECREATION PROGRAMS FOR PHYSICAL HEALTH

Therapeutic recreation activities for physical health include physical activity such as walking, gardening, aerobics, yoga, tai chi, and swimming. They also

Yoga has proven to be successful in reducing and managing pain.

Human Kinetics/Kelly Huff

include nutrition-oriented programs such as healthy cooking and nutrition education, which can be led together with a dietitian, and trips to restaurants. To promote awareness of positive physical health practices, special events should include healthy menus and food choices. Behavioral techniques such as writing a contract, values clarification activities, and support groups can also help clients change their behaviors. Assertiveness training may help them stand up for their rights to engage in physical activity and prepare and eat healthy meals. Treatment of obesity- and weight-related problems includes not only increased physical activity but also dietary management, stress reduction and relaxation programs, and cognitive restructuring techniques.

Many TR programs also address pain management as a component of physical health. Activities that have proven successful in reducing and managing pain include complementary or alternative therapies, such as yoga, acupuncture, therapeutic touch, meditation, and massage. Family and caregiver counseling that focuses on pain management techniques, recognition of triggers that can worsen pain, and coping skills for both caregiver and patient is an effective treatment approach. Additional techniques include restructuring how the client views the pain and implementing activities that support self-efficacy and increase positive coping skills. Chapter 6 provides more information on these TR programs.

CULTURAL COMPETENCE

The TRS demonstrates cultural competence in programming physical activities by having an awareness of the range of cultural views on issues such as pain, the range of, activity choices, and appropriate dress. Pain has different meanings in different cultures. People may see pain as due to evil spirits, as punishment for bad behaviors toward another person, or as an inevitable part of disease (Jeffrey & Morof Lubkin, 2002). These views affect a client's reactions to suggested pain management approaches.

Ideal body weight varies across cultures. The Western cultural ideal is for women to be thin, whereas Latin and African cultures value fuller figures. The TRS must respect a client's cultural values and determine, in consultation with the team, how to address weight issues that are affecting physical health. Participation in physical activities is also influenced by cultural preferences. The TRS should carefully assess clients' interests as related to their backgrounds. For example, a group of Latino teenage boys did not participate in a basketball program

because their interest was in soccer. Different cultures also view certain activities as inappropriate for females because of the exertion required or because they do not approve of the type of clothing associated with sport or exercise participation. Orthodox Jewish women do not wear slacks. Many religions require head coverings. The TRS must not embarrass a client by asking her to remove her hat or scarf. Religious beliefs are to be respected, and viable alternative choices can be selected to help the client achieve fitness goals. With some groups, males and females are not allowed to participate together in sports or to dance with partners. Sensitivity and creativity help contribute to an atmosphere of acceptance of varying beliefs and to the development of effective programs. When in doubt, it's better to ask someone about her cultural practices than to misinterpret behavior.

TEAM COLLABORATION

Collaboration with the team on a client's care and program implementation is a source of information and support, as well as a means to monitor the quality of TR services. The TRS may collaborate as part of a team approach with a physical therapist (PT) or exercise physiologist to design a physical recreation program to enhance the client's PT treatment or cardiac rehabilitation. The PT or exercise physiologist may be able to design exercises that strengthen the client's physical abilities or endurance, which can be incorporated into the recreation activities he chooses. A cotreatment group for persons recovering from stroke may involve use of recreation activities by the occupational therapist (OT) and TRS to increase range of motion. In long-term care, a falls prevention program may be implemented jointly with TR, physical therapy, and nursing; and a program to increase food intake may be a joint effort between dietary services and TR.

RISK MANAGEMENT

Working with people who have concerns in the physical domain presents a unique set of risk management considerations for the TRS. Whenever possible, clients should be fully informed about the programs they are going to participate in, and provide informed consent for participation. Medical clearance, which specifies any contraindications or limitations on the client's participation in physical activity, must be obtained. The TRS should have a detailed description of the program available for clients, caregivers, and medical staff. In order to properly address common physical concerns, the TRS must be knowledgeable about the specific diagnoses associated with these concerns, types of treatments, and any contraindications. Clients with intellectual disabilities may have difficulty understanding the expectations of the treatment or difficulty verbally communicating if they are feeling pain or discomfort.

Specific diagnoses may present unique risk management concerns. In a swimming program for persons with flexibility or mobility issues, the temperature of the pool may be a consideration. While there are no standard guidelines for exercising in water, a temperature between 83 and 88 degrees is considered tolerable. For a person with a diagnosis of multiple sclerosis, however, these water temperatures can trigger a relapse; the proper water temperature, between 71 and 75 degrees, can actually help reduce symptoms and improve range of motion (Levine, 2001). For those with cerebral palsy, these temperatures are too cold and can cause increased spasticity. A temperature of 90 degrees is optimal for aqua-exercise classes for people with arthritis. Regulating body temperature may also be a problem for individuals with progressive muscular impairments, such as muscular dystrophy, because of the absence of or limited sensation in lower limbs (Mobily & MacNeil, 2002); and careful monitoring is recommended.

Individuals with allergies to latex may be at risk during TR programs because latex is often used in sport equipment and latex gloves are often used in cooking and art classes. Latex balloons used during special events are sometimes an overlooked source of allergic contact for participants.

The TRS should research each diagnosis she encounters in her clients to determine all the possible activity contraindications and modify her programs and equipment as necessary.

In addition to diagnoses that warrant risk management procedures, the following conditions and precautions should be noted:

● Physical activity in the outdoors can lead to heat exhaustion.

● Clients taking medications that may cause sun sensitivity, such as thorazine or tetracycline, should wear visors and sunscreen when participating in outdoor activities (see table 5.2 for a list of drugs that cause photosensitivity).

● Certain medications can cause dry mouth, and clients should have water or ice available to them at all times.

● Dehydration can occur very quickly in older people who are exercising even moderately, as well as in persons of any age who are taking medication.

● People who have low levels of physical fitness or excess weight may be more prone to injuries during a physical activity program and should be monitored closely. Clients who are obese may be at high risk for stroke if they have high blood pressure, as well as for heart attack, while exercising.

● Activities that are too strenuous for someone who is experiencing chronic pain can trigger the original source of the pain.

TABLE 5.2

Common Drugs That May Cause Sun Sensitivity

Type	Name
Antianxiety	Librium, Xanax
Antibiotics	Bactrim, Cipro, tetracycline, Vibramycin
Antidepressants	Effexor, Elavil, Sineqan, Zoloft
Antihistamines	Benadryl, Claritin
Anti-inflammatories	Daypro, ibuprofen, naproxen
Antipsychotics	Haldol, Risperdal, Thorazine
Cancer chemotherapy	DTIC, 5-FU, Mexate, Velban
Cardiovascular	Cardizem, Mevacor, Pravachol, Procardia
Diuretics	Lasix
Miscellaneous	Ambien, Neurontin

● When exercise equipment is being used, appropriate adaptations should be addressed with the client. All equipment should be checked for steadiness, reliability, durability, possibilities for injury, and overall good working order. Equipment should be disinfected after each use.

ETHICAL PRACTICE

Ethical practice requires that the TRS understand the risk management concerns associated with physical activities and obtain accurate information and relevant training. The competence of the TRS is of particular importance in the context of common physical concerns due to the risk of physical injury or exacerbation of conditions. Therapeutic recreation specialists can obtain additional training and certification as needed in the areas of personal training, fitness, aerobics, adapted aquatics, tai chi, yoga, and nutrition to ensure that clients are receiving the proper and safest instruction. Table 5.3 lists available certifications that the TRS may obtain to enhance her knowledge and skill in physical activity interventions. For example, a TRS working with cardiac patients should be trained to take and monitor blood pressure and pulse rate, be cognizant of target rates established for fitness standards, and watch for signs of fatigue or dizziness. Knowledge of medications and their side effects is imperative when one is working in the physical domain. The TRS follows the ethical principles of doing no harm, competence in professional practices, obtaining informed consent from clients, and diligence.

Case Study

The following case study describes two clients who share the common physical concern of low level of physical fitness and receive TR services according to the Therapeutic Recreation Service Model (Carter et al., 2003). In this model, the TRS can set rehabilitation, education, and health promotion goals. Following a brief case history, common goals are presented along with specific objectives (also known as measurable goals as discussed in chapter 3).

BACKGROUND

Charles is a 45-year-old man in a hospital cardiac rehabilitation unit after a heart attack and triple bypass surgery. He is an investment broker and has been married for 20 years to Joan, a schoolteacher, and is the father of two teenage children. Charles is described as the classic workaholic personality who typically works an 80-hour week. Prior to the heart attack Charles was 20 pounds overweight, was a moderate smoker, and engaged in little to no exercise. Joan has expressed fear and anxiety about her husband's recovery process. Charles needs to learn how to improve his physical fitness and eating habits, manage stress, and stop smoking and also learn to appropriately express his emotions. Joan wants to learn how to support his recovery and cope with the lifestyle changes.

TABLE 5.3

Professional Fitness Certifications

American College of Sports Medicine (ACSM)	American Council on Exercise (ACE)	National Federation of Personal Trainers (NFPT)	National Council on Strength and Fitness (NCSF)	National Academy of Sports Medicine (NASM)	National Strength and Conditioning Association (NSCA)
Personal Trainer	Personal Trainer	Personal Trainer	Certified Personal Trainer	Personal Trainer	NSCA-Certified Personal Trainer
Health/Fitness Instructor	Advanced Health and Fitness Specialist	Master Trainer	www.ncsf.org	www.nasm.org	Certified Strength and Conditioning Specialist
Exercise Specialist	Group Fitness Instructor	Sports Nutrition Specialist			www.nsca-cc.org
Registered Clinical Exercise Physiologist	Lifestyle and Weight Management Consultant	Endurance Trainer Specialist			
www.acsm.org	Peer Fitness Trainer	Weight Trainer Specialist			
	www.acefitness.org	www.nfpt.com			

Mr. Jones is 67 years old and a retired police officer. He also is in the hospital for rehabilitation after a stroke caused by atrial fibrillation. He has high blood pressure, gets minimal exercise, and has limited leisure interests. He needs to improve his muscle strength and range of motion. His wife needs support to manage her husband's physical limitations caused by the stroke. Mr. Jones is mildly depressed and is experiencing low self-esteem due to the change in his capabilities. The effects of the stroke have stirred up some feelings about being unproductive since his retirement. The doctor's orders are for Mr. Jones to change his lifestyle by developing an exercise routine and improving his eating habits.

Charles and Mr. Jones share a common concern associated with the physical domain—low level of physical fitness—despite the different causes of their illnesses. Following the TR Service Model, the TRS assessed the clients and developed a TR plan with each of them that addressed their needs to improve their fitness levels and develop leisure interests to promote and sustain improved health. The hospital has a swimming pool with an adapted aquatics program. The TRS recommends this program for both clients, and they are both willing to attend an initial session.

GOALS AND OBJECTIVES

Rehabilitation Goal: Improve physical fitness

Objective for Charles

Improve cardiovascular endurance by increasing participation in an adapted aquatics program to three days a week, 30 minutes each session, after three weeks.

Objective for Mr. Jones

Improve range of motion and strength 50 percent by participating in adapted aquatics three days a week, 30 minutes each session, for three weeks.

Education Goal: Acquire skills that support a healthier lifestyle

Objective for Charles

Acquire skills to maintain a heart healthy diet by designing a healthy menu for the weekly luncheon group, according to the guidelines of the American Heart Association.

Objective for Mr. and Mrs. Jones

Acquire skills to design a low-sodium diet as demonstrated by writing a weekly food shopping list, according to the guidelines of the American Dietetics Association.

Health Promotion Goal: Engage in ongoing healthy lifestyle behaviors

Objective for Charles and Mr. Jones

Enroll in a community fitness program that is accessible to their homes, is within their budgets, and has a schedule that accommodates their daily routine.

THERAPEUTIC RECREATION LEADERSHIP

To help Charles and Mr. Jones progress toward their overall goal of improving physical fitness, the TRS assists in the following ways:

- Offers emotional support as they cope with their health issues and the need for change in their lifestyles
- Provides instruction in adapted aquatics
- Provides guidance on healthy food choices
- Selects topics in the support group that address their specific issues such as their relationships with their spouses and the stress they are facing (on the job for Charles and in retirement for Mr. Jones)
- Guides them in practicing a range of relaxation techniques, evaluating their effectiveness, and selecting appropriate ones to use
- Models appropriate expression of feelings
- Provides opportunities for their wives to engage in TR with their husbands
- Collaborates with the PT to obtain ongoing evaluation of the clients' physical improvements, and with the dietitian to ensure that dietary guidelines have been followed

Charles' Progress and Discharge Plan

After three weeks of TR, Charles has improved his endurance during adapted aquatics as demonstrated by increasing his time in the activity from 10 to 20 minutes. He can state the guidelines for a healthy heart diet and has begun to assemble a recipe file. He has stated his willingness to join an exercise program near his home.

Charles will continue his fitness activities three times a week and cook dinner twice a week for his family, according to the healthy heart guidelines.

Mr. Jones' Progress and Discharge Plan

After three weeks of TR, Mr. Jones has increased his muscle strength 50 percent as demonstrated by being able to lift 5-pound water weights. He is able to state the guidelines for a low-sodium diet, although he has said, "This food doesn't taste as good as my wife's cooking." He has told the TRS that a senior center near his home has a fitness program and he would be willing to "check it out if my wife goes with me."

The TRS will assist Mr. and Mrs. Jones in making a plan to attend the local senior center and enroll in an exercise program as well as one additional activity. She will provide them with resources on cooking tastier meals and transportation options.

ECOLOGICAL PERSPECTIVE

From an ecological perspective, the TRS directs his attention to how the client's home and community environments can support physical health. In certain work settings the TRS may be able to visit the client's home and community. If this is not a practice of the agency, the TRS can advise the client and the family or work with other professionals. Typically, social workers and physical therapists are the team members who provide in-home and community-based services. If the client lives in or will return to his own home, the TRS can make recommendations to him on how he can maintain the progress he has made in the TR program. For example, the TRS can discuss guidelines for in-home exercise within the available space, use of in-home resources such as DVDs, and the importance of adequate ventilation and safety precautions. The TRS also works with the client and family to identify accessible facilities, indoor and outdoor, and transportation to the desired locations. The TRS should have knowledge of available community resources and skill in finding resources in the client's community. With the client's permission, the TRS can contact facilities to determine if their services will meet the needs and interests of the client. The TRS may provide facility staff with information on adaptations and equipment, as well as training to promote inclusion. The TRS can also be an advocate in the community for the development of a range of accessible programs and facilities. The TRS can lead or colead a family support group.

COGNITIVE DOMAIN

Cognition is the ability to learn and process information in order to engage optimally with one's environment (Lahey, 2001). This domain is associated with a person's abilities to think clearly, reason, and develop insight into factors affecting his own health status and behaviors and adjust lifestyle decisions accordingly. Cognitive abilities include attention span and concentration, **memory**, ability to follow instructions, comprehension, and executive functioning. **Executive functioning** refers to the higher-level cognitive skills required to perform daily activities that involve planning, organizing, making connections, self-monitoring, judgment, and decision making (National Center for Learning Disabilities, 2008). The cognitive skills associated with executive functioning also include the ability to adapt to different situations, initiate activities, complete tasks, and demonstrate perseverance. Cognitive abilities significantly influence a person's ability to function in all of the other behavioral domains. Playing a competitive sport requires problem-solving and concentration skills; social activities require the ability to make connections and pay attention to others. A person with affective or emotional concerns benefits from the cognitive ability to manage stress, develop insights, and think critically. Many forms of leisure participation involve executive functioning skills, including planning, decision making, organizing, concentration, and memory.

Common Cognitive Concerns

People with a range of conditions and of all ages can have the common concerns of limited attention span and concentration, forgetfulness and memory loss, poor executive functioning, difficulty following instructions, and poor or limited comprehension. Cognitive concerns are associated with intellectual disabilities, learning disabilities, attention-deficit disorders, Alzheimer's disease and other dementias, traumatic brain injury, psychiatric conditions including depression and obsessive compulsive disorder, and central nervous system disorders such as AIDS and Parkinson's disease. The impact of these conditions on cognitive functioning may be limited and of short duration or pervasive and long-term, as well as progressive. Whatever the origins, people who have cognitive limitations may experience frustration; low self-esteem; anxiety; and difficulty with age-appropriate activities, interpersonal communication, and lifestyle management. They may also engage in unhealthy or inappropriate behaviors.

LIMITED ATTENTION SPAN AND CONCENTRATION

Attention span refers to the amount of time and effort a person can focus on a single activity. It is associated with achieving goals and is often longer when a person engages in something he enjoys, such as recreation. Attention implies single-mindedness, which is fundamental to learning because the more we can concentrate on a task and ignore distracting stimuli, the more enhanced our learning will be (Mobily & MacNeil, 2002). The ability to concentrate can be impaired due to organic factors, such as a developmental disability, learning disability, head injury, or Alzheimer's disease; but it can also be affected by medications, sleeplessness, environmental conditions, psychiatric and emotional problems, substance abuse, and stress. **Attention-deficit disorders** are a group of conditions characterized by patterns of inattention or hyperactivity.

FORGETFULNESS AND MEMORY LOSS

Memory is the ability to store, retain, and retrieve information. Short-term memory refers to the ability to learn new information, and long-term memory is the ability to recall information learned in the past (Mobily & MacNeil, 2002). Difficulty in learning and retaining new material and forgetfulness are a normal part of the aging process and should not be confused with a disease or disorder. Memory impairments are seen in clients with dementia, head injuries, stroke, brain tumors, psychiatric and substance abuse disorders, and extreme stress. Memory impairment can occur suddenly as a result of emotional trauma, physical injury, or stroke. It may also have a gradual onset; for example, people may begin to forget names of family members, may not remember how to get to a familiar place, or may forget to do simple things like turning off the stove. Medications, poor nutrition, and sleep deprivation can also affect memory. People who are forgetful or memory impaired may become confused, disoriented, fearful, anxious, and frustrated and be reluctant to participate in recreation.

POOR EXECUTIVE FUNCTIONING

Executive functioning refers to the ability to plan, organize, initiate, sustain, and complete actions or a course of behavior. Being able to think critically in order to make connections among ideas, information, and concepts is a significant component of executive functioning. It includes making decisions, exercising judgment, and monitoring one's own behavior. More complex recreation activities require these higher-level cognitive skills. Problems with executive functioning may manifest as poor motivation, inability to act in a healthy and responsible way, making poor choices or an inability to choose or decide, poor time management and procrastination, and lack of progress toward personal goals.

Poor executive functioning is associated with learning disabilities, intellectual disabilities, attention-deficit hyperactivity disorder, depression, stress, and head injuries.

DIFFICULTY FOLLOWING INSTRUCTIONS

Difficulty following instructions is a common concern of many clients due to auditory processing and other learning disabilities, intellectual disabilities, dementia, head injuries, depression, psychosis, or stroke. Being able to proceed according to a step-by-step, logical plan of action is essential to daily functioning. Clients may be able to follow a few steps but become confused or lose their focus with more complicated sets of instructions. Many recreation activities, such as games or arts and crafts, involve following a series of steps or instructions.

POOR OR LIMITED COMPREHENSION

Comprehension refers to the capacity to fully understand an idea, a concept, or information. Literal comprehension involves identifying facts, whereas inferential comprehension is "reading between the lines." To fully comprehend anything requires a combination of literal and inferential comprehension. Many of us have taken reading comprehension tests that measure our ability to understand and interpret what we have read. But comprehension is also important for effectively handling social situations and relationships, achieving goals, and exercising autonomy. The ability to comprehend can be affected by intellectual and learning disabilities, psychiatric and substance abuse disorders, dementia, head injuries, and sensory impairments. Engaging in recreation activities can help clients develop comprehension as they apply a variety of skills to accomplish an activity.

The TR Approach to Cognitive Concerns

When working with a client who has cognitive concerns, the TRS may find it frustrating to remain patient and provide the repetition needed to help him succeed. It is helpful to remember that in many cases learning *can* happen—it just may take longer. The TR approach may focus on restoring previous abilities, acquiring new abilities, or maintaining existing abilities for as long as possible. These are the key strategies the TRS uses in addressing cognitive concerns:

● Planning activities of short duration
● Using task analysis to break complex activities into a series of simpler steps

- Providing instructions verbally and in writing
- Demonstrating actions
- Providing visual as well as verbal cues
- Having clients use to-do lists, organizers, and color-coding systems
- Reducing environmental distractions
- Providing ongoing monitoring, constant support, and praise
- Using behavior management and modification techniques
- Maintaining consistency of approach

Games like checkers have many cognitive benefits.

When giving people an activity they are capable of doing, it is important to break it down into smaller steps and also to provide opportunities for challenge. Acknowledgment of strengths is very important for clients with cognitive concerns in order to reduce the impact of **secondary conditions** such as depression and emotional problems, which may have been triggered by the initial medical condition as in the case of a traumatic brain injury. Improving one of the cognitive functions can have a positive impact on other skills. For example, a person who as a result of TR participation has increased her attention span may now also demonstrate improvements in controlling impulsive behaviors, tolerating frustration, and interacting with others.

THERAPEUTIC RECREATION PROGRAMS FOR COGNITIVE HEALTH

Therapeutic recreation programs to address cognitive concerns include games, writing, reminiscence, horticulture therapy, arts and crafts, and social skills training. For example, when playing a trivia game with children who have learning disabilities, the TRS could both read the question and also have each child read it from the card and play with a partner. She can also give ample time for the child to comprehend the meaning of the question. With use of these strategies, the children have a greater chance for success because the TRS's leadership has been tailored to their particular cognitive needs. Activities such as aerobic exercise, swimming, martial arts, yoga, meditation, and drumming, which involve repetitive motor actions, help promote cognitive functioning and the development of cognitive skills. When cogni-

tive concerns are progressive, as in people with dementia, the role of the TRS is to maximize the client's current cognitive abilities by using techniques to help elicit actions and responses. Choices offered should be concrete and clear. For example, instead of asking "What do you want to do today?" the TRS should ask, "Do you want to paint today or play cards?" Utilizing pictures, models, and visual cues is an important teaching approach with clients who have cognitive concerns. The TRS should actively promote these clients' independence and self-regulatory behaviors in order to prevent the development of learned helplessness.

CULTURAL COMPETENCE

Language barriers may present an obstacle to communication that becomes even more pronounced in individuals with cognitive concerns. Staff may conclude that a client has more severe limitations in cognitive functioning than she actually does due to difficulties in comprehension, following directions, or concentration brought on by not understanding the language spoken by the TRS. Physical prompts used by the TRS to assist a client during a program may be misinterpreted as inappropriate touch, either because of culture or because the client does not understand the meaning of certain gestures. Another culturally based action is lining up to wait one's turn or to enter a facility. In some cultures, lining up is the accepted practice, but in others people just gather in a group. The TRS should be careful not to misconstrue these types of actions as indicative of a cognitive concern.

TEAM COLLABORATION

As a member of the professional team, the TRS collaborates to develop a consistent approach to addressing clients' needs and concerns. The TRS coordinates with other disciplines to plan activities that would support TR goals and programs. For example, in a day program for adults with intellectual disabilities, clients participated in a leisure education program to plan a trip to a restaurant. This community reintegration activity involved planning, making decisions, following instructions, paying attention, comprehension, and memory. The clients were learning how to select a restaurant, dress appropriately, practice good hygiene and good manners, use the bus system, and order from a menu. Physical therapy assisted with mobility issues; the travel trainer addressed use of public transportation; and the OT taught activities of daily living skills with a focus on grooming. In addition, a speech therapist worked with the clients on articulating their food order. This comprehensive approach maximized the opportunities for the clients to experience success and apply this experience to their daily life. The TRS organized the program based on the clients' interests and goals, which gave them the opportunity to integrate all their skills in the natural environment, while incorporating fun and emphasizing the benefits of the experience.

RISK MANAGEMENT

Safety is a major consideration with clients with cognitive concerns, particularly if they have confusion, memory loss, or impairments in judgment. A person with cognitive concerns fluctuates in her abilities; therefore, behaviors may not be consistent. This inconsistency must be recognized and planned for so that the client is not placed in a potentially harmful situation. The TRS should be sure that clients understand directions and remember rules, safety precautions, and the parameters of acceptable behavior and that they have the abilities to make the decisions required for participation. The TRS should gear the activity to the level of the client's functioning while providing opportunities to meet challenges. Repetition, written instructions, pictures that illustrate procedures, and adequate supervision will help maintain a safe TR program. When planning out trips into the community, one should consider selecting clients for participation according to their ability to control inappropriate behaviors, follow directions, and stay with the group. If members of the group are "wanderers," have problems following instructions or directions, or have a limited attention span, an adequate number of staff should go along. This allows the opportunity to remove a client temporarily from a situation or to provide one-on-one support.

ETHICAL PRACTICE

Respecting and protecting the autonomy of the client is a major ethical issue with clients who have cognitive concerns. The TRS must be diligent and conscientious in making sure that clients and their caregivers understand, to the best of their abilities, the nature of the TR programs and the reasons they have been selected. Because cognitive concerns affect a person's decision making, the TRS may also assume a role as advocate. The TRS models appro-

---

Rising Incidence of Traumatic Brain Injury

Traumatic brain injury is considered the "signature injury" of the wars in Iraq and Afghanistan. Major causes are blast injuries from incendiary devices or bombs, as well as motor vehicle and helicopter accidents. The number of service personnel affected is astounding. Approximately 300,000 or 20 percent of all the combat veterans have suffered at least one form of traumatic brain injury affecting attention span, ability to find the right words to use in conversation, judgment, and memory. In addition, thousands are suffering from posttraumatic stress disorder, which has similar symptoms as well as causing sleeplessness, agitation, anxiety, and depression. One of the long-term impacts of these injuries is a dramatic increase in the number of clients requiring myriad health-related and counseling services. Therapeutic recreation professionals are addressing these concerns through initiatives that focus on training veterans' hospital staff, military personnel, and community recreation providers; delivering appropriate TR interventions; and facilitating community reentry.

priate social interaction skills and is vigilant about boundary issues. Many times clients with cognitive concerns, particularly those with head injuries, are similar in age to the TRS. There may be situations in which clients confuse the client–professional relationship with friendship or a romantic attachment. Telling jokes or kidding around with clients can easily be misunderstood or misinterpreted. This can occur with clients of any age. An older adult may misinterpret the attentions of even a much younger TRS. Feelings and attitudes about the source of the client's condition may even cloud a therapist's judgment or behaviors toward a client (Lahey, 2001). A client who has had a head injury as a result of a high-risk behavior such as drunk driving may trigger a different reaction than a client whose head injury was caused by a drunk driver. The TRS can refer to the guidelines for ethical practice for support and guidance as she handles these situations.

Case Study

The following case describes two clients with similar concerns who are receiving services in different facilities. One common goal is presented, with three objectives for one client and one objective for the other, to illustrate various approaches to TR planning. Applying the Self-Determination and Enjoyment Enhancement Model (Dattilo & Kleiber, 2002), the TRS's intent is to provide opportunities for both clients to engage in recreation that they will find enjoyable, thereby leading to improvements in functional skills. In these cases, the specific executive functioning skill the TRS is addressing is decision making.

BACKGROUND

Eddie is a 27-year-old adult with mixed-type cerebral palsy that has affected his mobility, fine motor skills, and speech. He is nonverbal and also has mild intellectual disabilities. He uses a wheelchair. Eddie attends a day program for adults with developmental disabilities and resides in a group home. The group home members report that Eddie requires substantial assistance from the staff to help with his activities of daily living (ADLs) and most activities and is often bored. Although he expresses an interest in art, his fine and gross motor control has been a barrier to participating. Thus his primary recreation activities are listening to music and watching TV. The TRS consultant to the group home assessed Eddie and identified the following needs: a suitable means of communication, skills in making choices and following directions, and improved concentration.

Jin is a 29-year-old woman who is a returning war veteran. She was injured in Iraq and has been diagnosed with a traumatic brain injury. Jin currently attends a transitional day program for people with similar injuries. As a result of her injury Jin has problems with balance, interpreting social cues, and cognitive abilities. Her cognitive limitations include problems with decision making, memory, following instructions, and concentration. Prior to her injury, Jin enjoyed listening to country western music, dancing, and socializing with friends. After assessing Jin, the TRS identified the following needs: to improve skills in following directions, concentration, and making choices.

GOALS AND OBJECTIVES

**Goal:
Increase the ability to make choices**

Eddie's Objectives

Objective 1: When presented with a choice of three art activities, Eddie will select one activity to participate in for 30 minutes.

Objective 2: During art class, Eddie will demonstrate the ability to make choices by selecting a subject to be painted and three colors of paint.

Objective 3: After completing one painting, Eddie will select a new activity from a list of five provided by the TRS.

Jin's Objective

Objective 1: After two weeks of leisure education, Jin will select two country western line dances to learn.

Objective 2: After six weeks of dance instruction, Jin will complete a line dance with no more than two missteps.

Objective 3: After eight weeks of practice, Jin will demonstrate a line dance during the day program talent show.

THERAPEUTIC RECREATION LEADERSHIP

The TRS selects activities that are of interest to the client and provides the adaptations necessary to allow the client to successfully complete the required tasks. The TRS allows time for each client to express his or her interests, providing verbal and physical prompts as needed. The TRS supports Eddie's and Jin's efforts by providing pictures or samples of options from which to make choices. For Eddie, she presents pictures and examples of possible subjects to paint and helps him use an adapted paintbrush so he can pursue his interest in art, thereby supporting his choice. She offers appropriate praise to help maintain his motivation and continued independence. For Jin, the TRS presents a number of country western line dances to learn and helps her evaluate her perceived competence to learn the steps in the dance. This helps Jin practice how to go about making wise decisions. Based on the TRS's understanding of common concerns associated with the cognitive domain, the TRS practices patience, demonstrates adapted equipment, uses props, breaks tasks into smaller units, asks clients to verbally repeat procedures and guidelines, and offers consistent directions and praise.

Eddie's Progress and Discharge Plan

After four sessions in the TR art program, Eddie selected primary colors and completed one painting of a sailboat. With verbal cues from the TRS, he selected cooking and water skiing as activities he would like to learn.

The TRS will provide a starter kit of art supplies to the group home where Eddie resides so he can paint at home. She will help the group home staff plan easy cooking activities he can do in the home.

Jin's Progress and Discharge Plan

After two weeks of leisure education, Jin was able to select a line dance to learn. With physical prompts from the TRS, she learned the steps and performed with a group of clients at the talent show. Jin appeared pleased with her accomplishment, smiling and giving a "thumbs up" to the audience.

The TRS will work with Jin to identify two additional activities she can do in the community. They will explore three recreation facilities where she will be able continue her dancing as well as pursue new interests.

ECOLOGICAL PERSPECTIVE

Both Eddie and Jin live in the community, and the TRS works with them to identify community resources and make the necessary adaptations to continue the progress they made during TR programs. The TRS could offer training to the staff in Eddie's group home so they can learn techniques to assist Eddie to engage in more activities. Techniques include giving him enough time to make appropriate choices, using visual aids to enhance communication, and providing adapted equipment. For Jin, who lives at home with her family, the TRS invites them to participate in the family support group and encourages them to be patient with Jin, to allow her to act on her choices, and to support her age-appropriate behavior. The TRS has identi-

fied the local recreation department as a resource for dancing and has determined that it is an accessible and welcoming environment offering a range of activities. This case study is an example of how clients' personal sources of enjoyment are used as motivators to improve cognitive functioning, thereby contributing to overall well-being. It also demonstrates how the TRS can use similar teaching techniques with different activities in order to reach a goal.

AFFECTIVE OR EMOTIONAL DOMAIN

The **affective or emotional domain** includes a person's capacities for enjoying life; successfully managing life's stressful situations; and experiencing healthy self-esteem, motivation, and control over one's actions. This can be considered emotional intelligence (Goleman, 1995), known as the ability to understand and handle emotions critical to success in life and to feel empathy for others. Emotional intelligence is a component of good mental health. People with good mental health have a positive self-image, get along well with others, can cope with stress, respond appropriately to negative emotions, and have a positive outlook on life (Long, 2008a). To be mentally healthy allows one to see the possibilities of living a full, rich, and satisfying life (Mobily & MacNeil, 2002), as well as to fulfill one's potential and make a contribution to the lives of others. A person can have problems in the emotional domain without receiving a diagnosis of a mental illness or psychiatric disorder. These problems include anxiety, depression, anger, difficulty with relationships, and engaging in unhealthy behaviors. For example, the phrase "stuffing one's feelings" means overeating to repress feelings that are too painful or difficult to address in an appropriate manner.

Many clients present difficulties in the emotional domain that may manifest as an unwillingness to engage in programming; worry and anxiety about what the future may hold; angry outbursts; self-defeating behaviors such as substance abuse, overeating, or anorexic or bulimic behaviors; risk taking; and verbal put-downs of self. Other people and even family members may not understand when a client can't "snap out of it," leading to additional frustration and conflict. **Stigma**, the labeling of a particular group of people as less worthy of respect than others based on their health condition or disability, is also an issue. When an individual's behaviors are misunderstood or are frightening to others, they may stigmatize the person, which can cause the individual to feel ashamed. Clients with emotional concerns often feel devalued and as a result are stigmatized, excluded, or rejected by society. Participation in inclusive recreation can help reduce stigma.

Common Affective Concerns

Common concerns associated with the affective or emotional domain include the inability to handle stress, low **self-esteem**, inappropriate expression of emotions, depression, and anxiety.

INABILITY TO HANDLE STRESS

Stress is a natural part of life that everyone experiences. Stress can help motivate a person to act and achieve goals. The sense of control people perceive over life's events affects how they handle stress (Leitner & Leitner & Associates, 2004). Stress causes both physiological and psychological responses. In order to cope successfully with stress, the individual must identify the cause of the stress (known as the stressor), identify how he responds to stress, and determine the costs or benefits of allowing the stressor to exist in his life. Some stressors may be beyond the individual's control, such as catastrophic events, death of a loved one, loss of a job or home, or an illness or disability. Other sources of stress may be lifestyle choices, such as risky behaviors, poor health practices, unhealthy relationships, and unwise decisions. When a person is faced with more stress than he can successfully handle, he may experience stress overload and negative consequences. Inability to manage stress can lead to high blood pressure, chronic pain, heart conditions, gastrointestinal problems, changes in appetite and sleep patterns, substance abuse, anxiety, depression, self-defeating behaviors, problems with relationships, and difficulty expressing emotions in an acceptable manner. Recreation participation is an effective means of handling stress. Many recreation activities can be incorporated into a person's lifestyle as an ongoing stress management strategy.

LOW SELF-ESTEEM

Simply put, self-esteem is one's opinion of one's self. A person with healthy self-esteem is self-motivated and enjoys life. On the other hand, "few problems have more diverse behavioral manifestations than low self-esteem" (Mundy, 1998, p. 31). Low self-esteem is associated with beliefs that one is unworthy and undeserving, feelings of guilt and embarrassment, fear of trying new things, a tendency to do what others want one to do, difficulty saying no, and an inability to set and attain

Participating together in recreation can help promote understanding between people with and without disabilities and reduce stigma.

goals. Improving self-esteem is a very common goal in TR practice because many clients, due to their illness, disability, or life experiences, may not have developed positive self-perceptions. People develop their self-esteem through their experiences with other people (Sylvester et al., 2001). Negative and unsatisfying experiences contribute to low self-esteem, which is often noted in clients with eating disorders, anxiety, depression, social isolation, substance abuse, unfulfilling relationships, physical or emotional abuse, and behavioral problems. People with low self-esteem may feel they do not deserve to enjoy themselves in recreation activities or take time for themselves. They may be unwilling to try new activities because of fear of being ridiculed or judged, whereas high self-esteem is connected to experimentation with new activities. Those with low self-esteem often respond to compliments by saying something negative, such as "It was nothing" or "Anyone could do it" (Mundy, 1998). They may also be unwilling to ask for help or to have others make efforts on their behalf. Participation in recreation can contribute to enhanced self-esteem as people perceive that their successes are due to their own efforts and abilities.

INAPPROPRIATE EXPRESSION OF EMOTIONS

What is considered appropriate or inappropriate behavior is often hard to describe in concrete terms, yet people often use the word with a fairly accurate sense of what it means to them. Appropriateness is rooted in the context of the situation. What is appropriate in certain circumstances may be unacceptable in others. Professional, social, and private settings have different standards of acceptable or appropriate behavior. When behaviors are related to expressing emotions, there are socially accepted modes of doing so. Society has expectations about how to express the four main emotions of anger, fear, sadness, and joy. Public displays of extreme emotions are generally frowned upon, and the person may be seen as out of control or in conflict with social norms. Misreading social cues can lead to inappropriate expression of emotions. Expressing anger through aggressive behavior such as hitting, spitting, threatening, shouting, cursing, or making obscene gestures is seen as being out of control and even dangerous. An angry person may appear agitated or suspicious. Others may consider his anger out of proportion to the apparent cause. Fear may cause a person to engage in self-destructive behaviors, withdraw from interaction with the world, or verbally or physically lash out at others. Societies also have expectations of how long a person should mourn, because ongoing sadness is seen as depression or an inability to overcome losses. Even expressing joy and happiness with too much enthusiasm can be considered inappropriate. The ability to regulate the expression of one's feelings is developed over the life span, beginning with learning from the family and other role models. It is a sign of emotional intelligence and promotes healthy relationships.

The inability to express emotions appropriately, in the context of a given situation, can be due to stroke, head injury, multiple sclerosis, ALS, Parkinson's disease, dementia, depression, schizophrenia, personality disorders, conduct disorders, substance abuse, physical or emotional abuse, intellectual disabilities, or autism. Certain conditions are accompanied by emotional **lability**, which is the sudden and uncontrollable expression of emotions (such as excessive laughing or crying) or mood-incongruent emotional expressions (such as laughing when one

is angry). Inappropriate expression of emotions often causes social rejection, embarrassment, or anxiety, which in turn lead to isolation and loneliness. Relationships are affected because of the disruption to healthy interaction, misunderstandings, and hurt feelings.

DEPRESSION

Most of us have experienced feeling "down" or "sad" at some time in our lives. We may have even described ourselves as depressed. Not all depression is a reason for concern; but when these feelings become persistent and interfere with the ability to function in everyday life or limit recovery from a primary illness, then intervention is desirable. Depression is distinguished by extreme feelings of sadness, hopelessness, and helplessness; loss of interest in life activities; and impairments in thinking and the ability to concentrate. It also has physical manifestations such as fatigue, aches and pains, slow body movements, and troubled eating and sleeping patterns (American Psychiatric Association, 2000). Depression may be a primary diagnosis or a condition secondary to another primary problem. As a primary diagnosis, depression may take several forms, including major depression, bipolar disorder, dysthymia, postpartum depression, and seasonal affective disorder. A secondary condition is any condition to which a person is more susceptible by virtue of having a primary disabling condition (Simeonsson & McDevitt, 1999), such as cancer, HIV/AIDS, diabetes, dementia, multiple sclerosis, Parkinson's disease, stroke, or heart attack. For example, Mrs. Kelly, whose primary diagnosis is stroke, also has a secondary diagnosis of depression due to her loss of physical functioning and fear of not being able to regain her mobility. The depression contributes to her lack of motivation during participation in treatment. The depression must be treated in order to support her ability to participate in treatment to improve her mobility.

On the other hand, clients with chronic disability may experience depression at any point in their lives as they encounter new challenges or situations or changes in their status. Depression can also be a logical reaction to a very difficult or trying event; but when it continues to the degree that a person cannot carry out daily activities within a reasonable period of time, he may benefit from treatment. Other behavioral manifestations of depression that the TRS will observe in clients are isolation and withdrawal, sadness or crying, an unwillingness to participate, agitation, making negative comments about self, somatic complaints (complaining about physical aches and pains), or suicidal statements or gestures.

ANXIETY

Many of us experience anxious or nervous feelings that we are able to cope with using our own methods and techniques. Anxiety like this is normal and may even be viewed as a coping mechanism because it allows us to identify a situation that is causing us concern and that we wish to address. Sometimes this anxiety leads to enough distress that a person can benefit from intervention to help manage or reduce it. It can even become overwhelming, a response out of proportion to the cause, and interfere with daily functioning. Physical manifestations of anxiety that the TRS will observe in her interactions with clients include shortness of breath, dizziness, trembling, sweating, nausea, headaches, backaches, chest pains, insomnia, and digestive problems. Clients with anxiety may experience feelings of unreality or fear of dying or of losing control (Kinney & Kinney, 2001).

As with depression, anxiety can be a primary or a secondary diagnosis. Primary diagnoses of anxiety include panic disorder, phobias, posttraumatic stress disorder (PTSD), obsessive-compulsive disorder, and generalized anxiety disorder (Mobily & MacNeil, 2002). Anxiety is a feeling of intense fear or panic with no apparent reason or cause (Kinney & Kinney, 2001), except in the case of PTSD, which is a reaction to a specific traumatic event. As a secondary diagnosis, anxiety is feeling anxious or nervous regarding a health crisis, one's ability to function, one's life situation, or a specific event (e.g., an exam, a job interview, a new relationship, a move to a new location, meeting new people). A client who is anxious may be jumpy, restless, or fidgety; seek constant reassurance; express incessant worrying; and be unwilling to attend activities. Other clients with anxiety may be too embarrassed to talk about it. In TR settings, clients may feel anxiety about their abilities because of their health condition or disability, concerns about acceptance by others, or fears of being stigmatized. Physical disabilities, heart conditions, AIDS, psychiatric illness, dementia, learning disabilities, attention-deficit hyperactivity disorder, and autism are among the diagnoses that can generate anxiety.

The TR Approach to Emotional Concerns

When working with clients who have affective or emotional concerns, the TRS should seek to establish a relationship based on mutual respect, trust, and cooperation. The TRS should display patience, empathy, and consistency in interactions and approaches. Goals should be developed whenever possible with input and direction from the client, and may target behaviors specific to the client as well as issues related to the client's social or physical environment (Kinney & Kinney, 2001). The TRS should carefully plan and consistently apply strategies and facilitation techniques. A client may appear unwilling to help himself and be difficult to motivate. The TRS should recognize that progress may be slow because of the nature of the client's condition; interpersonal skills are often impaired by emotional difficulties. Realistic praise and reassurance should be offered to clients on a regular basis, and clear rules should be established so clients understand what is expected and what behaviors are acceptable. Clients should have the rules explained to them so they understand the purpose of the rules as well as the importance of following them. Whether working with a group or an individual, it is important that the TRS provide regular feedback so that the client develops insights into and awareness of her behaviors. This insight can be a prelude to changing negative behaviors and engaging in healthy lifestyle activities. The

Emotional health can be promoted through exercise as well as group activity.

Monkey Business/fotolia.com

group experience is often emphasized with these clients because it offers an opportunity to develop relationships that are reflective of the client's typical interactions (Kinney & Kinney, 2001).

THERAPEUTIC RECREATION PROGRAMS FOR EMOTIONAL HEALTH

Therapeutic recreation approaches to the common affective concerns include stress management, anger management, assertiveness training, and social skills training to learn appropriate ways to express emotions. Physical activity and exercise, martial arts, tai chi, yoga, and meditation help individuals develop self-control. Opportunities for self-expression through the arts, discussion groups, and writing activities contribute to developing insight into emotions and offer alternative means of expression. Through horticulture and pet care, clients can learn to nurture a relationship. In leisure education, clients learn how to have fun, express emotions in a healthy way, and discover satisfying activities. Techniques such as role playing, creative visualization, and homework assignments help clients practice new behaviors.

CULTURAL COMPETENCE

Cultural considerations are always a factor in interactions with clients. Some behaviors that appear unusual or even deviant in the context of the situation or to the larger group may actually be a reflection of cultural differences and not indicative of inappropriate behavior. For example, a client who spits on the ground may come from a culture where this is an accepted cultural practice. A person who uses large hand gestures while speaking may be considered threatening, but this may be a form of cultural expression. Behaviors that are grounded in a cultural context include how people mourn in public, engaging in loud arguments, making positive statements about oneself, crying in men and boys, and showing anger in women and girls. Client and professional boundaries, social role expectations, and use of personal space are also affected by cultural background. The TRS should be mindful of the possible factors that underlie behavior in order to determine how best to address affective concerns.

TEAM COLLABORATION

As with the concerns identified in other domains, the TRS works with the team to form a consistent plan of action to support the client's positive growth. It is important that all members of the team agree on how to best interact with the client, ensuring that the client gets a clear message about behavioral expectations and requirements. The client should not feel embarrassed because of the reaction of any team member to his behavior. Sharing information among team members is particularly important because clients often act differently with different staff and even at different times of the day. Individual staff members may observe behaviors that indicate a reaction to medication or a potential suicide attempt, and reporting this to the team is critical.

RISK MANAGEMENT

Clients with affective or emotional concerns can display challenging and even dangerous behaviors. The TRS must clearly document all risk management issues and consult with the team or appropriate staffperson to discuss any ongoing problems. The TRS must observe clients for suicide risk, self-injurious and violent behaviors, acting out, or unauthorized attempts to leave a program or the facility. The program environment should be safe and must include supervision in connection with potentially hazardous equipment and supplies. A client may attempt to harm himself with sharp objects. Clients should be monitored for medication side effects, misuse, or abuse or failure to take medications. Side effects of medications such as sun sensitivity should be considered with outdoor activities, and hats and sunscreen provided. Clients who display poor judgment or even delusional or psychotic behavior require stricter supervision, especially in more open environments. Appropriateness for group participation and outings should be evaluated and behavioral expectations clearly defined.

ETHICAL PRACTICE

Clients with emotional concerns are facing very challenging personal situations. The TRS has an ethical responsibility to take care of his own mental health needs, as working with clients who have emotional concerns can be stressful (Drench et al., 2007). The TRS should actively engage in a process of ongoing self-awareness and guard against transference. If he is struggling with his own emotional issues, he might inappropriately project feelings on his clients and detrimentally affect the way he provides services. The TRS should maintain a calm demeanor and be prepared to cope with unexpected events. Clients with emotional issues also may display sexually inappropriate behaviors. The TRS has to handle these professionally and tactfully. He must demonstrate professional behavior and make sure expressions of support and praise are not being misinterpreted by the client.

Case Study

The following case study describes two clients with similar concerns, despite differing diagnoses and manifestations, with emphasis on a team approach. A discharge plan is included. The TR department follows the Health Protection/Health Promotion Model (Austin, 2004), which has three components: prescriptive activities, recreation, and leisure. The TRS sets one goal for each component.

BACKGROUND

Paulette is a 32-year-old woman who has been admitted to a short-term psychiatric unit for depression and anxiety. Paulette's assessment identified that in addition to depression she was facing significant medical issues. In the last six months she had experienced two major events: (1) the death of her mother from kidney cancer, which doctors related to obesity; and (2) being newly diagnosed with a prediabetic condition, which necessitates that she lose weight. Paulette also has a low level of physical fitness. Her history revealed that she has had weight problems since childhood and has been unsuccessful in dieting. The consequences of her ongoing problems with weight have led Paulette to a sedentary and isolated lifestyle. Paulette revealed that because she was embarrassed by her weight she withdrew from social activities. She demonstrates low self-esteem. Her major leisure activities include watching television and playing computer games. Her diet consists of fast foods that can be easily delivered to her house. Paulette's strengths include awareness of the seriousness of her health problems and cognitive abilities that allow her to comprehend what needs to be done to improve her health. Prior to her mother's death, Paulette planned and prepared the family meals and coordinated her mother's care. The stress of her mother's care added to her ongoing weight problems and increased social isolation. Paulette expressed to the TRS her desire to change her behaviors in order to develop a healthier lifestyle. Her community environment, including public and private recreation agencies, does offer opportunities for participation.

Debbie, 44, is another patient on the same psychiatric unit as Paulette. Unlike Paulette, Debbie was admitted for alcohol abuse and is very thin, but they share common concerns. Her alcohol abuse caused her to neglect her physical health and develop poor eating habits and a sedentary lifestyle. Despite their differing diagnoses and conditions of depression and anxiety, they share the common affective concern of low self-esteem, as well as poor physical fitness and social isolation. The TRS, in consultation with the team, determined that Paulette's and Debbie's unhealthy lifestyle behaviors contributed to their low self-esteem and that these would be the target of the TR plan. The TRS recommends the walking, "Chef for a Day," and leisure education programs.

GOALS AND OBJECTIVES

Prescriptive Goal: Increase feelings of control

Objective for Paulette and Debbie

Increase feelings of control over behavior as demonstrated by daily participation in the walking program for 30 minutes after two weeks.

THERAPEUTIC RECREATION LEADERSHIP

Because Paulette is embarrassed about her weight and her low level of physical fitness, initially she will need much encouragement and support from the TRS to join the walking group. The TRS introduces Paulette to the other members to facilitate her social interaction with them. As Paulette begins the program, the TRS praises her efforts in order to encourage and support her continuing involvement. As part of the orientation to the program, the TRS informs the group that aches and pains are not uncommon when someone starts or increases exercising. The TRS carefully monitors Paulette and the other group members for any signs of distress, such as breathing difficulty or fatigue. At the end of week 1, Paulette is rewarded for her participation with a pedometer to keep track of how much she is walking and to motivate her to continue. Whereas Paulette is overweight, Debbie is underweight. Although Debbie is willing to join the walking program, she makes negative remarks about her ability to walk for very long without resting. The TRS uses a firmer approach with Debbie, not allowing her to make excuses and setting strict parameters on how long she should walk before she can take a break.

Recreation Goal: Incorporate healthy eating habits into daily lifestyle

Objective for Paulette and Debbie

Demonstrate the ability to maintain a healthy lifestyle by planning and cooking a healthy meal for the weekly lunch group.

Both Paulette and Debbie need to develop healthy eating habits, Paulette so she can lose weight and control her prediabetic condition, and Debbie to overcome her nutritional deficiencies as a result of alcohol abuse. They both expressed some interest in cooking as an enjoyable experience they had had in the past. The TRS recommends the "Chef for a Day" healthy eating habits TR program, which consists of learning about good nutrition and planning and preparing a healthy meal to serve at a luncheon for the other patients. This also fulfills the purpose of enhancing appropriate social interactions with peers. During the educational portion of the program, the TRS, coleading with the dietitian, helps the group learn the principles and practices of good nutrition and healthy eating. The TRS also helps Paulette to develop and practice assertive behaviors so she can say "no" politely and effectively to offers of unhealthy foods. Debbie also practices assertiveness so she can stand up for her right to become a healthier and happier person. Once the luncheon takes place, Paulette and Debbie receive praise from the group for the delicious meal they have prepared according to the guidelines. They both report that they had fun planning, preparing, and sharing the meal and would enjoy inviting friends to their respective homes for a dinner party. They also stated that they felt better about themselves because they were able to successfully put on the luncheon.

**Leisure Goal:
Plan independent leisure pursuits
that support a healthy lifestyle**

Objective for Paulette

Demonstrate the ability to maintain a healthy lifestyle by joining the Parks and Recreation Center's Step-Up-to-Health program near her home.

Objective for Debbie

Demonstrate the ability to maintain a healthy lifestyle by joining the local YMCA and attending the weekly cooking club at the local kitchen supply store.

Progress Report

The TRS assisted Debbie and Paulette in identifying programs near their homes and within their financial means that would support their new behaviors. Paulette wanted to continue the healthy lifestyle choices she began in the hospital. As she saw that she could engage in these behaviors, her self-esteem increased. This allowed her to feel more comfortable in community settings. Debbie, on the other hand,

learned that she had a right to replace her former activities and choice of friends, which reinforced her unhealthy drinking behaviors, with a positive environment. In leisure education, both Debbie and Paulette learn about local resources for leisure that will promote their health. Paulette selects the Step-Up-to-Health program, which is low in cost, is near her home, and offers a social environment. At the end of week 3, she visits the center with the TRS, is introduced to the leader of the program, and signs up to join. Paulette expresses pride in her abilities and newly acquired behaviors. Debbie has selected the local YMCA fitness program and the weekly cooking club. Debbie visits the YMCA and joins a yoga class. The TRS offers praise and encouragement to Debbie to continue the positive choices she has made.

Discharge Plan

Paulette will continue her walking at the mall with members of the Step-Up program, which she will attend regularly. She will make a weekly shopping list and menu to follow, and at the end of one month she will host a small dinner party for her new friends. She will investigate other fitness and exercise programs that she may join in the near future. The TRS will make weekly phone calls to Paulette and the Step-Up program leader for one month to check on Paulette's progress. Debbie will attend the yoga program at the local YMCA two times a week and attend the weekly cooking club. She will explore additional exercise opportunities at the Y and other community agencies. Debbie will identify two additional recreation activities for twice-weekly participation that utilize her strength in the area of creativity.

ECOLOGICAL PERSPECTIVE

For clients with emotional concerns, ecological considerations often center on issues of stigma and acceptance. Clients and family members may benefit from attending support groups in the community. Family and friends, while well-meaning, may ask clients to engage in behaviors that are unhealthy and do not support their recovery. The TRS not only works with the clients, but also can help their loved ones understand the client's needs and what constitutes appropriate activities. The TRS can offer education to local organizations to assist them in being more welcoming and understanding toward those with emotional concerns. Paulette and Debbie both demonstrated a lack of self-esteem and unhealthy lifestyle behaviors. Through the application of prescriptive activity, recreation participation, leisure education, and a focused discharge plan, both clients were able to achieve specific outcomes and develop ways to maintain gains made during participation in TR. The TRS provided the leadership and expertise to support clients' achievements and long-lasting effects.

SOCIAL DOMAIN

The **social domain** encompasses the individual's social behaviors. Social behaviors are most often "displayed during group experience" (Carter et al., 2003, p. 120). A person with good social health possesses the abilities necessary to live in society interdependently and engage in reciprocal relationships. Recent studies have shown that healthy social relationships are important contributors to a person's level of happiness (Chadsey, 2007). **Social intelligence** involves making judgments about how to enter a new group of people, when to speak and what to say, and how to react in a range of social situations on a daily basis in order to establish and maintain relationships in all the environments of a person's life. Social concerns can be associated with intellectual and developmental disabilities such as autism spectrum disorders, Down syndrome, or fetal alcohol syndrome; learning disabilities; attention-deficit disorders; childhood conditions such as conduct disorder, being sheltered or overprotected, or not having adequate social experiences with peers; child abuse; social anxiety; and traumatic brain injury, depression, addiction, schizophrenia, stroke, and dementia.

Common Social Concerns

Common social concerns can be grouped into three categories: social isolation, poor social skills, and inappropriate social behaviors.

SOCIAL ISOLATION

Social isolation is often a component of chronic illness, as well as a reaction to acquiring a disability or health problem or experiencing an event that the individual finds uncomfortable or embarrassing. The isolation may be initiated by the person with the illness or by friends and family who have problems coping with the illness. These are behaviors associated with social isolation:

Healthy social relationships are important contributors to a person's level of happiness.

Image Source

- Withdrawal from other people and situations that require interaction
- Lack of support networks
- Limited friendships
- Shyness
- Worry that one does not know what to say or how to act
- Fear of rejection or trying new activities

POOR SOCIAL SKILLS

Social skills encompass a person's ability to initiate social interactions, sustain a conversation, listen, participate as a member of a team or group, cultivate new social opportunities, behave in ways that are satisfying and fulfilling to the individual and his network of friends, and support and maintain friendships and relationships. A person with poor social skills behaves awkwardly in social situations. Clients with poor social skills misread social cues and nonverbal communication, interrupt others' conversations or demonstrate awkwardness when joining a conversation, laugh at the wrong point in a conversation, engage in inappropriate touching, and either stare at others or do not make eye contact. Some people with disabilities or chronic conditions may never have had opportunities to interact in a broad variety of social situations and consequently lack experience with how to navigate these situations. They often perceive themselves as separate or different from others (Luskin Biordi, 2002).

INAPPROPRIATE SOCIAL BEHAVIORS

Much as with inappropriate expression of emotions, inappropriate social behaviors may be defined by the context in which they occur. In general, extremes of behavior are deemed inappropriate and may be closely related to a specific diagnosis. For example, a person with Tourette syndrome may shout obscenities, a behavior that they have no control over and that is a manifestation of the condition. An individual with autism may engage in self-stimulating behavior in public, touch others, or sniff their hair. People with Down syndrome are very affectionate and may hug strangers. Other inappropriate behaviors may be due to emotional problems or be a characteristic behavior of a peer group. Being overly aggressive or belligerent in social interactions, acting too young or too old for one's age, dressing inappropriately for one's age or for a particular situation, and disrupting a group are other examples. Often adults with intellectual disabilities have been dressed as children, which has been a barrier to their social integration and inclusion. Or, a client may refuse to attend activities or may sit quietly and not interact with others in a group. If he is the only one to do this, he may be viewed by the other group members as behaving inappropriately.

The TR Approach to Social Concerns

Most TR programs are inherently social and require degrees of social interaction, whether on a one-to-one, small-group, or large-group basis. The TR setting is an ideal situation for clients to learn and practice new social skills. The TRS is a role model of appropriate social behaviors. These include displaying good manners, carrying on a conversation, listening, dressing appropriately, handling criticism and expressing anger in acceptable ways, giving and receiving compliments, and initiating actions. Whenever possible the TRS should help clients to form friendships; friendship is considered one of the most essential and valuable types of social relationships (Chadsey, 2007). Communication skills are just one component of the development of friendships, which also involves having common interests, being in physical proximity to each other, having time available for a relationship, and reciprocity (Chadsey, 2007).

The TRS should motivate the socially isolated client by approaching her on a regular basis in a nonthreatening manner, starting to talk about a simple, familiar topic, and attempting to identify a need or interest that may prompt the client to engage with others. For example, an elderly woman in a nursing home refused to leave her room. At some point the TRS asked her, "Is there anything you would like?" She replied, "I would love a good cup of coffee." The TRS told her, "I have a coffee pot in the TR room. If you come down, I will make you a great cup of coffee." The next day, she went to the TR room. The TRS had identified a powerful motivator, based on something that mattered to the resident. If a client is withdrawn because she is embarrassed by her condition or situation, the TRS should acknowledge her feelings. He could then introduce her to a peer who has a similar concern or involve her in a one-to-one activity that might build her confidence and lead her to eventually share her interest with a small group. The TRS can also work with the client's family, who may become isolated from their own social relationships as they address their family member's health issues.

To help clients develop appropriate social behaviors and social skills, the TRS can teach specific skills utilizing role playing, demonstrations, homework, and watching and critiquing television shows and movies. As clients develop and utilize these skills

Cultural Influences on Social Behaviors

Greeting someone
When working with people from Asian backgrounds (Chinese, Japanese, Vietnamese), avoid physical contact, particularly during initial meetings. Instead, nod to the person and give a verbal greeting.

People of Middle Eastern descent avoid physical contact with the opposite sex, but hugging and kissing between men are considered acceptable.

People from European cultures (France, Portugal, Spain, Italy) expect to be kissed on both cheeks.

Eye contact

In Western cultures, maintaining direct eye contact is viewed as positive.

In Native American and Asian cultures, it is considered disrespectful to look directly at a person of higher authority.

Smiling

In Korean cultures, smiling implies shallowness.

In some Asian cultures, smiling may actually convey anger, frustration, or confusion.

For someone from Puerto Rico, a smile has several meanings, including "Thank you" or "How may I help you?" depending on the movement of the forehead and the expression in the eyes.

Native Americans may avoid smiling.

Expressing yes and no nonverbally

In Eastern European cultures (Albania and Bulgaria), people express "yes" by turning the head from side to side and express "no" by nodding.

In American culture, it is the exact opposite.

Friendliness

In Ethiopian culture, being open and friendly with a stranger is considered misleading and inappropriate.

Giving praise

In Asian cultures, praise is often seen as a sign of criticism and makes people feel uncomfortable or embarrassed. Public praise or criticism is seen as demeaning. Speaking about one's strengths and positive attributes is seen as bragging and is considered inappropriate.

Attitudes toward weight

Cultures have different views about what represents a desirable weight.

In some African, Middle Eastern, and Mediterranean cultures, a woman who is plump or is gaining weight is considered desirable, and the weight is a sign of readiness for marriage.

In Hispanic cultures, a full-figured woman is considered very attractive.

Holding hands

Most Asian cultures disapprove of public displays of affection by males and females. However, in Asian, Middle Eastern, and Mediterranean cultures, same-sex hand holding is considered acceptable and a symbol of friendship.

In Latino culture, women often walk arm in arm.

Time

The concept of what it means to be on time also differs by culture.

In Indian and Nigerian cultures, saying that a meeting or social event is at one o'clock may mean that the meeting will take place anywhere between one and three o'clock.

Filipinos say "American time" to indicate promptness.

Asian and Middle Eastern cultures in general place less value on being on time than most Western cultures (the French, though, are very casual about meeting times).

Personal space

People from the Middle East and Latin America tend to prefer close spacing between people who are interacting, within 12 inches.

Americans maintain an arm's-length distance from people when they are socially interacting.

The Dutch prefer even more space between themselves and others in a social situation.

Data from Dresser 2005.

Props can be useful when leading social activities to stimulate excitement and conversation.

Photo courtesy of Robin Kunstler.

THERAPEUTIC RECREATION PROGRAMS FOR SOCIAL HEALTH

Programs that have been shown to be successful in work with people who have social concerns include games, sports, dancing, creative dramatics, animal-assisted therapy, social skills training, assertiveness training, leisure education, community outings, and family support groups (see chapter 6). These activities require social interaction on some level and can be led by the TRS to help clients overcome social concerns, feel more comfortable in social situations, and be more accepted by others. For children, play opportunities are essential for social skills development. Participation in small play groups and club activities are effective in promoting social intelligence. Social activities such as parties, coffee hours, or group games are venues for clients to practice their newly acquired skills in the safe environment of the TR program. More recently, the Internet has served as an avenue for making social connections and diminishing social isolation through e-mails, blogs, chat rooms, and social networking sites. Clients may wish to utilize text messaging as a means of communication with members of their social network.

CULTURAL COMPETENCE

Culture influences behaviors. Actions that are expected in the dominant culture may be contrary to how a person was raised and now lives, in accordance with his cultural practices. Being aware of these influences will give the TRS insight into why a person is displaying particular social behaviors. Behaviors that are culturally based include amount of eye contact, giving of gifts, touching others, shaking hands, decision making, use of personal space, and identifying strengths or "bragging" about oneself. The TRS may help the client understand cultural differences and navigate how to interact in situations that may be at variance with the client's social customs and personal cultural values. Cultural differences may also apply to clients' expectations during interactions with a staff member. Touch is considered inappropriate and frowned on in many cultures and also in some treatment programs; but in certain cultures and populations, touch can help to reduce social isolation and provide comfort and reassurance (Luskin Biordi, 2002). The TRS should assess the appropriateness of using touch in his interactions with clients and discuss this with the team before initiating any behavior using touch. Touch with older adults can be very comforting but may convey a different meaning when used with teenage girls.

during TR programs, the TRS provides feedback and reinforcement to encourage them to continue to utilize newly acquired behaviors. Verbal cues or prompts may be needed to produce a behavioral response (Dattilo & Guerin, 2001). Age-appropriate activities have been discussed in relation to many different client groups, including the elderly, adults with intellectual disabilities, and young adults with physical disabilities. While the concept has evolved to "person-appropriate" activities, the TRS should endeavor to provide activities and programs that are typical of the client's chronological age yet adapted to his level of cognitive functioning. When a person engages in an activity that is suitable for a much younger person, this isolates him from his peers and perpetuates negative stereotypes.

TEAM COLLABORATION

Addressing social concerns is a team effort. The TRS works with the members of the team to develop a consistent plan for each client that is culturally sensitive and age appropriate. All staff must follow the guidelines for how to interact with the client so that he is not receiving mixed messages about what is acceptable behavior. The causes and consequences of inappropriate behaviors are best addressed by a team that shares observations of clients' behaviors. A uniform behavior management plan should be developed and followed by all disciplines. All staff members engage in social interactions with clients and bear the responsibility of modeling appropriate behavior. Clients even observe staff-to-staff interactions, so staff should be mindful of the powerful influence their actions have on clients. Often clients with social concerns live in the community and receive services at home, in school, or in a day program. The TRS may be asked to collaborate with the IEP (Individual Education Plan) team in the school, with local parks and recreation staff, or with group home or day treatment personnel. Parents may also be involved in the social skills training and work closely with the TRS to ensure that the training approaches are carried over into home, school, or work situations and that new behaviors and skills are reinforced.

RISK MANAGEMENT

Social concerns can pose a risk for clients during TR programs. Inappropriate behaviors may be misunderstood by others, leading to arguments or altercations. Rules specifying acceptable and unacceptable social behaviors should be established and followed for all programs. Clients with intellectual disabilities, as well as children and teenagers, need to be taught how to differentiate among friends, acquaintances, and strangers and to learn appropriate social boundaries. Clients who have not developed social intelligence or judgment in social situations may be victimized by others. The TRS also has a responsibility to identify the appropriate behaviors and skills required for participation in community programs. The clients' readiness for the community experience should be carefully assessed. A client may be able to function well in the safe environment of the TR setting but not be ready for the challenges of the community. For example, many clients in substance abuse treatment do very well in the closed setting, but when discharged they cannot cope with the responsibility of structuring their own time. The TRS is responsible for continually monitoring a client's behavior on community

outings or assessing community reentry skills to determine what skills need improvement, as well as to prevent embarrassment to the client or untoward incidents. The TRS should have a plan in place for how to handle behavioral problems on a trip and, when necessary, have support staff available for addressing such incidents. A client may get lost or "elope" from a trip or outing, and the TRS must have a set of procedures to follow in case this occurs. The TRS must be observant of the client's needs because he may be unwilling or afraid to speak up if he is having a problem or even be unaware of a problem. The TRS should also be knowledgeable about the medications clients are taking and the side effects that may affect behavior.

ETHICAL PRACTICE

The TRS maintains appropriate social boundaries and self-awareness of her own needs so that she does not send mixed messages to clients who have social concerns. Clients with cognitive limitations, including those with intellectual disabilities and traumatic brain injuries, may have problems distinguishing different types of relationships. Clients may call staff members "girlfriends" or "boyfriends" or make inappropriate sexual remarks or gestures. The TRS should monitor her own behavior and that of staff to ensure that clients are not infantilized. When clients are in a dependent situation in an institutional setting, staff often view them as children in their care and may pat them on the head, offer false reassurance, or dress them in age-inappropriate clothing. The TRS also needs to behave in a socially appropriate manner, dress professionally, use proper language, and be well groomed. Often in TR the relaxed atmosphere is more accepting of a range of social behaviors, and the TRS may inadvertently neglect aspects of a client's plan that relate to overcoming social concerns.

Case Study

This case study describes two female residents of a nursing home who share the common social concern of social isolation. The TR department follows the Therapeutic Recreation Outcome Model (Carter et al., 2003) because it focuses on quality of life, which is of primary importance in the long-term care setting. One goal is set for both residents, followed by three objectives.

BACKGROUND

Mrs. Kelly and Mrs. Garcia are residents in a long-term care (LTC) facility. Mrs. Kelly recently moved into the nursing home because she was displaying mild confusion, limited mobility due to a stroke, and social isolation while living at home. Mrs. Garcia is a long-term resident of the nursing home who recently engaged in one-to-one programming with the TRS due to confinement during a long illness. Now that her health has improved, she is being encouraged to participate in group programs. At the comprehensive care planning (CCP) meeting, in which both women are discussed, the TRS reports that they seem receptive to becoming involved in group activities. Despite their differing diagnoses (Mrs. Garcia with physical illnesses and Mrs. Kelly with mild dementia), they share common concerns of social isolation and a need for friendship development.

GOALS AND OBJECTIVES

Goal: Increase social interaction with other residents

Objectives for Mrs. Garcia and Mrs. Kelly:

Objective 1: Participate in one activity of interest per day selected from the weekly TR calendar, for a minimum of three consecutive days, with the guidance of the TRS.

Objective 2: After two weeks of participation, initiate a 3-minute conversation with two other group members during each of the three activities.

Objective 3: By the fourth week, invite one other resident to the weekly tea party.

THERAPEUTIC RECREATION LEADERSHIP

The TRS visits Mrs. Garcia and Mrs. Kelly on a daily basis to build rapport and a trusting relationship. During these daily motivational visits, the TRS reviews the weekly TR calendar with the women. She respects their need to take their time to make a decision about activity engagement. The TRS suggests activities from the calendar based on the women's leisure interests as identified during the assessment process. She focuses on music, which is a common interest of the women. She offers to take each of them to the activity for 10 minutes and explains that if they want to leave, she will have them escorted back to their rooms. The TRS answers their concerns about getting to the activities, proximity to the rest room, and not missing meals, medications, or visitors while at the activities. These concerns reveal their anxieties about attending the program and their need for reassurance.

On arrival at the activity, the TRS places both women next to more talkative members. The TRS leading the activity engages Mrs. Kelly and Mrs. Garcia in conversation and refocuses their attention when they appear to be losing interest or their attention is drifting. When the activity is finished she praises Mrs. Kelly for her knowledge of the different types of music. Other residents also give Mrs. Kelly compliments. Mrs. Kelly feels a little more comfortable as she has connected with familiar music and shared a mutual interest with others. The TRS also praises Mrs. Garcia for her active involvement in the group by acknowledging that Mrs. Garcia clapped her hands and tapped her feet to the music.

Progress Report

At the quarterly review, the TRS reports that Mrs. Kelly and Mrs. Garcia have met their goal. They are now attending Italian club, a movement to music program, and the afternoon tea party each week. Mrs. Kelly demonstrates increased social interaction and participation; she initiates conversations with other residents and is able to express opinions and choices about activities to do with her family. As her social skills have improved, so has her cognitive functioning. Mrs. Kelly's family has reported that

Dorot's University Without Walls

Dorot is a multiservice agency founded in 1976 in New York City to meet the needs of older adults living in their own homes and coping with the challenges of aging. With a network of over 10,000 volunteers, Dorot provides a wide range of programs. Dorot offers hundreds of classes each year that appeal to a wide range of interests, including "a unique community via telephone conference calls that enable those with limited mobility to join in lively, stimulating classes, make new friends, get and give emotional support, and celebrate the holidays—all within the comfort of their homes. Classes and support groups are led by professionals and volunteers who enjoy sharing their expertise and learning from class participants. Topics include the arts, history, health, current events, and more. Seniors and facilitators can be connected from any location in the U.S. equipped with a telephone, and all participants can speak to and hear each other." For more information, visit www.dorotusa.org.

she appears to be more animated during their visits and is able to concentrate longer on the conversation. Mrs. Garcia has no family, but nursing staff state that she is more conversational, spends less time in her room, and shows an improved mood. As their health improved in several domains, both women achieved the outcome of improved quality of life.

Mrs. Kelly's Discharge Plan

The TRS will collaborate with the social worker and Mrs. Kelly's family to determine the feasibility of Mrs. Kelly's moving from the nursing home to her daughter's home. If this occurs, socialization and exercise will be essential to maintain her optimal level of functioning and quality of life. The TRS will provide family leisure education to help the family identify leisure activities that can be pursued in the home and in the surrounding neighborhood by Mrs. Kelly, family members, and a home health aide. She will provide a DVD of an in-home exercise program and contact information for organizations providing teleconference classes and games. Mrs. Kelly's improved social interaction and activity participation should be reinforced frequently with praise, and she should maintain daily activity involvement.

ECOLOGICAL PERSPECTIVE

Although Mrs. Garcia and Mrs. Kelly live in a long-term care facility, the TRS has the ethical responsibility to advocate for their right to be actively engaged. The TRS ensures that the environment is supportive of their participation by offering meaningful choices and easy access to program locations, promoting a home-like atmosphere, and ensuring that staff treat them with respect and dignity. The TRS may need to educate the staff and the family to interact socially with the residents as adults with a lifetime of experiences and to offer support and encouragement in the context of their limitations. In any setting or with any population, the TRS may encounter families who interact inappropriately with the client, or demonstrate social concerns themselves, and who may need intervention to learn new patterns of behavior. Families may encourage or enable inappropriate or unhealthy behavior. The TRS may be able to refer the family for services. The TRS can also educate personnel in local community settings about behaviors associated with different cultural practices or behaviors resulting from illness or disability, to further understanding and acceptance.

● Summary ●

The TR profession can make a significant contribution to helping clients achieve good health and, potentially, optimal wellness by supporting their efforts to make healthy lifestyle choices. In developing and providing the most appropriate TR plan for a client, the TRS should consider both the common concerns the client faces and his strengths. The client's strengths are assets that he can use to overcome or minimize the common concerns. Common concerns are evident in all the functional domains: leisure, physical, cognitive, affective or emotional, and social, and occur across diagnoses and age groups. The TRS should be cognizant of the particular limitations or problems that may be associated with clients' conditions.

The challenge to the TRS is to provide programming that can have meaning and value to an entire group of individuals, each with their unique needs. By focusing on the common concerns, regardless of diagnosis, the TRS can more successfully design relevant programming. To do this, the TRS must be familiar with cultural influences on clients' beliefs, values, and behaviors and incorporate culturally appropriate behaviors into her own TR practice. The TRS collaborates with other professionals as a team member and with community agencies to develop and implement programs that are comprehensive and effective in supporting a client's improved health and maintenance of well-being.

The TRS must be vigilant about respecting clients' confidentiality and implementing person-appropriate and safe activities. Risk management is a priority in the provision of TR leadership. The TRS, in accordance with the TR principle of the ecological perspective, recognizes that the physical and social environment influences and is influenced by clients' behaviors. The practice of TR is complex and multidimensional. The ability of the TRS to recognize and understand common concerns and implement effective programs is essential to the ethical practice of TR leadership. Chapter 6 describes the TR toolkit, which includes the activities, resources, and techniques used by the TRS to deliver programs.

● **Learning Activities** ●

1. To what extent do you practice the behaviors associated with a healthy lifestyle? In a small-group discussion compare your behaviors with those of others. Brainstorm changes you can make to promote your health.

2. Discuss in a small group the ethical implications of trying to change a client's freely chosen *unhealthy* behaviors.

3. Pick two of the common concerns in the chapter. For each one, identify simple activities you can use to assess functioning. What types of programming could you offer in collaboration with other disciplines?

4. Choose one of the clients from the case studies. Investigate your own community for agencies, organizations, and support services for this client. What barriers to inclusion exist in the community? Write a discharge plan, similar to the one in this chapter for the clients with affective and emotional concerns, that incorporates the resources you have identified in order to overcome these barriers.

5. Select any TR activity and develop a risk management plan that addresses the risks associated with equipment and supplies, physical environment, needed skills of the TRS, and client behavioral and health considerations.

6. Pick another case study from the chapter. For each of the clients in the case, identify an additional goal and a set of three objectives, with appropriate TR programs. Ask a classmate or coworker to review your goals and objectives to see if they are clear and relevant to the clients' needs and interests.

7. Discuss in a small group how each person's cultural background has influenced choices of leisure participation. What similarities do the group members share? What differences stand out?

The Therapeutic Recreation Toolkit: Programs, Benefits, and Implementation

In this chapter you will learn about:

- The TR toolkit
- Selecting and analyzing recreation activities
- Five categories of TR programs:
  - Arts-related programs
  - Cognitively oriented programs
  - Health-related programs
  - Nature-oriented programs
  - Social activities
- The benefits of participating in activities and the skills required for participation
- Risk management practices for all TR programs

The TRS plans and implements TR programs in order to address clients' needs, help them reach their goals, and reinforce their strengths. The TRS selects from a range of recreation activities that, when combined with the TRS's interactions and communication skills, become TR programs or experiences (also known as **therapeutic recreation interventions**) that help the clients achieve functional and existential outcomes. Recreation activities are the "bread and butter" of TR services, the fundamental methods used to achieve the goals of TR. "Enjoyable, freely entered into, and health promoting, these activities recreate a positive sense of the inner self" (O'Keefe, 2005, p. 81). Recreation activities can be powerful vehicles for learning new skills, adapting existing abilities to new circumstances, developing new behaviors in order to function in one's chosen environment, and maintaining functioning to minimize decline (Bullock & Mahon, 2000), as well as for personal fulfillment and overall quality of life. "It is through direct experience in carefully chosen activities that the majority of therapeutic benefits" (Austin, 2001, p. 53) are obtained. Almost any recreation activity can be used for therapeutic purposes (Austin, 2001). It is the TRS's ethical responsibility to develop knowledge and competence in a wide variety of activities so that she can select the most appropriate ones for her client. The TRS's ethical obligation is to do good for clients, to respect their personal values and beliefs in providing programs, to be competent in TR programming, and to treat everyone fairly.

THE TR TOOLKIT

The **therapeutic recreation toolkit** is a collection of information, resources, and activities that the TRS uses in his work. This chapter focuses on the activities included in the toolkit. While there are as many different TR activities as there are recreation activities, a fairly standard group of TR program offerings are used in many settings and with all types of clients. These programs can be loosely grouped into five areas: arts related, cognitively oriented, health related, nature oriented, and social. These are the activities in each area:

- Arts related: arts and crafts, the arts (fine or visual arts, performing arts, and technology or new arts)
- Cognitively oriented: discussion groups, leisure education (including values clarification, assertiveness training, and social skills training), intellectual and literary activities, and games

- Health related: cooking and food preparation, physical activity (exercise, fitness, sports, aquatics), relaxation and stress management, hobbies, and humor
- Nature oriented: outdoor recreation, horticulture and gardening, and animal-assisted programming
- Social activities and special events

Looking over this list, we can see that every TRS has had experience in her own life as a participant in specific activities in each program area. Every TRS should be able to lead programs in each of these areas as appropriate to the particular client population. While the TRS does not have to know how to play every single type of game, for example, she should know at least several that can be used or adapted for her clients. Initially, the TRS needs to be comfortable and secure with the basics of the activity. Over time, she can add to her knowledge and repertoire to deliver imaginative and motivating activities that maximize the benefits to the clients. In addition to the activities, the TR toolkit contains resources such as exercise tapes, CDs of relaxing music, magazines, and Web sites that exponentially increase the range of activity choices. The TRS's ethical responsibility is to do what is best for her clients and to be competent in her work. Participating in TR should be enjoyable, meaningful, and therapeutic for clients. Fulfilling the blended role of TR leadership entails being a role model, enjoying and actively engaging in the recreation experience, and displaying enthusiasm and energy that are contagious and motivating to clients.

SELECTING ACTIVITIES

Knowing which TR activity to select for a particular client or group of clients is part of the TRS's professional expertise and judgment. In health and human service agencies, each professional utilizes the interventions and strategies of his own discipline to produce desired outcomes. These interventions may be "high tech," with state-of-the-art equipment or supplies, or as basic as a card game. Just as a doctor may prescribe either a sophisticated antibiotic for a particular illness or recommend only bed rest and plenty of fluids, a physical therapist may utilize elaborate equipment such as an electrotherapy muscle stimulator or simple walking. So too, the TRS may choose a Wii game system or the standard board game of Scrabble. All of the TR program areas described in this chapter are supported by evidence of their effectiveness and guidelines for implementation with different client groups. The TRS should select the TR program based on the evidence, taking into account the client's strengths, needs, preferences, cultural background, and future desires. Activity selection is influenced by

- the mission of the agency;
- regulations of government agencies and accrediting bodies;
- the TR model followed by the TR department;
- budgetary availability;
- the physical environment;
- staffing; and
- strengths, preferences, and goals of participants.

For activities to be considered therapeutic, certain characteristics should be present (Austin, 2001). Activities should

- be goal directed, done for a reason or purpose;
- require active participation by the client;
- have meaning and value to the client;
- offer potential for pleasure and satisfaction;
- provide opportunities for mastery and success as well as feelings of competence and enjoyment; and
- be carefully selected with the guidance of the TRS.

As in our personal recreation pursuits, all activities should be enjoyable and fun for the participant. "Recreation services are purely enjoyable, while therapeutic recreation services are enjoyable but intentionally more goal-oriented and treatment-oriented" (Bullock & Mahon, 2000, p. ix).

Creativity and ingenuity on the part of the TRS can maximize the experience for the clients and enhance the benefits. "Creativity is the ability to see things in a new way, to recognize what is significant; to relate meaningful observations, and to pull them together into some new whole" (Streitfeld, 1993, p. 120). Being creative is exciting for the TRS and helps keep programming fresh.

ACTIVITY ANALYSIS

To determine which activities are the most suitable for a client or group of clients in a particular setting, the TRS conducts an **activity analysis**. Activity analysis is a systematic procedure for identifying the specific behaviors needed to participate in a given activity. These behaviors can be categorized according to the four behavioral domains: physical, cognitive, affective or emotional, and social. Within each of these domains are specific skills and behaviors that are used in doing the activity. For example, playing a game of cards requires

- cognitive skills—knowing the rules and strategy of the game;
- physical skills—fine motor manipulation of the cards and visual acuity;
- social skills—taking turns and engaging in conversation with other players; and
- emotional skills—feeling positive, enjoying the experience, and coping with competition and winning and losing (Mobily & Ostiguy, 2004).

It is critical to analyze the activity as it is typically played or engaged in, and not for any particular disability or condition (Stumbo & Peterson, 2009). Once the TRS understands the skills needed to do the activity, she can select the activity for a particular client to help improve his current functioning, develop new skills, and utilize his strengths. A card game can be selected for a client whose goals include improving fine motor skills, cognitive functioning, or social interaction. Also, the client may have enjoyed playing cards in the past, and being able to play again may have significant meaning to him and contribute to his quality of life. The activity analysis has revealed that card games can help meet these goals. At this point the TRS can determine the **adaptations** necessary to enable the client to participate in the activity. A client who does not have the fine motor skills to hold the cards can use a piece of adapted equipment, such as a card holder, to enable participation. A client who has difficulty processing information quickly can be given more time to take his turn. Activity analysis serves as a means to understand both what skills are needed in order to do the activity and which skills can be developed or enhanced by participation in the activity. Through the process of analyzing an activity, the TRS obtains essential information that leads to modifying or adapting activities to the functioning level of the particular client (Shank & Coyle, 2002).

One of the most valuable aspects of activity analysis is that it provides the TRS with a rationale for selecting a particular activity. The rationale can be used to communicate the benefits of participating in a given activity to the clients, their families, and the other professionals. The TRS should have a thorough understanding of why she has selected an activity for the client and be able to articulate this rationale in a clear and comprehensible manner so others see its value. Even bingo can be played for its therapeutic value, as shown in the activity analysis presented by DeVries and Lake (2002). See figure 6.1 for their activity analysis of bingo and table 6.1 for a list of the knowledge and skills to examine when conducting an activity analysis (Sylvester et al., 2001).

Let's look at another game, checkers. Checkers requires vision and fine motor dexterity to grasp and move the playing pieces, cognitive skills for knowing the rules, use of strategy to make decisions about

moves, and concentration. It also requires social skills of taking turns and sitting quietly while the opponent contemplates his moves and emotional control during the game and when responding to winning or losing (Stumbo & Peterson, 2009). Checkers might be a good choice for a client who is overcoming social isolation and is more comfortable interacting one to one. If needed, the pieces can be modified to be easier to grasp. When modifying activities, keep the activity as close to the original as possible. By making only the necessary modifications, the activity is more similar to the way it is typically engaged in. This is more fun for clients and

TABLE 6.1

Knowledge and Skills to Examine in an Activity Analysis

Domains of knowledge	Examples
Physical	What body parts are used when doing the activity?
	Does the activity require independence in mobility?
	What types of movements: reaching, pushing, bending?
	Does the activity require flexibility?
	Does the activity require upper or lower body strength or both?
	Does the activity require coordination?
	Does the activity require speed?
	Does the activity require fine motor skills?
Cognitive	Does the activity require ability to follow directions?
	Does the activity require an understanding of numbers?
	Does the activity require reading and writing skills?
	Does the activity require long- or short-term memory or both?
	Does the activity require concentration?
	Does the activity require sensory abilities? Which ones?
	Does the activity require abstract or concrete thinking or both?
Affective	Does the activity allow for expression of feelings? (e.g., happiness, sadness, frustration)
	Does the activity require control of feelings? (e.g., anger, frustration)
Social	Does the activity require one-to-one, small-group, or large-group interaction or some combination of these?
	Does the activity require communication?
	Does the activity require competition, cooperation, or both?
	Does the activity require participants to provide leadership?
	Does the activity require close physical proximity or contact among participants?
Feasibility	How realistic is it to conduct this activity? Are the appropriate equipment, location, and staff expertise and time available?

Adapted from C. Sylvester, J. Voelkl, and G. Ellis, 2001, *Therapeutic recreation: Theory and practice* (State College, PA: Venture). By permission of C. Sylvester.

Activity Analysis

Therapeutic Recreation Program: *Bingo*

Group Size: Small (<12) _____ Large(>12) *X* _____ One-to-one _____

Time required: *45-60 minutes* _____ Location: *Recreation Room* _____

Equipment needed: *Bingo set, cards, chips, scoreboard, microphone, prizes*

Frequency: *One time per week* _____ Staff-to-resident ratio: *1:40*

Skills Required

Physical: *Arm extension and flexion, crossing midline, fine motor grip, trunk and head control, hand-eye coordination, gross motor control*

Cognitive: *Recall, number and letter recognition, reading ability, following directions, processing, attention to task, initiation*

Social/Communication: *Verbal expression, socially appropriate behavior, self-control*

Sensory: *Auditory comprehension; visual scanning; visual tracking; tactile, auditory, and visual discrimination*

Emotional: *Self-control, ability to cope with losing*

Leisure: *Knowledge of game, sportsmanship*

Goals and Objectives

Physical: *Grasp objects, maintain sitting position, demonstrate control of upper extremities and fine motor movements*

Cognitive: *Maintain attention to task, recognize numbers and letters, follow directions, recall information, initiate and complete task*

Social: *Express self, self-control, demonstrate appropriate social behavior*

Emotional: *Appropriately express emotions related to winning and losing*

Leisure: *Enjoy game and group activity*

Figure 6.1 Bingo activity analysis.
Based on DeVries and Lake 2002.

also facilitates their transfer of skills to more typical environments. Modify only as necessary to enable the client's successful engagement. Individualize modifications to the needs of each participant. Modifications may be temporary, used only until the client develops the skills and knowledge necessary to participate as fully as possible. For example, as a client's ability to concentrate increases, he will no longer require extra time to take his turn. For a comprehensive discussion of activity analysis, see *Therapeutic Recreation Program Design* by Norma Stumbo and Carol Peterson (2009); any edition of this classic TR textbook is highly recommended.

This chapter presents the five broad categories of TR programs, with descriptions of specific activities, their benefits and applications to a variety of clients, and risk management concerns. Each TR program is supported by evidence from research findings and the literature demonstrating the efficacy and value of the activity in producing the desired outcomes and providing the client with a meaningful experience.

Arts-Related Programs

Arts-related activities have long been recognized as worthwhile programs in recreation agencies for their universal appeal and wide range of benefits. The therapeutic value of participation in arts and crafts, the fine arts, the performing arts (music, dance, and dramatics), and arts that use technology makes these ideal programs for TR participants.

Arts and Crafts

In an **arts and crafts** activity, people make, by hand, objects that typically have a useful purpose but are also decorative. It is distinguished from **art**, which involves creation of an artwork as a form of aesthetic expression (Kraus, 1997). For thousands of years, people from various cultures have produced craft objects using clay, wood, metal, paper, fabric, plants, and found objects or scrap materials. Arts and crafts projects range from the very simple to the very complex and can be done by people of all ages and with a wide variety of physical and cognitive limitations. Arts and crafts can be done alone or with others; they are offered within classes or as workshops or can be done at home, and are often featured in exhibitions and displays or offered for sale. Many types of arts and crafts can be developed into hobbies that are very satisfying to the participant and can be continued after treatment (Williams, 2008).

Benefits of Arts and Crafts

Arts and crafts have benefits in all the behavioral domains, making them an excellent choice for a TR program. Arts and crafts provides an opportunity for self-expression without the use of verbal language, gives participants a sense of control over the outcome of their efforts, and facilitates interaction between the TRS and the client (Chow, 2002). Mastering the use of materials and specific techniques strengthens the client's feelings of accomplishment (Levine, 2001) and self-esteem. There are also group projects that promote positive communication and cooperation (Williams, 2008), such as quilting.

Arts and crafts utilizes the following skills and can produce a number of benefits:

- Physical: fine motor coordination and dexterity, pincer grasp, range of motion in upper limbs, eye–hand coordination

- Cognitive: following directions, concentration, task sequencing, decision making, counting, measuring, reading instructions
- Affective or emotional: creativity, feelings of success, self-expression, relaxation
- Social: cooperation in sharing supplies, giving and receiving compliments on efforts

Risk Management

Implementing a safe arts and crafts program requires

- a large enough surface to arrange the supplies and to work on the projects;
- adequate lighting;
- sufficient ventilation, especially if materials that have odors are being used;
- access to a sink for washing up afterward;
- storage containers and areas; and
- a range of equipment and supplies that can be used successfully by participants with varying limitations.

Be sure to have plenty of supplies on hand so when mistakes are made it is easy to provide additional materials (Peniston, 1998). Arts and crafts programs give rise to particular risk management concerns, necessitating careful monitoring of the use of sharp tools such as scissors, needles, and craft knives; toxic materials (because of the risk of ingestion); spills (which should be wiped up immediately because of the risk of slipping and falls); and power equipment.

Programming

Arts and crafts activities include decoupage, making yarn dolls, puppetry, making flowers and holiday objects, quilting, scrapbooking, mosaic tile work, ceramics, and woodworking, to name a few. The TRS may choose projects that can be completed in one session, which gives more immediate gratification, or projects that take several sessions to complete, which may contribute to developing patience to work toward a goal. Arts and crafts can be offered in a variety of program formats: as instruction on an individual basis or in a group, as a drop-in activity, as a special event with a demonstration by a local

ARTS

COGNITIVE

HEALTH

NATURE

SOCIAL

141

Arts and Crafts Web Sites

www.abcteach.com
www.amazingmoms.com
www.artistshelpingchildren.org
www.crayola.com
www.enchantedlearning.com
www.familyfun.com
www.recreationtherapy.com

craftsperson, or as a craft show with or without prizes. Clients who are skilled at arts and crafts may also want to sell their work. Many facilities have sales of clients' craft projects that raise money for the TR department or other causes. Also, some clients may go on to sell their work commercially or start a business. At a shelter for homeless adults with AIDS and mental illness, making handmade note paper and wrapping paper was selected as an arts and craft activity that would have commercial value (Fazio, 2008).

Arts and crafts activities should be age appropriate and meaningful to participants. The TRS should present the activities with the attitude that this is not just busy work but can be a satisfying experience (Streitfeld, 1993). While most children enjoy making things, as people get older they seem to decrease their involvement in arts and crafts unless they have developed it into a hobby. However, this interest can be rekindled if the projects selected are of interest to the participants. The TRS should have a completed object available to show participants in order to give them a sense of direction and motivate them to do the project. Having a display of crafts or a one-time workshop to introduce new crafts projects can attract new participants. Rancourt (1989) reported an excellent example of a TRS's use of ingenuity to develop an age-appropriate program that promoted inclusion. An older adult member of a senior citizen center who had mental retardation (MR) enjoyed coloring with crayons. The typical seniors saw this as a childish activity, and in fact it reinforced the differences between the group and the individual, rather than promoting social interaction based on commonalities. The TRS decided to provide the older adult with MR with stenciling supplies, rather than crayons, for coloring. Both activities involve using coloring agents to create a picture or design.

Yet stenciling is popular as a way of decorating objects such as canvas tote bags and caps, is also used in interior design, and was perceived by the typical seniors as age appropriate. They also began stenciling and social interaction with the individual with MR increased greatly. Thinking about the ways to make an activity relevant and meaningful is the TRS's responsibility when selecting activities to help clients meet their goals.

Adaptations

There are many easy ways to adapt an arts and crafts activity to enable participation by people with disabilities. Clients who had a prior interest in arts and crafts but now have a condition that affects their ability to participate can learn adaptations to be able to continue their hobby. The equipment can be adapted. For clients with poor hand control due to tremors, lack of coordination, poor grasp, and limited movement, small pieces of sponge can be held by clothespins, foam can be used to build up handles of brushes and other implements, or a Velcro band can be used to attach a paintbrush or other tool to the wrist or head (Levine, 2001). For clients with poor vision, using larger supplies, so that they can string big beads on leather rather than small beads on wire, is helpful. Soft clay is an excellent medium that responds to mild pressure and does not require keen vision. An occupational therapist could be a useful resource for collaboration on adaptations to fine motor limitations for people with stroke, multiple sclerosis, Parkinson's disease, or arthritis. Clients themselves can figure out ways to enable them to do something they love. An elderly man who had a stroke supported his weak right hand, which held his paintbrush, with his strong left hand (Streitfeld, 1993) in order to continue to pursue an interest that had become vital to his well-being. Clients may also have difficulty understanding and following directions or measuring or counting supplies, the number of steps in a process, or the number of times an action needs to be taken (Peniston, 1998). The TRS, a volunteer, or peer can give one-to-one assistance in these areas.

Case Study

In a case report, Chow (2002) described a successful TR arts and crafts intervention with an elderly woman, Mrs. P., age 91, who lived at home with her husband and had diagnoses of Parkinson's disease and dementia. Based on her assessment, the TRS identified the goals of improving fine and gross motor skills and increasing attention span. She selected two arts and crafts projects, decoupage and making a yarn doll. Mrs. P. chose the picture for the decoupage and the color of the yarn for the doll. The decoupage project was completed first because it helped Mrs. P. develop skills that she then used in making the yarn doll. For the decoupage, she was given lightweight scissors and a fat, short-handled brush because of her small hands and limited fine motor skills. With verbal prompts by the TRS, Mrs. P. was able to cut out the picture using the scissors. When making the yarn doll, Mrs. P. was able to wind the yarn around the cardboard model, also with verbal prompting by the TRS. Building on the skills she had developed using the scissors on the decoupage project, she was able to use the scissors to cut the yarn without prompts. When she completed the doll, she showed it to her husband, saying "I cannot believe it went from nothing to something." She told the TRS, "It made me happy to know I was able to do things despite my age . . . I like to make things" (Chow, 2002, p. 209), which demonstrated that she felt worthwhile because she had completed the tasks required to finish these projects.

Based on Chow 2002

Arts and crafts have been around for thousands of years, which demonstrates their universal appeal and the multiple satisfactions that come from creating a useful and attractive object bearing the mark or personality of the person who made it. Arts and crafts is a "back to basics" activity in a fast-paced, technological world. The TRS will find that arts and crafts activities are an essential component of the TR toolkit.

Visual, Performing, and Technological Arts

The arts are very popular; one survey showed that 63 percent of Americans participate in the arts (Carpenter, 2006). Almost all TR services include arts programming, as it has considerable value to clients. In 2004, the Joint Commission on Accreditation of Healthcare Organizations conducted a survey and found that 2000 hospitals in the United States offered some kind of arts programming (Stewart, 2006). Arts programming in TR is not the same as art therapy, music therapy, dance therapy, or drama therapy. Those disciplines use arts in therapy for diagnosis and treatment; to analyze and interpret clients' behaviors, reactions, and expressions; and as forms of nonverbal psychotherapy. Professionals in these fields require extensive training in the psychological aspects of behavior, in therapeutic methods, and in a single art medium. Other terms that may be used are creative arts, an umbrella

term covering the use of multiple art forms, and expressive arts, which has similar meaning. In New York State, creative arts therapists are licensed as mental health professionals who practice nonverbal psychotherapy using art, music, dance, or drama. Therapeutic recreation specialists should be very careful not to use these terms for their programming. While not required to be an artist, dancer, musician, or actor, the TRS should have sufficient knowledge and resources to provide the leadership the program requires. To lead arts programming, she should be able to demonstrate, assist, instruct, and give feedback that enables clients to progress both in the process of the activity and in achieving their goals.

Benefits of the Arts

The rationale for using the arts in health care settings relates to their ability to promote well-being, encourage social interaction and participation in rehabilitation, and address unmet needs (Higgins, McKevitt & Wolfe, 2005). Arts activities in TR should be conducted in "a non-judgmental atmosphere of unconditional regard" (Baglin, Lewis & Williams, 2004, p. 100). They can be presented at many levels of proficiency and to groups of diverse members (Kraus, 1997); or people can do them alone in order to relax, compose themselves, or express the feelings of the moment, as well as to develop a personal leisure interest (Baglin et al., 2004). Engaging with the arts can help clients manage pain, alleviate stress and anxiety, and cope with upsetting events (Arts Council of Wales, 2007). The arts offer an alternative means of self-expression and communicating emotions, as well as an aesthetic experience in appreciating or creating beauty. The arts are a creative activity characterized by feelings of freedom and control, and they allow us to feel in touch with our real selves (Carpenter, 2006). The arts embody the customs and traditions of a culture and can help bridge cultural gaps as participants learn about each other's creative expressions (Kassing & Jay, 2003). The arts can be categorized as visual or fine, performing, and technological.

Fine or Visual Arts

Fine or **visual arts** may be defined as "visual-arts expressions in painting, sculpting and photography" (Carpenter, 2006, p. 337) that are intended to be looked at. Whereas arts and crafts involve making a useful object, "fine art may be viewed as the use of materials to demonstrate a concept or perception" (Russell & Jamieson, 2008, p. 53). A TR fine arts program can combine an aesthetic experience with the process of creative expression (Shank & Coyle, 2002). This suggests how meaningful clients might find the opportunities to engage in fine arts programming. In contrast to the TRS's art programming, an art therapist uses art as a tool to help clients develop insights and resolve emotional conflicts. On the other hand, the TRS can utilize art programming for self-expression, relaxation, self-esteem, and enjoyment. The TRS can work in collaboration with an art therapist to provide additional opportunities for a client to engage in artistic expression.

In TR, visual arts programs include (a) painting with different types of paint including tempera, watercolor, oil, and acrylics; (b) drawing with pencils, pens, charcoal, crayons, oil sticks, and pastels; (c) sculpture using found objects, fabric, natural materials, clay, wood, metal, wire, plaster of paris, or papier mâché; and (d) photography using different types of cameras. Group art projects such as painting a mural, creating an abstract collage from cut-up paper and pictures, or working on a life-size human figure drawing allow each person to contribute what he can, regardless of level of skill or functioning (Harlan, 1993). As part of the art program, the TRS can organize an exhibit of artwork or a juried art show, invite local artists to demonstrate and teach, and offer art appreciation through viewing images of artwork and films about artists or taking clients to galleries and museums.

Clients might discover that arts-related programs help them to feel in touch with their real selves.

Simone van den Berg/fotolia.com

Benefits of Fine and Visual Arts

The benefits of participating in the fine arts can be emphasized according to the client's needs: for relaxation, as a way to express oneself without words, for novelty and variety, and as a way to enjoy a positive group atmosphere. Art activities have the advantage of providing a group experience without the demand for ongoing social interaction, yet they can also be done on an individual basis.

Visual arts require the following skills and can produce these benefits:

- Physical: ability to manipulate art materials, which can include fine motor skills, use of the arms for reaching, or ability to utilize adaptive devices to carry out the art activity

- Cognitive: decision making that can include choice of colors, choice of materials, and conceptualizing an art piece; knowledge of how to use materials or equipment, such as a camera for photography

- Affective: aesthetic appreciation, nonverbal expression of emotions, experiencing joy and feelings of achievement

- Social: cooperation in group projects, giving and receiving a critique of artwork, teaching others, interaction, working toward a common goal

Art also can be used to help foster self-esteem, self-control, and expression of emotions (Mobily & MacNeil, 2002). For clients with eating disorders, art may be a way in which they depict their body image. It may be healthy for them to bring out their internal images on paper. The TRS is advised to consult with mental health staff on how to interact with clients regarding these images. Women with cancer have also been shown to benefit from art. In a study of a group of 111 women with cancer, the women engaged in art projects that included sketching self-portraits and sculpting with clay. Their improvements were reductions in stress level, less pain, better sleep, fewer physical complaints, and improved health-related quality of life (Larson, 2006). Art is also beneficial for reducing stress in health care providers. As medical care becomes increasingly technological, the human factor has been set aside, and art can bring it back for both the patients and those who care for them. Having an art space for staff, or allowing staff and visitors to participate in art activities with clients, can foster a human connection.

Risk Management

To provide a successful fine arts program, the TRS may wish to have a range of materials and resources of good quality to meet varying abilities. The TRS's role is to stimulate creativity and free expression, yet some technical expertise in art is helpful (Russell & Jamieson, 2008). Risk management concerns include the use of art supplies as weapons or the ingestion of art materials; clients may also have allergies to certain art supplies. Other aspects of risk management include having adequate ventilation, having clients wear smocks to protect clothing, and availability of a sink for cleaning up. An ample supply of paper towels and rags is essential. Adequate storage is needed to maintain and preserve materials.

Art With Children

The TRS can be very creative in developing art projects for children that draw on their spontaneity, creativity, and willingness to engage in art. For children, art can promote emotional and physical development, provide a sensory experience, be a means of self-expression, and become a leisure interest (Baglin, Lewis & Williams, 2004). Sensory art materials such as marshmallows, sponges, cotton balls, or fabrics dipped in paint can be more enjoyable and easier for younger or immature children, who may find pastels or watercolors too challenging or hard to control. As children get older or improve their skills, they may be able to use markers and crayons; make collages from magazine pictures; and work with clay, yarn, or tissue paper. Eventually, good choices may include making mobiles; papier mâché; sand art; and constructing with wood or with wire or pipe cleaners. Finally, clay is highly recommended for teenagers because it allows them to alter their projects as they go along. For children with psychological issues, the TRS should carefully monitor their responses. Some may require a more structured approach, and others are capable of self-direction.

Art for Adults With Mental Health Issues

Art has been used for many years with people with psychiatric illnesses and eating disorders, as well as for those suffering from trauma. Art is a powerful means of expressing feelings, especially when verbalization is difficult. Art can be used to reawaken

creativity or for continuity of lifestyle in clients who have been artistic in the past. Some adult clients may say "I can't draw a straight line" or "I never was any good at art." The TRS can encourage clients to try by showing pictures of nonrepresentational or abstract art and pointing out that a straight line is not essential to creating an art object. The availability of art materials, including paper, sketchbooks, and a range of media, can encourage a solitary person to create, can promote group support for clients who wish to create artwork, and also promote trust and cooperation when people work together on projects. The role of the TRS is never to judge a client's artwork but to facilitate the art process using both verbal and physical prompts as needed (Freeman, 2006).

An example of a TR art intervention with a woman in a mental health hospital, diagnosed with paranoia and rheumatoid arthritis, shows how the TRS was able to help the client improve her fine motor skills, verbalize her choices, build trust, reduce anxiety, increase self-esteem, and even sell her pictures (Freeman, 2006). As the client used increasingly challenging media, progressing from felt pens to watercolors and sponges and then to pastels, her skill and confidence increased. The team observed her progress and perceived her increasing ability to trust them. She received praise from others when her artwork was displayed. Key to this success was the TRS's attitude of respect for the client's autonomy in making her own choices as she created, as well as acceptance that the artwork was complete when the client was finished. The TRS also did not interfere with the integrity of the artwork by altering or adding to it in any way unless invited.

Art With the Elderly

Art can be a successful and meaningful program for the elderly, including those with dementia. Older adults may have the same reaction as younger adults to participation in an art group. Art is very absorbing and gives clients a chance to forget about their pain and other physical problems. It also has reminiscence value as clients remember when they were creative in the past. Art can be a means of reducing isolation as people connect through viewing a work. Former artists may be shocked or upset that they cannot create in the same way they once did. Looking at artworks by famous painters such as Henri Matisse, who used assistants in his later years to help him produce beautiful collages, can help people see that they can still create, but in a different way. Eventually they may teach others what they know. Art can reaffirm one's identity. A one-person art show can provide recognition and

ARTS

> Henri Matisse, 1869-1954, was a French painter who became very famous for using extraordinarily bold colors. Considered one of the giants of modern painting, as his health began to fail later in life Matisse turned to making mixed-media collages. He arranged boldly colored paper cutouts into striking compositions and added text in his own handwriting to produce a book that has been referred to as "the visual counterpart of jazz music."

pride in one's self and one's accomplishments. Other people, including family and staff, may see the client in a new light.

To create is empowering and can increase self-determination. People with Alzheimer's can work as a group using a drip technique to paint large sheets of paper (Stewart, 2006). Another activity for people with Alzheimer's was described by Streitfeld (1993). She set up a large easel and pad, recited a simple haiku, and then asked the clients what she should paint. Sometimes they took the brush themselves. Even if clients do not engage in the creative act, they can benefit from visual arts by looking at artwork, watching art films, or listening to artists talk about or demonstrate their work. It has also been reported that art is a viable intervention for terminally ill clients as a means of expressing and coming to terms with their feelings about dying and death (Mobily & MacNeil, 2002).

Performing Arts

The **performing arts** include music, dance, and drama. In the performing arts, the participant is a performer and is the mode of artistic expression. The performer sings or plays an instrument, dances, or acts out a part or role. The performing artist may also be the creator of the art form, composing a piece of music, choreographing a dance, or writing song lyrics or a play. Music therapists, dance therapists, and drama therapists all are skilled and talented artists in their discipline. They use their art forms to develop insights and bring forth nonverbal and verbal expressions of feelings from clients who have been unable or unwilling to express themselves. In TR, the performing arts are used to communicate emotions and a wide range of themes and are suitable for all ages and levels of ability (Kraus, 1997). Programs can be offered in a class or club format, or

groups can meet regularly over an extended period or only occasionally. There are also many activities ancillary to the actual performing, which for dance and drama can include making costumes, designing sets, arranging the space, and designing a program. The many components reach across a wide range of abilities and interests.

Music

Music programming can include listening, singing, or performing; it can serve as a basis for a discussion group, or serve as accompaniment to an exercise or relaxation program as a means of maximizing the potential outcomes of those activities. It can be utilized on an individual, small-, or large-group basis and may require minimal supplies and equipment. All human beings respond to music in some form. Music can be used to set a mood, express emotion, develop group cohesion, and control behavior (Russell & Jamieson, 2008).

Benefits of Music

Music can contribute to improving motor skills, stimulate cognitive functioning, reduce agitation and stress, and promote reminiscence. People with Alzheimer's disease can remember the words to a song even in the late stage of their disease (Mobily & MacNeil, 2002). Music can reinforce identity as clients listen to, sing, or play music associated with their cultural background or personal history. The skills required for participation in music vary based on the specific behavioral requirements of the activity, which may include listening, singing, or performing.

Participating in music involves the following skills and potential benefits:

- Physical: vocalization, hearing, fine motor skills, range of motion, respiratory functioning
- Cognitive: attention span, following instructions, making choices, memory, learning lyrics and how to play an instrument
- Affective: enjoyment, feeling and expressing emotions, aesthetic appreciation, experiencing success
- Social: cooperation, sharing a group experience, interaction

Even if music isn't the main focus of an activity, it can be a powerful enhancer of another experience. In one study, four nursing home residents with dementia attained outcomes of decreased agitation at mealtime and increased food intake when CDs of relaxing music were played for an hour at dinnertime (Richeson, 2004). Music has been found to enhance the benefits of acupuncture and to increase physical stability. Therapeutic recreation specialists can collaborate with other professionals to introduce music into treatment.

Risk Management

Risk management concerns center around the ability of music to trigger emotions that may be upsetting and require understanding on the part of the TRS. The TRS also needs to monitor the volume level so that the music is loud enough to be heard but not so loud as to be disturbing. This may require repositioning people's seating or adjusting the sound system to ensure the comfort of all participants.

Listening

Listening to music is a great comfort to people. It can connect us to a deeper part of ourselves as it expresses our emotions; gives voice to our thoughts; relieves our pains; relaxes, energizes, and inspires us; and links us with others. Listening can be a solitary pursuit or a shared social experience. For the individual, the TRS can provide music for listening or invite a strolling musician in to give a private performance. For example, cancer patients in the hospital responded to the playing of songs such as "Bridge Over Troubled Water" by Simon and Garfunkel and "The Long and Winding Road" by the Beatles, which led to reflection and comfort during a one-to-one visit (Meyerstein & Ruskin, 2007). The TRS can prepare a CD or download preferred music for a client for individual listening. She can work with the client or the family to choose music that can provide a particular benefit such as comfort, relaxation, or motivation. As with all programming, giving clients the choice of what music to play is essential. If they are not able to communicate their preferences, family or friends can probably give suggestions.

For groups, listening to music can serve as the basis for a discussion on themes represented in the songs, such as relationships, dealing with hardship, hope, or life goals. The TRS can select songs that address an issue the group is having, such as independence. After playing the songs, she might ask if anyone has experienced the fears or struggles that the singer expresses or ask how the group would suggest

resolving the issue the song presents. Other group music activities can involve cognitive stimulation, for example playing "Name That Tune" or trivia, reminiscing, or learning the words to a song. Participants can create playlists of songs and put together a concert for others. Listening to music has been shown to reduce pain, improve sleep, and reduce agitation.

Singing

Singing is one of the oldest of the arts. Singing has physical, cognitive, and social benefits for clients. Physical benefits include exercising the lungs. Clients with aphasia may be able to sing even if they can't talk, thereby enhancing their communication. Attention span, learning, and following directions are cognitive benefits of group singing. The social value of singing in a group or chorus is in sharing the experience with others. In one study, a year of participating in choral groups led to better health, fewer doctor visits, less medication, decreased falls, lessened loneliness, and an improved outlook on life for older adults (Music for your health, 2004).

Sing-alongs have been a staple of TR programming for many years. Using songbooks or familiar favorites, the TRS and the clients can choose songs that represent people's fondest memories or favorite tunes or singers, or songs related to a particular

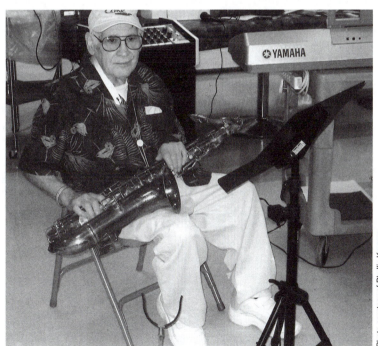

Anthony used to play saxophone professionally, but hadn't played for years until CTRS Arnie Idelson suggested that he return to this leisure interest as a method of pain management.

topic. When choosing music for a singing group, the TRS should be careful not to stereotype, for example in thinking that older people like only "oldies" and are not interested in contemporary music. She should also be familiar with the music of all age groups and cultures. Clients can put on a performance for other clients, staff, and visitors. Being a member of a singing group or chorus can give purpose and meaning to a person's life. Performing is empowering and motivating, can increase self-esteem, and creates excitement. It promotes the outcomes of improved cooperation, teamwork, and social skills. The TRS can also assist those who are unable or unwilling to participate in a singing group to sing along to Web sites that play music while displaying the lyrics.

Karaoke

Karaoke has become a very popular activity for people of all ages. It involves singing into a microphone while music is playing and lyrics are displayed on a screen, which provides both auditory and visual prompts. Newer versions of karaoke also display on-screen images to accompany the songs. Karaoke started in Japan as a way for people to relax after work. In addition to relaxation, karaoke has been found to have physical, social, cognitive, and psychological benefits for people with disabilities. In nursing homes, karaoke can help people with language deficits due to stroke or dementia improve their articulation. Karaoke has been used with people with high-level quadriplegia who have compromised respiratory functioning, including respiratory strength and endurance, breath control, and lung capacity. It also lets them take a more active role in their recreation (Batavia & Batavia, 2003), decreasing their social isolation as they participate in a fun activity with family and friends. Reading the words to the songs can have educational value for children with developmental disabilities. For patients with schizophrenia, karaoke can be more effective than simply singing for improving social interaction (Leung et al., 1998). Karaoke allows people to "let their hair down" in a relatively intimate setting, which can improve their mood and provide a catharsis or emotional release. This may be beneficial for those in treatment for substance abuse. Not only can people benefit from the singing, but they can be recorded and have their images projected on-screen. This can have the added value of reinforcing identity and promoting a positive self-image as people see and hear their own performance. It is also a source of laughter and fun. One group who may not respond well to karaoke is

psychiatric patients who suffer from anxiety (Leung et al., 1998) or paranoia.

Playing Music

Most TR settings have a piano, guitar, or rhythm band instruments that can accommodate varying levels of knowledge and skill. Even clients who do not know how to play an instrument can create music. If a client does know how to play an instrument, it can be beneficial to apply the continuity of lifestyle and strengths-based approaches in a TR program. The client may wish to practice and play for his own satisfaction, perform for others, or accompany a sing-along or choral performance.

An inexpensive, easy-to-use music program is a hand bell choir. A major advantage is that hand bells require no musical ability but can help a person learn music skills and have the experience of creating music with a group. Hand bells are rung in a sequence in order to play a song. A hand bell choir fosters cooperation, teamwork, and socialization. Knowledge of music, confidence, and success are easily achievable with hand bells. Hand bells appeal to all ages, and are very beneficial for a person who may be visually or hearing impaired (or both).

An increasingly popular program is the drumming circle. Drumming circles bring together a group of people to play handheld drums and other percussion instruments. These programs have been used with people who have Alzheimer's disease, autism, substance abuse, emotional problems, and trauma and those who are in prison or are homeless. Drumming circles have been shown to boost the immune system, produce relaxation, have a calming effect, and foster connections with others (Winkelman, 2003).

Another way to create and play music is with a movement-to-music computer system. Using this type of system, six children ages 2 1/2 to 7 years with spina bifida, cerebral palsy, and spinal muscular atrophy, who had been limited to passive forms of play, were able to develop skills, have fun, and "forget about therapy" (Tam et al., 2007). These approaches to playing music foster inclusion as people with disabilities are able to engage with others as equals in age-appropriate activities.

Dance

Dance is a form of personal expression through movement, usually in rhythm to sound or music. It "is the most fundamental of the arts, involving direct expression through the body" (Barksdale, 2003, p. 95). Dance is used to express emotion and release tension, as well as improve physical fitness, balance, and coordination. It is also used as a means of interaction with others, creative and cultural expression, and aesthetic appreciation. Dance differs from movement in that movement is conscious or unconscious nonverbal communication whereas dance is a constructed, artistic movement. Both are a response to an internal or external stimulus (Edginton et al., 2004). We may begin to move unconsciously when we hear music or in response to a noise or the sound of someone's voice. To become dance, movement must be a conscious reaction that is intended as an artistic creation. The many types of dance include ballet, jazz, modern, and free form; ethnic, folk, and square dancing; tap, social, ballroom, line, disco, and hip-hop; and wheelchair dancing. Some people shy away from dance because they think they don't have the coordination, grace, or talent to be "a dancer." The many types of dance, however, make it available to just about anyone.

Benefits of Dance

Dance requires the following skills and produces these benefits:

- Physical: gross motor skills, range of motion, balance, coordination, endurance, posture, body movements such as stretching or bending
- Cognitive: following a sequence of movements, knowing the steps in a dance, concentration, memory
- Affective: respecting personal space and boundaries, creativity, aesthetic appreciation, emotional response, joy
- Social: partnering skills, group cooperation, comfort with physical proximity, appropriate comments to others, social etiquette

Risk Management

Risk management for dance programs requires careful attention to safety, and will vary based on the degree of effort and complexity. Clients should be observed for fatigue, pain, breathing difficulty due to exertion, and injury or stress to their legs and feet in particular. Proper attire is important. Clothing should be comfortable, allowing for ease of movement, and footwear should be suitable for the type of dancing. Drinking water and towels should be available, as well as a place to sit down and rest. A successful TR dance program requires adequate space for people to move comfortably, a well-ventilated area, a decent sound system, and appropriate flooring. The TRS should also be mindful of the importance of teaching the clients about

appropriate touching during dance activities. It may be necessary to explain that touching another person in the context of dancing is a component of the activity and not an indication of an emotional connection between the dancers.

Dance Activities for Different Age Groups

Children and youth can develop self-confidence, a healthy body image, and a valued social skill by learning ballet, jazz, modern, and contemporary steps and dances. Dance activities include creative dance, especially for children, who can make up or act out a story, or for teenagers, who can use dance to act out situations they encounter. Dances for children and movement games help them learn directional concepts (Shank & Coyle, 2002). Teens with developmental disabilities can learn social behaviors through an inclusive dance program in which they partner with nondisabled peers (Frye & Peters, 1972). They can emulate the grooming, dress, and manners of their partners, which facilitates social acceptance.

Children and teens with physical disabilities can experience dance as "their own form of freedom of movement" (Goodwin, Krohn & Kuhnle, 2004, p. 231). Those with extreme limitations can "dance" with their hands or have a partner move his wheelchair. In a multiple case study of five children ages 6 to 14 with spina bifida, the children participated in a wheelchair dance program consisting of a warm-up to music that emphasized floor movement in the wheelchair, flexibility, technical exercises for posture and upper body strength, and choreographed dance movements. The children reported feeling a sense of belonging and pride in their accomplishments. They came to perceive their wheelchairs as more than a means of transportation; the chairs had become part of their dance. They also developed a stronger sense of identity (Goodwin et al., 2004).

For adults in an inpatient facility, ballroom, line, and contemporary dancing on a Friday or Saturday evening can help them develop and maintain appropriate social skills and can provide a healthy means of satisfying their needs for physical and emotional intimacy. Dance involves both body and mind, so it helps people experience a sense of wholeness and increase their self-understanding. Dance forms such as jazz and ballet have clear structure and technique and can help people increase their concentration (Ravelin, Kylma & Korhonen, 2006).

Another group who can benefit from dance is those with Parkinson's disease. Parkinson's is a movement disorder that can cause isolation and depression. To help themselves move, individuals with Parkinson's may put their hand on a wall or on another person to help them turn their body, or listen to music in their head to help them get up from seated positions. These techniques also are used in dance. Participating in a real dance class gave adults with Parkinson's disease confidence in their balance and stability and encouraged their movement. They especially found joy in the sense of community, with one participant saying, "The pleasure of the experience is that it's not a therapy session" (Sulcas, 2007, p. B9). While neurologists are cautious about whether the effects of dance on Parkinson's are long-term, they feel that the short-term benefits are very worthwhile. In another study of people with Parkinson's disease, the group that received 20 tango classes improved more in their balance than the group that participated in 20 exercise classes (Nagourney, 2008). The tango classes were more vigorous than the exercise class. Learning the tango involved focusing on stretching, balance, footwork, and timing, whereas in the exercise class the group members sat in chairs or used chairs for support. These results also show that we should not underestimate our clients' capabilities or desires for a more complex activity.

Older adults and nursing home residents find dance a source of fond memories, physical activity, and exercise. It stimulates communication, requires concentration, and has meaning for people with dementia and their spouses and other family members. People with dementia retain their dance abilities (Palo-Bengtsson, Winblad & Ekman, 1998), and the TRS should capitalize on this strength in programming. "Senior proms" for nursing home residents are also popular. People enjoy watching dancing even if they don't participate and may join in by clapping, nodding, or moving in their seats. Dance is an area for collaboration between the TRS and the physical therapists to design dance programs that improve physical functions.

Dramatics

Dramatics activities can be classified as creative (or informal) or as formal. Formal dramatics activities involve a director, a written script, staging, and costuming, resulting in a performance to an audience for their entertainment and reactions. Formal dramatics incorporates not only actors, but also writers, directors, producers, costumers, set designers, and a construction crew, as well as front-of-house staff handling tickets and seating. If a TR program puts on a play or dramatic production, it can be an engrossing and creative activity

that draws on a broad range of client skills and abilities. A less structured and more easily achievable program is creative dramatics, which can take many forms including make-believe, role playing, puppetry, improvisational theater workshops, and even a game of charades.

Benefits of Dramatics

Drama is very satisfying because it gives people the opportunity to try out new personalities and behaviors in the safety of a role or part. It encourages people to use their imagination and creativity. Through dramatics, a person may gain new insight into a situation, develop new social behaviors through role playing, and learn about other lifestyles. Among the advantages of drama programs are that they can range from the simple to the complex, be relatively quiet or very lively, and can take place in many types of locations.

Dramatics requires the following skills and provides these benefits:

- Physical: ability to express oneself through either physical movement or the senses
- Cognitive: comprehension, following directions, memory, attention span, learning ability
- Affective or emotional: expression of feelings, imagination, creativity
- Social: group cooperation, interaction, giving and receiving feedback

Risk Management

Risk management issues of safety center around using a stage, building sets, and making costumes. The TRS should carefully monitor the environment and supplies to minimize injuries. Emotional risk may be present as clients respond emotionally to a dramatic activity, either as actors or as observers. Clients who cannot separate fantasy from reality should not participate in dramatics.

Drama for Different Groups

Children who are facing surgery or other medical procedures can act out their fears using puppets, dolls, play medical equipment, and other props. Known as **medical play**, this activity helps them cope with their emotions and learn about what will be happening to them. They may enact scenarios that involve other people, such as their families and medical staff. By using a puppet or doll, the child can more safely convey and express his fears and concerns than if he is asked direct questions about his feelings. This helps the child gain some control over a frightening and confusing situation (Dickason & London, 2001). The TRS can learn what the child understands about his hospitalization and care. Puppets can be used to make up a story, and eventually the child may make his own book, which can give him a sense of accomplishment (Carter et al., 2003). Puppets can be very simple, like homemade finger or hand puppets, or large and lifelike. Human beings of all ages respond to puppets because they are nonthreatening and their interactions are controlled by their handler. People with dementia can use puppets to replay stories from their own lives (Streitfeld, 1993), which stimulates their memories.

An unusual application of dramatics was a theater workshop for young adults with autism, ages 16 to 39 (Kelley, 2007). Using a strengths-based approach, the workshop leader determined that the participants all had an interest in theater. The group members, who due to their autism often remained socially isolated or noncommunicative, were able to work together toward a common goal, share their fears and embarrassing situations, and create their own works through writing, movement, and storytelling. Drama groups for people with AIDS that range from producing plays about living with HIV disease to role playing are recommended for the feelings of empowerment they generate (Grossman & Caroleo, 2001).

Arts That Use Technology

Arts that use technological apparatus to create artwork, known as "**new arts**", include photography, computer-generated art, and film, video, or DVD making (Edginton et al., 2004). The advantage of incorporating technology into TR programs is it enables clients to be creative in an up-to-date format. Digital photography, **digital storytelling**, computer art, and making films (or videos, CDs, or DVDs) give immediate feedback and allow for modifying and changing one's creation with little cost in time and effort. Participants can depict their emotions through manipulating images, colors, design, and graphics. Using technology may require learning new skills that are adaptable to many situations. Putting together a photography exhibit, showing digital stories, or burning a CD can bring recognition, increase self-esteem, encourage social interaction, and be a meaningful form of personal self-expression for all types of clients.

Benefits of Arts That Use Technology

Arts that use technology require the following skills and can produce the following benefits:

- Physical: fine motor skills; sensory perception either visual or auditory, with or without adaptive devices; degree of range of motion in hands and arms
- Cognitive: comprehension of the technical requirements of the equipment, understanding directions, concentration
- Affective or emotional: expression of feelings, coping with frustration, feelings of accomplishment
- Social: giving and receiving feedback, cooperating on group projects

Risk Management

While there is little danger of physical risk with technology, the TRS should be sure to obtain releases to use images of clients in order to protect their privacy. Theft of equipment may also be a concern, and the TRS should have secure facilities for storage.

Photo courtesy of Ragen E. Sanner.

Drama can be a satisfying creative outlet for clients of any age.

Digital Storytelling

With the growth of the Internet, Web2, and the availability of digital technology, individuals and groups are harnessing the power of storytelling to find common ground and build community in exciting new ways.

Digital storytelling (DS) is the process of combining the spoken word, images, sound, and motion to tell a story in a short (2-4 minute) video. A DS workshop typically begins with each participant writing a short, reflective script, which is then shared in a group "story circle." Using presentation or video editing software, the recorded voiceover is then layered with production elements to construct a personal narrative. The interplay of words, images, and music enables the individual or group to express meaning with more emotional directness, subtlety, and complexity than words alone can.

Digital storytelling groups are led by a facilitator whose role, beyond teaching the technical skills, is to nurture the delicate and sensitive process as each storyteller creates a story to make sense of the events and people in his or her life. When working together in a supportive group setting, participants experience the benefits of enhanced communication skills (both technical and interpersonal), validation, connectivity, and even catharsis.

Therapeutic recreation specialists who wish to use DS will find it a powerful technique for people of all ages and abilities. Storytelling projects have been tailored to meet the needs and goals of many different individuals and groups:

- Young people with disabilities raising public awareness about the challenges they face
- Older people coming to terms with life-transforming changes
- People with chronic illness sharing their experience to empower others
- Teens exploring how their identities are shaped by others' perceptions of them
- College students helping senior housing residents give artistic form to their memories
- Political refugees advocating for their rights
- Young immigrants feeling caught between two cultures
- Students taking a public stand on breaches of environmental justice in their neighborhoods

For more information, resources, and training opportunities and to view digital stories, visit these Web sites:
www.creativenarrations.net
www.storiesforchange.net
www.storycenter.org
www.umbc.edu/blogs/digitalstories/

Reprinted, by permission, from H. Pope, *Digital Media Arts trainer and consultant to schools, professional organizations and nonprofits* (Boston, MA).

When using technology to explore sensitive issues and emotional situations, clients may react with a range of feelings that the TRS needs to handle with sensitivity, understanding, and respect.

Photography

Most people enjoy using a camera and taking it along on outings. For individuals with severe multiple disabilities, equipment such as cameras that can be operated by pressing a button, or with an adaptive switch, provide immediate feedback and expand their interactions with their environment (Schlein, Fahnestock & Miller, 2001). Photography may be a less intimidating way to produce artwork than the traditional fine arts. Clients in treatment for substance abuse who took photos of themselves and described them to others used photography as an effective form of communication and overcame the secrecy that tends to surround the issue of substance abuse (Glover-Graf & Miller, 2006). Having a display of the photographs also can increase clients' self-esteem. In another example of the benefits of photography, four adults with schizophrenia were able to use cameras to take pictures that conveyed "hope." The fun of taking pictures helped them articulate this concept (Miller & Happell, 2006). Photography has also facilitated communication in nursing home residents with dementia (Mitchell, 2006).

Film-making activities are particularly appealing to adolescents. In a shelter for adolescents who were homeless, filming their life stories helped them develop writing, videotaping, communication, and time management skills, as well as explore their talents and interests (Fazio, 2008). Children in hospitals also benefit from making videos of stories they create or of their own experiences dealing with illness (Austin, 2009).

———————

Arts-related activities offer myriad opportunities for TR programming, ranging from projects that can be completed in one session to those requiring long periods of time to produce, and from projects that can be successful with a minimum of skill to those utilizing a great deal of talent. The TRS will find that arts activities are an indispensable component of the TR toolkit, as they can provide both short-term outcomes and a lifetime of enjoyment that can foster a sense of community (Carpenter, 2006).

Cognitively Oriented Programs

Cognitively oriented programs are those that involve thinking and intellectual skills, including expressing ideas and opinions through oral, written, or graphic communication. Discussions, writing, educational activities, and many games rely on a person's ability to think, reason, comprehend, and mentally organize and share information. Cognitively oriented activities often require the participant to acquire and apply information, as in discussing or writing about a topic, learning new material, and playing a game that requires following directions, strategy, and concentration.

■ Discussion Groups

Discussion groups are small gatherings of people with a similar need or interest who come together for the purpose of sharing ideas, information, opinions, and feedback on various subjects. Discussion groups are popular TR programs because they provide the support and social interaction of a group and also involve a topic or focus that is of interest and relevance to participants. Discussion groups can be conducted on any issue, such as current events, books, history, or the arts, or with any focus, such as women's issues, health concerns, coping with stigma or recovery, caregiving, or parenting. What is unique about a discussion group as a TR activity is that the medium or vehicle is not tangible as in arts and crafts, cooking, or sports; rather it is the social interaction that is the recreation experience. As with other social occasions, refreshments may be served to contribute to a friendly atmosphere, conducive to sharing.

Discussion groups can be either therapeutic, with emphasis on gaining insights and solving problems; or educational, with the intent to learn new information and skills or strategies; or recreational, with fun and socializing as a primary goal. They can be either highly or loosely structured, with the TRS as leader or with peer leadership. The size of the group can be as small as three clients or as many as a dozen. Beyond a dozen, it is doubtful that all participants will have a chance to contribute. To conduct a discussion group, the TRS needs to be knowledgeable about the topics under discussion and skilled at facilitating group interaction. The TRS's role is to encourage input from all participants, ensure that all have a chance to speak and that no one person

dominates the discussion, and keep the conversation going. Group members should be seated in a circle or semicircle so they can see or hear each other clearly. Those who are nonverbal may wish to listen; those with vision or hearing impairments can participate using their typical accommodations. The group can meet indoors or outdoors.

Benefits of Discussion Groups

These are skills required for participation in a group discussion and the benefits to participants:

- Physical: ability to communicate either verbally, via American Sign Language, or in written form; ability to tolerate physically being part of a group, from either a seated, a standing, or a reclining position
- Cognitive: understanding the topic under discussion, following the discussion, formulating comments, attention span, concentration, memory, and judgment
- Affective or emotional: controlling and expressing emotions appropriately, such as anger, frustration, annoyance; enjoyment; feelings of competence; increased self-esteem
- Social: communication skills, teamwork, enhanced feelings of having commonalities with others, cooperation, conflict resolution, taking turns, giving and receiving feedback

Many TR departments offer current events groups, reminiscence, discussions on general topics, support groups, or group meetings about living in a facility, depending on the nature of the setting and the wishes of the clients.

Risk Management

There are few physical risks inherent in discussion groups. The TRS may wish to set rules for the group that include taking turns, not interrupting, not being rude, treating each other with respect, not shouting, and any others that seem appropriate and contribute to a positive group atmosphere. Depending on the nature of the discussion, some members may react strongly with sadness or anger or have a disturbing emotional reaction, or an argument may break out. The TRS needs to know her participants, be aware of how comfortable they are discussing

Did You Know That?

A TRS in a long-term care facility in New Jersey was looking for a new approach for the reminiscence program that would stimulate conversation. He came up with a game called "Did You Know That?" He researched a number of facts about the state of New Jersey and incorporated these facts within a question format. The participants in the TR program were a diverse group with varying levels of cognitive ability. The TRS asked the first question: "Did you know that New Jersey is called the Garden State?" Many of the residents responded, "Yes, I know that." The TRS then went on to the next question: "Did you know that Thomas Edison was born in New Jersey?" Once again the residents responded "Yes!" After each response the TRS would say, as if in amazement, "I didn't know that!" Finally, after 10 questions and no real discussion, one resident said in a loud voice, "What exactly do you know?"

What was wrong with this program?

Even with the structure created by the TRS, how could he have encouraged conversation among the residents?

may make the selections themselves. For those in an inpatient or residential facility, current events provide a means for conversation with families and visitors, thereby reducing the perception of the client in the "sick role." Participating in current events programs can reinforce feelings of still being a part of the larger world. In long-term residential or day care settings, current events can be part of a daily morning program that orients residents to reality, stimulates memory, encourages socialization, and follows a morning stretch or coffee hour. In this setting, recreating a normal morning routine has many benefits. For clients in recovery, or for those reintegrating into community life, current events discussions enhance the sense of being a part of the everyday world. For children and young people, current events groups are educational and can stimulate their interest in various topics.

A current events group requires few supplies, just a daily newspaper. Large-print editions are available; the *New York Times Weekly*, for example, reprints articles from the daily paper, with color pictures, in 16-point type, and is available by subscription all over the world. The TRS can also have the group watch a morning TV news show or view clips projected from a computer to stimulate discussion. It is imperative that the TRS has read the news! The TRS should be familiar with current events so she can facilitate discussion, encourage expression of views, and contribute to the participants' understanding. She should vary her leadership style according to the needs of the group. With a high-functioning group, participants themselves may take on the role of leading the discussion. Lower-functioning clients will require more direct questioning and prompting by the TRS.

Apart from economic and political news, many social and cultural events attract a lot of interest and can be the focus of programs. The Olympics, the Academy Awards, and the Super Bowl are examples. These are also events that generate a great deal of media attention for weeks at a time, thereby lending themselves to themed programming (see chapter 9). Participants may also want to read and comment on comic strips or advice columns. Additionally, the TRS can encourage clients to relate topics to news events they may remember or to events in their own lives. She can bring in pictures or other items, such as maps, that have to do with the news of the day.

A skilled TRS will know how to engage participants in a meaningful discussion rather than just read articles aloud from the paper. There may be clients who prefer to read or watch the news on

various issues, and be able to provide assistance if someone is upset. Certain topics can be considered controversial, such as politics, religion, and sex. A lively discussion is of course desirable, but opposing views may emerge and need to be handled tactfully. Still, some people may be offended by a topic and wish to change the subject or leave. These situations can be addressed by the TRS.

Current Events

Current events groups are discussions focused on the latest news and events, which can be as local as the clients' community or as broad as the global environment. Staying up-to-date with current events keeps participants in touch with what is happening in the world and for many is a continuation of a lifelong practice (Hart, Primm & Cranisky, 2003). Depending on the setting and the needs of the clients, the TRS can initially select topics and issues that clients will find appealing, and eventually they their own and not enter into a discussion. Their wishes deserve respect. The mere fact that someone reads or watches the news does not mean he wants to talk about it!

Reminiscence

Reminiscing is the structured verbal interaction process or act of recalling long-term memories, generally with a focus more on positive memories than negative ones. Reminiscing enables people to reflect over their lives, view events and relationships from a new perspective, and make connections with other group members and younger generations. **Reminiscence** groups are offered in almost all programs serving older adults, especially in nursing homes, because long-term memories can remain intact even when short-term memory is lost, making this type of program a valuable choice for residents who are confused. Reminiscence is life affirming as people acknowledge their past accomplishments and meaningful experiences (Sylvester et al., 2001). In a reminiscence group, the TRS can select a topic or theme that has relevance to everyone and can be discussed within a relatively informal structure. Topics can include childhood, family, work, recreation, marriage, historical events, holidays, or vacations. The TRS's role is to facilitate pleasant recollections and socialization. Props and visual aids, such as pictures, music and songs, old newspapers, household items and other everyday objects can be used that stimulate the memory and bring excitement to the discussion. For example, a group of older men might enjoy seeing and handling tools used in home repairs, such as hammers, screwdrivers, pliers, and wrenches.

When selecting a topic for reminiscence groups, be sure that it is relevant to the participants' ages and the events and experiences of their younger days. These are some possible topics:

- Life cycle events: births, bar mitzvahs, quinceañeras, sweet sixteens, senior proms, graduations, weddings
- Childhood memories
- School days
- Family vacations
- Holidays and celebrations
- Foods
- Jobs
- Favorite recreation activities
- Historical events

- Popular culture of a time period: music, movies, cars, clothing, celebrities, fads
- Favorite places
- Major historical events of a time period

Reminiscence can also be done as a one-to-one program for those who either are too frail or are unwilling to join a group. In an in-home reminiscence program with an elderly woman who had dementia and her husband, the TRS used pictures of famous events that had occurred 50 years earlier, in combination with family photo albums and souvenirs of the couple's travels during that time (Chow, 2002). The woman was able to recall information about people in the photos and concentrate for a 10- to 15-minute period, whereas previously her attention had drifted very quickly. She and her husband were able to converse about a trip they had taken. The reminiscence stimulated her memory and enhanced her relationship with her husband as they were once again able to share treasured experiences.

However, reminiscence is not just for nursing home residents and people with dementia. Other adult populations also can benefit from this type of program. Community-based older adults attending senior centers (Atkinson et al., 1999), older adults fighting alcohol and drug problems (Dunlop, 1990), aging people with developmental disabilities (Van Puyenbroeck & Maes, 2006), adults with chronic mental illness (Quam & Abramson, 1991), and those who are terminally ill (Jonsdottir et al., 2001) have all participated in reminiscence programs.

To maximize the success of a reminiscence group, the TRS can utilize three types of leadership roles (Van Puyenbroeck & Maes, 2006).

- Facilitator: A creative leader who stimulates creativity in the group. The facilitator's job is to make it easier for people to join in and to share memories. She elaborates on what is said by asking questions to elicit additional memories and to obtain more details. Her focus is on content.
- Coach: A personal assistant who is supportive of each group member. She helps members find the right word or name and may need to slow the pace of the discussion to give an individual time to recall. Her focus is on individual attention.
- Moderator: A leader who guides the conversation, pointing out similarities and differences among people's stories. She may choose to use rounds, having each person speak in turn. Her focus is on the group process.

Suggested Questions for Guided Reminiscence

1. Tell me what you did for work when you were well and what you liked most about your job.
2. When you were not working, what did you enjoy doing with your spare time?
3. Tell me about a past accomplishment you are particularly proud of.
4. What would you describe as *the happiest day of your life* and why?
5. Tell me about a happy memory of your childhood.
6. Tell me about a particular holiday that holds special meaning for you. How did you celebrate it?
7. Can you tell me about a *first* (e.g., first date, kiss, job)?
8. Tell me about a time when you helped someone in need. How were you useful to that person?
9. Tell me about a home or place you once lived or visited, or your favorite one and why?
10. Tell me about someone you once thought of as a *best friend* and some of the good times you shared.

Based on Wholihan 2004.

COGNITIVE

Although older adults with intellectual disabilities may be viewed as having inadequate verbal skills or limited life experience due to spending many years in institutional settings, they can also benefit from reminiscence. Careful and thorough planning can result in a successful reminiscence group and demonstrates respect for this population as a group with life experiences worthy of being shared. Successful themes for this group include games and toys, school, food, religious worship, and holidays. Mixing past and present events, providing more structure, and using visual triggers can enable the group's communication. However, one study showed that sharing photo albums was boring to everyone except the individual the album belonged to (Van Puyenbroeck & Maes, 2006).

An interesting issue related to the delivery of reminiscence programs is whether participants from non-Western backgrounds will respond well to a program centered on the Western cultural value of recognizing individual achievements. Older adults of Asian or Latin descent might feel that a focus on individual success conflicts with their traditional cultural values of group accomplishment and cohesion and could feel uncomfortable reminiscing. Yet a study of Mexican Americans, European Americans, and Chinese Americans at nine senior centers showed that all were good candidates for reminiscing (Atkinson et al., 1999) and were equally willing to share past experiences and resolve problems. Nor did they have a preference for the ethnicity of the group leader.

Life review is a more structured approach in which participants review their entire life span with the goals of resolving issues, conflicts, regrets, and disappointments (Austin, 2004); reducing depression; and decreasing social isolation. In life review, drawing a time line, chart, or map can help depict events in the client's life. Through reviewing the events of their past, it is hoped that people can resolve negative life experiences and make sense out of their lives. Life review also can be conducted with the client's family. The role of the TRS in life review is oriented toward helping the client develop insight in order to resolve conflicts and to see positive aspects of their lives. Negative outcomes are very rare with life review, but this type of program should not be conducted with those who are psychotic, paranoid, or grieving the loss of a loved one (Jonsdottir et al., 2001). Life review can be appropriate for people of any age who are terminally ill and wish to engage in **"legacy building,"** which involves creating a story of one's life on tape, on DVD, or digitally to share with loved ones (Shank & Coyle, 2002). This provides a meaningful experience for both the client and those who receive the legacy. Clients can also create stories, poems, songs, and artwork as part of the life review process.

As the TRS conducts reminiscence programming, regardless of population, she has the responsibility to be sure that all members are comfortable with the process, do not suffer any undue emotional stress, and have an equal chance to contribute and participate. Participants in reminiscence can take a great deal of pleasure from sharing memories, reinforcing their own identity, receiving recognition for their accomplishments, creating bonds with others, and feeling competent as they are able to recall the past (Austin, 2004). Sharing memories is fun, not just for the individual who is speaking but also for the listeners who enjoy the story, increasing their self-esteem and life satisfaction and possibly reducing the risk of depression.

General Topic Discussions and Support Groups

General topic discussions and **support groups** are appropriate for all ages and settings as a means for clients to get together and talk. Social contact in a discussion group can contribute to feelings of health and well-being. It is an enjoyable experience that can lead to creating a network of social connections, friendship, and support. For those who are readily communicative and sociable, these groups offer a setting for socializing and conversing that reinforces their strengths. Clients can benefit from sharing their knowledge and opinions, receiving emotional support, and acquiring new information and ideas. The TRS can vary the name of the program, the format, and the topic to make the group relevant to the clients' particular needs and interests. Many discussions operate as an open forum, in which the TRS provides an opening statement and the participants respond (Shank & Coyle, 2002). Most institutional settings offer regularly scheduled discussion groups. Regardless of setting, these are some of the forms discussion groups can take:

● A coffee or tea and conversation, or an open forum, that can cover a wide range of topics, perhaps based on a suggestion from someone in the group

● A women's or men's group that may deal with issues best discussed in a same-sex environment

● A group designed for support on topics such as living with a disability, growing old gracefully, coping with recovery, dealing with stigma, or handling family issues

● A group dealing with adolescents' concerns of responsibility, independence, relationships, and future plans

For clients who live in the community, a discussion group that meets regularly as part of TR in a day program, at a community center, or in someone's home can be a substantial component of their socialization and help to overcome feelings of isolation and stigma. Such groups provide a formal opportunity for those who are depressed, withdrawn, shy, or socially isolated, or those who feel stigmatized by their illness or disability, to overcome their barriers to social interaction. It can be a relief to be in the company of others who are similar to you and understand your life experience. Clients can enhance their self-esteem as they share insights or lessons from their own experience with the purpose of helping another or share knowledge of a particular subject.

The roles of the TRS leading a general topics discussion group are similar to those described for reminiscence. The TRS moderates the discussion to keep it flowing, contributes to the content with helpful information, and helps members express themselves. Coleading discussion groups can be enlightening to the professional from another discipline such as social work, nursing, or mental health. She may hear things from the clients that are not revealed in the normal course of her interactions with them. Her perspective may be welcomed by the participants in the context of a group discussion. As with all TR programs, the possibilities are limited only by the TRS's creativity and flexibility as she anticipates and responds to the needs of the clients.

One example of a men's discussion group focusing on health and lifestyle topics illustrated that young men were willing to discuss health-related issues (Davies et al., 2000). A cross section of male college students representative of the college student population participated in groups of three to nine members, conducted by a male leader. Contrary to what might have been expected, the men from all groups reported feeling comfortable with the small groups, found them enjoyable and therapeutic, and gained a sense of peer support. Their major health concerns were alcohol and drug use, physical fitness, anger management, and relationships. Their preferred coping strategy was physical activity. This report demonstrates the success of a men's discussion group centered on issues and concerns that can be addressed by a TRS. These results could be used to encourage the implementation of similar groups.

Support groups centered on living with a common issue or concern related to health condition, disability, or challenges in daily life are offered to clients and their families for emotional support and socialization. The primary focus of support groups is to increase coping ability in the face of stress by providing advice and feedback, sharing information, and building interpersonal skills (Perese & Wolf, 2005). While support groups can be conducted by professionals from any discipline, TR may be a logical sponsor because the nature of the group is to provide a positive atmosphere of hope and comfort, as well as to encourage people to share struggles. Participants can discuss strategies and resources for handling situations, including participation in recreation. One of three "leisure coping strategies" has been identified as leisure companionship, which is "shared involvement in leisure activities to buffer effects of stress" (Hutchinson et al., 2003, p. 148). The support group can function as a form of leisure companionship, as well as preparation to engage in recreation that has the effects of reducing stress. Participation in the support group can motivate participants to sustain coping efforts and to attempt to be more socially active in their everyday lives (Hutchinson et al., 2003). The support group can help members learn friendship-building behaviors of sharing information about oneself and having feeling and empathy for others (Perese & Wolf, 2005). The TRS can model the behaviors and skills associated with making friends.

The TRS can also offer support groups to family members, such as caregivers, spouses of stroke patients, parents of children with a disability, adults with a parent in a nursing home, or children with a sibling or parent in the hospital. In one study of people with traumatic brain injuries (TBI) and their families, "feeling extremely isolated, alone, confused and cast adrift" (Leith, Phillips & Sample, 2004) were common reactions to the occurrence of the TBI. A local support group helped decrease social isolation and led to making friends. In expressing his strong feelings about the value of the support group, one participant with TBI said "We're home" (p. 1204). As another example of how the value of the support group can extend beyond the discussion itself, a support group for emotionally disturbed teenagers participated in an intergenera-

tional group with low-income community-dwelling older adults for discussions and recreation activities (Jones, Herrick & York, 2004).

Intellectual and Literary Activities

Intellectual and literary activities encompass the acquisition and personal expression of ideas and opinions through reading, writing, and discussion. These activities have many variations, are appropriate for all ages and populations, and can be done alone or in small groups. They include reading literature, **creative** or **expressive writing**, journaling, putting out a newsletter, book clubs, adult education, bibliotherapy, and cinematherapy (also called videotherapy).

Benefits of Intellectual and Literary Activities

Intellectual and literary activities require the following skills and produce the following benefits:

- Physical: fine motor dexterity for writing, vision for reading, hearing to listen to others
- Cognitive: attention span, concentration, comprehension, memory, language skills
- Affective: expression of emotions, experiencing joy, feelings of accomplishment
- Social: sharing with others, cooperation, giving and receiving feedback, interaction

Support groups offer a safe environment for discussing issues and sharing common concerns.

Intellectual and literary activities provide a wealth of programming opportunities along the continuum from therapy or clinical intervention to education to recreation participation to independent leisure. Technology has expanded access to reading materials with devices such as the Kindle electronic reader with hundreds of thousands of books available.

Risk Management

Risk management concerns related to intellectual and literary activities are mostly in the area of emotional reactions. While writing has many positive effects, some clients may experience sadness, anger, and frustration as they relive an experience through their writing. The TRS should always acknowledge the validity of these feelings. Once the clients experience this empathy, they may be able to move past the most painful moments to begin to resolve these issues. The TRS may wish to colead the group with a counselor or psychologist. Confidentiality is also an issue when clients are writing. If they are sharing their writing, either by reading aloud or allowing others to read what they have written, all participants should be informed about the need for confidentiality of what is shared. Respect for privacy and the personal feelings and experiences that are shared is paramount. The TRS must also be sure to explain that there is a difference between real life and the fantasy life depicted in a book or film.

There may be some physical risks. Clients may experience pain in their hands from writing, or eye strain or fatigue. While these risks are minimal, the TRS should carefully observe clients for any signs of physical stress. Adjustments of one's physical position, physical supports, and lighting can alleviate discomfort.

Writing Activities

The benefits of writing are evident across cultures, languages, education levels, and socioeconomic status (Smyth & Helm, 2003), making it an ideal activity for a TR program. Writing as a therapeutic intervention has been found to decrease the number of doctor visits and improve physical health (McArdle & Byrt, 2001) in people with asthma, rheumatoid arthritis, and breast cancer (Smyth & Helm, 2003). While supplies for writing programs are minimal, be sure to have plenty of paper, pens, pencils, and erasers, including items ergonomically designed to reduce stress on the hand. Unusual pens or inexpensive notebooks or journals can be distributed to get clients excited about writing. Lap desks can be used for clients who are in a chair or in a bed and cannot reach another writing surface. Writing activities include creative writing, journaling, and letter writing.

Creative Writing

Creative or expressive writing is "the use of writing to enable people to enjoy and express themselves, develop creativity and empowerment, affirm identity and give voice to views and experiences" (McArdle & Byrt, 2001, p. 517). Writing can take many forms: poems, stories, songs, letters, newsletters, and plays. The use of creative writing as a TR intervention (Gillespie, 2003) has been reported primarily with clients who have behavioral health issues such as substance abuse, stress, depression, anxiety, or trauma. Yet it can be used with all ages, from children to older adults, and is effective in promoting learning, cognitive functioning, resolution of personal issues, self-expression, and social relationships. Creative writing can be done in groups, with the TRS establishing an atmosphere of trust and respect. It is important that clients feel they can share their feelings and writings without being judged (Lahey, 2001).

The TRS can begin the writing activity with a prompt such as reading a poem, showing a picture, or playing a song; clients write their reactions or whatever thoughts the prompt has triggered. The prompt helps clients who have difficulty with verbal expression put their feelings and thoughts into words. In a group, clients typically are asked if they would like to read what they have written. The TRS respects the clients' choice whether or not they wish to share their writings. The TRS can facilitate a discussion with questions (e.g., "How did this piece make you feel?"; "How can you relate your own experience to what James wrote?"; "Do you have any questions for James?"; "What does this piece make you think of?"). She may use a specific format as a prompt, such as an **alphapoem**, a 26-line free verse poem in which each line begins with a letter of the alphabet (Gillespie, 2003). A line can be one word or a phrase. Depending on the needs of the clients and the focus of the group, topics like "my personal qualities," or "things I like to do for fun," or "grief and loss" can be presented. Other popular formats for a poem are haiku and cinquains. A haiku is a three-line poem, usually with images of nature, that expresses a single feeling. The format is 5-7-5 (five syllables in the first and last line and seven syllables in the middle line). A cinquain is a five-line poem in this format:

- Line 1: one word, a noun that is the subject of the poem
- Line 2: two words, adjectives that describe the subject
- Line 3: three words, action verbs that relate to the subject
- Line 4: four words that denote feelings or a sentence that relates to the subject
- Line 5: a one-word synonym of the subject or a summary of the poem

Members may collaborate to write as a group or may combine parts of their own writings to create a work. The group can engage in open-ended or free writing, in which they write whatever they want.

Journaling

Another writing activity is journaling. Journaling usually is done alone. However, a client may wish to share what he has written with the TRS, or the TRS can form groups in which people read to each other from their journals. The TRS may suggest topics for the client to write about; but journal writing is a very personal form of self-expression, and clients should feel they can write freely without rules or regard for use of language. Writing helps us to get in touch with our thinking through seeing our thoughts in writing (Lahey, 2001). One study of older people showed that journal writing had three benefits: coping with day-to-day situations as individuals sorted out their feelings, thereby helping with decision making and memory; experiencing the joy of discovery about oneself and finding oneself more observant and more attentive to details; and nurturing one's own voice and spirit by setting aside a time to reflect (Brady & Sky, 2003). Sharing journals can help clients develop more meaningful relationships with others, combining psychological benefits with desired social outcomes (Gillespie, 2003).

COGNITIVE

Examples of Poems

Alphapoem
Ways I Cope

Arguing
Bullying
Crying
Dancing
Eating
Fighting
Going shopping
Having a bath
Imagining
Joking
Kissing
Looking for answers
Making meaning
Not
Opening doors
Pretending
Quiet time
Reading

Singing
Talking
Undoing old hurts
Visiting friends
Walking
Xenophobic behavior
Yelling
Zoloft

Haiku
Summery morning
Watching the breeze in the trees
Limitless choices

Cinquain
Painting
Emotional relief
Designing, coloring, admiring
I make my world
Identity

Poems by Robin Kunstler

Letter Writing

Letter writing can also promote social relationships. A pen pal program can be set up with clients at another facility. In one nursing home, residents became pen pals with adults in a nearby day program who had developmental disabilities. The TR group can come together to read the letters they have received and write their responses. A pen pal program can be a foundation for other activities as well, including friendship development. A group may write letters to people they wish to contact. A buddy system can be set up to help those with an impairment that affects their ability to write, whether it is visual or fine motor. The physical act of writing can be rehabilitative in itself. Many people consider letter writing a lost art, with the advent of e-mail; but it has much therapeutic value, including the excitement of receiving a letter.

Other Writing Activities

Other TR program ideas include having clients produce a literary magazine to distribute to staff and families, which fosters self-esteem and pride of accomplishment. The TR department can sponsor a poetry reading, which gives clients an opportunity to share their poems and receive recognition for their achievements. They can write a play and perform it. Writing fosters an interest in reading, which can be nourished through a book club. Book clubs have become very popular. The group decides on a book to read and comes together to discuss it. Many books today include discussion guides for use by book clubs. In one case, a 96-year-old woman living in her own home attended a weekly book club at the local senior center (Kunstler, 2004b). Due to a visual impairment, she had difficulty reading fast enough to keep up with the pace of the club. An in-home TRS discussed the books with her so she would be prepared for the weekly meetings. She enjoyed the intellectual stimulation and the continuity of lifestyle that the TR program provided. A related activity is storytelling, "the oral narration of fact or fiction" (Shank & Coyle, 2002, p. 167), either via personal stories or from literature, which is used for conversation, reminiscence, or life review. The TRS or a client can start by telling or reading a complete story, or members of the group can join in to create a story. This can enhance oral communication, creativity and imagination, and cognitive skills, as well as being an enjoyable experience. Having clients read aloud is also therapeutic. The TRS can suggest storytelling to family members as an activity to do during visits (Beland, 2004).

Educational Programs

Many people enjoy attending educational programs—the presentation of material in lectures and other learning formats—covering a wide range of topics including history, travel, the arts, culture, science, and current events. Adult education classes, after-school programs, college or continuing education courses, and lectures are sources of intellectual stimulation and ongoing cognitive development, and may provide an opportunity to interact with others who have similar interests. In a TR program, educational activities can help clients experience the joy of learning for its own sake, reinforce their abilities to learn new things, and encourage them to share what they have learned or know about a particular topic. The TRS can organize a lecture series by contacting a local college or a speakers' bureau. One of the clients can write up a summary for the facility newsletter or magazine. Encouraging intellectual stimulation is of particular benefit to clients with stroke and head injury. Intellectual and literary activities can help clients build skills they may use on a job, if that is part of their plan. Exploritas (formerly known as Elderhostel) is an organization that offers educational vacations or "adventures in lifelong learning" for adults. Each trip provides a full schedule of programs including lectures, tours, outdoor activities, and volunteer opportunities built around several themes. One Day University has developed a single-day format for adults of all ages that includes lectures on contemporary topics given by college professors. The TRS may wish to implement a similar program in her facility.

Bibliotherapy

Bibliotherapy is a therapeutic program based on reading that has been used effectively with a number of different client groups. Essentially bibliotherapy involves guiding a person's reading in order to foster an understanding of oneself, help solve therapeutic issues and provide solutions to personal problems, develop life skills, and enhance self-image (Vare & Norton, 2004). It can be offered in a one-to-one or a group format for those with common concerns (Austin, 2004). Bibliotherapy has been used successfully with children in pediatric settings to cope with illness and with children who have suffered physical or sexual abuse. These programs have also been used with youth at risk from bullying, those dealing with their own homosexuality, those with academic struggles and chronic misbehavior (Schreur, 2006), and those with eating disorders. Adults with alcohol problems, panic

Reading is more than great entertainment and education—it can be a means of guiding growth.

attacks, anxiety, and depression have responded positively to this technique. Having parents read to their children to improve their communication and the child's learning is another form of bibliotherapy.

Most researchers feel that the guided use of selected readings accelerates the learning process because clients realize they are not alone and can begin to better understand their problems. Clients can safely identify with fictional characters when their own situation may be too painful to discuss in the first person. The bibliotherapy process has three steps: identification, catharsis, and insight (Gregory & Vessey, 2004). The TRS can guide clients through this process to first identify with the character in the reading and then express feelings surrounding the issue or the situation, thereby gaining insight and the realization that a challenging situation can change. This process can be combined with dramatization and role playing or puppetry, in which a situation in the reading is acted out, or with writing a letter or creating a picture, in which one responds

to or illustrates a theme in the reading (Nicholson & Pearson, 2003).

The TRS can offer a selection of books for clients to choose from. The TRS will be most effective when she can personally take enjoyment in the reading so as to reinforce the appropriateness of the choice. Clients with memory problems and poor attention span may not respond well to bibliotherapy; however, using children's books that take only 5 or 10 minutes to read has worked well with nursing home residents with dementia (Beland, 2004). The TRS should also choose books that represent the diverse cultural backgrounds of her clients to enhance their identification with the characters and to correspond to their value systems. Clients may feel proud that their culture is depicted in a book or story. Participation in bibliotherapy also improves literacy skills and critical thinking and can foster an interest in reading. Apart from literary works, self-help books also can be used.

Cinematherapy or Videotherapy

A variation on bibliotherapy is **cinematherapy** or **videotherapy,** in which films are selected for clients to view for therapeutic purposes. Film or video may help them talk openly about topics that they are uncomfortable discussing and can be a model of therapist–client interaction (Wedding & Niemiec, 2003). Another version of this technique is **soap opera therapy**, which developed when therapists realized they could take advantage of their patients' interest in soap operas to guide them to develop insight about their own issues and apply their problem-solving skills to their personal situations. The emphasis on relationships in soap operas makes them a resource for exploring emotions that is effective for clients from various cultures (Breen, 2007). Soap opera therapy was successfully used with a 14-year-old boy with autism to help him learn to recognize various emotions and improve social skills (Breen, 2007). Watching the shows fostered an alliance between the therapist and the boy, which is often a challenge in autism. The boy became animated discussing the characters, improved his eye contact and speech, and increased his participation in school. It's important to realize that these approaches not only are useful in clinical settings, but also can be used successfully in community settings to help people deal with everyday problems and challenges (Dole & McMahan, 2005). In school settings, videotherapy has been successful with students who have learning disabilities and behavior problems. For young people who don't like to read,

Comstock

COGNITIVE

COGNITIVE

Questions for Cinematherapy Discussions

1. What was/were the major theme(s) of the movie?
2. What feelings/emotions did the movie evoke in you?
3. What lessons/values/important facts can be taken away from the film?
4. Does the movie relate in some way to you personally or your life? If so, how?

For an annotated list of films for cinematherapy discussions, visit www.recreationtherapy.com/history/film.htm.

movies are a natural medium for facilitating discussion. Visit www.cinematherapy.com for an excellent list of movies by topic. The TRS also can prepare a list of questions or discussion topics, based on the film, that relate to the needs and interests of the group or individual client.

■ Leisure Education

Leisure education is not a recreation activity in the same way as the other activities in the TR toolkit. However, it is included here because providing leisure education is the obligation of the TR profession and part of TR's unique contribution to health and human services. Leisure education is a program that educates people on the meaning, value, and benefits of leisure experiences and also on the recreation options available to each individual. Additionally, it assists in the development of skills needed for healthy and meaningful participation. All of the TR service models either have a specific educational component or imply that education about leisure is a vital part of the TRS's intervention. Leisure education also is included as a specific component of recreation as a related service in special education under the **Individuals with Disabilities Education Act (IDEA)**, which defines leisure education as follows (Bullock & Johnson, 1998):

Instruction to improve school and community involvement and social connectedness through

- the development of positive attitudes toward leisure,
- the development of skills necessary for recreation participation,
- knowledge of recreational resources, and
- recognition of the benefits of recreation involvement.

The TRS can provide leisure education in a recreational format by utilizing group discussions, games, paper-and-pencil activities, role playing, and other experiential approaches. In a leisure education program, the TRS could lead clients in

- a group discussion of the meaning and benefits of leisure;
- completing a leisure attitude or recreation interest survey;
- engaging in a paper-and-pencil activity to determine barriers to leisure participation;
- selecting and practicing recreation activities;
- role playing leisure-related situations;
- learning a decision-making process for leisure choices;
- participating in leisure planning; and
- engaging in a recreation activity and evaluating the outcomes of participation.

Therapeutic recreation specialists can implement a leisure education program with any population (Sylvester et al., 2001). We cannot emphasize enough that leisure education can be tailored to the needs and functioning levels of just about any client, his family, or the service setting. Leisure education is a service that TR can offer not only in health care settings, but also in community settings to any member of the public who feels he may benefit from learning more about leisure. Public recreation departments, adult education programs, YMCAs and YWCAs, community centers, libraries, and schools may welcome a leisure education program as a service to their community. How to use free time, choosing among an overwhelming array of options, and facing the challenges of living a healthy lifestyle are concerns of many consumers (Edginton et al., 2004) that can be addressed in a leisure education program.

To provide leisure education in any setting requires an in-depth understanding of its purposes and methods and a specific program or set of activities. There are many books and resources available to the TRS who wishes to develop an appropriate leisure education program. Materials have been developed for leisure education programs related to developmental disabilities, substance abuse, children and youth, and retirement planning. Information is available on leisure education for those who are in prison, individuals with an acquired physical disability, people with AIDS, and older adults. Guidance is available for leisure education programming from a multicultural perspective (Dieser, 2004). The *Therapeutic Recreation Journal* has published a number of articles over the years on the relationship between leisure education and various outcomes for different populations. These articles describe a variety of leisure education interventions that can be implemented by TRSs. While research on leisure education has produced inconclusive results, most studies have noted varying degrees of positive outcomes such as increased participation, socialization, and awareness of leisure opportunities (Sylvester et al., 2001).

Leisure Education Resources

Books

Leisure Education Program Planning: A Systematic Approach (3rd ed.), by John Dattilo (Venture, 2008)

Leisure Education Specific Programs, by John Dattilo (Venture, 2000)

Leisure Education: Theory and Practice (2nd ed.), by Jean Mundy (Sagamore, 1998)

Leisure Education Manuals by Norma Stumbo

Leisure Education I: A Manual of Activities and Resources (2nd ed., Venture, 2002c)

Leisure Education II: More Activities and Resources (2nd ed., Venture, 2002b)

Leisure Education III: More Goal-Oriented Activities (Venture, 1997)

Leisure Education IV: Activities for Individuals with Substance Addictions (Venture, 1998)

Leisure Education Activity Ideas

www.recreationtherapy.com/tx/txleised.htm

Benefits of Leisure Education

Leisure education rests on the assumption that as people acquire new knowledge, skills, abilities, and attitudes, their behavior will change for the better (Stumbo & Peterson, 2009). By participating in leisure education, individuals learn how recreation can enrich their lives and contribute to their well-being. In leisure education, participants

- explore their attitudes toward leisure;
- develop positive attitudes toward leisure engagement;
- appreciate the contribution leisure can make to them, their families, the community, and society;
- acquire knowledge of leisure options and resources;
- develop skills for successful participation; and
- participate in a variety of recreation activities in order to evaluate them for ongoing involvement.

Leisure education also promotes inclusion: Individuals learn how to engage in recreation, what recreation facilities are available to them, what types of adaptations they may use, and how to interact with others in the inclusive recreation setting. Lack of leisure partners, or "I don't have anyone to go with," is a barrier to engaging in inclusive recreation. How to make, be, and keep a friend has been recognized as a significant need of people with developmental disabilities and with behavioral health problems. Leisure education is also a logical intervention for clients whose behavior has contributed to problems with substance abuse, stress-related ailments, diseases that are exacerbated by lack of exercise or poor nutrition, and risky or even dangerous pursuits. When mental health issues or substance abuse is present, the TRS can help the family identify maladaptive recreation patterns and positive recreation activities that everyone can do together. For families who have the attitude that their family member with a disability is helpless or dependent, leisure education may reveal the strengths the client possesses as he demonstrates them in a recreation activity. Families with a child who has a disability can benefit from sharing a fun recreation experience that promotes family cohesion and helps parents develop their child's healthy leisure behaviors.

The following are examples of goals that can be addressed in a leisure education program.

For those with a life-changing injury such as spinal cord injury, heart disease, or amputation (Long & Robertson, 2008):

- Understand the importance of recreation and fitness in maintaining health
- Increase knowledge of resources available for participating in recreation
- Acquire skill in using adaptations to facilitate preferred recreation participation

For those with developmental disabilities (Foose & Ardovino, 2008):

- Expand the range of recreation opportunities
- Successfully use adaptations of recreation activities
- Improve recreation-related social skills
- Master activity skills

For individuals in treatment for substance abuse (Kunstler, 2001):

- Identify barriers to leisure participation
- Improve ability to choose healthy alternatives
- Develop a supportive social network

Leisure education is primarily a cognitive activity. Its success relies on the client's willingness and ability to explore issues and make plans related to successful leisure participation. There are also social aspects to a leisure education group as clients discuss the various topics and share experiences.

Skills required for participation in leisure education and the benefits include the following:

- Physical: mode of communication, physical skill development
- Cognitive: comprehension, attention span, concentration, memory, decision making, problem solving, devising strategy, following directions, planning
- Affective or emotional: appropriate expression of emotions, ability to experience feelings of competence and increased self-esteem, willingness to reflect
- Social: interpersonal interaction, communicating effectively with others, sharing ideas and reactions

Risk Management

The risks in leisure education are minimal. As with any activity in which clients discuss personal issues, an emotional reaction may occur. As a result of leisure education, clients may make decisions that cause conflicts with family members and loved ones. The TRS needs to be vigilant regarding this possibility and work with the client to resolve these issues. This may involve other staff as well. In addition, if clients practice new activities or experiment with adaptive equipment, it is important to take care to ensure safety when they are using unfamiliar devices.

Leisure Counseling

Clients whose leisure-related problems are more deeply rooted may benefit from **leisure counseling**. Leisure counseling is the development of a counseling relationship between the counselor (TRS) and the client to address leisure-related attitudes and behaviors that are detrimental to the client's health and well-being. This relationship progresses through the use of interpersonal communication and counseling skills and techniques that help the client develop insight, awareness, and understanding regarding his issues and problems. Leisure counseling also involves selecting and applying strategies to develop and implement new lifestyle behaviors. The TRS who provides leisure counseling should have thorough knowledge of counseling approaches and skill in using a variety of counseling interventions. Although there is little formal training available for leisure counseling, this is an approach that requires additional education and practice. Leisure counseling can be provided one-to-one or in a group format; coleadership with a psychologist or social worker may be a desirable option.

Two interventions that are often applied in a leisure education context are values clarification and assertiveness training. Although both of these can be applied to other types of behavior, they are very effective when used to address changes in leisure-related behaviors.

Values Clarification

Values clarification is a process by which clients explore their values and how their values influence their behaviors, and make decisions to act in accordance with their values. Lack of clear values can lead to loss of motivation, poor decision making, and dissatisfaction (Mosconi & Emmett, 2003). As a result of values clarification, an individual begins to understand and embrace what he believes to be true. The process is not an attempt to align a person with a set of morals or beliefs held by any particular group about what is right or wrong. For this reason, values clarification is appropriate for people from diverse cultures (Mosconi & Emmett, 2003). A person may state that he values family but does not spend time with them. Another may state that she values leading a sober lifestyle but cannot turn down offers to go drinking with friends. Through values clarification, the TRS helps these clients to recognize that they are not living in harmony with their own values and to consider other options and make more fulfilling choices.

Activities such as "Two Ideal Days," "Twenty Things I Love to Do," and "Pie of Life" are fun and lead to discussions of choices, options, values, and behaviors. They also lead to reflection when clients complete sentences that begin with "I learned . . ." or "I was surprised that . . ." or "I plan to. . . ." Values clarification can be a fun group activity that promotes interaction and increased understanding of others' choices as well. The TRS can choose a poem or song that presents values-related themes as a springboard for the process. Issues and concepts that are relevant to everyone are presented in songs like "Honesty" by Billy Joel and "Another Day in Paradise" by Phil Collins, as well as in the poems "If" by Rudyard Kipling, "Hap" by Thomas Hardy, and "The Road Not Taken" by Robert Frost. The TRS should come up with his own file of songs, poems, stories, and films that are relevant to the needs and concerns of his clients.

Assertiveness Training

Assertiveness training helps people learn how to communicate their feelings, desires, and needs in an honest and straightforward fashion. Assertiveness is the ability to directly express one's feelings, needs, and desires to the appropriate person in an appropriate manner (Melillo & Houde, 2005). Many people have learned to express themselves in a style that is counterproductive to meeting their needs in a healthy way. Nonproductive communication includes passive, aggressive, and passive-aggressive behaviors. Passive behaviors include poor eye contact, soft voice, slumped posture, inability to say no to unreasonable requests, having difficulty addressing conflicts, or inability to make reasonable requests of others. Aggressive behaviors include interrupting, shouting, name calling, physical threats or attacks, making demands, and being sarcastic or hostile. Passive-aggressive behavior includes showing up late, using a tone of voice that implies the opposite of what one's words mean, procrastinating, complaining, making excuses, and appearing sullen or resentful. Passive-aggressive behavior is an indirect form of resistance. Passive, aggressive, and passive-aggressive behaviors are nonproductive forms of communication and are the opposite of **assertiveness**. When people do not assert what are considered their "legitimate" rights (to be listened to, to have their wishes respected, and to be able to take the time to make decisions), they may feel frustrated, devalued, angry, or anxious. By learning to express themselves appropriately,

they may feel more confident, reduce their stress, increase their self-esteem, and engage in more satisfying behaviors and relationships. Although demonstrating assertiveness is not a guarantee that a person will always get what he wants, it can result in clearer communication and increase others' understanding of the individual's needs and wishes (Peniston, 1998).

Assertiveness training helps people develop the social skills needed for interpersonal interaction in a variety of situations, including recreation. Assertiveness training can help clients in TR assert their rights to engage in recreation activities of their choice, to make decisions that they feel are in their best interests, and to advocate for themselves. Assertiveness training has been used with clients who have problems related to mental health, bulimia, cancer, chronic pain, midlife crises, and low self-esteem, as well as women with visual impairments, survivors of sexual assault, elderly nursing home residents at risk for depression, college students, and persons who are incarcerated. An assertiveness training program can incorporate instruction, role playing, modeling, feedback, and homework assignments. The activities can be fun to do and can allow clients the opportunity to explore new behaviors in a safe environment. An assertiveness training program has been developed around reading works by Homer, Shakespeare, and Toni Morrison. These

Biosketch of Toni Morrison

Toni Morrison was born in 1931 in Ohio to a family proud of its heritage, and growing up she heard many tales of Southern folklore. Her love of literature led her to become a college English instructor and a book editor. Active in the Civil Rights Movement of the 1960s, she began writing stories based on memories from her childhood of strong male and female characters.

Morrison's novel *Beloved*, which won the Pulitzer Prize for Fiction, told the story of a slave who chose to go to prison rather than give up her right to self-determination. In 1993, Morrison became the first black woman, and the eighth woman, to win the Nobel Prize in Literature.

COGNITIVE

great authors depict heroic characters who have struggled to meet their goals (Blackwell, 2003). This approach combined a skills training component with a recreation experience.

The TRS can help clients enrich their lives by learning listening skills and using verbal problem-solving abilities in order to express themselves in a manner that is direct and fulfilling. Clients receiving TR services may very well have been put in positions in which they could not express themselves openly, or were not expected to, due to disability, illness, or destructive environments. Honest expression of feelings in a direct, nonthreatening way is a powerful component of human interaction. Teaching clients how to paraphrase what another person has said, reflect the other's feelings, and summarize what they have heard will help increase the quality of their interpersonal communication. They also can learn how to share their own thoughts and feelings by making "I" statements, such as "I feel lonely when you go out and don't ask me to come along." "I" statements help people take responsibility for their feelings without attacking the other person. Compare the "I" statement just cited to "You never ask me to go with you. You're mean!" This puts the other person on the defensive and can lead to an argument rather than to a conversation that might increase mutual understanding. Another example is "I have the right to take time for myself to exercise." By getting to the main message, the client demonstrates respect for the other person as well as for himself. He also demonstrates respect by extending the same assertive rights to the other person.

In addition to expressing one's feelings, being a good listener is a vital social skill that can facilitate clients' relationships and progress. Listening includes nonverbal techniques of encouraging the speaker with nods, having a facial expression that shows interest, leaning slightly toward the speaker, and using paraverbal expressions such as "um-hmm." As with values clarification, assertiveness training has to be culturally sensitive to the values of the client. Expressing feelings indirectly or not talking about feelings can be based on cultural background, and the TRS must demonstrate sensitivity to clients' cultural values.

Social Skills Training

Social skills are addressed in leisure education programs because recreation participation is inherently social and can lead to the development and strengthening of friendships and relationships, which are significant aspects of quality of life (McCormick, 2002). An individual may never have learned effec-

tive social skills or may have experienced negative reactions that affected his using them properly (Austin, 2004). Social skills include knowing how to greet others appropriately, following a conversation, choosing an appropriate topic for conversation, knowing when it's one's turn to speak, making a joke or laughing at the right time, and judging the mood of a situation. Many of us do this instinctively; but for clients who do not, social skills training can teach communication skills and create learning opportunities using demonstrations, modeling, role playing, rehearsal, feedback, and homework to practice skills in a real-life situation. Many clients in Alcoholics Anonymous (AA) or other 12-step programs may not have the social skills of listening, taking turns in speaking, controlling their temper or impulses, or smiling and nodding appropriately. They could benefit from social skills training prior to attending AA so that they can derive maximum benefit from their participation. Other benefits of social skills training include increased self-esteem, social confidence, more satisfying relationships, and a greater range of options and choices.

Clients may also need to learn to differentiate among social relationships that require different types of behaviors. For example, communicating with friends, interacting with coworkers, and engaging in casual conversation involve different levels of familiarity and different interaction styles. Social intelligence or social competence is the ability to understand the social dynamics of the interactions that guide people's behaviors. Lack of social intelligence due to developmental disability, psychiatric illness, traumatic brain injury, or substance abuse, among other conditions, can be a barrier to inclusion. A socially competent person understands the impact of his own behavior on others, and can balance the demands of the social environment and make effective responses. Social intelligence acts as a guide when we enter a new group of people and become a member, make others feel comfortable, and handle difficulties that may arise. It combines the social skills of verbal and nonverbal communication, such as using and interpreting body language and personal space, initiating and carrying on a conversation, listening, using humor appropriately, and giving and receiving compliments, with knowing how to read between the lines in a social situation.

Understanding **proxemics**, which is the study of how human beings use space, can contribute to the development of social competence. The principles of proxemics give valuable insight into use of personal space and acceptable distances between people who are interacting. Personal space is the invisible zone that surrounds a person and which he considers his own. Territory is similar to personal space but includes the physical area surrounding the person. Always sitting in the same seat at the table, at bingo, or in front of the TV is an example of territoriality. Crowding relates to our tolerance of how close people are to us in different situations. Sensing and respecting personal space and a person's territory are valuable social skills. The TRS may work with clients who are not aware of the prevailing cultural practices regarding proxemics and who can benefit from guidance in this area.

When one is implementing social skills training, it is important to consider that newly acquired social skills are not always generalized from the training setting to the real world. Therapeutic recreation offers many opportunities for generalizing newly learned skills of all types, including social skills, and should be promoted as a preferred environment for social skills training. All TR groups involve social interaction. Once clients have learned new social skills, they can be coached to try them out and use them in TR programs. The TRS can provide feedback and support as participants carry on conversations, make friends, and socialize with a variety of people. On a community outing, real situations present themselves in which people can practice social skills.

A newer approach that has been recommended for use with social skills training is **replacement behavior training (RBT)**, in which participants learn to replace an inappropriate behavior with an appropriate one that meets the same need (Maag, 2005). By observing the behaviors of high-status peers to see how they meet their needs in a situation, people can identify and learn an effective replacement behavior. For example, a child who head butts others to keep them away from her can learn to hold her arm straight out with her hand palm outward (similar to a traffic officer indicating "Stop"). She has replaced the head with another body part, the arm, and maintained the forward

COGNITIVE

Proxemics

E.T. Hall, the cultural anthropologist, wrote his landmark work, *The Hidden Dimension,* in 1966. In this book he presented his theory of proxemics, discussing how people use space in their personal relationships and their physical environments, and even the use of space in urban planning and design. Hall identified four interpersonal distances, which can vary by culture:

Intimate space: 0 to 1.5 feet (.3 to .46 meters)
Indicates probability of intimacy, used for whispering and embracing

Personal space: 1.5 to 4 feet (.46 to 1.2 meters)
Used among family and friends and when waiting on line

Social space: 4 to 12 feet (1.2 to 3.7 meters)
Used for routine social interaction, among coworkers and acquaintances, and to separate strangers in public spaces

Public space: 12 to 25 feet (3.7 to 7.6 meters)
Refers to the distance between an audience and a speaker, the space beyond which interaction is anonymous and impersonal

Effects of cultural variations

Saudi Arabians' social space = Americans' intimate space, so the Saudi thinks the American is "standoffish," and the American thinks the Saudi is "pushy."

The Dutch's personal space = Americans' social space, so the American seems like the "pushy" Saudi to the more reserved Dutch.

Americans use more space; they like big cars, big offices, and big houses.

The Japanese use small spaces, perhaps due to the shortage of usable space in their small country.

COGNITIVE

movement of a body part while conveying the same message, "I need space," in a more acceptable manner.

Leisure education is a comprehensive program that has many facets. The TRS is strongly encouraged to avail herself of the many resources that can be used to develop and implement leisure education interventions that are appropriate to the needs of the clients. The TRS's ethical practice is to ensure that the benefits of leisure are available to her clients by assisting them in overcoming barriers posed by lack of awareness or information, lifestyle factors, and personal circumstances.

■ Games

Games have been played for thousands of years by people all over the world. Games have several characteristics: rules that govern how they are played and who wins, some degree of structure or format, an interactive quality, and an element of luck or chance that adds to the uncertainty of the outcome. The challenge in a game lies in determining strategy and figuring out what move to make or what action to take. The degree of challenge depends on the level of skill needed to play, and also involves the role of luck or chance. Games range from simple card games like Go Fish and paper-and-pencil games like tic-tac-toe, to memory games such as Concentration or Trivia, to very complex ones such as bridge or chess. There are tabletop games, designed to be played on a table or similar flat surface, such as board games, card games, and puzzles, as well as electronic handheld games and games available on a computer like solitaire and Scrabble. Computer game systems such as video games, XBOX, and Wii require more space. Online games and virtual worlds, which players either play by themselves or with any number of people, open up a range of possibilities for recreation participation. Active low-organization games (e.g., tag; hide-and-seek; jump rope; Giant Steps; Duck, Duck, Goose; Red Rover; Red Light, Green Light) and relay races are typically engaged in by children and are seen as precursors to more complex sport activities. Games may require equipment such as a game board, dice, cards, play money, a computer system, or a large space or open area. Whatever level of complexity games possess, they are fun to play and offer many benefits to participants in a TR program. The TRS also can create games to meet specific goals for which he hasn't found another activity (Stumbo, 2002b). Creating the game can even become a TR group program.

Benefits of Games

In a TR program, games have the advantage of being available for every age group and for every level of physical and cognitive functioning. Many games can be easily adapted to meet the skills of the participants. Games are also a wonderful tool for learning new skills and enhancing existing skills. Games that almost everyone has played offer the comfort of a familiar experience; but also there are many new ones to learn, and there is always the challenge and excitement of the unknown outcome. How well will I play? Will I win? Games are a leisure activity that families can participate in together and that can also lead to new friendships. "The practicing of familiar games and the learning of new, and possibly adapted, games can be carried over into the home and school following the client's discharge" (Carter et al., 2003, p. 465). There are games that can be played alone, with one other player, or with a group. In many TR programs, decks of cards, puzzles, board games, and computers are readily available for independent participation. Clients often play games such as cards, dominoes, or Scrabble or do a jigsaw puzzle on their own, or gather with others to play in their free time.

Games utilize the following skills and can produce the following benefits:

- Physical: fine motor skills; manual dexterity; grasping and releasing; reaching; range of motion in fingers, wrist, elbow, and arm; crossing the midline to transfer objects from one hand to the other; visual tracking and scanning
- Cognitive: understanding and following rules, strategy, concentration, attention span, memory, verbal language skills, reading, arithmetic, number recognition, matching and sorting, sense of direction, problem solving, decision making, knowledge
- Affective or emotional: sense of fair play, concern for others' feelings, self-esteem, relaxation, experiencing joy and fun
- Social: cooperation, competition, teamwork, social interaction, taking turns, giving and receiving verbal feedback

Risk Management

Risk management concerns for games involve both the playing surface and the equipment or pieces. Playing games requires a surface that is large enough to accommodate the activity. If the participants are in wheelchairs or in bed, the TRS needs to be sure that the players are comfortably positioned, that lighting is adequate, and that they can reach as far as necessary. Be sure the playing surface is balanced so that pieces such as dice don't roll off and become difficult to retrieve. Depending on clients' functioning levels, the TRS should be sure that they do not put playing pieces in their mouth, that there are no sharp objects, and that arguments do not break out. Small pieces often go missing. The TRS should check the games inventory regularly to make sure that sets are complete. Many adaptations are available for different needs. Adaptive equipment such as large-print playing cards and board games, magnifiers, HI-Mark paint (which is raised so that lines can be distinguished by touch), and card holders and shufflers can facilitate participation, as can the use of partners or teams. In active games, the TRS must ensure that the play area is safe, without hidden obstacles, and of ample size to allow for unrestricted movement. Boundaries of the playing area need to be set and explained clearly to children. Games such as dodgeball have become very controversial due to the risk of injury from being hit with the ball. However, many active games can be played without equipment, which is a great advantage. In the more active games that involve running, players can collide or fall, and the TRS should be prepared with a first aid kit. The competitive aspects may lead to arguments, which need to be handled quickly and effectively.

Selecting Games

When selecting a game for a client, the TRS must be mindful of providing activities that will be challenging but not unduly frustrating. The client may have a preference for a particular familiar game, or the TRS may suggest one that will help the client meet his goals and offer a new interest to expand his repertoire. When the activity requires two or more participants, the TRS needs to be sure that participants are of equal capabilities so that no player is either bored or overwhelmed. Games that can be played in teams, such as charades, Trivia, and Pictionary, promote group cohesion and cooperation and alleviate the stress of competition on a single person. The TRS also needs to know how to play a variety of games so she can choose the appropriate games for her clients, teach them how to play, settle disputes about rules, and facilitate the clients' desired behavioral outcomes. See table 6.2 for a list of well-known games that provide cognitive benefits. It also is very valuable for a client to have the opportunity to teach others, including the TRS, how to play a game.

Preferred games may vary according to one's cultural background. For example, the game of dominoes is very popular with men from the Dominican Republic. Mexican American children enjoy Loteria, a bingo game with pictures instead of numbers. On the other hand, some cultures view certain games as forms of gambling and do not approve of playing them. As with all programming, the TRS must be sensitive to the cultural practices of her clients.

Games for Different Groups

Much of the research on the therapeutic value of games has been done with children with autism spectrum disorders, including Asperger's syndrome. Games can help children learn positive social behaviors, serve as a vehicle for parent–child interaction, and promote friendships. Carefully observing clients' preferred activities can help the TRS select games that incorporate their interests, thereby promoting desired behaviors. In one study of preschool children, researchers used games that incorporated the children's preferences for numbers and letters, such as puzzles with letters, board games, and Uno. This helped them increase their intrinsic motivation to interact and develop socially appropriate play activities with typically developing peers and siblings (Vismara & Lyons, 2007). Children with learning disabilities can successfully play card games such as Crazy 8s, table games such

TABLE 6.2

Cognitive Benefits of Well-Known Games

Concentration	Eye–hand coordination	Language	Matching	Spatial organization	Strategy and problem solving
Concentration	Darts	Boggle	Dominoes	Erector sets	Checkers
Password	Pick-up sticks	Monopoly	Lotto	Etch A Sketch	Chess
Yahtzee	Tic-tac-toe	Scrabble	Uno	Legos	Clue
		Zingo		Othello	Rummikub

as Yahtzee and dominoes, and knowledge games including Trivia, Jeopardy, Wheel of Fortune, Scattergories, and Outburst. If needed, adaptations can be made. The following are accommodations that can enable successful participation in games:

- Extending the amount of time per roll
- Repeating questions and information
- Having people play in partners
- Using an electronic spell checker or dictionary and a calculator for scoring (Peniston, 1998)

Clients with cognitive impairments due to stroke and head injury can benefit from games of chance and strategy, gradually progressing in the processes of organizing information, decision making, and planning a course of action (Lahey, 2001). Games can be modified so that they use pictures instead of words, or can be combined with physical movements to create a multisensory experience. Older adults can benefit from doing a group crossword puzzle, enlarged for easy viewing, to stimulate memory, word retrieval, and problem solving. Memory games such as Trivia and Jeopardy have similar benefits (Hart, Primm, and Cranisky, 2003). Thirteen nursing home residents with dementia successfully played a game in which they solved anagrams (Phillips, 1993). An anagram consists of a set of scrambled letters that when rearranged correctly spell a single word. The player moves one letter at a time to eventually spell the word correctly. The residents' ability to come up with the correct word (DRESS) when given a category as a cue (such as "article of clothing" for REDSS), demonstrated their capacity for participating in a challenging and fun activity and overcame misperceptions of their cognitive skill level.

Bingo remains a popular activity offered by TR departments, especially to older adults, although some professionals view it as being offered too frequently and not having enough therapeutic value. However, clients may find it comforting to engage in a familiar and undemanding activity when they are in times of stress and change. Newly admitted residents to a hospital or long-term care facility, or newcomers in a day care program, can often be encouraged to join a bingo game. As with any TR program, the TRS can use her skills to maximize the quality of the experience and the outcomes for the participants. Knowing how much time to give players to mark their cards, who needs assistance, and how to encourage and instruct are all skills the TRS can apply during bingo. An activity analysis of bingo is shown on page 139. One common misconception is that bingo is a social activity; although it is a group activity, play does not *require* interaction with others, except with the caller. This makes it a good choice for those who are in the initial stages of joining group activities. The prizes also seem to be meaningful to the players. The TRS should offer a range of games that have qualities similar to those of bingo. In music bingo the caller plays fragments of the songs, and the players mark the song titles on their bingo cards, instead of numbers. This variation of bingo also stimulates memory and can lead to a sing-along (Hart et al., 2003).

Electronic Games

The first video game was introduced to American homes in the 1970s. As of 2005, it was estimated that 60 percent of all Americans played interactive games on a regular basis (Baglin, Lewis & Williams, 2004); 92 percent of 2- to 17-year-olds play video and computer games and spend 6.5 hours per day in front of television, video, and computer screens (Simpson, 2005). The widespread popularity of interactive electronic games makes them practical options for TR programming. The TRS should be at the forefront of introducing and using electronic games in her setting. While the benefits and drawbacks of electronic game playing are much debated, there is no doubt that there are therapeutic advantages to using electronic games in TR, as well as other rehabilitative therapies. Electronic games involve rules and clear roles; both competition and collaboration are required; and trial and error is a viable course of action (Simpson, 2005). In these games, the player has control over how the action unfolds; players realize that nothing is impossible, there is always an answer to a problem, and with effort there will be results. Playing involves decision making, strategy, and reflection on the consequences of one's actions and can lengthen attention span (Norton-Meier, 2005). The controls on these games are easily adaptable to enable participation by individuals with developmental and multiple disabilities, and the clear feedback and multisensory stimulation promote sustained involvement. Electronic games are nonthreatening to children with emotional and behavioral disabilities (Baglin et al., 2004). Children as young as toddlers can play video games on the iPhone (Stone, 2010), making it a very convenient activity that can be played in any situation.

Research has been conducted on the benefits of video games. In one study, video games were shown to reduce the stress of children undergoing chemotherapy treatment for cancer (Ell & Reardon, 1990). Older adults also are responding to these games.

In another study, because video games require memory, concentration, and quick responses, nursing home residents played on the Super Nintendo Entertainment System 5 hours per week for five weeks. Playing improved the participants' reaction time and also provided a topic of conversation that promoted interaction and friendship development (Goldstein et al., 1997). Video games can motivate intergenerational participation as well.

Another use of video games is to provide health information and promote healthy behaviors, especially for teenagers. Games have been found to be an effective tool in educating young people about the effects of drugs. A CD-ROM–based arcade-style computer game was designed to simulate driving a motorcycle while drug free as well as while using cocaine (Noble et al., 2000). The player who is not using drugs wins, while the one using cocaine sees a progressive deterioration in his performance, has to make more frequents stops for drug purchases, and always loses. Each player plays the game under both conditions so they can see the effects of drugs on their performance. It is also believed that involvement in a structured experience increases learning. Kaledo, a game developed in Italy, significantly increased nutrition knowledge and vegetable intake in 11- to 14-year olds. For wounded war veterans, other video games, such as Guitar Hero 2, can improve hand strength and dexterity; handheld games such as Brain-Teaser can improve cognitive functioning; and persons with quadriplegia can hold a controller in their mouth to play and restore a sense of normalcy (Musgrove, 2007).

One of the criticisms of electronic game playing has been that it discourages participants from engaging in physical activity and promotes a sedentary lifestyle. However, Dance Dance Revolution (DDR) is one example of the use of technology to encourage exercise. Players stand on a dance mat or pad and move their feet according to arrows that indicate direction as songs requiring increasingly complex and strenuous patterns are played. Dance Dance Revolution is becoming popular in physical education classes because it is a fun and novel way to get exercise. Research shows that DDR participation improves overall fitness and blood pressure (Schiesel, 2007). In an international survey, 556 respondents ages 12 to 50, from 22 countries, indicated that DDR improved both their physical fitness and their social life in that they made new friends while playing (Hoysniemi, 2006). The Wii video game system is making a huge impact in physical rehabilitation and long-term care facilities for those of all ages recovering from strokes, broken bones, surgery, and combat injuries (Associated Press, 2008). Wii uses a motion-sensitive controller that allows the player to make the same arm movements required in a sport to direct the actions of animated athletes on the screen. The game aspect motivates patients to engage in both fine motor and arm movements that promote their recovery by improving endurance, strength, and coordination.

Cognitively oriented programs can be geared to any level of intellectual functioning and can provide the participant with the joys of learning, self-expression, and healthy competition. Cognitive recreation activities can be effectively implemented in any TR program, and their potential to help clients achieve critical outcomes is vast.

COGNITIVE

Health-Related Programs

While all the activities in the TR toolkit have a relationship to promoting health, those more widely recognized as having direct physical and mental health benefits include cooking and food preparation; physical activity, exercise, sports, and aquatics; relaxation and stress management; hobbies; and humor. With the never-ending concern regarding the personal and societal costs of health care, as well as the growing emphasis on a holistic approach to health as essential to quality of life, health-related programs are a significant component of TR programming. Many variations of these programs can be included in the TR toolkit.

■ Cooking and Food Preparation

Cooking and other activities involving food preparation and consumption are probably among the few universal recreation activities since every human being eats and has undoubtedly done at least the most basic food preparation. Cooking involves preparing food for eating by choosing and planning what is to be prepared, obtaining ingredients, organizing the environment for maximum efficiency, and effectively carrying out the sequence of steps involved in the chosen recipe (Ho et al., n.d.). Other key components of cooking are understanding safety, operating within a time frame, and using appliances and utensils. Once the food is cooked, serving, eating, and cleanup are part of the overall activity. Cooking is an activity that requires skills in all four behavioral domains. A number of adaptations are available to facilitate cooking by people with disabilities. The almost infinite number of recipes, from the simplest to the very complex, enables successful participation by people of any age, from toddlers to the very old, and by those with severe physical and cognitive limitations. Even without a kitchen or an oven, the TRS can conduct a food preparation group using microwaves, toaster ovens, or cold foods. Opportunities abound for collaboration with occupational therapists for adaptive equipment, with dietitians for healthy recipes, and with kitchen staff for supplies.

Benefits of Cooking and Food Preparation Programs

Cooking as part of a TR program is an extension of real life. While occupational therapy (OT) may focus on helping clients develop cooking skills to promote independent living or a return to a normal routine that has been disrupted by illness or disability, TR can focus on cooking as a social and recreational experience as well as a learning tool. Food preparation can also be a very creative activity as people prepare meals, follow or adjust recipes, decorate cakes, or set an attractive table. Cooking can be adapted to any age group, from toddlers who find the multisensory experience exciting to older adults living in nursing homes who are thrilled to cook again. For those with emotional or cognitive impairments, cooking and food preparation aid in improving executive functioning—"being able to think about what you're going to do, being able to make the plans and being able to carry through with these plans to completion" (Sutin, 2005)—and time management. The focus and concentration on a concrete task can help reduce feelings of anxiety and confusion.

Cooking also can stimulate memory as people reminisce about foods they have eaten, meals they have cooked or that their mothers prepared, restaurants they ate in, and food from their travels. Cooking can reinforce one's identity because it can give people the opportunity to share a favorite recipe, participate in a former activity, and maintain contact with foods of their cultural background. Cooking can strengthen family ties as family members see that their loved one can still make a valued contribution to home life. Food is recognized as a social lubricant that can make communication and interaction flow more easily. Coffee hours, tea parties, and happy hours are popular social activities offered by TR. Clients may also develop cooking as a leisure interest that they pursue following discharge. For clients living in group homes or other residential settings, cooking and food sharing are a normalizing activity. The TRS can also be a role model for a healthy relationship with food (Carter et al., 2003).

No-Cook Snacks

Ants on a Log: Stuff celery with peanut butter or cream cheese and push in raisins.

Candy Bird Nests: Mix cereal with peanut butter, blend in chocolate chips, shape into a nest, and press in M&Ms for birds' eggs.

Crispy Candy Sushi Snacks: Use fruit roll-ups, gummy worms, rice cereals, and marshmallows; shape into sushi.

Grape Caterpillar: Skewer green and red grapes on pretzel sticks; add carrot strips for antennae.

Strawberry Shortcake: Spread lady fingers with whipped cream and add berries.

Cooking utilizes the following skills and produces the following benefits:

- Physical: range of motion in the entire arm including the fingers, wrist, elbow and shoulder, and neck; some muscle strength for lifting, chopping, mixing, cutting; balance for standing; sensory awareness of hot and cold and of sharp utensils; sensory stimulation

- Cognitive: following directions, sequencing of steps, memory for safety and for following through on procedures, time management to complete tasks in the allotted time frame, attention span, decision making, knowledge of nutrition, math skills for measuring

- Affective or emotional: feelings of competence and mastery, pride in accomplishment, self-esteem, creativity, anticipation of eating the finished product, reminiscing

- Social: cooperation, sharing the food, receiving compliments, building relationships

Adaptations

Many modifications can be used to enable clients to participate in cooking. Even those who do not want to do the actual cooking may be willing to help with setup, serving, or cleanup. Cooking lends itself to varying degrees of complexity. The TRS can plan to bake using a cake mix that requires adding only a few ingredients or a very complex recipe. The TRS

can perform several steps in advance, including gathering the utensils and ingredients, if that is required to meet the level of clients' functioning. Pictures can be used to explain the steps in a recipe or to help clients learn what the various supplies are. Be aware that clients may misread directions or make mistakes in measuring ingredients and calculating the time needed to cook an item (Peniston, 1998). For those with physical limitations, mixing bowls with a suction base and nonslip mats are available, as are utensils with built-up foam handles and book holders for recipes. The OT may have suggestions for clients on how best to position themselves or lift objects and move around in the kitchen area. The nutritionist can help adapt recipes to the dietary needs of the clients.

Risk Management

A cooking program requires careful planning and supervision. There are endless possibilities of meals that can be prepared safely, but clients may need assistance in any of the tasks involved in cooking, for safety reasons as well as because of their degree of functional ability. Risk management concerns in a cooking program include monitoring hot stoves, ovens, and pots and pans; sharp utensils such as knives and cooking shears; breakable containers and bowls; and food restrictions and allergies among participants. Clients who are using a wheelchair may be working on an attached tray that offers limited space, and may need assistance in managing supplies. There may be participants who eat ingredients due to confusion or a low level of cognitive functioning.

Cooking Activities With Different Groups

Current attention to nutritional needs of people with varying illnesses and conditions that are affected by foods has broadened the scope of cooking programs from addressing physical and cognitive skills to improving overall health outcomes. Many cooking programs today emphasize healthy eating guidelines, weight loss, and exercise and fitness. Conditions such as diabetes, hypertension, AIDS, and cancer entail dietary restrictions and recommendations that the TRS should address in a cooking and nutrition program. Helping clients understand that they can still enjoy food by learning to cook tasty and healthy meals can be a focus of a TR cooking program. Individuals with developmental disabilities who tend to be overweight can learn about healthy meals and snacks and how to prepare them. Cooking can stimulate eating in

HEALTH

Cooking can stimulate memories, reinforce identity, and promote socialization.

clients with poor appetites. For people with AIDS, "social events that offer high caloric snacks and meals in a leisure environment can often result in increased food consumption" (Grossman & Caroleo, 2001, p. 304). Children who are in the hospital may find it difficult to comply with nutritional or dietary requirements, and TR can take the opportunity to offer food that is appealing and teach about proper eating in a fun way (Carter et al., 2003).

Women in particular experience family as a significant influence on choices about what foods to eat. In one study, both healthy women and women with breast cancer reported that they wanted to eat a more healthful diet but were influenced by the preferences of their husbands and children. Those who received a diagnosis of breast cancer, however, placed a higher priority on healthy eating (Beagan & Chapman, 2004). The TRS can help women learn to prepare healthy meals that are appealing to their families and invite families to share a meal. For female nursing home residents, who tend to equate preparing and serving family meals with love and nurturing and may miss this experience (Bruck, 1999), preparing a meal with others leads to "talking, reminiscing, having fun and feeling at home" (p. 37). In addition to the actual cooking or preparation of food, TR activities can involve discussions

on healthy eating, ordering in restaurants, accessibility issues, and writing up shopping lists; trips to the market and dining out; and luncheon clubs and other social events involving food. A TR group can prepare the food for an event or activity such as a holiday party, summer barbeque, or picnic. Cooking also has great value for sensory stimulation because of the aromas, tastes, colors, and textures of foods.

There are also innovative techniques that the TRS can use to help clients learn to cook. Clients with traumatic brain injuries have been successfully taught cooking skills using videotapes. As they received instructions and feedback, they were videotaped while cooking and then were able to watch the videos to improve their cooking skills (McGraw-Hunter, Faw & Davis, 2006). A popular program, conducted by one of the authors in a psychiatric facility, was making homemade ice cream. This activity had several aspects that enabled participation by a number of clients. First came preparing the mix, including measuring and combining the ingredients, and then cooking the mixture on the stovetop. The next step was adding the ice and rock salt to the ice cream maker and taking a turn at the hand crank. The use of an old-fashioned model rather than an electric ice cream maker motivated the involvement of many men who were typically reluctant to participate in group activities. The hand cranking not only triggered youthful memories, but also required physical effort and provided an opportunity to display pride in one's physical prowess. Once the ice cream was ready, tables were set with toppings, dishes, spoons, and napkins. Finally, there was cleanup. Families and other visitors were able to share in the finished product. Making the ice cream promoted a positive social experience as well. This experience demonstrates the many benefits of cooking and food preparation programming.

Cooking activities can also be an excellent opportunity for the TRS to observe behaviors that are relevant to the client's overall treatment. Monitoring whether a client eats, how much, and what types of food might stimulate someone's appetite provides useful data to share with the treatment team. When working with people who have eating disorders, the TRS can note whether the client has any unusual rituals regarding food and eating (Carter et al., 2003) and also report this to the appropriate team members. Certain situations may trigger eating, and this may be another concern.

■ Physical Activity, Exercise, Fitness, and Sport

A goal of all TR programs is to prevent worsening of health conditions, and **physical activity** is a key element in reaching that goal. Physical activity should be an integral part of every TR program (Carter et al., 2004) due to its wide-reaching impact on health and well-being. In fact, physical activity may be one of the most effective means of increasing functioning and independence in people with disabilities (Santiago & Coyle, 2004). In addition, specific treatment programs for obesity, known as **bariatrics,** are becoming more prevalent; and TRSs are providing services to these patients. Adequate amounts of physical activity have been proven to result in reduced rates of cardiovascular disease, diabetes, and some cancers; improvements in mental health and hypertension; decreased risk of falls; and prevention of osteoporosis (Meriwether et al., 2008). Despite these findings, in the United States alone, 250,000 deaths each year are attributed to a lack of physical activity; furthermore, over 60 percent of American adults are not regularly active, and 25 percent are not active at all. Compared to people without a disability, a smaller proportion of people with a disability meet national standards for physical activity (Rimmer et al., 2007). Both ATRA and NTRS have developed initiatives to support the objectives of Healthy People 2010, which outlines a national health agenda aimed at preventing threats to and promoting health, including increasing the number of people with disabilities who engage in physical activity and improving their access to community health and wellness programs (Howard et al., 2004). See table 6.3 for benefits of physical activity. The obesity "epidemic" has prompted thousands of community and public health initiatives. It has tremendous implications for the development of health problems and the need for health care.

Definitions of Types of Physical Activity

Most experts define physical activity as *bodily movement produced by skeletal muscles which results in an increased expenditure of energy* (Austin, 2002a; Broach, Dattilo & Loy, 2000). Physical activity can be divided into four categories: leisure-time physical activity (LTPA), planned and structured exercise, household activity, and occupational activity. Therapeutic recreation focuses primarily on LTPA and exercise (Swann-Guerrero & Mackey, 2008). Leisure-time physical activity includes **sports, gardening,** walking, active games, and any other physical activity done for recreation. Exercise, on the other hand, is planned, structured and repetitive bodily movement with the objective of improving one's physical fitness (Austin, 2002a; Broach et al., 2000). Exercise

TABLE 6.3

Benefits of Physical Activity

Disease prevention benefits	Wellness benefits
Exercise lowers the risk of:	**Physical activity promotes:**
Heart disease	Weight loss
Stroke	Oxygen consumption and blood flow
Hypertension	Stress reduction
Type 2 diabetes	Improved mood
Obesity	Longevity
Back pain	Improved sleep
Cancer, 12 types	Increased flexibility and mobility
Osteoporosis	Energy
Gallstones	Memory and learning
Diverticulitis	Quality of life
Falls	Positive self-image
Peripheral vascular disease	Increased self-confidence
	Reduced fatigue, pain, morning stiffness, and anxiety
	Improved immune function

is voluntary and occurs due to the anticipated positive physical, psychological, or social benefits or some combination of these (Nowicka & Flodmark, 2007). Exercise includes activities such as aerobics, tai chi, yoga, weight training, bicycling, dancing, and swimming.

The U.S. government has issued guidelines recommending 30 minutes of accumulated, moderate-intensity physical activity on five or more days per week, which can be in 10-minute increments. For those just beginning to be physically active, 10 minutes is a more realistic goal and a safer way to get involved in exercise. Sports are among the most popular forms of physical activity and are characterized by physical exertion; competition involving physical skills; and rules (Rossman & Schlatter, 2003), both formal and informal, such as standards of etiquette and fair play (Kraus, 1997). Whatever type of physical activity one chooses, becoming physically active "is an essential component of wellness and a healthy lifestyle, and it is critical to the development of physical fitness" (Swann-Guerrero & Mackey, 2008, p. 201). Physical fitness is defined as "the ability to carry out daily tasks with alertness and vigor, without undue fatigue and with enough energy reserve to meet emergencies and to enjoy leisure time" (*Mosby's Dental Dictionary*, 2008). While physical fitness may be seen as subjective, varying by age and physical condition, striving to improve physical fitness is a process that can benefit all participants. The vast array of activities that promote physical fitness ensures that there are satisfying options for everyone.

Benefits of Physical Activity

Besides the obvious and well-researched physical benefits, physical activity has been shown to have significant positive effects on mental health and social behavior (Bullock & Mahon, 2000; Mobily & MacNeil, 2002; McKenney, 2004). As clients develop their physical fitness, they may begin to perceive themselves as having a healthier identity, as a "fit" individual, rather than someone who is sick or limited in some way. As they increase their physical capabilities, they can be encouraged to apply their self-management skills to other aspects of their lives that they wish to improve. Participation in sport can help adolescents with disruptive behavior disorders develop **prosocial behaviors** (McKenney, 2004). Prosocial behaviors include helping others, offering compliments and encouragement, sharing, cooperating, and resolving conflicts. The TRS can use role plays of situations that occur during sport participation to help clients learn prosocial behaviors, as

well as take advantage of "teachable moments" that occur during sport activities. Participation in Special Olympics and wheelchair sports has been found to contribute to psychological well-being (Bullock & Mahon, 2000). Aerobic exercise has been shown to reduce anxiety and depressed mood, and weight training increases self-esteem and feelings of control (Mobily & MacNeil, 2002). The popularity of sport and other forms of physical activity makes these pursuits a natural for promoting inclusion. Clients who have developed a repertoire of interests in LTPA and exercise have many opportunities to participate in the environments of their choice. Inclusive sport opportunities can also improve the attitudes of people without disabilities toward people with disabilities (Bullock & Mahon, 2000).

A common misperception is that if one has not been physically active for most of one's life, it is too late to start and to experience the benefits of physical activity. This is absolutely a fallacy! Research has shown that even older adults in their 90s made gains in a weight training program (Fiatarone, O'Neill, Ryan, Clements, Solares, & Nelson, et al., 1994). For older adults, physical activity can reduce the risk of developing chronic disease, aid in the management of chronic disease, and improve the ability to function and stay independent. Since 80 percent of older adults have at least one chronic condition (Richeson et al., 2006), physical activity is essential to their health and well-being. In a study of 178 adults ranging in age from 55 to 94 years, participants were encouraged to increase their daily activity, wore pedometers all day, and recorded the number of steps they took at the end of each day (Richeson et al., 2006). Results showed that they increased their lower extremity strength and walking ability. Having realistic short-term goals and wearing the pedometers, which provided immediate feedback, were seen as key motivators. This study demonstrates that people of all ages can be encouraged and supported to increase the amount of physical activity they do on a daily basis.

These are the benefits of physical activity and the skills required for participation:

- Physical: gross motor skills, fine motor skills, balance, flexibility, range of motion, coordination, muscle strength, cardiovascular endurance, respiratory capacity, posture
- Cognitive: attention span, concentration, decision making, following rules and instructions, sense of direction, memory, judgment, learning
- Affective: feelings of joy, accomplishment, pride; releasing stress and frustration; coping with win-

HEALTH

ning and losing; experiencing healthy competition; relaxation; positive mood

- Social: teamwork, cooperation, working toward a mutual goal, social interaction, peer relationships, giving and receiving praise and feedback

Risk Management

Risks are inherent to participation in physical activity. Risks may be due to the environment, the equipment, or the physical condition of the participant. The TRS has the ethical responsibility to accurately assess and inform the clients of risks inherent in an activity. Many individuals with disabilities and health conditions have been overprotected by well-meaning family and staff and denied the right to risk and to take chances. Their rights to engage in a range of physical recreation programs should be safeguarded, yet safety and qualified supervision are paramount concerns in programming. The TRS must educate clients on the safety procedures and behaviors relevant to each activity. She should maintain the integrity of the activity yet be prepared to adapt aspects as needed to facilitate participation. Adjusting rules, shortening distances, giving more time or chances, using lead-up activities to build skills, and providing written information are all methods that can help clients improve their abilities to engage in sport and other physical activities.

Prior to the start of the TR program, the physical environment must be inspected for any hazards, such as slippery floors, poor ventilation, inadequate lighting, stray electrical cords, or physical obstructions. The TRS should have water, towels, a first aid kit, and a quick guide to emergency procedures available. In an outdoor setting, the ground surface should be checked for loose gravel, stone, branches, or other objects that can cause a person to trip or fall. Other safety precautions in the outdoors include sunscreen, hats, and first aid for insect bites and allergies.

Equipment used in physical activity should be in good working order and should be checked for sharp edges and loose parts. Balls, rackets, bats, and hand weights should be provided in a range of sizes and weight to accommodate all needs. Adaptive equipment is available for most sports, and many companies market these products. Exercise mats that provide adequate padding are required for floor exercise and yoga. Protective equipment such as helmets, knee and elbow pads, goggles, swim caps, and gloves should be supplied. Clients must wear proper clothing. Generally, comfortable clothing that does not restrict movement and sneakers or other specialized footwear are recommended. Some departments keep on hand an assortment of sneakers, hats, and appropriate clothing for use by clients who do not have their own. The TRS should have a checklist to follow to inspect the facilities and equipment on a regular basis.

As always, the TRS must closely monitor the participants' performance and behavior. If a client experiences undue pain or physical discomfort, shortness of breath, dizziness, or any concerns out of the ordinary, the TRS must immediately intervene and seek assistance. Some agencies or organizations require all TRSs to be certified in First Aid and CPR and be trained to handle medical emergencies. All this is not to suggest that there are many injuries in TR physical activity programs, but to encourage the TRS to be as prepared as possible to handle situations that may arise. An excellent guide to disability-specific recommendations and considerations is provided by Swann-Guerrero and Mackey in their chapter "Wellness Through Physical Activity" in *Foundations of Therapeutic Recreation* (Robertson & Long, 2008).

Physical activity improves the health of the whole person—body and mind.

HEALTH

Checklist for Safety Inspection

The TRS can use the following checklist to inspect a space or location for safety prior to beginning the TR program.

Space

- Free of hazards
  - No obstructions to ease of movement
  - Indoor floor: clean and swept, not wet or slippery
  - Outdoor ground: clear of debris, stones, branches
- Adequate lighting
  - Replacement bulbs available
  - Extra light sources available
- Adequate ventilation and comfortable temperature
- Adequate acoustics or voice amplification system so participants can hear the TRS clearly
- Receptacles to dispose of garbage and recyclables

Furnishings

- Arranged to allow ease of movement and use
- Arranged to facilitate either interaction or privacy
- Furniture: not ripped or torn
- Tables and chairs: stable, not "tippy"
- Tabletops and other surfaces: clean, not sticky
- Chairs: comfortable, able to provide support

Equipment

- Electrical cords: not frayed
- No loose parts or sharp edges
- Adequate storage to avoid "runaway" balls, clutter, and misuse
- Exercise mats: not worn too thin
- Functional smoke alarms and carbon dioxide detectors

Protective Gear and Equipment

- Hats, sunscreen, long-sleeved tops
- Helmets, knee and elbow pads, gloves, goggles, swim caps
- First aid kit
- Hand sanitizers
- Drinking water

Location

- Proximity to rest rooms
- Emergency procedures clearly posted

Barriers to Participation in Physical Activity

Despite the benefits of physical activity, the TRS may encounter resistance among clients as he encourages them to engage in exercise, sport, or other LTPA (Williams, 2008). The word "exercise" may elicit the reaction that it is boring, is repetitive, and requires too much physical effort. Barriers to participation include lack of confidence; lack of motivation; laziness; misperceptions about exercise; poor body image; beliefs held by older women that "it isn't ladylike to sweat" or by people from cultures that view exercise as inappropriate for females; or one's negative past experiences with exercise and sport. The creative TRS will be familiar with the range of physical activities, exercise, and sports that can promote health and fitness; will have resources to expand programming, such as DVDs, electronic systems like Wii and DDR, and specialized instruction; and will enlist the support of other members of the team and the client's family to encourage exercise participation. Changing clients' attitudes toward physical activity and helping them develop a habit and routine of ongoing exercise may be one of the most challenging responsibilities the TRS faces in promoting healthy behaviors. The TRS is also a role model of healthy behavior. She should be engaged in her own efforts to attain and maintain physical fitness and can share her experiences with her clients.

External barriers to participation in physical activity also exist. People's efforts to participate can be hampered by lack of accessible, affordable community-based facilities; family members who do not support or encourage the client's physical activity; and staff who do not understand the importance of physical activity or lack the knowledge or skill to assist people with disabilities. But providing opportunities can have valuable results. For example, a group that may have had few opportunities to participate in physical activity is clients with severe mental illness. In one study, 62 adults diagnosed with schizophrenia were assigned to two groups (Perham & Accordino, 2007). The experimental group participated in at least 30 minutes of exercise twice a week for three months. Compared to the control group, they improved their hygiene and their pursuit of independence, supporting the hypothesis that improved physical fitness could lead to increased feelings of control over one's life. To be sure that all clients have opportunities to participate in physical activity, the TRS can promote family-friendly physical activities; can serve as an advocate for clients' rights and needs to exercise,

---

5As Approach to Encouraging Physical Activity

Assess
Advise
Agree
Assist
Arrange

---

to participate in sports, and to have access to inclusive programs that are welcoming and inviting; and can educate the family, staff, and community on effective methods and techniques to facilitate participation.

Programming Guidelines for Physical Activity

Five steps for physical activity programming (Rimmer, 1998) have been adapted for TR to help the TRS plan and conduct safe, stimulating, and effective physical activity programs:

1. **Get physician approval.** Before beginning any physical activity, exercise, or sport program, the TRS should obtain physician referrals for his clients. This not only ensures that the client has no contraindicating conditions for a particular activity but also serves to motivate the client to be active. Research has shown that physician support increases adherence to exercise (Kunstler, 2000). Physicians are being encouraged to recommend physical activity to their patients using the 5As approach (Meriwether et al., 2008): Assess, Advise, Agree, Assist, Arrange. Briefly, this approach involves assessing the individual's physical status, advising her to become physically active, getting her to agree to do so, assisting her with referrals, and making arrangements if necessary. Taking this approach, coupled with identifying the patient's stage of change (see chapter 7), can increase exercise participation and adherence. The TRS may find it helpful to use the 5As as well. In addition to working with the medical provider, the TRS may find it valuable to consult with the physical therapist to reinforce the

actions and skills addressed during physical therapy in TR programs.

2. **Increase physical activity throughout the day.** Opportunities are available to increase the amount of physical activity people engage in on a daily basis. Although the measurable benefits of these changes are not always apparent, they help to create a mindset and a momentum that encourage being physically active. Taking the stairs instead of the elevator, moving one's arms and legs while one is seated, lifting light weights periodically, and incorporating a few minutes of movement into any TR program are easy ideas to implement. Engaging in active play, walking a dog, doing chores, and taking up a hobby are ways to get more physical activity on a daily basis.

3. **Choose the right exercise program.** An important TR goal is the development of lifelong participation in physical activity. The TRS can use the benefits-based approach to determine what aspects of a particular activity would motivate and sustain participation. Physical activities, exercise, and sport can be done alone, in small or large groups, or as a member of a team. They can be cooperative or competitive. They range in skill from very low to very high. They can be as structured as counting repetitions and sets in weight training to as free form as creative dance. Any sport or activity can be adapted for participation by a person with a disability, be it physical, cognitive, social, or emotional. Different activities provide opportunities to socialize and to be part of a group, or to compete, or to be outdoors, or to relax. The TRS's assessment and knowledge of the client will help guide him to the right choices. People's needs and interests may change over time and with variations in health, functioning, and social supports. By exploring a range of options, the TRS helps the client keep the door open for adjustments in his choices. Many books, DVDs, CDs, and other resources are available on the market that provide step-by-step instruction in fitness programs. A quality comprehensive fitness program clearly outlines a routine that begins with basic movements and stretches, engaging the entire body, and gradually increases the number of repetitions, level of difficulty, and rigorousness of the routine.

4. **Exercise a minimum of three days a week.** The TRS should offer daily physical activity programs. Structured exercise can be alternated with sports or physical activities such as gardening, walking, biking, in-line skating, or dancing. Weight training should be performed on at least two days with a day of rest in between. Daily activity helps develop the habit of engaging in physical activity as a part of one's regular routine. Setting goals, time management, stress management, and use of motivational techniques will motivate clients to adhere to a physical activity program (Nowicka, 2005).

5. **Keep the program fun and rewarding.** A TR physical activity program should be fun and enjoyable. Depending on the needs of the clients, some may enjoy variation in their exercise routines and others may prefer more consistency. For those with impaired cognitive skills, consistent routines work best because they are familiar and easily understood and followed. Change may produce frustration, may decrease interest, and could lead to dropping out of the program. The TRS must gauge the participant's willingness for change and adjust the program accordingly. For others, repetitive routines can get boring. Using a variety of music and movements maintains interest, creates excitement, enhances motivation, and adds challenge. Keeping up with new trends in exercise ensures that programs are timely and can ease a client's transition to community-based programs because she knows the latest activities. Programs such as yoga, tai chi, qigong, karate, and aquatic exercise may have been outside of a client's experience, so conducting different types of activities can help clients experiment to see what best fits their needs and interests. Active games such as relay races and obstacle courses are popular with children and teenagers but can be fun for adults as well. Fun aerobic activities such as ultimate Frisbee and circus acrobatics are ways to encourage and sustain involvement in physical activity (Leitner & Leitner & Associates, 2004).

Combining physical activity with a cognitive component that teaches its relationship to health, well-being, and one's desired outcomes enables clients to understand its value and connect it to their quality of life. Clients may feel more engaged in physical activity if they learn how to take their pulse and calculate their target heart rate (Broach et al., 2000). Dropping out of fitness programs is a widespread phenomenon that has led to the growth of personal training. The TRS can function as a personal trainer, offering individual guidance and coaching. Personal trainers also work with pairs of people; some find this more fun because they can participate together and cooperate on exercises and movements. The TRS should give frequent encouragement and praise. Measuring improvements in physical status and functioning is easy and provides concrete feedback to participants. To make the physical effort rewarding, the TRS can track clients' progress, distribute pedometers, take before and after photos, have a recognition ceremony, or publicize results on a bulletin board or in a newsletter.

Based on Rimmer 1997.

Aquatics

Aquatics is a very popular form of physical activity. Aquatics are activities that take place in or on the water. While boating and fishing are also considered aquatic activities, this discussion focuses on participation in the water for exercise, swimming, or just experiencing the benefits of being in a water-based environment. One major benefit of the aquatic environment is that it is "freeing," allowing movement that could not be accomplished on land (Carter et al., 2003) and that does not cause pain (Broach & Dattilo, 2000). Another benefit of aquatics is that it is enjoyable and promotes socialization. In a recent study of people with multiple sclerosis who participated in aquatic therapy, they all reported that it was an enjoyable intervention (Broach, Dattilo & McKenney, 2007). People tend to gravitate to water, and it provides a setting for social interaction (Edginton et al., 2004). A third benefit is that aquatics supports inclusion. Swimming usually ranks as one of the most popular leisure pursuits in the United States and Canada (Kraus, 1997), and being able to swim or enjoy the water is a normalizing experience for people with disabilities. If clients develop interest and skills in aquatics in the treatment setting, they will find many opportunities to participate in this type of activity in the community. While many TR programs may not have a pool within the facility, the TRS could develop a collaborative program with a pool in a site such as another health care facility, a school, or a community or recreation center. Water is a universal environment that can provide multiple benefits to any participant. The TRS has the obligation to extend this opportunity, if available, to her clients.

Benefits of Aquatics

Aquatic activities require the following skills and produce the following benefits:

- Physical: gross motor skill, sensory perception, breath control, range of motion, relaxation of muscles, circulation, strength, endurance
- Cognitive: awareness of surroundings, ability to follow safety precautions and instructions, sense of direction, counting skill
- Affective: experiencing enjoyment; increasing self-esteem; relaxation; feelings of empowerment, mastery, and control; fun, challenge, and excitement
- Social: cooperation, social interaction, maturity

Risk Management

There is little physical risk in carrying out the physical movements in aquatic activities. Water provides a natural support and puts minimal stress and strain on the body. There is a risk of skin irritation as a reaction to the chlorine in the pool. Also, some people are bothered by the smell of chlorine. Clients may wish to wear goggles to keep water out of their eyes. The major risks inherent in aquatic programming are the risk of drowning and risks related to conditions in which aquatic activity is contraindicated or conditions that require specific safety procedures, such as seizures (see Broach & Dattilo). A sufficient staff-to-client ratio must be maintained to provide adequate supervision.

Whether indoors or outdoors, in a swimming pool or a natural body of water, all aquatics programs must be supervised by qualified lifeguards who are trained in all first aid and safety procedures. A client's head may go under water and he may swallow water or become frightened or disoriented. Swallowing excessive amounts of water or breathing in water through the nose can cause drowning in rare instances. Staff need to be able to reach a client in a few seconds to minimize any adverse physical or emotional reactions. Safety equipment should be within arm's reach. Flotation devices can be placed at regular intervals around the pool. Personal flotation devices or life jackets may be recommended depending on the clients' abilities and the location of the program. Clients should be instructed or guided to wear appropriate swimwear that provides sufficient coverage of the body. They should not wear dangling jewelry that may become tangled. Some participants may wish to wear swim shoes to cushion their feet or provide traction. The TRS should also dress appropriately. The pool deck should be checked periodically for excess water to reduce the risks of slipping and falling. Glass and other breakables should not be allowed in the pool area.

Clients may experience emotional risks if they are afraid of the water or of putting their head under water, or as they transition into the aquatic environment, which permits more physical freedom than they may be accustomed to. The TRS should offer words of encouragement, a reassuring presence, and physical support as needed.

Aquatic Programming

Most aquatic programs have three goals: to provide a safe aquatic experience, to encourage fun and enjoyment, and to develop skills (Edginton et al., 2004). These goals can be addressed in the three types of aquatic programming that can be offered by TR:

● **Adapted aquatics.** An adapted aquatics program is ideal for any client who wishes to learn to swim. Swimming has many health benefits, including improved cardiovascular fitness, muscle strength, balance, easing of stiff joints, relaxation of stiff muscles, and overall relaxation and stress reduction. Swimming "is regarded as an almost perfect form of exercise, improving the strength and flexibility of everything from one's neck to one's toes, without the injuries and strains that often result from other kinds of exercise" (Kraus, 1997, p. 135). It also has social benefits, enabling people with disabilities to interact in an environment in which they are free from wheelchairs, crutches, braces, canes, and other physical supports.

To teach clients to swim, the TRS must have appropriate Red Cross certification as a Water Safety Instructor (WSI) and must be knowledgeable about teaching methods to use with people with limitations. Two teaching methods, the Halliwick method and the Dolan method, are currently used by TRSs. The Halliwick method is safe for people of all ages and with any type of disability. The Dolan method was developed specifically for people with autism (see Broach & Dattilo, 2000). Teaching swimming to children under 4 years old is not recommended, because they are not developmentally ready for formal swim lessons, and should not be promoted as a means to reduce the risk of drowning. However, there are classes geared toward enjoyment of the water for this age group and for infants and toddlers; adults should provide "touch supervision" at all times (Preboth, 2001).

● **Aquatic fitness.** Aquatic fitness programs involve exercising in the water. Frequently provided as a half-hour group session, this type of program is appropriate for swimmers and nonswimmers as a way to engage in a fun and beneficial physical activity, usually accompanied by music. Participants stand in waist- to chest-high water, with the instructor in the pool or at poolside. Pool temperature should be warm, 83-88 degrees, and flotation devices can be used. The participants need a swimsuit; waterproof shoes for cushioning and traction are optional according to preference. Traditional aerobic exercise routines can be followed. Ai Chi, a program designed to increase range of motion, mobility, and relaxation, combines deep breathing with slow, full movements (Broach & Dattilo, 2000). There are also one-to-one aquatic fitness interventions, such as Watsu and Bad Ragaz, in which the TRS moves the client through movement patterns to enhance typical functioning. The TRS utilizing these methods should be thoroughly trained to do so. The Arthritis Foundation also offers training and certification to any individual who wishes to conduct an aquatic exercise program for individuals with arthritis and related conditions. This is a recreational program designed to improve flexibility and muscle strength and to reduce pain and stiffness. The potential for harm to consumers in aquatic fitness group activities is considered low (Salzman, 2007).

● **Aquatic therapy.** Although "aquatic therapy" is sometimes considered the umbrella term for all three types of aquatic programming for people with disabilities, the American Medical Association views aquatic therapy as a therapeutic modality and procedure that is not restricted to practice by any single profession. The potential for harm in providing aquatic therapy as a treatment modality exists. Therefore, any practitioner conducting an aquatic therapy program must be certified or licensed by her profession as well as certified in aquatic therapy. A TRS so qualified could bill third-party payers to be reimbursed for her services. However, for aquatic therapy treatment to be a reimbursable service, documentation must specify that the water environment is necessary for the client and that the goal of the treatment is to produce functional gains. Conditioning and improving overall fitness are not considered reimbursable outcomes (Salzman, 2007).

Besides these three types of aquatic activity, the TRS should consider using the pool as a setting for other types of programs. A pool party could introduce reluctant people to the pool environment and get them used to the atmosphere in order to encourage them to try aquatics. The novelty of the environment can promote socialization. The TRS can organize games in the pool. The pool area also can be set up for relaxation, with soothing music, aromatherapy, and dim lighting. Some clients may just enjoy lounging in the water with its calming motion. The TRS can combine several activities in one program, such as aquatic exercise to warm up, swimming instruction, free swim, water games, and a relaxing cool-down (Levine, 2001). An activity protocol for aquatics that combines stretching, aerobics, and relaxation is available (Carter et al., 2003). Outdoor aquatic activities for people with disabilities now include scuba diving and surfing (Fazio, 2008), which enhance the aquatic experience by providing novelty and adventure.

In addition to the 5As used to encourage physical activity, there are 5As for successful aquatics programming for people with disabilities (Stein, 2002):

1. Total accessibility of all facilities
2. Appropriate accommodations for full participation
3. Positive attitudes on the part of people with disabilities and all service providers
4. Advocacy for aquatics and self-advocacy by people with disabilities
5. Assimilation into environments with nondisabled family, friends, and peers

These guidelines will help ensure that all people have opportunities to experience the joys and benefits of aquatics programming.

Aquatic programming encompasses far more than just swimming.

Photo courtesy of Robin Kunstler.

The TRS's responsibility is to educate, promote, and advocate for a physical activity program for all populations for whom she is providing services. The values of exercise and physical fitness cannot be underestimated and must be appropriately included in a comprehensive TR program. It is the role of the TRS to provide physical activity and exercise programs that address the current needs of the clients and that will improve their present conditions, address their future goals, and endorse healthy lifestyles. The TRS should be knowledgeable about the various programs available and about which health conditions they most effectively address.

Relaxation and Stress Management

Everyone has a need for **relaxation.** Being relaxed means being in a calm and peaceful state of mind, with minimal bodily tension. The TRS will find that many of his clients have a need to reduce the stress and tension that accompany their illnesses and disabilities in both acute and long-term care settings (Kraus & Shank, 1992), in addition to the typical causes of stress in everyday life. Stress is very subjective. What is stressful for one person may not be the least bit stressful for the next. Although stress was originally conceptualized by Hans Selye as the nonspecific response of the body to any demand for change, it quickly took on a negative association as a cause of strain or tension (American Institute of Stress [AIS], 2008). Selye actually believed that stress could have a positive effect, up to a point, in increasing a person's productivity; this may help explain why not everyone reacts to a particular situation in the same way. However, once a person reaches that point or peak, the negative effects of stress may occur. It is estimated that stress-related problems account for 75 to 90 percent of visits to physicians (AIS, 2008). Stress is a possible contributor to heart disease, high blood pressure, atherosclerosis, irritable bowel syndrome, ulcers, anxiety disorders, and substance abuse, as well as a trigger of nausea, headaches, hair loss, and fatigue (Ford-Martin, 2005).

Benefits of Relaxation and Stress Management

Programs that help clients relax and learn effective and feasible personal relaxation strategies are becoming more and more prevalent in TR as contemporary life continues to have negative effects on health and well-being. Selye emphasized

HEALTH

enjoying life's pleasures, social interaction, and self-expression as ways to manage stress (Leitner & Leitner & Associates 2004); these also are outcomes of recreation experiences. Clearly, helping people develop a repertoire of recreation activities that promote relaxation and reduce stress may relieve health problems and contribute to clients' well-being. Many recreation activities bring about relaxation, which is a major motivation for participation. Although each of us will find our own foolproof method—music, dancing, walking, reading, talking, exercise, yoga, tai chi, meditation, or knitting—there are several programmatic approaches a TRS can take. She can conduct a formal stress management group, introduce clients to a variety of relaxation techniques and a range of recreation activities, or collaborate with other disciplines to offer a comprehensive wellness program.

Relaxation and stress management activities use the following skills and produce the following benefits:

- Physical: gross motor skills, circulation, respiratory functioning, release of muscle tension, pain relief
- Cognitive: concentration, memory, abstract thinking, learning
- Affective: relaxation, anxiety reduction, improved coping, feelings of well-being, positive attitude, relief of anger, fun
- Social: communication, bonding, being part of a group, easing social discomfort

Risk Management

The physical risks involved in relaxation and stress management are no greater than those associated with any physical activities. Emotional risks can occur if participants feel increased anxiety or become upset when discussing the causes of their stress. Also, clients who are not used to engaging in "quiet" activities, such as meditation or yoga, may become uncomfortable and anxious. The TRS should reassure the client, remind her that the purpose of the activity is to reduce the stress, and could suggest an alternative technique.

Programming

Depending on the cognitive functioning level of the clients, the TRS can implement a stress management program using paper-and-pencil activities, group discussion, experimentation with different relaxation techniques, homework exercises, and feedback. Discussion topics could include

- identifying the sources of stress in one's life and physiological and psychological reactions to stress;
- developing coping resources such as relaxation techniques, social supports, and recreation interests; and
- learning strategies for effective use of coping mechanisms, including making a personal stress management plan.

Sources of stress may be real events and situations, such as illness, job, family, or finances, or negative thoughts that create unnecessary stress (Carruthers & Hood, 2002). Reactions to stress include rapid heartbeat, dry mouth, headache, nausea, and feelings of panic. Developing coping resources involves experimenting with different stress management strategies, evaluating their effectiveness, and recognizing when to use them. There are three types of coping strategies:

1. Changing the way one thinks about a situation so that one sees it as challenging rather than intolerable
2. Reducing physiological tension resulting from stress
3. Altering the stressful situation

One often-overlooked strategy that is of great value is learning how and when to ask for help (Grossman & Caroleo, 2001). Successful stress management incorporates not only a set of particular strategies, but also positive social relationships and satisfying recreation interests.

Relaxation Techniques

Relaxation is a process by which people retreat mentally from their surroundings by quieting their thoughts and relaxing their muscles, and maintaining this state long enough to decrease anxiety and tension (DeMarco-Sinatra, 2000). **Relaxation techniques**, which are methods to deal with excess tension brought about by stress, are used to achieve a state of relaxation (Austin, 2009). Therapeutic recreation is a natural venue for practicing relaxation techniques because their effectiveness depends on one's willingness to engage and because engagement in TR is characterized by feelings of control and enjoyment. Many relaxation techniques can be taught by a TRS with a reasonable degree of preparation. Visualization, guided imagery, breathing, self-massage, and meditation are at the forefront of self-help relaxation methods that the TRS can introduce to his clients.

"Doing nothing" and the **minute vacation** (Leitner & Leitner & Associates, 2004) are other examples of relaxation techniques that can be done anywhere and can produce a relaxation effect very quickly. A minute vacation involves simply stopping what you are doing, sitting still with your eyes closed, and letting your mind relax or drift. It's surprisingly refreshing. Other techniques involve only minor preparation or equipment, such as aromatherapy, shoulder massage, and listening to music. More complex relaxation systems include yoga, qigong, and tai chi. These involve a series of gentle exercises and breathing that have the beneficial effects of centering a person's breathing and mental focus, stretching and exercising the body, and producing physiological and psychological relaxation. Research findings on the success of these approaches are very extensive. For example, using meditation, guided imagery, and breathing techniques in conjunction with self-expression through words, drawings, and movement, 82 adolescents with posttraumatic stress disorder from war-torn Kosovo were able to significantly reduce their symptoms (Gordon et al., 2009). Therapeutic recreation specialists may wish to become trained in these techniques so they can conduct their own groups.

A different type of relaxation program is a **relaxation room** (Foose & Ardovino, 2008), a soothing environment designed for individuals who are particularly susceptible to overstimulation, such as children with autism. A room with beanbag seating, pillows, soothing music, soft lighting, and aromatherapy can offer a respite from environmental stimuli. If a facility cannot designate a specific room to be set up permanently for relaxation, the TRS can set one up at designated times using portable equipment and supplies.

Physical Activity and Exercise

The body's natural response to stress is to move. Sustained and repetitive total body physical activity such as stretching, walking, aerobics, swimming, running, biking, or engaging in sport is effective in stress management. Activities range from simple to complex and vary in the amount of preparation required for participation. Regular participation in physical activity can help people keep their negative stress reactions at a manageable level.

Hobbies

Hobbies that require concentration and repetition of action have been found to promote positive health outcomes. Recently, the traditional activities of knitting and crocheting have resurged in popularity,

with one in three American women (53 million), and more and more men, participating. The relaxation effect these hobbies produce has been found to be similar to that of meditation, tai chi, or yoga, with decreases in heart rate and blood pressure. Knitting and crocheting have been introduced at Gilda's Clubs, for families coping with cancer, and at the Duke University Fitness and Diet Center to help weight loss clients reduce their stress (Ford-Martin, 2005). Journaling and other writing activities also are an effective form of stress release. Helping clients develop a hobby may be one of the best gifts we can give them. The benefits inherent in recreation participation can be realized through a hobby. Physical health, skill development, improved self-esteem, positive attitude, enhanced social interactions, and ongoing engagement in a fulfilling and meaningful leisure experience can all result from participation in a hobby. Helping a person find a suitable hobby should entail several considerations (Bartalos, 1993):

- The need the activity might fulfill, that is, to be physical, to experience solitude, to be productive and of service to others
- The type of activity a person might want to pursue over the long term, which may be different from the activity used to produce a functional outcome in the treatment setting
- Availability of resources to pursue a hobby that is appropriate to one's age, health, and financial capabilities
- The enjoyment the activity gives a person, so that it is not a chore but a truly significant experience

Knitting uses fine motor skills, offers opportunities for creativity and relaxation, and provides the satisfaction of a finished product.

Photo courtesy of Patrick Brune.

HEALTH

Humor

"Laughter is the best medicine." This may be a cliché, but it is one that is supported by scientific evidence. Incorporating humor into activities, as well as implementing a therapeutic humor or humor therapy program, can help clients relax, reduce anxiety, and distract them from their pain (Williams & Dattilo, 2000). Telling jokes or funny stories, comedy CDs and movies, clowning, and even laughter yoga are used in humor programs. Laughter, the body's response to humor, is usually a spontaneous physiological response with no negative side effects, which is similar to the response produced by exercise (Leitner & Leitner & Associates, 2004). Laughter also changes the emotional climate, serving as a transition from negative feelings to a more positive outlook, as well as promoting improved cognitive functioning, such as memorization skills (Williams & Dattilo, 2000). It also facilitates communication and creates a bond among people. Besides a humor therapy group, the TRS can create a "humor corner" or center with a bulletin board on which jokes, cartoons, and humorous photographs and pictures are posted. "Toys" that make people smile or laugh such as bubbles, puppets, or whoopee cushions can create a welcome diversion or break the ice in a new situation or group. A humor cart can be stocked and taken around to various locations, including bedside. Humor is beneficial for families and visitors as well. Staff can also use humor as a way to reduce their own stress and to cope with the emotional demands at work. A comedy club can be a creative way for clients, staff, and families to perform as comedians and create as well as respond to humor. Clowning has become popular in pediatric hospital units and in long-term care for the elderly and terminally ill. Clowns can make room visits and do magic tricks, and their costumes can stimulate laughter and reduce tension.

Another activity used in TR is laughter yoga, which was developed in 1995 to extend the benefits of laughing to people in the absence of a humorous stimulus (www.laughteryoga.org). Laughter yoga consists of a 15- to 30-minute session combining simulated laughing or laughter exercises, rhythmic clapping, chanting "ho, ho, ha, ha, ha," yoga breathing, and stretching. This can be helpful for people who say they don't have a sense of humor in that it will still provide the benefits of laughter. Engaging in laughter yoga for more than 30 minutes is not recommended. Some people may experience pain or discomfort in attempting certain yoga positions; however, yoga practice emphasizes listening to your own body and not going beyond what is comfortable.

While many humorous situations are universal, there are cultural views on what is funny. The TRS should reduce the risk that a humor group will offend people or make them uncomfortable. He should begin the group by asking clients what makes them laugh, when they laugh and with whom, and whether they can laugh at themselves or at difficult situations (Austin, 2009). He should take care to explain a joke that anyone finds bewildering or misunderstands. There's a reason "Just kidding" is a common phrase. Clients who are paranoid, or people who are extremely sensitive that others may be making fun of them, may not be good candidates for humor therapy. Also, some people are frightened by clowns. The TRS has the ethical responsibility to do no harm to clients, to treat them with respect, and to be competent in his use of stress management approaches. He should be sure to laugh "with" clients, not "at" them, and serve as a role model of appropriate behavior.

Health-related activities offer the potential to promote positive health as participants learn new activities or variations on familiar ones. They also provide a multitude of benefits as well as the opportunity for clients to achieve critical health outcomes. The TRS should incorporate health-related activities into daily TR programming.

Nature-Oriented Programs

The outdoor environment, nature, plants, and animals offer myriad programming ideas with substantial benefits to TR clients in all types of settings. Even for those with limited access to the outdoors, the TRS can provide programming that captures the qualities and elements of nature to provide benefits and help clients achieve a number of outcomes.

■ Outdoor Recreation

Outdoor recreation refers to activities that require "a meaningful and intentional relationship with the natural environment" (Russell & Jamieson, 2008, p. 55). In outdoor recreation, the participant interacts with the natural setting (Edginton et al., 2004). Although it may be pleasant to read or play basketball outside, these activities are not dependent on the natural environment and so are not considered outdoor recreation. This is not to deny the value of engaging in recreation outside. A national survey of Americans showed that 90 percent believe that being outdoors reduces stress and gives them a sense of accomplishment; 79 percent believe that doing outdoor activities with their families has strengthened their family relationships (*Journal of Physical Education, Recreation and Dance*, 2004). Outdoor activities, however, also should contribute to the development of an appreciation and respect for the environment and its natural beauty. People can experience the beauty of nature directly by being outdoors; however, viewing nature through a window, or in films or paintings, is very valuable for those who cannot go outside. Research has shown that hospital patients whose beds were next to a window looking out on trees, compared to those viewing a brick wall, recovered faster (Relf, 2005). The TRS should take every opportunity to bring the outdoors in to clients, as well as bringing them outside.

Benefits of Outdoor Recreation

There are many benefits of outdoor recreation participation for clients in TR programs. Caring about nature and the environment can develop feelings of nurturing and self-worth; seeing oneself in the context of the larger environment can give perspective on problems; feelings of relaxation and harmony are promoted through contact with the outdoors; and outdoor recreation promotes physical health through active participation with the natural world.

Outdoor recreation requires the following skills and produces the following benefits:

- Physical: gross motor skills, cardiovascular endurance, muscle strength, fine motor skills, balance, ability to use equipment
- Cognitive: attention span, concentration, strategy, problem solving, awareness of one's surroundings, ability to follow safety procedures, memory, sense of direction, judgment, respect for the environment
- Affective: enjoyment, frustration tolerance, coping with stress, relaxation, appropriate expression of emotions, aesthetic appreciation, self-esteem, internal locus of control
- Social: teamwork, group cooperation, ability to give and receive feedback, appropriate social behaviors, leadership

Risk Management

Risk management takes on a whole new meaning in the outdoor environment. Safety of participants is paramount, but the element of risk is also a meaningful characteristic of outdoor recreation. Despite the physical risks involved, preparedness goes a long way toward minimizing unnecessary risk while maintaining the excitement of the outdoor experience. The TRS should be sure that clients are capable of the physical demands of the activity, with or without assistance and adaptations, but must respect the client's right to risk. Buddy systems are very effective in the outdoors in enabling participation by those with physical and cognitive limitations. Participating in outdoor recreation involves rules that the TRS should review with the group before they embark on their experience. She should provide training to participants on safe use of equipment, first aid, and proper procedures for carrying out the activities. She should be well equipped with maps, cell phones, flashlights, extra batteries, drinking water, a first aid kit, rain gear, and blankets. All equipment must be inspected before the program to ensure that it is in good working order. If clients have dietary or nutritional needs, such as the need to snack frequently, these must be provided for. Other considerations are allergies to plants, pollen, or insect bites. Sunscreen, hats, long-sleeved shirts, long pants, proper footwear, and bandanas may be required.

Another risk to consider is emotional risk. To test oneself against nature is challenging and thrilling. Some will find it frustrating, and others will respond with overwhelming emotion. Sensitivity and the ability to judge how to address clients' reactions are the responsibility of the TRS. The TRS must also monitor clients' interactions. Social risks involve being made fun of due to lack of skill, being the object of a trick or practical joke, someone pretending to get hurt, or someone being left behind. Depending on the social maturity of the group, the TRS should step in to redirect socially inappropriate behaviors and help participants see the consequences of these actions (Ewert, Voight & Harnishfeger, 2002).

Outdoor Recreation Programming

Outdoor recreation that can be incorporated into TR programs includes nature walks, bird watching, hiking, bicycling, boating, fishing, gardening, camping, and wilderness activities, depending on location, availability, and facility regulations. People with disabilities can participate in any type of outdoor activity: walking, kite flying, hiking, mountain biking, canoeing and rafting, skiing and snowboarding. Staff who are knowledgeable about the needs and characteristics of people with disabilities can promote success in and enjoyment of outdoor programs by using adapted equipment and by carefully planning and organizing programs (Peniston, 1998). Many organizations, such as Outward Bound, Project Adventure, Wilderness Inquiry, and the National Ability Center, provide a wide variety of outdoor recreation programs. These organizations offer staff training as well as a range of activities, from segregated to inclusive, to meet the needs of clients as they learn new skills and improve their abilities in the outdoor environment.

Camps have been designed for people with all types of needs, including people who are blind or visually impaired; people with muscular dystrophy, diabetes, physical and intellectual disabilities, and cancer; and those recovering from emotional trauma. The value of the camp setting is that it is democratic; everyone encounters the same environment, opportunities, and challenges. For children, camp may be exciting in its novelty; for adults there may be elements of nostalgia as they remember their childhood experiences. An inclusive day camp run by the city of Los Angeles set a goal to help children ages 5 to 8 develop their interpersonal

and social skills. With a TRS and OT collaborating, a full round of activities was developed and successfully offered to the children (Fazio, 2008). In a camp with professional therapeutic staff, the children's individual therapy goals from their individualized education plans (IEP) can be addressed, rather than being abandoned, over the summer. Sleep-away camps often include activities such as sleeping in a tent, animal care, hiking, water sports, and singing around the campfire. These types of activities are normalizing and provide opportunities for fun, challenge, and freedom.

Therapeutic Outdoor Programming

Mastering the challenges of the outdoors is very empowering, builds confidence, and provides the exhilaration of being in nature. These values are the basis for **therapeutic outdoor programming**, an umbrella term for **adventure therapy** and **wilderness therapy**, which utilize direct experience of the outdoors as a treatment intervention as well as structured interventions in the outdoor setting for treatment purposes (Ewert et al., 2002). In adventure therapy, the participants engage in recreation in novel physical and social settings. This atypical environment requires them to develop new skills and behaviors to master the challenges inherent in the situation. The intention is that the new skills and behaviors will carry over to other aspects of their lives. While most adventure therapy takes place outdoors, there are indoor versions with ropes courses, climbing walls, and initiative games that utilize the elements of adventure.

Adventure therapy is a popular technique used with adolescents who have behavioral or criminal problems or psychiatric issues to build trust, teamwork, and problem-solving skills. Teenagers with obesity, eating disorders, delinquent behaviors, and a history of sexual abuse have responded well to the positive use of stress and emphasis on solutions and success, not problems and failure, that is a hallmark of adventure therapy. Adventure therapy also has been used in family counseling as it promotes cohesion and group problem-solving. Facing the challenges of a new environment, working together to overcome obstacles, and reflecting on struggles and accomplishments help to achieve the goals of adventure therapy. People have the opportunity to see themselves and others in a new way. Processing the experience, or debriefing, is a vital component of adventure therapy. As participants reflect on what they have learned and how they can apply this to other issues they face, they develop new insights and strategies. The format "What, So What, and

Now What?" (Austin, 2004) refers to discussing what happened during the program, how participants felt about the experience and their involvement, and how they will use what they learned.

Wilderness therapy is very similar to adventure therapy. The distinction between the two may be that wilderness therapy requires adapting to and coping with the wilderness environment, whereas adventure therapy does not necessarily take place in what is considered a wilderness area. While most TR programs probably will not include opportunities to take clients on a high adventure or wilderness experience, the TRS can utilize the concepts of challenge, positive stress, group problem-solving, and taking initiative in the outdoors to promote positive outcomes.

For example, in a substance abuse treatment program for women, Peggy and Debby go on a nature hike in the state park with the TR group. During the program, Debby gets very frustrated because her feet hurt; she throws down her small backpack and cries out, "I'm not going another step." Peggy supports her, saying "Debby can't go on because she's in pain." The TRS implements a stop-action technique, stopping the group to discuss what is happening (Austin, 2004). She then uses reframing to provide an alternative interpretation of Debby's behavior and reactions. In this way, the outdoor activity becomes a window through which Debby can gain perspective on how she usually handles situations (gives up and starts drinking) and, with the help of her group, find another way to cope (discussing options with members of her support network). The TRS gives Debby the feedback that she is making progress by choosing to problem solve with the group, and encourages her to continue the process. She also guides Peggy to see how she is enabling Debby's less productive behaviors. It can be seen that to lead these programs effectively and safely, the TRS requires the technical skills to do the outdoor activities and the ability to use the techniques of processing and debriefing effectively (as discussed in chapter 7).

The research on the benefits of adventure and wilderness therapy shows that these programs do produce desired outcomes, but that the changes do not usually last over time (Sklar & Autry, 2008; Weston, Tinsley & O'Dell, 1999). It may be helpful to view these interventions as "jump starts" to change, which need to be reinforced with other programming on a long-term basis. However, in one study, adolescents with obesity did maintain their weight loss six months after the completion of an intervention combining adventure therapy and

Robert Cocquyt/fotolia.com

Mastering the challenges of the outdoors is very empowering, builds confidence, and provides the exhilaration of being in nature.

cognitive-behavioral treatment (CBT) as compared to those receiving an aerobic exercise intervention and CBT (Jelalian et al., 2006). It may be that the changes brought about by the adventure therapy had a more profound psychological effect on the adolescents than did the aerobics, thereby promoting their maintenance of healthy behaviors over the long term. Results from another study of 25 youth who participated in an eight-day wilderness canoe trip (Sklar, Anderson & Autry, 2007) point to the need for ongoing programming after the wilderness experience is over. Youth-directed volunteer projects and recreation activities, as well as parental involvement, could maximize the positive benefits the youth attain from wilderness recreation experiences.

■ Horticultural Activities

Incorporating horticulture into a TR program includes the use of plant life and gardening activities to bring about therapeutic outcomes and improve physical and mental health. To be considered true **horticultural therapy,** a program must have a client in treatment for a defined problem, must include a goal that the client is trying to achieve, and must give the client responsibility for the care of living plants (Relf, 2005). Nonetheless, the TRS can

NATURE

conduct numerous horticultural activities: planting seeds and seedlings; growing and nurturing house plants and herb gardens; flower arranging; making bird feeders from pine cones and potpourri from flowers; cooking with foods and herbs grown in gardens; crafts, such as stationery and collages that use dried flowers, leaves, and branches; and making a terrarium or planter as a living legacy. Programs can incorporate aromatherapy using herbs, spices, and flowers or include visits to a garden for purposes such as meditation and relaxation. Given the range of activities related to plant life, it's no coincidence that gardening is considered the most popular leisure activity of Americans. The TRS can organize a regularly scheduled gardening program; have a month-long themed program of crafts and cooking related to the plants, flowers, and foods of the season; use an indoor greenhouse for a relaxation program; and provide sensory stimulation using the colors, aromas, and textures of plants.

Benefits of Horticultural Activities

Caring for plants can help a client see beyond himself and his own issues. Anecdotal evidence demonstrates a wide range of benefits. Growing food plants helped a client with an eating disorder learn to value food because she grew it herself; gardening gave an elderly man a sense of purpose and a means to reconnect with life after the death of his wife; and a client with addiction learned to look after himself in a caring way as a result of gardening (Young, 2007). Making a legacy garden for a loved one helped a woman dying of cancer (Sourby, 1998). Children in the hospital can learn to take their medicine by giving plants their "medicine" of plant food and water. A very simple and popular horticultural activity is making a pine cone bird feeder; the pine cone is smeared with peanut butter, rolled in birdseed, and hung outside a window. Benefits include not only the satisfaction of making something useful, but also sensory stimulation (smelling the peanut butter, seeing the colors of the birds, and hearing them sing). Another benefit may be cognitive stimulation if clients can identify the birds. The TRS may offer other horticultural activities by showing films, inviting garden club members to give lectures, having a flower arranging demonstration, or taking clients on a trip to a botanic garden. The array of options and the varying levels of complexity of the tasks involved in gardening make it an ideal TR program. A program protocol for gardening emphasizes its value as a structured program that can produce physical, cognitive, psychological, and emotional benefits (Grote et al., 1995).

Horticulture requires the following skills and provides the following benefits:

● Physical: fine and gross motor skills, manual dexterity, sensory stimulation, strength

● Cognitive: concentration, following directions, knowledge of plant care and the value of plants, attention span, observation skills, problem solving, weighing alternatives, sense of responsibility, orientation to time, eye–hand coordination

● Affective: caring and nurturing, sense of purpose and feeling needed, self-esteem, sense of accomplishment, appreciation of beauty and the cycle of life, improving mood, experiencing joy, motivation, hopefulness, expression of emotions, fun, relaxation, trust, self-expression, creativity

● Social: teamwork, social interaction, working with a group toward a common goal, networking

Horticultural Therapy Activities

- Pine cone bird feeders: smear pine cone with peanut butter and roll in birdseed
- Planting seeds and cuttings in pots or garden beds
- Flower arranging
- Decorating containers to use as planters
- Herb gardens
- Sachets
- Aromatherapy
- Terrariums
- Nature prints
- Collages from natural objects and pictures
- Jewelry making
- Plant care
- Picking flowers
- Garden club speaker
- Horticulture-themed reading of poetry and other literary works
- Virtual garden tours
- Trips to gardens

NATURE

Risk Management

The TRS should help the clients choose the types of plants and the size of garden that are feasible and within the capabilities of the clients and the program. Risk management concerns include monitoring clients in the outdoors for exertion and sun exposure; knowing poisonous plants and allergic reactions to plants; monitoring for ingestion of soil, plants, or seeds; and safe use of equipment. Hats, sunscreen, drinking water, shaded rest areas, insect repellent, and gardening gloves and shoes are recommended. Clients with learning difficulties or time management or memory problems may forget to tend to the plants or overwater them (Peniston, 1998), which may lead to sadness or guilt. If plants die, the TRS should help the clients accept their responsibility and the cycle of life, which includes the inevitability of death. There is an abundance of adapted equipment that can facilitate participation in gardening by people with disabilities. Raised flower beds and wide, gently graded paths provide access to gardening for people in wheelchairs. It is easy to obtain gardening tools with extended handles, safety grips, and C-clamps and Velcro straps for affixing tools to a participant. A garden bed can be installed on a wheeled cart so that it can be brought to those who are not able to get to a garden (Austin, 2009).

Gardening

Gardening is growing and caring for plants as an enjoyable leisure activity, for the production of food, or for the creation of beautiful landscapes. There are many types of gardens that have therapeutic and health benefits (Relf, 2005):

- Meditation gardens for relaxation, solitude, and contemplation
- Healing gardens that help restore visitors to health
- Therapeutic gardens that are part of a treatment program for physical or psychiatric rehabilitation
- Wandering gardens for people with dementia for the reduction of symptoms such as purposeless wandering
- Horticultural therapy gardens, designed for the care of plants by patients as part of treatment goals, including fun

The TRS may have access to a garden or be able to develop a garden at her facility. Gardens can be of any size. For a meditation or healing garden, a quiet location that has seating and access for wheelchairs

Caring for plants can help a client see beyond herself and her own issues.

peejay - Fotolia

is recommended. A therapeutic or horticultural therapy garden requires more space so that clients can be actively involved in the physical aspects of gardening. A wandering garden requires pathways that facilitate the safe movement of clients. A garden has tremendous potential for programming. A greenhouse can be used during the day for gardening activities that contribute to functional outcomes and during the evening for relaxation to music (Shank & Coyle, 2002).

Recognition of the health benefits of gardening has led to the development of community gardens. **Community gardening** takes place when a group of community members grow flowers and foodstuffs on plots of urban land for personal or collective benefits (Glover, Parry & Shinew, 2005). Benefits include physical exercise, purposeful involvement, stress release, and strengthening of relationships among community members (Worden, Frohne & Sullivan, 2004). As community gardens are now being developed to promote physical and mental health and contribute to creating strong, healthy communities, an inclusive community garden would be an ideal venue for developing and maintaining social networks for clients. The TRS can take the opportunity to develop an inclusive garden that brings together community members and clients. Fazio (2008) identifies benefits of community gardening for diverse client groups:

NATURE

- People with chronic mental illness and developmental disabilities can find a niche in their communities and develop prevocational skills.
- Retirees can contribute their skills and knowledge and feel a sense of purpose.
- People with dementia can experience multisensory stimulation.
- At-risk youth can engage in productive activity.

Older adults choose gardening for the physical and mental health benefits of the exercise, access to fresh food, the sense of accomplishment, and cognitive stimulation through the use of problem-solving strategies (Austin, Johnston & Morgan, 2006). The community garden is also a natural setting for intergenerational programming. The TRS should seek out other community groups to collaborate on a community gardening program. The success of a garden project results from the social interaction of the members as they garden together and share resources, information, and a leisure experience, thereby contributing to a sense of community (Glover et al., 2005). The TRS will find that gardening has great potential to meet a number of functional and existential outcomes.

■ Animal-Assisted Therapy

The human–companion animal bond has long been recognized as a source of comfort and companionship that also provides the benefits of relaxation and stress reduction. Its roots go back to work with psychiatric patients in the 18th century (Zamir, 2006). Florence Nightingale, known as the pioneer of modern nursing (Carter et al., 2003) who cared for wounded soldiers during the Crimean War (1853-1856), wrote in her *Notes on Nursing* in 1873 that "a small pet is often an excellent companion to the sick." Pet therapy, as it was originally named, has grown into the practice of **animal-assisted therapy** (AAT), also known as pet-facilitated therapy (PFT). Since pet therapy implied the used of pets, AAT is seen as a broader definition (Dattilo, Born & Cory, 2000). Animal-assisted therapy can be defined as the "introduction of an animal into an individual's or group's immediate surroundings, with therapeutic intent" (Brodie & Biley, 1999, p. 329). Many articles on the benefits of various formats for AAT, for people of all ages and with all types of health conditions, show that AAT has positive effects on human health (Velde, Cipriani & Fisher, 2005). Although researchers still cite a need for better-designed research, there is ample evidence for the inclusion of AAT in TR programming. "A health professional working within the scope of his or her profession" can utilize live animals in treatment (Curtright & Turner, 2002, p. 61).

Types of Animal-Assisted Therapy Programming

Animal-assisted therapy can involve pet visits, having a resident pet or animals in a facility, taking care of pets, or incorporating an animal into a specific goal-directed intervention. Clients should not be required to interact with animals. Those who do not wish direct contact with animals may get pleasure from looking at them; or they may enjoy watching movies or television shows about animals, reading stories involving animals, or looking at paintings and sculptures of animals. Zhu Zhu is a smart electronic pet, a hamster who may bring the experience of interacting with a pet to someone who has no other means to do so. Animal-related activities can also involve stuffed animals, collecting animal objects, and reminiscing. Dogs, cats, rabbits, birds, and fish are commonly used in AAT. The TRS can do both one-to-one and group programming with animals. Animals can go on room visits or spend time with an individual in a common setting. A TR group can be organized that involves petting animals, playing with them, talking about them, and reminiscing about other animals. The TRS can have clients learn and practice animal care. Animals that are trained and certified as therapy dogs or companion dogs are usually brought to programs by their handlers to provide motivation, sensory stimulation, relaxation, and improved quality of life (Long & Robertson, 2008). Caring for farm animals, **therapeutic horseback riding** (including **hippotherapy**), and swimming with dolphins are forms of AAT that involve more elaborate facilities than are typically available to the TRS; however, there may be opportunities to provide these activities as well.

Benefits of Animal-Assisted Therapy

Animal-assisted therapy provides the following benefits and requires the following skills:

- Physical: fine and gross motor skills, manual dexterity, grasp, reaching, sensory stimulation
- Cognitive: attention span; focus and concentration; knowledge of proper handling, care, and interactions with the animals; learning; problem-solving; judgment; following safety procedures; respect for animals; awareness of environment
- Affective: feelings of caring, nurturing, joy, relaxation, competence, mastery
- Social: interaction with animals and others, cooperation, sharing a mutual experience

NATURE

Risk Management

Risk management concerns relate to protecting both the human participants and the animals. Policies, procedures, and protocols regarding AAT are very important. Adequate space is necessary to allow for ease of movement of the animals and the people. Beware of someone tripping over an animal or moving a wheelchair over a tail or paw. In institutional settings, if animals are allowed on beds or other furniture, a protective covering can be put down (Jalongo, Astorino & Bomboy, 2004). After a visit with an animal, hand washing or use of sanitary hand wipes is essential, although there are no reported cases of animals passing infections to humans (Cullen, Titler & Drahozal, 2003). However, allergies to cats, dogs, rabbits, guinea pigs, birds, and horses are not uncommon; and people should be screened for allergic reactions. Although therapy animals are trained and certified, a visiting animal may be provoked to scratch or nip. Despite the perception that horseback riding is a risky activity, there are extremely low incidences of injury at therapeutic riding centers (Benda, 2005). Children with emotional and behavioral disorders should be carefully supervised to prevent them from teasing or otherwise annoying an animal.

In addition to physical risks, there are emotional risks. People become emotionally attached to animals. If an animal dies, moves out of the facility, or leaves the AAT program, clients may experience loss and grief. The TRS should be sensitive to the depth of the feelings of clients toward animals. A client can become upset if animals are visiting others. On the other hand, some clients may be afraid of or not interested in animals. Their wishes should be respected. Some people from Middle Eastern and Southeast Asian cultures believe that dogs are unclean or a nuisance. Working with people from these regions, the TRS should determine their wishes regarding AAT prior to implementing the program. A warm-up activity can be conducted prior to the visit of an animal to get people ready for the visit. The TRS can ask clients about their previous experiences with animals, whether they had pets, and how they feel about the upcoming pet visit (Dattilo et al., 2000).

Although many populations with physical and emotional concerns have effectively participated

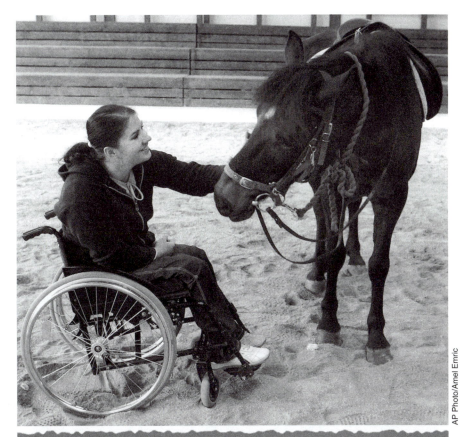

Interacting with animals is a normalizing experience for clients.

AP Photo/Arnel Emric

in horseback riding, there are groups for whom it is contraindicated, including those with severe psychiatric symptoms, severe mental retardation, uncontrolled epilepsy, scoliosis with a curvature of more than 30 degrees, or a tendency to develop decubitus ulcers (Bliss, 1997). Clients on medications that impair concentration and balance should not ride (Bizub, Joy & Davidson, 2003). Protective equipment such as helmets and safety belts or body harnesses attached to the waist, saddle pads, special stirrups and reins, and mounting ramps is available (Sausser & Dattilo, 2000).

Animal-Assisted Therapy With Children and Youth

Interacting with animals is fun—a normalizing experience for children whose lives are constrained by illness, disability, or life circumstances—and can help a child develop a sense of responsibility and feelings of love and nurturance. Children with pets have been found to have better coping strategies than children without pets. When dealing with trauma from war or sexual abuse, children found more support from animals than from people, were more motivated to interact, and were better able to deal with stress (Delta Society, 2008). Being with animals also improves children's moods and has a calming effect. Children who are fearful and resistant to receiving medical and dental care become more relaxed and compliant even if a therapy dog is merely present in the treatment room.

Interesting results have been obtained in children with autism and pervasive developmental disorders (PDD). An in-depth study of three children with autism and their families demonstrated that the children displayed behaviors toward their pets that they rarely showed toward their families (McNicholas & Collis, 1995). The children hugged their pets, confided in them, and took comfort from their presence; yet these behaviors are contrary to the criteria used to diagnose autism! In another study, 10 children with PDD, ages 3 to 13 years, were more playful, more energetic, more focused, and more aware of their environment when they played with a dog, as compared to a ball or a stuffed animal, after having completed 45 sessions of 15 minutes each (Martin & Farnum, 2002). Children are now participating in programs with dogs that have been trained as Reading Education Assistance Dogs (R.E.A.D.). Children with weak reading skills may feel anxiety and stress as they try to improve their skills. However, in a study of children with Asperger's syndrome (Jalongo, 2005), children read aloud to a dog to practice their reading skills, which stimulated their interest, decreased disruptive behaviors, and lowered their blood pressure and heart rate. In other R.E.A.D. programs, teachers reported that children were less intimidated about reading, showed greater confidence, forgot about their limitations, decreased absenteeism, and improved reading scores (Delta Society, 2008). Animals provide unconditional love, nonjudgmental acceptance, and affection (Austin, 2004), which makes them ideal companions for children who feel lonely and insecure, who lack confidence, who are uncomfortable around adults, and who are unable or unwilling to interact with peers.

For older children and adolescents, taking responsibility for the care and training of animals may be a form of vocational training as well. Researchers in one study taught youth in a juvenile facility how to train dogs. These young people had histories of violence, substance abuse, and learning disabilities; they also had poor sense of self, chronic low self-esteem, and difficulty forming and maintaining relationships and were suicidal (McDongall & Jones, 2007). Despite their extensive problems, they were able to develop a sense of responsibility, caring, and patience through their interactions with the dogs. This study demonstrates the powerful impact of human–animal interaction.

The TRS working with children and youth should pursue AAT programming, including animal visits, animals-in-residence, pet care, and animal training. A community-based program for at-risk youth or teens with disabilities could have the teens start a dog walking and grooming service, bring their pets to visit nursing home residents, or volunteer to help elderly or ill people take care of their pets.

Animal-Assisted Therapy With Adults

As much as children are drawn to animals and pets, so are adults. The major benefits of AAT for adults are social support, stress reduction, and relaxation. Various studies have looked at the relationship between dog ownership and high blood pressure, cholesterol levels, anxiety, and social interaction (Delta Society, 2008). Overall, it has been concluded that having a pet can reduce stress and anxiety, increase social interaction with others, and contribute to general quality of life. In one study of almost 6,000 people in Australia, pet owners had lower blood pressure and cholesterol levels than non-pet owners (Delta Society, 1992). Hospital patients got out of bed and spoke for the first time since their admittance when their pets were brought in to visit them; the physiological evidence showed that their stress levels were reduced (Cullen et al., 2003). Four separate studies showed that cancer patients had reduced fear and anxiety as a result of animal visits. The presence of animals in the health care setting also had beneficial effects on reducing stress and burnout in staff (Brodie & Biley, 1999).

Animals can be a means to start up conversations with new people even if those involved don't have direct physical contact with the animal. People often derive comfort from petting an animal on their lap and at the same time can be exercising their fingers and arms. There are several examples of how AAT can be used with a people who have had a stroke (Dattilo et al., 2000). Grooming a dog can improve coordination, grasp, and range of motion; playing catch with the dog can improve eye–hand coordination; and giving commands is a way to practice expressive language skills. The novelty and excitement of interacting with a dog can help increase attention span and provide a topic of conversation between the TRS and client to practice social interaction and memory skills. These effects of interacting can also motivate clients to engage in behaviors that promote their health, such as physical activity as they play with the dog. In another study with stroke patients, patients with aphasia spoke more easily to a dog than with the therapist and had more spontaneous communication (McCauley, 2006). Although AAT in this study produced the same results as traditional therapy, it was more enjoyable for the patients and they looked forward to it more. The comfort and love that a pet provides is indispensable to people with AIDS, cancer, and other debilitating and terminal illnesses. Services have been established to help these patients care for their pets and to obtain homes for their pets after they die, which reduces the worry and anxiety they may have over what will become of a beloved companion.

An adapted saddle horn allows Geri (far right) to ride a horse.

Photo courtesy of Geri Pinciaro Mariano.

Animal-Assisted Therapy With Older Adults

Having a pet or maintaining contact with animals can be very valuable for many older adults for whom aging brings illness, loss of a spouse, and new living arrangements. Many long-term care facilities have adopted the Eden Alternative, an approach that creates an environment of people, plants, and animals (Shank & Coyle, 2002). In an "Edenized" nursing home, indoor and outdoor plants, gardens, dogs, cats, birds, and rabbits receive care from the residents and in turn provide the biodiversity found in everyday life. The Eden Alternative seeks to transform an institution dedicated to professional care into a community of living things. Staff may initially be resistant to these changes. However, the Eden approach closely reflects the aims of TR to promote well-being and quality of life (Shank & Coyle, 2002). Facilities using the Eden approach note increased family involvement and satisfaction, with greater communication among the families, residents, and staff. While the Eden Alternative represents a major shift in thinking regarding how nursing homes often operate, elements of this approach can be incorporated through the integration of plants, animals, intergenerational programming, and more opportunities for residents to take responsibility for caring for other living things.

Animal-Assisted Therapy With Clients With Dementia

Much research has been conducted on AAT and older adults with Alzheimer's disease (AD). In one case, an older man with AD refused to take a bath (DeGeest, 2007). He was usually observed clutching a small book. The therapist got him to show her the book, which turned out to be a photo album with pictures of his dog, including some of the dog taking a bath. The therapist engaged him in conversation about the dog, and eventually he agreed to take a bath himself. This case illustrates the powerful attachment people may have to a pet and suggests how that bond can be used to move someone toward a healthy behavior. People with dementia have demonstrated less agitation and more social interaction as a result of AAT and more purposive interaction during puppy visits (Curtright & Turner, 2002). These visits were a vehicle for reminiscence, socialization, sensory stimulation, communication, and emotional expression. The TRS can ask questions, encourage petting, and reflect the feelings of the clients as they interact with the animals. Photos of these interactions can be taken and displayed. Clients can make pet treats to serve to their animal visitors. Even if there is no contact with an animal during a pet visit, the animal can become a topic of conversation. Another intervention that does not utilize direct contact is an aquarium. In one study, having an aquarium in the dining room resulted in increased food intake and weight in persons with AD (Edwards & Beck, 2002). An aquarium, bird habitat, or bird feeders outside the window can add a great deal of sensory stimulation, increase social interaction, and become a natural gathering place. Computer programs and CDs also are available that visually display an aquarium, with accompanying bubbling sounds.

Therapeutic Horseback Riding

The recognition that horses have therapeutic value goes back to the ancient Greeks, who offered horse rides to people with illnesses that were considered

NATURE

untreatable and incurable (Bizub et al., 2003). Therapeutic horseback riding is a broad term that includes equine-assisted activities (E-AA) and equine-assisted therapy (E-AT). Equine-assisted activity involves learning horse-related skills, such as riding and grooming, to improve one's quality of life; in E-AT, a therapist uses the horse as an intervention in goal-directed treatment. Hippotherapy is a specific form of E-AT in which physical, occupational, and speech therapists utilize equine movement as a treatment to meet goals. It does not include teaching horseback riding; rather, the movement of the horse is a form of therapeutic intervention. Given these definitions, we can see that TR can both offer therapeutic horseback riding as a TR program and collaborate with other therapies to help clients achieve therapeutic goals. Contrary to what might be assumed, there are hundreds of facilities in the United States that offer these opportunities. Therapeutic horseback riding has been used successfully with children and adults who have physical, developmental, and emotional difficulties. Its use is now being expanded to wounded war veterans.

Several recent research studies illustrate the benefits of this activity. In one study of children with cerebral palsy, hippotherapy was compared to sitting astride a barrel to see which approach improved muscle symmetry (Benda, McGibbon & Grant, 2003). The positioning of the child was the same in the two approaches, but with the hippotherapy the movement of the horse was a factor in the intervention. The results showed that riding the horse produced more improvements than did sitting on the barrel. Riding a horse provides a precise, rhythmic, and repetitive pattern of movement similar to the mechanics of the natural human gait. A disability such as cerebral palsy may prevent a child from developing a natural gait, which often takes place during children's play. This research demonstrates that being on a horse is a viable intervention. Other studies have shown that hippotherapy improves posture, balance, breathing, and speech (McCauley & Gutierrez, 2004).

In addition to the actual physical stimulation the client receives from being on the horse, the emotional and psychological benefits are extensive. On a horse, people are free from the adapted devices and equipment they may use for mobility and postural support. They improve their self-concept as they gain a sense of mastery over their fears of being on horseback and begin to perceive that

they have been successful at a sport activity that is thought to be risky (Benda et al., 2003). In children with language-learning disabilities being on horseback triggered spontaneous communication, motivation, and attention, aspects that were seen as factors contributing to the success of hippotherapy over traditional speech therapy (McCauley & Gutierrez, 2004). In one study of children mourning the death of a family member, hippotherapy brought about three important outcomes: increase in overall communication including talking about the deceased, increased self-confidence as the children expressed pride and joy in their riding accomplishments, and greater trust in others (Glazer, Clark & Stein, 2004). The nonclinical environment, the nonjudgmental relationship with the horse, the horse's response to the child's commands, and the trust the horse places in the child were all seen as factors contributing to the outcomes. Similar outcomes were obtained in adults with schizophrenia who rode for 2 hours a week over 10 weeks (Bizub et al., 2003). Overcoming their fears of horseback riding contributed to feelings of empowerment and increased self-esteem and actually led them to make changes in their lives. Venturing into a new environment to do a typical activity reduced the stigma of mental illness and increased their feelings of joy and acceptance. Overall, therapeutic horseback riding is more like play than therapy, and it provides all the benefits and motivation of recreation experiences.

Ethical Issues Regarding AAT

An important ethical issue in AAT relates to the rights of the animals. The TRS and animal handlers must be very vigilant about stress on the animal from too much handling, attention, or commotion. The animals may need quiet time between visits; they should not be forced to participate if they are reluctant, and animal welfare should be a primary concern. Human beings are entrusted with the lives of animals, and a stressed or unwilling animal should not be part of an AAT program. There is a distinction to be made between use and exploitation of animals in AAT (Zamir, 2006). One animal ethicist feels that because dogs and horses have a mutually beneficial and interdependent relationship with people, their participation in AAT is consistent with their welfare (Zamir, 2006). However, he believes that other types of animals, such as rodents, birds, reptiles, and dolphins, gain little from AAT and that their involvement may be considered exploitative. Dolphin-assisted therapy is a controversial area in AAT. There is very little research on swimming with dolphins that has demonstrated its effectiveness over the long term; many believe that the expense and the absence of any standards or regulations preclude recommending it as a therapy. An analysis of six studies on dolphin-assisted therapy with young children with disabilities found no evidence that it was any more effective than other treatments (Humphries, 2003). As respect for living things is consistent with the ethics, principles, and values of TR, the TRS delivering AAT programming must take every action to protect the health and welfare of the animals.

—————

Nature-oriented programs can take place both indoors and outdoors and can impart to participants a respect for nature as they experience its joys and benefits. Interacting with animals, plants, and other aspects of the natural environment fosters a sense of harmony, feelings of accomplishment, and respect and can strengthen a number of skills. The TRS should endeavor to make nature activities a vital part of TR programming, regardless of physical setting.

NATURE

Social Activities

Social activities are probably the most universal of all forms of recreation and interaction. Ranging from the casual and informal conversation to a highly organized trip or special event, social recreation activities give participants opportunities for meaningful communication, the joy of relating to others, and a fun and relaxed atmosphere. They can promote group cohesion, expose participants to new skills, and provide a welcome reprieve from preoccupation with health concerns.

Social recreation "is comprised of the familiar, casual and enjoyable experiences conducted by a leader to promote relaxed and appropriate social behavior within groups" (Valentine, 2006, p. 9). Most TR activities take place in groups that incorporate social interaction as a strength of the TR experience; however, in social recreation the primary purpose of the event is the socializing rather than the activity itself (Edginton et al., 2004). Participating in social recreation makes minimal demands on participants to plan ahead or to possess specialized skills (Valentine, 2006). Social recreation activities are a large part of TR programming because they provide opportunities for interaction, relaxation, and trying out new skills. Social recreation activities can include group games such as charades, relay races, or cards; outings and trips; all types of parties including costume parties, tea parties, and pizza parties; occasions centered on the Super Bowl or other sporting events; holiday celebrations; coffee hours or happy hours; dances, sing-alongs, talent shows, picnics, or barbeques. Social recreation "stresses the informal mixing of people and the enjoyment of casual, noncompetitive socializing activities that are often traditional or folk-like" (Kraus, 1997, p. 139). Electronic socializing using Skype video chats and social networking are only the latest manifestation of this age-old recreation experience. Participation in social recreation generally requires minimal skills, and typically people can join the activity or leave at any point. Icebreakers or mixers are frequently used to promote feelings of comfort and social ease among the participants.

Benefits of Social Recreation

The TRS's main purpose in providing social recreation is to facilitate socialization by designing programs around active participation and interpersonal contact. Many social recreation activities take place in a large group and offer fewer opportunities for the TRS to interact with clients individually to promote achievement of therapeutic goals or outcomes. However, during social recreation, the client experiences a more natural, relaxed setting than the typical treatment environment and may apply skills, such as conversation skills and appropriate social behavior, that he has learned in smaller TR groups. Group interaction in social recreation activities can enhance teamwork, feelings of belonging and loyalty, and cooperation skills. Clients may be able to develop or contribute unique talents to a social recreation event or carry out planning and leadership functions. For some clients, the value of the activity may be in enjoying it as a spectator without being actively involved. Because social recreation encompasses so many types of activities, it has the potential to utilize all types of skills and produce all types of benefits. Benefits particular to the social aspect include the following:

- Physical: use of senses, sensory stimulation, release of muscular tension
- Cognitive: attention span, memory, following directions, awareness of surroundings
- Affective or emotional: fun, enjoyment, relaxation, self-esteem, positive attitude, feelings of well-being, excitement, mastery
- Social: interaction, group identity and cohesion, cooperation, teamwork, sharing, conversation skills, social maturity

Risk Management

Risk management concerns for social recreation and **special events** include all the procedures that cover games, food activities, physical activities, and any other program elements that are involved. However, the large-group nature of these programs means that supervision must be adequate to ensure the safety of all participants. The most successful social recreation activities are those in which the leader has control of the group and the physical arrangements (Valentine, 2006). Close monitoring is needed regarding dietary and activity restrictions, exposure to the outdoor environment, and working order of all equipment. Indoors, hazards from spills must be cleaned up and hazards like slippery floors and blocked thoroughfares attended to quickly. A checklist should be developed for each event to facilitate planning and smooth operations.

Programming

These are three useful guidelines for social recreation programming (Russell & Jamieson, 2008):

- Programs should be appropriate to the characteristics of the participants and the purpose of the group.
- Programs should follow the "social curve" with a definite beginning and end, starting with a low level of excitement that builds to a higher level about midway through the program and gradually subsides toward the end of the activity.
- The leader of the program must be able to recognize when to directly intervene to control the flow of the activity and when to let the program take its natural course. This "reading" of the event's energy and the participants' needs contributes to the success of any TR event.

The mere fact that an activity is social does not necessarily mean everyone will naturally interact; this is important for the TR leader to keep in mind. The TRS's role is to facilitate socialization by introducing clients to one another, making connections between those with common interests, incorporating into the environment the types of stimulation that will promote social interaction, and organizing a sequence of smaller activities to achieve the TR goals. As much as possible the TRS should observe the behaviors of clients during social recreation activities in order to report and document beneficial outcomes. For people with AIDS, for example, social activities offer opportunities to overcome social isolation, develop social support, reduce stress, promote family relationships, and increase food consumption (Grossman & Caroleo, 2001). Social recreation is an excellent opportunity to include family and loved ones in typical activities.

Special Events

Special events may be seen as one type of social recreation. A special event is an opportunity outside of the usual range of choices and beyond typical daily experiences (Edginton et al., 2004). Special events are out-of-the-ordinary activities that generate interest, excitement, enthusiasm, and participation by creating a "buzz." Because of their large scale, special events may give the appearance to other staff, and even clients and their families, that they are diversional rather than therapeutic. The TRS should be mindful to emphasize their therapeutic

In social recreation the primary purpose of the event is the socializing rather than the activity itself.

Human Kinetics/Kelly Huff

SOCIAL

Checklist for Special Events

To ensure a safe and successful special event:

Draw up a list of all planning activities with due dates and contact information for persons responsible for each activity.

Be sure everyone in the facility is well informed in advance about the event, all activities, and how the event will impact their work.

Determine extra staffing needs for escorting participants and for ensuring safety.

Ensure that all areas and facilities are accessible to all. Wheelchair seating should be integrated into typical seating areas. Ensure that people with disabilities can see and hear the events.

Reserve use of all space and equipment well in advance.

Arrange for refreshments, including pickup, delivery, and cleanup.

Be sure that refreshments are available to meet all dietary needs and restrictions.

Ensure a sufficient number of conveniently located receptacles for trash and recyclables.

Post clearly written and easy-to-read signs.

Check for clear pathways for emergency evacuations. Be sure aisles and exits are not blocked.

Be sure that entertainment is age appropriate and meets the prevailing norms and values of the participants. Call entertainers to reconfirm several days prior to the event.

Have an alternative activity available for those who choose not to participate.

Provide all staff with a list of participants who wish to attend. Include any special instructions, such as supplies or clothing participants should bring or location for pickup and drop-off.

Ensure sufficient seating and supplies, extra extension cords, batteries, flashlights, cameras, and keys.

If guests are coming, reserve parking, provide maps, and provide a phone number for them to call if they are lost or have an emergency.

Have a foul-weather backup plan: If the event is to be postponed or canceled or relocated in the event of bad weather, publicize the time by which the decision will be made and how people can find out this information.

Clean up event area, return all equipment and supplies, and replace all furniture and other objects that were moved.

Send thank-you notes or e-mails to all who assisted. Pay all bills.

values. In TR, special events are often used to break up the routine of institutional life or ongoing care, to provide a normalizing experience, to promote common bonds among participants, and to encourage clients to contribute their unique strengths and skills. It can be challenging to provide goal-directed TR leadership in this situation. A way to address the therapeutic value of a special event is to debrief clients who had specific goals that were supported by their participation.

A special event can include a range of activities so that there is something for everyone to do. These can include Olympic-type competitions, art shows, musical or theatrical performances, film festivals, ethnic festivals, graduations or proms, holiday or seasonal celebrations, carnivals, or open houses, to name just a few. It's obvious that special events require extensive and careful planning, but clients can attain benefits in the planning stage and after the event is over. Clients can be members of a planning committee, take on responsibilities during the event, and record the event by taking photos and videos that can be given to families as mementos. These opportunities provide the clients with memories that can be shared in subsequent programs. Special events can involve an entire agency or facility as well as the local community and family and friends. Special events are often used as a marketing or public relations tool to draw attention to the quality, value, and types of services that the sponsor provides. Chapter 9 provides more detail on special events and themed programming.

■ Outings and Trips

Outings and trips are organized activities in which the TRS accompanies an individual or group on an excursion in the community setting. Parks, bowling alleys, swimming facilities, shops, restaurants, museums, theme parks, movies, and concerts are among the many possible destinations. Major trips for vacations such as trips to Disney World, cruises, and visits to national parks and other tourist attractions can be a part of TR programming, depending on the agency. Trips can be scheduled on a regular basis, such as weekly or biweekly, or less frequently, such as once a month or once a year. Going on an outing requires special permission and has been used as a "reward" for accomplishing one's goals.

Outings are the means by which the TRS addresses **community reintegration** for clients and promotes inclusion. Outings can be used to assess how the client functions in the real world, as an opportunity to apply new skills, and as a way to explore community resources and new forms of recreation. The purposes of community reintegration outings (Williams, 2008) are to

- reduce stigma associated with a disability,
- practice in a real-world setting the skills that have been learned in treatment, and
- gain familiarity with community resources.

Benefits of Outings and Trips

Outings are unique in that the clients are participating in the typical environment, outside of the service setting. They provide a normalizing experience as clients engage in the activities common to their peers and families. An outing can also be a special occasion that lends excitement and novelty to the client's daily routine and provides a source of conversation and connection with others. Outings and trips require the following skills and produce the following benefits:

- Physical: mobility skills, sensory skills, endurance
- Cognitive: attention and concentration, memory, strategy, comprehension, judgment, sense of direction, problem solving, decision making, learning

- Affective: sense of accomplishment, frustration tolerance, anger management, feelings of self-confidence, fun, enjoyment
- Social: appropriate social behaviors, interaction skills, tolerance of crowds, respecting personal space of others, appropriate dress, sense of belonging to a community

Risk Management

A trip off-site involves many risks that can be reduced with careful planning. The TRS should be sure that all clients have permission to participate and are prepared for the outing. They need to be well informed regarding appropriate behaviors, the length of time and the destination, and any personal items they need to bring with them. A client may need medication, something to eat or drink, or sunblock. A policy should be in place regarding staff-to-client ratios and the need for a nurse, nursing assistants, or support staff to accompany the group. Safe and reliable transportation, a first aid kit, emergency procedures, plenty of money, cell phones, and backup plans are all required. Risks that can occur include illness or injuries, breakdown of a vehicle, a client "eloping" or running away from the group, other inappropriate behavior such as shoplifting or harassing a member of the public, lack of accessible bathrooms, getting lost, or a destination that is closed unexpectedly. When clients are being taken on an overnight trip, all these preparations are even more complicated, and thorough assessment of the participants' readiness to go on the trip is required. Emergency contact information for the destination and permission to obtain emergency treatment are mandatory. Anything the TRS has encountered on her own trips, and probably more, can happen. Being thoroughly prepared is the best risk management procedure. Ethically, the TRS must do no harm and must be competent and professional in conducting outings and trips. They are often the highlight of a client's routine.

Programming

Outings and trips are a valuable form of leisure education. The TRS can expose clients to a range of leisure resources, such as parks, museums, theaters, restaurants, and malls that are sources of recreation for all people. In addition, the TRS can help clients identify and visit appropriate facilities to be used after discharge, such as recreation centers, Ys, senior centers, Boys' and Girls' Clubs, and fitness centers, in order to develop and continue a healthy lifestyle. This can be considered transitional TR as the TRS helps the client transition back to the home community (Sylvester et al., 2001). As a component of transitional TR services, the TRS can contact the professionals who work at facilities that clients will be attending after discharge in order to facilitate their smooth transition to community involvement. The TRS can work collaboratively with other professionals to develop the necessary support and recreation services for successful participation by clients in their home communities (Schleien et al., 2001). Clients should be involved in planning the outings, and the TRS should discuss with clients their challenges and successes in managing the trip. Afterward, a discussion of their strengths and the skills they would like to develop further is a valuable aspect of the community experience. Outings promote inclusion as clients take their place in the community and as the community recognizes them as full community members.

The TRS can work with clients to identify barriers to their successful return to their home environment, to help them master the necessary skills, and to help them develop strategies for positive involvement (Long & Robertson, 2008). For example, those recovering from a physical injury can test their mobility skills and their ability to use transportation, explore community resources for accessibility and availability of programs, and build self-confidence in managing the "real world." Clients can apply skills developed through physical therapy and occupational therapy. For those in recovery from substance abuse or psychiatric illness, outings are an opportunity to apply new social, money management, and transportation skills and to develop a sense of direction, as well as to test their ability to handle the challenges of the real world with appropriate stress management techniques. Residents of long-term care facilities can maintain the continuity of their former lifestyles by going on outings. Clients with developmental disabilities can practice new social skills, money handling, and use of transportation, as well as explore community resources for recreation participation. In one such program, adults with developmental disabilities attended a community recreation center for physical fitness (Carter et al., 2004). The other center members assisted them with the fitness equipment and asked after participants who missed a session.

Social activities are the mainstay of TR programming, as group interaction is a significant portion of TR activities. Promoting a relaxed atmosphere, group cohesion, and the reassurance of the easy and familiar, social recreation has great value in supporting the achievement of meaningful outcomes. As with all the major categories of TR programs, there are countless variations on social activities that can be included in the TR toolkit.

● **Summary** ●

The TR toolkit includes dozens of types of recreation programs that are engaged in by all people. When implemented by the TRS, the programs in the toolkit become both a means of attaining the desired goals and outcomes for clients and a means of providing opportunities for meaningful and satisfying participation. With experience, the TRS will develop and refine her personal toolkit, which becomes a hallmark of her professional services. The TRS is encouraged to be creative and flexible, well prepared, quick to adapt to the needs and interests of her participants, innovative, and open-minded. Attention to risk management and ethical concerns is essential to the successful and safe implementation of all TR programs. The specific strategies the TRS uses as she delivers TR leadership are discussed in chapter 7.

● **Learning Activities** ●

1. In a small group, discuss the contents of the TR toolkit. Brainstorm the contents of a TR toolkit for a group of children with developmental disabilities, for nursing home residents, and for adults in psychiatric treatment. How do the toolkits differ? How are they similar?

2. In a small group, discuss the factors that influence activity selection that were presented in the chapter. Can you think of any others?

3. Visit the Web sites for arts and crafts activity suggestions. Select one activity and complete an activity analysis. Conduct the activity for a group of classmates or coworkers. Discuss the skills they used and the benefits they received from participation. How do these compare to those you identified in your activity analysis?

4. Compile a list of songs for a sing-along or karaoke program that is age appropriate and meets the needs and interests of a group of teenagers. Create a list for adults. Compare the two lists.

5. Pick a theme for a bibliotherapy program for a group of your choice. Select appropriate readings and develop discussion questions. Do the same for a cinematherapy program, using movies.

6. Practice three new relaxation techniques mentioned in the chapter. Evaluate how you feel as a result of each one. Which would you choose to use for your personal stress management technique?

7. In a small group, discuss ethical issues regarding animal-assisted therapy. Do you feel that AAT is an ethical use of animals? What procedures could ensure that the animals' rights are protected?

8. Develop a list of places for outings and trips in your area. Contact the sites for information on hours, admission, and accessibility.

9. Examine the risk management guidelines presented in the chapter. Identify the aspects that are common to all TR programs, as well as those that are unique to a particular program area.

10. Select one of the TR programs discussed in the chapter and update the research and evidence that supports its use and effectiveness with selected groups.

11. With your classmates or coworkers, plan a special event using the checklist in the chapter.

Therapeutic Recreation Leadership: Strategies for Growth and Learning

In this chapter you will learn about:

- The TRS's responsibility for promoting client learning and growth
- How the TR environment facilitates teaching and learning
- Learning styles and their effect on the acquisition of new information and behaviors
- Motivational strategies based on readiness, needs, flow, self-efficacy, and intrinsic and extrinsic factors
- Applying activity analysis and task analysis to prepare for instruction
- Six teaching techniques
- Using instructional materials, collaboration, and positive teaching behaviors
- Facilitating positive growth and change through processing and coaching
- Cultural and ethical considerations for instruction and facilitation

The application of TR leadership is guided by theories, philosophy, and a comprehensive understanding of the value and benefits of leisure and recreation. Building up from this foundation, the TRS develops goals and objectives, selects activities, and implements TR programs using specific instructional strategies and facilitation techniques. These strategies and techniques are selected by the TRS based on her knowledge of the purpose and benefits of the techniques and the information she has gathered about the clients. The merging of this body of knowledge with her interpersonal skills and qualities is known as clinical judgment or judgment-based practice of care, which was discussed in chapter 3. Clinical judgment is utilized in the development of the individual client's plan and in choosing the appropriate techniques and strategies. Clinical judgment gets stronger as the TRS practices in real settings, beginning with the internship experience and continuing throughout her career. The TRS must think analytically, strategize to create the best programs, be able to solve problems as they arise, and design a dynamic and supportive TR environment.

THE CONTEXT OF TR LEADERSHIP

As we examine the strategies and techniques used by the TRS to implement TR programs, it is important to grasp the full scope of the TR environment. Understanding has increased over the last few years of the role that both the physical and social environments play in treatment, education, and health promotion. An environment that is "designed not only to support and facilitate state-of-the-art medicine and technology, patient safety, and quality patient care, but to also embrace the patient, family, and caregivers in a psycho-socially supportive therapeutic environment" (Smith & Watkins, 2008, p.1) can significantly contribute to achieving positive client outcomes. An understanding of this perspective of the health care environment is an important element in the practice of TR, but particularly in the application of TR leadership. The TRS must practice from the perspective that the TR environment is not just a specific place; it is also a viewpoint, an attitude, and a *mindset* that the TRS expresses in her daily interactions and encounters. The TR environment is extended to formal and informal interactions with other staff, both professional and paraprofessional, including dietary, housekeeping, maintenance, security, and aides; volunteers and members of

outside organizations in the community; and family members.

Having the mindset that you "carry" the TR environment with you in all your encounters is a component of TR leadership. A TRS must be acutely aware of the opportunities presented each day for the practice of TR leadership and capitalize on these opportunities to encourage, support, and ultimately influence clients' health and well-being. Therapeutic recreation leadership does not start and stop with the delivery of a TR program but is always present and active before, during, and after the program as the TRS motivates, encourages, and reinforces engagement in TR. The TRS creates and "carries" the **therapeutic recreation environment** with her whenever she encounters and interacts with clients, including greeting them in hallways and elevators, thereby creating opportunities and experiences that encourage and support them. The TRS should be mindful of the effect of the TR environment on enhancing the clients' learning. Learning can be defined as "a relatively permanent change in behavior or knowledge that is the result of experience" (Sylvester et al., 2001, p. 186).

HOW WE LEARN

Learning means gaining new insight, developing the skills to do something new, or acquiring new knowledge (Niepoth, 1983). Learning is not just an experience that occurs in childhood but one that continues throughout life. How one learns and how one is motivated to learn are influenced by many factors: family history, age, life stage, health status, personal learning style, previous experiences with learning, resources, and lifestyle. Many conditions that the TRS addresses in his work affect individuals' behavior and learning capacity, such as cognitive limitations, autism, traumatic brain injuries, psychiatric disorders, and dementia. In addition, many behaviors that impede the learning process are learned responses or coping mechanisms used to handle stress and difficult situations. These behaviors, however, are often not the most useful actions individuals can take in order to cope. Clients also come to a learning situation with preconceived notions about the learning process and the teacher or instructor (Burlingame & Singley, 1998). The TRS should be aware of clients' attitudes toward learning in order to best help them reach their goals. Many people do not recognize that recreation participation can help them learn new skills and behaviors that have relevance to many aspects of life. They may not recognize the TRS as a viable teacher or the potential of TR participation in meeting their goals. The TRS is responsible for educating clients about the value of TR and its potential contribution to their learning and progress. When the TRS conducts the individual client assessment, he may gain insight into clients' barriers to learning. In order to facilitate learning and most effectively assist the client, the TRS can work with the team to develop positive behavioral supports, behavior management interventions, and instructional plans that best meet clients' needs.

The way we learn changes over the lifespan. Children are in the process of learning from the moment they are born. It comes as no surprise that families are a major influence on a child's ability to learn. The majority of information learned is provided to them by adults (parents, grandparents, and teachers). Children who have a supportive and caring family that values education have a greater chance of being successful learners than children who do not. How children are taught within the family also influences their learning style. Some children are taught to be quiet and observe what is being demonstrated, others to work side by side with the parent, and others to follow directions given by their parents.

Once children enter the educational system, they understand that their responsibility is to be a student or learner. Children learn more quickly and more readily change their views than adults because they have more limited life experience and less entrenched views about the world. Initially children learn what they are told they must learn, and they learn in the way they are told they should learn. They are often motivated by rewards, praise, and recognition. By the time they reach adolescence, children begin to challenge what they are told and engage in a process of making choices about what they want to learn and who will teach them (Cave, LaMaster & White, 2006).

Adults learn differently than children. Adults are autonomous and self-directed and generally tend to expect their learning experiences to be goal oriented. They want to know not only what their goals are but what is expected of them to achieve these goals. What they are being taught or asked to do must have value to them, must relate to what they already know, and must have application to work or to everyday life. They seek, in the process of learning, to be recognized and respected for the value of their life experiences. Because of these experiences, adult learners are more likely to initially reject new information if it goes against their already

developed ways of viewing things. The older we get, the longer we may take to learn something, but we can learn it just as well as a younger person (Cantor, 2008).

Learning Styles

How well people learn a new skill or behavior may have more to do with their learning style than with how well they do on an intelligence test. **Learning style** refers to the process by which people gain and retain knowledge, analyze information, and demonstrate what they have learned. Individuals perceive and process information in very different ways. When one is working with clients in situations that require instruction, identifying an individual's learning style can be very significant in helping him learn. Generally people fall into one of three categories of learning styles: auditory, visual, and tactile or kinesthetic (Niepoth, 1983).

AUDITORY LEARNERS

Auditory learners are responsive to both the words the instructor uses and the tone and inflection of the speaker's voice. The TRS should speak clearly, repeat important points, look directly at clients, encourage them to repeat the information aloud (Vance, 2003), and provide opportunities to talk through a problem or situation. Discussion groups, instructional CDs or DVDs, and lectures are generally positive instructional strategies for auditory learners. In a leisure education group, the TRS can give a lecture on community resources, have the group discuss a challenge that may arise as they try to go to a community event (such as lack of wheelchair accessibility), and provide a CD that explains how to navigate the local transportation system. The auditory learner learns best by listening.

VISUAL LEARNERS

Visual learners learn best when they can see the instructor while he is talking. They benefit from observing the instructor's body language and are typically the people who are in the front of the room or sitting close to the TRS so that they have an unobstructed view. The visual learner responds to diagrams, models, written instructions, reading materials, and samples that help them visualize the skills and information being taught. They learn by writing notes and use the word "see" to show understanding. They may look as though they are daydreaming but may actually be visualizing a situation in their mind. They may close their eyes to visualize or create a mental image of what they

Visual learners learn best if they are sitting close to the TRS so they can see her while she's talking and easily view any objects she shows.

have seen or read. They respond to colorful, flashy images (Vance, 2003). For the leisure education group, the TRS could show colorful brochures on places to go in the community, provide a diagram of the bus route, and encourage participants to write down directions to various sites.

TACTILE LEARNERS

The tactile or kinesthetic learning style is the least prevalent. Tactile learners learn by exploring their environment and acquiring new information hands-on. Tactile learners have short attention spans, have difficulty sitting still, and almost always have a part of their body in motion (such as foot tapping). They benefit from taking in small amounts of information and then actively doing the new skill or practicing the new behavior. They may underline while reading, take notes when listening, or keep their hands busy as they are learning. They respond to an instructor who uses movements and gestures. In the leisure education session, practicing getting on and off an accessible bus and role playing how to handle a challenging situation in the community would be valuable strategies for these learners.

Cultural and Ethical Considerations for Learning

The TRS's ethical responsibility is to adjust his instructional strategies to best accommodate the influence of cultural background on clients' learning

styles. This is known as an inclusive approach to instruction (Coelho, 1998). If the TRS and the clients do not share a common background, miscommunication can occur. As mentioned in previous chapters, certain Asian cultures do not value talking about their strengths. They see this as bragging. In a group focused on increasing self-esteem, a client may be viewed as having a poor self-perception of her strengths if she does not feel comfortable discussing them. In fact, she may be behaving in accordance with her cultural beliefs and practices. If the TRS is culturally competent, he can tailor his approach to the client's cultural background. He can ask the client to make statements about things that she can do, rather than about her positive qualities. The ethical responsibility of the TRS is to be responsive to the needs and learning styles of all participants, using a range of techniques to facilitate their success. It is important to help clients extend their range of responses so that they can succeed in a number of settings, not only in their own environment.

STRATEGIES TO PROMOTE LEARNING AND GROWTH

Numerous strategies, techniques, and methods are used to teach people new information, skills, behaviors, and concepts. All types of professionals, from educators to therapists, apply the strategies that can best facilitate learning in a variety of clients with their particular needs and goals. The three categories of strategies used by TRSs are motivational, instructional, and growth-promoting strategies. "Strategies can be classified into many different categories. . . . Classification is unimportant as long as you can identify the strengths and weaknesses of each available technique" (Anspaugh & Ezell, 2007, p. 48). The TRS will find that the terms strategies, techniques, methods, and tools, among others, are often used interchangeably and should not be confused by this.

MOTIVATIONAL STRATEGIES

One of the primary roles of the TRS is that of motivator, as discussed in chapter 4. As a motivator, the TRS utilizes his knowledge of what motivates human beings, combined with his unique talents and abilities, to create a motivating environment that will help clients move toward change. Each person may need a unique combination of strategies and supports to make change, but believing that all individuals have the potential to change reflects the core TR principle of the humanistic perspective. Many factors influence an individual's desire and ability to change, in addition to personal beliefs and attitudes. Family and friends, education and economic levels, religious and cultural background, health status, medical condition, and living environment can all influence a person's motivation level.

Client motivation is often facilitated through the process of negotiating the pros and cons of participation between the client and the TRS (Rollnick, Mason & Butler, 1999). When someone is motivated to change, the TRS supports that motivation with information, feedback, and resources to ensure success. When faced with a person who does not appear motivated to change, it is the responsibility of the TRS to come up with effective motivation strategies. The TRS should assist clients to cultivate long-term and continuing motivation, as well as to experience immediate and momentary enjoyment (Frye & Peters, 1972). In addition to being skilled in strategies that motivate client participation, the TRS uses motivational strategies to promote family involvement and increase inclusive options in the community.

Enjoyment

Enjoyment of the TR experience is the TRS's most powerful motivational strategy. People want to engage in recreation because it is inherently fun and enjoyable. This is a unique characteristic of TR. A TR program should have the qualities of a recreation experience; it should be voluntary, should be enjoyable, and should allow participants to use their strengths and reinforce their identity. "One of the potential joys of participating in therapeutic recreation is that individuals have an opportunity to explore their true selves in a challenging, accepting, supportive and conscious environment" (Howe-Murphy & Murphy, 1997, p. 47). Enjoyment can keep people involved in the face of challenges and barriers. "In other words, people will try longer and harder when they enjoy themselves" (Hutchinson et al., 2006, p. 234). Fun and enjoyment are motivators that can enhance clients' progress toward the achievement of functional outcomes. The TRS's own enthusiasm and joy in participating in recreation can also be a major factor in motivating clients. Thera-

peutic recreation in groups gives people the chance to interact with others in familiar activities. To the extent that the TR experience distracts participants from their problems and is relaxing, it can serve as a coping resource (Hutchinson et al., 2006). Therapeutic recreation specialists should not underestimate the power of the recreation experience to promote clients' willingness and ability to learn.

Readiness

The first step in motivating a client is to assess him for his **readiness** to change, which was also discussed in chapter 3. Readiness from the health perspective refers to an individual's state of mind and level of preparedness to take action. Failure to fully understand a client's readiness can contribute to his resistance to participate and frustration with the demands placed upon him in the service setting. The concept of readiness for change is the basis of the Stages of Change or **Transtheoretical Model** (Prochaska & DiClemente, 1982), which identifies key stages in the change process.

The stages of change are precontemplation, contemplation, preparation for change, action, and maintenance. Termination may be included as a sixth stage, at which point the client has acquired positive behaviors that have become fully incorporated into his lifestyle.

- **Precontemplation.** In this stage a person is not planning or likely to make any changes in behavior now or in the future. The reason may be that the person is unaware of the negative consequences of his behavior, or that the experience of trying to change a behavior in the past was too difficult or painful or was unsuccessful.

- **Contemplation.** At this stage the person is not yet ready for change but is considering changing in the near future (within the next six months). The person may be gathering information about the potential benefits of changing his behavior and weighing pros and cons of the consequences of the change.

- **Preparation.** At this stage the person may have developed a plan of action and is intending to implement that plan in the immediate future (within the next month).

- **Action.** In this stage, the person is totally engaged in the process of behavior change. Small changes in behavior do not count at this stage. If the person is attempting to stop drinking by just reducing the number of drinks, instead of not drinking at all, he is not yet in the action stage.

- **Maintenance.** At this stage the person is continuing to engage in the changed behavior and is focused on preventing relapse and integrating this new behavior totally into his lifestyle.
- **Termination.** The client has acquired new behaviors that are fully incorporated into his lifestyle.

Based on Prochaska and DiClemente 1982

The Transtheoretical Model also addresses the concept of situational temptations. Situational temptations are triggers that may occur at any of the stages and interfere with a client's progress toward reaching her goals. Helping a client to recognize the triggers that can cause relapse into negative or destructive behaviors, and to develop coping strategies to address the triggers, can be a major contributor to the client's success. Using this model, the TRS can develop and implement plans and programs tailored to the client's stage of change. The TRS may be treating two clients who have come into a drug rehabilitation unit with similar functional limitations due to substance abuse; but their motivation to accept and respond to treatment may be markedly different due to age, former interests, social support, or degree of impairment. For example, a client at the precontemplation stage would not be ready for change. If presented with specific reasons to change her behavior or invitations to attend particular groups, she would not be receptive and might respond to any efforts to engage her by withdrawing from all interaction. At this stage, the role of the TRS should be to provide information without trying to persuade the person to take particular actions. The TRS should emphasize actively listening to and engaging the client in conversation and then offering helpful information. The information does not have to be the same at each session but should reinforce common themes.

The case of Debbie illustrates the themes of alternative coping skills and health-promoting behaviors. Debbie is a 44-year-old woman who has entered a behavioral health unit for a six-week treatment program for acute alcoholism. Even with numerous drunk-driving arrests, Debbie does not believe she has a problem and has no motivation to change. She does not feel that she needs treatment and has come to the unit only to fulfill the judge's order. The TRS engages Debbie in initial conversations in order to understand her better and to conduct the TR assessment. The TRS determines that Debbie is at the precontemplation stage. Because the TRS believes that Debbie lacks knowledge about the damage her alcoholism is causing, he decides to provide her with information regarding the disease

and its effects. During one conversation, Debbie explains to the TRS that she is under a great deal of stress and that drinking relaxes her. The TRS mentions that he practices yoga to relieve stress and offers Debbie information about the yoga program he leads on the unit.

Debbie decides to attend yoga, which shows that she has moved into the contemplation stage. However, she doesn't feel she is benefiting from yoga. Additional stress reduction techniques are then explored during the stress management group. In the contemplation stage, the client has recognized that there is a problem and is considering making changes, but action on these changes is still projected into the future. The client is weighing the pros and cons of changing behavior. As Debbie moves through the treatment process, receiving TR and other services, she develops new insights into her condition. Debbie's problem is not a lack of confidence that she is capable of change; rather, change is not yet important enough to her to prompt active engagement in behavior change. Once Debbie begins to believe that the benefits of change outweigh the benefits of *not* changing, she moves into the preparation and action stages. It is in the preparation stage that Debbie will start to make concrete plans to change her life after discharge. Motivators that can help her progress in the behavior change process include obtaining information on resources, developing new skills, and identifying and learning how to cope with triggers in her environment.

During leisure education, the TRS helps Debbie and the other participants develop behavioral contracts for their future recreation lifestyle. Group support is also a motivator to Debbie as she sees that others share her challenges. Together, they identify community resources through which Debbie can engage in recreation activities that can help her reduce stress, enhance her mood, and have fun without the benefits of alcohol. In the action stage, she is attending the full range of activities offered at the facility, which include yoga classes, stress management activities, and AA meetings. Her discharge plan includes identifying new social situations and activities that she can participate in after discharge—that do not focus on alcohol—and developing a support network. After discharge, in the action stage, Debbie is fully engaged in implementing the changes in her life. Once she has been sober for at least six months, she moves into the maintenance stage. Continued support to reinforce Debbie's success is needed at this stage to avoid relapse and help her handle situational temptations in her environment. For Debbie a trigger might be an important social event, such as the annual holiday party at work, where alcohol is served. Debbie prepares herself for this by practicing relaxation breathing before she joins the gathering. At the party she makes her own nonalcoholic drink and does not stand near the bar. In this way, she utilizes the techniques she role played during her inpatient stay in order to avoid relapse.

By understanding the stages of change, the TRS can adapt motivation strategies to the client's frame of mind. These strategies include

- sharing information,
- providing encouragement,
- helping the client to develop skills and resources, and
- providing opportunities to practice new behaviors.

The case of Sheri illustrates a client at another stage of change. In contrast to Debbie, Sheri enters the drug rehabilitation unit because she is ready to change her drug abuse behaviors. She is already at stage 3, the preparation stage. She is eager to explore a variety of coping skills that will help her maintain her new behavior of not using drugs and alcohol, but needs the services of the TRS in order to understand the range of opportunities. The TRS shares information with Sheri about the TR program options and the benefits of each. The TRS then develops a plan that includes stress management to give Sheri the tools for coping; leisure education to help her develop new interests; physical fitness for the promotion of a healthier lifestyle and self-image; and assertiveness training to help her learn how to handle situations that may trigger relapse. By recognizing that Sheri is at this stage, the TRS can plan a program to capitalize on her motivation to change. The TRS encourages Sheri as she engages in the TR programs and guides her toward developing new skills and acquiring resources that will help her in her recovery. In accordance with her TR plan, Sheri practices newly acquired behaviors. A potential pitfall for Sheri, because she is so eager to embrace a new lifestyle, may be that she is overly confident that she can resist temptations to relapse and so may be less vigilant during the maintenance stage. The TRS can help Sheri develop strategies to stay motivated to adhere to her new behaviors, such as journaling, friendship development, and exercise. Assessing a client's readiness to change can help the TRS develop effective strategies and programs to best meet the client's needs.

Needs-Based Strategies

One group of motivational strategies is based on understanding human needs. Chapter 4 presented several theories of motivation according to human needs. As with all types of human endeavor, people participate in TR programs to meet their needs. Understanding what needs a person is seeking to fulfill gives the TRS insight he can use to motivate clients to participate. Often TRSs do not fully understand what needs people are seeking to fulfill, and they frequently say that motivation is their biggest challenge. Therapeutic recreation specialists should use their knowledge of human behavior to try to decipher the complex dynamics of need fulfillment in order to use the most effective motivation strategies. The following examples identify the possible needs expressed by clients and the strategies the TRS may use to address those needs:

- People who do not want to attend a TR program may say they are expecting a visitor, or will miss a phone call, or need to be near a rest room. They may be experiencing an unmet need for emotional safety and security in the facility. The TRS could seek to reassure the client that the program is located near a rest room, that the client will be called to the phone, or that a visitor will be directed to the TR room so the client feels more secure that she will not miss something of importance.
- A client who is constantly asking the TRS for assistance in a group or making provocative comments to the other group members could be attempting to meet needs for attention, belonging, or acceptance. The TRS could give this client leadership responsibility, ask the client to help him set up and clean up after the activity, or give the client praise for positive behavior.
- Clients may not wish to attend a program that is not challenging or stimulating to them because it does not meet their needs to be productive or feel confident in their abilities. Bingo is considered universally popular, but many clients may not find it a particularly demanding game. The TRS should plan a range of programs that meet varying levels of cognitive needs and abilities.
- A person who is terminally ill may display anxiety as he tries to express his needs to maintain his unique identity and to be remembered. The TRS can help him select photos, create a piece of art as a legacy for friends and family, or create a journal or video diary of his life experiences.

For terminally ill clients, selecting old photos can be a means of establishing a legacy for their loved ones to remember.

Bill Crump/Brand X Pictures

Human needs are such powerful motivators of behavior that people may seek to meet their needs in unhealthy, destructive, or socially unacceptable ways, including substance abuse, criminal activity, self-injurious actions, not taking care of their physical health in the presence of disease, or staying in an unhealthy relationship. A person with a substance abuse problem may be motivated to find his next drink even when he is medically or financially compromised. It may be that he attends a TR program but that his motive is to pretend he is doing well so he can get a day pass to go drinking. The TRS should try to understand the client's motives so she can address this with the client. In this case, the client's motives are in conflict with the purpose of the group, which is to learn healthy strategies for successful recovery. To address these negative expressions of unmet human needs, the TRS can help the client develop insight into what

needs he is trying to meet and can acknowledge his feelings. On the other hand, clients may refuse to attend TR programs. The TRS and other staff may view these clients as unmotivated to participate, but the clients may be feeling that TR is not meeting their needs. An individual with a developmental disability who bangs his head may be bored and seeking stimulating activity; he could benefit from more challenging programming. Other clients may behave in ways that are seen as inappropriate. For example, in a nursing home a resident may gain a reputation as a "dirty old man" because he makes suggestive comments to the female staff. He may have a need for companionship, intimacy, or recognition of his identity as an attractive man. Meaningful alternatives that meet clients' needs for challenge and stimulation, intimacy, and positive friendships should include activities that are intellectually stimulating, challenging, and age appropriate.

Most people have a need to feel in control of their lives. The TRS should always provide activity choices for clients in order to promote their sense of control. People with disabilities and limitations often have had their choices made for them or have not been recognized as capable of making choices. A key TR value and ethical principle is autonomy. In TR, this may mean having the power to make decisions about attending or not attending a program. Other decisions may be about the degree of involvement to have in a program, games to play, materials to use in arts and crafts, songs to sing during music group, or topics to bring up in a group discussion. Providing and reinforcing an individual's freedom to make decisions is a powerful motivator. According to Glasser (1998), combining the power and control to make choices with fun experiences is essential to a healthy and happy life. For a client whose physical and cognitive functioning are very limited, such as an individual with severe developmental disabilities, a choice may be between two colors of paint. If the client is nonverbal and has extremely limited motor skills, he may be unable to indicate a preference for blue paint rather than red. He may glance toward the blue jar of paint. The TRS will reinforce the choice by saying, "Eddie, you picked blue." Then Eddie may make a sound that the TRS should try to interpret as either agreement or pleasure or disagreement or discontent. The TRS should continue to offer choices and reinforcement as a means to increase the client's sense of control over his life, thereby enhancing motivation. She also could be playful, making the choosing of the colors and the painting activity itself fun and enjoyable, which will increase the client's motivation.

On the other hand, for a very high-functioning client like Kenneth, in cardiac rehabilitation, decisions may be related to which stress management techniques he finds most effective, enjoyable, and feasible to incorporate into his day-to-day routine. The TRS offers information on different techniques, provides an opportunity to learn and practice each, and discusses with Kenneth the pros and cons of each technique in order to help him decide which is best for him. Feeling vulnerable as a result of his heart attack, Kenneth regains a sense of control as he goes through this process and is motivated to continue his rehabilitation. The TRS can apply knowledge of human needs to help motivate clients to engage in TR programs that have been designed and implemented to meet their needs and interests and help them achieve their goals.

Flow

Another group of strategies used to enhance motivation is based on *flow theory*. Flow theory, put forth by Mihaly Csikszentmihalyi (1990), describes the psychological state of an individual when he is fully absorbed in an experience. When a person experiences flow, several components join together to contribute to an optimal experience. The degree of skill of the individual and the challenge inherent in the activity must be balanced so that the person perceives he has the ability to do the activity successfully. All activities possess a degree of challenge and skill, but the challenge must not be so overwhelming as to discourage participation. Too much challenge results in anxiety and frustration. Conversely, too little challenge leads to boredom. The best condition is when the activity provides just enough challenge to cause the participant to strive more than he would normally be asked to. Flow can be compared to experiencing a "natural high," being "in the moment" or "in the zone," or having a "peak" experience. People seek this flow state in many ways. It can be experienced through work, recreation, human interactions, or any endeavor, and even negative behavior.

Therapeutic recreation specialists can help clients find recreation pursuits that produce flow. Recreation activities are ideal for producing flow because they require skills for participation, have rules and goals, provide immediate and concrete feedback, and offer novelty and opportunities to experience control. When the TRS chooses recreation activities for clients that are fun, pleasurable, challenging, and within the client's perceived skill level, they can be structured so as to have a high likelihood of producing flow. Participating in a flow-producing recreation activity can motivate clients to change their behaviors, improve their health, and participate in other positive activities. The experience itself provides feedback to clients on their performance and reinforcement of their efforts. As the individual makes a move in a game, carries out a step in a recipe, or makes a statement in a discussion, the response or outcome is a form of feedback. The client quickly knows the results of his action. This feedback gives the individual a feeling of a high degree of control and empowerment. The flow experience is intrinsically rewarding and therefore highly motivating.

As already mentioned, sometimes activities are not challenging enough to participants. Residents of nursing homes, people with developmental disabilities, and clients with physical ailments who are cognitively intact are often viewed as less capable than they really are of engaging in stimulating activities. As a result, programming is not appealing to them because it is boring. They either do not participate or act out in inappropriate ways during a program. The TRS can motivate participants by choosing exciting recreation activities and adapting these activities so that the client is challenged but also has the supports necessary for participation. For example, Eddie would become very frustrated during painting sessions because he could not hold and control the paintbrush. Eddie's day program has hired a new TRS, Stuart, who obtains an adaptive device that allows Eddie to hold the brush. With Stuart's assistance, Eddie is able to paint. Eddie is absorbed in the activity, which reduces his boredom and allows him to overcome the limitations of his disabilities. Eddie's excitement at being able to master the challenge of a new activity has increased his attention span and degree of involvement in the day program. Now he is motivated to try other activities. In manipulating the degree of challenge in the painting activity by enhancing Eddie's skill at holding the brush, Stuart has used flow strategies to create a meaningful and motivating experience.

Another motivation lesson from flow theory is that people seek a balance between novelty and stability. Each of us has needs for excitement and variety in our lives, as well as a need for the familiar and comfortable. Some people are bigger thrill seekers, and others prefer a greater degree of comfort and security. However, both needs exist along a continuum from stability to novelty, and the TRS can motivate participants by altering the degree of each in programs. Familiar activities can provide a sense of continuity with one's former lifestyle during a period of turmoil and change caused by a health crisis. This may be the reason bingo is so popular. Its familiarity brings comfort to new residents of nursing homes or older adults with depression who have been admitted to a psychiatric unit. On the other hand, activities that are different or presented in a new way can provoke interest. Use of unexpected props and decorations can capture people's attention. When leading a familiar activity, such as cooking, Stuart, the TRS, adds an element of the unexpected by wearing a chef's hat and apron. He uses colored lightbulbs and scented candles to alter the usual environment to enhance a creative writing program. Therapeutic recreation specialists should be mindful not to simply provide clients with activity choices based on their former participation patterns, but to make available a range of opportunities that are both typical and novel. The flow experience itself is considered intrinsically motivating. The *doing* of a flow-producing activity is rewarding in and of itself and is motivating to the individual.

Use of Intrinsic and Extrinsic Motivators

The experience of flow is intrinsically motivating. However, people may initially be motivated more by extrinsic factors, whether tangible or intangible, than by intrinsic factors. Extrinsic motivators include tangibles such as money, food, prizes, desired objects or items, or tokens that can be exchanged for something of value. Intangibles include praise and attention, as well as opportunities to make choices, take control, challenge oneself, and experience freedom. The TRS initially may have to use extrinsic motivators to involve a person in a program. Many TR programs include refreshments to entice people to attend. Often it is easier to use extrinsic motivators because they appeal to people on a very basic level and are easy to supply. Some facilities, perhaps a children's psychiatric center or a day program for people with developmental disabilities, operate on a token economy, whereby desired behavior is rewarded with extrinsic motivators such as points or tokens. But even though extrinsic motivation may keep a person involved in a particular behavior, if that behavior is motivated solely by extrinsic factors it will not in and of itself contribute to long-term happiness and fulfillment. Over time, the extrinsic motivator may lose its appeal. Therapeutic recreation specialists should be wary of relying too much on extrinsic motivators. Identifying the situations and experiences that intrinsically motivate each individual takes skill and practice because of people's unique needs and

Extrinsic Motivators

There are a wide variety of extrinsic motivators, but their effectiveness depends upon the preferences, likes, and dislikes of the individual. These are some extrinsic motivators:

- Food
- Gold stars
- Points
- Stickers
- Tokens
- Certificates of achievement
- Medals or trophies
- Name mentioned in the paper or posted on a sign or bulletin board or in an online forum
- Baseball cards or other desired objects
- Opportunity to engage in preferred activity, such as listening to music, watching a favorite TV show, or playing a game
- Money
- Prizes or gifts

personalities. The TRS should attempt to move the person along the continuum from being extrinsically motivated to being intrinsically motivated. By giving feedback to the client about his participation, identifying and reflecting the client's nonverbal reactions, and structuring the activities to meet the client's needs, the TRS can increase the client's intrinsic motivation.

Intrinsic motivation can be seen as "something that sparks an interest so powerful that a client would act in spite of pain, boredom, fear or poor self-esteem" (Shank & Coyle, 2002, p. 142). The meaning of this quotation is illustrated in the story of Mrs. Kelly, a nursing home resident of Irish heritage. Without a conscientiously conducted TR assessment, an assumption might have been made that Mrs. Kelly would enjoy the Irish Club. However, she refused to attend that program and chose instead to attend the Italian Culture Club because of her long-standing love of Italian art, opera, and food. She had taken a memorable trip to Italy for her 80th birthday. Her motivation to attend the club was intrinsic and intangible. During the club meetings, she was able to display her knowledge of Italian culture and reinforce her identity as an intelligent and worldly woman, expressed through her past interests and experiences. Mrs. Kelly was highly intrinsically motivated to attend the Italian club, and the TRS's role in this type of situation is to provide ongoing leadership to keep the program at the level that continually challenges and sustains meaningful participation. The TRS is a catalyst who stimulates the client to action by cultivating her intrinsic motivation. The TRS may invite Mrs. Kelly to deliver a lecture on her travels or do an Italian cooking demonstration. The TRS can organize a trip to see Italian art in the local museum or offer Italian language lessons. This results in the client's new or enlightened perspective about her ability to experience meaning in her life at this stage and to promote her quality of life.

"All individuals are intrinsically motivated toward behavior in which they can experience competence and self-determination" (Stumbo & Peterson, 2004, p. 20). This was true of Mrs. Kelly, who was not in fact a "joiner" of groups. But in this case, she was motivated to overcome her shyness and less outgoing personality and participate in a group activity that she perceived as meaningful and appealing. From an ethical perspective, the TRS's service to Mrs. Kelly reflects respect for her autonomy to make her own choices regarding which program to attend, demonstrates the TRS's competence in providing quality TR services, and manifests his efforts to promote her well-being. After a few months, though, Mrs. Kelly started complaining that other residents were attending only for the Italian pastries served during the meetings. These people were motivated by the refreshments. The lesson is that people can attend the same program based on very different motivations and obtain very different benefits from participation. The TRS can use both concrete, tangible items and internal, intangible, nonmaterial factors as motivators to encourage clients to attend and participate in TR programs. Once the clients are actively engaged in TR, the TRS can begin to facilitate their participation in the direction of reaching their goals.

Strategies for Self-Efficacy

Each person has a perception of how effective he is at completing a task or reaching a goal. This is known as self-efficacy, which has been identified as a significant factor in how motivated people are to change. Many things influence one's perception of self-efficacy, including family history and environment. Once established, a person's sense of self-efficacy may be difficult to influence (Shank & Coyle, 2002) because psychological beliefs about himself and his ability to succeed at a given task or challenge (Bandura, 1997) are very deeply rooted. Four specific approaches have been identified as effective in increasing perceptions of self-efficacy:

- Vicarious experiences
- Mastery experiences
- Control of physiological responses
- Social or verbal persuasion

Vicarious Experiences

According to the vicarious experiences approach, the client observes the behaviors of others who she perceives as facing similar challenges and uses these observations to form perceptions about her self-efficacy. This is a guiding principle of 12-step programs. People are best helped by others who have mastered similar challenges. For example, Paulette has struggled with a weight problem since she was a young child, has been on numerous diet programs, and has been unsuccessful at losing weight. She has a hard time losing weight even when confronted by a diagnosis of prediabetes. Her life experience has demonstrated to her that she does not have the ability to successfully follow a weight loss program. Paulette has formed a cognitive appraisal of her self-efficacy. She thinks she is not competent to lose weight. The TRS can help increase Paulette's perception of her competence to adhere to a weight loss plan by using a vicarious experience approach. In this approach, Paulette observes other obese patients in an exercise class and listens to them discuss how they have lost weight and handled the pressures of dieting. Vicarious experiences can teach people more effective ways to approach their own problems. The effectiveness of changing cognitive appraisals of self-efficacy through vicarious experiences depends on how much the client can relate to and identify with the others. James presents another example of this.

James, a 19-year-old college freshman and member of the college basketball team, suffered a severe spinal cord injury as the result of a serious car accident. As a result of the accident, James has paraplegia with full use of his arms and hands. James believes that he will never be able to actively engage in sports again. The TRS has discussed adapted sport programs with him, but James has rejected any participation. The TRS arranges for James to attend a wheelchair basketball game and to meet with the team after the game. James listens to the players discuss their disabilities, the challenges they face, and the benefits they derive from playing basketball. James even gets to work out with a few players. He meets Tommy, a 13-year-old boy who inspires him because of the similarity of their situations. Once a confident athlete, James realizes that he still has the capability to participate in sports

and upon discharge joins a local wheelchair sport program. Observing and interacting with a variety of role models of the desired behavior may have a strong impact and increase the chance of success for the client. The result of this approach is to move the client from "I can't do that" to "If he could do that, then I can do it."

Mastering the Experience

Actually mastering an experience is the most powerful influence on a person's self-efficacy. The power of mastery experiences is influenced by an individual's past history and perceptions of success and failure. The client's cognitive appraisals of his ability to succeed can be useful to the TRS as she tries to motivate the client. Identifying the appropriate activity or experience to offer the client becomes extremely important when we are trying to provide mastery opportunities. In the case of James, vicarious experience succeeded in motivating him to try out wheelchair basketball. As he mastered this experience, he enhanced his perception of his self-efficacy that he could now do other activities despite his disability. Adventure-based programming, as discussed in chapter 6, is a very effective program used in TR to enhance self-efficacy. Adventure activities are often so far removed from the client's typical life experiences that when she is successful in accomplishing them, her cognitive appraisals of her abilities are dramatically affected. The TRS can use processing (discussed later) to help the client generalize her success in a mastery experience to other aspects of her life.

Controlling Physiological Responses

Challenging situations can produce physiological responses that are indicators of a lack of self-efficacy. Rapid heart rate, aches and pains, fatigue, sweating, and panic attacks are examples of physiological responses to stressful situations. If a person can control his physiological responses, he may perceive that he is better able to cope with stress and challenges. Kenneth is a 45-year-old man who had a heart attack and is in a cardiac rehabilitation program. Prior to the heart attack, Kenneth was active in competitive sports and attended a local gym. He always viewed himself as physically fit. Now, during the early days of the outpatient cardiac

Rehabilitation programs offer clients the opportunity to work toward better controlling physiological responses.

Human Kinetics/Kelly Huff

rehabilitation program, he experiences fatigue and nervousness during exercise and attributes these responses to the effects of the heart attack on his physical capabilities. He is afraid to continue the program, believing that these symptoms reflect just how physically frail he has become. Kenneth's partner, Howard, is afraid that Kenneth will never be able to return to his old self and is afraid of losing him to another heart attack. Howard doesn't feel that Kenneth should participate in the exercise program because it is too risky. Howard has begun to experience panic attacks as a result of his anxiety about Kenneth's condition. Howard's negative attitude has also increased Kenneth's resistance to treatment.

The TRS encourages Howard to join the spouse support group and to observe the cardiac rehabilitation program. She lends him a DVD about what to expect during recovery from a heart attack, and invites both Kenneth and Howard to join the nutrition group, which she coleads with the dietitian, to discuss diet and menu planning for Kenneth. As Howard becomes more informed, he is more supportive of Kenneth's steps toward recovery. The TRS works with Kenneth to help him understand that the pains associated with exercise are natural in the early stages of the rehabilitation program. The TRS helps him see that he can control and reduce his physiological responses to stress by learning the stress reduction techniques of meditation and yoga. This reduces his anxiety about participating in the program, thereby increasing his self-efficacy. In the family support group Howard meets Joan, whose husband is also in cardiac rehabilitation. Joan shares with Howard some of the stress management techniques she has used to control her own stress successfully, thereby providing support and encouraging Howard to utilize similar techniques.

Verbal Persuasion

Verbal persuasion is the use of words to convince a client that he is capable of a certain action, including that he is able to reach a goal. Verbal persuasion is most often used with people who have some degree of self-efficacy and believe that their actions can affect their outcomes. The success of the verbal persuasion approach is only as strong as the client's confidence in the TRS. The trust between the client and the TRS is central to the effectiveness of the approach. The therapist, as the persuader, provides encouragement to the client to engage in a course of action and gives her meaningful and realistic feedback on her performance, as well as praise for real accomplishments. For example, Paulette is attending a family wedding and is concerned that she will

not be able to resist the temptation to overeat. The TRS uses verbal persuasion to reinforce Paulette's newly learned behaviors of refusing unhealthy food choices. After the wedding, Paulette reports to the TRS that she did not have any wedding cake. The TRS praises Paulette for using her strategies to adhere to her weight loss program, and makes motivating statements about Paulette's positive actions in pursuit of her goal.

The TRS can motivate clients using needs-based strategies, flow strategies, intrinsic and extrinsic motivators, and the four self-efficacy strategies. These effective and powerful methods can enhance learning and promote growth and change. These strategies also maximize the quality and meaning of TR experiences for the clients.

GUIDELINES FOR MOTIVATION

The following general guidelines for motivation can be applied to any TR situation to enhance the motivating qualities of the TR program:

- As a TRS, recognize that your behavior is central to the motivating experience. Your behavior should be supportive, reassuring, reinforcing, and genuine. The TRS is a role model not only of how to behave but also of how to *enjoy* an activity and have fun. The TRS should have a positive and enthusiastic approach but should tailor his interaction style to the mood and needs of the individual client.

- The TR experience should be fun and enjoyable. This "fun factor" should not be underestimated as both a motivator and an outcome of participation. One of the most important aspects of the recreation experience is that it provides opportunities for fun and pleasure.

- Provide clients with opportunities to make choices as often as possible. Choices can range from the very basic, such as choosing what color paint to use, to more complex decisions such as setting goals. If clients feel empowered to make their own choices, they will be more motivated than when activities and goals are imposed upon them.

- Offer opportunities for clients to be challenged. Teaching skills in sequence and at a level that is slightly above their current capabilities offers clients opportunities to strive to meet an attainable challenge. On the other hand, while experiencing some frustration can be expected and learning how to deal with frustration is a positive learning experience, too much frustration can quickly demotivate a person. By providing feedback to clients regarding their competence to learn a new skill, the TRS can help them navigate challenges and frustrations.

- Identify positive reinforcers or motivators, both intrinsic and extrinsic. While food is one of the most commonly used motivators, there are important considerations when snacks are part of an activity.

- Make sure that the environment in which the TR program occurs is appropriate and maintains the integrity of the activity as well as the dignity of the clients. Contributors to motivation include

adequate space, seating, lighting, acoustics, ventilation, proximity to equipment or facilities that may be needed such as a sink or rest room, decorations, supplies, equipment, and privacy. A well-designed and sufficiently equipped space promotes engagement in the TR program.

ETHICAL CONSIDERATIONS WHEN PROVIDING MOTIVATION

One of the challenges of working with people who have motivation problems, health issues, or inappropriate behaviors is making sure that our own

Guidelines for Using Food as a Motivator

Food is often used to attract clients to an activity. It is important to remember that the purpose of the session is the *activity*, not the food.

Have a set time when the food will be available and make that clear to participants. People often come to an activity only for the food. Participation in the activity can be interrupted or diminished by preoccupation with when the food will be served.

Serve healthy food whenever possible, or limit the amount of food people can indulge in.

Be aware of clients' dietary restrictions and arrange for appropriate foods for clients who have a restricted diet. Common alternatives include sugar-free desserts for people with diabetes, soft foods for people who have trouble chewing, low-salt foods for people on sodium-restricted diets, gluten-free or lactose-free foods for those with food allergies, and low-calorie foods for those on weight loss diets.

Consider cultural preferences in food choices and accommodate them as much as possible.

Consider the time of day when food is being served. Try not to serve food too close to lunch or dinner.

People may need assistance when eating. Arrange for an aide or volunteer to help out.

Use appropriate safety precautions and proper food-handling methods.

The Downside of Using Food as a Motivator

There is a downside to using food as a motivator. According to behavioral theory, positive consequences reinforce a behavior.

When Paulette got a good grade in school, her mother rewarded her with cookies and milk. Now every time something good happens she wants to eat, because she perceived the cookies as a positive consequence of her good grades. But she also eats when she's feeling unhappy, because she associates eating with the positive consequence of getting attention from and being comforted by her mother.

This example shows that in addition to being motivated by needs, people may be motivated by the consequences of their behaviors. Unfortunately, this has led to Paulette's poor eating habits and obesity. In adulthood the cookies still are associated with positive feelings, even though the positive behavior (good grades) that earned her the reward is no longer part of her life. For the TRS to use food as a motivator might motivate Paulette to engage in a particular behavior, but it would not be an appropriate reinforcer given her current health condition.

Behavioral theory also states that negative behavior, in this case overeating, can be changed with the appropriate reinforcers and rewards. The TRS can work with Paulette to explore alternative activities that would be rewarding to her.

attitudes and assumptions do not cloud our interactions with them. The following are assumptions or actions on the part of a TRS that are *not* ethically responsible:

- Ignoring or overlooking clients who do not appear motivated to participate
- Assuming that a client is not interested or capable of doing certain activities
- Believing that the client must change without regard for her readiness to change
- Trying to impose his own activity preferences on the client
- Acting as if he is the expert and knows what's best for the client rather than respecting the client's autonomy
- Focusing his efforts only on people who are responsive to him

From a humanistic perspective and a person-centered approach, the TRS is ethically responsible to use a range of strategies to motivate his clients. He should be ready to employ a wide range of motivational techniques and seek to continually expand his repertoire of skills and knowledge related to motivating human behavior. In addition to understanding what motivates a client, the TRS should understand how clients learn and process information.

INSTRUCTIONAL STRATEGIES

Teaching is a process that supports an individual's ability to learn. Teachers are "change agents, that is, someone who changes the behavior of others through the educational process" (Cantor, 2008, p. 2). Therapeutic recreation specialists in the TR leadership role are teachers who guide students (clients) in the experience of acquiring the knowledge, skills, and abilities necessary to achieve their goals. In TR, clients learn new skills and behaviors in order to improve health and well-being (Sylvester et al., 2001). The TRS recognizes that each learner is unique and comes to the learning experience with his own history, set of needs, and potential for learning (Cantor, 2008). The individual's diagnosis and learning style, and the environment in which the instruction occurs, have an impact on his ability to learn. An effective teacher uses the same skills and abilities as an effective leader or therapist: communicating; assessing participants' needs, capabilities, and learning styles; developing goals and objectives; selecting strategies; and managing the environment.

Teaching is a partnership that can be effective only when the teacher and the student join together in the experience. As a teacher the TRS may be engaged in direct skills instruction, including instruction in how to develop activity, coping, social, decision-making, and problem-solving skills. Education is a major aspect of TR practice, as shown in many of the TR practice models. For example, in the Leisure Ability Model, one of the three components is leisure education. Therapeutic recreation emphasizes actively engaging the client in an experience he enjoys. Learning new skills and improving functional abilities are enhanced when clients' personal leisure interests and desires for enjoyment are incorporated into TR programs (Hutchinson et al., 2006). A person who loves baseball will participate in a game with a higher level of intensity, feelings, and focus than a person who is only moderately interested in the sport. From playing baseball the client can learn or further develop his skills in such areas as teamwork, handling competition, eye–hand coordination, and gross motor functioning. A woman who enjoys cooking may improve her skills in following directions, concentration, and social interaction as she experiences feelings of accomplishment from serving her finished product of a gourmet meal.

Instructional Ethics

Seek and share truth.
Govern behavior by ethically sound principles.
Maintain high standards of professional integrity.
Recognize unique human personalities and strive to help each learner reach full potential.
Deal impartially with all learners.
Strive to broaden your understanding and knowledge to become a better instructor and leader.
Contribute to and loyally support your organization and its mission and standards.
Be conscious of the privilege and responsibility to preserve and strengthen the integrity of the organization.

Reprinted, by permission, from J. Cantor, 2008, *Delivering instruction to adult learners*, 3rd ed. (Dayton, Ohio: Wall & Emerson, Inc.), 7.

To help the client learn new skills and behaviors, the TRS can follow a procedure that is similar to the TR process. For each new skill, the TRS sets a goal of what the client will learn, establishes a baseline of the client's current skill level, specifies a detailed and organized program of instruction, and evaluates the client's progress as he moves toward achieving the outcome. For example, as part of the implementation step of the TR process, Stuart, the TRS, develops a procedure to help Eddie paint. First Eddie must learn how to use the adapted paintbrush (goal); Stuart takes a baseline measure to identify Eddie's current skill in using the paintbrush. The baseline measure shows that Eddie knows which hand he will use to hold the brush but does not know how to hold or manipulate the brush. Next, Stuart will devise a strategy to help Eddie learn to hold and use the paintbrush.

Preparation for Teaching

The TRS should be thoroughly prepared to use a wide range of instructional strategies to teach new behaviors and specific skills to clients. The choice of strategies reflects the client's needs, learning style, and motivators, as well as the resources and space available. Once these factors are considered, an instructional plan for the client can be developed. To teach clients new skills and activities, whether or not within a formal instructional plan, the TRS should use activity analysis and task analysis to provide the most effective instruction.

ACTIVITY ANALYSIS

Activity analysis is a procedure for identifying the behaviors in the cognitive, physical, and affective domains required to do an activity, as well as the social aspects involved. Activity analysis is used to select the appropriate activities for a particular group or an individual client that will lead to meeting goals. In order to use an activity to reach a specific goal, the TRS chooses an activity based on the behaviors involved in the activity and matches the activity with the client's particular goal. For example, Mrs. Kelly, who has arthritis in her hands, had an interest in crafts prior to her admission to the nursing home. The TRS sets the following TR goals for Mrs. Kelly:

● To continue aspects of her prior lifestyle
● To increase her involvement in daily activities of the nursing home
● To maintain her fine motor flexibility and coordination

Arts and crafts is selected as an activity for Mrs. Kelly because it requires fine motor skill, is offered in a group format that encourages socialization, and is based on her prior interests. However, the activity analysis indicates that arts and crafts does not require social interaction. Verbal interaction is not necessary to working on a craft project. The TRS can do several things to modify the arts and crafts group to promote socialization in a nonthreatening way. He can require the clients to share supplies, lead a group discussion on the craft while the group members are working on their projects, or ask Mrs. Kelly direct questions as well as having her partner with another resident who shares her interests, Mrs. Garcia. Mrs. Garcia had a large family for whom she made many craft items. The two women have several things in common, and a new friendship is formed. In this way the TRS has addressed Mrs. Kelly's goals as well as her interests.

Activity analysis is also used to identify the adaptations needed as a result of a client's limitations in order to facilitate participation. Due to her arthritis, Mrs. Kelly demonstrates difficulty manipulating the scissors. The TRS has three options for adaptation:

1. Supply Mrs. Kelly with adapted scissors
2. Have her work with a partner who does the cutting
3. Provide precut materials

In the selection of an appropriate adaptation, it is a principle of activity analysis to modify or adapt only the aspect of the activity that needs to be adapted. "The best modification is the least modification" (Austin, 2004, p. 225). Option 1 gives Mrs. Kelly the most control, option 2 only moderate control, and option 3 the least amount of control. Adapted scissors would give Mrs. Kelly the most control over her participation. A partner would contribute to social interaction. The precut materials would perhaps be the choice that makes the activity easiest. The TRS, based on her knowledge of Mrs. Kelly and her needs, selects the adaptation that will promote Mrs. Kelly's ability to do as much of the project as possible on her own, contribute to her feelings of accomplishment, and increase her perceptions of self-efficacy. The TRS chooses option 1, use of the adapted scissors, and also provides physical assistance for Mrs. Kelly to enable her to successfully use them.

These are the principles to follow when selecting adaptations or modifications (Stumbo & Peterson, 2004):

● Keep the activity as close to the original as possible, so the client is having as authentic an experience as can be provided and obtains the widest possible range of learning opportunities.

- Modify only the aspects of the activity that need adapting based on the behavioral domains, such as the means of carrying out a physical action, a cognitive process, or the degree of emotional or social demands made on the client.

- Individualize modifications according to the unique needs of the client in order to maximize her ability to learn.

- Implement the modification for only as long as needed in order for the client to become capable of doing the activity on her own, so she does not become dependent on the adaptation.

Adaptations can be made in rules and procedures, materials, equipment, the environment, and teaching methods. In arts and crafts, adapted equipment can be purchased or made using everyday objects; for example, a paintbrush handle can be wrapped with a sponge to make it easier to grip. Another modification might involve the environment. For example, if the TRS observes that Mrs. Kelly seems to have difficulty hearing, although this is not noted in her medical chart, he stands closer to her when giving instructions and provides her with a written set of directions.

TASK ANALYSIS

Task analysis is a procedure for identifying the steps or behaviors needed to complete a task or activity and the sequence in which the steps should occur. Every activity is made up of a set of steps or behaviors. Whether the steps are simple or complex, task analysis provides a logical method for teaching the needed skills. These are the advantages of task analysis:

- It can serve as an assessment tool of a client's skill proficiency.

- It allows for individualizing of adaptations.

- It provides a consistent teaching sequence that can be used by many different staff members (Schlein et al., 2001).

The complexity of the activity and the skill level of the individual determine how many steps may be needed to complete a task. The general rule is that if completion of an activity requires more than eight steps, it should be broken down into the component skill sets. The steps should be easily teachable and observable (Schlein et al., 2001). The fact that a client may be able to complete only some of the steps in a task independently should not be a deterrent to

teaching the client the activity. Supports such as adaptations, prompts, and cues are to be provided as needed. However, assistance should be provided only when the client has made an unsuccessful attempt at performing the task in the specified time (Dattilo & Guerin, 2001). Once the client has mastered the step, assistance is phased out. For example, Eddie wants to go bowling. An assessment of his skill level reveals that he needs to learn how to use the adapted bowling ramp. The task analysis has identified the steps in this process and the assistance and instructional strategies necessary in order for Eddie to learn this task:

1. Lift the bowling ball from the ball return.
2. Place bowling ball on lap.
3. Position wheelchair at the head of the foul line behind the bowling ramp.
4. Place both hands on the ball.
5. Using both hands, slide the ball off the lap onto the top of the ramp.
6. Position the ramp toward the desired pins.
7. Release or push the ball down the ramp.

The TRS models the procedure for using the adapted ramp. While Eddie understands the procedure, on the basis of the task analysis the TRS finds that Eddie needs physical assistance to lift the ball and place it on his lap. He is able to move independently to position himself in front of the alley, but also needs physical guidance for lifting and positioning the ball on the adapted ramp. He is able to push the ball down the ramp himself.

Teaching Techniques

To best facilitate learning in clients whose ability to learn or change may be impaired by their health condition, disability, or life circumstances, the TRS selects teaching techniques based on the learning style of the client and the nature of the particular task or skill. The TRS can use techniques such as forward and backward chaining, total or whole task instruction, instructional prompts, positive reinforcers, environmental strategies, and opportunities for practice and generalization (Gardner & Chapman, 1993). By developing the ability to select and apply the six teaching techniques, the TRS can help clients to learn new skills, achieve desired outcomes, and have more satisfying and rewarding experiences.

FORWARD AND BACKWARD CHAINING

Forward chaining involves teaching a person specific skills in a logical sequence from the first to the last step, moving from one step to the next as each step is mastered. For example, for an individual to learn how to complete a puzzle requires cognitive abilities as well as fine motor skills. Using forward chaining, the TRS would have the client start by putting in the first puzzle piece and then continue until the puzzle was completed. This process may be too complex for some clients because they don't know what the finished product will be. If they cannot anticipate the reward of completing the puzzle they may experience frustration, which can impede learning. In this case, the TRS can use the technique of **backward chaining**. The TRS places a completed puzzle in front of the client with the exception of the last piece. She instructs the client to place this piece into the empty spot. The advantage of using backward chaining is that the client completes the task on the first trial and feels successful. After this, the client is asked to place the last two pieces, then the last three, and so on until he can eventually complete the puzzle on his own from the first piece to the last.

TOTAL TASK INSTRUCTION

Total task instruction (TTI), also known as **whole task instruction**, refers to teaching all the steps of a task at once. By observing or understanding the entire sequence of steps, a client may be able to duplicate or perform the behavior. To teach clients bowling, the TRS could prepare them by first explaining how to bowl the ball down the alley. For clients with an auditory learning style, she could say, "Pick up the ball, walk to the line at the top of the alley, holding your arm straight down at your side with your palm facing the pins, swing your arm back, then forward, and release the ball." She could ask the client to repeat these instructions out loud. For visual learners, she would combine verbal instruction with demonstration of how to bowl the ball down the alley, from the first step of picking up the ball to the last step of releasing it. She might also give the clients a picture or diagram that shows the process. The kinesthetic or tactile learner may learn best by actually picking up the ball and carrying out the entire set of steps. As the TRS verbally guides him, she positions herself next to him and demonstrates. Total task instruction is related to modeling. People learn through observing and imitating a behavior because they want to acquire a new skill or because they admire the person who is teaching them.

INSTRUCTIONAL PROMPTS AND CUES

Prompts (sometimes called instructional prompts) and cues help an individual remember what to do in a given situation and increase the probability of

Types of Prompts

The TRS uses prompts to elicit the desired behavior or response from the participant. There are several types of prompts.

Verbal prompts are spoken words that provide information to help direct the client's behavior to carry out a task or an action appropriately. The TRS might say "It's your turn" as a prompt to a client who is learning to play a game.

Gestures are movements of the instructor's hands or body to suggest or elicit a response. Pointing is an example of a gestural prompt.

Shadowing involves following the movements displayed by the participant with your hands but without touching the participant. This provides guidance but allows for more independence.

Physical prompts include a range of supports, from minimal physical assistance (placing a hand lightly on the client's arm to provide direction) to manual guidance including hand-over-hand assistance (placing a hand over the client's to move him through the actions) in order to guide the client through the complete movement or activity.

Modeling or demonstration typically involves actually showing clients the behavior to be learned. It is generally used with visual learners and people who are capable of following steps and have the physical ability to actually duplicate the behavior.

Adapted from Schlein et al.1995.

the occurrence of a target behavior. Instructional prompts include gestures, verbal directions, modeling of behaviors, physical assistance, and hands-on guidance, the latter of which involves moving the client's hands through the actual doing of the behavior. When using a prompt, the leader directly helps a client to make the correct response, for example by physically helping him pick the correct puzzle piece. Although often used interchangeably with the word "prompt," a cue is a form of prompt used to indirectly help the client refocus his attention to an action; an example is redirecting a client's attention by saying, "James, it's your turn." Prompts and cues are important to the teaching process and are used frequently. Clients' skill levels, levels of functioning, learning styles, and the complexity of the task itself determine what type of prompt is necessary.

The degree of prompting used to teach a client a task should be as minimal as possible. Prompts are not meant to be permanent; they are a tool for teaching. James, who is learning how to maneuver his wheelchair in order to play wheelchair basketball, is practicing on the basketball court. The TRS initially models for James how to control the wheelchair when moving quickly during a game. While James is practicing this skill, the TRS leaves the court and gives James only verbal directions on how to control the wheelchair. These prompts help him learn and master the skill. As another example, a client who is visually impaired may require hand-over-hand support when first working with scissors on an arts and crafts project. As the client becomes more familiar with the materials and their location on the table, only verbal cues may be needed to support the client's completion of the activity. The TRS might say, "Now use the scissors." Once the task is learned, the cues should be faded out. When developing an instructional plan, the TRS should take into consideration when to fade prompts or eliminate supports. Stopping a prompt too early can lead to loss of skill or feelings of frustration. Using a prompt when it is no longer needed can lead to the client's developing dependence on the cue for success. Fading out prompts involves the TRS's clinical judgment and, when appropriate, consultation with team members.

REINFORCERS

"**Reinforcers** are events that occur following a desired response, which increase the likelihood that the behavior will occur again" (Schlein et al., 2001, p. 171). We all respond to reinforcers, whether they are in the form of attention, praise, a tangible reward, or an internal feeling of satisfaction. Reinforcers help to

Corbis RF/age fotostock

The minimal physical assistance used here is a physical prompt.

ensure that a response or behavior will be repeated. When our behavior is reinforced, we do it again to receive the positive response. While the reinforcers just mentioned may seem universal, each of us may or may not respond to a particular reinforcer given our own personal history and preferences. Reinforcers can be intrinsic to an activity, as when you eat a cookie you have baked, or external, as when you receive an award in a cooking contest.

The use of reinforcers—when needed—should be identified for a client, based on her specific likes and interests, in the instructional plan. A cookie would not be a positive reinforcer for Paulette, but winning a prize in a healthy cooking contest might be a powerful reinforcer. In one TR program, when a particular client completed his task without leaving the table, he was given a picture of his favorite baseball player to hold in his pocket for the rest of the session. This was an object he desired, so it was an effective reinforcer of his positive behavior. A client also can be offered a group of reinforcers and select the one he wants, rather than receiving the same one every time. This choice gives the client a greater sense of control and also limits the possibility that he will get bored with a reinforcer. An effective approach is to "catch people doing something good and recognize them for it." Too often, bad behavior gets attention and positive behavior is overlooked. This results in repetition of the bad behavior because that is what has been reinforced by the attention.

The use of reinforcers and the choice of potential reinforcers should be discussed with the team to ensure consistency and avoid conflict with any preexisting plan. Recreation activities are an effective source of reinforcement because they are enjoyable, provide feedback on clients' actions, and give them opportunities to make choices and be in control.

ENVIRONMENTAL ARRANGEMENTS

The environment can play a major role in supporting learning. Environments that are safe, comfortable, and accepting facilitate participation and the attainment of goals (DeVries & Lake, 2002). The TRS should seek a balance between an environment that provides stimulation and one that is soothing and calming, depending on the needs of the clients and the tasks to be learned. Similar to needing a balance of skills and challenge in order to experience flow, people need a balance between their capabilities and the demands of the environment. A mismatch can lead to boredom or stress (Shank & Coyle, 2002), which are counterproductive to learning. Some people prefer a formal, structured classroom-type setting for learning; others prefer a more informal, relaxed setting such as a lounge or even prefer to sit on the floor (Anspaugh & Ezell, 2007).

How supplies and materials are set up on a table, the shape of the table, the brightness of the lights, and the types of equipment available all affect participation. Round tables and lighting that enable people to see each other are more conducive to social interaction, which can facilitate learning. However, dimmer lighting can be used to set a certain type of mood or facilitate discussion of sensitive topics. Too much background noise, cluttered space, and poor organization of materials often diminish a client's capacity to stay focused and learn. Using adaptive equipment such as a bigger ball initially to teach how to hit a baseball, or a baseball tee to hold the ball, can provide environmental support for a person with a visual impairment or gross motor concerns. The environment itself can be designed to simulate a real-life situation, such as a model apartment or a facility store where clients can work and shop, In a facility library or coffee shop, clients can practice their newly acquired behaviors. The environment should promote the maintenance, application, and transferability of new learning.

OPPORTUNITIES FOR PRACTICE AND GENERALIZATION

Once a skill is learned, opportunities for maintaining skills, applying them in the natural environment, and generalizing to other settings should be provided. Maintaining newly learned skills and behaviors requires practice and repetition. The TRS should offer programs that give clients the opportunity to use their new skills, both in the service setting and in the community. A leisure lounge with appropriate and preferred recreation materials that is accessible to all clients and that fosters opportunities to make choices and exercise control is an excellent example of a supportive learning environment (Buettner & Martin, 1995). Opportunities for clients' families and friends to participate with them promote generalization. Application in the natural environment involves demonstrating the new skill or behavior in the real-world setting. Hitting a baseball in a gym is not the same as hitting a baseball on a ball field. Practicing a golf swing in the recreation room is different than playing on a commercial miniature golf course where many others are playing and time is a factor. It is important for clients to be able to transfer what they have learned to a variety of settings. Generalizing a behavior from the TR environment to other settings where this skill can be used is vital to clients' success. Learning to take turns in a game can be applied to waiting in line to purchase a movie ticket or to order lunch at a fast food restaurant. The TRS should also report a client's accomplishments to the team members so they can reinforce the client's new learning in the context of the services they are providing.

Use of Instructional Materials

The TRS can use a variety of instructional materials to teach clients new activities. These materials include supplies and equipment such as paints, brushes, paper, balls, food, video games, computers, exercise equipment, board games, and playing cards—and the list goes on. Sometimes these materials are used exactly as intended; at other times the TRS can adapt materials or purchase them in an adapted form so that they are appropriate to clients' needs and capabilities. Activity analysis and task analysis help the TRS determine what materials are necessary for teaching an activity. When the materials are not readily available, the TRS should determine if the budget allows for purchase, whether the potential for donations exists, if alternate materials are available, and how long it will take to get materials. Sometimes materials already available can be adapted. A game board from a children's game can be adapted to create an adult leisure education game. Cardboard paper towel holders can be used to make easy-to-hold game pieces. Numerous online resources offer free computer shells for games as well as game boards and materials. Commercially available kits and games can be purchased by TR departments or donated to a facility for use with clients. Preparation is the key when one is using any instructional materials.

The TRS should be thoroughly familiar with the materials available for activities at her facility. She should have completed the activity herself to determine, for example, if a craft could actually be made by the clients in the allotted time. If the activity is part of an arts and crafts class, the TRS should have a sample ready to show clients. The TRS also needs to consider the adaptations that need to be made. For example, in an adult medical day program the group is working on creating leather eyeglass holders as holiday gifts for family members. Sewing the parts of the case together requires well-developed fine motor skills and eye–hand coordination. Depending on the skills of the clients, adapted large-size needles may be needed. The leather strips used for the stitching may be replaced by yarn, which is easier to handle. Following instructions may be difficult for persons with dementia or for visual learners, so a sample of the finished product as well as a picture should be available.

Specialized instructional materials, such as board games, are often used in TR programs to stimulate discussion and help clients focus on specific issues such as leisure education, decision making, or coping skills. These games are generally easy to play and readily available. A good source for games is www.idyllarbor.com. However, not all games or game questions are appropriate for all clients and situations. The TRS must familiarize herself with the purpose and rules of the game and the types of questions in order to best match the questions to the needs and abilities of the clients. For example, Emily, a new TRS, chooses a commercially produced board game to encourage the members of a group to practice speaking as well as to stimulate memory and promote self-awareness. Emily has not used or reviewed the game but has heard from other TRSs

The TR specialist should be familiar with a wide range of common games, including card games.

that the clients like this game, and she decides to use it. In the group are three clients over the age of 40 who have had a serious head injury. The first card Emily selects has the question, "Who is your favorite teacher in school?"; the next card has "How do you get to school: bus, walk, or does your mother drive you?" Failing to prescreen the game results in asking questions that are age inappropriate for several members of the group. Therefore the activity does not produce the desired result of the clients' engaging each other in conversation. The TRS should be familiar with all the materials and equipment available at the facility and consider creating her own games, kits, and special activities when commercial materials are not available or are too expensive. Being properly prepared and offering organized and well thought-out programs are part of being a positive and effective leader and teacher and can involve collaboration with other professionals.

Positive Teaching Behaviors

For the TRS to successfully apply teaching strategies, he must also demonstrate positive teaching behaviors. His teaching methods, belief in the clients' capability to learn, and his patience as they struggle with challenging new behaviors and attempt to master unfamiliar environments are key elements that promote client learning. Consistency of approach in teaching and instruction means making your expectations clear and treating all participants fairly and equally (Kassing & Jay, 2003).

The TRS needs to be alert to clients' responses to learning, as well as develop the essential skill of addressing the goals and learning needs of each individual within the context of a group program. The TRS should be careful not to become frustrated if clients seem unwilling or unable to learn. Trying different motivation and teaching strategies to find the most effective approaches exemplifies our ethical practice to do our best to meet the needs of our clients. The TRS promotes a learning environment that is fun; that communicates acceptance and understanding; that emphasizes strengths, identity, and free choice; and that offers opportunities for clients to be successful in their efforts (Frye & Peters, 1972).

A crucial element in learning is consistency. Clients should know what to expect when a skill is being taught. The TRS should use the same language and approach when teaching a skill or an activity over a number of sessions. This should be written in the form of an instructional plan so that another leader will be able to maintain a consistent approach in case the TRS is absent. Because of differences in styles and paces of learning, the TRS also must be prepared to present an activity in multiple ways without causing confusion. She could say, "Let's try another way to do this" if she needs to change teaching methods to facilitate learning. Clients deserve to be taught in an environment that supports positive behaviors, and the TRS needs to be able to provide a consistent response when they are having difficulties or are not achieving their goals.

Collaboration to Enhance Learning

Collaboration is the sharing of information and working together to achieve a goal or outcome. It requires collegiality and active listening between two or more people. Collaboration can occur on a number of levels (Shank & Coyle, 2002). The TRS collaborates with a client to develop goals and objectives and, when appropriate, with family members to ensure that clients are being assessed appropriately and have family support. The TRS works collaboratively with other professionals as a member of the team to ensure that clients are receiving appropriate interventions and getting the best treatment possible. Working with clients is a team effort, not a competition, and collaboration is an ethical responsibility of the TRS. As well as collaborating with professionals such as physicians, occupational therapists, physical and speech therapists, nurses, social workers, dietitians, and other staff, the TRS may collaborate with paraprofessionals and support

personnel when planning and organizing programs.

Collaboration related to learning occurs when the TRS cotreats or coleads with another professional. Cotreatment provides the client with an integrated approach to learning and strengthens the impact of the treatment or learning experiences. For example, Emily, the new TRS, cotreated with a speech therapist during a board game. The two professionals supported each other's goals utilizing techniques from both disciplines to maximize the clients' achievement of outcomes. The clients' TR goals included working on the ability to follow instructions and to interact with other group members appropriately, and speech therapy goals focused on articulating words and expressing thoughts effectively. In a cotreatment session, clients have the opportunity to transfer and integrate skills that have been developed in individual speech therapy sessions to the cotreatment environment. Both the TRS and the speech therapist share responsibility for the success of the group. While each professional works on the goals of her own discipline, they interact with the clients to reinforce the integration of the newly learned behaviors. The ability to cotreat with another discipline requires that the TRS be knowledgeable about her own discipline and respectful and knowledgeable of other disciplines. The TRS deserves and expects the same level of knowledge and respect from her collaborators. Collaboration can enrich the clients' learning experience.

Summary of Instructional Strategies

The TRS blends instructional strategies with motivational strategies in an environment designed to promote learning, growth, and the achievement of desired outcomes. It is a challenging but vital aspect of professional practice to plan and organize the TR program so that all clients can learn and make progress toward their own goals in the context of a group setting. The TRS has to be skilled in order to address multiple goals in a single group using the strategies discussed in this chapter. Because of staff shortages and time limitations, the TRS may need to focus on one or two primary goals when leading a TR group. However, she has to be sure to pay attention to every individual in order to enhance each one's learning in the context of the group experience. She should not fall into the habit of engaging only the people who are more verbal and responsive. Therapeutic recreation leadership requires the TRS to engage all the members of the group. The following example illustrates many of the instructional strategies we have discussed.

Case Study

A bowling group in a day program for young adults with intellectual and developmental disabilities was developed and implemented according to the core TR values and principles. First, based on the clients' assessments, the TRS determined that the needs of the group members included developing leisure interests, learning to follow instructions, increasing cooperative behaviors, and learning social skills for functioning in the inclusive environment. Next, in order to decide what group activity would best meet the needs of all the members of the group, the TRS considered the following questions:

- What activities were of interest to the individual members of the group?
- What activity could be used to address multiple needs in the most efficient and organized way?
- What resources were available in the facility and the community?
- What activity had real-life applications for the participants and provided opportunities for future inclusion and community involvement?

In answering the questions, the TRS and the group selected three possible choices: bowling, swimming, and gardening. Access to a pool and space for a garden were limited, so the TRS decided to investigate bowling as the recreation experience. He then completed an activity analysis of bowling and concluded that bowling was indeed a potential activity for the group. For those participants who had no or minimal experience with bowling, the TRS developed a task analysis of bowling. Since bowling is a complex activity to learn, requiring more than eight steps, the TRS broke the steps into smaller components. He selected the teaching techniques of total task instruction (TTI) and modeling to help the clients learn the skills they needed to go bowling. He would use these techniques at the day center before taking the group to a community bowling alley. He simulated a bowling lane with pins, balls, and gutters to maximize transferability or generalization of skills from the treatment to the community setting. Using TTI, the TRS did not break the skill of bowling the ball down the alley into smaller steps but modeled the entire task, from picking up the ball to aiming to releasing the ball toward the pins. He used the same language and approach at every session to provide consistency of instruction.

The TRS also used prompts and cues to promote learning. He initially provided physical assistance to those clients who needed guidance to develop the correct stance and hold the ball. As he observed that the clients were learning these skills, he faded the prompts from physical to verbal, such as "Stand up straight" and "Swing your arm back, then forward, and let the ball go." Eventually the clients learned to execute the skill with the verbal cue "Your turn to bowl." The TRS also provided verbal praise as a reinforcer for the clients when they successfully completed each step. The clients practiced the skills until they were confident that they knew them and were then ready to go to the community bowling center. We can see that a number of instructional strategies and techniques were used successfully to prepare the clients for the activity: activity analysis, task analysis, total task instruction, modeling, physical and verbal prompts, fading, generalization, and practice.

GROWTH-PROMOTING STRATEGIES

As the client is learning new skills and behaviors, the TRS uses the range of instructional strategies we have described. During and after the learning process, the TRS also takes "opportunities to facilitate personal growth through skilled dialog" (Long, 2008b, p. 90). This skilled dialog is known as **therapeutic communication**, which is a goal-directed, focused dialogue between the TRS and a client specifically fitted to the needs of the client (Austin, 2004). Therapeutic communication involves the exchange of ideas, feelings, and attitudes oriented to the desired health care outcomes, using the range of verbal and nonverbal communication behaviors described in chapter 4. By using therapeutic communication, the TRS promotes the clients' personal growth along with their learning of new skills and behaviors. This heightens the therapeutic value of TR. Therapeutic communication is closely related to "processing." "Processing the experience" helps the client internalize the experience, thereby gaining more insight and benefits that can be applied to everyday life. If the TRS does not process with the client, there is a risk that activities will be diversional rather than educational (Austin, 2009).

Processing

Processing is a "therapeutic technique primarily involving verbal discussion of client behaviors, as well as their thoughts, feelings, and other external factors that relate to the behavior" (Shank & Coyle,

2002, p. 219). Processing aims to have a client accurately describe an experience, reflect on the impact the experience had on her, and communicate this to the TRS and—when appropriate—to group members or other clinicians. Processing helps a client to increase her awareness of what she has accomplished and contributes to her new learning. For example, if a client can successfully master a particular activity that requires a high level of skill, the ability to take a risk, and a degree of self-confidence, perhaps she can also accomplish successful outcomes in other aspects of treatment and after discharge.

Processing has several specific components: framing or frontloading, providing feedback, and debriefing, which correspond to the beginning, middle, and end of an activity. Each component or technique can be used to promote the TRS–client relationship and to enhance the learning experience of the client (Mobily & Ostiguy, 2004).

FRONTLOADING OR FRAMING

Frontloading, or **framing**, is a technique the TRS can use to explain the purpose of the activity before the clients begin participating in the program. Frontloading is the means by which the TRS informs clients of the goals of the program and provides information relevant to participating in the activity. It helps clients focus on the important aspects of the experience while they are engaged in it. The TRS creates a frame of reference for the clients so they can see the relevance and value of an activity. Too often, TRSs don't explain the therapeutic value of a TR program; instead they try to motivate clients to attend by saying, "It's fun, you'll have a good time." Although fun is a core TR value, it is only one aspect of the TR experience. Many clients are motivated to participate when they see the relevance of the TR program to their goals. For example, in short-term physical rehabilitation, in which clients focus on overcoming their functional limitations, the TRS can explain how arts and crafts can improve motor skills. In this way the TRS provides a rationale for why a particular TR program is being offered to the client. Frontloading can also be used to review clients' progress to a given point and discuss any barriers or obstacles to further learning (Mobily & Ostiguy, 2004).

Another use of frontloading is to "brief" clients before the start of the program to enhance their ability to focus on the activity (Russell, 2004). When organizing a game of Uno with a group of clients who have cognitive limitations, the TRS may tell the clients up front that the purpose of the program is to enhance cognitive skills such as following instructions, number and color recognition, and strategic thinking. This helps the clients pay attention to addressing their goals. Thinking about what you are doing and why you are doing it is what a personal fitness trainer is getting at when he tells you to "think about the muscle you are working" in order to get the best results. But while frontloading is valuable, too much frontloading can confuse and distract a client. To avoid this, it is best to frontload only periodically and to provide only enough information to target key points (Hutchinson & Dattilo, 2001). Clients' thoughts and feelings about the activity should also be discussed to relieve anxiety and reduce stress about their abilities and interactions with others in the group (Shank & Coyle, 2002).

FEEDBACK

Feedback refers to "teaching moments that occur during the activity" (Mobily & Ostiguy, p. 192) when the TRS gives supportive and informative comments to clients regarding their efforts and actions. When provided skillfully, feedback is a powerful tool. The goal of feedback is self-awareness (Niepoth, 1983). Feedback helps clients understand what they have experienced in TR, learn how they are perceived by others and what they themselves are communicating, and develop a positive self-concept. It gives them information and guidance to use to improve their skills or change their behaviors. Therefore it is essential that providing feedback be a *conscious* act. The TRS may be giving feedback unintentionally through nonverbal communication, not only in structured TR interactions with clients but also in informal interactions, as expressed in the saying, "You can never *not* communicate." The TRS must be aware of his own nonverbal behaviors so he can be sure he is communicating what he intends to and that his body language is not misunderstood. Nonverbal communication in the form of a smile, a nod, a pat on the back, or an encouraging gesture sends powerful messages about one's actions or behaviors. Conversely, rolling one's eyes, turning away from a client, or not consciously providing feedback may unintentionally send a message that the client misinterprets as failure, disapproval, or rejection.

Some people are uncomfortable receiving feedback, either because they feel they don't deserve "compliments" or they perceive it as criticism. To help those clients be more receptive to feedback, it should be directly linked to their goals and objectives. On the other hand, overloading clients with too much feedback can be overwhelming, resulting in frustration and anxiety. To be effective, feedback should be informational, contingent, and motivating:

- Informational feedback is descriptive, providing specific information on the behavior being addressed.
- Contingent feedback means feedback given as soon as the action occurs.
- Motivational feedback is feedback given to encourage continued learning.

While James is learning how to play wheelchair basketball, as soon as he performs a new move correctly the TRS tells him that he has done so (contingent) by saying "You really were able to control the wheelchair during practice (informational). I bet you'll be a big help to the team at Friday's game" (motivational). When given well, feedback is clear, affirms the client's abilities, and focuses on an attainable goal. Feedback statements should be honest and direct but offered in a way that is reinforcing, motivating, and supportive of change.

DEBRIEFING

The conclusion of an activity also offers the opportunity to promote clients' growth through use of the strategy of **debriefing**. Debriefing occurs at the end of an activity to help clients reflect on the meaning of the experience for both the individual and the group as a whole (Hutchinson & Dattilo, 2001), as well as on what they have learned as a result of their participation. Debriefing answers the questions "What happened? So what does it mean? And now what comes next?" (Shank & Coyle, 2002; Austin, 2009).

- To answer the question "What happened?" clients are asked about what went on in the group, what they learned, what they observed, what they did that was "right" or "wrong," and how they reacted.
- The question "So what does it mean?" refers to understanding the consequences and results of what happened in the group and what clients learned from these consequences. Participants are encouraged to consider how they might use what they learned in other situations.
- Finally the question "And now what comes next?" leads participants to set goals for applying their newly learned skills and behaviors in other aspects of their lives.

The TRS should design questions to facilitate the client's successful use of the debriefing process as a learning tool. The TRS can ask the clients to describe how what they did today reminds them of a previous experience and what insights they developed about how they might handle that situation in the future. For example, David, a 12-year-old boy with cancer (see chapter 5), has a goal of learning to use adaptive devices for video games to compensate for fine motor skill weakness. After the training session with the TRS, she asks him to review what he was able to accomplish, how he felt about his progress in learning, how he thought this new skill would help him, and what he wants to do in the future based on what he has learned. David replies that he learned how using the devices could help him play games with the other kids; he felt a little clumsy, but was confident (thanks to the TRS's feedback) that he could master use of the tools with a few more sessions. See table 7.1 on page 232 for descriptions of debriefing techniques that could be used by the TRS.

For nonverbal clients or those for whom the primary language of the service setting is not their native language, written responses and observations, drawings, or reflective journals can be used. A significant multicultural consideration for using growth-promoting strategies is that not all cultures believe in or are familiar with engaging in reflection to develop and share insights. The TRS should explain the purpose and value of processing activities to all participants, yet must be respectful of an individual's comfort level about engaging. Kenneth, the patient in cardiac rehabilitation, feels uncomfortable verbally sharing in a group. The TRS suggests that he keep a daily journal to reflect on the causes of his stress and on his efforts to identify helpful stress management techniques. The TRS meets with Kenneth every other day for debriefing, reviewing what he has written in order to help him determine effective means to reduce his stress and cope with his feelings of vulnerability surrounding his health.

Debriefing would seem to be essential to making meaning out of the TR experience. Without the process of reflection and developing insight, new learning may not occur as easily or may not be maintained over time. Therapeutic recreation specialists should develop their skill in using all the types of processing approaches in order to maximize what clients learn and enhance the value of the TR experience. Ethically, it is the TRS's responsibility to be aware of her own needs and competent in using growth-promoting strategies that can have a powerful effect on clients. The TRS protects the well-being and safety of clients, and respects their autonomy and choices about engaging in learning and growth-promoting experiences.

TABLE 7.1

Debriefing Techniques

Technique	Description
Go Around	Each client contributes a descriptive sentence or word regarding the activity or a portion of the activity. The TRS could ask each member of the group to share an emotion she experienced during the program.
Whip	Similar to Go Around, but each client completes a sentence stem presented by the TRS. Examples: "One thing we did well today was . . ."; "I feel good about. . . ."
Memory game	Clients recall the events of the session in chronological order, with each client taking up where the previous client left off. The facilitator indicates when to pass the story off to the next person.
Gestalt	The client closes his eyes, recalls an event, and describes it as if he were actually going through the event again. Essentially the client mentally relives the experience. The facilitator questions the client about the experience when appropriate: for example, "What do you see as you stand in front of the group?"
Props	Props are used to stimulate discussion, including "talking sticks," playing cards, and other commercially produced processing products.
Artifacts	Physical items created or related to the experience are used to stimulate discussion. Examples: T-shirts, medals, craft projects, and self-assessments such as the colors personality test.
Videos and photographs	Videos, photos, or audio recordings made during a session are used as a prompt for recollection and discussion of the experience.

Reprinted, by permission, from T. Long, 2008, The therapeutic recreation process. In *Foundations of therapeutic recreation*, edited by T. Robertson and T. Long (Champaign, IL: Human Kinetics), p. 95.

Coaching

Coaching is one of the more recent developments in leadership strategies. Coaching is based on several approaches but particularly on the work of Stephen Covey, who wrote *Seven Habits of Highly Effective People*. Coaching is usually thought of in the context of sport, but job and lifestyle coaching now have become popular. Coaching is a person-centered approach to helping individuals develop and reach their goals. The technique of coaching is based on specific therapeutic approaches and focuses on the client's developing practical lifelong skills to help her lead a more successful and balanced life. Coaching is not therapy, but is seen as the next step after someone gains insight and awareness into her problems or limitations. The intent of coaching is for the client to take on a leadership role in her change process. The coach–client relationship is action oriented. The coach assists the client with specific skill development, provides ongoing support to help her "reframe" her life by looking at it in a new way, and creates a nurturing environment that facilitates progress towards achieving goals.

The TRS can take on the role of coach as clients gain insight into their problems and begin to take greater control over their lives. For example, Sheri has completed her alcohol treatment and is in recovery back home. Her former friends enjoyed going to bars and playing in a softball league where the beer flowed freely, which reinforced Sheri's drinking behavior. She knows that new friends and leisure interests are necessary to support her recovery, but is not ready to make those changes on her own. The TRS can use coaching to help Sheri envision this new lifestyle and develop strategies to meet new people who have healthier leisure interests. The TRS's style of interaction has shifted from the therapist's approach of helping Sheri to gain insight, to that of coach as he assists her in identifying the next steps in the recovery process, and finally to that of a leader as he helps her learn new recreation activities.

Ethical Considerations for Using Growth-Promoting Strategies

Fulfilling the more therapeutic aspects of the TR leadership role with clients places an even greater responsibility on the TRS to monitor her own behavior and operate from a sound ethical mindset. Processing and coaching are powerful strategies that can be very effective at promoting growth and change when used conscientiously. The TRS is ethically obligated to be self-aware; to screen her interactions and responses for inappropriate, irrelevant, or harmful content; to be honest, fair, and competent in applying these strategies; to protect the well-being of clients and safeguard their privacy; and to cooperate with and support colleagues in their efforts. The TRS should endeavor to improve her understanding and skill in professional practices of applying these strategies, as well as to inform clients thoroughly of the nature and purpose of all professional practices in language and modes that are comprehensible to them.

● Summary ●

Therapeutic recreation leadership is delivered successfully when clients learn new behaviors and skills to support a healthy and happy lifestyle. The TRS should develop and use a repertoire of strategies to motivate and teach and to facilitate learning and growth in clients. Therapeutic recreation participation is active and experiential; clients are involved in *doing*. Learning by doing is one of the most powerful modes for learning. Recreation is an ideal experience for learning because it is the venue in which all a person's skills can come together in a set of freely chosen behaviors and activities that are pleasing and satisfying to the individual. Our ethical responsibility to our clients is to protect and promote their well-being, to be competent and up-to-date in the methods we use, to make efficient and effective use of resources, to be diligent in meeting our clients' needs, and to respect their self-determination. Ethical leadership embodies use of the strategies in a sincere and equitable manner and the exercise of sound clinical judgment. To be sure that our actions are just, we evaluate ourselves, our programs, and the progress of our clients.

● Learning Activities ●

1. In a small group, discuss the concept of the "TR environment" and its impact on clients.

2. Reflect on your personal learning style. Do you tend to learn visually, auditorily, or kinesthetically? Compare your style to those of your classmates or coworkers. What similarities and differences exist?

3. Think of a behavior or new skill you would like to learn but have put off doing. Analyze your readiness for change by identifying the stage of change you are in. How could you use flow technology to promote your learning of the new skill?

4. How aware are you of your personal needs and how they affect the choices you make? What role do intrinsic and extrinsic motivators play in your behavior?

5. Prepare a task analysis of a simple board game or card game.

6. Based on the task analysis you prepared for question 5, teach the game to another person using the six teaching techniques discussed in the chapter. Be sure to give feedback to your student. At the end of the activity, discuss how effective your feedback was in promoting learning. Evaluate the accuracy of your task analysis and the effectiveness of your techniques.

7. Select the case of either Mrs. Kelly or Debbie from the chapter. With a partner, take turns role playing the TRS and the client engaged in processing the client's experience in the TR activity. How comfortable were you as the TRS processing the activity with the client? What effect did the processing experience have on the client's responses?

8. Make arrangements to observe a TRS conducting a TR program. Identify all the motivational, instructional, and growth-promoting strategies he or she uses. Write a brief report, as if you were the TRS's clinical supervisor, to give feedback on his or her use of strategies.

Evaluation of Practitioners, Programs, and Participants

In this chapter you will learn about:

- The purposes of evaluation
- The three sets of skills the practitioner should possess
- Clinical supervision
- Formative and summative evaluation
- Program protocols
- How to evaluate the effectiveness of TR programs
- Evaluating program structure; scheduling; and the physical, human, and administrative resources used to deliver programs
- Measuring outcomes by observation, interviewing, and using standardized instruments
- Procedures for documentation
- How to schedule evaluation activities
- Evaluation according to standards of professional practice, regulations governing health care, and performance improvement processes
- The value of research for the practitioner and the profession
- The purpose and use of action research and logic models

How do TRSs know that their work has meaning and value? By carrying out a comprehensive process of evaluation, the TRS can better understand and describe the outcomes and effects of her work. Evaluation helps to determine TR's contribution to clients, agencies, the profession, and society. Yet many TR departments fall short on collecting and utilizing data to demonstrate the outcomes and effects of TR programs, perhaps because staff are in need of more concrete knowledge of how to conduct evaluation. It's important to understand *why* we evaluate, *what* we evaluate, and *how* we evaluate. Evaluation is necessary for the following reasons (Vander Molen, 2007):

- To demonstrate that programs are worthwhile
- To improve service delivery
- To determine program effectiveness
- To provide evidence to stakeholders, who are the individuals or groups who have an interest in the activities and outcomes of an organization and its programs and services (Commission on Accreditation of Rehabilitation Facilities, 2008).

From an ethical perspective, TR professionals are obligated to provide services that promote their clients' well-being according to the highest standards of professional practice. Evaluation contributes to fulfilling the profession's ethical responsibility.

Evaluation can be defined as determining the value or amount of something. In TR, evaluation refers to a systematic process of collecting and analyzing data for the purposes of making decisions about programs and services. These data may be related to the clients' progress as a result of TR intervention, the effectiveness of TR programs at meeting the goals of the TR department and achieving desired outcomes, and the performance of the TR staff in providing TR services. Analysis of the data results either in decisions to make changes in services or in the conclusion that no changes are needed. For many years, the emphasis in TR was on collecting attendance statistics. It was believed that the number of clients who attended programs was an indicator of the success of the program. But attendance tells only one small part of the evaluation story. Do people attend a program because it is the only choice offered at that time? How meaningful is their participation? Is the program addressing their needs and goals? What are the outcomes of their attendance at the program? How effective is the TRS at leading the program? Does the TRS possess the skills to conduct the program? Answering these questions gives a fuller picture of the qual-

ity and worth of TR services. The value of the TR programs themselves is measured by the effects on the individuals who participate, as well as the participants' satisfaction with services. In addition, today, programs are evaluated to determine if they are an efficient use of resources. A good TR evaluation plan should assess the effects of programs on the clients and determine how efficiently and effectively programs are delivered.

EVALUATING THE PRACTITIONER

The first area we will address is evaluation of the TRS, since this is a book about how the TRS can deliver competent TR leadership. "The quality of programs and services depends to a large extent upon the caliber of the professional leadership" (Frye & Peters, 1972, p. 128). It is the premise of this book that the interaction of the TRS with the client in the provision of services is the essence of TR practice. This interaction frequently occurs in the context of providing TR leadership of a program. How effectively the TRS conducts the program and interacts with the clients is, to a large extent, what leads clients to achieving outcomes and having meaningful experiences in TR. Several approaches can be used to evaluate the performance of the TRS. The TRS is undoubtedly evaluated formally by her supervisor at regularly scheduled intervals as part of an agency's human resource management process. This is known as performance appraisal or evaluation and typically involves filling out a form with a rating scale and a section for comments. This form should reflect the specifications of the job description for the TRS's position. The supervisor may base the evaluation on his observations of the TRS in action, discussions with the TRS, the TRS's fulfillment of various responsibilities, and feedback received from other staff, clients, and families. Many management textbooks discuss this procedure, including *Effective Management in Therapeutic Recreation Service* (Carter & O'Morrow, 2006).

In addition to the administrative supervisor's evaluation, the TRS also has responsibility to evaluate herself on an ongoing basis. As the TRS plans and leads TR programs, she should engage in self-monitoring. According to the codes of ethics of the TR profession, TRSs adhere to the ethical principle of competence. We have an ethical responsibility to be competent at what we do and to engage in ongoing education to improve our knowledge and skills. The TRS may use a checklist of skills and behaviors to evaluate her knowledge and professional practice. In addition to the knowledge and skills presented in chapters 4 and 7, the TRS can use the skills identified in the job analysis conducted by the National Council for Therapeutic Recreation Certification (NCTRC), which describes the tasks that Certified Therapeutic Recreation Specialists (CTRSs) are performing on their jobs. However, the TR profession is dynamic, and new knowledge is being created all the time; new skills may be needed to maintain a high level of service. The TRS has the responsibility to stay current and up-to-date with the latest professional developments.

Other methods of evaluating the TRS include peer review and customer satisfaction surveys. Using peer review, TRSs may observe and evaluate each other's performance to give feedback and suggestions for improvement. They can sit in on each other's groups and observe the TRS's leadership and facilitation skills, as well as review each other's documentation. In addition, many agencies use customer or patient satisfaction surveys, which are given or mailed to clients. These surveys ask a number of questions regarding the services clients received and the personnel who delivered those services. Therapeutic recreation departments should be sure that TR is included as a focus of these surveys in order to obtain valuable feedback that may help demonstrate as well as improve the performance of the TRS, the effectiveness of TR programming for the clients, and the overall value of TR services.

Table 8.1 shows a sample TRS effectiveness survey. Therapeutic recreation specialists can use these and similar items to construct a simple survey for their department's use. Compare this survey to the items in the rating scale shown in table 8.2 on page 238. This behavioral expectation scale is developed for supervisors to evaluate a TRS's performance in selecting TR programs and interventions. Using these two types of evaluation together provides a fuller picture of the TRS's performance and useful feedback for the improvement of services.

Practitioners' Skills

The TRS, in fulfilling the TR leadership role, must possess a level of skill sufficient to effectively plan and deliver quality TR services. A helpful approach to evaluating the skills of the practitioner is to examine three subsets of skills: mechanical, intellectual, and interpersonal (Hebert, 1997). Just as the TRS fulfills the blended TR leadership role, these three sets of skills are blended in the provision of TR programs.

MECHANICAL SKILLS

Mechanical skills are those used in carrying out the TR program. Mechanical skills are related to the practitioner's performance: having the ability to conduct a range of TR programs and to use equipment and supplies in a skillful manner. While a TRS

TABLE 8.1

Therapist Effectiveness Survey

Therapist's name:		
1. My therapist was interested in me.	Yes	No
2. Therapist kept the activity interesting.	Yes	No
3. Therapist was usually on time.	Yes	No
4. Therapist took an active part.	Yes	No
5. Therapist cared about me.	Yes	No
6. Therapist helped me feel better.	Yes	No
7. Therapist talked to me.	Yes	No
8. Therapist was courteous.	Yes	No
9. Therapist was knowledgeable.	Yes	No
10. Therapist showed respect for me.	Yes	No
11. Therapist won my trust.	Yes	No
12. Therapist was sensitive to my needs.	Yes	No

Reprinted from L. Buettner and D. Martin, 1995, *Therapeutic recreation in the nursing home* (State College, PA: Venture Publishing), 185. By permission of L. Buettner.

TABLE 8.2

Behaviorally Anchored Rating Scale

CTRS criterion: selection of programs and interventions	Rating
Could be expected to select services that enable each client to achieve program or treatment plan objectives	5
Could be expected to recommend services that enable client achievement of program or treatment plan objectives with occasional supervisory guidance	4
Could be expected to identify alternative services appropriate to client objectives for staff review and program determination	3
Could be expected to seek approval for recommended services to achieve objectives from staff and manager	2
Could be expected to seek assistance from staff and manager for identifying appropriate alternatives to achieve	1

Note: 5 is the highest rating the CTRS can attain to demonstrate competence in selecting appropriate programs and interventions.

Reprinted from M. Carter and G. O'Morrow, 2006, *Effective management in therapeutic recreation service*, 2nd ed. (State College, PA: Venture Publishing), 222. By permission of M. Carter.

cannot possibly be highly talented in every type of activity, she must understand the nature of the activities and how to conduct them. The greater her knowledge, the less chance of things going wrong and the more smoothly the program will operate. Mechanical skills also include using leadership techniques: applying motivation strategies, organizing the group, giving directions and instructions, using reinforcers appropriately and effectively, and facilitating the flow of the activity. These skills are used in the actual leading of the program, which is the vehicle for producing changes in clients and strengthening their areas of competence.

The TRS can engage in self-monitoring to evaluate and improve her mechanical skills by asking herself these questions:

- Do I know how to do this activity?
- Do I know how to use the particular equipment and supplies the activity requires?
- If the equipment breaks or I run out of supplies, do I have a backup plan?
- Am I competent to lead the broad range of activities that should be part of a good TR program?
- Do I know how to select and apply appropriate leadership strategies?
- Am I familiar with the resources available to me to expand my programming?

Now, you may be thinking, "I don't play a musical instrument, so how can I lead a music program?"; or "I'm not artistic, I can't do arts and crafts"; or "I'm not athletic; how can I run a sport program?" Remember, learning the steps in an activity does not require talent. Being able to provide instruction does not require a high level of performance. It does not matter if the TRS is not an expert in an activity. What matters is that the TRS is effective in leading the program with sufficient knowledge to make it worthwhile and that she possesses the energy, commitment, and sincere desire to help her clients. Playing a musical instrument or swimming or skiing involve skills that a TRS could probably not learn in a short time. But there may be clients, other staff, family members, or volunteers who can assist the TRS with these activities. The TRS has the responsibility to continually develop new skills, utilize resources, and be creative in offering programs. This leads us to the next set of skills.

INTELLECTUAL SKILLS

Intellectual skills refer to the ability to select the appropriate and relevant TR interventions and programs for a client based on his needs and goals, in the context of the setting where services are provided. This can be compared to diagnosing and prescribing. The TRS does not actually make a medical diagnosis, but does "diagnose" what a client needs and "prescribes" a TR plan. This plan may also include reinforcing clients' strengths. To possess a sufficient degree of competence in this area, the TRS needs extensive knowledge of what the clients' status and conditions are, how the conditions affect the clients' behavior, and how best to address these issues. For example, for a patient in a long-term psychiatric hospital who has an interest in gardening, a gardening group in which clients nurture plants may be an excellent choice to meet goals of increasing self-esteem and taking on a responsibility. For a client on an acute care unit with a short length of stay, there would not be enough time for those goals to be achieved in a gardening program. Thorough knowledge of TR interventions and when to use them, keeping up-to-date on new approaches, and the ability to analyze activities are part of the

TRS's intellectual skills. An essential intellectual skill for the TRS is knowing how to adapt an activity in order to produce an outcome. The TRS should know how to shape the TR experience to maximize the opportunity for the client to achieve his planned outcomes or have the desired experience.

The following are self-monitoring questions regarding intellectual skills:

- Do I understand the purposes of the TR activities I am providing?
- Do I know what the actual experience of doing a particular activity may feel like to my clients?
- Do I understand how the recreation experience may affect a client?
- Do I have the skill to facilitate my client's attainment of outcomes?
- Am I confident in my knowledge of program planning?
- Are there new interventions that I should learn to best help my clients?
- Do I understand the new trends that are affecting services in my agency?

Intellectual skills reflect the knowledge obtained in academic degree programs, continuing education, and in-service training. Ongoing professional development and lifelong learning are essential to quality services and professional viability. As TRSs increase their collaboration with other disciplines, intellectual skills will be needed to demonstrate and convey the role and value of TR. Effective communication is included in the next group of skills.

INTERPERSONAL SKILLS

Interpersonal skills are the heart of the TRS's services to the client. Putting a client and an activity together may produce an outcome by chance; but it is the nature of the relationship between the TRS and the client, manifested in the TRS's interpersonal skills, that facilitates the change and growth of the client. Interpersonal skill includes the ability to provide information to clients in a manner and format that are understandable to them. The TRS must ascertain that the client understands the real meaning of what is being said. If common understanding is not present, communication may not be successful. Moreover, communication occurs not only through the spoken word but also through body language, sign language, writing, pictures, the computer, or other means. The TRS must determine the appropriate means of expression, be skilled in communicating in that way, and gauge the amount and level of complexity of the information provided to the client and his family members.

Lisa Petkau/First Light/Getty Images

Tailoring communication to the client might include learning and using American Sign Language.

Besides giving information to clients and their families, the TRS provides encouragement and emotional support in a sensitive and caring manner. These skills are utilized in one-to-one conversations with clients as well as in facilitating the client's participation during the TR program. The TRS's interpersonal skill is what she uses to create the "TR environment" that enables clients to experience the benefits of recreation, have meaningful experiences, and attain valued outcomes. With the proper use of interpersonal skills, the TRS develops a rapport with the client, gains his trust, and facilitates his growth and positive experiences within the context of almost any TR program. This is the essence of TR leadership.

Self-monitoring of interpersonal skills includes answering these questions:

- How do others perceive me?
- Am I patient? Do my clients feel comfortable with me? Am I treating everyone fairly?
- Am I keeping my personal needs separate from my work with clients? Am I maintaining appropriate boundaries?
- Are there any new modes of communication I can learn to facilitate my interaction with clients?

- Is my nonverbal communication being misinterpreted?
- Am I altering my leadership style to suit the changing needs and abilities of my clients?
- Am I successful at creating TR experiences that are both fun and therapeutic?
- Do I demonstrate passion for and commitment to the TR experience and communicate this to my clients?

A high degree of interpersonal skill is essential to fulfilling the ethical obligations of protecting and promoting clients' well-being, demonstrating respect for their autonomy and privacy, and developing and maintaining appropriate and meaningful relationships that will serve their best interests.

While TR practice is based on a body of knowledge that is reflected in the skills the TRS possesses, the practitioner's personal characteristics may affect the quality and type of services offered (Hebert, 1997). Age, gender, amount of experience, type of training, professional philosophy, and personal interests play a role in how a TRS practices skills and how clients may respond. While the uniqueness of each TR practitioner contributes to the personal nature of the TR experience, the TRS should be diligent in self-monitoring to provide services that are relevant, appropriate, and meaningful. An increasingly important concern for TRSs is cultural competence. Cultural competence is "the lifelong pursuit of increasing personal awareness of other cultures" (Getz, 2002, p. 154). Getz (2002) has designed a self-evaluation tool that TRSs can use to assess their knowledge of cultural issues. No matter how one scores on this self-evaluation, it can help the TRS identify areas to develop to be a culturally competent practitioner.

Clinical Supervision

Besides the formal evaluation of the TRS and the TRS's self-monitoring of his knowledge, skills, and performance, there is another very helpful method that can be used to evaluate the practitioner for ongoing professional growth. **Clinical supervision** is a well-recognized practice in the mental health fields, such as psychiatry, clinical psychology, psychiatric social work, and psychiatric nursing; however, it is less frequently provided to TRSs (Austin, 2004). Clinical supervision refers to an ongoing relationship between a clinical supervisor and a practitioner, focused on helping the practitioner develop his knowledge and skills in order to provide the highest-quality services. It is not a perfor-

mance evaluation for human resource management purposes. In fact, the clinical supervisor should not necessarily be someone who has administrative authority over the TRS, but rather a professional who possesses expertise in the areas addressed in the clinical setting. The clinical supervisor could be another TR professional or a professional from another discipline. In psychiatry, a psychiatric nurse practitioner, psychiatric social worker, or psychologist could provide clinical supervision to the TRS. In clinical supervision, trust is an essential element. The TRS is sharing what she sees as her limitations or weaknesses regarding practice with the expectation that the supervisor will understand and help her develop a plan for professional growth. The feelings and beliefs that the TRS shares with the clinical supervisor are *not* to be used as part of a performance evaluation. All professionals probably have doubts about what they know or about the adequacy of their knowledge and skills. The TRS may be confronted with a challenging client, or a task that she doesn't feel prepared for, or a situation involving another department. It is essential to successful clinical supervision that the TRS feel comfortable about sharing these feelings with her clinical supervisor.

Let's look at the example of the TRS who is working with Debbie in treatment for alcoholism. The TRS becomes frustrated and feels angry with Debbie for her lack of willingness to address her problems. The TRS brings this up with the clinical supervisor and also reveals that Debbie reminds her of her sister-in-law, who struggles with a similar problem. The clinical supervisor can help the TRS by discussing countertransference issues, suggesting readings related to interacting with people with alcohol abuse, demonstrating verbal techniques to use with Debbie, role playing interactions between the TRS and Debbie, and directly observing the TRS in her interactions with Debbie. The feedback that the supervisor gives the TRS can help her learn how to keep her personal feelings in check and work more effectively with Debbie. As a result of this clinical supervision process, the TRS has increased her self-awareness, identified an area she needed to learn more about, and learned new methods for her practice. With the assistance of her clinical supervisor, she may make a plan to learn new facilitation techniques to use with clients in recovery from alcoholism. This plan could include doing specific readings, attending a conference, and receiving coaching from the psychologist. The TRS may plan to develop two new TR programs to address issues that Debbie and other clients have. She can set target dates by which to accomplish these goals and specify the outcomes that will indicate successful completion. In this way, evaluation of the practitioner contributes to determining the value of the work the TRS has done and to the ongoing improvement of her services.

Done right, clinical supervision is an excellent tool for professional development and can lead to improved services. It can be effective when provided in particularly challenging settings or to new practitioners weekly or even monthly. All departments are encouraged to incorporate clinical supervision as an ethical practice. Unfortunately, in many agencies today, time pressures make it difficult to schedule clinical supervision. One approach to finding the time is a peer support group. In one psychiatric hospital, the TR director allotted time for the staff to meet on their own in order to share issues and problems, such as addressing the challenge of completing paperwork in a timely fashion. The group came up with their own solution, which they then presented to the director. In this way, they were able to freely express their concerns without fear of being judged by their supervisor and to develop a course of action that they felt would be workable and effective. This approach can help practitioners develop their skills and feel empowered in their work through group problem solving. The director demonstrates his commitment to the process by authorizing the group and allowing them to test out their solution.

Today, evaluation of the leadership provided by the TRS has moved beyond rating a set of optimal skills and behaviors to evaluating on-the-job effectiveness. Evaluation should be used to improve professional practice (Kraus, 1997) and not viewed solely as a tool to judge professional performance. Through the evaluation process, the TRS can identify her strengths and weaknesses to help make a plan for professional development. A true professional always seeks to further develop his skills and knowledge in order to be more effective. Competence is an ethical principle of the TR profession.

EVALUATING PROGRAMS

In providing competent TR leadership, the TRS carries out program evaluation to ensure the highest-quality services that meet needs and provide benefits to the clients. Evaluation is a continuing process that occurs at all points of the programming process, in the form of summative and formative evaluation. The TRS carries out formative and summative evaluation as part of her regular job responsibilities.

Formative and Summative Evaluation

Formative evaluation is evaluation that is ongoing, that occurs during the actual activity, and that leads to immediate changes in an activity as needed. Just as the TRS monitors his own conduct, he is continually adjusting his programs, when necessary, to facilitate successful experiences. For example, if the TRS is conducting an activity and needs to adjust the rules, offer more one-to-one assistance, or obtain additional supplies, he can make these modifications as the need arises. If at the end of a single session of a multisession program he determines that the time of day the program is offered or the size of the group should be adjusted, he makes these changes if possible. Formative evaluation leads to immediate improvements in the program.

Summative evaluation refers to evaluation done at the end of a program, whether it is a summer camp, a three-month once-weekly art program, or a twice-a-week fitness program that runs for two months. At the conclusion of the total program, the TRS conducts an evaluation of all the elements to determine if the program was a success, if any changes are needed to improve the program, and if the program should be offered again. Conducting summative evaluation at regular intervals maintains the quality of the TR program. The following examples illustrate formative and summative evaluation.

Therapeutic recreation specialists may offer a single activity on a regular basis, such as a weekly bingo game or arts and crafts three times a week, or a program that is ongoing and consists of multiple sessions, such as a summer gardening program or winter sport program. During each session the TRS conducts formative evaluation to make necessary changes or improvements. Perhaps the bingo prizes are no longer valued or the craft activities are too complicated for a client population that is in functional decline. The TRS should obtain different prizes or conduct simpler craft projects. Then, at the conclusion of the entire program, the TRS conducts summative evaluation to determine if the program met the clients' goals, interests, and needs; if it was successful in helping clients achieve their outcomes; and if it was an efficient use of resources.

Ongoing programs that are offered on a continual basis also should be evaluated periodically to ensure that they are still meeting the needs of the clients and adhering to the best program design and leadership principles. It is easy to fall into the habit of scheduling the same program week after week; but in long-term care settings, group homes, or residential facilities that serve the same clients for extended periods of time, often years, programs can get stale. It is vital to schedule regular summative evaluation to mix old favorites with new activities. The client mix can change as well. Nursing home populations have an older and frailer elderly population, as well as younger clients with traumatic brain injuries, AIDS, multiple sclerosis, and developmental disabilities. A more diverse program is required to meet their varied needs. In psychiatric and physical rehabilitation units, length of stay has decreased, so a different type of programming is needed to achieve goals in a shorter span of time. The TRS is responsible for ongoing review of the clients' needs and characteristics to insure the provision of programs that are relevant and timely.

Program Effectiveness

The purpose of program evaluation is to determine program effectiveness and improve services. Improving services is "the most important function program evaluation plays" (Widmer, Zabriskie & Wells, 2003, p. 203). In both the NTRS and ATRA standards of practice, one of the standards is to conduct routine program evaluation for the purpose of determining the appropriateness and efficacy of programs. The TRS's ethical responsibility is to do what is in the best interests of the people she serves. "Far too often, programs are offered because of tradition, precedent, popularity, demand, or other reasons" (Sylvester et al., 2001, p. 253). The TRS must carefully select a TR program to meet the interests, needs, and abilities of the clients and not her own interests. Her personal preferences should not dictate choice of programming. In addition, TR programs should be designed and selected in accordance with research findings. "No TR program should be proposed without a serious search of the research literature for support" (Patrick, 2001, p. 404). This is a form of evidence-based practice. The TRS should review the professional literature for research articles related to the programs being planned. Most research articles include a section on practical implications of the findings for implementing TR interventions. Once the TRS has reviewed the evidence and decided to offer a specific program, she should develop a program protocol. A **program protocol** is a standardized set of procedures used to carry out a program or intervention in order to attain a predetermined client outcome (Hood, 2001).

PROGRAM PROTOCOLS

A protocol should represent the "best practice" of TR. Protocols present a rationale for TR services and a guide for selecting interventions (Hood, 2003). Program protocols outline

- who is to take part in the program,
- the specific details about the treatment that will be offered within the program, and
- what changes the client should see as a result of the treatment (Grote et al., 1995).

The TR profession has begun to develop program protocols to be used to establish a common basis for effective practice by all TR departments. By following an established protocol, the TRS can be more confident that the program selected for a client can bring about the desired changes. Protocols can be written with enough flexibility to accommodate the professional's judgment-based practice of care, which means combining research evidence with her own judgment based on her experience, knowledge, and caring for her clients. A very useful format for program protocols is provided in *Behavioral Health Protocols for Recreational Therapy* (Grote et al., 1995). This format includes seven components:

I. The name of the program

II. A rationale for offering the program based on the needs of the clients, using citations from efficacy research that supports the choice of the program

III. Identification of the types of clients who will be referred to the program, based on diagnosis, need, or symptoms; and any contraindications to participation in this program

IV. Risks of participation for the organization and the clients and suggestions for risk management

V. Three sets of program criteria:
- Structure for conducting the program, including length, frequency, and duration; and specific modules or components of the program
- Process the TRS utilizes, including program content, leadership styles and strategies, and therapeutic intervention techniques
- Outcomes the client can expect from program participation

VI. Credentials needed by the TRS, such as special certifications or training, in order to carry out the program

VII. Bibliography of references used to develop the program protocol

Designing protocols according to this format is very useful for program evaluation. It enables the TRS to focus on precise, individual aspects of a program during the evaluation process, which makes it easier to analyze exactly what should be adjusted to improve a program's effectiveness.

Evaluating the Structure, Process, and Outcomes of TR Programs

Chapter 3 presented guidelines for program planning that help to ensure that TR programs are appropriate, relevant, and meaningful. Nonetheless, all TR practitioners can share a story of a time they followed sound program planning principles and practices yet felt their program was a failure. To determine what went wrong in such a situation, the TRS can use the **discrepancy evaluation** model. Discrepancy evaluation looks at the discrepancy, difference, or gap between what the program was intended to accomplish (the desired outcomes) and the actual outcomes. The TRS can examine the difference between what was planned and what was actually carried out in the delivery of the program to determine why the desired outcomes were not attained. By examining the structure of the program (also known as inputs), the process (or what goes on during the program), and the outcomes (or outputs), the TRS can compare *what was planned* to *what actually occurred* in order to identify what might have influenced the program's effectiveness and to make necessary improvements or modifications.

PROGRAM STRUCTURE

The first component to evaluate is the structure of the program. Structure is also known as **inputs** in discrepancy evaluation. Structure refers to scheduling the program; selecting and arranging the setting, which includes the facility, space, and furnishings; and ensuring adequate resources, both material and human.

Scheduling

Scheduling includes the time the program is offered, the length of each session, and the number of sessions. The TRS may not always have control over scheduling programs and will have to work cooperatively with other departments. Yet it's

---

Sample Program Protocol

I. Yoga

II. Rationale

Stress is a leading cause of health problems including anxiety and depression (Bonadies, 2004). Yoga has been identified as an appropriate treatment for stress, anxiety, headaches, and back pain (Long, Huntley & Ernst, 2001). Yoga is associated with a variety of physical and mental health outcomes, including improved mood and reduced anxiety and depression (Malley & Dattilo, 2000).

III. Referrals

Clients will be referred to this program if they report stress, demonstrate symptoms of anxiety and depression, or express an interest in yoga. Adaptive equipment and posture modifications are available for clients who require adaptations.

IV. Risk management

Yoga is a low-risk activity. Participants are instructed to "listen to your body" and to work within their own capabilities. Groups will be limited to eight so the TRS can check individuals for proper positioning and comfort levels. Mats are used. Clients who are actively psychotic are not appropriate for the program.

V. Criteria

(continued)

Criteria for Sample Yoga Program

Structure criteria	Process criteria	Outcome criteria
The yoga group will meet twice a week for 30 minutes each session in the dance studio and include the following modules:	The TRS will check that all clients are medically screened for yoga and that the room is free of risks. The TRS will:	The clients will:
Monitoring stress, mood, pain, and anxiety	Introduce benefits of yoga Assist clients in identifying symptoms	State three benefits of yoga Identify symptoms and their causes
Breathing	Demonstrate and explain proper breathing techniques	Demonstrate proper breathing
Postures	Demonstrate each posture and explain its specific purpose Provide one-to-one physical guidance as needed to help clients do the posture correctly Encourage participation and give positive reinforcement for efforts	Demonstrate proper postures State benefits of each posture
Meditation	Explain that the purpose of meditation is for relaxation and to bring closure to the session Verbally guide clients through the meditation process	Demonstrate ability to meditate State the effect of the meditation
Debriefing	Lead clients in discussion of the feelings they experienced from the yoga Ask clients if they would continue yoga practice Give positive feedback	Discuss feelings and the effects of yoga on symptoms State intentions regarding yoga practice

VI. Credentialing

The TRS should be a certified yoga instructor or highly skilled in the practice of yoga.

VII. Bibliography

Bonadies, V. (2004). A yoga therapy program for AIDS-related pain and anxiety: Implications for therapeutic recreation. *Therapeutic Recreation Journal*, 38(2), 148-166.

Long, L., Hunt, A. & Ernst, E. (2001). Which complementary and alternative therapies benefit which conditions: A survey of the opinions of 223 professional organizations. *Complementary Therapies in Medicine*, 9(3), 178-185.

Malley, S. & Dattilo, J. (2000). Stress management. In J. Dattilo (Ed.), *Facilitation techniques in therapeutic recreation* (pp. 251-244). State College, PA: Venture.

This protocol format is from Grote, et al. 1995. The yoga protocol was adapted from a format developed by Angela Williams, MSEd.

important to keep principles of normalization in mind when scheduling. Most people don't watch movies at 9:00 a.m., right after breakfast, exercise after lunch on a full stomach, or begin a new project when faced with a major life change. The TRS should consider the following when evaluating the program schedule:

- Is the program offered at a time that would be typical for most people?
- Is the best time to offer the activity in the morning, afternoon, or evening; right before or right after a meal; early in the week or on the weekend?
- If attendance is low, is it because the program conflicts with too many other things that are going on at the same time?
- Is the length of the individual session too long or too short? Thirty minutes may be ample for a one-to-one activity or for a group with a short attention span. One hour may be optimal for most activities or for a group that requires a lot of assistance. Longer sessions can be held for more independent clients, for complex projects, and for community-based programs.
- Is the number of sessions in a program adequate to meeting its purpose and goals? Perhaps a program needs to meet more often than once a week or for longer than four or eight weeks.

Reflecting on these questions, observing participants for their reactions, and determining what is accomplished in each session will help the TRS plan the best schedule.

Physical Resources

Careful evaluation of the physical resources of a program: space, furnishings, equipment, and supplies is also necessary. Having a therapeutic group in a small, intimate setting can promote the values of the experience. Having a social activity in an open area that permits many people to attend and observe can maximize the excitement. Institutional and residential settings in particular should be decorated as much like a home as possible (Hart et al., 2003). A TR room in a hospital should have a unique ambience that differentiates it from the more impersonal and sterile environment of the medical setting where other staff, announcements over a public address system, televisions that are on, or visitors can interrupt the "flow" of a program. If a program is held in a community facility, the TRS may have less control over the setting and may wish to enhance the space in some way for each session. Props and decorations, music, and aromatherapy can be welcoming touches. Furnishings, equipment, and supplies need to be inspected for safety as one component of risk management. If there are clients who are confused or at risk of leaving the facility when they are not supposed to, the space should be secure or should be set up to minimize the chance that this will occur.

To evaluate the setting, the TRS should ask the following questions:

- Is the facility where the program is being held warm, inviting, and well ventilated, and is the temperature comfortable? What can I do to improve the ambience?
- Does the setting contribute to or distract from the purpose of the program?
- Are rest rooms and drinking water easily accessible?
- Is the setting barrier free, permitting easy movement and maneuverability of wheelchairs and other mobility devices?
- Is the space conducive to the type of activity?
- Are there too many distractions, including noise, odors, and interruptions?
- Does the décor enhance the space, and is it relevant to the participants?
- Is the furniture arranged to promote positive group interaction and performance?
- Can participants see and hear each other, as well as the TRS?
- Is seating comfortable, and are work spaces ample enough for all the group members?
- Are adequate and appropriate equipment and supplies available so clients can carry out the activity in a timely fashion?
- Are assistive devices needed for clients to participate?
- Is all equipment in good working order?
- Does the facility minimize risks to confused clients and those who are prone to wander or take off on their own?

Human Resources

The human resources for a TR program are the qualified staff who will lead TR activities, because without leadership there is no program. While programs are planned according to clients' needs, utilizing the individual strengths and talents of staff and volunteers is an asset in TR programming. A good leader can overcome the barest and least-appealing environment and run a program without

This group meets in a home-like environment that is bright and cheerful, with seating arranged to promote interaction.

Monkey Business/fotolia.com

equipment and supplies. Many TR departments do not have the luxury of being able to assign staff members to programs according to their personal skills and interests. Each TRS on staff has the responsibility to lead a variety of programs. Program evaluation may reveal that more staff are needed or that a program requires fewer staff than planned. Evaluation can also highlight whether staff need to develop skills in certain areas. Staffing evaluation questions include the following:

● Does the TRS have the skills to lead the program?

● How many staffpersons are needed to assist the participants?

● Are volunteers available who can contribute to the success of the program?

● Can the clients perform certain leadership tasks? Am I letting them take on enough responsibility for the operation of the program?

● Are there enough staff to ensure the safety of the participants? Are staff trained in emergency procedures?

Administrative Resources

The final elements related to the structure of a program are administrative: budget, transportation, promotion, and backup plans. Adequate funding is essential to carrying out certain programs. Weather also may be a factor in running a scheduled program. Alternative programming should be in place in case transportation falls through or the weather

causes cancellation of a program. Making sure people are informed of programs so they can decide to attend and have enough time to plan is critical. This can be a key factor for clients who are either responsible for getting to a program themselves or dependent on others to assist them in getting to a program. A system should be in place for participants to sign up or send notification if they cannot attend. Clients also may need time to prepare to be ready for a program. These are questions to ask regarding administration:

● Was the budget adequate to operate the program and cover unexpected but essential costs?

● Was sufficient, reliable transportation or staff assistance available to help clients get to the program?

● Were people informed of the program in a timely manner?

● Was enough information provided to enable participants to make decisions about attending?

● Were adequate channels of communication in a variety of formats used to promote and advertise the program?

● Was there a backup plan to carry out a comparable program, if needed, due to weather, a scheduling conflict, or a last-minute cancellation?

While the structure is not the essence of what we think of when we plan a TR activity, it is the framework within which the activity takes place and can enhance the experience, benefits, and outcomes for the clients.

PROGRAM PROCESS

The second component in program evaluation is evaluation of the process. This refers to the leadership style, skills, and methods used by the TRS to "animate" the program or bring the program to life and to enhance the quality of the overall experience for the participants. These skills and methods were presented in chapters 4 and 7. The skill with which the TRS facilitates the program and guides the clients to the attainment of benefits and outcomes is her successful and effective application of TR leadership. Participating in TR should be a positive experience for clients.

Therapeutic recreation programs should be fun and enjoyable. Fun can be motivating and creates an atmosphere in which clients want to continue to grow, change, and fulfill their potential. Yet TRSs may feel that fun is not therapeutic, or that other professionals do not consider TR a clinical practice because fun is emphasized in programming. This view is being challenged more and more (Dattilo & Klieber, 2002; Hutchinson et al., 2006). Fun and enjoyment are the unique qualities of the TR experience. Enjoyment, while similar to fun, reflects "a considerable degree of psychological involvement" in an intrinsically motivated activity that engenders "concentration, effort and a sense of control and competence" (Dattilo & Klieber, 2002, p. 84). An observer of a TR program should see participants enjoying the experience: A TR group should look as if they are having a good time. "The instrumental value of TR is jeopardized if the activity is not enjoyable, and if the TR is too directive and prescriptive" (Mobily & Ostiguy, 2004, p. 183). The TRS should display warmth, should be a role model of a person enjoying herself, and should use humor to promote a relaxed atmosphere (Hutchinson et al., 2006). A good TRS can make any activity a beneficial experience. What goes on among participants during the activity is as important as the product or tangible accomplishment of the group—some would argue more important. Participation in TR may be emotional, challenging, and thought provoking, bringing about feelings of satisfaction and self-worth as the client experiences personal fulfillment. It is how the TRS conducts the program that produces the benefits and outcomes for the client. This comes more naturally to some TRSs than others, but it is a skill that can be developed with practice and commitment and is at the heart of TR practice.

To evaluate the program process, the TRS needs to ask the following questions:

- Are the clients having fun and enjoying themselves?
- When I interact with the clients do I talk to all of them, use their names, and give support, encouragement, and positive feedback?
- Am I using appropriate motivation, teaching, and reinforcement techniques?
- Am I aware of the participants' individual learning styles and providing a balance of challenging and success-oriented opportunities?
- Is my leadership style appropriate for the activity, and do I vary it according to the clients' needs and levels of functioning?
- Do the clients have opportunities to take on responsibility for assisting with leading the activity, helping others, organizing the materials, cleaning up, and planning?
- Am I creating linkages and connections among clients so all feel included and may develop relationships that go beyond this group?
- Am I focused too much on product, as opposed to process?
- Does the group format contribute to the clients' experiences and progress?

PROGRAM OUTCOMES

Outcomes can be defined as "observed short- or long-term changes in a client's status as a result of interventions and interactions or some aspect of providing and receiving services" (Wilhite, Hodges & Peebles, 2003, p. 90). Therapeutic recreation programs are offered so that clients will achieve certain outcomes as a result of participation. The TRS wants to determine if the program has made an impact on the client and led to attaining outcomes. Evaluating clients' progress to see if they have achieved their desired outcomes is inseparable from evaluating programs. The following are categories of outcomes (Wilhite et al., 2003):

- Functional changes in the clients' physical, cognitive, psychological, and social behaviors
- Experiential improvements in the clients' adjustment to illness and disability, development of social networks and support systems, and development of leisure interests and satisfaction
- Societal advances that overcome barriers in the lives of people with disabilities and limitations, such as inclusiveness of the community, environmental supports, and positive attitudes toward people with disabilities.

Most TR programming focuses on functional and experiential outcomes. However, TR has a significant role to play in addressing barriers in society that inhibit the inclusion of people with disabilities, and can offer services to the community in order to achieve these outcomes as well. Measuring the changes that occur in clients as a result of TR participation can strengthen TR services by identifying effective programs, eliminating weaker ones, improving quality of care, and increasing the visibility of the value of TR (Carruthers, 2003).

EVALUATING THE CLIENT'S PROGRESS

In carrying out the TR process, the TRS has conducted an assessment of the client's level of functioning to establish a baseline measure of his status. The TRS has also specified goals and objectives in the client's individual plan. She determines if the client has met these goals and objectives as a result of participation in the TR programs specified in the plan. To accomplish this, she compares the client's functioning at set points during programming, and at the conclusion of programming, to his baseline measure. If clients demonstrate measurable changes in behavior or functioning, this can be taken as an indication that the program was effective in making progress toward or achieving the outcomes.

Measuring Change

"Therapists are required to use sound measurement tools to help guide and assess the effectiveness of practice" (Botner-Marigold & Miller, 2007, p. 256). Means of taking measurements are making observations, interviewing the client, and using standardized assessment instruments for pretesting and posttesting (Widmer et al., 2003). This use of multiple methods is known as **triangulation**. In addition to triangulating the methods used to collect data, the TRS can triangulate the sources of data. She can use herself, her client, the client's family, and other staff as sources of information. By using multiple methods and multiple sources, she strengthens the accuracy of her findings.

MEASUREMENT BY OBSERVATION

As the TRS is conducting TR programs, she is also making observations of her clients' behaviors. The purpose of observation as an evaluation tool is to determine if the client is making progress toward his goals or if there are any unexpected changes in the client's behavior. Observations are both casual and more formal or structured. Casual observations are the things we happen to notice about people and their actions. While everyone makes casual observations throughout the day, the TRS should not rely on this as the sole source of evaluation information. Casual observations are filtered through our

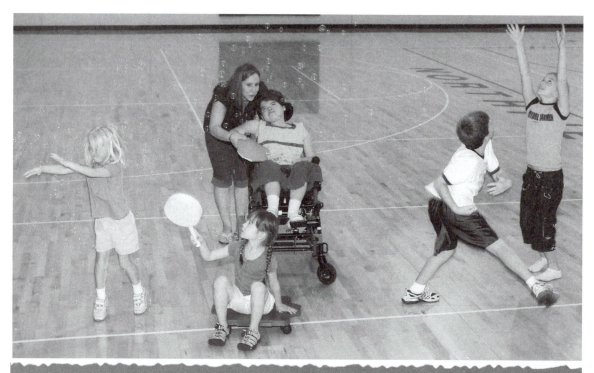

Therapeutic recreation programs should be fun and enjoyable.

own biases and interpretations of what people's behaviors mean. For example, if the TRS observes a client having a loud argument with his family, she may view this as a sign of a serious problem because in her own family, yelling was very hurtful. However, for this client, loud arguments are just the family's style of expressing their disagreements, and moments later they are talking normally and laughing. If the TRS happens to observe something that she feels may be noteworthy, she should verify it by speaking to the client and discussing her observations with other team members.

Formal observation is systematic; it involves deliberately observing, at regular intervals, a specific behavior that has been identified as a target of TR intervention. This targeted behavior, identified in the client's individual plan, may include social interaction, performance on task-oriented skills, problem-solving and decision-making actions, and level and type of participation (Shank & Coyle, 2002). The TRS may also observe the client's appearance, grooming, body language, and general demeanor. The TRS observes whether the client's functioning level is improving and whether there are changes in his behavior. If the TRS has an impairment that affects her ability to make visual observations, she may rely on what she hears and confer with other staff to make accurate observations. She is responsible for making careful notes that describe the client's behavior in order to document the progress the client is making. The TRS compares the level of functioning or the behavior the client demonstrates at the time of the observation to his performance at the time of assessment. Observation does *not* include the TRS's interpretation of the client's behavior and actions (Stumbo, 2002a). This is particularly relevant in regard to observing behaviors of people from different cultures. The TRS should be culturally competent in understanding that people's behaviors may have different causes and meanings based on cultural background.

Let's look at how the TRS conducts her observation of Mr. Jones, who has had a stroke. With the help of the TRS, he made a plan to attend aquatic fitness to improve his endurance and range of motion. This choice of activity was based on his previous enjoyment of swimming (reflecting the continuity of lifestyle approach to planning). He now also needs to learn how to use a flotation device to enable him to continue swimming, given the effects of the stroke. The TRS has "prescribed" adapted aquatics three times a week, for a half an hour each session, for four weeks (planning based on active treatment). She based this "dosage" on evidence in the research literature (evidence-

based practice). During the sessions, she casually observes that Mr. Jones seems comfortable and is benefiting from the program. She makes systematic observations of his progress in the areas of endurance and range of motion, as well as his learning to use the flotation device. At the end of the four weeks, she compares his current functioning level to his baseline measures prior to the start of the adapted aquatics program. She observes that he has learned to use the flotation device correctly, that he is able to make larger circles with his arms in the water (range of motion), and that he can now participate in the program for a longer period of time (endurance). On the basis of her observations, she concludes that Mr. Jones has made progress toward his goals. However, it is vital to rely on more than one source of information to determine progress. In order to provide corroborating evidence that Mr. Jones has improved, the TRS can also interview him.

MEASUREMENT BY INTERVIEWING

Initially, the TRS interviews the client as part of the assessment process, which leads to the development of the individual plan as discussed in chapter 3. Similar to observations, interviews can be used as a means to gather information about a client's progress. Interviews, like observation, can be casual or more highly structured. Casual interviews can occur while the client is participating in TR services; the TRS and the client will be talking and discussing how the client is doing, what progress he feels he is making, and any issues he may be having, while carrying on social conversation. At regular intervals, much as with structured observations, the TRS may ask the client precise questions related to his progress toward his goals. She should phrase these questions objectively so that the client can give as accurate a response as possible. She should be careful not to "lead" the client to say what he thinks she wants to hear, as in, "Mr. Jones, you seem to be much stronger since you started the aquatics program. What do you think?" A better way to phrase the question is, "Can you describe any physical changes you have observed in yourself since you started the aquatics program?" These are other interview questions appropriate to measuring Mr. Jones' progress:

● "What actions can you perform now as compared to four weeks ago?"

● "Can you demonstrate how to use the flotation device?"

● "How does using the flotation device affect your ability to carry out the aquatic movements?"

In addition to obtaining objective feedback from Mr. Jones, the TRS should question him about the value and quality of the experience he is having. It may be that he does not make significant progress in his targeted areas of functional improvements as a result of participation in the aquatics program. But he enjoys the program and feels more confident because he is able to engage in an activity that is meaningful to him, thereby improving his experience as a person with a disability. This qualitative evaluation, regarding how a client feels during and after an experience, is being recognized as valuable information about the outcomes of a TR program, in addition to quantitative evaluation, which measures the amounts of changes in the client from the baseline as a result of participation.

When conducting an interview for evaluation purposes, the TRS should have the questions prepared ahead of time. The questions are geared toward gaining information on the client's progress toward his goals or outcomes. Questions focus on what behavioral changes the client has observed about himself, what new information he has acquired, and how he feels during and as a result of TR participation. The TRS can ask him what he has learned and what new things he would like to learn or changes he wants to make. Interview responses can lead to new goals for a client. In interviewing, the TRS needs to use language the client understands, inform the client that she is asking these questions to determine his progress, and reassure him that she wants his honest answers and that his responses will not have negative repercussions. A client may feel that if he gives the "right" answer he will be able to leave the treatment facility sooner or earn privileges. He may be trying to please the TRS. The TRS relies on the rapport she has established with the client to conduct the interview as objectively as possible in order to obtain valuable evaluation data. She records the responses as given, as fully as possible, and without her own interpretations.

Just as with observations, the TRS does not rely solely on the interview to determine the client's progress. This is particularly significant in work with clients who are not able to fully communicate their responses or whose cognitive level of functioning precludes them from giving completely informed and rational responses. The TRS can interview parents, guardians, and significant others as well, but must do so with the same degree of caution regarding any biases that may be affecting responses. When interviewing a client or the family, the TRS may need an interpreter or translator if she does not speak their language (Sylvester et al., 2001). Mr. Jones' wife may give the TRS relevant information: She may have observed that he can now reach objects farther away, and Mr. Jones may have told her how happy he is that he can go swimming. This additional information lends support to the TRS's observations and the responses Mr. Jones gave during the interview.

MEASUREMENT USING STANDARDIZED INSTRUMENTS

The third method used in evaluation is a standardized instrument. Standardized instruments, also known as tools, assessments, scales, or questionnaires, can provide objective, accurate measures of a client's performance or behavior. These tools have been developed to deliver reliable and valid information that can be accepted as accurate and as a true representation of what they are measuring. They can be used as both a pretest, prior to the beginning of the treatment or intervention to establish a baseline, and as a posttest, at the conclusion of treatment. Results on the posttest are compared to scores on the pretest to determine how much progress has been made. It's crucial to select the tool carefully so that it will measure what you are intending to measure, is easy for staff to use and incorporate into their daily routine, and is comprehensible to the client. The TRS also has to consider any cultural bias that may be inherent in the instrument. Standardized tools come with instructions on how to administer them and guidelines regarding whom their use is appropriate with. However, "one of the major criticisms of TR assessments is that there are few available assessments that have undergone rigorous testing necessary to ensure confidence in the results" (Botner-Marigold & Miller, 2007, p. 256). Instruments that have undergone some degree of testing as reported in the literature include the following:

- Leisure Diagnostic Battery (LDB)
- Comprehensive Evaluation in Recreation Therapy (CERT)
- Idyll Arbor Leisure Battery's four scales: Leisure Attitude Measure, Leisure Motivation Scale, Leisure Satisfaction Scale, and Leisure Interest Measure
- Leisure Competence Measure (LCM)
- Functional Assessment of Characteristics for Therapeutic Recreation, Revised (FACTR-R)

Most of these tools are available in *Assessment Tools for Recreational Therapy and Related Fields* (Burlingame & Blaschko, 2002). While results have indicated that these scales can be used with both confidence and caution, more testing is needed. The

LDB (Witt & Ellis, 1989) and the LCM (Kloseck & Crilly, 1997) are the most widely researched tools in the field (Stumbo & Peterson, 2004). Therapeutic recreation practitioners are encouraged to explore the use of standardized instruments in the evaluation of their clients. Chapter 3 discusses the LDB and the FACTR-R in more detail. In addition to these instruments, which are specific to TR, TRSs may also use the Functional Independence Measure and Functional Assessment Measure (FIM + FAM), the Mini-Mental State Examination (MMSE), the Beck Depression Inventory (BDI) or Geriatric Depression Scale (GDS), and the Rosenberg Self-Esteem Scale (SES) in conjunction with professionals from other disciplines. These instruments may be viewed at the listed Web sites. Many other instruments are available that measure a variety of constructs, including attitudes, behaviors, feelings, knowledge, and skills.

In the case of Mr. Jones, the TRS administered the Leisure Competence Measure, which was developed to align with the FIM (see Carter & O'Morrow, 2006, p. 331). The FIM uses a seven-point scale ranging from 7 *(Complete Independence)* to 1 *(Total Dependence with Total Assistance)*. Prior to his participation in aquatic fitness, Mr. Jones scored 3 *(Modified Dependence with Moderate Assistance: initiates choosing community-based leisure activities (swimming); requires assistance planning and following through)*. Mr. Jones was able to choose swimming as an interest

Web Sites for Assessment Instruments

Beck Depression Inventory and Geriatric Depression Scale
www.neurotransmitter.net/depressionscales.html
Mini-Mental State Exam
www.alzheimerprediction.ca
Rosenberg Self-Esteem Scale
www.selfesteem2go.com/rosenberg-self-esteem-scale.html
Functional Independence Measure and Functional Assessment Measure
http://birf.info/home/bi-tools/tests/fam.html

he wanted to continue; but because of his physical limitations resulting from the stroke and his lack of knowledge of adaptive equipment, he stated that he felt insecure about pursuing this activity and unsure if he had the capabilities. After participating in the aquatics program, he scored 6 *(Modified Independence: with the provision of necessary resources, client initiates, plans and follows through with chosen community-based activities)*. That is, from the pretest to the posttest, Mr. Jones increased his score from 3 to 6. As a result of the TR intervention, he overcame some of his physical limitations and learned how to use adaptive equipment; his confidence increased and he was able to initiate community participation.

In agencies in which the TRS follows up on clients to see if they have maintained their gains and need any further assistance, as in the OLH-TR model (see chapter 2), she can contact the client at regularly scheduled intervals. This could be after one week or one month, with subsequent contacts on a monthly and then a quarterly basis. If clients maintain their new behaviors, this is further validation of the program's success. If the client is not engaging in new behaviors, the TRS can question him to ascertain what the barriers are. In Mr. Jones' case, he needed more time in the locker room to change, and this reduced his swim time. The TRS can use this information to provide guidance to the client and to make changes in programming in order to improve services to other clients as well.

One additional outcome that the TRS evaluates is the societal changes that have been made as a result of her efforts to provide transitional TR services. To facilitate Mr. Jones' use of community resources, such as the pool at the local YMCA, she has met with the staff to discuss access issues and to educate them regarding his use of his flotation device in the pool and his need for extra time to get ready for swimming. She asks them to let him into the locker room 15 minutes earlier than it is scheduled to open. With these accommodations, he is able to make maximum use of the open swim hours. This change also accommodates other individuals who require similar adjustments. The TRS can check back after one month, and then after two months, to ensure that these procedures are still in place and are serving those who need the accommodations. She also can ask the staff if they require any further assistance in providing access. An excellent example of addressing access in the community is provided by Hodges and colleagues (2004). These authors reported how a TRS, working with a man with autism, met with staff in the local senior centers to discuss his needs and the accommodations that would facilitate his participation in their programs.

This ramp is an example of an adaptation that could enhance a recreational experience for anyone who would choose to use it.

Bold Stock/age fotostock

Reasons for Lack of Progress

Despite the TRS's best efforts, it is still possible for a client not to attain outcomes or have meaningful experiences in TR. The reasons can be grouped into four categories, relating to the client, the TRS, significant others, and team members (O'Morrow, 1976). Reviewing these four possibilities can provide insight into a client's lack of progress.

The following reasons related to the client himself may contribute to lack of attainment of outcomes:

- His physical or psychological condition may have worsened.
- His living, job, or family situation may have changed.
- He may have experienced a loss of self-esteem, may lack interest in addressing his problems, or may be withholding important information.

These situations can occur before or during the time the client is receiving services and can have an impact on his response to TR.

The following may be reasons related to the TRS:

- She may have overlooked relevant information.
- She may have failed to validate information that she received.
- She may have lacked knowledge about the client's situation.

- She did not recognize the client's strengths.
- She selected an inappropriate program.
- She did not obtain input from others.
- She failed to recognize her own limitations, which could have affected the services she provided.

These reasons relate to significant others in the client's life, such as family members, friends, or loved ones:

- They not be available or may not be interested in or understand the client, his problems, and possible solutions.
- They may have fears and anxieties regarding the client's condition.
- They may possess moral, cultural, or religious beliefs that are at odds with the treatment approaches.
- They may lack transportation or resources that facilitate their involvement.

The following are beliefs and actions of the members of the professional team that can affect the success of the TR plan:

- The TRS has conflicts with other team members regarding the client's goals.
- Team members do not take a holistic approach to the client's plan.
- Team members fail to see the value of the TR plan.
- Team members function ineffectively.
- Team members take other actions that depersonalize the client or lead to an inconsistent approach to services.

By examining these four categories of reasons the plan did not work, the TRS can take the necessary steps to address the issues. The TRS always behaves in an ethical and professional manner when approaching significant others and fellow professionals, demonstrating respect and the attitude that the client's well-being is uppermost in providing services. Whether or not the client has made progress, the results of TR services must be recorded, or documented. Documentation is an essential component of the evaluation process.

Documentation

Documentation is "the written (or electronic) record of the client's experience in the agency" (Mobily & Ostiguy, 2004, p. 214). An adage often quoted in TR is "If it isn't written down, it didn't happen." The work of the TRS, as with all health and human services professionals, must be recorded to demonstrate accountability for the quality of care provided to recipients of services. Regardless of setting, the TRS is responsible for accurate documentation, which constitutes evidence that services were provided, specifies the manner in which they were provided, and identifies the outcomes or effects of those services on clients. The TRS may keep a variety of records of her work: assessments and individual client plans, progress notes, attendance statistics, program evaluations, and periodic reports that summarize the TR services provided in a given period. The information the TRS collects is systematically recorded in the client's record or medical chart, which is considered a legal document. Documentation may be handwritten or computerized, depending on the practices of the individual agency.

Documentation has several vital functions (Austin, 2009; Mobily & Ostiguy, 2004; Shank & Coyle, 2002; Stumbo & Peterson, 2009; Sylvester et al., 2001):

- As a means of communication among staff so they are informed of the services provided to the client and how the client has responded
- As evidence in legal proceedings
- As a requirement of regulatory and governmental agencies and third-party payers to provide a record of services rendered and a database for reimbursable services
- As a source of data and topics for conducting evaluation research and improving services
- As a standard of practice of the TR profession

Documentation can be used to evaluate the client's progress and the effectiveness of TR programming. A primary documentation responsibility of the TRS is to write **progress notes** on each of his clients. A progress note can be either a single narrative or several short sections written under a series of headings, or categories. Regardless of the system the agency uses, the note will cover the same areas:

- The client's participation in TR programming and his responses to it, both positive and negative
- His progress toward achieving the goals and objectives set in the original plan
- Future directions for TR intervention
- Any unusual events

Progress notes may also be referred to as charting or documenting. Charting occurs according to a predetermined schedule depending on the agency and the regulations that govern services. This can be weekly, biweekly, monthly, or every three months (quarterly). The TRS is responsible for compliance with the regulations by staying up-to-date with his documentation and writing honestly and accurately. By reviewing the TR progress notes, the TRS can determine if clients are making progress, which TR programs are successful at helping clients meet goals in a timely manner, and what types of needs clients have that are being met successfully and which needs may require different approaches. Chart reviews are conducted regularly to ensure that the needs and goals specified in the client's original treatment plan are being addressed and that progress notes are written as scheduled. All notes must be signed and dated as a testament to their veracity and authenticity.

An example of a progress note on Mr. Jones, written after one month of participation in adapted aquatics, might read as follows:

> Mr. Jones was assessed by the TRS 6/1/09 and scored a 3 on the FIM scale for his ability to participate in community-based recreation activities. Mr. Jones was reassessed on 6/30/09 after attending adapted aquatics for four weeks, three times a week. He scored 6 on the FIM. He demonstrated proper use of the flotation device, and verbally stated two benefits to using the device and that he will continue to use it when he attends the YMCA swim program after discharge. He has increased his endurance as demonstrated by increasing the amount of time he participates in aquatic exercise from 5 minutes to 25 minutes. His wife reports that he told her he feels confident about being able to go to the Y. The TRS observed less hesitation by Mr. Jones when he entered and exited the pool. He was smiling and laughing when he discussed his progress. He stated, "Now I believe I will be able to go to the pool with my grandson this summer, like we used to do." The TRS will meet with Y staff on 7/5/09 to discuss accommodations for Mr. Jones. Mr. Jones has met his goals of increasing endurance and range of motion. He is ready for discharge from the TR program.

> Robin Kunstler, CTRS, 7/1/09

A review of the note shows that Mr. Jones met his goals through adapted aquatics. Both quantitative measures (scores on the FIM, amount of time) and qualitative data (comments of Mr. and Mrs. Jones) were documented. The note indicates how much time it took for Mr. Jones to make this progress. A reasonable conclusion about the success of the TR intervention was that it was effective in meeting the client's goals in a timely fashion. If Mr. Jones had not made progress, the TRS could explore the reasons the plan didn't work and make needed changes.

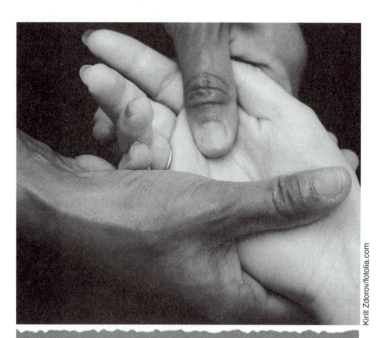

Kirill Zdorov/fotolia.com

Documenting the outcomes of a hand massage intervention could include both quantitative and qualitative data.

The TRS also can analyze data on all the clients in the program to determine program effectiveness (Carruthers, 2003). If a number of clients do not show gains through the aquatics program, as an example, the TRS could then, through the evaluation process, determine if the program was the wrong choice, if it was not conducted in the prescribed manner, if there are errors in the measurement process, or if there are other reasons the plan didn't work. Therapeutic recreation specialists should not overlook progress notes as a valuable source of evaluation data. Progress notes written about all the clients, or a sample of clients, can yield strong evidence of TR's effectiveness or provide information that can be used to revise and improve services. Therapeutic recreation specialists can report percentages of clients meeting goals, types of goals that TR is most successful at addressing, TR programs that are effective, and any unanticipated outcomes and benefits of TR participation. The TR plan includes outcomes that the client hopes to achieve. But the client also may obtain unexpected benefits or outcomes, and the TRS should not overlook their significance. In a study of the effects of aromatherapy and hand massage on chronic pain, it was hypothesized that these interventions would reduce residents' perception of pain and blood pressure (Kunstler et al., 2004). An unexpected outcome of the study was that the residents reported they slept better after receiving the intervention. Although unanticipated, this out-

come was meaningful to the participants and could influence the design of future programs that address improving sleeping patterns.

Quantitative and Qualitative Measures

Quantitative data are data that can be counted, or quantified in numbers. They allow us to compare scores on a pretest and a posttest and, in more sophisticated analyses, to use statistical tests to determine significance of the results. Results that are based on quantitative measures are easy to grasp, are well suited for interpreting large amounts of data or for evaluating large numbers of people, and are highly valued because they present in very clear-cut terms the outcomes of a particular program or intervention. In a well-designed study, results expressed in quantitative terms can allow the researcher to make inferences and generalizations to a larger population. In TR, quantitative methods are well suited for evaluating functional outcomes.

Qualitative data, on the other hand, provide rich verbal descriptions of people's experiences within a program or as a result of an intervention, leading to a deeper understanding of the impacts the programming has on a person. Qualitative methods are particularly useful for evaluating existential outcomes that focus on the meaning of a person's experience. They cannot be used to generalize findings to others but can give direction for further study. The use of qualitative data is becoming more highly valued by researchers because it puts a human face on services and supports the current focus on customer satisfaction. Ideally, evaluations that combine quantitative and qualitative findings provide the fullest picture of the effects of a program. In TR research, although there have not been as many well-designed quantitative studies as in some other fields, the use of well-designed research involving both quantitative and qualitative methods has been increasing. Therapeutic recreation programs should be evaluated using a combination of methods.

EVALUATION SCHEDULE

In accordance with regulations of governmental and accrediting agencies, progress notes must be written as scheduled. Evaluation should also occur on a regular basis. There are evaluation tasks that should be completed daily, weekly, monthly, quarterly, and annually. The following schedule is suggested as a guide that could be adjusted according to the planning and evaluation cycle of the agency.

- Daily:
  - Record attendance at TR programs.
  - Complete individual TR planning form (see figure 10.1 on page 306); record number of hours of programming offered.
  - Identify any risk management issues.
  - Observe clients for degree of involvement, response to programs, and any unmet needs.
- Weekly:
  - Review daily records.
  - Compile statistics on attendance and number of hours of program offerings.
  - Identify any unusual occurrences and risk management problems.
  - Complete balanced programming checklist (see chapter 9).
  - Determine if clients are making progress toward goals.
- Monthly:
  - Compile monthly attendance statistics.
  - Summarize balanced programming checklist.
  - Analyze whether client goals are being met.
  - Consider whether program placement is still appropriate for individual clients.
- Quarterly:
  - Summarize attendance data, number of programs offered, percentage of clients meeting goals, percentage of goals clients met.
  - Analyze the types of goals being met.
  - Identify program successes.
  - Identify weaknesses or problem areas and devise a plan to address them.
- Annually:
  - Summarize data from four quarters.
  - Present data-driven plans for requests and allocations for programming, budgeting and staffing, staff training, and purchase of equipment and supplies.

The data collected according to the evaluation schedule can be used to assure the quality of services to clients and aid in ongoing performance improvement. Quality assurance (QA) and performance improvement (PI) are two terms closely associated with evaluation.

Management Approaches to Evaluation

Quality assurance began as an inspection procedure to ensure that health care facilities met minimal standards set by government regulatory agencies. A general belief was that QA was a process mostly undertaken to satisfy these regulatory agencies (McCormick, 2003). The focus of QA was on identifying and correcting errors that came to light during medical chart reviews or audits, so it was seen as essentially a punitive process that uncovered problems rather than as a proactive approach to preventing problems before they occurred (Kelly, 2008). However, QA was successful at monitoring how well agencies were meeting the regulators' standards. Subsequently, continuous quality improvement (CQI), also known as total quality management (TQM), became the preferred approach to delivering quality services. The underlying principle of CQI was that there should be an ongoing process of improving services rather than simply a focus on mistakes after they occurred.

Just as QA evolved into CQI, so did CQI evolve into **performance improvement** (PI), reflecting the shifting focus from the quality of the *structure* of services, to the quality of the *process* used in delivering services, to the quality of the *outcomes* produced. Performance improvement is seen as a total management process that should be integrated into the overall operations of the agency on a daily basis. The philosophy of PI is that the entire organization's effectiveness influences the achievement of outcomes. These outcomes are not limited to the outcomes clients attain as a result of care, interventions, and programs but also include outcomes valued by stakeholders who have a vested interest in the quality of services. Stakeholders include outside groups, such as government agencies, accrediting organizations, advocacy groups, and philanthropic organizations, that provide funding and oversight of agencies where TR is offered and are concerned that clients are protected and that funds are not wasted. In a PI environment, efficient and effective delivery of services is expected, and all staff members are encouraged to view themselves as partners striving to achieve organizational outcomes.

Performance improvement goes hand in hand with the management focus on customer satisfaction. In PI, clients or patients are viewed as "customers" who expect and deserve quality services. This view has a powerful influence on the design and types of services offered. In an increasingly competitive environment for the resources needed to fund agencies and services, a satisfied customer is seen as a repeat customer or one who recommends a particular facility to others. Many agencies have become proactive in measuring customer satisfaction with their services. Rather than waiting for complaints and addressing them, agencies are conducting patient or customer satisfaction surveys. Areas typically included in these surveys are convenience, technical quality, staff interaction, cost, environment, and length of treatment (Widmer et al., 2003). A high predictor of overall satisfaction with services is the communication between staff and patient (Maciejewski, Kawiecki & Rockwood, 1997), which is often a strength of TR. Therapeutic recreation should be included in these surveys to evaluate whether customers used TR services, whether they found them beneficial, and whether they have any recommendations to make. Customer input can be very valuable for learning what works effectively. Results of these surveys could lead to a heightened image for a successful TR department, more resources to support TR services, and concrete suggestions for improving TR programming. Marketing of health care organizations today often includes images of clients participating in TR programs because these present a positive, life-affirming impression of the organization. See table 8.3 and figure 8.1 for examples of patient satisfaction surveys. Therapeutic recreation specialists are encouraged to develop their own surveys with items relevant to their setting. The following (Rhodes, 1991) are examples of items that the TRS can use in a form of her own design:

The TRS helped me learn new skills.

TR gave me the opportunity to try games/activities/sports I hadn't done in a long time.

The TRS gave me ideas for new activities to use after discharge.

I enjoyed having fun in a group.

The TRS helped me look at problems in the ways I use my leisure time.

We visited new community resources.

Regardless of the terminology used in any given agency, there is a widespread movement to measure performance; and TR departments will be expected to evaluate the delivery and outcomes of their services. Too often, evaluation has been seen as an added burden rather than as an essential professional practice. Following a schedule makes it easier to collect the needed data and to integrate evaluation procedures into the regular routine of the workday. By collecting, reviewing, and using evaluation data according to the evaluation schedule, the TRS is complying with the PI principle of using data to make improvements or changes in services. With the outcome in mind as the goal, the TRS uses his expertise to combine the structure of the TR program and the process of providing TR leadership to bring about positive change. See table 8.4 on page 258 for an example of a performance improvement project.

STANDARDS OF PRACTICE

Standards for practice were first discussed in chapter 3. The standards of practice present guidelines for minimal acceptable delivery of services as established by a profession. They are based on expert

TABLE 8.3

Patient Satisfaction Survey

Therapeutic Recreation Survey Form

Circle the number that best represents your feelings.

	Very poor	Poor	Fair	Good	Very good
The courtesy of your therapeutic recreation therapist	1	2	3	4	5
The degree to which you were able to participate in setting your therapeutic recreation goals	1	2	3	4	5
How well did the therapeutic recreation specialist explain your treatment and progress?	1	2	3	4	5
The adequacy of your therapeutic recreation program	1	2	3	4	5
The availability of recreational activities (e.g., crafts, games, entertainment)	1	2	3	4	5
The helpfulness of the instruction and information given about your postdischarge recreational activities	1	2	3	4	5

Reprinted from M. Carter and G. O'Morrow, 2006, *Effective management in therapeutic recreation service*, 2nd ed. (State College, PA: Venture Publishing), 334. By permission of M. Carter.

Resident Satisfaction Survey

Resident name: _____ Building/room:_____

TR leader/specialist: _____ Date: _____

SECOND QUARTER SUMMARY

ITEM	YES	NO	COMMENTS
Do you know who your TRS is?	X		*Yes, she is very pleasant and accessible.*
Do you know how to contact your TRS?	X		*Yes*
Do you feel your TRS is responsive to your needs? If yes, in what ways: If no, why not:	X		*Yes* *She helps find activities I enjoy doing.*
Do you enjoy the activities you are currently attending?	X		*Yes*
What do you like about the activities you are currently attending or those you have attended?			*They are entertaining and relaxing.*
What don't you like about the activities you are attending or those you have attended?			*Elevators are too slow.*
Are there activities not offered which you would like to participate in?	X		*Yes*
What activities would you like to see that are not offered?			*More classical music concerts*

FOURTH QUARTER SUMMARY

ITEM	YES	NO	COMMENTS
Do you feel that therapeutic recreation has helped you get better or recuperate while on the subacute unit?	X		*Yes*
If yes, in what ways has therapeutic recreation helped you to feel better? If no, what could the TRS do to help facilitate your rehabilitation process?			*I feel more relaxed.*
Do you feel that your participation in therapeutic recreation (activities, trips, etc.) will help to make it easier for you to return to your home and the community?	X		*Yes*
If so, in what ways will it help you to make it easier to return to your home or community?			*They teach us how to get on and off the bus when we go on trips.* *We do cooking which helps us.*
Other:			

These surveys show the responses of the patient after the second quarter of services and then after the fourth quarter. Sample responses are included.

Figure 8.1 Sample completed patient satisfaction survey.

Reprinted, by permission, from Fred Greenblatt, CTRS.

TABLE 8.4

Performance Improvement Report

Discipline:	Therapeutic recreation
Review period:	October, November, December 2008
Plan:	Increase opportunity for resident input and planning of recreation activities to ensure resident satisfaction with recreation programs
Methodology:	Resident community meetings Resident satisfaction surveys
Do:	*Each TRS will conduct a monthly resident community meeting to plan activities with residents and receive suggestions and input from residents regarding the activity programs. *Each TRS will conduct a resident satisfaction survey on a quarterly basis. *Therapeutic recreation job description and performance appraisal will be revised to indicate residents' satisfaction with TRS and activities.
Check:	Continue monthly resident community meetings. Continue quarterly resident satisfaction surveys.
Act:	Revise activities based on input from resident community meetings and satisfaction surveys.

The PI report uses the Plan-Do-Check-Act format.

Prepared by Fred Greenblatt, CTRS, MA, MPA, Quality Care Consultants

opinion, research findings, client preferences, and regulations of government and accrediting bodies. As such, they can be considered "official" recommendations of what constitutes the practice of TR. Following these standards ensures consistency and a unity of purpose among all TR departments and helps establish the credibility of TR practice. The standards for practice also can be used as an evaluation tool to determine if programs are meeting the accepted conditions and levels of performance of quality TR services. Both the ATRA and NTRS standards address the area of evaluation of TR services. For example, ATRA's Standard 12 reads, "The therapeutic recreation department engages in routine, systematic program evaluation and research for the purpose of determining appropriateness and efficacy" (ATRA, 1991). The TRS can consult the standards for practice of both professional organizations for details on the professional practices that demonstrate meeting the standards. Therapeutic recreation specialists can use the standards to compare the structure of their services, as well as the processes used to deliver their services, to the types and levels stated in the standards. Designing, implementing, and evaluating TR services according to the standards of the profession are essential to quality practice.

REGULATIONS AND LEGAL MANDATES

Adhering to the regulations and legal mandates of accrediting organizations and government agencies is a requirement of all TR departments. The major national regulatory bodies are the **Centers for Medicare and Medicaid Services (CMS), the Joint Commission (JC)**, and the **Commission on Accreditation of Rehabilitation Facilities (CARF)**. These bodies carry out a survey process in each organization that they accredit to see if performance standards are being met. Passing government surveys is required in order for an organization to receive federal reimbursement for health care services, and meeting the standards of accrediting organizations is recognized as a hallmark of quality.

The Centers for Medicare and Medicaid Services is a U.S. federal agency that oversees Medicare, Medicaid, and the Health Insurance Portability and Accountability Act (HIPAA), among other programs. All health professionals and the general public are familiar with HIPAA, which regulates the privacy of patient information. Before seeing a medical professional, everyone signs a form to attest that he or she is aware of and informed about the

HIPAA regulations. See chapter 1 for information on HIPAA provisions relevant to TR practice. The mission of CMS is to ensure health care security for patients whose services are paid for by CMS. Because Medicare and Medicaid are the largest reimbursers of health care services in the United States, CMS's regulations and guidelines are very influential on the types and quality of health care services provided nationwide. Private insurers often follow CMS's lead in these areas. Regulations issued by CMS in 2006 specified that all staff, not just TR, should help residents in long-term care settings participate in activities. This has influenced the delivery of TR services in all long-term care settings, because personnel from all departments are supposed to conduct and assist with activities to enhance the residents' lives.

The Joint Commission, formerly known as the Joint Commission on Accreditation of Healthcare Organizations, is a private, not-for-profit organization that accredits over 19,000 health care programs in the United States, including hospitals, addiction services, rehabilitation centers, and long-term care facilities. The Joint Commission emphasizes quality of health care, patient safety, establishing and attaining performance measures, and continuing quality improvements. When JC sets a new goal or standard, it affects all health care settings. Recent JC priorities that have had a direct impact on TR services are patient safety, falls prevention, pain management, active involvement of patients and their families in patient care, and ethics education for staff.

The Commission on Accreditation of Rehabilitation Facilities accredits over 5,000 health and human services providers in the United States, Canada, South America, and Western Europe. The purpose of CARF is to improve the quality of services and enhance the lives of the people it serves. The commission characterizes quality as customers' satisfaction and "delight" with the services they receive, planning that is individualized to the patient's needs, and inclusion of the patient as a critical partner in the planning process. The TR profession, as well, believes in the importance of client involvement in and satisfaction with services.

The National Committee for Quality Assurance (NCQA) accredits health care organizations according to its standards for quality of care and services. The Committee uses HEDIS, the Healthcare Effectiveness Data and Information Set, which provides measures of services. Many employers

Web Sites for Regulatory Bodies

Centers for Medicare and Medicaid Services
www.cms.hhs.gov
Commission on Accreditation of Rehabilitation Facilities
www.carf.org
Joint Commission
www.jointcommission.org
National Committee for Quality Assurance
www.ncqa.org

select managed health care plans using HEDIS standards (Stumbo & Peterson, 2009). The National Committee for Quality Assurance is dedicated to health care quality and works to improve organizations' performance according to a process known as "measure, analyze, improve." It is obvious that the emphasis on quality, continuous improvement, and delivery of outstanding services is a widespread phenomenon affecting all settings where TRSs are employed.

In addition to these national government and private agencies, state and local governments have standards and regulations for health and human service agencies. In most states the Departments of Health, Aging, Mental Health, and Developmental Disabilities, among others, each carry out a survey and regulatory process. The TRS must familiarize herself with the standards of each accrediting body and ensure that her services are in compliance. This is a form of evaluation, is a testament to the quality of the TR department, and demonstrates ongoing and continuous improvement of services. Ethical principles of the TR profession are to comply with local, state, and federal laws governing TR practice and to protect and promote the health and well-being of the people it serves. Adhering to these ethical principles is an indicator of quality improvement. Another method used to determine quality is conducting research on the effectiveness of professional practices and services.

RESEARCH

Conducting research that demonstrates the efficacy and effectiveness of TR has been seen as the responsibility of researchers and college professors. Nothing could be further from the truth! All practitioners share in the professional obligation to advance the profession by engaging in the research process. From reading research findings, to applying the results in the design of program protocols and evidence-based practice, to evaluating TR services, to the actual carrying out of a research project, all TRSs can participate in research. Basing TR intervention on the results of sound research investigations contributes to the body of knowledge of the profession, demonstrates the viability of TR as a service, earns the respect of other professionals, and is seen as essential to obtaining third-party reimbursement.

Efficacy Research

Both efficacy and effectiveness research relate to evaluating whether programs are successful in changing client behavior (Stumbo & Peterson, 2009). **Efficacy research** refers specifically to a methodologically rigorous experimental study aimed at determining whether there is a cause-and-effect relationship between the TR intervention and client outcomes (Carruthers, 2003). Efficacy research also is concerned with comparing the success of a treatment with its cost; in other words, determining which intervention produces an acceptable amount of change using the least amount of resources (Malkin, Coyle & Carruthers, 1998). It is crucial that members of the TR profession conduct efficacy research to provide evidence that TR services "work" and are a cost-effective intervention, which is needed to obtain reimbursement for TR services.

In the case of Mr. Jones, an efficacy research study might be designed to determine whether the adapted aquatics intervention was truly responsible for the changes in range of motion, endurance, and quality of life that Mr. Jones experienced. A control group and an experimental group of clients with similar characteristics and needs would be used in the research study. The experimental group would participate in the adapted aquatics and the control group would not, at least until after the completion of the study. The variables under study would be carefully measured during the pretest and posttest. Obviously, carrying out this study would require having adequate numbers of participants, using very precise measurement instruments, applying a consistent treatment intervention, and minimizing

the effects of any outside factors that might affect the clients' functioning levels. This type of experimental research is difficult to carry out in most TR settings because of the time required and the difficulty in controlling so many different factors. It also requires precluding members of the control group from receiving the intervention during the course of the study. Once the study is over, we are ethically obligated to offer members of the control group the opportunity to participate in the same program. Therapeutic recreation textbooks and articles describe single-subject research, case study research, and qualitative methods that can be used more feasibly in TR practice settings, as compared to more rigorous experimental research designs.

Effectiveness Research

In contrast to efficacy research, "**effectiveness research** evaluates interventions as they are actually practiced with clients" (Stumbo & Peterson, 2004, p. 393). Program evaluation is a form of demonstrating effectiveness of interventions. Collecting and analyzing data as explained in this chapter can contribute to effectiveness research. A research study could be designed to formally evaluate the adapted aquatics intervention as it was provided to Mr. Jones and other participants. Multiple case study or multiple single-subject research designs would be appropriate methods. Disseminating the results of TR practice to others, by presenting at conferences and writing articles for publication, can provide evidence and information leading to engagement in further or more rigorous research. Therapeutic recreation specialists can write for a range of publications, from newsletters of local and state organizations to scholarly journals.

Action Research

One type of research that is being used more in fields such as teaching, community development, and occupational therapy, as well as TR, is **action research**. Action research is designed and conducted by practitioners to improve the quality of their own practice. "Action research involves regular people conducting evaluations in a systematic and organized manner" (DaGama & Hironaka-Juteau, 2002, p. 38). In action research, the TRS explores her own work, discusses possible new approaches, implements them, shares feedback with others, reflects on the results, and decides on which innovations she will implement to benefit the people with whom she is working (Haasen, Hornibrook & Pedlar, 1998). She can work in collaboration with other members of the

How to Read a Research Article

Reading research is the first step in both applying the results of research and conducting research studies. However, it is not uncommon for people to have feelings of intimidation or inadequacy when first reading research articles in scholarly journals. As with any skill, the more we practice, the better we become. So it is with reading research articles. Here are some brief guidelines to ease the process.

1. Be prepared to take notes or use a highlighter to emphasize points that are meaningful to you.

2. Read the title.

3. Read the abstract.

4. Thumb through the report quickly, reading the headings and subheadings to get an idea of how the research is presented and what is covered.

5. Read the discussion section. While the contents of this section are not totally consistent from one study to the next, they typically include the following:
   - A brief summary of the study
   - Concluding statements about the results
   - Factors that may have affected the results (known as the *limitations* of the study)
   - Discussion of the implications and significance of the findings
   - Recommendations for future research and practice

6. Go back to the beginning and read the introduction and literature review:
   - What is the problem that is being investigated?
   - What are the broader areas that have been studied that provide context for the research?
   - What previous work has been completed in the area (review of literature)?
   - The author or authors are saying there is a need for this investigation. What reasons are given for conducting the study?

7. Now read the methods section. This is generally the most difficult section because it describes the research methodology used in the study and, if relevant, the statistical analyses of the data. Read slowly and try to understand the researcher's decisions about who the subjects were, how the study was designed, whether quantitative or qualitative methods were used, and what types of analyses were conducted.

8. Read the findings or results. Do they make sense? What type of information is reported (demographic, simple statistical information, more complex analyses)?

9. Review the conclusion, discussion, recommendations, and implications. Do the conclusions follow logically from the problem statement? How do the authors relate their findings to the information presented in the introduction and review of related literature?

10. Finally, apply your clinical judgment:
   - Do you accept the conclusions?
   - Was the study worth doing? What is the significance of this work to the field?
   - Is the study useful for practice? Can you apply the findings to your own work?
   - Are there any risks to changing practice based on this study?
   - Do you have any unanswered questions about the study or the findings?

From Leedy 1981; Hudson-Barr 2004; Santelman 2001.

community, sharing ideas, information, strategies, and skills as a form of practical problem solving (Fazio, 2008). The action research process can also foster a collaborative approach with clients, who can participate as members of the community in identifying needs and possible solutions. This reflects the person-centered, benefits-based, strengths-based, and inclusion approaches to TR program planning. Again, referring back to Mr. Jones, what if the clients were not making enough progress as a result of participating in adapted aquatics? The TRS had read the evidence and believed the intervention should have been effective. To conduct an action research investigation, she might assemble a team of collaborators including clients and other staff to brainstorm possible strategies that might yield better outcomes. She could then implement the changes, reflect upon and discuss the results with the team, and decide on a course of action to improve the program. It is essential for TR students and practitioners to learn methods such as action research that are well suited to the real world of practice. The logic model is another method deserving of attention for use in evaluation.

Logic Model

The logic model is an increasingly popular tool for program evaluation. A **logic model** is a chart or visual representation that displays how an organi-

zation's day-to-day activities are connected to the outcomes it is trying to achieve (Coffman, 1999). Logic models are designed to be short, one or two pages at most, and are useful for both planning and evaluating. Logic models can be created by anyone with knowledge of the organization or program. Using a logic model puts the focus on the structure, process, and outcomes of a program. The TRS may notice slight variations in formats, but the overall concept and design are the same in most examples of logic models. Logic models consist of

● inputs, which include resources such as funding, staff, supplies, equipment, facilities, and participants;

● processes or activities to be provided; for example, recruiting participants, training staff or volunteers, or specific TR programs;

● outputs, which are the specific goods and services generated by the processes such as a written manual, or a number of staff trained in a new technique;

● outcomes, which are the specific accomplishments of the program and can be divided into short-term and long-term; a short-term outcome might be development of an intergenerational program and the long-term outcome could be an increased number of student volunteers in the nursing home; and

Grant-Funded TR Research Projects

The following projects were funded by the ATRA Foundation. They are examples of research investigations into the effectiveness of various TR program interventions at producing outcomes.

■ Leisure education with homeless persons with mental illness (M. Keogh-Hoss)

■ Efficacy of prescribed TR protocols on falls and injuries in nursing home residents with dementia (L. Buettner)

■ Efficacy of animal-assisted therapy—a TR intervention using AAT: Effects on the subjective well-being of older adults (N. Richeson)

■ The effects of aquatics on depression (B. Berlin)

■ Air mat therapy for the treatment of agitated wandering and depression (M. Shalek)

■ The effectiveness of a recreational modality (Tai Chi Chuan) in enhancing health status and reducing health care costs in an elderly population (A. Paterno)

■ Magic as a therapeutic intervention (L. Bedini)

■ The use of relaxation techniques for management of pain and blood pressure (C. Graziano-Perez and C. Jones)

● impacts or goals, which refer to the broad-level changes brought about by the program such as changed attitudes of teenagers toward nursing home residents, or more teenagers selecting gerontology-related fields as a college major or career.

Table 8.5 presents an example of a logic model developed for *FreshenUp*, a therapeutic recreation and fitness program for teenagers with developmental disabilities in order to develop skills for participation in typical community recreation environments, that we described in chapter 3. Logic models are valuable to use in grant applications because of the direct link between the inputs, activities, outputs, and outcomes, which presents

a clear picture of concrete actions and the tangible results they are expected to produce. The TRS can apply for a grant to fund a new TR program or service, or collaborate with other professionals in an agency or organization to develop a comprehensive new program that includes TR. Grants are awarded by government agencies, foundations, organizations, corporations, and even some individuals. Both NTRS and ATRA have had research award programs to fund small TR research projects. Using a logic model both to plan the activities to be funded by a grant and to be an evaluation tool for the grant's outcomes, demonstrates the TRS's ability to utilize current, respected processes common to many professions.

TABLE 8.5

FreshenUp Logic Model

Inputs/Resources	Activities	Outputs	Outcomes	Goal
A. College course	A. Design and offer three-credit course.	A. New course developed	A. 20 students passed course.	Teens with disabilities regularly participate in inclusive recreation and fitness opportunities in their chosen communities in a socially and age-appropriate manner.

Community awareness of the rights and capabilities of people with disabilities is raised through interaction with people with disabilities in positive activities. |
| B. College students | B. Train 20 college students. | B. 20 students enrolled in courses | B. Students report increased awareness and knowledge of recreational and fitness needs of people with disabilities. | |
| C. Fitness facility Sport facility Supplies and equipment | C. Perform fitness testing of 20 teens | C. 20 teens fitness tested, 10 weeks of team sports, one-to-one fitness, socialization | C. College students give skilled support and assistance to teens with disabilities who know their fitness levels and increase fitness. | Progress is made toward creating inclusive communities. |
| D. Staff: project coordinator, course instructors | D. Offer 10 sessions of recreation, fitness, and sport activities to 20 teens. | D. Teens learned to use fitness equipment and facility, learned new sport and recreation activities, practiced social skills in natural setting, and acquired information on community recreation resources. | D. Teens demonstrate proper use of fitness and gym equipment, identify healthy behaviors.

Teens and families report positive outcomes including participant satisfaction and increased self-esteem.

Teens report regular participation in fitness activities; families report ongoing participation and improvements. | |
| E. Financial resources | | | | |

● Summary ●

Evaluation is an exciting and satisfying process because it validates the work of the TRS. A comprehensive evaluation program that examines the practitioner's skills, the TR programs, and the effects on clients should follow a realistic schedule and provide information required by the TR department's stakeholders. Through evaluation, professionals obtain concrete evidence of the value of their efforts and information that is helpful in further developing services and providing clients with rewarding experiences. Becoming familiar with and skilled in the use of a variety of evaluation tools and procedures, including administering standardized instruments, designing logic models, grant writing, and conducting research, is both an ethical responsibility of the TRS and respected professional practice. When incorporated into the design and implementation of programming, evaluation will come to be viewed as less of a burden and more as a key function of TR leadership.

● Learning Activities ●

1. Conduct a self-evaluation based on the three sets of practitioner skills. Which skills do you possess? Which do you need to develop? Discuss your results in a small group.

2. Make a plan with a clinical or internship supervisor to develop the skills you identified in answering question 1.

3. Write a program protocol for a TR program of your choice.

4. Select a program you are familiar with, perhaps one you have recently conducted. Evaluate the program structure according to the guidelines in the chapter. What changes would improve the program?

5. Observe a TR program in progress. What observations can you make of the participants' behaviors? If possible, interview one of the participants using the questions in the chapter. Write up the results of your interview and share it with the TRS leading the program. Does he or she agree with your observations?

6. In a small group, design an evaluation schedule for a type of agency the group is familiar with, such as a nursing home, a group home, or an after-school or day program.

7. Brainstorm possible research topics in a small group. Select one and discuss how you would conduct an action research study.

8. Read a research article according to the guidelines given in the chapter. Summarize what you have read for an oral report in class or for a presentation to fellow staff members.

9. Develop a logic model for a new TR program you would like to implement.

PART III

Applications of TR Leadership

Applying TR leadership and programming principles to groups and individuals is the majority of the daily work of the TRS. Creating a schedule of TR programs that are relevant, feasible, and enjoyable is an ongoing challenge that utilizes the creativity and flexibility of the TRS in addition to the many skills already discussed. Working with groups is the primary mode of delivering TR leadership and necessitates an understanding of group dynamics, TR group structures and processes, and effective interaction strategies. One-to-one programming and private practice TR are growing rapidly as innovative TR leadership formats with some unique characteristics. Finally, what will be the role of TR leadership in the 21st century? Direct leadership of clients in TR programs is only one of multiple levels of professional TR leadership. All TRSs have a responsibility to be dedicated to the process of professionalization and evolve as professionals who contribute to the emergence of TR as a mature profession.

Unit-Wide Programming

In this chapter you will learn about:

- Planning balanced unit-wide TR programming
- The TR environment
- The power of the TR group
- How to use program formats to enhance the unit-wide TR schedule
- How to incorporate behavioral domains and social interaction patterns into TR programming
- The importance of program names, varying group size and leadership style, and coleadership
- How to schedule unit-wide programming in different locations and for different periods of time
- The value of special events and themed programming

The TRS is responsible for planning a schedule of TR programs that includes the full continuum or spectrum of TR services offered by the TR department in order to meet the needs of all the clients in her caseload on a regular basis. Depending on the setting, as a TRS you could work with as few as a handful of clients or as many as 80. Implementing programs for up to 80 clients in one setting, such as a single unit or ward or a day center, can be challenging. The term **unit-wide** refers to the single setting for which the TRS plans the TR schedule. This chapter presents guidelines for creating a total schedule that addresses the range of common concerns, needs, and interests identified in the clients' individual plans, taking into account a number of factors that affect programming. This schedule of programs should be presented in a weekly or monthly calendar, in a variety of formats, that is distributed to participants and is available to all the staff in the facility, family members, and visitors. In order to develop a comprehensive and well-balanced schedule, the TRS builds on the foundations of TR programming.

FOUNDATIONS OF BALANCED PROGRAMMING

The programs and activities that TR provides in a given setting occur in the context of the services of the overall agency and the TR department, as well as the needs and wishes of the clients. Therapeutic recreation programming is built on a foundation that includes governmental mandates; standards of accrediting bodies; codes of ethics; the agency's mission and goals; the TR department's mission, goals, and practice model (see chapter 2); and the input of the clients. A TR department may have only one staff member or as many as 25; but regardless of the size of the department, this foundation influences the types of programs that are offered and the benefits and outcomes emphasized by the TRS as he is implementing activities. For instance, if the mission of an agency is to prepare clients for independent living and discharge, the TRS could provide leisure education with a focus on how to use community recreation resources. If the mission is to improve quality of life for terminally ill patients, the programs could provide spiritual comfort through music and creating legacies. Regardless of the specific TR model followed, all of the models incorporate a continuum of services that

- build on the strengths of the individual,
- encourage the client to take greater control over her choices and actions as the TRS decreases his control, and

- promote the client's participation in the natural community.

The programs that are offered, therefore, can be

- therapeutic and rehabilitative in addressing limitations or health problems;
- educational in teaching new attitudes, skills, and behaviors;
- recreational in providing opportunities to experience fun, enjoyment, autonomy, and feelings of competence and control; and
- inclusion oriented in helping clients overcome barriers to participation in the activities and environments of their choice.

Therapeutic recreation programming addresses the challenge of focusing on the process or experience of the participants in the program versus the product of participation. Therapeutic recreation generally is a more process-focused service than other disciplines in the agency. It is concerned with how people feel during TR participation and how the experience is affecting them as much as, if not more than, what they produce or complete. Therapeutic recreation focuses on people's relationships and interactions with others, as well as the sense of achievement and accomplishment in coming up with a finished product or learning a new skill or activity. Developing a unit-wide TR program that balances the focus between process and product can be based on professional decisions about which focus best serves the needs, strengths, and interests of the clients.

To build a TR program based on the foundations of **balanced programming** requires planning. The efforts devoted to planning a meaningful and relevant schedule require time. Many TRSs feel pressured to conduct activities before they have had adequate time to plan. It is essential to put thought and care into designing programs in order to help clients achieve desired outcomes and have fulfilling and satisfying experiences. Following the guidelines presented in this chapter will facilitate the planning process. To build the program upon the proper foundation, the TR staff uses two unique resources: the TR environment and the TR group.

THE TR ENVIRONMENT

One unique TR resource for the provision of TR services in any setting is the TR environment. The TR environment is the distinctive atmosphere that exists in a TR room or space, surrounds a TR program, or is present in the structured or unstructured contact between a TR and a client or group of clients. The TR environment promotes interaction; offers opportunities for self-expression, feelings of control, making choices, taking chances, creativity, and enjoyment; and demonstrates respect for the autonomy of the individual. The TRS should create this environment whether or not TR has its own room or uses a variety of spaces in a larger facility or unit. The TR environment is one in which clients should feel comfortable, welcomed, and encouraged, as if they are in a more natural and relaxed space compared to settings in which they are receiving other treatments or services. Clients should experience TR as a place to be themselves, without the pressure they may feel in the clinical milieu, regardless of whether or not they are actively participating in an individual or group activity. It is as if the TRS is bringing a special aura to her programming. The qualities, attributes, and skills of the TRS create this aura.

Any encounter a TRS has with a client, even a casual interaction, can be an opportunity for the client to experience the qualities of the TR environment. For instance, when the TRS meets Patty in the hallway, he knows she needs encouragement to join social activities because she is shy about engaging in active recreation. The TRS says, "I saw you watching the Ping-Pong game yesterday. We are having a tournament tonight. Perhaps you can come and keep score or serve refreshments, even if you don't want to sign up to play." In this brief encounter, the TRS has demonstrated that he knows what Patty has been doing, has given her information she can act upon, and has offered her several choices for participation based on her treatment plan. Patty perceives the TRS's recognition of her strengths, concern for her needs, and sensitivity to her social and emotional issues. Utilizing the positive assets of the TR environment, even in a brief interaction, can augment the benefits of unit-wide programming. Specific suggestions for enhancing the TR environment with physical, psychological, and social modifications are presented throughout the chapter and outlined in table 9.1 on page 270.

THE TR GROUP

The second unique resource of TR is the TR group. It may seem from the emphasis in TR practice on individual program planning that groups are not as effective or as valuable as one-to-one activities. Yet groups are a natural part of life (DeVries & Lake, 2002) and an ideal setting for TR. "Social interaction in groups has long been regarded as one of the strongest assets in the leisure movement" (Gunn &

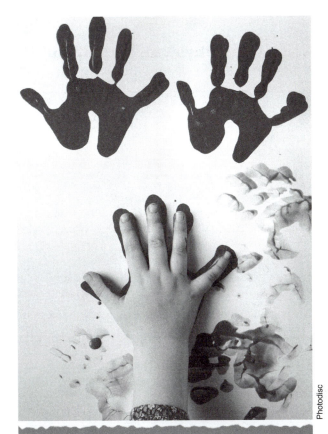

Therapeutic recreation programming generally emphasizes process rather than product.

Peterson, 1978, p. 94). In TR, clients benefit from interacting with other group members and taking on various roles and responsibilities within a group, in addition to benefiting from doing the activity. For example, Patty may not play Ping-Pong, but by keeping score or helping with refreshments she can perform a valuable function for the group and can receive acceptance, recognition, and appreciation from other members. This will increase her comfort level and willingness to participate in other activities. Clients themselves offer support, assistance, and friendship to each other as they share a mutual experience and common concerns. This synergistic effect within the TR group heightens the power of the TR environment.

The scheduling of clients into groups is also affected by regulatory guidelines for when initial assessments must be completed and by the length of stay. All clients are entitled to TR services and an individual plan, based on an assessment, that specifies appropriate TR programs. In short-term care settings, such as an acute care psychiatric unit, there may not be time to complete a comprehensive assessment prior to clients' joining a TR program. Or in a long-term care facility, with 14 days to complete

TABLE 9.1

Physical, Social, and Psychological Enhancements for the TR Environment

Physical	Social	Psychological
Provide information in a variety of formats: written, auditory, graphic, electronic.	Offer small-group programs.	"See the person in the patient" with a life history.
Create a homelike décor, using preferred colors and seasonal decorations as relevant.	Provide opportunities for structured and less formal social interactions.	Reinforce individual identity.
Display recreation projects and favorite objects.	Maintain a caring and supportive staff.	Provide opportunities for self-expression, creativity, and taking on responsibility.
Use a variety of spaces for programs.	Involve family and caregivers in programming.	Provide challenges and success-oriented activities.
Arrange furniture to create "conversation nooks."	Use humor—it's not just a joke, it's an attitude; remember, "You don't have to be funny to have fun."	Promote choice and decision making.
Position seating to take maximum benefit of daylight and windows.	Use buddies, clients as volunteers, and sometimes pair higher- and lower-functioning clients.	Give feedback.
Incorporate nature: plants, animals, natural light.		Reflect feelings.

an assessment, the client may begin attending programs before the assessment has been completed. Whether or not an assessment has been completed and an individual plan developed, the TRS should be prepared to incorporate all clients into any group that is scheduled (Shank & Coyle, 2002). To accommodate all potential group members, it is essential to know their common characteristics and concerns and the TR programs that are typically used to meet their needs. As discussed in chapter 8, program protocols indicate the specific criteria for participation in a TR group. However, in most TR programs, a client is not usually denied access to a TR group unless she is unable to behave appropriately or does not have the level of functioning required, or unless the program is one that would not meet her needs. Clients who are not appropriate for a scheduled TR program should have alternative activity choices on the schedule. In many settings, however, clients are free to attend any group that is scheduled. This may present challenges for the TRS, but the air of acceptance contributes to the TR environment. One can develop a variety of options for participation by thinking creatively about how to engage clients in activities and achieve their goals and aims.

GUIDELINES FOR BALANCED PROGRAMMING

The guidelines for balanced TR programming can transform the foundations of TR programming, the TR environment, and the TR group structure into a viable TR schedule. A balanced program of unit-wide TR may not address all the needs and issues of all clients on any given day, but implementing the guidelines will ensure that the TRS has made every effort to reach as many clients as possible. A balanced schedule should provide programs that

● build on clients' previous interests and also offer opportunities to learn new activities;

● emphasize all the behavioral domains and the eight social interaction patterns;

● vary in the number of participants;

● use a variety of rooms, spaces, and facilities (whenever possible);

● are offered at varying frequencies, intensities, and durations; and

● utilize a range of leadership styles and program formats.

The TRS should offer some programs that lead to immediate success and others that provide for longer-term efforts, continuing interest, and delayed gratification. Therapeutic recreation programs can also be led together with staff from other disciplines to draw on an array of professional skills and maximize the benefits to clients. Specific TR activities, especially those that are recreational, should be normalizing and should offer opportunities for inclusive recreation participation. In other words, to the extent possible, the activities should be the same as or as similar to the activities people do in the "real world" and should take place in the everyday world. This helps clients apply their skills and behaviors in a setting as much like their optimal living environment as possible, leading to a smoother transition from the service setting to their home or residence. What's more, it is vital to name TR programs so that they attract participants' interest and convey the intent, content, and benefits of the program.

This may sound like a lot of factors to juggle, but using the balanced programming guidelines will help the TRS develop a meaningful schedule of fulfilling activities that addresses the needs and interests of the clients in the TRS's caseload. The TR schedule should have a balance between the stability of routine, familiar activities and the excitement and novelty of the unexpected and of special events. These guidelines can also be used to evaluate weekly and monthly schedules to determine if a well-balanced program is being offered. The guidelines are divided into structural aspects, leadership aspects, and scheduling aspects.

Structural Aspects

The structural aspects of balanced programming include the behavioral domains, social interaction patterns, program formats, program names, and group size.

BEHAVIORAL DOMAINS

During the course of a day, clients should have the opportunity to participate in programs that emphasize each of the behavioral domains: physical; cognitive, mental, or intellectual; emotional or affective; social; and spiritual. While leisure is sometimes described as a behavioral domain, leisure is the domain in which all of the person's behaviors are integrated into one experience; therefore, any TR program could emphasize the leisure experience aspects for the clients. Programs can be physically active; be cognitively stimulating; allow

for expression of emotions, creativity, and aesthetic appreciation; promote mental health; contribute to managing stress; encourage socialization; and offer a recreation experience. The spiritual domain is now receiving more attention in TR programs. Typically, religious activities have been sources of spiritual meaning, but individuals may express and fulfill their spiritual needs through many different experiences, such as meditation, contemplating nature or art, listening to music, or caring for another. TRSs should be mindful of the diverse experiences that can be spiritually meaningful for participants. Although any activity incorporates more than one behavioral domain, the TRS may find it useful to identify the primary domain to aid in the selection of appropriate leadership strategies and needed modifications. Through activity analysis, discussed in chapters 3 and 6, the TRS can determine the primary behavioral domain used in an activity, as well as the specific behaviors and skills involved, and acquire the knowledge to make modifications in and influence the activity to promote specific behaviors and outcomes.

In TR programs, clients also demonstrate their strengths, reinforce their identity, and experience joy and fun. While this may seem like a tall order, many activities combine several of these elements:

- An exercise group can reduce stress, teach a new skill, promote feelings of self-confidence, and also be a fun activity with informal socializing.

- An arts and crafts program is an opportunity for creative expression, can strengthen cognitive skills of concentration and the ability to complete a task, can improve fine motor skills, and may promote social interaction as people share supplies or assist one another.

- A word game can provide competition, mental stimulation, excitement, socialization, and a normalizing experience.

Success in any activity, and in any aspect of an activity, helps reinforce the client's strengths and self-concept. Feedback from the TRS as he fulfills the TR leadership role helps clients achieve these benefits and outcomes. To cover all the domains, the TRS could schedule in one day a physical activity, a cognitive activity, an expressive activity, and a social activity for the unit. These are some examples:

- In a nursing home or a geriatric day care program, the TRS schedules a morning stretch and exercise activity to promote physical fitness, then a current events discussion for cognitive stimulation, then an arts and crafts activity to encourage creativity and feelings of accomplishment, horticulture to promote fine motor skills, music in the afternoon for relaxation, and finally a card party for socialization.

● In a children's psychiatric hospital, active games or martial arts can provide exercise; woodworking or model building addresses concentration and fine motor skills; a games tournament supplies socialization and healthy competition; and dance or music facilitates self-expression.

● In a substance abuse treatment program, the TR schedule includes an outdoor walk for physical fitness, a leisure education group for identification of leisure interests, a creative expression activity for dealing with feelings, a stress management program for the development of coping skills, and an evening social in which group members make homemade ice cream.

By providing a balanced daily program that covers all the behavioral domains, the TRS is doing his best to address all the needs of the clients. Although programming is planned for the unit as a whole, individuals may have varying degrees of skills and limitations in any one or more of the behavioral domains. The TRS can facilitate individual participation by using adaptive equipment, modifying the activity, and providing assistance. As discussed in chapter 6, behaviors from all the domains are used to some degree to carry out any given activity, and participation can increase skills in several of the domains.

SOCIAL INTERACTION PATTERNS

Closely related to behavioral domains are the eight **social interaction patterns** (see table 9.2). From moments of solitude to competitive team sports or games, TR programs should involve the full range of social interaction. It is beneficial for people to be

● comfortable alone,

● successful in solitary pursuits,

● at ease doing something in the company of others,

● able to enjoy social interaction,

● comfortable with different levels of competition, and

● a member of a group with a common goal or activity.

It is important for many TR clients to develop interests that they can engage in when they are alone,

because they may have a lot of free time; these activities can keep them mentally healthy, reduce stress, and serve as a source of fulfillment. Activities such as reading, painting, yoga, and collecting can be done on an individual basis and also serve as a gateway to interacting with others (e.g., book club, painting or yoga class). Aggregate activities, which do not *require* social interaction, can be structured so that participants do need to interact. When clients share supplies, assist one another, or discuss their projects or experiences, an aggregate activity becomes an intragroup activity, requiring a higher level of social interaction and cooperation. Clients also enjoy and benefit from engaging in competitive activities, either facing a single competitor in a game such as chess, or as a member of a sports team. These activities may become interests that clients can share with their families so they have something positive they can do together, which may not have been the case in the past due to the client's condition or other factors. A group activity may lead to a new interest that a person may subsequently pursue on her own. Also, it may be necessary to modify a favorite activity, due to an individual's newly acquired illness or disability, in order for him to continue participating with family or friends. The TRS can offer programs with varied social interaction patterns to help clients develop their socialization and group participation skills. The examples previously mentioned include aggregate (crafts, exercise), intragroup (discussions, making ice cream), and competitive activities (card party, Ping-Pong tournament, chess, basketball). Social skill requirements also differ depending on the type of **program format** used.

PROGRAM FORMATS

Program formats, often studied in recreation program planning, are the organizational structures used to present activities. Several different groupings of program formats have been developed. The most useful grouping for TR programs includes instructional classes; clubs and interest groups; open and unstructured facilities where participants can "drop in" either to participate or to just "hang out"; competitions such as contests or tournaments; spectator activities; outings; and special events.

● Instructional classes: These programs teach clients new activities or skills, such as arts and crafts, swimming, games, writing, American Sign Language, or computers. Classes may also provide training for clients to become lifeguards, volunteers, or recreation assistants.

TABLE 9.2

Social Interaction Patterns

Interaction pattern	Type of action	Degree of interaction	Examples
Intraindividual	Action taking place within the mind of a person or action involving the mind and a part of the body	Requires no contact with another person or external object	Twiddling thumbs or playing with hair, daydreaming, fantasizing, meditation, yoga
Extraindividual	Action directed by a person toward an object in the environment	Requires no contact with another person	Watching TV, doing a crossword, playing solitaire, using the computer, reading, making a craft, gardening, cooking
Aggregate	Action directed by a person toward an object in the environment while in the company of others who are also directing action toward objects in the environment	Action is not directed toward another, and no interaction between participants is required or necessary; but interaction may occur.	Spectator activities, such as concerts, plays, sports; craft programs; exercise class; working out in the gym, lectures
Interindividual	Action of a competitive nature	Action is directed by one person toward another.	Chess, checkers, card games, tennis, Ping-Pong, racquetball
Unilateral	Action of a competitive nature among three or more persons with one antagonist	Action is directed toward one person as the antagonist, or "it."	Tag, hide-and-seek, charades
Multilateral	Action of a competitive nature among three or more persons with no single antagonist	Action is directed at all others; no one person is the antagonist.	Scrabble, poker, Monopoly
Intragroup	Action of a cooperative nature by two or more persons intent upon reaching a mutual goal	Action requires positive verbal and nonverbal interaction.	Bands, choruses, putting on a play, membership on a committee, partner dancing, volunteer or service projects, cooperative games, producing a newsletter
Intergroup	Action of a competitive nature between two or more intragroups	Action requires positive verbal and nonverbal interaction, as well as competition.	Team sports, Bridge, relay races

Data from Avedon 1974; Stumbo and Peterson 2009.

- Clubs and interest groups: A club can be organized around a particular interest or common characteristic, such as Italian culture, Latin dance, or environmental issues. As another example, a club could be formed for siblings of children in the hospital.

- Open or drop-in facility: An art or craft room, game room, library, or fitness center can be used as an open facility with hours of operation allowing for clients to drop by at their convenience, perhaps with visitors, and either participate or just watch what's going on.

- Competition: Competitions may involve sports and games tournaments, talent shows, or a judged art show. They could also take the form of contests to name a team or newsletter, decorate a cake, or paint a T-shirt.

- Spectator activities: Activities may include movies, plays, sport events, concerts, art exhibits, or any form of entertainment or performance.

- Outings or trips: These may be walks in the community, bus trips for sightseeing, visits to museums and places of historic or cultural interest, or boat rides. Clients may go to restaurants or to a mall, take weekend trips, or go on leisure education outings to learn about community resources and practice newly learned skills.

- Special events: These may be parties, summer barbecues, holiday celebrations, carnivals, fairs, or special entertainment.

These program formats provide the stability of a known activity along with the novelty of experiencing the activity in a different way. Program formats can be adjusted to enhance the variety of the unit schedule. Diversifying program formats can meet a greater range of needs (Kraus, 1997):

- Arts and crafts can be offered as an instructional class in yarn crafts, such as knitting and crocheting, to learn and develop a recreational skill. A special event in which the finished projects are displayed gives the creators feelings of pride and accomplishment. The craft show is a spectator activity for those who attend and may trigger interest in learning the activity. Awarding prizes adds the excitement of a contest. Issuing invitations and serving refreshments help to make a craft show a special social event.

- The weekly bowling trip can become a tournament. Lessons can be offered to build skills for competition. Presenting prizes at an awards luncheon and inviting families will make the tournament a special event.

- The creative writing group can become a literary magazine project. Those who say they can't write may be able to design, type, illustrate, or distribute the magazine. Suddenly there is a focus and an excitement and the activity is more like life in the real world, which supports the principle of inclusion.

In TR, programming takes an experiential approach, with clients actively engaged in *doing* something. Taking time to plan what type of format will best meet the needs of the group demonstrates the TRS's ethical responsibility to "do good" for clients by promoting their well-being. Too often, clients are sitting in a circle or at a table for most of their TR activities or are offered the same types of programs over and over. For instance, youth are frequently offered mostly sports and active games, and elderly long-term care residents may have a steady diet of bingo. In these situations, the TRS serves as the leader and directs the activity rather than facilitating the experience and empowering clients to take more responsibility and control. A variety of formats can increase clients' motivation to

participate in TR programs and enhance the benefits they derive from participation.

Using the range of program formats enables the TR staff to be more creative and keep the programming fresh and appealing while increasing the number of benefits offered by any given activity. Depending on the setting, certain formats may be preferable or more frequently used; for example, a group home typically schedules more community outings than would a nursing home or a psychiatric hospital. See table 9.3 for more examples of how activities can be varied by format.

PROGRAM NAMES

Closely connected to selecting the format for a program is creating a program name or title. Naming TR programs so that they generate curiosity, or "buzz," can increase attendance. Client motivation is probably the biggest complaint of TR staff. But as we have said before, all people are motivated—they just may not be motivated to do what the TRS wants them to do. This may bring up the ethical principle of autonomy. A client may say "I don't want to do anything" or "I just like watching TV"; statements like these are considered expressions of preference. In fact, they may reflect habits of behavior that have formed because individuals are fearful, depressed, or bored. It may be also that people don't understand the value of participating in recreation, don't have the skills, lack confidence, or have never developed any interests. The TRS has the duty to use her professional knowledge and ability to motivate clients, expose them to a range of leisure experiences, and help them make choices that fulfill the purposes of TR, thereby increasing their exercise of autonomy. The goal is for these activities to be meaningful and beneficial to clients, and this goal can be reinforced through the names of TR groups. Naming groups according to the benefits they offer, rather than using the name to identify the activity, helps clients understand that a given activity has particular meaning and relevance to them. This is an application of the benefits-based approach to TR program planning, discussed in chapter 3. Knowing your clients' concerns and what motivates them will help you create names that convey to them the value of TR programs.

Program names also communicate the purpose of TR programs to other staff in the facility who may complain that the programs' names don't sound "therapeutic" enough. Therapeutic recreation has the ethical obligation to educate the other staff about the purposes and benefits of TR groups, their value to clients, and the reasons TR designs and implements programming in certain ways. The TRS's professional demeanor and ability to interpret TR to others influence the perception of TR services in his agency. "Chair Aerobics" merely identifies what the program is. "Functional Exercise" may appeal to people in a physical rehabilitation setting with very clinical, treatment-oriented TR services, because the name relates to the agency goal of improving physical functioning and communicates this as the purpose of the program. "Jump Up, Jump Out" may attract participants in a transitional setting for young adults with developmental disabilities because it indicates the direction people are headed in, back to the community, and sounds like a fun approach to engaging in exercise. "Yomenco," which combines yoga movements, breathing exercises, and flamenco dance and music, is a great example of an attention-getting name that sparks curiosity. Catchy titles grab people's attention in having a "hook" that conveys the benefits people seek from a program (Russell & Jamieson, 2008). The following are four guidelines for naming programs (Russell & Jamieson, 2008):

● Names should be distinctive so the program stands out as unique.

● Names should convey the relevance of the program to the target audience.

● Names should be memorable.

● Names should not be so specific that they restrict the content of the program rather than allow for easy changes in the program content over time as needs and interests change.

The TR department should be creative about naming programs to liven up the schedule and convey the fun of TR activities. Contests can also be held to come up with names for programs.

GROUP SIZE

Groups vary most obviously by size. Programs can balance the desire to have as many people as possible involved in TR with the real need to achieve therapeutic goals by controlling the size of the group according to its purpose.

Large Groups

Large-group programs tend to be diversional and are often similar to common recreation activities engaged in by the general public. Large-group activities do not require social interaction, can accommodate a wide range of abilities and levels of functioning, and are often open to visitors. Examples include special events, sing-alongs, parties, movies, entertainment, and some trips. While large-group programs have the highest attendance, they usually do not produce therapeutic outcomes because the TRS cannot provide each client with personal attention. Large-group activities are valuable to clients because they are normalizing and

TABLE 9.3

Ways of Varying Activities by Program Formats

	Instruction class	Club or interest group	Open or drop-in	Competition	Spectator	Trip	Special event
Basketball	Ball-handling skills	Collecting sports memorabilia	Pickup game	League play	Watching play-offs on TV	Going to a pro game	Invite a pro athlete to visit
Exercise	Learn latest craze	Open dance sessions	Open gym	5K race	Watching a marathon	Fund-raising walk	Put on a demo
Music	Learn an instrument	Jazz lovers' club	Jam session	Talent show	Listening to a performance	Going to a concert	Putting on a concert
Board games	Learn to play board games	Scrabble club	Game room	Scrabble tournament	Watching a match	Visiting a game store	Make your own board game
Pets	Dog training class	Bassett hound owners' club	Dog park	Funniest dog contest	Going to a dog show	Zoo	Blessing of the animals

fun, providing relief from the treatment or institutional environment. Although an essential part of TR programming, they may not require the direct leadership of a qualified TR professional. The TRS's main responsibility in large groups is to plan and supervise the program and to train the staff members who will be assisting her.

With large groups, a risk management concern is having an adequate number of staff at the program to ensure the safety of all participants. Safety includes supervision, assistance for clients who wish to go to the rest room or leave, and coverage in an emergency or other situation that might take the TRS away from the program temporarily. Therapeutic recreation departments may find it valuable to work within their facilities to establish staff-to-client ratios for particular groups and procedures to handle these situations. Safety procedures should apply to all programs, regardless of size.

Small Groups

Smaller groups are more therapeutic and educational because the TRS can give personal attention to each client based on his needs and abilities. In a small group, each participant has more responsibility and opportunity to be actively engaged. In a group of four to 12 participants, the TRS can

● consider the stage of change of each client,
● use learning principles to help develop new behaviors,
● facilitate active engagement and goal-directed behavior using therapeutic intervention techniques,
● provide feedback tailored to the strengths and needs of the individual, and
● provide participants with assistance based on task analysis.

Therapeutic recreation programs that are effective in a small-group format include educational programs such as leisure education, stress management, assertiveness training, community reintegration, and social skills training; they also include therapeutic groups such as expressive arts, discussions, cognitive games, and task-oriented activities. Groups oriented to functional improvement, which may include exercise, basic communication skills, or cognitive retraining, are also best in a small group.

In the course of a day, clients who participate in group programming should be able to attend both large and small groups. Many TR specialists find themselves running large groups because of lack of staff and the pressure to have as many clients as possible in programs. One way to gain support for smaller TR groups that are more therapeutic and goal oriented is to propose a pilot program for a limited period of time. Select a focus for the program that is valued by the agency, such as falls prevention in a nursing home, anger management in a psychiatric facility, or social skills in a group home. Suggest offering the pilot program to a small group for a short period of time to determine effectiveness. If the clients can demonstrate positive outcomes as a result of participation, this will help you to gain support for offering more small TR groups. One-to-one TR programs are also growing in popularity in settings such as long-term care where they are required to provide TR to all clients whether or not they can join a group or are candidates for rehabilitation (see chapter 11).

An example of a TR program that incorporates groups of different sizes is the Innovations approach (DeVries & Lake, 2002). The Innovations program is conducted by the TRS with at least one additional staffperson. This approach uses a five-track program that was found to be effective in meeting the needs of the clients. The five tracks are large-group (12-40 participants) activities; smaller groups for 4 to 12 participants; one-to-one visits; cotreatments led by the TRS with physical, occupational, or speech therapy staff (or some combination of these) for clients in a subacute or rehabilitation unit; and a restorative program for 4 to 15 participants who are no longer eligible for physical, occupational, or speech therapy. With this approach, clients can experience the benefits of large groups, smaller groups, individual attention, and enhanced therapeutic intervention. Group size also affects the leadership aspects of balanced programming.

Leadership Aspects

The leadership aspects of balanced programming relate to choosing an appropriate leadership style for the group and coleading with other disciplines.

LEADERSHIP STYLE

Leadership style is another variable in delivering TR programming. The TRS should plan programs over the course of a day that require different styles of leadership. Therapeutic recreation leadership ranges from a strong, directive approach in structuring group activities and processes to a very relaxed and informal approach. It is important to remember that choosing the appropriate leadership style should be part of the TRS's repertoire of therapeutic techniques. A program should not be conducted in a certain style simply because that is the one the TRS is most comfortable using. Leadership style affects the degree of control and decision making of both the TRS and the participants.

Authoritarian Style

The most controlling style of leadership is known as an **autocratic or authoritarian leadership style**. When using this style, the TRS reserves the right to make all the decisions and choices about the activity and the individuals' participation. While this may seem inconsistent with the TR value of autonomy, an autocratic style may be necessary when clients are low functioning, are in a compromised state of health, are confused or psychotic, or are unable to control their behavior and make appropriate decisions and choices about their actions.

The TRS should allow the participants to make choices, but ultimately the TRS has the final word. Some practitioners feel uncomfortable in this role; however, clients who are at low levels of functioning may welcome the structure and control the TRS imposes if they are unable, physically, cognitively, or emotionally, to handle certain tasks and expectations. On the other hand, in some types of programs they may be able to handle more responsibility. For example, in a morning arts and crafts group for elderly nursing home residents with varying degrees of dementia, the TRS may need to give a great deal of instruction on how to do the project, provide physical assistance for carrying out the fine motor movements, carefully monitor use of supplies such as scissors for safety, and monitor all participants' efforts in order to keep them on track to complete the project. Yet during the monthly birthday party in the afternoon, with music and refreshments, it may be beneficial to the residents to just relax and enjoy the stimulation the activity provides without continual intervention from the TRS. The TRS needs to carefully observe the clients for their readiness to take on more control, make choices, and function more independently in an activity. The authoritarian style is necessary in a crisis situation, such as a fight, a client's running away, a medical emergency, or a safety problem in the facility.

Closely related to the authoritarian style is the **paternalistic leadership style** in which the leader protects and guides the clients. This style may foster dependency in that the leader is seen as a benevolent protector, but it may be useful for clients who are newly admitted to a facility, very fearful, or traumatized by events or illness. The TRS needs to carefully monitor himself when using this style so as to know when it is no longer needed. The danger is that it may become comfortable for the TRS and the client rather than beneficial.

Democratic Style

Farther along the continuum of leadership styles, to a style in which the TRS begins sharing control and decision making with the clients, is the **democratic or shared leadership style**. This works well with clients who are motivated and are capable of making choices and decisions on their own and with the group with guidance from the TRS. The group functions like a team, giving input into the design and implementation of the activities. This may be appropriate for many clients in TR programs in which they are learning new skills, planning and carrying out a group project or activity or event, or participating in a game. The participants may select the game, choose teams, decide how long the game will last, and what the rewards might be. In a community reintegration group in a rehabilitation setting, the democratic style may be well suited to

The broad range of programming in therapeutic recreation requires a wide array of leadership styles and techniques.

clients who are capable of understanding the scope of the project and the planning process and are able to carry out many of the steps independently, with minimal assistance from the TRS. In planning a community outing, the TRS may need to provide a balance between minimal and maximal control in order to help the group make a feasible plan. The TR professional's responsibilities, in accordance with ethical practice, are to enable the clients to take as much control as possible over their participation, as well as to maintain a safe environment while protecting their rights to take risks. The TRS may find himself in the role of advocate as he defends and promotes a client's rights to engage in certain activities that other members of the professional team consider unsafe or unnecessary.

Another example of a situation in which democratic leadership is the preferred style is seen when a group of clients decides to put on a talent show, write a poetry magazine, or volunteer in a nursing home. Their ability to direct their own actions is supported by the TRS, who facilitates the functioning of the group as a team with shared leadership. This style enables clients to become more responsible and accountable for their own actions. It may be difficult for the TRS to gradually fade the degree of control she maintains over a group. She may be afraid that the members are not ready for or capable of making wise decisions, or she may be accustomed to a stricter style of leadership. However, the ability of individuals to exercise their full potential for self-direction, and to learn how to do this within the protection of the TR environment, is vital for their growth, health, and well-being and also related to their right to leisure. It is sound ethical practice to do what is in the best interests of the clients, and not what is more comfortable or convenient for the professional.

Laissez-Faire Style

The third style along the continuum is the **laissez-faire leadership style** (*laissez-faire* is French for "allow to do"). It implies a more lenient or relaxed style of leadership, letting people act without interference from the leader. This style is appropriate for high-functioning clients who are very motivated and capable of self-direction. The TRS is supportive, provides only minimal direction, answers questions as needed, and may supervise the program space or facility as in a drop-in program. This is often the leadership style in a large spectator or entertainment activity in which the TRS is not providing individual or small-group direction and facilitation. The TRS may also choose laissez-faire leadership as a therapeutic technique to enable the group to take on responsibility in the absence of strong direction from a leader so that the members can practice newly learned skills and behaviors. A group of youth at risk may put on a play, or residents of a group home may go out to the movies. A very clear example of laissez-faire leadership is the role of the TRS with a residents' council. These councils are a form of resident government in nursing homes and other residential facilities. The council serves as a voice for residents, communicating with staff and administration, gathering information, discussing issues, inviting speakers, and conducting whatever business they deem necessary to promote the quality of life in the facility. The TRS often serves as liaison for the residents' council, facilitating meetings and activities as required.

The continuum formed by three leadership styles, autocratic, democratic, and laissez-faire, can be viewed as parallel to those in several of the practice models, including the Leisure Ability Model, the Health Protection/Health Promotion Model, and the TR Service Delivery Model (see chapter 2). As clients grow in their skills, abilities, health, functioning, or degree of independent participation, the TRS gradually reduces her degree of control over them by moving from an autocratic to a democratic and finally to a laissez-faire style. In models using an approach that is more circular than linear, such as the OLH-TR model, the TRS moves back and forth among leadership styles. This is necessary in any model, depending on the needs of the clients. While the TRS predominantly uses a democratic style of leadership, styles can be varied in unit-wide programming to enable and encourage degrees of freedom in clients during daily activities. In this approach, known as situational leadership, the TRS chooses his leadership style based on the situation. The approach can also be considered eclectic, in that the TRS selects, from the range of styles, the one that best fits the situation. Leadership style can also be affected by the type of facility or space in which a program is provided.

The TRS's leadership style can be varied to emphasize process or product. For some groups, an authoritarian style will facilitate completion of a product, and for others a democratic style can enhance the process. Coleadership of groups can affect the degree of emphasis placed on process and product in a particular program.

COLEADERSHIP

Coleadership with other disciplines is worth considering when one is planning balanced programming.

Cooperating with and supporting colleagues for the benefit of clients are included in the NTRS Code of Ethics (National Therapeutic Recreation Society, 1990). In most health care and human service settings, the TRS is a member of a team made up of all disciplines working with the clients. Depending on the type of agency, the team could include teachers; psychologists; nurses; physical, occupational, and speech therapists; rehabilitation counselors; and medical doctors from a number of specialties. Each profession focuses on its own area of expertise. For example, TR focuses on recreational needs and the benefits of recreation activities; physical therapy (PT) focuses on physical functioning using movement and exercise; psychologists address psychological and emotional issues of clients; dietitians plan menus based on dietary needs and restrictions; and vocational rehabilitation counselors help clients with job skills and placement. Other professionals may have excellent suggestions for the TRS based on their expertise and insights about the clients. Paraprofessionals such as nursing assistants, dietary aides, mental health workers, and PT or occupational therapy aides, who know clients very well because of the direct services they provide to them, also are active team members.

Collaborating with other disciplines can enrich and expand TR programming. Programs provided by two or three team members who work together to lead a group could maximize the benefits the clients receive from group participation and improve their progress toward achieving desired outcomes. As an example, improving physical functioning is the specialty of PT; but developing and maintaining fitness is the responsibility of physical educators and fitness trainers, and exercise is also a major form of recreation. Accordingly, the PT, the physical educator or fitness specialist, and the TRS could collaborate on planning and leading a comprehensive physical fitness program, recognizing that each discipline has unique expertise and knowledge to offer but that the knowledge bases of the disciplines are also similar in some ways. The TRS, however, is skilled in bringing together all the components into a meaningful program. In the TR group, all aspects of the activity and the total person are integrated, which can enhance the impact of participation on the client. As emphasized throughout this book, TR programming is inherently recreational and therefore fun for participants. This may motivate clients to follow an exercise regimen prescribed by PT that could otherwise seem tedious. As examples of other popular collaborations, the TRS and a dietitian may colead a healthy cooking group; the

TRS and a nursing assistant may offer a grooming group; and a psychologist and a TRS may conduct a stress management program together. For themed programming, such as a Wellness Month, every one of these professionals could work together to design pertinent activities. Falls prevention for older adults is one area in which collaboration and coleadership are being encouraged.

A successful team and effective coleadership are based on mutual respect and trust among the coleaders. Communication is essential as coleaders plan the content and process of a group. Careful planning, coupled with the ability to be flexible, helps the group run smoothly. The planning should include how the group will be carried out and what the roles and actions of each leader will be. Leadership does not necessarily have to be equally divided. A benefit of coleadership is that group members receive more attention and assistance than they would from only one group leader. But regardless of how the work is allocated, the experience can be enriching for the coleaders and the participants. The other staff will better understand the purposes and processes of TR through their direct involvement in coleading because the TRS is the primary facilitator of a TR group. Coleadership can foster unity among the team members and a spirit of collaboration in the best interests of the clients. However, scheduling programs with shared leadership may present its own challenges. Staff availability is affected by each person's schedule of programming, meetings, and other responsibilities. Meetings with department heads may be helpful for setting up workable and mutually satisfactory procedures to facilitate coleadership and staff involvement in TR.

Even when a group doesn't have more than one leader, it is obviously beneficial to have other staff assist the TRS. The TRS should work with nursing, social work, education, rehabilitation services, and other departments, depending on the setting, to have direct care staff and other specialists lend a hand. The TRS is responsible for educating other staff about how their presence at TR programs will benefit clients. Clients will benefit from the extra attention, assistance, and care; and the staff themselves can benefit from interacting with and observing the clients in the more natural setting of the TR environment. An obstacle is often that the staff are too busy to help out. To overcome this obstacle, indicate exactly when the group is scheduled and how long the staff involvement would be, and allow people to choose when they can assist. Point out that assistance from just one staffperson will allow for a larger group, thereby freeing up other staff to attend to other clients or responsibilities. In addition, the guidelines from the Center for Medicare and Medicaid Services (CMS) for long-term care facilities specifically indicate that all staff should be involved with activities as a contribution to quality of life.

Scheduling Aspects

The scheduling aspects of balanced programming include the locations and spaces in which programs are held and the time frames of programs, including their frequency, duration, and intensity. Programming life cycles, time-limited programming, and programming themes are closely related to program time frames.

LOCATIONS FOR PROGRAMS

Over the course of the day and the week, the TRS should use a variety of spaces as appropriate to the purposes of the TR programs. It is helpful to vary the locations, whether programs take place indoors or outdoors, on or off the unit, in different buildings, or away from the facility altogether. This is an effective way to stimulate interest in attending TR groups, increase the range of programs offered, and promote **normalization**. When clients can try out new skills and behaviors in a range of locations, transfer of learning from one setting to another is enhanced. A change of setting provides novelty and stimulates interest in finding out "what is going on"; however, some clients, such as those with autism or dementia, may function better if a specific program, or most of their TR participation, takes place in the same room or space. These clients benefit from a familiar routine that is comforting and provides structure in their lives (DeVries & Lake, 2002). Knowing client characteristics and needs affects the choice of location for programs.

The first step in designating the appropriate location for a program is to inventory the types of spaces and environments available in the facility. There may be a room designated exclusively for TR use, an activity room that is shared with OT, or an all-purpose room that has multiple users. In some settings, a day room or common area may double as a dining room and also serve as the main space for TR programming. Apart from the obvious locations, there may be rooms or areas that can provide an atmosphere or ambience that facilitates group participation. In addition to location, the size of the space can affect participation. Perhaps there is a way to subdivide a large space with a portable divider, such as a screen, or to group the furniture to create a smaller, more intimate area. Large spaces may be distracting, or too many stimuli and other activities going on interfere with clients' ability to focus on the TR program. Small meeting rooms or lounges, even those used by staff, or outdoor spaces may be available. Special areas such as a garden, PT gym, OT kitchen, tennis court, park, or library may be used for TR programs. And the benefits of being outdoors cannot be overstated. The outdoor environment provides relief from the treatment setting, puts people in contact with nature, and reflects the rhythms and patterns of typical life.

PUBLIC VERSUS PRIVATE SPACE

Both public space and private space have advantages. Typically, public spaces are larger than private spaces. You can create privacy if you subdivide larger spaces by rearranging furniture or using privacy screens.

● **Public spaces** are those that have open access to anyone. In service settings that include TR, this can include a day room, outdoor area, dining area, gym, or lounge. There is no single designated use for this type of space; even in an eating room, people are able to sit and socialize and TR programs may take place. Although public spaces may present many distractions, a program in a public space may be appropriate if it is large group, is socially oriented, has a recreational emphasis, and sets a tone of positive interaction and goodwill. In a public space, more people, including clients, staff, and visitors, can be exposed to TR programming. Clients can take time to observe a program until they feel comfortable joining in. If they see others participating and benefiting from the group, this may encourage them to want to be involved. They can take time to become familiar with the process and more willing to try the activity. Families and other visitors can observe and even assist if needed. They may begin to see their family member in a new light in the context of the client's positive, active participation in recreation. Other staff also can see aspects of clients that are not revealed during other forms of treatment or services, as well as enhance their understanding of TR as they observe or assist with the TR program. The TRS may wish to consider programming the whole space even if the group itself is small. Playing music, adding decorations or props, and rearranging the furniture can expand the TR environment beyond the borders of the group itself.

● **Private spaces** are those with restricted access, such as a TR room, small meeting room, or specialty area like a dance studio or craft room. Programs in smaller, more private areas are critical to creating an atmosphere of trust and emotional safety, security, and privacy. This mood is crucial for conducting educational and therapeutic TR groups in which clients explore their issues and feelings, learn and try out new skills and behaviors, and struggle with difficult challenges to their health and well-being. It is critical for them to feel safe and secure in a trusting environment. A smaller space conveys the helping nature of the TR program to clients because the TRS is able to focus his attention on a smaller group and provide more individualized attention. A sign on the door can indicate that the group is in progress and should not be interrupted. In certain settings, the names of the participants should also be listed so that staff members know who is attending the program.

The outdoor environment provides relief from the treatment setting, puts people in contact with nature, and reflects the rhythms and patterns of typical life.

TIME FRAMES

Scheduling a balanced program involves decisions about the program time frame. Plugging the activities into the schedule may seem like the final step in putting the program together, but it also relates to the concept of TR as active treatment. In order for a program to be considered active treatment and therefore a reimbursable service according to the guidelines of the federal government and health accrediting organizations, TRSs must indicate on the individual treatment plan the frequency, duration, and intensity of the TR intervention provided to the client. Varying frequency, duration, and intensity of TR programs is a guideline for balanced program planning.

Frequency

Frequency may seem to mean simply "Can I ethically offer bingo more than once a week?"; however, varying the frequency of programs can be a significant element in programming. Clients may come to rely on TR as a source of stability in their lives, based on their positive relationship with the TRS, their enjoyment of a particular routine of activities (for example, daily exercise at 9 a.m.), and the opportunity to engage in familiar and beloved pastimes. Clients may also look to TR to provide excitement, novelty, a break from the routine, and something to anticipate with pleasure. The psychologist Mihaly Csikszentmihalyi (1990), in his discussion of flow, points out that human beings have a need to strike a

balance in their lives between stability and novelty, the routine and the unexpected, and comfort and risk. One way TR can address this need is by varying the frequency with which different programs are offered. Programs that provide physical exercise, cognitive stimulation, and social interaction should be offered every day. These programs are essential to good physical and mental health. Frequent and ongoing involvement helps clients maintain continuity and a focus on the content of a particular program. Reinforcing the learning of a new skill can best be done in the context of a regularly scheduled program. Repetition can help cognitively impaired clients, for example, to remember and relearn how to do certain activities, such as playing a game or finding one's way to a particular location.

Special events are activities that are offered infrequently, according to the length of stay or **duration** of service provided by the department. Special events may be offered less than once a week, whether biweekly, monthly, or at longer intervals. Because they occur less often, special events generate a mood of expectation and excitement. A restaurant trip could occur once a week, a themed party once a month. It has been said that a recreation experience is not just the *doing* of the activity: It is the anticipation, the doing, and the recollection. Therapeutic recreation can build eagerness and enthusiasm for a special event by talking it up; hanging flyers and posters; making announcements; and sending out messages via e-mail, text messages, or an in-house intranet system. Eagerly anticipating a program that doesn't occur all the time triggers people's curiosity and contributes to the TR environment. Once the program is over, show pictures, write articles, and talk about it. Let people enjoy the memories. Special events should be scheduled at least once a month in a long-term care facility; in settings where the length of stay is several months or less, the TR staff should plan special events more often. However, the more frequently they are offered, the less elaborate they may have to be because of the degree of planning and staff time and effort needed to produce a quality event.

Duration

Duration refers to the length of time a program is offered—a month, eight sessions, three months, a season, and so on. When one is planning program length, reviewing the research on specific activities may give a guide as to how much time is needed to produce change. Many research articles in TR journals discuss limitations that may have influenced the results of the study. One frequently mentioned limitation is that the TR intervention program was not offered for a long enough period of time to produce desired results. Careful review of the evidence on the effectiveness of specific TR interventions will help determine the optimal duration of a program.

A Lesson From Community Recreation Community-based recreation programs adhere to certain programming procedures related to duration that could be useful in TR program planning. In community-based programs, people usually sign up for an eight-week session, a holiday program, a summer season, or some other defined time frame. This allows a recreation department to offer programs of current interest, evaluate their success, and then schedule them again with or without changes. On the other hand, too many TR programs are typically scheduled and run every week, week after week, *forever*, without any evaluation of their effectiveness and appropriateness for the particular group of clients. Yet every program has a life cycle that encompasses growth and decline. Once a new program is introduced, it grows in acceptance or interest and then reaches a healthy peak or plateau of participation, and finally interest and participation begin to decline (Kraus, 1997).

At this point in the program's life cycle, the TRS has to determine if it is possible to revive the program by changing some elements or if it should be terminated. Some activities are fads that fade out quickly; others have enduring interest. Fads can attract notice and participation for a time because "Everyone is doing it." Games like Twister and Trivial Pursuit were once ubiquitous; they are no longer trendy, but playing similar active group and trivia-type games still interests people. The TRS can maintain the benefits of these activities by introducing the latest version. Listening to music is timeless, but Walkmans have been replaced by iPods because people like new and improved equipment. Children still like collecting dolls or stuffed animals, just not Beanie Babies or Cabbage Patch dolls. Fitness activities such as Tae Bo and spinning are still offered but the "buzz" surrounding them has faded. Laughter yoga and Zumba are the current trends. They, too, may not last but can provide variety to engage a greater number of people. Keep in mind, though, that fads may not warrant a big financial investment. If people are losing interest in a program, analyzing the possible reasons will help determine the course of action to take regarding keeping or changing the program.

Offering programs for only a limited period of time is another strategy to consider in determining the duration of a program. While we certainly may want to offer exercise every day, varying the duration of different types of exercise programs may increase clients' motivation to participate. Scheduling boxing, Yomenco, or aqua ballet for only one month or 10 sessions creates a sense of urgency not to miss out on something new and different and also maintains a level of excitement about the program. Themed programs are another form of time-limited programming.

Themed Programming Themed programming is a means of offering a group of related programs of both short and longer duration. Selecting a theme around which to build a week's or month's worth of programs helps focus attention on the particular set of benefits TR is promoting and creates the "hook" to rouse people's interest. This hook also extends to the TR staff, other professionals, all of the unit's employees, and clients' families and friends. Most TRSs will tell you that their biggest programming challenge is motivating clients to attend programs. As staff begin to notice and talk about the programming, the clients become more interested and motivated to find out what's going on. Themed programming also encourages TRSs to use their creativity in conceiving new programs, themes, titles, and slogans. Clients may intellectually understand the value of health promotion activities, but designating the month of March as a time to "March for a Fresh Start," with a message to "shape up for spring," can build up people's enthusiasm about participating. This month-long program could include the following components:

- A four-session series on good nutrition and healthy eating that culminates in planning, preparing, and eating a meal or going to a restaurant
- Daily exercise groups with a different type of exercise each week, such as tai chi, chair aerobics, boxing, Pilates, aquacise, Zumba, or Yomenco
- Weekly movies about athletes who overcame their obstacles to participation and competition
- Sessions with a personal trainer for fitness testing and creating a personal fitness plan
- A "stress-buster" day with a "spa" offering hand massages, relaxation techniques, and wellness consultations

The same types of activities that are usually part of a TR schedule may seem new and different if they are organized around a theme and if formats, locations, and time frames are varied.

Another theme could be created for a month of art programming, in a group home, called "Release Your Inner Artist." The culminating event could be an art show with an exhibition of artwork and crafts projects completed in various art and crafts groups that have been offered over the month. The art show also could involve making refreshments (in a cooking group), interviewing the artists and writing articles for the newsletter (social interaction and writing groups), dressing up for the art show opening (grooming and ADL skills) and inviting families. Clients could go on a trip to an art museum. The theme gives the typical programs more meaning and purpose. Creating programs around a theme can also work for a single program, such as movies. Rather than just a different movie every week, sports movies or Broadway musicals could be shown for one month. See the flyer created for a program which invited participants to "travel around the world" as a guest at a different wedding each week of the four-week program (figure 9.1). This program was designed to promote awareness of selected cultures as well as show the universality of human experience. Serve refreshments, wear the style of clothing, and decorate the space to correspond to the theme. The more the

environment mirrors real life, the more relevance the programs will have to the clients' lives.

By creating themed programming, the TRS is integrating more behavioral domains, social interaction patterns, locations, and time frames into the unit-wide programming. There are more opportunities for a greater number of people to be involved. Time-limited, themed programming doesn't have the feeling of the same calendar week after week, month after month, even *year after year*, which can be boring to TR staff as well as clients. If the TR staff is bored, the clients will be too. If the program is always the same, a client doesn't necessarily feel the need to go *this* time; he can just as easily go the next time. But if staff are motivated, their enthusiasm and excitement will be contagious.

Intensity

The final factor in determining time frames for programs is **intensity**, which refers to how long a

Figure 9.1 Flyer promoting themed movie month.

single session lasts. This can be influenced by the scheduling of meals, medications, and services provided by other disciplines. Even the change of shift can affect when a program starts or ends. Visiting hours, naps, and the times a space is used for something else have bearing on the length of time of TR programs. Ideally, the TR activity should last for the amount of time that provides maximum benefit to the clients within the realities of the unit. Usually a group program is at least a half hour long, excluding setup and cleanup. Some clients require assistance getting to and from an activity. If escorting clients to and from programs requires a lot of time and effort, be sure that the program is long enough to be worth the trip.

On-unit programs lasting longer than 1 hour are appropriate for higher-functioning clients with the physical stamina, patience, concentration, and attention span to participate for that length of time. Programs that have a club, workshop, or drop-in

Project NOISEE: Naturally Occurring Interactions in a Shared Environment, Everyday

NOISEE is not a project name that one would naturally associate with a nursing home. Nonetheless, NOISEE is a nationally recognized, award-winning, highly innovative intergenerational program that has brought benefits to the children, residents, and staff of Isabella Geriatric Center in New York City.

NOISEE was created by Janet Listokin, CTRS, the director of therapeutic recreation, and Karen Ellefsen, the director of child day care, at Isabella, a 700-bed long-term care facility. Day care is also provided for 40 children, ages 3 months to 6 years. Realizing that intergenerational activities could contribute to both the development of the children and the quality of life of the residents, Janet and Karen turned the 3-acre setting into a shared environment, renaming the offices and physical spaces. The Recreation Suite became Marshmallow Sky; the Physical Therapy Gym became the Raisin Rain Forest; the staff cafeteria was renamed Yum Yum Hill; and the ninth-floor dining room is called Chocolate Chip Jungle.

Rather than just bringing together the generations for regularly scheduled programs, NOISEE brings the children into all areas of the facility to interact with the residents. Games, snack time, rhythm band, and special events are ongoing. The children's story hour takes place in Peppermint City; their snack time is on Mashed Potato Mountain; and spontaneous play time can occur anywhere. Some residents volunteer by rocking the infants, reading to the toddlers, and playing piano or doing puzzles with the children.

The goals of NOISEE reflect TR principles and values, as expressed in programming:

- To facilitate daily natural interaction between the generations
- To utilize the entire facility and grounds as the children's classroom
- To provide active and passive daily activities for the residents
- To provide opportunities for residents to feel useful through nurturing children
- To develop the children's awareness of, sensitivity to, and appreciation for the elderly
- To promote staff's understanding of the value of recreation

The natural, relaxed, and spontaneous presence of the children boosts the morale of residents and staff alike and creates a more homelike environment. It is not surprising that NOISEE received the NTRS Jean Tague Innovative Programming Award and was cited by the American Association of Homes and Services for the Aging as one of the Best Practices in Aging Services.

In the words of one resident, "The therapeutic component is so subtle that all the events are just fun, unless you really think about the cumulative feelings of well-being you experience. If a sense of lasting value is a therapeutic goal, NOISEE gives us its living, breathing, noisy manifestation."

*NOISEE is a registered service mark of Isabella Geriatric Center.

format (e.g., open game room, art or crafts room, gym or fitness center, library) or involve a more laissez-faire leadership style can run longer, such as for 1 1/2 to 2 hours. Therapeutic recreation should provide programs within a daily and weekly schedule that vary in the amount of time they last, from 15-minute one-to-one sessions to 2-hour movies to half-day outings. Most group activities, however, are optimal at 30 to 90 minutes depending on the population. The TRS wants to be sure that there is enough time for the client to have a worthwhile experience.

EVALUATION OF UNIT-WIDE PROGRAMMING

Planning the structural, leadership, and scheduling aspects of TR programming helps TR personnel fulfill the potential of TR to make a contribution to clients' lives. The key to balanced programming is to vary the components of each aspect of the total program in accordance with the availability of facilities and resources and the clients' needs. Incorporating all the behavioral domains, levels of social interaction, and program formats and varying

the size of the group, time frames, and leadership styles enable clients to benefit from TR services and achieve their outcomes. Attracting potential participants' attention through creative naming and innovative use of space and locations maximizes the possibilities for engagement. All these aspects can provide a framework for evaluation of unit-wide programming.

The guidelines for balanced programming can also be used to evaluate weekly and monthly schedules in order to ensure that the needs and interests of clients are being met on a regular basis. The TRS may determine that it is desirable to emphasize particular components of programming rather than others. For example, the TRS may find it best to offer small-group programs rather than large ones, or more physically active activities rather than sedentary ones, or may discover that activities of shorter duration are preferable. The TRS's professional skill and judgment will contribute to these planning decisions.

The checklist of balanced programming guidelines is useful for planning and evaluating the unit-wide program schedule. For more information on evaluation, see chapter 8.

Balanced Programming Checklist for Evaluation of a Weekly Schedule

Total number of activities per week_____

Indicate the **number** of times a week you offered the following:

Activities according to purpose
_____ Therapeutic/rehabilitative/treatment-oriented/functional improvement
_____ Educational/skill development/health promotion
_____ Recreational/diversional/leisure
_____ Inclusion

Activities according to primary behavioral domains
_____ Physical
_____ Cognitive
_____ Affective
_____ Social
_____ Spiritual

(continued)

Balanced Programming Checklist for Evaluation of a Weekly Schedule *(continued)*

Activities according to size
_____ Large group
_____ Small group
_____ One-to-one

Activities by location
_____ Large, public space
_____ Small, private space
_____ Indoor
_____ Outdoor
_____ Special facility (gym, kitchen, library, etc.)
_____ Off-site

Activities by time frames
_____ Ongoing
_____ Time-limited

Activities offering
_____ Immediate gratification and short-term successes
_____ Delayed gratification requiring long-term effort

Activities in each format
_____ Instructional classes
_____ Clubs and interest groups
_____ Open or drop-in
_____ Competitive
_____ Spectator
_____ Outings or trips
_____ Special events

Suggestions for next week's schedule:

From R. Kunstler and F. Stavola Daly, 2010, *Therapeutic recreation leadership and programming* (Champaign, IL: Human Kinetics).

● Summary ●

The concept of balanced programming is crucial to meeting the unique needs and interests of all clients who constitute the defined "unit." Planning and implementing the unit-wide TR schedule is influenced by the regulations and standards of government agencies and accrediting organizations that oversee the organization, the mission and goals of the organization and the TR department, the TR service model that the department follows, and the assessed needs and interests of the clients served. Understanding what each client needs and carefully observing their reactions and responses will contribute to planning a meaningful schedule. It is *how* the TRS puts all these pieces together that fulfills the purposes of TR services. The TRS fosters a TR environment that conveys warmth, acceptance, opportunity, facilitation of growth, the unique value of each individual, and meaningfulness to all participants. The power of the TR group to enhance the lives of clients is discussed further in chapter 10.

● Learning Activities ●

1. In a small group, discuss the behaviors of the TRS in promoting the TR environment and the power of the TR group.

2. Select three TR activities and analyze the various behaviors, according to domains, that are involved in participating in each activity. Select one of those activities and explain how it could be offered in at least five different program formats.

3. Describe the behaviors of a TRS using an authoritarian versus a democratic versus a laissez-faire leadership style. How comfortable would you be using each of the styles?

4. Visit a TR department and make a list of all the possible locations for TR programs. What opportunities exist for coleadership?

5. Discuss in a small group when you experienced the effects of public space versus private space on your own behaviors.

6. Design a month-long theme program for a setting of your choice including different activities, locations, and time frames. Name each activity.

7. Apply the balanced programming checklist to a weekly or monthly schedule from a TR department. What do you conclude about how balanced the schedule is? What changes would you recommend?

8. Draw up an outline for a presentation at a team meeting on "Why non-TR staff should assist at TR programs."

Leading Therapeutic Recreation Groups

In this chapter you will learn about:

- The TR group experience
- Therapeutic recreation leadership styles
- Stages of group development
- Characteristics of groups
- Planning and preparation for TR groups
- How to lead a TR group
- Three phases of the TR group
- Typical leader mistakes
- Dealing with challenging situations
- Postsession responsibilities of the TRS

Most TR practice is done in **group** formats, which is one of the unique strengths of TR service; in no aspect of the TRS's work is the synergy created by the blended role of therapist and recreation specialist more apparent than in work with groups. The TRS brings an added dimension to the typical group leader experience, that is, an understanding of the nature of the recreation experience and the conduciveness of this experience to growth and change for all participants. Therapeutic recreation group leadership begins with creating a group environment that is nurturing, growth enhancing, goal driven, and process oriented. The TRS must have a professional *mindset* that reflects an in-depth understanding of the complexity and impacts of TR, the benefits of group programs, the process of group development, and, most significantly, her roles and responsibilities in working with groups. Unlike TR practice, much of the practice of professions such as physical therapy, occupational therapy, speech therapy, and social work is done on a one-to-one basis. Yet groups are a powerful

Groups provide clients with social support and opportunities to learn from each other.

milieu. In chapter 4, we discussed the knowledge, skills, abilities, and qualities associated with being both a recreation specialist and a therapist. These include self-awareness, professional beliefs about the value and power of recreation participation, the ability to influence others to achieve goals, communication skills, organizational skills, and cultural competence. Chapter 7 presented the important facilitation techniques and instructional strategies used in the application of TR leadership.

Therapeutic recreation groups have several purposes, including therapeutic growth, education and skill building, recreation participation, and community reintegration. The purpose of TR groups varies depending on the setting. When thought and skill are applied, every group a TRS leads has the potential for enhancing the health and wellness of participants and positively influencing their quest for goal attainment. In addition, "particularly important to clients within therapeutic recreation groups are the fostering of hope through optimistic leadership" (Austin, 2009, p. 324). The TR practice models provide a guide to the type of TR leadership that should be delivered in each setting and with different clients.

GROUPS IN TR

In a long-term care facility, residents gather in the common area around the nurses' station and typically react to passersby with an occasional comment. Is this a group? In the day room on a psychiatric unit, a handful of patients are watching TV. Is this a group? One of the simplest definitions of a group is a "collection of people" (Russell, 2004, p. 88). However, defining a group as a collection of people is not really sufficient to answer these questions. A more comprehensive definition of a group suggests that the individuals who are gathered together

- have a unifying relationship,
- acknowledge that they are members of a group,
- interact with one another in a meaningful and continuous way,
- seek a shared goal, and
- meet members' needs (Beebe & Masterson, 2000; Engleberg & Wynn, 2000).

In the preceding examples, what would turn these people sharing the same physical space into a group? They would need to recognize that they have a common purpose, perhaps socialization, which requires their interaction with each other and their willingness to create a positive relationship among the members. Effective groups have members who are seeking the same benefits and thus share common goals. Some people join groups to meet needs to gain or experience affection, recognition, control, or acceptance through membership in a group. Others may join groups to fulfill their need to be self-actualized (Beebe & Masterson, 2000) or to contribute to the well-being of others. Therefore, a group can be defined as two or more people who acknowledge that they share a common purpose and interact with each other to achieve it.

The ability to function as a member of a group is critical in a person's development and also a factor in one's potential success in later life. Learning how to function as a group member and experience the benefits of being in a group is a highly valued outcome of TR participation. Groups provide clients with social support and opportunities to learn from each other. For a client, as for anyone else, realizing that he is not alone and that others share similar concerns, experiences, and problems can help him to feel less isolated and to gain insights that might not have been possible in a one-to-one environment. The group experience can be motivating to clients as they share a positive experience and learn new skills and behaviors. They have the opportunity to practice these skills in an environment that is more like the "real world" than other treatment-oriented settings, but in a safe haven—a place where trial and error, success and failure, and problems are dealt with in a supportive, nonthreatening, and nonjudgmental way. Participating in a successful group experience can be very rewarding and satisfying. When members of a group work together, they can accomplish more than when working alone because of the collective energy that is available to meet the needs and carry out the actions of the group. In successful groups, members have the skills to meet their individual needs while supporting and attending to the needs of other members and the group as a whole. Positive social interactions support the development of interdependence among group members, leading to the creation of synergy. When a group achieves interdependence, it has the potential to maximize the benefits for all participants.

Working with clients in a group format is a natural outgrowth of the recreation experience. From an agency perspective, because staff and time are often limited, working with clients in groups can be considered cost-effective. A larger number of people can receive services in a group format than on a one-to-one basis, and in a shorter period of time. This is often one of the primary arguments used in discussions of why TR is a valued service. But cost-effectiveness is far from the most important or most compelling argument for employing a TRS. Therapeutic recreation has its own unique benefits for clients and the agency. Therapeutic recreation supports the overall health goals of all participants, contributes to client satisfaction, and creates a climate that is conducive to client success.

The TRS is responsible for making clear to the TR group members the purpose and goals of the group, how the group can meet the members' needs, and the roles of the members as they interact with each other to meet their needs and achieve the goals. The TRS is ethically obligated to convey this in formats and language that are meaningful and comprehensible to the members. Since working with groups is a central component of what a TRS does, it is important for the TRS to increase his group leadership skills, starting by exploring his own group experiences and how they affect both his TR leadership ability and his capacity to be an effective group member. Like all of us, the TRS belongs to many groups in his life, some by choice and others by circumstance. To better understand what a group is and what benefits one can obtain from being a member of a group, explore the groups in your own life.

List the groups.

Why are you a member of each group?

How did you come to join each group?

Was membership voluntary or obligatory, or was the group one you were born into?

Pick one of the groups and explore your group membership further.

What is the group's purpose?

What are your roles and responsibilities in the group?

How has your behavior in the group changed over the time you have been a member?

What benefits do you derive from being a member of each group?

If there are no benefits, why do you continue to belong to this group?

Is there a group you are not currently a member of that you would like to join?

This understanding of the TRS's own personal group experiences can help her develop and apply the skills, knowledge, and abilities needed to create effective groups. Group work is a powerful

The Power of the Family Group

People will belong to many groups throughout their lifetime, but it is "the experiences as a member of the family that initially teaches the individual how to cope with the stress and the challenges of daily life" (Ridgeway, 1983, p. 331). It is in the family unit that people are introduced to the behavioral expectations of society, learn how to solve problems, deal with conflicts, and experience affection and security.

Some families are better than others at creating a climate for positive growth for each family member; some struggle with the dynamics of family responsibilities and relationships. Whatever form the family group may take, being part of a family generally involves an emotional commitment by the members that is intense and permanent. There are family traditions, styles of interacting and communicating with each other, and specific codes of behavior that people maintain throughout life.

While family isn't the only source of group experiences, it is the primary source for almost everyone.

approach to helping individuals maximize the treatment they are receiving and as a result transform their lives (Agazarian, 1999). The key to capitalizing on the benefits of the group experience for the clients is the TRS's group leadership.

GROUP LEADERSHIP

Therapeutic recreation group leadership is a multifaceted responsibility for the TRS due to the variety and complexity of the health issues and life concerns of the participants, the many different types of groups offered, and the diverse settings in which TRSs work. Developing and implementing a quality TR group can be compared to putting on a major event, with the TRS as producer, director, designer, and even the lead performer. In addition, focusing on the needs of the individual, as well as those of the entire group, is a balancing act involving ongoing observation and continuous monitoring of the progress of the group and of the individual members' behaviors. Success for the TRS as group leader lies in his ability to be a skilled communicator and to determine the type and intensity of leadership required for each group and for each stage of

the group's development. Group leadership is not static. What works for a TR leader with one group of people may not work with another. Leadership is affected by the purpose of the group, the members of the group, and the context in which the group occurs. The challenges of TR leadership are compounded by the fact that the TRS often works with people who either have little or no successful group experience or have limited skills due to illness or disability or life circumstances. In order to address the various demands presented by these challenges, the TRS as group leader is involved in a continual decision-making process about what leadership style is most appropriate to the given group or situation.

Applying Leadership Styles

The TRS's leadership style has a significant impact on the functioning of the TR group. The three primary leadership styles—autocratic, democratic, and laissez-faire—were discussed in chapter 9. Some groups may initially require an autocratic approach in which the TRS assumes responsibility for developing the purpose and goals, selecting the members and the content of the group, and identifying and assigning roles and responsibilities to the members. Other groups may require that the TRS be more democratic, engaging members in the decision-making process. In the third style, laissez-faire, the TRS turns over the leadership of the group to the group members. She steps back, allowing the group to function independently, and provides coaching and support when requested. The TRS may utilize one, two, or even all three of these styles with a single group. In a Friday night group for teens at risk, she may begin in a more authoritative manner but quickly become democratic so that the teens feel as if the group is truly theirs. She may shift to a laissez-faire style if the group begins to perform at a high level and demonstrates maturity in making decisions and resolving conflicts.

No one leadership style is "better" than another; what matters is which is the most appropriate depending on a number of factors in the given situation. Fiedler's Contingency Theory (Fiedler, 1967) states that "no one style of leadership is effective in every situation" (Lesser & Pope, 2007, p. 138). "Situational variables" include the type of group, the background and experiences of group members, the structure and location of the group, and the skills of the TRS. The style of leadership for a bingo game open to all the residents of a nursing home for recreation participation and held in the dining room would be different from a therapeutic reminiscence program on the Alzheimer's unit meeting in a small lounge. Choice of leadership style is also influenced by the TR model followed in the agency.

Leadership Roles According to TR Models

The TR models offer insight into the versatile role of the TRS as group leader. All the models approach the role of the TRS from the perspective of the client's actions during their participation in TR experiences. These actions reflect the client's degree of control over his behaviors and decisions. The models all emphasize that clients should have maximum opportunities to be in control of their own leisure and health behaviors (Sylvester et al., 2001). Some of the models, such as the Leisure Ability Model, clearly demonstrate that the TRS's degree of intervention moves along a continuum. The TRS exerts the greatest control (autocratic) in the role of therapist in the early stage when the client needs the most assistance. Once the client moves beyond this initial phase, the TRS's role is not so much diminished as changed from therapist to instructor (more democratic). The role of the TRS as group leader then changes to facilitator (laissez-faire) as the group becomes more cohesive and takes more control of its actions. These shifts in the group from dependence to greater responsibility for its own operation may not occur for each member at the same time, but do occur for the group overall.

Working with clients who have chronic or lifelong disabilities presents other challenges for the TR group leader. The Optimizing Lifelong Health Through Therapeutic Recreation Model addresses this situation in recognizing that for some clients, the TRS may have to wield greater leadership or control in order to support and enhance functioning (Sylvester et al., 2001). In such cases the TRS maintains ongoing control of the group for most activities, and smaller opportunities provided within the group experience allow clients to exercise independence and self-determination. In most TR practice models, the TRS may be required to take primary control of the group by offering guidelines and direction and even assigning roles within the group to initiate some movement toward the goals. As the group members become more skilled, the TRS may continue to facilitate the process but shifts the operation of the group to the members. As a facilitator and monitor, the TRS observes and encourages the ongoing work of the group. She supports the members of the group who may need individual attention or direction. She also helps the group process the experience, allowing the members to gain maximum benefit from each session and also to assume more responsibility for their individual and group success.

Another framework for understanding group leadership is task orientation versus process orientation. A group may have either a **task orientation**, focused primarily on completing a task or producing a "product," or a **process orientation**, focused on developing and promoting interpersonal relationships. Therefore, the primary purpose of a group may be either to complete a task or to experience positive interactions. Many TR groups try to accomplish both a finished product and a meaningful experience. This may be quite different from what occurs with groups in other disciplines, which are often single-purpose groups. In more therapeutic or process-oriented groups, the insights, expressions of feelings, and interpersonal relationships of the group members may be the primary focus; the TRS acts primarily as a facilitator. In groups with a goal to develop a skill or to produce a tangible result, completing the task may be the primary focus and would require the TRS to use a more directive or controlling leadership style. Knowing the various leadership styles and applying them as needed and relevant to each group situation is valuable in helping clients reach their goals.

Photo courtesy of Ragen E. Sanner.

In putting on this performance, the group members participate in a process and produce a product.

Clients will respond to differing leadership styles by altering their behavior and in this way develop their own abilities.

The application of TR leadership is most apparent when the TRS leads a group. In TR, precisely because of the value of the recreation experience, the TRS must be just as much a therapist as a leader in order to help clients achieve successful outcomes. This point is well illustrated in the TR Service Delivery Model (Carter et al., 2003). The dotted line in the model represents the continuum of services. However, it is dotted to indicate the flexibility of the TRS to emphasize either the intervention aspect of the group or the leisure experience aspect. The TRS places the emphasis on the intervention aspect in order to achieve goals, or places the emphasis on the leisure aspect to help clients experience fulfillment, satisfaction, and well-being. The group principles analyzed in this chapter apply to all TR groups, regardless of the type of activity or the degree of emphasis on either purposeful intervention or leisure experience. What the group experiences is a function of the TRS's application of the blended role of TR leadership.

The TR Group Leadership Responsibilities

As a group leader, the TRS should be enthusiastic, energetic, optimistic, flexible, creative, and highly motivated. She is a role model of how to communicate, demonstrating attentiveness, effective listening skills, and patience, and provides feedback, direction, and insights. She sets the tone of the group, establishes group morale, and creates a supportive environment that is conducive to productive interaction among the group members. The TRS has significant planning responsibilities, including developing specific goals and objectives for the group and its members and identifying and organizing activities that will have the greatest impact on the clients' success. Working to achieve specific goals can be a stressful and anxiety-provoking experience for the client and the family. The TRS has to have an optimistic attitude and utilize the client's strengths so that he can move beyond his limitations and commit to the group experience. Getting well or enhancing or maintaining one's abilities is a serious concern for most people. But, because the TRS uses recreation as the primary mode of activity and treatment in groups, she is also responsible for creating a fun environment or an enjoyable experience for the participants. Enjoyment is a key factor in members' development and maintenance of group membership. The TRS actively seeks to engage members; helps them accept roles and responsibilities; resolves conflicts; and responds to the members' needs, concerns, and issues.

CULTURALLY COMPETENT TR GROUP LEADERSHIP

A person's cultural background is a factor the TRS must take into consideration when leading the group. Clients come from diverse cultures with their own communication styles. The meaning of words, body language, eye contact, tone of voice, use of silence, and terms of address are different according to one's culture. How close to or far apart from each other the group members sit can be a product of culture. Touch is also culturally specific. The easy way North Americans have of slapping someone on the back or grabbing him by the arm, or even shaking hands, can be offensive to people from a different culture. Some Europeans believe that kissing is an appropriate greeting between casual acquaintances. Interpreting body language and reading social cues may be a problem for clients with learning disabilities, traumatic brain injury, autism, or dementia. Attitudes toward and ways of dealing with illness, disability, and family problems also differ by culture. In the United States, many people talk openly about their difficulties and challenges, whereas people from Asian cultures are more reticent.

While the TRS has an ethical responsibility to be culturally competent, clients themselves may not be aware or respectful of cultural differences due to lack of knowledge or the effects of their own illness or disability. This can lead to miscommunication and misunderstandings during the group session, and the TRS must be prepared to address these respectfully. Another cultural variation is attitude toward time. Most groups are scheduled to begin at a particular time. Western culture values promptness, while people from Hispanic and Middle Eastern backgrounds are more relaxed about arriving on time. This can create a dilemma for the TRS who is trying to balance the need to adhere to a schedule, minimize disruptions, and ensure that all clients are "on the same page" with showing respect for cultural differences. As with students arriving late to class, latecomers miss out on information, directions, and activities that promote group cohesion, and are also a distraction. The TRS should explain the expectations for group participation and the reasons behind them. For more information on cultural influences, see chapter 5.

THE TR GROUP LEADER AS COMMUNICATOR

The TRS is the central communicator in the group and is responsible for managing and influencing group communication to maximize the outcomes and benefits achieved. Effective communication is critical in order to motivate clients and to attain outcomes (Drench et al., 2007) and is the "vehicle that allows a group to move towards its goals" (Beebe & Masterson, 2000, p. 37). The TRS's role as communicator is to establish the purpose and maintain the focus of the group, institute guidelines for group behavior, and protect the members from harm. In TR group leadership, the communication skill and style of the TRS contribute to the group's feelings of cohesion, trust, self-efficacy, and willingness to rely on and help each other. The TRS accomplishes this through active listening; providing information clearly, sincerely, and honestly; using sensitive or "person-first" language; and checking both that she understands what her clients are saying and that they understand what she is saying. This can be a formidable challenge. Poor communication can cause misunderstandings, impede progress, and lead to stress and frustration in both the TRS and the client. Participants in TR groups may have limited communication skills, often due to their disability, limited experience as a group member, or inability or unwillingness to express problems and concerns. Groups cannot grow and develop, reach their goals, or become a significant factor in clients' care if the communication is dysfunctional, meaningless, or nonexistent (Ridgeway, 1983).

Dysfunctional or nonproductive communication behaviors are both verbal and nonverbal:

- Verbal distractions such as mumbling, whispering, interrupting, or talking out loud when another person is speaking, can cause conflict and stifle individual and group growth.

- Offensive and disrespectful language, vocabulary that is not familiar to the participants, or speaking too fast (or too loudly or in a monotone) can negatively affect communication.

- Negative nonverbal responses, such as grimacing, rolling one's eyes, looking at one's watch, turning around when someone is speaking, or refusing to speak, can be disruptive as they break the flow of the group, distract people from their interactions, and decrease motivation.

These behaviors send the message that the speaker or the group isn't important or is not a priority. On the other hand, a reassuring glance, a smile, or a pat on the back from a member or the leader may offer the simple reassurance that a person's efforts in the group are recognized and valued. Each act of communication is complex and is influenced by many factors. The TRS has an ethical responsibility to be competent in her communication skills and to conduct groups that demonstrate respect for persons and are sensitive to each member's unique needs and characteristics. Understanding your own communication behaviors can help you understand the communication styles and challenges faced by your clients. Take a moment to examine your own communication skills by referring to table 10.1 on page 296.

The TRS teaches and models good communication skills. She may call on members to speak, ask questions about their responses so they can elaborate or develop insight, moderate the conversation so that one member does not dominate the group, engage quiet members, and provide empathic listening and appropriate feedback. The TRS facilitates the group's communication using selected recreation activities and facilitation techniques that promote interaction and sharing of ideas and feeling. Therapeutic recreation groups vary in the amount of verbal interaction required. Obviously a discussion group will require much more interaction than an arts and crafts group. Therapeutic recreation groups should be structured so that all participants have opportunities to be engaged in the activities and interactions.

GROUP DEVELOPMENT

The TRS leads groups that meet for one time only, meet only for a specified number of sessions, or meet on an ongoing basis. Groups may consist of the same people every time or vary with each session. In any case, groups do not happen in TR just because a number of people get together, even when they have common goals. It takes time and effort on the part of the TRS and the participants for a group to become fully functioning. Understanding the stages of group development and characteristics enable the TRS to move the members from a simple gathering to fulfilling their purpose as a group, be it new learning, task completion, or a leisure experience. These stages and characteristics are more likely to be evident in groups that meet over time; however, they can be apparent and are deserving of the TRS's attention even in a single session.

Group Development Theories Applied to TR

Numerous theories have been aimed at explaining how groups develop. Many of these theories view group development as strictly linear (the group starts and moves through the stages of development in a straight line to its end), while others combine

TABLE 10.1

Assessing Your Communication Skills

There are many self-tests you can take online or in paper-and-pencil format to assess your communication skills. This one is geared toward working in the health fields and assesses valuable skills for the TRS.

Communication Self-Assessment Scale

Rate yourself from a 4 (very skilled) to 1 (not skilled).	4	3	2	1
1. I feel good about my communication skills.				
2. I smile at clients, family, and staff.				
3. I make good eye contact.				
4. I introduce myself and wear my name tag.				
5. I learn names and use correct pronunciation.				
6. I seek clarification if I don't understand.				
7. I take a moment to calm myself before interacting with clients.				
8. I explain procedures clearly.				
9. I encourage questions.				
10. I encourage feedback.				
11. I thank those who help me.				
12. I listen, knowing it is OK to be quiet and not have all the answers.				
13. I use good attending skills.				
14. I am aware of how the environment may affect communication.				
15. I use open-ended questions appropriately.				
16. I avoid asking "why" questions of clients.				
17. I respect client confidentiality.				
18. I use touch appropriately.				
19. I listen with a "third ear."				
20. I know how to structure the parts of an interview.				
21. I dress appropriately.				
22. I pay attention to my grooming.				
23. I give compliments to clients, family, and staff.				
24. I understand that I am still learning and that it is impossible to be perfect.				
25. I try to be myself, bringing my own special gifts to my TR practice.				

Scoring: Add up the numbers you have selected.

77-100: High awareness of necessary skills.

52-76: Average awareness of skills. Review low scores and identify areas for growth.

25-51: Low awareness of necessary skills. Pay more attention to skill development.

From R. Kunstler and F. Stavola Daly, 2010, *Therapeutic recreation leadership and programming* (Champaign, IL: Human Kinetics). Adapted from Balzer-Riley 1996.

a linear approach with a cyclical perspective. Still others theorize that each group has its own unique pattern of development, with different activities occurring at various points in the life of the group. The development of therapeutic groups is sometimes viewed as distinct from the development of team or work groups. In the next section we briefly present several theories and viewpoints on group development that will help the TRS understand the behaviors of her clients in group situations.

THE STAGE APPROACH

A very well-known theory of group development is known as the **stage theory**, most often identified with Tuckman who presented it in 1965 (Harris, 1998). According to this theory, groups develop in five stages: forming, storming, norming, performing, and adjourning.

- **Forming.** All stage theories follow similar phases and uniformly agree that the first stage, forming, is a time for group members to begin to get to know one another. The goal at this stage is to build acceptance and trust between and among the members and the leader and to create a shared sense of group purpose. During this stage, the interactions in the group tend to be tentative and relatively calm as the leader and members get acquainted with each other. The group members begin to develop an understanding of the skills and interests each person brings to the group, as well as the expectations of the group members. For example, in a group of teenagers with and without disabilities in a Friday evening community recreation program, the TRS may start by describing the group's purpose, conduct icebreaker activities to help members get acquainted, and lead trust-building games to begin to develop acceptance and rapport among the members.

- **Storming.** In the next stage, storming, conflict and chaos may initially dominate the interaction patterns of the group members as they start to assert their own beliefs and personalities and attempt to take on a particular role or position in the group. As the teenagers begin to display their personalities and express their ideas and opinions, conflicts may emerge. The TRS can intervene with conflict resolution strategies.

- **Norming.** As the group members begin to establish patterns for interaction to fulfill the purposes of the group, norming occurs, with both implicit and explicit rules of behavior emerging. The TRS may assist the group in establishing norms to

regulate relationships. The teens may begin to express how they think members should behave in the group, including how to handle disagreements, how to make decisions, and what rituals or traditions they would like to establish.

- **Performing.** Successful resolution of the issues in the early stages moves the group to the performing or productivity stage, which is when the actual activity of the group can begin to happen. It is at this stage that the members focus their energy and move toward completion of the task or toward achievement of both individual and group goals in an atmosphere of mutual respect and cooperation. The teens may plan a monthly calendar of activities, put on a tournament, engage in a service project, or create a Web site. If true acceptance has not been reached, group members may behave in ways that are counterproductive, such as arriving late, having arguments, dropping out, or acting apathetic or indifferent during the group meetings. If the group does not develop in a healthy way, group members may make poor decisions or even fail to make decisions and take too much time to accomplish projects and goals. The teens who show up late, don't join in, or disagree with everyone else just to be difficult can impede the group's successful functioning. The TRS can intervene to address this behavior.

- **Adjourning.** Finally, in the adjourning stage, the group has accomplished its task or purpose and is ready to disband or move on to a completely new task. This is an important phase in which the leader needs to help the group bring closure to the experience in a way that is beneficial and positive. The TRS processes the group experience by encouraging the teens to review their accomplishments, discuss their feelings and reactions to the group experience and activities, and make plans for the future. She may help the members solidify friendships that have developed, commit to new leisure interests, and reinforce newly acquired positive behaviors as the group draws to a close.

The stage theory views the group as moving step by step from beginning to termination. Many of the stage theories of group development have been criticized for being too linear, because in reality, groups may skip a stage or progress in a different order than presented here. Supporters of an alternate view, the cyclical view of group development, recognize that group development is a dynamic process, having starts and stops and ups and downs based on the needs of the group members and environmental factors that may influence their actions. A related concept, **downshifting**, is based on the recognition that the leader must continuously monitor the progress of the group to ensure that the stages have been fully developed. The leader may decide to utilize downshifting to move the group back and forth among the stages of group development in order to resolve problems that have not been fully addressed at each stage (Brocklebank & Maurer, 1990).

ECOLOGICAL PERSPECTIVE ON GROUP DEVELOPMENT

An ecological perspective on group development suggests that within different service delivery settings and populations, many factors from within and outside of the group influence group development. These factors must be understood and, when possible, managed in order for groups to develop successfully. The ecological perspective is one of the four core TR principles (see chapter 2). It states that a person's health and well-being are influenced by all his interactions with the people and systems in his environment. Group members exist within communities and as part of families, workplaces, and circles of friends that may continue to exert influence and demands on them in addition to the demands of the group. The client does not come to the group alone but carries with him this entire network of factors that influence his behavior in the group. These factors also include the physical and social environments; culture; lifestyle; and biological, psychological, spiritual, and social dimensions in a person's life (Shank & Coyle, 2002). The ecological perspective emphasizes the interactive and reciprocal relationship among these different factors (Howe-Murphy & Charbonneau, 1987). A TRS leading a leisure education outpatient group for clients with alcohol addiction should work not only with the client but also with family and friends whose behaviors may counteract, or work against, the client's efforts to remain sober. The TRS conducting a group for people with early-stage Alzheimer's disease, who are working on maintaining cognitive skills, may also have to help caregivers by teaching techniques that will enhance communication.

The TRS will probably be more successful at addressing internal factors, such as the size and location of a meeting room, staff and group membership, and interruptions during the group sessions, than external factors that are out of her control. The TRS should work closely with administration and other team members so that they understand and respect the TR group's rights to privacy, a safe and conducive environment, timely information about the group, assistance in attending the group on time, and appropriate membership and adequate staffing. There may be ethical implications if these rights are not protected, resulting in a negative impact on members' participation.

YALOM'S THERAPEUTIC GROUPS

Yalom (1995), the noted psychiatrist, studied the development of therapeutic groups and identified three phases of group development: orientation, conflict, and cohesion. As with stage theory, the success of the first stage, orientation, is crucial to helping the clients see the relevance of the group to their progress. Recognition of the value of the group is a significant step in motivating clients to join, to attend, and to actively engage in the group experience. It is also during the orientation stage that members learn about the purpose of the group and begin to develop a sense of security, trust, and acceptance within the group, and that the leader begins to lay the foundation necessary for the group to develop cohesion, or a sense of unity (Kinney & Kinney, 2001).

Processing the group's experience is extremely important as the group develops but particularly during the conflict phase. Conflicts are opportunities to help clients become more aware of their behaviors and develop appropriate skills for dealing with disagreements, as well as to foster relationships between and among members. The conflict stage presents one of the greatest challenges for the TRS. Conflicts may be simple or complex. Clients may argue over seating, feel that someone is trying to take over the group, or even suggest that someone is cheating during a game. Members may challenge other members' commitment to the group or express that a member is not being honest. Personality conflicts may arise, and a struggle for leadership of the group or for recognition from other group members or the leader may ensue. Conflicts are a natural evolutionary occurrence in most groups as members begin to assert their own feelings and ideas. The purpose of the group may be to address clients' maladaptive behaviors, and teaching them how to handle differences becomes a central responsibility for the TRS.

The TRS is essential to the attainment of group cohesion. The features of a cohesive group include hope, a feeling of closeness and that members are not alone, a sense of acceptance, positive interaction, and openness to expression of negative and positive emotions. The cohesive group affords the client the opportunity to clarify negative behaviors

Therapeutic Group Factors

The following factors are associated with therapeutic groups and can enhance the therapeutic value of the group for the individual members.

Altruism: By supporting other members of the group, one can feel a sense of purpose.

Catharsis: Through the group experience, members are able to release stressful emotions.

Corrective recapitulation of the family group: The group often serves as a place where people who have unresolved issues from their family relationships can work out these issues. Consciously or unconsciously, the group and leader remind the individual of his family group experience.

Development of social skills: The group provides opportunities for direct and indirect learning of new ways to talk about and share feelings and to interact that can facilitate personal growth.

Didactic interaction: In some cases, instruction and education can help people understand their circumstances; such information relieves anxiety and offers feelings of power and control over their situation.

Giving advice: In some groups, advice giving can be beneficial if one individual has more experience than another and can truly help. On the other hand, too much advice giving can impede the group.

Group cohesion: Members feel they belong to the group and value the group; the group provides nurturing and support.

Imitative behavior: The group offers opportunities for members to model positive behaviors and to learn new effective coping techniques.

Instillation of hope: Members should feel hopeful that this group's experience will be therapeutic and effective.

Universality: Members learn that they are not alone and may share similar concerns and issues with other group members. Although each individual is unique, there are common denominators that allow for connections and reduce feelings of being the only one with a particular problem.

Adapted from Kinney and Kinney 2001; Shank and Coyle 2002; Pederson and James 2008.

and feelings, allowing the client and the group as a whole to move in a more positive direction (Kinney & Kinney, 2001; Yalom, 1995). As the group progresses through the orientation, conflict, and cohesion stages, the TRS applies her skills to help the members gain a greater understanding of themselves, thus benefiting from many of the factors Yalom has identified.

Summary of Group Development

All groups, including TR groups, go through several stages and are subject to multiple factors that influence their performance and activities. By understanding the range of factors that affect the participants in a group and the possible issues that are having an impact on the members, the TRS can

deliver effective group leadership. All theories share the perspective that

● each group is unique,

● group development is an ongoing process, and

● the skills and abilities of the leader are significant factors in helping move the members of the group and the group as a whole toward the attainment of their goals.

CHARACTERISTICS OF GROUPS

Whether you are leading a single session or working with a group over the long term, groups possess certain characteristics including goals, norms or rules of behavior, cohesion, morale, member roles, and interdependence. The first of these characteristics, common goals, is one of the most important because without a goal or purpose, a group does not exist.

Common Goals

A goal is a "purpose or objective" that gives direction to the group. Every TR group is designed for a reason, but the reason may not always be clear to the members. Lack of purpose or direction is the major reason why groups fail (Engleberg & Wynn, 2000). The TRS as group leader is responsible for articulating a group's purpose in the early stages so that all participants have a clear shared understanding and common direction. Understanding the group's purpose can help members feel more committed to the group as they see it as an avenue toward their own health and well-being. In TR groups the TRS must be mindful of both individual and group goals. Each individual client has a set of goals he is trying to achieve within the context of the group. Addressing individual goals within the context of a TR group is a major responsibility of the TRS. A current events group in a psychiatric facility is designed not only to keep clients in touch with the world by being informed of the news of the day; it is also the setting in which to practice newly developed communication skills, learn how to express feelings and opinions appropriately, and share a common interest with others. Any particular client in the group may have one of these specific goals, but working within the group addresses all of the goals. A daily current events group in an assisted living facility may help members maintain awareness of world affairs, but it can also contribute to enhancing memory, increasing attention span, and promoting socialization. The size of the group could affect goal attainment. The larger the group, the more complicated the process of facilitating progress toward goals becomes for the TRS.

The TRS must be able to link group participation with the client's movement toward recovery, functional improvements, new learning, or improved quality of life. Clients often ask why they are assigned to a certain activity or group. Initially they may be resistant to attending the group because they do not see how it will contribute to their recovery. While TR is appealing because it has an element of enjoyment that other therapies may not have, clients who are experiencing a medical or other crisis may dismiss TR precisely because it appears frivolous or they don't see how it may help them improve their health or situation. Clients will give many reasons why they resist group participation: They are not joiners, they are uncomfortable with being in a group with strangers, they don't have the same problems as the other clients, they are here only to focus on therapy, and so on. For a client who has experienced a stroke, spinal cord injury, or traumatic brain injury, physical therapy, speech therapy, or occupational therapy may have a higher priority. The client wants to return home and be able to do all the things she did before, such as drive a car, cook dinner, or simply dress and climb stairs. To the client, the goals must be practical, reality based, and relevant. The client may not understand how TR activities are related to her overall goals. The TRS's role is to communicate to the client how the group can help her progress.

Norms

Once the clients come together for the group experience, a pattern of behavior emerges that should contribute to the successful functioning of the group. To promote smooth and productive group functioning, **norms** are established. Norms are the rules by which a group operates. Norms represent a standard of behavior for the members of the group. Norms may or may not be written down but should be understood by all group members. Norms may be explicit, which means that they are either written or stated, or implicit, which means that they are understood without being stated or visible.

EXPLICIT NORMS

An **explicit norm** or rule might be no smoking in the group. The norms that should be explicit will vary depending on the level of performance of the group members. A lower-functioning group may need more explicit norms. The norms depend on the setting, the population, and the purpose of the group. They may be established by the TRS initially and then revised or modified by the members as the group develops. If the TRS posts the rules, they should be easy to read and hung in a spot that is readily visible. Written copies can be handed out to the group members. Large-print, Braille, and alternate language versions of the rules should be made available, as needed. Having acceptable behaviors written down and available to all members or read at the beginning of each group is a sound risk management practice. It reduces the chances of unacceptable behaviors that will have a negative impact. Not all groups have preestablished rules. Rules may evolve out of the experiences of the group members as the group develops (Lesser & Pope, 2007).

IMPLICIT NORMS

Implicit norms represent a shared set of beliefs or values of a group. Such norms tend to focus on specific aspects of the group's operation, including appropriate ways in which members interact with each other, handle conflict, complete tasks, and determine status of members in the group. An implicit norm might be that everyone has her own "reserved" seat at the weekly bingo game. Understanding an implicit group norm can be challenging at first for a person with a cognitive disability or psychiatric illness who has difficulty interpreting social cues used by the group to convey the preferred standards of behaviors. This is a particular concern when one is preparing clients for participation in inclusive settings. Social behaviors are a major barrier to successful inclusion for individuals with cognitive limitations, as well as for children with problem behaviors. Failure to follow group norms, either implicit or explicit, can result in disapproval from other members or in sanctioning by the group. When members fail to adhere to the group's norms, opportunities for group growth and member insights are diminished, and chaos or group dysfunction can increase. For example, at the end of a sport skills group for teenagers with behavioral issues, it becomes a custom for members to "high-five" each other to acknowledge team spirit and share positive feelings. When Tommy leaves the gym floor without giving a high-five, the other group members interpret this as a slight or a sign of a problem.

The TRS can help group members not only to understand and conform to group norms, but also to learn tolerance for a wider range of behaviors that fall outside of what is considered acceptable. This may also lead to revision of existing norms. The TRS monitors group norms, assists members in understanding accepted behaviors, and supports the revision of norms when necessary and appropriate. When the norms are fair, appropriate, and acceptable to the group and are revised and adapted as needed, a positive atmosphere is created that supports the development of the group as a whole and its individual members. Generally, norms have some range of acceptability or latitude

Every group has implicit norms.

for members to follow (Ridgeway, 1983). Effective norms contribute to the cohesion, morale, roles, and interdependence of the group.

Cohesion

Review your personal groups list that you compiled on page 291. In at least one of those groups the group experience was very positive, flowed smoothly, and accomplished its shared goals. The members seemed to have a commitment to each other and a sense of belonging and of being effective. This quality is known as **cohesion**. Cohesion has been defined as "the mutual attraction that holds a group together" (Engleberg & Wynn, 2000, p. 170). Cohesiveness enhances and fosters communication among group members, and in turn, communication promotes group cohesion. In cohesive groups, members are supportive and communicate positive feelings to each other, and more is accomplished because members are motivated and productive. Acceptance of each member for who he is and what he can contribute is a significant feature of cohesive groups. When groups lack cohesiveness, members operate independently and are often at odds with the goals of the group. Cohesion can be a significant factor in accomplishing group goals for TR groups such as a sport team, a drama group putting on a play, a writing group producing a newsletter, or a special event planning committee. Conflicts in the group, when resolved, can lead to enhanced cohesion; but conflict can also foster negative attitudes and behaviors. When unresolved, conflict can result in the deterioration of the group and the failure of both the individual and the group to attain desired goals.

Cohesion does not result from one specific behavior or action but from numerous factors that interact together in the group experience. These factors include age and history of the members, attraction of group members to one another, leadership style, and location of the group. Cohesion is a desirable characteristic for all groups, but sometimes groups can be too cohesive. In these instances, "groupthink" may develop. **Groupthink** (Janis, 1982) is a style of thought seen in groups that develop a faulty decision-making process and seek unanimity on all decisions to prevent disagreements among members or to resolve a situation quickly. Groupthink can reflect two attitudes in a group. Members may believe that their way is the right way and fail to seek out alternative ideas and opinions that may alter a decision for the better; or they may conform to decisions because of lack of confidence, lack of commitment, or a desire to avoid conflict (Engleberg & Wynn, 2000; Russell, 2004). Groupthink is generally seen in groups that are highly cohesive and under pressure to make a decision or in groups whose members have limited experience working in groups, such as recovering substance abusers, or those with cognitive limitations. A meal planning group may be putting on a luncheon for family members and need to decide on a menu. Three of the eight members have come up with a four-course menu. The other members do not express an opinion. The TRS knows that some of the items on the menu are contraindicated for two members due to dietary restrictions. However, to avoid conflict, these members do not raise the issue. The TRS's responsibility is to enable every member to express his views, guide the group to use the optimal decision-making process, and ensure that there are fair alternative ways for members to express their opinions, as needed.

The TRS's responsibility is to help a collection of individuals develop into a successfully functioning cohesive group that provides mutual support and benefits for all members. The TRS helps members accept and trust one another, understand the purpose of the group, and value their own identity as a group member. The TRS emphasizes the success of the group as a whole, recognizing its efforts and accomplishments with praise and reinforcement. The TRS is a role model of behaviors that promote cohesion, such as demonstrating respect for each member's needs, cultural background, and interests and communicating effectively with all members. Cohesion is a significant contributor to the next group characteristic, morale.

Morale

All groups have a certain mood or feeling that is displayed by the group members. This mood, known as morale, reflects how the group members feel about the group as a whole. The more positive the morale of the group, the more satisfying the group experience is for everyone. When participating in recreation experiences, "the degree of morale becomes a thermometer for the degree of recreation satisfaction" (Russell, 2004, p. 92). This aspect of the recreation experience, that is, the fun factor or positive tone of the experience, is one of the defining characteristics of TR groups. The tone in a TR group is established by the leader. Recreation groups are inherently social and provide a positive and upbeat atmosphere that supports enhanced morale of the group members (Russell, 2004). The TRS's attitude toward the group and its members, her way of handling the different personalities in the group and the situations that arise, and her style in presenting group activities (using props and other motivational techniques) have a major impact on group morale. Participants need to feel that the TRS believes in the group's purpose, need to feel her energy and commitment to the group activity, and need to be inspired by her creativity and the positive reinforcement she gives for their efforts. These elements, as well as the TRS's ability to facilitate relationships between and among group members and to infuse fun and enjoyment into the activity, are the building blocks of good **group morale**. Morale can be affected by the manner in which the group members take on and fulfill their roles in the group.

Roles

Roles are consistent behaviors based on a specific task or relationship function. Each member brings to the group a set of experiences and beliefs that affect his behavior in the group. Culture, gender, and age also affect the members' roles. Roles related to specific functions include the captain of a team, the scorekeeper in a game, the person who hands out supplies in arts and crafts, or the piano player at a sing-along. A client may take on a role based on his prior knowledge of the activity or his desire to fulfill the role, or the TRS may assign him the role based on her knowledge of his needs and interests. The specific situation may dictate who assumes what role. In a group whose task is to construct an outdoor playground for children in the community, a member who has a background in construction, facility design, or children's play behaviors may assume a leadership role to support the completion of the task.

Roles related to group interaction or relationships, such as the peacemaker, the comedian, the person who is bored, the one who always disagrees, the know-it-all, or the bully, may be based on personality, habits of behavior, unmet needs for attention and recognition, or fear of conflict or rejection. In the playground project, one member may be the peacemaker who helps the group reach consensus on what equipment to purchase. Another member may think she knows what's best and disregard everyone else's opinion. While group roles are not meant to be static, it is very easy for people to be identified with one role and remain in that role for the duration of the group. The roles that people play in a group can be either disruptive or helpful to the group process. People behave differently in groups than they do in a one-to-one situation. The TRS should be mindful of this difference so that she can facilitate members' activities while taking into account that their behaviors vary in different situations. She needs to be able to help clients understand how their negative behaviors are affecting the group process and help them develop insight and interact more positively.

Even positive roles can eventually become negative when individuals fail to recognize that the behavior they have exhibited is no longer needed. For example, in a small-group discussion for individuals who have suffered a stroke, several of the more able members may take on the role of caregiver to the more seriously affected clients. As those members progress through their treatment and begin to improve and recover their functioning, the members acting as caregivers may find it difficult to reduce the amount of support they are providing. The TRS acknowledges to the "caregivers" how valuable their assistance has been; she conveys that she knows they share her happiness about their fellow members' increased abilities to do more for themselves. This reinforces the meaningfulness and value of the role they have played and helps them develop insight that it is time to assume a different role in the group. The TRS's responsibility is to help people strengthen their abilities to assume

new roles and shed negatively stereotyped roles that may be due to life experiences or the impact of a disability. Table 10.2 describes the typical roles people play in groups.

Interdependence

Interdependence in groups means that the individual members can give and receive information, seek advice, ask for help when appropriate, and incorporate other people's opinions and ideas in order to support the group's efforts (Engleberg & Wynn, 2000). Interdependence should not be confused with dependence. When a person is dependent, he relies on someone else for support, which could be emotional, financial, physical, or some combination of these. A person with a disability may be dependent on others to meet specific needs and not perceive that she can contribute to the others' needs as well. For example, a person who uses a wheelchair may need a friend to drive him to the health club and be able to reciprocate by making phone calls for his friend, who doesn't have the time to do so. While the ability to act independently is highly valued, the ability to be interdependent is equally important. There are times when it is appropriate and necessary to ask for support and assistance. The key to interdependence is equality in the partner relationship. As the group members fulfill different roles, the group begins to generate interdependence. The TRS acts as a moderator, helping the group members stay on target and continue to develop insights, and facilitates ways to strengthen the bonds established by the group. When group members successfully participate with each other, success may be even greater than would have been anticipated if each had worked alone (Covey, 2004).

Summary of Group Characteristics

In many TR service settings, including physical rehabilitation, drug detoxification, or psychiatry, individuals may stay for only a few days. Is it possible for TR groups in these settings to take on all the characteristics of a group? Austin (2004) has raised this question, which should prompt the TRS to consider how she can most effectively create a meaningful group experience for clients within the given time frame. Regardless of the length of time the TRS will work with a particular group, she engages the clients in defining and communicating the group's goals, establishing and implementing the group norms, developing feelings of cohesion, contributing to positive morale, understanding and assigning roles to members, and fostering group

TABLE 10.2

Group Roles

As a member of a group, people fulfill roles that may be positive in promoting the group's experience or negative in impeding the progress of the group.

Typical positive group roles:	
Initiator	This person gets the group started on accomplishing its tasks.
Clarifier (also known as information seeker)	This person attempts to explain group activities and simplify complex tasks or activities by asking questions and seeking information.
Compromiser (coordinator)	This is a person who tries to get people to cooperate by seeking the common or middle ground. He is concerned that everyone's needs or opinions be acknowledged and understood.
Encourager (energizer)	This person supports group members and encourages them to do their best.
Gatekeeper	This person ensures that the group's goals are being met by monitoring group members to make sure tasks are progressing or completed.
Harmonizer	This person attempts to mediate differences in the group and helps group members to work together as a team.
Typical negative group roles:	
Blocker	This is a person who gets in the way of group progress. He uses an assortment of delaying tactics and negative comments and actions to block or derail group plans, ideas, or activities.
Clown	This person uses humor to detract from or prevent the progress of the group. She is more interested in entertaining people and "goofing off" than engaging in activities. At times humor can be positive, helping to create a relaxed atmosphere and defusing tensions; but the clown overdoes it.
Dominator	This person attempts to take over leadership of the group and monopolizes the conversation.
Instigator	This is a person who knows how to irritate group members, which results in frustration and conflict among them.
Recognition seeker	This person is preoccupied with impressing others by bragging about accomplishments and trying to become the center of attention.
Scapegoat	This person is blamed for everything that goes wrong in the group.

Data from Jordan 2007; Engleberg and Wynn 2000

interdependence. While this collaborative process may be more realistic, and these characteristics more apparent and influential, in groups of longer duration, the principles can be applied to maximize the benefits and outcomes of even a single TR session. For example, in a psychiatric unit where the length of stay was only three to five days, the TRS consultant helped the TRS identify three goals of his clients that he could best address in this time period. Stress management through recreation activities was a common concern of almost all of the patients. He developed a combined stress management and leisure education group that taught clients three techniques: relaxation breathing, walking, and utilization of low-cost community resources. In this way he maximized the time available to make an impact on his clients by identifying common needs and inexpensive, easy-to-use, and proven strategies. He quickly communicated the goals to the group, made the norms explicit, and utilized a more directive leadership style with a slightly greater emphasis on task than on process. As the TRS becomes more familiar with the range of leadership options, he will be more skilled and effective in facilitating group identity, cohesion and effectiveness within the realities of the service setting.

PLANNING FOR THE TR GROUP

In most health care settings, protocols are used to guide the delivery of the professional's services to clients. TRSs develop both diagnostic protocols and program protocols. **Diagnostic protocols** contain a standardized set of steps used to address the needs of clients with a particular diagnosis (such as dementia, schizophrenia, or depression) and identify the TR programs to be provided to the clients. Program protocols outline the implementation of a particular TR program or intervention (coping skills, gardening, leisure education, exercise) by specifying the content of the program, the clients who will benefit from participation, the expected outcomes of participation, risk management concerns, guidelines for facilitation, and the evidence used from the research to design the program. Every TR group should have a program or activity protocol. See chapter 3 for an example of a program protocol.

In addition to a program protocol, the TRS should develop an individual TR session plan that identifies the goals, activities, supplies, equipment, staffing needs, and physical arrangements to be used to carry out the program. If the TRS who is supposed to lead the group is not available, the daily plan can be used by another TRS so that the program does not have to be canceled or substantially altered. The daily plan is not static. Circumstances may change; a room may need to be changed or unforeseen events may occur, but the plan provides the TRS with a basis for conducting the group and adapting and making changes as necessary. The form also identifies who is to attend the program. Keep in mind that the most carefully planned program has to be feasible for the setting. Ask yourself if you can realistically implement the program as designed, given the staffing, supplies, equipment, space, and needs and capabilities of the population. Consider what elements can be adjusted in order to produce the program that is in the best interests of the clients.

At the end of the session, the TRS completes the evaluation portion of the individual TR session planning and evaluation form, described in chapter 8, which indicates who attended, any aspects of program implementation that differed from what was planned, other factors that may have influenced the group process, instructions for the next session, and comments. See figure 10.1 on page 306 for a sample blank form and figure 10.2 on page 307 for a completed form. The evaluation form serves as a valuable record of what went on in the group and as a general resource for all staff. Reviewing this form prior to the next session provides the TRS with valuable information for successful conduct of the group.

Group Membership

Membership in TR groups is based on clients' needs and goals, medical readiness, functional abilities, and preferences. In general, it is ideal to form TR groups whose members have common goals. Social skills groups are a frequent offering for children diagnosed with autism or attention-deficit disorder, or individuals with schizophrenia, as well as those recovering from spinal cord and traumatic brain injuries. Clients within these groups may differ widely in age, may be male or female, may be from different cultures, and may have different levels of functioning; yet all share the same purpose—to improve social skills so they can function more effectively and with greater satisfaction. The TRS's leadership ability enables him to emphasize the common goals of the members and the group as a whole. This facilitates the development of the group's cohesion. Groups that are formed around a recreation activity, such as arts and crafts, may consist of clients with differing goals that can all be addressed through engagement in the program.

Scheduling

A TR group should be scheduled to maximize attendance by the targeted group members. Time of day, length of session, and location of a program are all factors that affect a client's decision or ability to attend the group. The competent TRS should know the lifestyle habits and patterns of behavior of her clients. In a nursing home in New York City, where many of the residents are retired from the theater and entertainment industry, activities are scheduled until late in the evening to accommodate the previous lifestyle of the residents, who often worked until midnight. However, in large facilities such as psychiatric hospitals and nursing homes, it may not be feasible to be this accommodating due to the general rhythm of the facility, medical schedules, and daily care requirements. Mealtimes and staff shift changes can affect optimal scheduling. Although many clients with dementia become agitated late in the afternoon, at which time they would benefit from a structured program, this is often the end of the work day for TRSs in long-term care. After-school programs for school-age children may conflict with parental schedules. The TRS should work with the agency staff to design an appropriate and realistic schedule that meets the clients' needs.

The length of the session is a factor in planning that may be dictated by reimbursement systems or conflicts with other programs, and not just what's best for clients. Determining the length of a session

Individual TR Session Planning and Evaluation Form

Name of program: _____ Date: _____

Name of activity: _____ Location: _____

Purpose of the activity: _____

_____

_____

If the activity is not open to all, who should attend? _____

_____

Description of the activity: _____

_____

_____

_____

Materials, supplies, and equipment: _____

_____

_____

Room requirements and setup: _____

_____

_____

Risk management and adaptations: _____

_____

_____

_____

TR leadership process (how the TRS interacts with the clients to produce outcomes):

_____

_____

_____

_____

From R. Kunstler and F. Stavola Daly, 2010, *Therapeutic recreation leadership and programming* (Champaign, IL: Human Kinetics).

Figure 10.1   Individual TR session planning and evaluation form.

Specific client outcomes from participation: _____

_____

_____

_____

Comments on session:

Evaluation:

How many attended?

If a closed program, did all appropriate participants attend? If not, why not?

Did anything happen during the session that interfered with or especially enhanced the activity?

Was the location appropriate?

Were materials, supplies, and equipment sufficient? Were there any problems with these? Were clients able to use them successfully?

Did any risk management issues occur?

Were TR leadership techniques effective at facilitating the group process?

Did clients achieve outcomes? If not, why not?

From R. Kunstler and F. Stavola Daly, 2010, *Therapeutic recreation leadership and programming* (Champaign, IL: Human Kinetics).

Figure 10.1 Individual TR session planning and evaluation form.

Individual TR Session Planning and Evaluation Form (completed)

Name of program: *Horticultural Therapy*   Date: *12/21/08*

Name of activity: *Pinecone Bird Feeders*   Location: *Solarium*

Purpose of the activity: *Exercise fine motor skills, sensory stimulation, appreciation of nature*

If the activity is not open to all, who should attend?

Mrs. Kelly, Mrs. Garcia, Mr. Jones, Dr. Li, Mrs. Polinsky, Mrs. Greenberg

Description of the activity: *A pinecone is covered with peanut butter and rolled in birdseed. A string is attached to hang the pinecone from a tree outside the window in each resident's room.*

Figure 10.2 Completed individual TR session planning and evaluation form.   *(continued)*

Materials, supplies, and equipment: *Pinecones, plastic knives, peanut butter, birdseed, paper towels, colored yarn or string, pictures of native birds, sample of finished bird feeder, CD of bird calls, CD player, aprons or smocks*

Room requirements and setup: *Round tables, wheelchair accessible, six people to a table, outlet for CD player, access to water or sink*

Risk management and adaptations: *Screen for allergy to peanuts, monitor for safe use of plastic knives and eating of birdseed. Adapt knife handles for easier grasp.*

TR leadership process (how the TRS interacts with the clients to produce outcomes):

Explain purpose of activity

Show pictures of birds and play bird calls

Discuss local birds

Show sample of bird feeder

Pair higher- and lower-functioning clients

Ask for volunteers to give out supplies

Distribute materials equally

Circulate to give assistance

Give encouragement and feedback as needed

Stimulate discussion about birds

Encourage reminiscence

Specific client outcomes from participation:

Used fine motor skills; stimulated senses of smell, hearing, vision, and touch; stimulated long-term memory, expression of appreciation of nature; social interaction; cooperation

Comments on session:

How many attended? 5

Did all appropriate participants attend? If not, why not?

Mrs. Garcia could not attend because her family came for a visit.

Did anything happen during the session that interfered with or especially enhanced the activity?
Nurse's aide interrupted session to take Dr. Li's BP. However, she gave members lots of positive feedback for their efforts at making the bird feeders. Fire drill about 30 minutes after the activity began, but activity was almost over so it did not cause too much disruption.

Figure 10.2 Completed individual TR session planning and evaluation form *(continued)*.

Was the location appropriate?

Yes, although a bit hot. Ms. Greenberg complained about the heat, but it didn't seem to interfere with the activity.

Were the materials, supplies, and equipment adequate? Were there any problems with these? Were clients able to use them successfully?

Yes. Mr. Jones used the adapted knife successfully.

Did any risk management issues occur? *No*

Were TR leadership techniques effective at facilitating the group process?

Discussion was at first limited to birds, but the use of pictures helped to stimulate conversation. Mrs. Kelly and Mr. Jones both stated they had parakeets as pets and were able to identify bird calls. They received positive reinforcement from the group for this information. Volunteer was helpful but had to be reminded to let the clients do as much of the activity as possible. TRS will speak with volunteer coordinator about additional in-service for volunteers on working with clients with cognitive limitations.

Did clients achieve outcomes? If not, why not?

Yes, all clients were able to use their fine motor skills, responded to sensory stimulation, and verbally shared memories and information regarding birds.

Figure 10.2 Completed individual TR session planning and evaluation form *(continued)*.

should take into account the time needed to carry out the activities of the group. A program should be long enough to make it worth the effort to attend. In a community-based program that involves group members traveling to a site, the TRS should be sure that the time spent is long enough to make the trip worthwhile. On the other hand, sessions that go on too long may tend to become disorganized and disjointed as members get restless, lose motivation, or leave. A session should end on a high note while there is still a strong degree of group interest. If the program involves a large-scale project, it may have to be divided into smaller sessions to help clients cope with starting and stopping their work.

Scheduling also involves ensuring that the room or space assigned gives participants a sense of safety and feeling of comfort. Too small a room may make a participant anxious or aggressive. Too large a space may cause clients to lose their focus on the activities or may offer too many distracting stimuli. Noise from the nurses' station or the hallway can interfere with communication in a nearby room. A noisy area can present a major challenge for a child diagnosed with autism because she may experience too much noise as painful, or for someone with attention-deficit disorder because the noise interferes with concentration. Rooms that are too hot can put clients

to sleep or cause physical distress, and temperatures that are too cold can be distracting or uncomfortable. Realistically, the physical aspects of a space may not be within the TRS's control. While many facilities have designated spaces for TR, others have only limited or shared program space and thus certain activities may not be possible. Adaptations to the space should be discussed with the team and, when appropriate, with administration, housekeeping, and maintenance.

Materials, Equipment, and Supplies

Having suitable and adequate supplies, materials, and equipment contributes to a successful group. Planning for an activity occurs long before the group takes place. Taking an inventory of available materials and resources is essential to planning and implementing quality programs. The TRS should research the cost, availability, and ordering information for materials well in advance of the start of the group. She must be informed about the agency procedures for purchasing; the time required for submitting purchase orders; and if petty cash can be used, for what types of purchases. If financial support is limited, she should consider alternative resources, such as grants or donations, or having participants supply their own equipment and supplies. Having full knowledge of what is available and having potential backup plans can keep a group from deteriorating due to conflicts and frustration.

A rule of thumb for a TRS is to be knowledgeable about the material requirements of an activity, know how to do the activity, and ensure that all materials are in working order. If an electrical extension cord is needed, she should check to see if she needs an adaptor for a two- or three-pronged plug to fit the available outlet. The TRS should know how games are played and periodically check to make sure no pieces are missing. One TRS brought a new bingo set, all wrapped in plastic, to a waiting group and on opening the box discovered that the bingo numbers were missing. A TR student intern decided to shift a planned activity at the last minute because of a change in group membership. Unfortunately, he chose a game he was not familiar with, which resulted in an unproductive and unsatisfying group experience. The questions were not age appropriate for the participants, and the intern was not able to make adjustments as the game was progressing. Group members could not respond to the questions, and the goal of promoting conversation was not achieved.

Staffing the Group

The TRS should determine the most appropriate leader for the given group. The head of the TR department or a staff TRS may design a group that another TRS will conduct; newly hired staff may take on leading existing groups; or a student intern may assume the responsibility of leading a particular group. According to the codes of ethics of the TR profession, the TRS must be competent by virtue of training and experience to provide services. Optimally the TR group leader should be selected according to who has the best skills for conducting the particular type of group. Therapeutic recreation specialists may be required to obtain certifications such as CPR and First Aid, as well as additional training for working with people on ventilators and intervening with violent behaviors. There also may be support staff, assistants, or volunteers who are needed to assist the TRS and participants. Both the complexity of the activity and the nature of the participants' limitations and functioning abilities are factors in identifying additional staffing needs. An out trip to a restaurant with a group of clients who have dysphagia may require the presence of a nurse or other trained staff. Having the proper staff support is an important risk management consideration.

FINAL PREPARATIONS

At the end of each week the TRS takes time to review the plans for the upcoming week. Supplies should be checked, and staffing and room arrangements confirmed. This end-of-the-week check allows the TRS time to modify plans in case anything has changed, or to identify additional needed supports. Perhaps a staffperson has taken the coming week off for a vacation, or renovations will be starting in a space scheduled for TR program use. Maybe supplies have been used up, equipment has been broken, or balls or game pieces are missing. Perhaps a new client will be participating in the group. By conducting this brief review of programming for the upcoming week, the TRS can eliminate any surprises that may negatively affect his programs.

At the start of the new programming week, the TRS again conducts a review. While this may seem to take up a lot of time, ongoing review and planning actually reduce the amount of time spent on troubleshooting. The TRS plans at the end of each day for the next day's programs by doing whatever can be done ahead of time: checking space availability and setup, compiling and distributing names of clients who will attend each group, preparing equipment and supplies, and reminding staff in other departments of relevant arrangements. For example, has the dietary department confirmed the order for a birthday cake or the food needed for the barbeque? Are transportation arrangements in place for a trip? Will housekeeping set up extra chairs for the concert? Do nurses have the list of patients who are going out of the building? Is the first aid kit well stocked? This is especially important for early morning activities. Even when the TRS has planned in detail for a group, activities may have to be shifted at the last minute because of scheduling conflicts, changes in group membership, or unforeseen problems; and the TRS needs to know what is on hand.

Organizing Materials

Before the program begins, the TRS should prepare a cart or gather the required materials in a box and determine how materials will be transported to the session location. In some programs, the materials are the same for each session. Other types of programs use a variety of materials that change from session to session. For example, a quilting group uses the same supplies at each meeting. A social skills group may use several different games and role play various scenarios from one session to another. A list of required materials is included in the individual TR session planning form. Always bring extra sup-

Universal Precautions

Universal precautions are a set of precautions used to avoid contact with patients' bodily fluids to prevent the transmission of HIV, hepatitis B virus, and other bloodborne pathogens so that communicable diseases do not spread.

Substances and Items Requiring Use of Universal Precautions

- Blood
- Bodily fluids containing visible blood
- Semen
- Saliva
- Vaginal fluid
- Cerebrospinal fluid
- Synovial, pleural, peritoneal, pericardial, and amniotic fluids
- Needles, scalpels, and other sharp instruments

Universal Precautions

- Wash hands before and after each procedure in which contact with bodily fluids is possible (using a waterless hand cleaner is acceptable).
- Wear gloves whenever contact with blood or other potentially infectious materials (body fluids and tissues) is possible.
- Wear a full-body gown whenever there is a possibility of being splashed by fluids.
- Wear a face mask and eye protection whenever there is a possibility of fluids splashing onto the face.
- Dispose of all contaminated sharp objects in an appropriate puncture-proof container.
- Dispose of all contaminated personal protective equipment in an appropriate container marked for biohazardous waste.

plies! Pay attention to universal precautions and have available gloves, disinfectant, hand sanitizer, paper towels, and any other materials that may be necessary to ensure the safety of the clients.

Preparing the Space

Whenever possible, the TRS should set up the room where the program will be held before the activity is scheduled to begin. Setting up may be among the clients' responsibilities. Tables, chairs, or other furnishings should be placed in the appropriate arrangement for the group. The tables and any equipment should be cleaned. If any non-TR staff are using the room and the activity is closed, they should be informed that they cannot stay in the space after it begins. Be clear with staff and other

clients that prior arrangements have been made for this as a closed session and that client confidentiality must be preserved. With use of a smaller section of a common space such as a day room, it may be hard to control distractions and interruptions. A portable screen or furniture rearrangement can create a sense of privacy for the clients and indicates that a program is in progress. Providing alternative materials for self-directed activities for individuals who are not participants in the group can decrease or prevent interruptions.

When setting up a space for an activity, the TRS may play background music to attract participants, create a relaxed atmosphere, and maintain people's interest prior to the start of the program. When music is played as an accompaniment to other types of programs, it should have a specific purpose. In a painting class, various types of music may be used to inspire creativity. In a stress reduction class, music can serve to relax participants and create a calming environment. Depending on the activity and the functional abilities of the clients, music can also be a distraction that negatively affects concentration and attention span. Background music, radio, and television should not be used unless they are contributing to the process of the activity. Cell phones should be turned off, and this goes for clients and staff!

Reviewing Client and Group Goals

Before each session, in addition to reviewing the plan for the day, the TRS should review the goals for each member of the group. This is crucial for small groups with a therapeutic purpose. Although all members can benefit from the group experience, based on its purpose, each member has unique needs that require the TRS to tailor his intervention

to help the client achieve desired outcomes. The TRS should plan which leadership style, facilitation techniques, and instructional behaviors he will use to accomplish both the individual and group goals. Reviewing the goals also helps the TRS focus on the progress the clients make during the group, which will be documented according to the documentation schedule.

Readying the Staff

The staff assigned to assist the TRS at a group may not be the same every time the group meets, so the TRS should be sure to prepare the assigned staff members regarding the purpose of the activity and their roles and responsibilities. Client confidentiality must be respected at all times. The goals for the clients attending the program should be clear. Even non-TR staff can have a therapeutic effect on clients in a TR group. They are expected to interact with cli-

Guidelines for Working With Volunteers

Volunteers are a great asset to any program and help to enhance services. The following guidelines should be followed for a successful volunteer program.

- Establish or identify a volunteer coordinator.
- Identify specific areas in the program where volunteers are needed.
- Develop a specific job description or list of tasks and roles for the volunteer. Be clear about roles and responsibilities.
- Establish a formal interview process for volunteers.
- Do a background check on a potential volunteer if appropriate.
- Assess the volunteers' skills and experience so you can assign them to the most suitable tasks and responsibilities.
- Have proper training to orient volunteers to the agency, the TR department philosophy, and the needs of the population served.
- Have standards for behavior in place and review them with each volunteer.
- Provide ongoing training.
- Maintain appropriate time and attendance records.
- Supervise and meet with volunteers regularly and provide feedback on performance.
- Conduct periodic formal evaluations.
- Have a clearly defined set of reasons for dismissal.
- Identify risk management and insurance issues.
- Offer volunteer counseling when appropriate.
- Regularly review volunteer policies.
- Offer recognition opportunities and incentives.

ents in accordance with the client's individual plan. One of the most important things to discuss with staff is the type of assistance that should be provided to the client. The TRS must make it clear to staff that clients should be given as much opportunity as possible to complete tasks and engage in conversation or activities without unnecessary or unwanted assistance. Another issue to discuss is feedback. Staff should be advised if there are particular types of comments that should or should not be made to individual clients. It is easy to be spontaneous in one's interactions during a TR program, but care should be taken to interact appropriately. Review the agency's policy for volunteers before discussing the clients' needs with volunteers.

Ensuring That Clients Attend Programs

Whenever possible, the TRS should remind clients in advance about the group, contact the unit staff who are to assist clients to the program, and announce the program using a public address system, if appropriate. Clients who use wheelchairs, have mobility impairments, or have behavioral problems may require physical assistance or supervision to access the location. In a psychiatric setting, assisted living facility, or day program, clients may be able to come on their own. Whatever the procedure, the TRS should be familiar with it and plan accordingly. Escorting clients to the program may be the responsibility of either the TR, nursing, or transportation department, depending on the agency. Nursing or other staff should be reminded on the day of the activity that clients are expected to be at the TR program at a certain time and where it is located. Session time may be cut short if clients are not able to make it to the activity on time, or if the TRS is busy escorting clients or going from room to room to tell people that a program is starting in order to encourage them to attend.

Conducting motivational rounds to support clients' attendance at TR programs is an invaluable TR leadership technique. It can be specified in a client's individual plan that she should receive personal encouragement to attend and that invitations should emphasize her goals, interests and needs. The TRS might say, "Mrs. Garcia, we are having our music program today. I know you like jazz, and this is a chance for you to meet some other people who share your interest. Last week you told me you would come if I came to get you. By the way, refreshments will be served." It may also be part of a client's plan to take responsibility to arrive at a program on her own. With the program preparation complete, the TRS is ready to conduct the group.

CONDUCTING THE TR GROUP

The major impetus for writing this book was the authors' commitment to helping the TRS and TR students learn how to deliver high-quality TR leadership of group programs. The TR group session has three phases that call for TR leadership:

- Warm-up
- Experience
- Wrap-up

Warm-Up Phase

The warm-up or orientation phase of the TR group sets the tone for the rest of the session. With adherence to a consistent format, the group members will know what is to take place at each session. Routine promotes a safe and secure environment in which to experiment with new behaviors and can be a comfort to inexperienced group members.

The TRS should start by introducing himself if necessary, warmly welcoming the group members, stating the name and explaining the purpose of the group, and introducing or asking the members to introduce themselves. While giving an introduction is a good rule to follow, the TRS can decide to dispense with some aspects of the introduction on the basis of his knowledge of the members and their abilities and needs. However, a sincere greeting that motivates participants to want to be involved in the group is essential. Any new members, staff, or volunteers should be introduced: The presence of people who are not known to members can create an atmosphere of confusion or suspicion. The TRS might say something like this:

> Good morning, everyone. My name is Stuart. I am the Therapeutic Recreation Specialist. I'd like to introduce Rachel, a student intern starting with us today. I want to welcome all of you to the horticulture program. The purpose of this program is to exercise your fine motor skills, sharpen your mental abilities, and enjoy the experience of nature as we do our gardening and planting. Let's go around and introduce ourselves to each other.

By stating the purpose of the group, the TRS provides direction for the clients' participation in the program and a framework for their actions. While clients may enjoy a TR group experience and derive benefits from their engagement, unless the purpose of the activity is clearly articulated they may not focus on the outcomes they are trying to achieve. For example, in a psychiatric facility, the TRS engaged the clients in a game of Battle of the

Sexes. Clients were divided into male and female teams, and each team took turns asking the other team trivia questions that it hoped the opponents could not answer. The clients had fun, and most verbally participated in the game; but the purpose of the group was never discussed. When the group was over, the clients were asked what they learned from the activity. Each client who responded had a different answer. Some said they had learned a particular piece of information from the trivia questions. Another learned that "men are smarter than women." While the intent of the group was to increase their attention span and to improve communication skills, none of the clients identified those outcomes. Because the purpose of the group was not discussed at the beginning of the session, the clients were not focused on trying to reach their desired goals. The group experience was seemingly successful, but an opportunity may have been missed: An explanation of the purpose of the group might have helped clients direct their efforts and attention toward working on specific skills.

Next, if applicable, the TRS reviews what went on in the previous session or sessions. This serves to remind the members of what they have accomplished and to orient new members or a member who missed the previous session. The TRS may ask members to describe the previous session or use a questioning technique to elicit this information from them. For example, he might say, "Kenneth, can you tell us what you accomplished during the last session?" Engaging the clients as soon as possible in the warm-up stage is a valuable motivational technique and begins two-way communication.

Using multiple channels of communication ensures that everyone in the group is "on the same page." Communication involves the conveying of information clearly and articulately and in a voice that is loud enough for all members to hear. A microphone can be used to help members hear the TRS, but this is generally not necessary in a small group. If the TRS is soft-spoken, he must work to project his voice or use a microphone so that the group can hear him and maintain their focus on the group's activities.

Alternative communication devices such as communication boards should be used when appropriate. Picture boards, written instructions, and large print can supplement verbal communications. If clients speak a language other than the TRS's, an interpreter or written translations could be provided. If clients have cognitive limitations, use simple sentences, break instructions down into small steps, and use demonstration as much as possible. The warm-up phase builds and reinforces group cohesion, trust, and acceptance.

Warm-up Activities, Icebreakers, and Mixers

Signatures: On arrival, each participant is given a sheet with a list of things they might like to know about one another: hobbies, personality traits, experiences, etc. They then go around the room and find someone who fits one of the items and has him sign his name next to it. The object is to fill your sheet without getting the same signature more than once, learn names, and become better acquainted by learning new things about each other.

One-Word Conversation: As each participant arrives, a card is pinned on his or her back. Participants circulate around the room and write on each other's cards, using one word to describe their first impression of the person. This continues until each participant has written on 10 people's cards or until everyone's card is filled. Each person then reads his card. The object is to give positive reinforcement to other group members through positive statements.

20 Questions: Participants try to identify a person or object selected by the leader in 20 questions or less.

Trust Walk Activity: In pairs, one member is blindfolded and the other gives him verbal or nonverbal instructions for navigating an obstacle course (also known as Minefield).

Two Truths and a Lie: People write down two truths about themselves and a lie. Then they introduce the three "facts" to the rest of the group, who try to guess which "fact" is really the lie.

Commonalities: People get into pairs and try to find 10 things they have in common. They then share with the group to find out what they all have in common.

WARM-UP ACTIVITIES OR ICEBREAKERS

Warm-up activities, also known as icebreakers or mixers, are used to help members get to know each other better, to promote relaxation in people who may feel tense or uncomfortable about being in the group or the overall program, and to promote socialization and group cohesion. There are countless icebreakers to choose from, depending on the size of the group, the time available for the warm-up, and the skills and abilities of the members. The activities should be fun, engage members' interest, offer a challenge, be an opportunity for interaction, be a preparation for the group experience, and be relatively brief. In a single-session program, spending too much time on the warm-up may leave little time for the main group experience. However, with a closed membership group that will meet for a number of sessions, the TRS may want to spend the entire first session on getting-acquainted activities. For subsequent sessions, reviewing the previous week's session can serve as an informal warm-up activity, and formal mixers may not be necessary. Mixers can be used at any session if the TRS observes a need to revitalize the participants or break up cliques that may have formed, or if the activity itself relates to the purpose of the group. Icebreakers can be used before or after presentation of the rules of the group.

EXPLAINING THE RULES

During the warm-up phase, the TRS also explains the rules that have been established to facilitate the smooth flow of the activity and makes sure that everyone understands the rules. This happens at the initial meeting and in subsequent group sessions as needed. The rules should be discussed to make sure that everyone understands why the rules exist. If a new member joins the group, the TRS may review the rules with her prior to the session or assign someone to help her learn rules or behaviors that have not been explicitly identified. The TRS may develop a basic set of rules and then, as the group progresses, members can amend or enhance them. Group rules that are set by the members are preferable, but this is not always possible. A written set of rules should be posted or available, and the TRS can refer to the list to briefly summarize the key points. Risk management is a primary reason why the TRS has initial responsibility for developing the rules for a program. For example, in a cooking group, rules might state that all participants must wash their hands before cooking and that members must wear an oven mitt and have the permission of the TRS before using the oven. Rules should be limited to those necessary to guarantee that group interactions are respectful and appropriate for the task at hand. The clients should be informed if there are consequences for not following the rules. For example, a basic rule in many TR groups is that clients cannot physically touch another client without permission; violation of this rule can result in suspension from the program. In addition, individual clients may have their own set of "rules" or guidelines for behavior to follow. At a camp for children with autism, Danny is given a laminated rule card to carry with him at all times to remind him of the proper rules of behavior (see figure 10.3).

When I am at Camp Okee Sunokee...

I need to have quiet hands.
I do not hit, kick, or bite.

I need to follow my schedule and do what my counselors say.

I need to use nice words when I talk.
I do not use mean words.

It is okay to get upset, mad, frustrated, or angry. When I feel this way, I need to say, **"I need a break."**

My counselors and my family will be happy and proud of me when I use my words and ask for a break the right way!

Figure 10.3 This individual rule card helped remind Danny of the behavior he should exhibit.

Rules for an Arts and Crafts Group

At a summer camp for children with learning disabilities and Asperger's syndrome, the TRS created a list of rules for the arts and crafts program, which were hung on the wall. Because the children had problems with retaining as well as generalizing information, these rules were reviewed at the beginning of each session to reinforce acceptable behaviors and to prevent behavior problems:

- Stay in your own place during the activity.
- Share materials with other campers.
- When using the scissors, cut only the materials for the project. (Do not cut another person's clothing or hair, or your own, with the scissors.)
- Stay in your seat when working with scissors. (Do not run around the room or wave your arms when holding the scissors.)
- Use paint, glitters, glue, and markers only on the materials provided. (Do not put paint, crayons, markers, glitter, or glue in your mouth or paint on a fellow camper's clothing or body or on your own clothing or body.)
- Arts and crafts supplies are not food.
- Respect another person's space, and do not try to touch or take another person's work unless invited by the other camper.
- Keep your hands on your own body.
- Always say "please" and "thank you."

The TRS serves as the first role model of adherence to group rules and norms and should demonstrate all appropriate group behaviors in her interactions with the clients. During the group, the TRS helps members understand the implicit as well as the explicit norms of the group. Implicit norms refer to "the way things are done" and have developed and emerged over the course of the group's existence. In a leisure education program in a short-term rehabilitation center, after the first two sessions the members have established, without discussion, their preferred seating. One member who tends to be claustrophobic likes to be near the open door. Another member who has problems with incontinence prefers to sit closer to the rest room. Still another who has a hard time hearing the leader always sits next to the TRS. The seating was not discussed openly, but the members have accepted the current arrangement. When a new member joins the group and attempts to sit near the door, the group admonishes her. She responds that she was told to sit anywhere she wanted. While technically this may be true, in reality the group has informally established a seating arrangement that everyone has implicitly agreed to support. When necessary,

the TRS may intervene to explain an unspoken but accepted behavior or encourage a participant to help another member learn the ways of the group. By respecting each participant, listening carefully to what the clients are saying, and staying focused on clients' needs, the TRS models appropriate communication and social behaviors and creates opportunities for open discussion about members' fears, anxieties, or confusion about participating in the group.

The TRS should also clarify policies regarding confidentiality and reassure members that what they disclose during the group stays within the group, unless it is detrimental to the safety of the client or others. If photographs will be taken, she obtains a separate release from each client. The TRS reviews member responsibilities such as setup of the activity, distribution of supplies, providing assistance to a peer, and cleanup.

The Experience Phase

The end of one phase and the beginning of the next is not always clear. In the experience phase the TRS is applying all he has learned, combined with his professional expertise and clinical judgment, in order to make possible the maximum benefits and outcomes of the group experience for his clients. The planning and preparation that have gone into establishing the group are essential, but the true meaning of the TR work is revealed during the group experience when the TRS must be performing at the top of his game. Therapeutic recreation contributes uniquely to helping people in that the experience of participants as they engage in TR services is an enjoyable one, in the deepest sense. The responsibility of the TRS is to facilitate enjoyment while leading a TR program that enables the members to move toward achievement of desired goals.

GIVING DIRECTIONS AND INSTRUCTIONS

Once the group has been through the warm-up phase, the TRS leads the activity. Clients may require instructions on how to do the activity, which might include rules of a game, steps in a craft or cooking project, exercise moves, procedures for painting a mural, or a planning process for an out trip. They may need directions on proper use of materials or on how to complete certain actions. If this is the case, the TRS should have available all the necessary materials and illustrations. The TRS's leadership style in giving instructions can vary from highly directive to laissez-faire. It may be very directive with a group who have cognitive limitations, poor physical skills, or emotional immaturity. It may be democratic or even laissez-faire with a higher-functioning and more capable group who may quickly pick up on what they need to do. The instructional approach depends on the purpose of the group, the activity to be taught, and the individual learning styles within the group. Each person learns best in his own way, whether it's from verbal directions, demonstrations, written instructions, or some combination of these. These are some examples of ways to direct a group:

- When teaching a group of children with learning disabilities how to do the hula hoop roll, the TRS says, "The goal of this activity is to get your hula hoop to the opposite end of the gymnasium. To roll the hula hoop, place your hand on top of the hoop, palm down, pulling the hoop back and then forward to release" (Peniston, 1998, p. 158). The TRS can also demonstrate the hula hoop roll, have the children practice, go around to each one to provide individual assistance as needed, and give feedback and encouragement.
- In an arts and crafts class, sharing a finished product, having simple instructions written out on individual index cards, demonstrating how

to make the project, and having supplies clearly labeled can facilitate learning and engagement.

- In an exercise class, the TRS not only leads and demonstrates the exercise in the front of the room but also circulates to guide each individual as needed, correcting exercise moves and postures.

Patience is indispensable in giving directions. If the TRS knows an activity very well, she may have to place herself in the position of a beginner so she can help members cope with frustration as they learn or try it. She needs to juggle the different levels of competence in the group. When members know the activity or have learned it quickly, having them help others in need of assistance is beneficial for everyone. This promotes feelings of self-worth in the client who is helping, as he feels positive about contributing his knowledge. It can also facilitate learning, as the person receiving assistance may feel "If he learned this, so can I." Once the group members have learned the activity, the TRS should keep a watchful eye on their progress. Anyone can reach a snag or need assistance during the course of the program.

The TRS is responsible for scanning the group repeatedly either to see who needs support or intervention to carry out the activity or to promote positive interaction. This means that the TRS, depending on the nature of the program, is physically active in the group, moving from one client to another as required. He should walk around and go to each individual who needs assistance. It is important to establish direct eye contact with the client, which may mean bending down or sitting if the client is seated. In a group seated in a circle, the TRS may not actually move among the clients but should verbally interact with each one throughout the session. The TRS must speak in a clear voice and at a pace and volume adapted to the clients. Table 10.3 offers tips for effective interaction with clients.

ENGAGING IN THE EXPERIENCE

The TRS scans the group while actually leading the activity or supervising the actions of the members. When giving direct leadership, the TRS must be sure to include all participants. In activities that require verbal interaction, she must be sure to encourage all members to speak. She needs to control those who would dominate the discussion and encourage those who don't speak up. Tact and diplomacy are skills to use when these behaviors occur.

In a game of Name That Tune in a nursing home, with memory stimulation and emotional appreciation of the music as the purpose of the group,

TABLE 10.3

Do's and Don'ts for Effective Interaction

Client conditions	Cognitive concerns	Hearing impairments	Mobility impairments	Visual impairments	Affective concerns
Do's	Minimize distractions in the environment. Break down complex tasks into simpler steps. Use clear, concrete, and direct language. Use age-appropriate language. Phrase questions to elicit accurate information. Verify comprehension by repeating comments in a different way; but when giving directions, use consistent language. Be patient and allow the person to take time to make decisions or follow through. Redirect client when appropriate. Praise efforts.	Before speaking, make sure you get the person's attention by waving your hand, tapping his shoulder, or turning the lights on and off. A quiet, well-lit room is best. Always face the person, maintain eye contact, and talk directly to the person. Speak clearly. The person may be reading your lips. Rephrase rather than repeat. The use of a qualified sign language interpreter is recommended, especially for important discussions. You may use writing back and forth. Placing a mirror or two at eye level can enable the person to be aware of more of what is going on in the room.	When speaking with a person in a wheelchair, try to be seated also. If this isn't possible, stand at a slight distance so the person isn't straining to look up at you. Make eye contact. Ask the person if she needs assistance and how much. Place items within reach. Let the person set the pace. Paths of travel should be clear. Remove cords and wires from traffic flow. Ensure that mats and rugs don't bunch up. Wipe up spills immediately. When maneuvering a person's wheelchair, push down on one tilting rod and tilt chair back slightly to go from street to curb and onto sidewalk. Go down ramps backward. Seat belts may be used on wheelchairs. If a service counter is too high for the person to see or reach, ask the person providing service to come around.	Identify yourself by name and role before you make physical contact. Introduce the person to others who are present. When giving directions, give specific information. Offer to read written information, such as signs, labels, menus, instructions. Solid-colored tablecloths or tabletops should contrast with activity supplies. When placing many items in front of the person, use a tray to hold them. Use a clock face as a means to describe placement (e.g., scissors at 9:00). Place furniture against walls to allow freer movement. Square or rectangular tables provide better orientation than round ones. When walking, offer your arm for guidance and describe the setting, noting any obstacles. Be specific when giving warnings: Move to the right, stop. Guide the person's hand to the chair back or railing. If a person has a guide dog, walk on the side opposite the dog. At meals, offer to help cut up food. The food can also be cut up in the kitchen.	Face the person. Maintain eye contact. Speak in a calm manner. Present one idea or concept at a time. Give the person time to respond. Be a sensitive listener. Take a time-out if the person is getting frustrated, disagrees, or doesn't understand.

Client conditions	Cognitive concerns	Hearing impairments	Mobility impairments	Visual impairments	Affective concerns
Don'ts	Don't assume that the individual understands or has prior knowledge. Don't give too many choices. Avoid overstimulation. Avoid abstract concepts.	Do not obscure your face when communicating. Avoid chewing gum, smoking, or looking down. Avoid standing in front of light sources such as lamps, windows. Don't shout. Don't look at the interpreter; look directly at the person with whom you are communicating.	Don't lean on someone's wheelchair. Respect the individual's space. Don't push or touch a person's wheelchair without asking first. Do not use the armrests to lift a wheelchair. Do not grab someone's cane or crutches; they are needed for balance. Do not store or place them in aisles, ramps, or passageways. If the person puts down his cane, do not move it. Let him know it is blocking the pathway.	Don't worry about language; it is OK to say "Did you see the movie?" Do not point and say "over there." Don't leave the person in the middle of a room. Don't grab his arm to guide him, pull him, or push him into a chair. Don't stand behind him. Don't touch his cane, move it, or pet his guide dog. Avoid rearranging personal items.	Don't rush the person to respond or act. Don't interrupt.

Reprinted, by permission, from Janet Listokin, CTRS

the TRS might say, "Mr. Jones, I'm impressed that you know so many songs! Let's see if anyone else can name the next one. . . . Mrs. Garcia, do you recognize this?" In this way, she compliments Mr. Jones for his knowledge yet gently informs him that others need a chance too. By calling on Mrs. Garcia, the TRS encourages her to participate. If Mrs. Garcia doesn't know the name of the song, the TRS might ask if she knows the singer. If not, then the TRS can say "Let's see if anyone else knows." By scanning the group, the TRS can observe whether others look as if they know or want to speak up but need encouragement. These may seem like obvious tips, but it may be difficult to control dominant participants or just easier to let them take over. The TRS may need to use a more authoritarian leadership style. If too few people are participating, the activity may be inappropriate for the group because they aren't familiar with the songs. Or the activity may be a good choice but the participants can't hear the music or need verbal prompts to focus their attention. The TRS can say, "Mrs. Kelly, listen to this song. Does it sound familiar to you?" Perhaps Mr. Jones and some of the others need a more challenging activity and a more democratic leadership style so they can do more of the program planning and organizing.

Another technique the TRS should use to promote a positive group experience is to make connections and linkages among the members. The power of the group lies in the human interaction that goes on during the activity; otherwise a TR program is just a collection of people in the same space doing the same activity who could just as easily be doing it on their own. This is actually a viable program format, but it does not fit into the context of a TR group as discussed in the chapter. In the preceding example, if the TRS plays a song and Mrs. Garcia guesses the name correctly, the TRS can go on to ask if anyone knows who the singer is, knows another song on the same subject, attended a concert by the singer, can sing the song, and so on. This maximizes the value of the program by triggering memories, eliciting feelings of satisfaction and success, and demonstrating to the participants that engaging in this activity has meaning. The TRS must always demonstrate depth of involvement in the program and commitment to the activity. By expanding on a simple response of the name of a song, the TRS has made the activity more interesting and is getting the most out of what the activity itself has to offer. To motivate others, you must be motivated yourself.

As mentioned earlier, interaction among group members is an essential component of a successful group. Members of TR groups have individual goals, but they are also connected by a common goal and share a group identity. In a group whose goal is more therapeutic, interactions are cornerstones of the group experience and serve to heighten the individual outcomes of the group members. For example, in a therapeutic group such as a creative writing group for individuals in treatment for substance abuse, the TRS asks the members to write an "alphapoem," a 26-line free verse poem on a particular topic in which each line begins with a different letter of the alphabet (Gillespie, 2003). See chapter 6 for "Ways I Cope," an example of an alphapoem.

Once the group is ready, the TRS asks for volunteers to read their poems and then encourages the members to respond to the reader by asking questions, sharing a similar coping method, and reflecting on how they felt about what they heard. As the members interact, the TRS may be using a democratic leadership style because the members are verbal, the group has been ongoing for a period of time, and they are comfortable with each other. The members know that their roles and responsibilities in the group are to write the poem, read it to the group, listen, and verbally participate in the discussion. As the group matures, the TRS's behavior moves from controlling the activities to facilitating and coaching the group members, supporting the achievement of individual and group goals. She may not even need to be responsible for the discussion. She may assign this role to a member and facilitate the discussion as needed. The TRS, based on her knowledge of the participants, takes the opportunity to make a relevant point, share an insight, or increase self-awareness of a group member. She creates an environment that is both safe and productive through open communication, encouragement, and sharing of her insights to fulfill the purposes of the group. As the group engages during the experience phase, the TRS monitors the members' progress, provides feedback and support in terms of the group's purpose, and emphasizes the benefits of participating in this particular activity. There may be activities within the program that participants do not want to do or do not perceive the value of. Review the benefits of TR programs, as identified in chapter 6. If a group is well planned and purposeful, the TRS can help the participants understand the value of the activity.

PROCESSING AND FEEDBACK

As explained in chapter 7, the TRS not only leads a recreation activity but also creates a therapeutic experience, by processing what the clients are going through during their engagement in the TR program and by giving them feedback on their actions and performance of desired skills and behaviors. For example, in an Out-of-School Time (OST) program for youth with developmental disabilities, the members of the sport skills group believe that their primary goal is playing softball. However, the goals for the group also include developing teamwork and cooperation. To facilitate the clients' progress toward their goals, the TRS provides guidance and feedback as they participate in the activity. The TRS gives feedback throughout the course of the program as needed by the participant.

For example, one skill the clients are learning is to take turns at bat. Rosa tries to cut in line every inning so that she can bat more often. The TRS, in the role of coach, intervenes by saying "No, Rosa. It is not your turn," and guides her by the arm back to her place in line. When she returns to the right place, he compliments her by saying "Rosa, you are in the correct place in line. Good for you for knowing where your place is." When it's her turn to bat, the TRS says "Rosa, it's your turn to bat" and praises her efforts to hit the ball. The larger the group, the more challenging it is for the TRS to give individual attention to each member. In this case, the other members of the team also give feedback to Rosa, either yelling at her or telling her that she is in the wrong place. The TRS models how to interact with Rosa, encourages her new and more appropriate behaviors, and also uses the group's responses to shape Rosa's behavior. After the game, the TRS can lead a discussion on what behaviors represent teamwork, giving verbal praise for the right answers and asking for examples of who demonstrated teamwork. If someone answers "Rosa," he can compliment Rosa and reinforce her newly learned behavior: "Rosa, you displayed great teamwork by taking turns."

TYPICAL LEADER MISTAKES

A major mistake TRSs make in leading groups is not engaging all the members. The TRS's primary and most significant responsibility as she provides TR leadership is to ensure that each client is having a meaningful experience. As an example, a TRS decided that making fruit smoothies for residents in a long-term care facility would be beneficial. The residents enjoyed drinking the fruit smoothies; however, the TRS made the smoothies in front of the residents, and their only participation was drinking! Instead, the TRS could have the residents peel and chop the fruit, put the fruit in the blender, press the stop and start buttons, and pour the smoothies, as well as set up and clean up the supplies. Even one of these tasks would promote the residents' engagement. Discussion topics could include the types of fruits, colors, flavors, aromas, past experiences, and growing fruits and other produce. Even for clients who are only observing, the TRS could make comments to them about the fruits, the smoothies, and the sound of the blender and reinforce nonverbal expressions; for instance, she could say, "I see you are watching the blender spin, Mrs. Garcia. Doesn't it make a strange noise?"

The TRS's leadership should be focused on taking any opportunity to meaningfully engage the clients.

AP Photo/Dave Martin

There is truly no excuse for not finding a way for a client to be actively involved, on some level, in the TR program. The TRS's leadership should be dynamic and focused on taking any opportunity to meaningfully engage the clients. There are multiple ways in which different group members can be engaged. The TRS should provide enough assistance, adaptations, and supports to facilitate participation, but not so much that clients are not reaching their potential. During all phases of TR group sessions, the TRS facilitates the participation of the group members, giving clear instructions and directions; she also provides informational, motivational, and contingent feedback and offers emotional support. Task analysis (see chapter 7) can help the TRS identify steps at which clients need intervention in order to engage in an activity.

Another mistake leaders make is not adapting quickly enough to a change in circumstances. If supplies run out, equipment breaks, the van gets a flat tire, a sudden rainstorm comes up, an entertainer cancels, or a space becomes unavailable, the TRS must be able to implement another activity—not merely a time filler—with very little notice or preparation. The TRS has the ethical responsibility to be competent and engage in continuing education to further develop her knowledge and skills to build up her TR toolkit.

DEALING WITH CHALLENGING SITUATIONS

The experience phase can present a number of challenging circumstances. Changes in the group membership, location, or leader can occur and create anxiety and negative behaviors in any group. These are some examples:

- A member leaves or a new member arrives. The TRS can ease the transition of the arrival of a new member by having an attitude of warm acceptance and preparing the current members for a new participant.

- The location of the group may have to be changed due to a scheduling conflict, causing a disruption in the comfort level that has been attained.

- The leader or coleader may be replaced because the TRS is out sick. This can have an impact on the group as they take time to develop trust in the new leader and adjust to a different personality.

The TRS should be proactive in anticipating the unexpected. She can use these changes as "teachable moments" about situations that occur in real life. How the group handles change can be a learning experience for everyone. The TRS can present problem-solving strategies such as discussion, brainstorming, or a step-by-step decision-making process or use direct intervention if necessary to smooth over a challenging situation. Children with autism, individuals with traumatic brain injury or attention-deficit disorder, and older adults with dementia are particularly sensitive to these types of changes. With any population, the TRS can reduce negative behaviors stemming from these changes by practicing with the existing group how to greet a new member or how to get to the new meeting location in advance of the change. The TRS may be able to bring something from the former location, such as a picture or decorations that will provide the members with a sense of familiarity. By maintaining the routine already established for the group, she can help members accommodate to anticipated and unanticipated changes.

Disruptive Behaviors

Another challenge for the TRS is disruptive behavior and conflicts among group members, or between a member and the TRS. The type of leadership applied by the TRS to resolve a behavioral issue or conflict depends on the type of behaviors or conflicts that arise. When the normally quiet and polite Mrs. Kelly started to act out in the Italian club, the TRS became very concerned. These behavioral changes included yelling at new members and interrupting the TRS

and other participants when they tried to speak. The TRS reported these changes in Mrs. Kelly's behavior at the morning care planning meeting. During the meeting, two factors were identified as possibly influencing Mrs. Kelly's behavior. First, Mrs. Kelly's close friend, who had come with her to the group, had recently passed away. Secondly, with the introduction of refreshments to the program, new people had joined the group. The TRS identified that Mrs. Kelly's behaviors were directly related to the significant changes in her social environment and in the membership of the group.

The TRS implemented a plan of action developed with the team's input. First, she met with Mrs. Kelly privately and engaged her in a discussion about the Italian club. Mrs. Kelly complained that the new members were interested only in the food and not in Italian culture. They often arrived late and talked to each other when the group activities were going on. The TRS then asked Mrs. Kelly for some suggestions on how they could involve new members in the group and thanked her for her suggestions. She discussed with Mrs. Kelly the passing of her friend and arranged for another member of the group who was also friendly with Mrs. Kelly to stop by her room and go with her to the Italian club program. On the basis of her talks with Mrs. Kelly,

Understanding Disruptive Behaviors

You are a TRS at a day program for individuals with developmental disabilities. Clients attend TR programs twice a day. You have observed that Carmen, a client diagnosed with cognitive limitations in the moderate to severe range, acts out in the day room after lunch during the afternoon session. These acting-out behaviors include throwing equipment, attempting to turn over the table, and hitting staff and other clients. Carmen does not display these behaviors in the morning TR session.

Carmen does not speak or use assistive communication devices. Staff members have observed Carmen during lunch and do not notice any issues that could cause this behavior. The staff contacts her group home; the staff there say that they have also noticed this behavior in the evening after dinner but have not determined any specific cause. The TRS works with Carmen to identify whether or not it is the choice of activities that has caused Carmen's behavior to change. The psychologist works with the team and develops a behavior modification plan for Carmen. The plan is implemented, but Carmen's behaviors do not change.

Several weeks after first addressing this behavior, the staff is contacted by the group home and told that Carmen is in the hospital. Carmen has been diagnosed with gallstones. After the gallstones are removed, Carmen returns to the program and the behaviors have disappeared. The behaviors appear to have been a reaction to physical pain that Carmen could not communicate rather than a specific behavior trigger. When a sudden behavior change appears, it is important to rule out any physical causes or other changes or events that may have affected the individual.

the TRS discussed the purpose of the group with the members and established a rule that in order to have refreshments, you had to attend the entire session.

Some negative or destructive behaviors may be directly related to the interactions of the group as it goes through the stages of group development. Over the course of the group sessions, interactions among the members increase in quantity and intensity from the tentativeness of the early phase when people are getting to know and trust one another. At this point, members often begin to struggle with how they fit into the group, how much control they have over the group, and how to express their opinions more openly. Members may be experiencing anxiety or become defensive (Corey, Schneider Corey & Haynes, 2000). It is during this transition that confusion, negative behavior, and conflict may arise. Negative behaviors in groups can often limit the effectiveness of the group or affect the quality of the group experience. Clients with health problems or other limitations come to TR programs with many emotional needs that are nowhere more apparent than during a group session. Clients may come to the first session displaying negative or unproductive behaviors due to resistance to treatment, lack of self-esteem, poor coping skills, or negative roles they have assumed throughout their lives. They may be bored with the activity or in the process of having medications adjusted. There may be an undiagnosed medical issue that the client is not able to communicate.

Members also may begin to question assigned roles or be unclear about the purpose of the group and its potential benefits. Difficult behaviors and the issues that cause them may become a focus of the group's interactions. Learning how to handle these issues and to change behaviors may be the reasons the client is attending this particular group. For example, Sheri is in treatment for drug abuse. Her poor coping skills and low frustration tolerance cause her to snap at comments and suggestions made by group members. They begin to lose patience with Sheri, and an argument breaks out. The TRS calls for a "time-out" and stops the activities in order to openly address the effects of Sheri's behaviors on the group. The TRS reviews the group rules:

- Each member has the right to be listened to.
- Everyone speaks without shouting.
- Disagreements are resolved respectfully.
- Individuals who do not follow the rules may be asked to leave the group.

The TRS also may ask Sheri how she is feeling or ask the group members, once they have calmed down, to speak with Sheri concerning her behavior.

The following are typical client behaviors that arise during group interaction and can become the focus of TR intervention:

- Attention-seeking behaviors such as interrupting, telling jokes, speaking loudly, or touching
- Aggressive behaviors such as yelling, grabbing supplies or equipment, fighting, or cursing
- Withdrawal behaviors such as poor eye contact, turning away from the group, or nonparticipation
- Passive-aggressive behaviors such as arriving late, sleeping, or undermining others' participation

Minimizing Disruptive Situations

The TRS should try to understand what is motivating the client's behavior and use appropriate strategies to address it. First, review the group's norms and be sure that the rules of behavior are being applied to all members equally. Basic rules that focus on how clients interact with each other and the consequences of not following those rules should be defined and discussed at the start of the group. A typical group rule may govern taking turns when speaking: For example, when one person is speaking other members may not interrupt, or in order to be called on to speak, members must raise their hand. If a member does not follow the rules, the consequence may be that he loses a turn or, in the case of extreme behavior, may be asked to leave the group for a time. More serious behaviors such as acting aggressively and threatening another client could result in suspension from the group. If a participant is on a positive behavior support plan, the plan must be implemented immediately once a behavior occurs. Consistency of approach among the staff is critical to promoting positive behavior change. The TRS should be well prepared to apply the behavior modification procedures exactly as presented in the plan. For example, Eddie has a behavior plan to stop the spitting behavior that he displays when he is angry or upset with another client. The plan requires that when he spits he is immediately given a time-out. He can return to the group only after the time-out is complete and he has apologized to the person he spit at. If he gets through an entire session without spitting, the plan may also state that he receives a token that he can redeem for an item of his choice later in the week.

A more detailed approach to behavior management can be developed using a **Positive Behavior Support Plan**. This type of plan is designed to prevent a problem behavior from occurring or decrease the frequency of the behavior, and to teach a new, more positive behavior to replace the problem behavior. Typical problem behaviors include aggressive and destructive acts, tantrums, and repetitive and irritating behaviors that interfere with social interactions. The plan takes an ecological perspective by also addressing issues in the participant's environment that may be contributing to the negative behaviors. Plans should be developed collaboratively and should be family friendly as well as culturally relevant to the individual. Positive Behavior Support is an approach that reflects person-centered planning, as discussed in chapter 3, and has a long-term goal of improving one's social relationships and lifestyle. Figure 10.4 shows a Positive Behavior Support Plan for JP, who is a participant in a community-based recreation program. The plan provides detailed directions to staff on how to address JP's behaviors during the program and was developed in collaboration with JP's parents, teacher, and behaviorist in addition to the TRS.

Having a clear set of group norms and consequences from the beginning of the group will help to address many of the challenging behaviors that occur. Program protocols state the behavioral criteria for participation. The TRS may need to explain the specific behaviors that a client must demonstrate in order to be in a particular group. For example, having the capabilities to follow directions, sit still, cooperate with group members, comprehend a discussion topic, or demonstrate judgment in using equipment can be prerequisites to attending a particular TR group. These criteria should be set to protect clients from harm and to ensure that they can benefit from a particular TR program. They are not set to exclude people who may be difficult for the TRS to work with or who are unpopular with other clients.

Conflicts related to group roles may arise. The TRS may have initially assigned roles for members, and as members become more adept they may begin to question if these roles are suitable for them. Roles in the group are associated with

- carrying out specific tasks such as distributing supplies, keeping score, or serving refreshments;
- maintaining the social and emotional climate of the group, such as showing a new member the ropes or helping a member; and

- on the negative side, behaving in ways that can deter the success of the group (e.g., the comedian, or the member who disagrees with anything anyone else says) (Russell, 2004; Lesser & Pope, 2007).

The role of carrying out specific tasks is generally assigned by the TRS. The TRS may ask members if they wish to volunteer for a task role, or at some point announce that it is time to switch responsibilities among the members. Conflicts may arise when a client does not want to either volunteer or give up responsibility for a task assignment. On the other hand, roles related to the climate of the group tend to be filled unofficially by individuals who behave with kindness and warmth toward others; these clients may find it difficult to recognize when they no longer need to fulfill that responsibility. The TRS may need to help a relationship-oriented member alter his behaviors so others can take on more responsibility or feel more capable. At times, this behavior may be a way of avoiding one's own issues or problems. Individual counterproductive actions can be addressed through the use of behavioral principles of rewarding positive behavior and ignoring negative ones. In the case of Sheri, the TRS could also choose to ignore the snappish remarks and focus on giving frequent praise for specific positive behaviors in the session.

For most conflicts and disagreements, the TRS relies on her position of trust within the group to assist with the resolution of conflicts. The nature of the TRS's role is such that her relationship with clients may be considered that of a "professional friend" (Austin, 2004). The TRS is someone the client can talk to who cares about the client's well-being and has the best interests of the client at heart. Because of the recreation component of TR, the clients interact with the TRS in a more relaxed and less formal fashion than they do with other professionals. This contributes to clients' allowing the TRS to help them resolve difficulties. At the same time, the TRS has the ethical obligation to maintain appropriate professional boundaries. Effective communication skills and ongoing monitoring of the interactions and behaviors of the group members may serve to resolve potential problems before they escalate. The TRS, in his role as leader of the group, helps members develop insights into how their behaviors can help or hinder them in meeting their goals and ultimately lead to happier and healthier lives. The TRS may be in a position to help the members recognize their fears and anxieties,

Positive Behavior Support Plan

Name: *JP* **Date:** *October 11, 2007*

DESCRIPTION OF NEEDS	STRATEGIES	STATUS*
Attention to task	Family will provide a 1:1 each week. In conjunction with TR staff, JP will be redirected as needed.	
Transitions: JP has difficulty transitioning into an activity. He has problems when demands are placed on him.	1. JP will arrive 10 minutes before the start of program each week. 2. Program supervisor will sit with JP and the person who will be working 1:1 with him and review the schedule for the evening, as well as go over the rules of the program and of the activity center. Consequences will be explained. 3. Staff will have JP repeat back the rules and consequences.	
Limit setting: JP needs limits and boundaries set. He needs to know there are consequences. Staff must follow through with those consequences.	JP will get one warning. If JP doesn't comply he will be removed from the program for 2 minutes and sit in designated chair. His 1:1 will sit with him. After his 2 minutes, JP will be asked to rejoin the group. Use phrases such as "JP, this is your warning. Next time you will be asked to leave and sit in the chair for 2 minutes."	
Communication	JP will be encouraged to use his appropriate words and not actions or gestures when he gets frustrated or angry.	
Positive reinforcement	In conjunction with family, TR staff will establish a positive reward system for JP. Suggestions include earning stickers toward rewards JP gets at home such as dinner in a fast food restaurant of his choice. Use phrases such as "Are you working for your sticker?"	
Feeling overwhelmed	JP needs to express himself when he is feeling overwhelmed. He needs to request a break, or staff should offer him a break.	

*Status: **A** = attained; **C** = continue; **R** = revise.

Figure 10.4 Positive Behavior Support Plan.

(continued)

DESCRIPTION OF NEEDS	STRATEGIES	STATUS*
Sensory integration: JP needs a lot of sensory input especially through oral and body movement. Sucking appears to be soothing and calming for him.	1. Staff will allow JP to have a piece of candy or gum, which will be provided by the family. JP will be allowed to have it only when the activity allows for safe chewing or sucking on a piece of candy. 2. Staff will use the sit disc for him to stand on (or sit on) when he is working at table on an activity. 3. Use clay or a deck of cards; may be a part of his behavior plan—he earns stickers toward time to play with cards or clay.	

Additional comments:

JP does not like to be touched and may be defensive and become physical or aggressive if touched. He is to use the words "Please do not touch me." He will need reminders throughout the program to stay on task and reminders about the rules. Use phrases such as "Don't forget the rules" when working with him.

Behaviorist Carmen C. is in agreement that only one person needs to be with JP at program. Anything more is overwhelming to him. Family will decide whether it is his worker or a family member.

JP will eat prior to coming to the program. He will bring one or two snacks with him that may be used as part of his positive reinforcement plan. This plan will be discussed with Gwen, and a mutually agreed-upon plan will be implemented.

JP thrives on movement, and movement breaks should be included in his plan. After 15 minutes, allow him a movement break if he appears to need it. This can be incorporated into his positive reinforcement plan.

JP does better when he has a piece of candy in his mouth or is chewing on gum. This is especially important when he is receiving directions. JP is to keep candy and gum in his mouth; make this a part of his rules.

I agree to the above-listed behavior management techniques. I understand that they will be implemented in all TR programs that I attend or my child attends. Any change to the plan will be made by the TR staff in conjunction with the parent/guardian and the participant or participant's behaviorist, if applicable.

Participant signature: _____ Date: _____

Parent or guardian signature: _____ Date: _____

TR manager signature: _____ Date: _____

Figure 10.4 Positive Behavior Support Plan *(continued)*.

encourage them to address issues in the present, and help them see how their feelings affect their behaviors. Conflict can be used positively as the members learn new skills and behaviors through the process of conflict resolution. The group can become more cohesive as a result.

As the experience phase draws to a close, either because time is running out or the group activities for the session are coming to an end, the TRS has fulfilled the functions of TR leadership. He has interacted with the clients in order to help them to engage in the actions of the group experience. He has addressed each member of the group by being welcoming, giving instructions and assistance as needed, and providing feedback directed toward the client's goals. Finally he debriefs the clients to reinforce the carryover value of what they have accomplished in TR.

DEBRIEFING

Debriefing, as discussed in chapter 7, is a process that supports the client's ability to reflect on the experiences of the group, on what he has learned in the group, and on how he will use what he has learned. Debriefing should occur toward the end of every session. To debrief, the TRS asks the members a series of questions that focus on what the purpose and goals of the group were, what went on during the group, how the members feel as a result of the experiences, and what specifically they have learned. The TRS prompts the group members to consider how they can use what they learned in other situations. This sharing of experiences with the TRS and other group members is also an opportunity to promote cohesion and interdependence among and between group members. The TRS can identify and reinforce, through discussion and feedback, the positive changes that members have made in the group.

If this is the final session of a program, the TRS can facilitate closure for the group members by encouraging them to evaluate the overall group experience. He may provide additional resources and materials to support the members' newly developed skills and insights. For example, in a leisure education group with clients in substance abuse treatment, the TRS facilitates the final session by asking the clients to identify five positive things they have learned to do to cope with stress. Clients can respond by identifying some of the strategies talked about in the group, such as taking a walk, attending an exercise class, listening to relaxing music, painting, or journaling. The clients provide

feedback to the TRS on the usefulness of the group, particular activities that were especially helpful, and their plans to incorporate the benefits of this group in their lives. They also have created a resource list to use after discharge with specific information on programs available in the community. The group could also practice calling the local YMCA, gym, or another organization to find out about exercise classes or go on the Internet to seek out additional programs.

As part of the last session of an art group for the same clients, the TRS asked the group members each to create two collages about their inpatient experience. For the first collage, he asked them to cut out pictures and words from magazines to produce a visual representation of their feelings when they first entered the facility. Using the same materials, the members then created a second collage that showed how they saw themselves now as they were about to be discharged. Once the collages were completed, the TRS asked the members to share them with the group, discuss the changes in their feelings, and talk about why they thought those changes occurred. He encouraged the group members to bring the collages home as a reminder of their treatment experience. Group members also offered each other encouragement and discussed how they could cope in healthy ways with the pressures and stress of the outside world.

Wrap-Up Phase

As with the beginning of the group, the wrap-up or send-off plays a significant role in how clients interpret the group experience and the meaning it holds for them. Whether this is an ongoing group or one that meets for a limited number of sessions, wrapping up the group involves a specific set of actions on the part of the TRS. The TRS informs the clients that the group is drawing to a close. Ample time should be left at the end of each session for the TRS to

- summarize the key points of the session;
- identify homework or assignments for members to complete for the next session;
- provide comments on what to look forward to in the next session;
- provide feedback and one last opportunity for clients to discuss or ask questions about the experience;
- provide contact information so that group members can connect with the leader between sessions

in case they have any concerns or find themselves upset about the session;

● have members assist with room cleanup when appropriate;

● make sure all completed projects are labeled and placed in a safe location; and

● make sure there is a plan to escort clients to their next session, meal, or room or provide additional transportation after the session if needed.

After the group program is over, the TRS has the responsibility for

● seeing that clients get to their next destination,

● cleaning up after the program,

● evaluation,

● documentation, and

● preparation for the next session.

The TRS also reports to the team and follows up with clients' families, as appropriate.

ESCORTING CLIENTS FROM THE GROUP

The TRS is responsible for ensuring the safe and prompt return of clients to their designated locations. Once the session is over, some clients may need to be escorted or accompanied back to their rooms, to meals, or other treatments or locations in the facility or may need outside transportation to return home. If a client does not arrive promptly at the next location, the client may miss medications, be late for a meal or visitors, or have to wait until later to get ready for bed because the shift is changing and staff are not available to provide assistance. These challenges are exacerbated after evening or weekend programs when staff availability may be more limited. For a client who is struggling with an acquired disability, learning how to meet his basic needs is very important. A client who is recovering from a stroke and needs assistance with toileting, dressing, and bathing can become anxious if he returns to his room too late after an evening program and has to wait because of a shift change for an aide to help him get ready for bed. If a group session goes over its allotted time, a client may miss the bus and have to wait additional time to return home. These situations could result in a client's not coming back to the group even if he enjoyed it or wants to return.

CLEANUP

Whenever the TRS conducts a group, either large or small, cleaning up after the activity is required.

Cleaning up after arts and crafts, cooking, or a group discussion is different than cleaning up after a basketball game or a special event. Cleanup may include storing and reorganizing supplies, storing leftover food, washing or disinfecting materials, wiping down furniture and equipment, rearranging furniture, sweeping floors, or calling the housekeeping or maintenance department to come in and take care of heavy cleaning. Whenever possible, have the group participants take responsibility for helping with cleaning up as part of the session wrap-up. Make sure that any materials to be saved for specific clients for the following session are marked with the clients' names and stored safely. Completed projects, pictures, or written stories may be collected for display. Additional supplies may need to be ordered. While completing these tasks, the TRS is already in the process of planning for the next session or group, and the process begins again.

Evaluation of the Group

The TRS completes the individual TR session evaluation form (see figure 10.1 on page 306), indicating who attended, any changes in the original plan, the effects of these changes, and any recommendations for the next session or group. Briefly evaluating the session as soon as possible after the program ends will prevent the TRS from forgetting anything that may need to be dealt with for the next session. The activity might have been too easy or too difficult. Maybe the room was unusually hot, there was an out trip that day and attendance was low because some clients chose to go on the trip, there weren't enough supplies, or there was a problem in escorting clients. Serious medical or risk management problems may have occurred. Perhaps a group member had an allergic reaction or a seizure or injury due to misuse of supplies. The TRS may need to fill out an incident report and carefully follow all agency policies. All information should be recorded and reviewed so that needed revisions can be made for the next session.

Documenting Clients' Progress

Documenting the clients' progress may occur after the group has ended, depending on the policies of the agency. While different types of agencies have specific requirements regarding how often progress notes are to be written and what should be included, any unusual behavior should be recorded and reported in a timely fashion. Regardless of the documentation schedule, the TRS should make notes on clients' behaviors and progress to include in the formal progress notes. Some agencies even provide PDAs (personal digital assistants) so that the TRS may document the clients' experience as soon as possible after the group has concluded. The TRS also may keep a notebook or use a section on an individual session planning form to write notes. These notes are confidential and should not be left in the open or unattended. The TRS then uses or refers to these notes when documenting progress.

Reporting to the Team

One of the responsibilities of the TRS is to report on clients' progress at regularly scheduled team or care plan meetings, depending on the agency. She should review notes before the meeting and base reporting on how the client's participation related to his goals. If a client participated in cooking group, it is not adequate to report that Charles cooked today. Instead the report should specify that he attended cooking class to work on the goal of improving his social skills, and should provide details. For example, Charles may have discussed recipes with the other clients, responded to questions when asked, and in return initiated conversation with the TRS and the other group members. He may have made plans to attend the concert the next day with another member. If anything untoward occurred in the group, such as a change in a client's behavior as in the example of Mrs. Kelly earlier in the chapter, it should be reported to other members of the team or to other professionals such as the psychologist or neurologist.

Follow-Up With Clients and Family

After the group session, the TRS may follow up with some of the clients to discuss their behaviors or progress in the group. These conversations may be at the request of either the TRS or the client and should be documented. If the TRS promises to meet with a client, she is ethically obligated to do so within a reasonable period of time or at the appointed time. If the TRS is advised by the team not to have the meeting or has to cancel for any reason, she must be sure to notify the client with a reasonable explanation. If a client's behavior has been problematic, it is important to speak to him as close to the time of the behavior as possible and to apply consequences in an appropriate time period. A client may be concerned about relationships with other group members, and the TRS must also remember to safeguard confidentiality of all group members. In addition, family members may ask about the client's progress. The TRS must obtain permission from the client to speak to a family member about her progress unless she is under the age of 18 or the family member is the legal guardian. One must always consider client confidentiality and make every effort to ensure that appropriate approvals have been obtained before speaking to anyone other than the client or members of the team about the client's progress.

ETHICAL PRACTICE

The TRS's ethical responsibility is to be competent in providing TR group leadership. The TRS must protect the welfare of the clients in the group, ensuring their safety and privacy. The TRS is honest in providing accurate information about the TR program to the clients. She must be fair and equitable, ensuring that each client receives the attention and assistance he needs. The TRS promotes the core TR value of autonomy, encouraging and supporting clients' choices and decisions related to TR group participation. She endeavors to make each program a fun and beneficial activity for participants. The TRS collaborates with other team members and cooperates with clients' families.

Now the TRS has completed the full cycle of professional actions involved in creating and implementing a successful TR program by providing TR leadership. Therapeutic recreation leadership of TR groups entails creating a supportive and trusting environment. The TRS uses communication skills to develop a connectedness between and among members. Through asking questions, making linkages between members and concepts, and providing positive feedback, the TRS fosters cohesion leading to a successful group experience.

• Summary •

In this chapter we have examined how the TRS provides TR leadership to groups. Groups are the primary setting for the delivery of TR services. The TR group experience in and of itself, apart from the specific TR program, has benefits for clients as they interact with others with whom they share common concerns. Understanding TR leadership in the context of the TR models, applying the theories of group development, knowing the characteristics of groups, and demonstrating cultural competence are the ethical obligations of the TRS. The TRS should be well prepared with the knowledge and methods needed to conduct the wide range of programming in the TR toolkit. The TRS utilizes facilitation techniques and instructional strategies to maximize the benefits of the group experience and help clients achieve outcomes. At times the TRS will encounter disruptive behavior in the group arising from conflicts.

Conflicts are part of every group's development and when managed successfully can help to enhance the growth and success of the group. By processing and debriefing with the group, the TRS helps the group members reflect on their experience and its benefits, assess their own progress toward their goals, and integrate these experiences into their everyday lives. Wrapping up the group is an equally important phase of group implementation. It brings closure to the experience and ensures the safety of the participants and the environment. The TRS can apply many of the TR group leadership principles to one-to-one TR programming, which will be discussed in the next chapter.

• Learning Activities •

1. Review the TR group leadership styles. How comfortable are you in providing authoritarian, democratic, and laissez-faire leadership?

2. Select a group that you are a member of. Which stage of group development is the group in? Analyze the group leader's leadership style. What behaviors does the group leader demonstrate that have a positive influence on the group's progress? Does the leader demonstrate any behaviors that negatively affect the group members?

3. Observe a TR group. Write a set of rules for the group.

4. In a small group, design a TR group program including group membership, scheduling, materials, and staffing considerations. Write a welcome similar to the one used by Stuart, the TRS in the chapter. Select an icebreaker and participate in it with your group.

5. With a small group, conduct either an arts and crafts, exercise, or discussion group or another activity of your choice. Practice giving directions, providing feedback, and debriefing the group. Have two members simulate a conflict. What strategies could you use to minimize the disruption they cause? After the group activity, have the members discuss your performance as a leader.

6. Review the example of Rosa in the chapter and write down your "observations" based on her performance during the softball session described. What would you report to the team about her participation and progress?

7. Make a video or film clip of yourself leading a group. Evaluate your TR leadership skills according to the behaviors described in the chapter. What do you conclude about your TR leadership ability? What are your strengths, and what areas do you need to improve?

8. Obtain copies of catalogs of crafts, games, and sporting goods. Given a budget of $500, prepare an order for a summer camp program for 25 children with developmental disabilities. With a budget of $1,000, prepare an order for a nursing home of 200 residents. Draw up an order for a adult day program for behavioral health for a six-month period.

One-to-One Therapeutic Recreation Service

In this chapter you will learn about:

- The purpose and benefits of one-to-one TR programming
- Different settings for one-to-one TR programs
- Appropriate TR practice models for each setting
- One-to-one TR program ideas
- The TRS's interaction style during one-to-ones
- Guidelines for the use of touch
- Ethical issues that may arise in the delivery of one-to-one programming
- In-home or home-based TR services
- Private practice TR

Providing **one-to-one programs** can be among the most meaningful and professionally satisfying experiences for a TR professional. In a one-to-one program, the TRS works with an individual rather than with a group. By working closely with one person, a TRS can provide focused interventions because the program is tailored to only one's client's personal needs and interests. One-to-one programs, commonly known as one-to-ones, at times may be more effective than group programs in producing both a meaningful experience for the client and the desired treatment outcomes.

Interest in one-to-ones is growing in both institutional and community-based TR programs. This chapter examines the settings in which the TRS can provide one-to-one programming. These settings include long-term care, hospice, assisted living, residential settings for people with mental health and substance abuse concerns, group homes for people with developmental disabilities, rehabilitation hospitals, and home-based settings. We outline specific needs of clients in each setting that would make one-to-ones a suitable option and present a suggested TR practice model, guidelines for TR leadership, suggested activities, and any risk management and ethical issues particular to the setting. One-to-ones can be offered to those who are restricted to their beds, are unable (due to physical or behavioral factors) to join a group, are unwilling to participate in a group, or would benefit more from individual attention. One-to-ones are also a way to provide a special form of caring and attention to a person who may be lonely or shy, without family and friends, or otherwise isolated. One-to-ones reinforce the current Centers for Medicare and Medicaid Services guideline "to see the person in the patient" and reflect person-centered planning.

Clients in community settings also can benefit from one-to-ones, which provide them with opportunities to learn and apply new skills, as well as experience recreation, in their natural or typical environment. Providing TR in the context of the client's home environment enhances learning as the client practices new behaviors in the real world. Positive outcomes also may be more readily achievable due to the individualized attention from the TRS, particularly when an individual has cognitive impairments (Homes & MacNeil, 1995).

GENERAL GUIDELINES FOR ONE-TO-ONE TR

When deciding to provide TR to a client in an individual or a group format, the TRS needs to determine which format would best meet the client's needs and preferences in the given setting. She must take into consideration the feasibility and practicality of conducting an activity on a one-to-one basis. For certain clients, such as those confined to bed, one-to-ones may be the only viable option. For others for whom the one-to-one would be the most suitable format, the TRS may need to justify the allocation of resources to one individual rather than a group. Ethical principles of fairness, justice, and competence can help guide the TRS's decision making. The TRS should have a thorough understanding of why one-to-one is the most appropriate programming option and how best to implement it, and should articulate this reasoning to administration and the team if necessary. The TRS serves as an advocate for the most appropriate TR services for the client.

Providing TR leadership in a one-to-one format has some distinctive features. The TRS's full and undivided attention is focused on helping a single individual to achieve meaningful outcomes. Interaction is ongoing and continuous, requiring maturity, competence, patience, and an understanding of boundary issues as discussed in chapter 4. The TRS may be in a private space with the client and has to be sure that her actions are not misinterpreted as having inappropriate personal meaning for the client. The TRS herself must engage in self-monitoring so as not become overly emotionally involved as a result of the close working relationship. The highest standards of ethical behavior are paramount. Nonetheless the quality of the relationship between the TRS and the client can enhance the progress the client makes, and the TRS can take deep satisfaction from the success of her efforts, which may be more obvious than with a group program.

LONG-TERM CARE SETTINGS

Long-term care facilities are frequently settings for one-to-one programming. According to federal regulations, every resident of a nursing home is to be offered appropriate and meaningful activities to participate in even if she is nonresponsive, is restricted to bed, or has behaviors that make group participation unrealistic. The TRS who provides one-to-one programs at bedside may be working with a range of residents, from those who are alert but physically very limited, to those who are ventilator dependent, to individuals in semivegetative states (comas). Each one is capable of receiving services, even if not actively participating on an obvious level. The TRS in this situation draws greatly upon her creativity, patience, and compassion in order to conduct meaningful programs that demonstrate respect for the person. Because of the strong emphasis on quality of life in long-term care, we will choose the TR Outcome Model (Carter et al., 2003) for one-to-ones in this setting. In this model, the TRS focuses on improving health status and functioning in order to achieve a higher level of quality of life. Although physical health does not improve for many residents in long-term care, spiritual, emotional, and **social health** can be addressed to improve quality of life, according to the Outcome Model.

Nursing Homes

Nursing homes are one type of long-term care setting. Typically serving geriatric residents, some nursing homes have units of younger residents who may have AIDS, multiple sclerosis, or traumatic brain injury. Planning a one-to-one in a nursing home requires reviewing the client's chart for information on her specific health problems and the contraindications to participation in different types of activities. Physical pain, allergies, movement restrictions, and degree of cognitive orientation are areas that may affect participation.

moodboard - Fotolia

Providing one-to-one programs can be among the most meaningful and professionally satisfying experiences for a TR professional.

THERAPEUTIC RECREATION LEADERSHIP APPLIED

When beginning a one-to-one with a resident in bed, concern for protecting her privacy should be paramount. Be sure the timing of your visit is convenient and does not conflict with activities of daily living (ADLs). Inform the nursing staff that you will be starting the activity so that interruptions are minimal. If the resident has a roommate, determine if the one-to-one needs to be timed for when the roommate is out of the room or rescheduled if the roommate's presence is a barrier to providing the activity.

The TRS doing a one-to-one at bedside has entered the personal space of the resident. When you enter the resident's room, knock on the door, ring a little bell, or provide some other type of audible signal of your presence. All interactions should begin with a warm greeting. Introduce yourself every time, and state why you are there—for example, "Hello, Mrs. Garcia. This is Stuart, the TR specialist. May I come in? How are you feeling today? I'd like to spend some time with you. I thought we could listen to music and look at some pictures." Of course, give her time to respond! Whether or not the staff knows if the resident can hear or comprehend, always act as if she can. Hearing is the last of the five senses that a person loses; people who have come out of comas have reported that they heard what was being said while they were in the coma. On the other hand, if the person has a visual impairment, you may need to touch her to get her attention. Show respect for her privacy and possessions by asking if it is all right to move a chair or an object on a nightstand. Describe what you are doing if she cannot see you or seems confused: "I'm going to place some of the things I brought with me today on the table over your bed and pull up this chair so I can sit beside you. I'd like to play you some music on this CD player." Or, "I brought some poetry to read to you. Last week you told me you enjoyed modern poetry. This is a new collection I found in the library."

SENSORY STIMULATION ACTIVITIES

Bedside interventions can include **sensory stimulation**, storytelling, humor therapy, games, crafts, horticulture, and virtually anything that space and safety can accommodate. Sensory stimulation is often provided because even residents who appear nonresponsive may be aware of the stimuli, and those who can respond may enjoy and benefit from the sensations. One sense at a time may be stimulated or a combination. Sensory stimulation may be used to try to provoke responses, which may reduce the severity and duration of a coma, and to reactivate senses that have become dulled from illness or lack of use. Therapeutic recreation specialists should carefully record the stimulus provided and observe the response exhibited by the resident (such as movement of a body part, eye movements, changes in breathing patterns, facial expressions). Observe if the resident seems pleased or uncomfortable. The goal is not to provoke a negative reaction unless this has been agreed upon by the treatment team.

Auditory and Visual Stimulation

Forms of auditory stimulus include playing music or singing; reading aloud from stories, poems, letters, or other texts; telling jokes; and using a sound machine, bells, or chimes. Sounds that incorporate a resident's former interests may be stimulating,

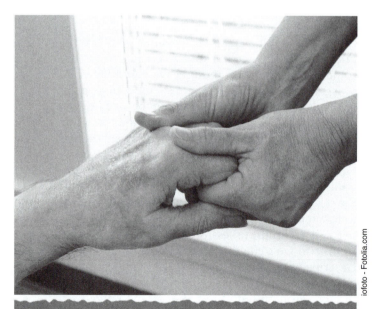

In a one-to-one, the TRS can show concern and caring through touch.

such as the sound of a nail being hammered for a woodworker, or applause for a performer. These can be recorded or produced live by the TRS. Visual stimulation should also be provided. Objects with bright, contrasting colors can be held up and moved in and out of the resident's visual field. A mirror or any object or picture that is colorful can be used. Images can be abstract or realistic. The TRS can describe the sounds and sights to the resident as he presents each one, allow time for the resident to experience the stimuli, and then state what just happened. "Mrs. Garcia, I see you moving your eyes to look at these bright pictures. That helps you look in different directions." In this way, the TRS motivates and gives feedback to the resident.

An unexpected visitor often means the end of the one-to-one. Always thank the resident for allowing you to share this time with her in her room, reiterate what you did and how she responded, and express your pleasure with her reactions, giving her specific examples as feedback. You might say, "Mrs. Garcia, it's time for me to leave. I enjoyed being with you and I'm pleased that you were able to recognize so many of the aromas and fabrics. I will see you tomorrow. Would you like me to bring some music to play for you? I know you like jazz and Broadway show tunes. Thank you for letting me come visit. See you tomorrow." In giving this feedback to clients, remember not to patronize. It's not what you say, but how you say it, that conveys respect for people's autonomy and accomplishments.

Stimulating Taste and Smell

The sense of taste can also be stimulated, but not with a resident who cannot give informed consent, as this is an invasive action in the mouth. For a resident who wishes to taste different flavors and feel different textures, the dietitian should provide input about what type of food would be acceptable given dietary restrictions and chewing and swallowing capacity. Jello, ice cream, yogurt, pudding, and mashed potatoes are soft and can provide a variety of flavor and temperature sensations. Care must be taken so the food is not too hot or too cold. Elderly people are more sensitive to temperatures than younger populations. Stimulating the sense of smell, however, is a popular form of sensory stimulation. Aromatherapy, incense, scented candles, floral sprays, and essential oils put in a diffuser, have become popular. (Essential oils should never be put directly on someone's skin). Items with particular smells, such as soaps, foods, spices, and flowers, can be held progressively closer to the resident's nose until she responds. Favorite perfumes and colognes can be offered. Less pleasing odors such as vinegar

Preparation and Procedures
for Aromatherapy and Hand Massage

Preparation for the TRS:

- Dress suitably in comfortable but professional-looking clothing such as slacks and lightweight tops that are not revealing. Tops with full-length, tightly fitting sleeves are preferred.
- Wash your hands prior to the session. Fingernails should be trimmed short and unpainted. The use of hand cream to soften the hands is advised.
- Remove all jewelry from your hands and wrists, as well as long necklaces and dangling earrings.
- Have long hair tied back to avoid inadvertent contact with the client.
- Bring clean towels; large and small pillows for support and positioning of the wrist, arm, and back; essential oils and diffuser; latex and nonlatex gloves; and any other supplies that may create a soothing environment (e.g., music, colored lightbulb).

Preparation of the environment:

- The room should be warm and airy, have good ventilation, and be large enough not to feel crowded.
- The door should be closed to ensure privacy, provided that this is consistent with facility guidelines and acceptable to the client.
- Televisions, radios, phones, and PDAs should be turned off to avoid interruptions.
- Lights should be dimmed.
- A "Do not disturb; session in progress" sign should be posted and staff informed.

Procedures:

- Make sure that the client is comfortable (warm enough, in a comfortable position; place pillows for support as needed).
- To get ready to perform hand massage, you should
  - be positioned comfortably in your seat, using good posture to avoid backache and fatigue;
  - sit facing the client with your chair on the client's left side;
  - avoid any contact with the client's body except the hands and arms;
  - perform hand exercises for strength, flexibility, relaxation, and sensitivity;
  - put on gloves, if required, for universal precautions; and
  - take a minute to breathe deeply and slowly.
- Use the client's own brand of hand lotion or cream to avoid allergic reactions.
- Support the client's wrist at all times (use pillow).
- Administer massage.
- Give the client 2-minute notice of conclusion of massage.
- Allow the client to rest for several minutes before restoring the original environment.

Adapted, by permission, from R. Kunstler, F. Greenblatt, and N. Moreno, 2004, "Aromatherapy and hand massage: Therapeutic recreation interventions for chronic pain," *Therapeutic Recreation Journal* 38(2): 133-147.

might be introduced. The sense of smell and taste lose their acuity as we age, much as with hearing and vision, so stronger scents may be necessary to provoke a response. The TRS must be aware of any allergies the client has to certain foods or odors so as not to trigger an allergic reaction.

Sense of Touch

The sense of touch is often neglected, especially for residents in long-term care, who may receive little in the way of caring touch while they are bathed, dressed, fed, and moved from one position to another. In a one-to-one, the TRS can show concern and caring through touch. Materials with different textures can be used to stimulate the sense of touch. Fabrics, feathers, and objects made of metal (or stone or smooth wood), even jewelry, can be applied to the resident's hand or forearm. The TRS can gently stroke the resident's cheek with a soft powder puff or piece of velvet. The TRS must determine if the client is allergic to feathers, wool, or other fabrics. Hand massage is a gentle and relaxing technique that TRSs can learn in a reasonable period of time. Even rubbing someone's hands with lotion is a simple form of massage. More intense massage or massaging other parts of the body requires specialized training. Stimulating more than one sense at a time can be very beneficial. The TRS can use an aromatherapy diffuser, apply a scented hand lotion, and play music all at the same time to provide both sensory stimulation and a pleasant experience. Using the client's own lotions will reduce the risk of an allergic reaction. For those who are medically cleared, animal-assisted therapy can be highly effective. Many long-term care facilities have resident pets that make bedside visits. The TRS can place a cat or small dog on a person's lap and physically guide the client's hand to pet the animal if needed. Listening to a bird chirp or watching goldfish in a bowl are other animal-related activities that stimulate the senses and also may be calming to the resident.

The Issue of Touch

Touch is a sensitive subject. Several forms of touch can occur between a client and the TRS. Touch may be (McNeil-Haber, 2004):

- accidental when two people come in contact (e.g., bumping into each another),
- used to get someone's attention (e.g., tugging on an arm),
- socially sanctioned (a handshake),
- an expression of a relationship (a hug), or
- used for therapeutic purposes (massage).

Touch between the TRS and the client can be very natural and positive when it is based on the client's needs and meets the criteria (Swade, Bayne & Horton, 2006) described. Certain cultures are comfortable with touch. On the other hand, some people may be very uncomfortable with being touched for reasons other than assistance with ADLs or by nonfamily members. A resident may have cultural proscriptions against being touched by a nonfamily member or a person of the opposite sex. *You should ask clients first if it is permissible for you to touch them.* You must also keep in mind that if you touch a patient appropriately during a TR session, the patient may feel comfortable touching you at another time. Touch can also be misinterpreted as sexual rather than therapeutic. As the TRS you must monitor yourself carefully so as not to send a mixed message, however unintentionally. Explaining what you are doing and why will help guard against misunderstandings. Nursing home residents may be confused and not always be in control of their behaviors. It is imperative to treat them respectfully. If a resident touches the TRS inappropriately, the TRS should say firmly, "No, that is not appropriate behavior. You cannot touch me that way."

It is an ethical responsibility of professionals to bring up issues of appropriate and inappropriate touching with administrative and clinical staff. A facility's ethics committee can take the leadership on this issue. Facilities should develop and implement policies and staff training related to sexual

Criteria for the Use of Touch

The client has consent, control, and choice over all aspects of touch.

The TRS and client engage in an open and detailed discussion, appropriate to the level of the client's comprehension, about touching and associated issues such as relationship boundaries.

Touch is congruent with the level of TRS–client intimacy.

Client's needs as perceived by the client are of primary importance.

The TRS is comfortable with touching.

The touch is authentic.

issues and needs of residents, the ways in which these needs and behaviors are to be addressed, and appropriate and respectful responses to inappropriate statements and gestures. Although the subject of sexual needs and behaviors makes some staff members uncomfortable, which can result in jokes and remarks that demean the resident, sexuality is a component of human functioning and deserving of attention. **Sexual assessments** to determine residents' needs and interests in this area, and to develop a plan to help them meet their needs appropriately and privately, are now a component of nursing assessments in long-term care (Wallace, 2008). There are also residents who may be aware of and offended by the inappropriate behavior of others, and they too can benefit from guidance on how to respond. The residents' council could also be involved. Nevertheless, most people can be touched with no sexual connotations. Hand massage is a good example of touch that is generally considered acceptable.

ADDITIONAL PROGRAMMING OPTIONS

For a resident who is confined to bed and alert, whether confused or not, there are many additional options. Conversation or discussion can be tailored to the resident's interests, past or present. Reminiscence incorporating objects, pictures, photographs, music, or reading is a staple of both one-to-ones and group programming. The possibilities for one-to-ones are endless:

- Discussing current events, the arts, sports, the activities of the facility, family or other topics; reading and discussing poetry, short stories, the newspaper, and magazines
- Writing letters
- Engaging in relaxation techniques of breathing, guided imagery, and meditation
- Playing games or cards
- Using a laptop computer
- Doing arts and crafts

The TRS may require assistance to position the resident for some of these activities. The resident also should be observed for signs of fatigue or discomfort. Our ethical responsibility is to protect the well-being of our clients and their decisions about participation.

ONE-TO-ONES FOR INDIVIDUALS WHO ARE MOBILE

In addition to the interventions already described with a resident who is confined to bed, one-to-ones

can be successfully implemented with a resident who is sitting up in any type of chair. There are several reasons for doing one-to-ones with a resident who is capable of joining a group:

- Certain activities, such as hand massage, can be done with only one person at a time. Doing these activities in a private area can enhance the relaxation benefits.
- One-to-one attention is beneficial for the resident.
- A one-to-one is more likely to produce an outcome because the TRS's attention is focused only on a single person.
- The TRS can make immediate modifications of the activity in order to meet the individual's assessed and expressed preferences and needs without having to consider the impact of changes in the program on other clients.
- By helping a resident become more comfortable interacting with one other person at a time, a one-to-one can also be used as a step toward getting people out of their rooms or helping them become more social with group members. This is apart from the use of one-to-ones during temporary confinement to maintain residents' level of participation in TR.

Hospice

Residents in long-term care settings may be on a hospice unit or receiving **hospice** services because they are dying. When hospice is provided in a facility, as opposed to an individual's own home, services are offered in the last few months of life. Although a client may be dying, as a member of the hospice care team the TRS has a significant role in addressing quality of life issues. The key application of the TR Outcome Model in hospice care is improving spiritual health by helping the dying person feel a sense of peace and comfort at this stage of life. A number of one-to-one interventions can be offered to hospice patients depending on their physical functioning, level of cognition, and interest. A calming presence, aromatherapy, gentle massage, reading, playing music, journaling or writing a letter for the patient, animal-assisted therapy, or conversation may all provide comfort. Horticultural therapy also has been used with excellent results, both to reinforce a dying person's sense of identity through participation in a former interest and to promote social interaction with the TRS (Sourby, 1998). **Legacy building**, in which the TRS helps the client create something that expresses his feelings and wishes to his family and loved ones, is being recognized as a very worthwhile activity to offer in the hospice setting. It can take the form of a letter, a poem, a picture, a plant, a CD, or any other item. The TRS should be sensitive to the moods and needs of the individual and family members, which may be unspoken and require intuitive understanding. All should be treated with respect and compassion at this challenging time.

A wonderful example of a hospice intervention in a long-term care facility is the CARE cart (Listokin, 2003). CARE stands for Comforting Alternatives for a Relaxing Environment. A beautiful wooden cabinet with a noninstitutional look was built on wheels so that it could be moved easily around the facility. It is filled with scented candles, inspirational readings, CDs of soothing music, candies, a blank journal and pens, and hand creams. There are also meal tickets for the family and information about where to get free coffee in the facility. A family member, resident, or staffperson can ask to have the CARE cart placed in the room of a resident who is on hospice or receiving palliative care. Anyone can then use the contents, including the TRS conducting a one-to-one with the resident. The CARE cart contributes to quality of life as the resident's and family's emotional and spiritual needs are attended to. Staff may use the CARE cart as they share in the emotional experience of hospice.

ETHICAL PRACTICE

Residents in nursing homes can derive substantial benefits from one-to-one TR programming. As an ethical practice, one-to-ones contribute to the well-being of residents, afford them privacy in treatment, and allow them autonomy by giving them more control during their TR sessions. In this type of program format the TRS may use more of her therapist skills than her recreation leadership skills, thereby maximizing residents' accomplishment of their goals. But while the TRS may believe that one-to-ones are a fair and just allocation of resources to meet residents' needs, she may have to justify them to administration. One-to-one programs are shorter than group programs and do not require escorting a large number of residents to a group setting. This time savings may help the TRS obtain permission to offer more one-to-one programming.

Assisted Living Facilities

Assisted living is a form of congregate housing in which older adults can have a private room, studio, or one-bedroom apartment, some with modified kitchen facilities, with 24-hour supervision (Voelkl & Aybar-Damali, 2008) and all meals and snacks. Residents can bring their own furnishings

and belongings to make their room or apartment more familiar and more similar to their own home (McGuire, Boyd & Tedrick, 2009). Health-related services, recreation and social activities, transportation, personal services such as laundry and housekeeping, and assistance with ADLs are typically provided. Assisted living facilities are sometimes affiliated with a nursing home to provide a smooth continuum of care for older adults and minimize the need to move as their health care needs become more complex. Of primary importance in this setting is maximizing the dignity, autonomy, privacy, independence, choice, safety, and family and community involvement of residents (McGuire et al., 2009). Assisted living facilities tend to provide a full schedule of daily activities and a variety of spaces for programming, including crafts, fitness, cooking, socializing, and outdoor activities, as well as transportation for outings and shopping trips. A recent trend in assisted living is specialty units for people with memory loss. Although one-to-ones would not be offered in assisted living as a rule, a TRS also working on the specialty unit may have the opportunity to do one-to-one programming to provide cognitive stimulation, physical exercise, socialization, and creative expression. These facilities also represent an option for private practice, which is discussed later in the chapter.

ETHICAL PRACTICE

The TRS should be aware that most assisted living facilities do not receive third-party reimbursements and that residents or their families are paying for the housing and care. Family involvement and financial resources may contribute to more creative and expanded programming. The TRS may be able to collaborate successfully with family members to enhance services. However, the family may have expectations for individually tailored services that the TRS must balance against the needs of all the residents.

ADULT HOUSING OPTIONS

There are several other types of residential settings for clients based on their disabilities or needs. These include housing for clients with behavioral health issues, such as substance abuse and psychiatric disabilities; supportive apartments for clients with AIDS; and group homes for individuals with developmental disabilities. All are settings where one-to-one TR services can be offered effectively. The major benefit of one-to-one TR programming for the client in a residential setting is that he receives an individually designed intervention, tailored to his specific needs, in order to improve functioning and skills for inclusive living and enhanced quality of life.

Housing for People With Behavioral Health Issues

In residential housing for people with behavioral health problems such as substance abuse and psychiatric conditions, TR may follow the OLH-TR Model (Wilhite et al., 1999). An important component of the OLH-TR model is that the client's health status and needs, and therefore the types of services he requires, will change over the course of his life. In this model, the TRS works with the client at different points in time to help him cope with and adapt to these changes. The TRS uses more of her therapist skills than recreation leadership skills. For this reason, the one-to-one format may be the most useful one for TR services in this situation. Carrying out the TR process in this setting will differ somewhat from what occurs in the institutional setting. The TRS could begin the process by asking the client what his goals are in order to assess which skills he has and which he needs to develop in order to meet his own goals. Typically, assessment precedes goal setting in the TR process. But here, starting with goal setting reinforces client autonomy, an important outcome for many clients as they try to readjust to community living.

In addition to assessing the traditional areas of interests and skills, it is useful to find out the client's negative triggers: what people, places, and things in the environment may produce stress or difficulty coping. Planning may need to take into account these negative triggers, fatigue levels, medication regimens, sudden mood changes, and other factors that can affect the client's participation (Kunstler, 2004a). For example, the client may need to rest more frequently, eat healthier foods, avoid certain acquaintances, make a daily schedule, and practice a relaxation activity in order to maintain healthy functioning. Implementing TR in the client's usual range of environments will help him to learn and apply new behaviors in the actual settings where he needs to cope successfully. As part of evaluation, the TRS should ask the client what he considers successful progress. It's important that the client learn to articulate for himself what his achievements have been and what behaviors helped him to attain them. Both the TRS and the client should evaluate the effectiveness of the TR program in helping him reach his goals.

LEISURE EDUCATION

Leisure education, which was discussed in chapter 6, is an ideal program to implement on a one-to-one basis to help a client develop and maintain a healthy lifestyle. Leisure education is a process directed toward developing awareness of the value of leisure, identifying potential leisure interests, learning new leisure skills, and acquiring knowledge of leisure resources and how to use them in order to achieve positive leisure functioning. The TRS working one-to-one with the client can identify the knowledge and skills he needs to effectively utilize the resources of his local community. He may need to find information on resources and facilities, select appropriate clothing to wear for different activities, identify transportation options, budget for the costs of activities, develop activity skills for participation in leisure choices, and learn social skills and ways of handling challenging situations. Individuals recovering from substance abuse may never have interacted positively without the use of drugs. Successful readjustment for this population often involves learning how to socialize with others. The one-to-one format may be a stepping-stone to developing social interaction skills. The TRS can model how to greet, converse with, listen to, question, and compliment another person to help the client learn how to have successful interaction with others. As part of the transition to inclusive participation, the TRS can accompany the client to selected sites. After trying out a variety of recreation alternatives, the TRS can help the client to evaluate possible choices and make and implement decisions about participation. As the client's health status changes over time, he can again utilize the TRS's services in order to select more appropriate recreation choices, learn about needed adaptations and new resources, and implement decisions based on an evaluation of the possible consequences.

Closely related to leisure education is leisure counseling. Although some authors contend that there is little distinction between the two (Austin, 2009), we agree with Stumbo and Peterson (2009) that in fact they have fundamental differences. Leisure education has specific program content, in the areas of leisure awareness, knowledge, skills, and resources, that the TRS provides to the client through TR leadership. On the other hand, leisure counseling, as in other forms of counseling, proceeds from the client's needs, interests, and goals and not from the program content (Stumbo & Peterson, 2009). Leisure counseling is an ideal one-to-one program for qualified TRSs to offer clients whose problems and concerns could be well served

Sample Leisure Education Process

The TRS, Stuart, is working with Sheri, a client in recovery from substance abuse. She lives in a transitional housing setting and needs to develop her leisure interests to support her recovery and healthy lifestyle. Stuart works one-to-one with Sheri, utilizing discussion and paper-and-pencil assessments and visits to local facilities. The four components of the leisure education process he uses can be adapted to any individual, based on her abilities and specific needs.

I. Awareness of leisure and recreation

Stuart begins the leisure education process by asking Sheri to identify experiences when she was having fun, or when she was totally engrossed in an activity. He asks her to describe her feelings at those times. He helps her to see the benefits she derived from these experiences and how these benefits can carry over into other aspects of her life. He and Sheri also discuss how recreation and leisure are perceived and valued by society in general. They might talk about major sporting events, the Olympics, the Academy Awards, Disney World, and other internationally known events and places that mean a great deal to millions of people. He has Sheri complete the Leisure Diagnostic Battery (LDB) to assess her leisure needs, barriers, and preferences.

II. Leisure interests

Stuart works with Sheri to help her identify recreation activities that she would like to pursue. They discuss the benefits of each activity, the skills required to do each one, and the "where, when, with whom, and how much": where will she do it, when will she do it, with whom, and how much it will cost. She completes the State Technical Institute Leisure Activities Project (known as STILAP) activity checklist and identifies physical, cognitive, social, and affective activities of interest. They plan a balanced program of activities that incorporate all the behavioral domains. Sheri chooses working out at the gym, painting, reading, and a book club.

III. Skill development

Once Sheri identifies the activities she would like to pursue, she and Stuart begin to address the needed skills. These include activity skills, time management skills, budgeting, and social skills. In particular, Sheri is concerned with how to deal with frustration during an activity without the use of drugs. Stuart recommends that she learn a stress management technique to use at any point during an activity when she needs to keep herself calm. He reviews a number of different techniques with Sheri and guides her to try out several that appeal to her. On the basis of her responses, she selects diaphragmatic breathing and visualization as techniques that can be done discreetly in public places.

IV. Leisure resources

Sheri is now ready to participate in her leisure activities of choice in the community. She and Stuart visit several facilities, including a local fitness center, the Y, the town recreation department, and the public library. She meets the staff, obtains schedules of programs, and gathers information on cost and registration procedures. She and Stuart draw up a weekly plan of activities with all the relevant information. After the first week of following her plan, Sheri reviews with Stuart what she did, how she felt, what the challenges were, and what her successes were. Stuart offers her support and encourages her to evaluate the various activities she has participated in. Sheri can make decisions about her choices and revise her schedule as desired.

by a counseling approach. Any TRS interested in conducting leisure counseling should have more specialized training in counseling theories, methods, and techniques.

In addition to leisure education, stress management could be successfully implemented on a one-to-one basis in this setting. The TRS can guide the client to identify sources of and responses to stress, explore and practice a range of stress management techniques, and select and utilize effective methods.

Each person should try out the stress management activities that seem appealing and then reflect on their effectiveness.

ETHICAL PRACTICE

Maintaining professional boundaries may be an issue when the therapist is working with adults similar to her in age. The TRS should set clear guidelines of acceptable behavior, conduct herself in a professional and friendly manner, and use ethical

---

Stress Management Activities

Any activity can be used to manage stress if it works for the individual. Some people find that working a crossword puzzle or reading reduces stress; others may prefer physical activity or listening to music. Getting deeply involved in any activity can help a person relax. People should have a few techniques that work for them in different situations. A breathing technique would be good to use in a public place when stress occurs unexpectedly or when someone is getting ready to enter a situation that he knows will be stressful. Engaging in stress-reducing activities on a regular basis is essential to promoting health and managing stress.

The body's natural response to stress is to get moving, hence the value of physical activity:

- Walking, jogging, hiking, running
- Biking, in-line skating, ice skating
- Dancing, tai chi, yoga, aerobics
- Weightlifting, martial arts, swimming
- Basketball, tennis, Ping-Pong

Relaxing, soothing activities:

- Listening to music, aromatherapy, massage
- Meditation, deep breathing, guided imagery, visualization
- Going to a spa, getting a manicure, sitting by the water
- Writing in a journal

Creative activities:

- Art, cooking, gardening
- Cleaning out closets
- Woodworking, pottery, knitting
- Doing a puzzle, playing solitaire, computer games

Social activities

- Talking to a friend
- Board games
- Dog walking
- Movies

judgment so as not to embarrass a client. "Respecting the subtle boundaries of treatment remains the cornerstone of competent care" (Pies, 2007, p. C5).

Group Homes for Individuals With Developmental Disabilities

Another form of residential housing in which one-to-ones are effective is a group home for individuals with developmental disabilities. This setting is amenable to implementation of the Interaction Model (Howe-Murphy & Charbonneau, 1987), based on the ecological perspective, in which the TRS can both support the efforts of the individual and address the needed changes in the environment to overcome barriers to inclusive community living. An excellent example of implementation of this model using one-to-one intervention was presented in *Therapeutic Recreation Journal* (Hodges et al., 2004). A TRS worked with Bradley, a 55-year-old man with autism, who lived in a group home and decided he would like to retire from his job in a sheltered workshop after 10 years of employment. His concept of retirement was to sit on the porch and read, as his father had done. However, the regulations of the group home required that he be out of the home for 6 hours each weekday.

Through one-to-one TR, Bradley was able to identify senior centers and various community facilities that had programs of interest to him. The TRS helped him write out questions to ask when he telephoned these places for information. The TRS accompanied him on visits to the sites, helped him select the ones he wanted to attend, taught him how to travel to the centers and how to budget, and helped him develop the appropriate social behaviors for successful participation. She also coordinated his transportation to the senior centers. The TRS gave training to the staff regarding Bradley's needs and interests and suggested strategies for addressing his challenging behaviors. Although this process was lengthy, the TRS was able to provide ongoing support and assistance that resulted in Bradley's successful transition to full retirement. At age 60 he was still participating in his leisure activities, was volunteering, and had revised his perception of what constituted retirement to include engaging in meaningful recreation choices.

ETHICAL PRACTICE

To facilitate inclusion using an ecological approach, the TRS must do more than work solely with the individual client. The role of the TRS in providing one-to-one intervention in a community-based setting is to address the needed changes in the environment. The TRS can provide staff training, ongoing support, and advocacy to expand accessible options, establish networks, and develop resources that promote an inclusive community. From an ethical standpoint, providing training to the senior center staff in the example of Bradley was an application of the principles of well-being and justice. The training was essential to the client's well-being as it ensured that staff understood the most effective means to interact with him. Justice was assured in that Bradley was treated fairly and had access to the resources of his community. Respect was demonstrated for his wishes regarding his vision of retirement. The very positive results of this case support the value of the one-to-one approach. This case also could be an application of the OLH-TR model, as the TRS worked with the client over time to adapt to his changing needs and stage of life.

REHABILITATION SERVICE SETTINGS

Rehabilitation services of several months duration, if not longer, are provided to individuals with physical conditions such as spinal cord injury, amputation, or severe nerve damage; to alleviate the effects of a physical disability; or to assist in recovery from head or traumatic brain injuries (TBI). In an inpatient rehabilitation center, the TRS can address the changes in patients' lifestyles that require adaptations as well as assist them with their readjustment to everyday living in light of their new level of functioning. After a period of inpatient rehabilitation, clients may also receive services on an outpatient basis. The Leisure Ability Model, which addresses three vital purposes of TR (functional intervention, emphasizing therapeutic outcomes; education to develop leisure awareness, skills, and resources; and recreation participation to facilitate inclusion and enhance quality of life), is particularly applicable to an inpatient TBI treatment center. Traumatic brain injury is the result of sudden trauma to the brain.

Traumatic Brain Injury Inpatient Care

The top five causes of TBI are car accidents, bicycle and motorcycle accidents, falls, sport injuries, and acts of violence such as assaults. The number of armed forces personnel who survive with head injuries also has risen rapidly due to advances in medical treatment. While these injuries affect different parts of the brain, resulting in a broad spectrum of symptoms and disabilities, there are some common manifestations. For a client with a TBI, attention span, frustration tolerance, and concentration, among other areas of functioning, may need painstaking intervention on a one-to-one level. Relearning cognitive skills may be especially frustrating for a client due to feelings of irritability and depression and the inability to process stimuli (Lahey, 2001). Therapeutic recreation specialists working with TBI clients must carefully adapt the programming for success-oriented activities and not set the clients up for failure, which can lead to the client's refusing treatment. Cognitive retraining can be a very slow process and requires effort, patience, and commitment on the part of the TRS, as well as collaboration between the TRS and the client. Because of the complex nature of head injuries, rehabilitation requires a considerable amount of time and intensity of intervention (Mobily & MacNeil, 2002). One-to-one recreation can help motivate the client to sustain the degree of involvement necessary to obtain optimal results (Kunstler & Sokoloff, 1993).

In a one-to-one program with a client with a TBI in a rehabilitation center, the TRS should select an activity based on the client's interests and assist him in learning or relearning the steps in the activity (using task analysis to determine at what step in the process the client needs retraining). A simple computer game or word game, such as solving anagrams using cues (Phillips, 1993), involves focusing on making a single move in the game and obtaining a response before proceeding to the next step. In solving anagrams, the client is presented with a five-letter word that is scrambled, such as TMUHO. He needs to move the letters, one at a time, to put them in the correct order to spell the word. If he moves the "H" in front of the "T," the TRS could say "Good try, you're getting there; let's try again." During this process, the TRS continually redirects the client to the activity to overcome his attention deficits, encourages him to withstand the frustration resulting from a wrong move, guides him to process the feedback resulting from the move or selection he has made, and supports him to persevere.

As the client continues to engage in the activity, he redevelops his skills to a level where he can enjoy the game as a form of recreation. He also can relearn the social skills that accompany playing the game, such as asking someone to play, taking turns, and making small talk. The TRS demonstrates and models these skills. In terms of the Leisure Ability Model, the desired outcomes for the client are improvement of cognitive skills (functional intervention), relearning a desired activity (leisure education), and enjoying a recreation experience with preferred leisure partners (recreation participation). The TRS capitalizes on the qualities of recreation to motivate the client to adhere to the treatment program. A TR activity incorporates physical, cognitive, social, and emotional behaviors; therefore it is an ideal vehicle through which the client can integrate all the skills he has been working on during rehabilitation. This sometimes painstaking but rewarding process is enhanced using a one-to-one approach.

ETHICAL PRACTICE

Guidelines for one-to-ones with people with TBI include collaborating not only with the client, as just discussed, but also with the treatment team. Although this is true with all populations, the lengthy and challenging rehabilitation of head injuries is eased with a consistent and interdisciplinary approach to services. The TRS has the responsibility to provide both treatment for the purposes of rehabilitation and a leisure experience to promote quality of life. From the first session, the TRS should build a relationship with the client based on mutual respect, trust, and honesty and should demonstrate a willingness to help the client reach his goals. Working with the client requires patience and empathy for his frustration and slow progress. It is critical that the TRS is nonjudgmental. Clients with head injuries or other illnesses or disabilities may be responsible for their own injuries or may have harmed others through their own actions, such as drunk driving. An ethical responsibility of the TRS is not to let her feelings about these circumstances affect the delivery of TR services.

Another sensitive issue involves boundaries between the TRS and the client. Clients with TBI often experience impairment in judgment that affects their social and sexual behavior. They may misinterpret the TRS's actions as representative of a personal relationship and may lack insight regarding the suitability of their own behaviors. The TRS must handle this firmly and professionally, but in a way that conveys understanding of the client's feelings and his manner of expressing his feelings. Much as with the long-term care setting, rehabilitation centers should have policies and procedures related to addressing the sexual needs and behaviors of clients with respect and consideration. This population is younger than the typical long-term care population; therefore, sexual issues may be more widely recognized, accepted, and addressed as integral to their overall functioning and readjustment. Other specific ethical principles that apply are maintaining confidentiality regarding the client's behaviors and promoting his autonomy in decision making as much as possible.

Physical Rehabilitation Outpatient Care

Despite the intensive physical and occupational therapy that some clients with physical disabilities receive for months or even years, they may not all make adequate progress to return to an optimal level of functioning and quality of life (Kunstler & Sokoloff, 1993). Clients who suffer catastrophic injury and trauma are not always successful in traditional treatment due to multiple physical and emotional problems. They may require intensive intervention, three to five days per week for several hours each day, for very lengthy periods. This level of participation is very demanding, and clients need to be highly motivated to persevere. With complex health problems, a client may become depressed and frustrated and not see any point in continuing treatment. Therapeutic recreation, however, may have several advantages over more typical physical therapy and occupational therapy treatments, as shown in the following example of TR in private practice.

A TRS in private practice, serving clients on an outpatient basis, was able to help five clients resume productive and fulfilling lives utilizing a holistic TR approach (Kunstler & Sokoloff, 1993). Four of the five clients had been in automobile accidents, and one had had a heart attack and brain injury.

TR is uniquely positioned to assist patients recovering from traumatic injury by holistically addressing a variety of needs in a wide range of settings.

AP Photo/David J. Phillip

All five had ambulation problems; three had cognitive deficits such as memory loss; and three had chronic pain. Other problems included depression, sleeplessness, and posttraumatic stress disorder. Each client had received from three months to three years of physical and occupational therapy. But they were unable to make satisfactory progress, and as a last resort they obtained the services of a private TR practitioner. The TRS conducted a comprehensive assessment of their leisure, lifestyle, and health and wellness practices. The goals set for the clients included improving physical functioning and cognitive skills, developing new interests, increasing self-confidence and independence, and decreasing depression. All clients received one-to-one TR services in their homes and the local community, including adapted swimming, walking, weight training, adapted games, arts and crafts, leisure counseling, and planning for community reintegration. All five improved over a 2- to 25-month period in the areas of ambulation, physical conditioning, cognitive skills, and social interaction. Two began attending college and obtained part-time jobs, and four developed new leisure interests.

Perhaps these results could have occurred with any type of treatment of such intensity. Yet TR has unique advantages over other forms of treatment. First, TR takes a holistic approach. In these cases, TR addressed the physical, social, cognitive, and emotional functioning of the clients in their leisure, home, school, and community settings. A client receiving physical therapy may certainly improve physical functioning but may still be depressed and socially isolated, wondering, "OK, now I can walk again. Where can I go?" TR can provide the answer. The second advantage TR has over other treatments is the motivating qualities of the recreation experience that help a person persevere in building skills and increasing functioning. Therapeutic recreation activities are fun, are fulfilling to the person, and reinforce strengths and unique identity. For example, one of the clients was very neglectful of his ADL skills, seeing little reason to maintain personal hygiene. The TRS learned that the client wanted to go swimming in the local pool. To enter the pool, swimmers first have to shower. This client now had a reason to take a shower and perform his ADL skills. This multiple-case study reflects the Self-Determination and Enjoyment Enhancement Model, in which the client becomes motivated to improve skills and functioning as a result of successful participation in personally rewarding recreation. Clients are successful, according to this model, when they are enhancing their self-determination and receiving services in an environment free of distractions (Sylvester et al., 2001), such as a one-to-one setting.

ETHICAL PRACTICE

The TRS conducting a one-to-one with clients in circumstances similar to those just described has to be creative in setting goals and selecting interventions that are meaningful and relevant to the client. The TRS has to be able to break the TR activities down into smaller, achievable steps to give the client hope and let him see early signs of progress. The successful TRS in this setting will give informational and motivational feedback, know when to push the client and when to step back, and use task analysis to teach skills and activities. The ethical principles of autonomy, respect, and well-being are crucial to interacting with the client in a supportive and encouraging manner that promotes his efforts.

IN-HOME AND HOME-BASED SETTINGS

One of the most innovative settings for TR is an individual's own home. In-home services may be provided to people of any age, with any type of illness or disability, including children with a developmental disability, adults in need of physical rehabilitation due to an accident, or elderly individuals in the early stages of Alzheimer's disease or with other limitations accompanying aging. Services provided in the home are usually referred to as "in-home." Because the TRS and the client may leave the home to use the neighborhood resources, these services can be called "home-based." To receive services in one's own home or neighborhood is very helpful to individuals for a number of reasons. Benefits include the convenience, feelings of security and comfort, and opportunity to receive services in familiar surroundings. Typically, nursing care, social services, and physical therapy have been available in the home for individuals rehabilitating from an illness or injury, such as a stroke or hip fracture, or from surgery. Other services offered in the home are hospice services which may include pain management, massage, music therapy, visits from volunteers, and pastoral visits; as well as the traditional nursing and household care. Therapeutic recreation has yet to be widely implemented as an in-home service, but the demand is growing.

Older Adults at Home

The huge growth in the aging population, particularly the baby boomers with their high levels of interest in health, fitness, and many forms of recreation, is a strong indicator that there will be a demand for one-to-one programming in a variety of homelike settings. Life span is extending as well, so that the increasing number of older adults living into their 90s and beyond will also require expanded services, including TR. As people age, there is a strong preference among many to stay in their own homes and comfortable and familiar surroundings. **"Aging in place"** means that as people grow older and health declines they do not have to move from their homes in order to obtain the support services they may need. As people age, they may become more socially isolated, less physically active, confused and forgetful, and unable to care for themselves. Nursing, social services, and housekeeping assistance may be available to address these changes in their lives and allow them to stay in their own homes. In-home TR services for older adults also have been increasing (Kunstler, 2004b) in part due to this trend. There is mounting evidence that when a TRS provides in-home services to aging adults, some of the negative effects of the physical, social, cognitive, and emotional declines of aging can be minimized. Some recent examples demonstrate the effectiveness of professional TR intervention in the home environment (Chow, 2002; Kunstler, 2004b; Stavola Daly, 2002). The Health Protection/Health Promotion Model, with its focus on recreation as a means to overcome threats to health and enhance the optimal health status of participants, can be applied in any setting or with any person who desires to maintain or improve his level of health (Austin, 2001), including the in-home setting for older adults.

Applying the TR process in the home setting has some special features. Unlike the client who is assessed in a health care facility, to which he has been admitted due to sudden illness or a drastic change in functioning, the older adult living at home is probably experiencing a slow decline. What is causing the changes in behavior and lifestyle may be less obvious, and a careful assessment should be used to try to uncover this information. Another critical area to assess is social supports. Are there family, friends, neighbors, visitors, Meals on Wheels deliverers, or home health care aides who come into the home? These people may be significant members of the client's network. Another type of assessment that is becoming standard practice is an environmental assessment. Take an inventory of the space, furniture, equipment, supplies, and objects in the home. What do these tell you about the interests and habits of the client? How can they be incorporated into a meaningful and relevant TR program? There may be a photo album for reminiscence, art that can be discussed, books of poetry to read, plants to be repotted, or a piano stool that needs to be adjusted. In-home TR allows the specialist to be creative in utilizing what is available. However, there may be loved activities that a client can no longer do because of declining functioning. Can these be adapted, or can meaningful alternatives be found? In the home setting, TR resources may be limited to whatever is already available in the home or can be easily transported and stored. Also, are seating, lighting, and ventilation adequate? The outdoor environment can be assessed for use by the client as well. It may be possible to accompany the older adult outside for a walk or to sit in a park. Older adults who are alone or declining physically are fearful of going out alone, which becomes a significant quality of life issue that TR can address.

When planning in-home TR activities, keep in mind that you are planning for a "group" of one. No matter how carefully you schedule a visit, there may be unanticipated events or situations. If the "one" client is unable or does not want to participate in the planned activity, what happens to the program?

Marcin Kempski/fotolia.com

Taking an older adult out for a walk is a simple way to improve quality of life.

Is "conversation and company" an appropriate intervention? (Yes.) Your role may be that of leisure companion, or it may be to identify other leisure companions from the client's social network. You may help him develop his interests in activities he can do alone and learn the needed skills and adaptations. Is there a budget for purchasing equipment and supplies that will belong to the client? Technology opens many doors for seniors. Access to computers and other electronic devices enables them to use e-mail and the Internet for entertainment, education, socialization, and information. An electronic reader, such as the Kindle, with enlarged print could be a very worthwhile purchase. Also, are your services time limited or ongoing? This will influence the programs that you design as well as the evaluation procedures.

One in-home TR program for older adults was initiated by a social worker and a nurse (Kunstler, 2004b) who were concerned that the elderly residents of an apartment complex, to whom they provided services, were becoming isolated in their apartments due to declining health and lack of companionship. They contacted a CTRS, who trained four senior college TR honor students, all of whom had work and internship experience with the elderly in long-term care environments. Each student was assigned three clients and visited them in their apartments to conduct an assessment, set goals, develop a treatment plan, and implement TR programs over an eight-week period. The results of the assessments showed that of the 12 clients in the program, nine had socialization needs, seven needed intellectual stimulation, six needed exercise, and six needed cognitive intervention for memory loss and mild confusion. Therapeutic recreation programs included arts and crafts, horticulture, exercise, walking, word games, reminiscence, reading and discussing literature, and creative writing.

Ms. H., a 96-year-old widow who lived alone, was one of the participants in this program. Although she had some visual impairment, she was able to ambulate with assistance and attended a senior center one day a week for her book club meetings. However, she was experiencing fatigue and was unable to keep up with her readings for the book club. The TR student who worked with her applied the three components of the Health Protection/Health Promotion Model:

● Prescriptive activity: exercise to protect Ms. H.'s physical functioning
● Recreation activity: discussing the book club's reading selections with Ms. H. to promote her sense of control and mastery

● Leisure: engaging a friendly visitor who would interact with Ms. H. to promote ongoing cognitive and social stimulation and quality of life (Kunstler, 2004)

At the end of the program, the students reported that the participants had become more verbal, expressed feelings of control, were excited to continue trying new activities, and enjoyed the companionship and conversation of the students. The students also observed that the participants' sense of control, as a result of being in their own homes, reinforced their desire to be involved in the activities. The older adults felt comfortable in their familiar surroundings and free to try new things. This study demonstrated that an in-home TR program can make a significant contribution to aging in place by providing individual services that may serve to reconnect the older adult with his community.

ETHICAL PRACTICE

Certain recommendations can be made for carrying out an in-home program compared to programming in the institutional setting. First, the TRS is entering an individual's home, a personal and private space with a unique set of "rules" of behavior. Social etiquette differs by cultures. An individual's cultural background can influence these rules. For example, the client may live alone and may be hesitant to have a stranger come in without a formal introduction from a mutual acquaintance or a professional known to both parties. The client may wish to offer food or drink and become offended if the TRS declines. The TRS needs to determine her boundaries for accepting these offerings and gently but firmly inform the client. She might say, "Thank you for the offer, Mr. Murray, but I prefer not to when I'm working with a client." However, the home environment is much more relaxed and informal than a hospital or nursing home. The client may wish to express his gratitude to the TRS by giving a gift (Pies, 2007). Professional judgment is warranted regarding what is permissible to accept. Also, the TRS may observe unsafe or unsanitary conditions that need to be corrected. If the TRS is part of an organization such as a visiting nurse service, or a department that has contracted to provide in-home services, she should report this to a nurse or social worker or to the family member who has arranged for the TR services.

The final element that distinguishes home-based TR is the termination of the relationship. Because of the intimate setting, a warm and friendly bond develops that may not be replaced by other professionals or visitors when the TR program is over. The client may feel hurt, angry, or abandoned. To minimize this possibility, be sure to be clear in the beginning, and repeat as often as necessary, how long you will be there and how many sessions are left. Try to develop linkages with others who can become part of the elderly person's daily life. Ethical principles of autonomy, well-being, and respect for persons are paramount in the home setting. Being respectful of the environment and of a person's cherished possessions, protecting his well-being, and promoting his control and decision making in his own space are essential. Attentiveness, supportiveness, patience, and caring are essential behaviors for the TRS to demonstrate in this setting. In-home TR for persons who are elderly can reinforce their identity and improve their quality of life.

Home-Based Service for Children With Disabilities

While the majority of in-home TR programs have been for older adults, younger people, particularly children, are becoming frequent recipients of home-based TR with positive results. A young person may be more motivated to engage in TR when she can learn and use new skills in her everyday life. Experiencing the benefits of participation in the context of the natural home environment reinforces the value of the TR experience. Family members, as well, may see the child in a new light as she participates successfully in recreation, thereby enhancing the family's relationships. Several TR models could be applied in the home setting depending on the population. An ecological perspective, in particular, can "provide a rich and supportive environment for clients" (Groff, Lawrence & Grivna, 2006, p. 270) as they develop recreation skills and interests for inclusive living. The ecological approach to inclusion focuses on empowering the client to achieve optimal interdependence (Groff et al., 2006); often with children this means improving their skills to engage in recreation with the family.

To illustrate the possibilities of a home-based, one-to-one TR intervention with a child with disabilities, let's look at the example of Chris, an ambulatory 11-year-old boy with cerebral palsy and vision impairments who was deaf and communicated in American Sign Language (ASL) (Groff et al., 2006). Doctors suggested to Chris' mother that he begin to exercise more as preparation for receiving a new form of treatment. His mother also was eager for Chris to develop his gross motor skills in order to participate more fully in recreation with his family, including his sisters. She contacted a local university with a TR degree program and obtained the services of a TR team consisting of a professor, who was a CTRS, and two graduate students in TR. The team completed an assessment of Chris, developed a plan of intervention to improve his physical functioning based on his specific interests in sports and physical activities, and implemented a program in his home environment. The program included walking, sit-ups, and push-ups; soccer techniques; strength building; and eye–hand coordination exercises. This varied program took place in Chris' real world, his home and neighborhood, where he would continue to play after he completed the TR program.

At the start of each session, Chris was excited to see the team and appeared happy to begin the program, smiling frequently. He seemed to respond well to the individualized attention and enjoyed his achievements in performing the activities. As a result of the six-week program, he made progress toward his initial goals of improved physical functioning. Evaluation of the intervention process underscored the significance of family involvement, not only to reinforce the value of the TR services to the client but also to promote the family's positive attitudes and hopefulness regarding the child's progress. This case also illustrated the importance of flexibility: Initial plans for transportation and possible use of a community recreation facility fell through, and alternate arrangements were made. Conducting TR in the home setting requires relying to a much greater extent on readily and easily available facilities and resources than in an institutional setting. But by selecting the familiar streets and grassy areas near Chris' home, the TR team was able to maximize the opportunity afforded by home-based programs to provide services in the child's own environment. This emphasizes the value of recreation as an indispensable part of the client's life, not just a temporary treatment. Implementing the program also involved following other one-to-one principles:

- Adjusting the specific activities to the child's interests and abilities
- Trying a variety of approaches over a short period of time to find out what works the best
- Giving immediate and informational feedback

Obviously, the amount of attention and intervention Chris received from three TRSs is highly unusual. With only one TRS, a volunteer, family member, or other caregiver could assist. However, services of this type are also highly effective with the customary one-to-one ratio.

ETHICAL PRACTICE

Often, as in Chris' case, it is the parents who are seeking TR services for their young or adult child with a disability, looking to provide them with a combination of skill development, social interaction, and quality recreation experiences. In these situations, ethical issues may arise that involve a conflict between what the parent wants the child to do and what the child himself wants to do. The TRS may feel caught between the two sides. She may wonder, who is my client? Is it the child who is receiving the services, or the parent who is paying for them? The TRS should carefully explain to the parents that she will do a thorough assessment and develop a plan that will then be reviewed with the family. She needs to present a thoughtful rationale for why she has selected the interventions in the plan. If the parents do not wish the child to participate in a given activity, the TRS should present options that will meet the same needs. If the child does not wish to participate in the TR program, the TRS needs to carefully discuss this with the parents. According to the ethical principle of autonomy, the child should not be forced or coerced to participate. If the TRS is unable to motivate the child to participate, and it is her clinical judgment that the child's wishes must be respected, it is her ethical obligation to inform the parents of this decision. Also, if the TRS is working as part of a team she could consult with the other professionals or her supervisor.

Boundary issues also can be a concern, particularly if the TRS and the child form a close relationship. The types of touch discussed in the context of work in a nursing home apply to children as well. Touch is almost inevitable when a TRS is interacting with children. The TRS must "have a way to think about touch with young children that considers the child's needs, boundaries, developmental level, and ability to communicate yet does not confuse the child with inconsistent responses or shame the child" (McNeil-Haber, 2004, p. 124).

The family may come to view the TRS as a member and wish her to be involved in family activities or ask her for favors. The TRS must maintain her professional identity and clarify up front what she will and will not do in order to help to minimize any conflicts of interest. The TRS is ethically bound to do what's best for the client; to do no harm; to be competent, honest, fair, respectful, and loyal; and to maintain confidentiality and protect privacy. If the TRS believes that the child is at risk in the home, she must report this to the proper authorities. The TRS may decide that she can no longer ethically

Use of Touch With Children

Training:

The TRS should be aware of cultural values and meanings related to touch and be well versed in the literature on the uses of touch with children.

Informed consent:

The TRS should obtain informed consent from the child's caretakers to use touch.

A signed release permitting physical contact may be used.

The TRS should give examples to the child and the caretakers of touch that can occur during TR sessions.

The child's physical safety should be ensured at all times.

Implementation:

The TRS should use touch only when it meets the needs of the child and is consistent with his treatment goals.

Touch should be appropriate to the child's needs and developmental level.

Supervision:

The TRS should consult with other professionals who are experienced in the use of touch.

Ethical considerations:

Sexual contact or erotic touch between the TRS and the child is ethically and professionally wrong, as well as illegal.

The TRS should not use touch when there is a risk of exploitation or coercion.

If the TRS is uncomfortable with touch, she should not use it.

The TRS should be very cautious when a child may perceive touch as aggressive, punitive, or seductive.

Special considerations:

Evaluate appropriate use of nonerotic touch such as spontaneous "high fives," hugs, or physical assistance.

Abused or traumatized children require vigilant monitoring in relation to the use of touch and should be assessed for touch on a case-by-case basis.

When working with groups, the TRS should establish and communicate rules regarding not hurting others and limiting physical contact among the members, and should stress that each individual has different needs for physical contact, distance, and space.

To use physical restraints when necessary, the TRS should receive training.

Documentation:

All forms of touch in a session, including who initiated it, how it was addressed and implemented, and what the consequences and reactions were, should be documented.

Adapted from McNeil-Haber, 2004

Guidelines for Conducting a Private TR Practice

Therapeutic recreation entrepreneurs who have successfully operated their own TR businesses say that TRSs have valuable skills for working with individuals and groups, planning programs, and conducting assessments, as well as creativity and a desire to help. These skills are assets for private practice. Most TRSs start their own practice because they want to use these skills, desire independence and flexibility, and seek to fill an unmet need. If you are planning to start a TR business, the following are steps you will want to take.

1. Be prepared for uncertainty.
2. Be ready to take risks.
3. Identify your niche: What are the unique services you are qualified to offer? What are trends in your area and on a national level that may indicate needs for services (e.g., youth fitness, inclusion, aging population, interest in complementary therapies)?
4. Obtain all the certifications for which you are eligible.
5. Obtain professional liability and malpractice insurance.
6. Develop your business skills: financing, budgeting, accounting, marketing, personnel management, and time management. Consult with an attorney.
7. Think up a catchy name for your practice that communicates your values and your services.
8. Develop a mission statement.
9. List the services you can offer, develop program protocols, assemble assessment toolkits, and have TR toolkits for several different situations.
10. Write policies and procedures related to handling emergencies, conducting assessments, billing clients, purchasing supplies and equipment, confidentiality, presence of others during TR sessions, and termination of services.

provide services to the child, given a particular family situation or conflicts that affect her ability to do her work professionally. She should terminate the relationship honestly but in terms that are tolerable to the family, are comprehensible to the child, and do not endanger the child's safety in the home.

Private Practice TR

With the trends toward community-based health care, emphasizing prevention and taking control of one's own health, as well as growing interest in health-promoting lifestyle practices, in-home TR can become a substantial component of home-based health care. Agencies may be able to offer in-home

TR as part of their services. A private practitioner can also provide in-home TR; in fact, this is a growing specialty within TR services that offers tremendous potential for expanding the field (Kunstler, 1999). A number of TRSs are developing small businesses to provide individual TR services to older adults, children with developmental disabilities, and adults with multiple sclerosis and other physical conditions. All the ethical obligations and issues that have been discussed apply to the TRS in private practice. Maintaining professional credentials and obtaining professional liability insurance are essential for the TRS with his own business in order to protect the consumer as well as the TRS.

● **Summary** ●

The benefits of one-to-one TR programming are many and varied, for both clients and TR professionals. No matter the population, diagnosis, functioning level, or setting, the relationship between the TRS and client can be a model of healthy caring and thoughtful interaction. Although boundary issues may arise in the more personal and informal setting of a one-to-one program, the TRS is always directed by the codes of ethics of the TR profession. In particular, the TRS must protect the privacy and well-being of the client and respect his choices and decisions as an autonomous human being. A dilemma may arise when family members, who may be more closely involved than in typical group programs, express wishes regarding the client's participation that are contrary to what the TRS or the client believes is the best approach. The TRS has the responsibility to be honest and respectful in dealing with the client and the family. Our obligation to be competent at what we do guides us as we present the reasons for the programming, explain why we believe it is a wise choice, and address the concerns and suggestions of the client, family, and other professionals. The ethic of care guides us to always see "the client as a growing person" (O'Keefe, 2005) and focus on the person at the center of the TR experience.

Implementing an intervention that is tailored to the unique needs, interests, and abilities of an individual creates a meaningful experience for the client and maximizes the possibilities for successful outcomes. The TRS is able to adapt and adjust the intervention to the client's immediate needs, skills, and progress. With the focus and attention on a single client, it is likely that positive results will occur. The TRS can experience a real sense of professional fulfillment when directly facilitating the worthwhile contribution of one-to-one TR to an individual's life.

● **Learning Activities** ●

1. In a small group, discuss the purposes and benefits of one-to-one TR services as compared to group TR programming.

2. Design a sensory stimulation toolkit that could be used in a one-to-one program at bedside. Conduct a sensory stimulation program, using your toolkit, with a classmate or fellow staff member.

3. Write a proposal to justify the need for TR in a hospice setting, including the value of TR and selected activities.

4. Write a protocol for a leisure education program that could be conducted on a one-to-one basis to facilitate community reentry for a client with behavioral health concerns.

5. Visit a group home or assisted living facility. Based on your observations, what potential exists for developing one-to-one TR services?

6. In a small group, brainstorm additional settings and populations, identifying specific TR programs, that could benefit from one-to-one TR.

7. As part of self-evaluation for professional growth, identify the knowledge and skills you need to develop, as well as those you already possess, in order to successfully deliver one-to-one TR services.

8. Reflect on how comfortable you are touching and being touched by clients. In a small group, role play potential situations that may arise in which touch could be an issue and possible responses the TRS could give to a client.

Therapeutic Recreation Leadership for the 21st Century

In this chapter you will learn about:

- The criteria of a profession
- Evaluating TR as an emerging profession
- The concepts of professional leadership and 21st century leadership
- The responsibilities of a mature TR professional
- Types of leadership opportunities
- How to develop a personal leadership action plan

Therapeutic recreation leadership, as discussed in this book, refers to the day-to-day practice of TR, the "how to" of the daily work of a TRS. The privilege of providing TR leadership is to contribute to improving functioning, health and well-being, and quality of life of the individuals who entrust their care to us. The TRS forms a relationship with each client that facilitates the meaningful experiences derived from TR participation. In chapter 1 we defined *therapeutic recreation leadership* as "the unique blending of the therapist's purposeful application of therapeutic strategies and facilitation techniques with the recreation specialist's abilities to create and facilitate leisure experiences to deliver TR services according to the highest ethical standards." The powerful impact of TR leadership comes from this combination of therapeutic methods and approaches with the leisure experience. The TRS can emphasize either a more therapeutic or a more recreational approach depending on the situational context and the characteristics of the participants, but *both elements are always present* in the delivery of TR leadership. We have also highlighted the obligation of the professional to practice with an ethical mindset, to do what is good for the clients, in accordance with their wishes, to the maximum extent possible. To be a professional means that people in the public trust you to act in their best interests. Every TRS should be dedicated to the values and principles of the profession, to lifelong learning, and to excellence in professional practice. Each TR professional is a member of the TR **profession** and should strive to meet the criteria by which all professions are measured.

CRITERIA OF A PROFESSION

In 1966, the National Therapeutic Recreation Society was formed from three professional organizations to consolidate professional activities into one association. Since that time, TR has evaluated itself according to the generally accepted criteria of a profession. These criteria are the conditions that a given occupation must meet in order to be considered a profession. They represent benchmarks that distinguish a job from a calling to practice. These are the criteria:

● A body of knowledge based on research that is disseminated through professional journals and publications

● A code of ethics that serves to protect the public

● A credentialing process that attests to the qualifications of the practitioners so that they are worthy of exercising autonomy of judgment

● Professional organizations that provide continuing education and lobbying efforts

● Standards for professional practice

● Established value and acceptance in the eyes of the public, which recognizes the profession's service motive

The TR profession has fulfilled these criteria to varying degrees. We have

● codes of ethics that guide the professional's daily practice;

● credentialing through national certification and state licensure;

● professional organizations that offer continuing education, networking, and publications; and

● standards for practice that give direction and a framework for designing services.

However, TR may fall short of meeting two other criteria. First, while there are many publications in TR, our body of knowledge is not based totally on research that meets the highest standards for rigor as demanded in many disciplines. Second, our value to the public has not been clearly established in the world of practice or clearly articulated. The general public has limited awareness of what TR is, what a TRS does, and how TR can benefit them. In addition, many employers do not recognize or require the Certified Therapeutic Recreation Specialist (CTRS) **credential** as a necessary qualification in hiring TRSs. This is the reason given by many people who identify themselves as working in TR for not pursuing professional certification. Unfortunately, by not being proactive in obtaining certification and thereby establishing themselves as professionals, they are waiting for recognition from the public *before* they go for certification. In this way, these practitioners slow down the process of professionalization. Fulfilling the final two criteria is a responsibility of all TRSs, regardless of their specific job functions, and can come about through carrying out professional leadership.

PROFESSIONAL LEADERSHIP

Professional leadership requires the TRS to step outside the confines of her service setting to network with other professionals and to be a voice in the community for the rights of all people to a life of dignity, freedom of choice, optimal living, and access to meaningful opportunities. Professional leadership also signifies being a role model and inspiration to other professionals both within and outside of one's own department and agency. Professional leadership involves being a member of professional organizations, serving on their committees and as an officer or board member, making presentations to community and professional groups, and advocating for the recognition of TR and the advancement of the profession. All actions of professional leadership have benefits for the TRS. Increasing one's knowledge, networking, developing skills, and contributing to the growth of other professionals and to the profession enhance the TRS's confidence, personal, and professional identity and bring a sense of satisfaction and well-being.

The commitment to establishing TR as a mature profession begins with the work the TRS does every day.

Photo courtesy of Kasey Stevenson.

The TR profession itself must embody leadership through proactive practice. The Center for Health Professions developed a template for evaluating emerging professions such as TR (Dower, O'Neil & Hough, 2001). This template guides professions to reflect on a number of factors in order to develop into a profession that is mature:

I. Definition and description of the profession: Can TR define succinctly the types of services provided, specific treatment modalities, and how TR compares to other forms of intervention?

II. Safety and efficacy: How safe are TR interventions and activities? Have they proven to be effective? What are the potential risks?

III. Education and training: How do individuals prepare to become TRSs? What types of educational programs and internship experiences are available? What are these TRSs prepared to do?

IV. Government and private sector recognition: How extensive are TR credentialing programs, and are they recognized by governmental entities and third-party payers? Is TR reimbursable? Is malpractice insurance required?

V. Viability of the profession: How will TR contribute to health care in the future? Is the profession growing or shrinking? Do TR organizations have enough members to adequately teach new professionals, conduct research, provide service, and lead the profession into the future? Is TR addressing issues of quality services, interdisciplinary teamwork, and culturally competent practice?

These questions represent fundamental issues that the TR profession should address in order to establish itself as a mature profession. A mature profession is characterized by members who

● are capable of revisiting decisions and making hard choices when necessary even at the risk of losing face;

● are updating their knowledge;

● are making a contribution through research, volunteering, advocacy, and public speaking and are continuing to grow; and

● are thinking about their legacy and the future of the next generation of TR specialists.

Each TRS must make a commitment to contributing to the establishment of TR as a fully mature profession that receives public recognition. This commitment lasts throughout the TRS's professional career, no matter what type of leadership the TRS delivers, starting with the work the TRS does every day. This fulfills our duty, as individual practitioners and as members of the profession, to help TR fully emerge as a mature profession in the 21st century.

TWENTY-FIRST CENTURY LEADERSHIP

The twenty-first century calls for "a new era of responsibility," as President Barack Obama said in his inaugural address in 2009. Therapeutic recreation, as all professions, must heed this call. Doing so will require understanding what changes are taking place globally, as well as in the agency and community, and taking advantage of these changes rather than falling victim to them (Peterson & James, 2008). "Changes in health care, economic pressures, social trends, demographic characteristics and technological advances are influencing society to focus on health promotion, independent functioning, quality of life and quality of services. These concerns present both challenges and opportunities for growth and innovation in the therapeutic recreation field" (Stavola Daly & Kunstler, 2006, p. 195). It will be incumbent upon every professional to take on the responsibility of articulating the value of TR and advocating for TR's place in health care, education, human services, and other community organizations. The TRS should help shape a vision of what the profession can be and can accomplish. The most effective way to address critical issues and move forward is to recognize the interrelatedness of all aspects of the organization and community and to work together. Twenty-first century leadership will require collaboration, flexibility, transdisciplinarity, the creation of environments to help people achieve success, and the rewarding of teamwork in addition to individual effort. Managing change, building relationships, and implementing participatory management will be more important than resourcefulness, decisiveness, and "doing whatever it takes" to get the job done (Martin, 2007). Honesty, dependability, trust, and transparency will be highly valued in the 21st century.

"To the extent that a profession has a clear view of its mission within society, it will be able to perform its role and continue to define itself through periods of social change" (Lahey, 1998, p. 489). In the 21st century, a mature professional will be one who bases her practice on knowledge, acts on behalf of her clients, develops structures for their participation, and renews herself and her organization.

A mature professional TRS

- thoroughly understands and is able to articulate the definition of TR and its principles and values;
- has a mindset for ethical TR practice based on the codes of ethics;
- "does" ethics every day in the delivery of TR leadership;
- applies a process to resolve ethical dilemmas;
- understands and utilizes TR models appropriate to the setting and needs of the clients;

- utilizes relevant elements of the eight approaches to program planning in program design;
- complies with standards for practice of the TR profession;
- develops proficiency in applying the TR process;
- engages in continuous self-evaluation according to the knowledge and skills of the blended role of TR leadership;
- increases self-awareness, interpersonal skills, and cross-cultural competence for effective practice in a diverse world;
- stays up-to-date with clients' common concerns;
- understands and embodies the dimensions of good health and wellness;
- employs best practices in risk management;
- assembles and continually improves his TR toolkit;
- develops skills in planning and implementing a wide variety of TR programs based on an understanding of their benefits;
- plans programs based on evidence of success and efficacy;
- uses motivating, teaching, and processing strategies in the practice of TR leadership;
- understands principles and practices of evaluation of the TRS, TR programs, and clients and engages in ongoing evaluation;
- reads and applies research findings to improve TR services;
- conducts performance improvement activities, seeks grant funding to expand programs, and uses logic models and action research to develop quality services;
- differentiates between the components of one-to-one, group, and unit-wide programming and plans accordingly;
- employs principles of balanced programming;
- values and facilitates the benefits of the TR group experience;
- develops expertise and skills in planning and leading TR groups to maximize the experience and outcomes for the clients;
- is creative and innovative in addressing clients' needs; and
- strives for the highest levels of professionalism.

These behaviors of the mature professional form the foundation of TR practice regardless of the particular job functions the TRS performs. There are several types of leadership opportunities TRSs may fulfill in their professional practice.

LEADERSHIP OPPORTUNITIES

Many TRSs will undoubtedly take on different types of leadership throughout their careers. While the focus of this book has been on direct leadership, it is only one of the types of leadership opportunities available. The range of leadership opportunities is as follows:

- **Direct leadership or the leadership of everyday practice** involves day-to-day contact with clients in one-to-one or group TR programs. The TRS also interacts with other staff and clients' families to provide the most appropriate services. Responsibilities of direct leadership include assessment, planning, documentation, and reporting of clients' progress to the team.

- **Team leadership**, which the TRS can provide in his work with practitioners from other disciplines. The TRS is an essential member of the team, responsible for explaining the client's TR plan and what it aims to accomplish and for providing a report of the client's functioning and behaviors as observed in TR programs. The TRS makes clear to the team the client's recreational needs and goals in the context of her overall status. The TRS has the ethical obligation to be accurate and competent and to advocate for the client's rights to the values and principles of TR. He contributes his knowledge and skill to team planning and resolution of issues. The TRS can serve as the team leader.

- **Supervisory leadership**, which includes overseeing the actions of other staff, volunteers, and interns; keeping an eye on the big picture of equipment, supplies, facility use, and safety; conducting in-service training; scheduling programs; and providing input to agency committees and other groups.

- **Administrative leadership**, which is provided by those who have risen to the top of their department or organizational structure. They have responsibility for management, operations, strategic planning, and policy development; budgeting, fund-raising, and grantsmanship; recruiting, hiring, training, and evaluating personnel; marketing; ensuring compliance with regulations; and functioning as a member of the administrative team.

The TRS may wish to create a plan to help guide her professional growth as she aspires to different levels of leadership. With TRSs at all levels of leadership, the viability of TR as a profession and its functions may be more effectively communicated, thereby contributing to the maturing of the profession.

PERSONAL LEADERSHIP ACTION PLAN

To build a "foundation for future professional growth" (LaBarre & Magnino-Rabig, 2008, p. 631), the TRS can develop a personal leadership action plan. A plan can help the TRS to maintain energy and enthusiasm in often challenging work environments by setting forth a clear professional path and a set of actions. The first component of the personal action plan is a personal vision or mission statement. This statement expresses the TRS's core values and principles in the context of being a TR professional. Once this statement is articulated, it serves as the basis for the actions specified in the plan. The TRS should reflect on what directions his career might take. An entry-level professional may identify potential ideal work settings; a more seasoned professional may identify alternative work opportunities she would like to pursue and new skills to develop, or existing skills in which to develop expertise. For example, the TRS may wish to learn tai chi or ceramics or become the "in-house expert" in American Sign Language.

Within her current job setting, the TRS should always seek challenges or new ways to be creative. The TRS will find it worthwhile to visit other units or settings, observe other professionals as they provide services and other types of programs, offer to supervise and work with volunteers and interns, join a work committee, or pilot a new TR program. Continuing one's education by attending workshops and conferences, acquiring cross-training (e.g., to become a substance abuse counselor), and working with a mentor or becoming a mentor present opportunities for learning and for "giving back" to the profession. The action plan also includes suggestions for stress reduction and health-promoting behaviors that can be incorporated on a daily basis. By taking these steps, the TRS fulfills his professional responsibility to strive for health and to be a role model to his clients. The TRS can review and revise his personal action plan periodically as he grows as a professional, gains new experiences, takes on responsibilities, and fulfills different types of leadership.

Example of a Personal Leadership Action Plan

My Mission

- As a TR professional my mission is to be a highly competent and ethical practitioner who seeks to provide person-centered care with sensitivity and skill.
- I will serve as a role model for other TRSs and will always be honest and trustworthy in my interactions with friends, family, clients, and coworkers.
- I continually seek to perfect my skills and abilities so that I may practice TR skillfully and effectively.
- I will advocate for my profession in all my interactions and maintain the highest standards of my profession.
- Most of all I will enjoy what I do every day.

Action Steps

- Identify one new skill, technique, or activity to learn and incorporate into my daily practice.
- Attend a local or state TR conference at least twice a year.
- Join my local and national professional associations.
- Read professional journals on a regular basis.
- Visit Web sites related to TR to review information and to interact with other professionals.
- Speak at a local university TR-related class.
- Offer to mentor a TR student or an entry-level professional.
- Join a committee of a local TR organization.

Additional Action Steps for Seasoned Professionals

- Colead a group.
- Present at a TR conference.
- Write an article for a professional magazine or journal.
- Conduct an in-service for non-TR personnel.
- Attend a national TR conference.
- Participate in legislative and advocacy activities.
- Develop and implement an evaluation or research study at my facility.
- Pursue a master's degree or postbaccalaureate certification.

Health-Promoting Actions

- Exercise at least four times a week.
- Keep a journal.
- Eat more fresh fruit and vegetables.
- Maintain a healthy weight.
- Take time for myself.
- Do something nice for others.
- Share my feelings.
- Practice stress management.
- Try something new.
- Have fun every day.

● Summary ●

"Therapeutic recreation is a profession that is easy to enter, but is difficult to excel in" (Richter & Kaschalk, 1996, p. 86). This chapter has explored how crucial it is that TRSs do strive to excel. This is no easy task, yet the dedicated TRS will be able to take the relevant steps to do his or her best. There will always be challenges that come from within and outside the profession. In the face of these challenges, the essence of TR remains constant: to facilitate leisure experiences as both a means to a better life and a viable end in themselves. Whether you are preparing to enter the field or have been practicing for a number of years, it is your ethical duty to develop a mindset for professional practice that will help you deliver the highest-quality TR leadership. The specific manifestations of TR leadership will undoubtedly evolve during the course of our own careers and beyond. Yet the unique role TR fulfills in its service to our clients will be the legacy of all professionals.

A life is not important except in the impact it has on other lives.—Jackie Robinson

● Learning Activities ●

1. In a small group, discuss the six criteria for a profession as presented in this chapter. Based on your reading of this book, how well do you think TR meets the criteria? What areas can you identify for improvement and further development?

2. Select one of the five factors presented in the template developed by the Center for Health Professions. Research the answers to the questions about that factor. What do you conclude about the status of the TR profession? Engage in a debate on the following issue: TR is a mature profession.

3. Evaluate how qualified you feel you are to carry out the responsibilities of a mature TR professional. Identify areas you wish to develop further.

4. Review the types of leadership opportunities. Interview a professional at each level of leadership. What are the challenges and rewards of carrying out each type of leadership?

5. Develop a personal leadership action plan as described in the chapter. In a small group, share your personal mission. Discuss similarities and differences among the mission statements.

6. Specify at least three action steps and two health-promoting actions you will take, with a timetable for their completion.

7. Read the quote from Jackie Robinson. Reflect on what you want your impact to be. Share in a small group.

NTRS Code of Ethics

Preamble

Leisure, recreation, and play are inherent aspects of the human experience, and are essential to health and well-being. All people, therefore, have an inalienable right to leisure and the opportunities it affords for play and recreation. Some human beings have disabilities, illnesses, or social conditions which may limit their participation in the normative structure of society. These persons have the same need for and right to leisure, recreation, and play.

Accordingly, the purpose of therapeutic recreation is to facilitate leisure, recreation, and play for persons with physical, mental, emotional, or social limitations in order to promote their health and well-being. This goal is accomplished through professional services delivered in clinical and community meetings. Services are intended to develop skills and knowledge, to foster values and attitudes, and to maximize independence by decreasing barriers and by increasing ability and opportunity.

The National Therapeutic Recreation Society exists to promote the development of therapeutic recreation in order to ensure quality services and to protect and promote the rights of persons receiving services. The National Therapeutic Recreation Society and its members are morally obligated to contribute to the health and well-being of the people they serve. In order to meet this important social responsibility, the National Therapeutic Recreation Society and its members endorse and practice the following ethical principles.

The Preamble to the Code of Ethics presents the central values and ideals of the Society which express the commitment of the profession to the common good. The professions differ from commercial enterprises because of the altruistic values which shape their relationship to society. These values are fundamental to an understanding of therapeutic recreation. Since the purpose of the profession is to serve the public interest, issues of personal advancement, or even the advancement of the profession are secondary to the purpose of the Society indicated in the Preamble.

In order to fulfill its obligations to promote leisure values in society and to facilitate the leisure, recreation, and play for persons with limitations, members of the National Therapeutic Recreation Society obligate themselves to be bound by specific ethical principles.

I. The Obligation of Professional Virtue

Professionals possess and practice the virtues of integrity, honesty, fairness, competence, diligence, and self-awareness.

A. Integrity: Professionals act in ways that protect, preserve, and promote the soundness and completeness of their commitment to service. Professionals do not forsake nor arbitrarily compromise their principles. They strive for unity, firmness, and consistency of character. Professionals exhibit personal and professional qualities conducive to the highest ideals of human service.

B. Honesty: Professionals are truthful. They do not misrepresent themselves, their knowledge, their abilities, or their profession. Their communications are sufficiently complete, accurate, and clear in order for individuals to understand the intent and implications of services.

C. Fairness: Professionals are just. They do not place individuals at unwarranted advantage or disadvantage. They distribute resources and services according to principles of equity.

D. Competence: Professionals function to the best of their knowledge and skill. They only render services and employ techniques of which they are qualified by training and experience. They recognize their limitations, and seek to reduce them by expanding their expertise. Professionals continuously enhance their knowledge and skills through education and by remaining informed of professional and social trends, issues, and developments.

E. Diligence: Professionals are earnest and conscientious. Their time, energy, and professional resources are efficiently used to meet the needs of the persons they serve.

F. Awareness: Professionals are aware of how their personal needs, desires, values, and interests may influence their professional actions. They are especially cognizant of where their personal needs may interfere with the needs of the persons they serve.

▌ II. The Obligation of the Professional to the Individual

A. Well-being: Professionals' foremost concern is the well-being of the people they serve. They do everything reasonable in their power and within the scope of professional practice to benefit them. Above all, professionals cause no harm.

B. Loyalty: Professionals' first loyalty is to the well-being of the individuals they serve. In instances of multiple loyalties, professionals make the nature and the priority of their loyalties explicit to everyone concerned, especially where they may be in question or in conflict.

C. Respect: Professionals respect the people they serve. They show regard for their intrinsic worth and for their potential to grow and change. The following areas of respect merit special attention:

    1. Freedom, autonomy, and self-determination: Professionals respect the ability of people to make, execute, and take responsibility for their own choices. Individuals are given adequate opportunity for self-determination in the least restrictive environment possible. Individuals have the right of informed consent. They may refuse participation in any program except where

their welfare is clearly and immediately threatened and where they are unable to make rational decisions on their own due to temporary or permanent incapacity. Professionals promote independence and interdependence as appropriate for each individual. They avoid fostering dependence and other behaviors that manipulatively control individuals against their will or best interests. In particular, sexual relations with clients is expressly unethical.

    2. Cultural beliefs and practices: Professionals respect cultural diversity and provide services that are responsive to the cultural backgrounds and needs of clients. They use person-first language to acknowledge and honor individual uniqueness above any disability, illness, impairment, or condition.

    3. Privacy: Professionals respect the privacy of individuals. Communications are kept confidential except with the explicit consent of the individual or where the welfare of the individual or others is clearly imperiled. Individuals are informed of the nature and the scope of confidentiality.

D. Professional practices: Professionals provide quality services based on the highest professional standards. Professionals abide by standards set by the profession, deviating only when justified by the needs of the individual. Care is used in administering tests and other measurement instruments. They are used only for their express purposes. Instruments should conform to accepted psychometric standards. The nature of all practices, including tests and measurements are explained to individuals. Individuals are also debriefed on the results and the implications of professional practices. All professional practices are conducted with the safety and well-being of the individual in mind.

▌ III. The Obligation of the Professional to Other Individuals and to Society

A. General welfare: Professionals make certain that their actions do not harm others. They also seek to promote the general welfare of society by advocating the importance of leisure, recreation, and play.

B. Fairness: Professionals are fair to other individuals and to the general public. They seek to balance the needs of the individuals they serve with the needs of other persons according to principles of equity.

IV. The Obligation of the Professional to Colleagues

A. Respect: Professionals show respect for colleagues and their respective professions. They take no action that undermines the integrity of their colleagues.

B. Cooperation and support: Professionals cooperate with and support their colleagues for the benefit of the persons they serve. Professionals demand the highest professional and moral conduct of each other. They approach and offer help to colleagues who require assistance with an ethical problem. Professionals take appropriate action toward colleagues who behave unethically.

V. The Obligation of the Professional to the Profession

A. Knowledge: Professionals work to increase and improve the profession's body of knowledge by supporting and conducting research. Research is practiced according to accepted canons and ethics of scientific inquiry. Where subjects are involved, their welfare is paramount. Prior permission is gained from subjects to participate in research. They are informed of the general nature of the research and any specific risks that may be involved. Subjects are debriefed at the conclusion of the research, and are provided with results of the study on request.

B. Respect: Professionals treat the profession with critical respect. They strive to protect, preserve, and promote the integrity of the profession and its commitment to pubic service.

C. Reform: Professionals are committed to regular and continuous evaluation of the profession. Changes are implemented that improve the profession's ability to serve society.

VI. The Obligation of the Profession to Society

A. Service: The profession exists to serve society. All of its activities and resources are devoted to the principle of service.

B. Equality: The profession is committed to equality of opportunity. No person shall be refused service because of race, gender, religion, social status, ethnic background, religious preference, or sexual orientation. Therapeutic recreation specialists support affordable health care services to persons currently without coverage or the means to pay for services. Additionally, they are committed to pro bono work that offers some relief for those unable to pay.

C. Advocacy: The profession advocates for the people it is entrusted to serve. It protects and promotes their health and well-being and their inalienable right to leisure, recreation, and play in clinical and community settings.

The NTRS Code of Ethics with Interpretive Guidelines is available from the National Parks and Recreation Association/National Therapeutic Recreation Society, 22377 Belmont Ridge Road, Ashburn, Va 20148-4501 / 800.626.NRPA (6772)

www.nrpa.org

Reprinted, by permission, from NRPA.

ATRA Code of Ethics

The American Therapeutic Recreation Association's Code of Ethics is to be used as a guide for promoting and maintaining the highest standards of ethical behavior. The Code applies to all Recreational Therapy personnel. The term Recreational Therapy personnel includes Certified Therapeutic Recreation Specialists (CTRS), recreational therapy assistants, and recreational therapy students. Acceptance of membership in the American Therapeutic Recreation Association commits a member to adherence to these principles.

■ Principle 1: Beneficence

Recreational Therapy personnel shall treat persons served in an ethical manner by actively making efforts to provide for their well-being by maximizing possible benefits and relieving, lessening, or minimizing possible harm.

■ Principle 2: Non-Maleficence

Recreational Therapy personnel have an obligation to use their knowledge, skills, abilities, and judgment to help persons while respecting their decisions and protecting them from harm.

■ Principle 3: Autonomy

Recreational Therapy personnel have a duty to preserve and protect the right of each individual to make his or her own choices. Each individual is to be given the opportunity to determine his or her own course of action in accordance with a plan freely chosen. In the case of individuals who are unable to exercise autonomy with regard to their care, recreational therapy personnel have the duty to respect the decisions of their qualified legal representative.

■ Principle 4: Justice

Recreational Therapy personnel are responsible for ensuring that individuals are served fairly and that there is equity in the distribution of services. Individuals should receive services without regard to race, color, creed, gender, sexual orientation, age, disability or disease, and social and financial status.

■ Principle 5: Fidelity

Recreational Therapy personnel have an obligation, first and foremost, to be loyal, faithful, and meet commitments made to persons receiving services. In addition, Recreational Therapy personnel have a secondary obligation to colleagues, agencies, and the profession.

■ Principle 6: Veracity

Recreational Therapy personnel shall be truthful and honest. Deception, by being dishonest or omitting what is true, should always be avoided.

■ Principle 7: Informed Consent

Recreational Therapy personnel should provide services characterized by mutual respect and shared decision making. These personnel are responsible for providing each individual receiving service with information regarding the services, benefits, outcomes, length of treatment, expected activities, risk, and limitations, including the professional's training and credentials. Informed consent is obtained when information needed to make a reasoned decision is provided by the professional to competent persons seeking services who then decide whether or not to accept the treatment.

Principle 8: Confidentiality & Privacy

Recreational Therapy personnel have a duty to disclose all relevant information to persons seeking services: they also have a corresponding duty not to disclose private information to third parties. If a situation arises that requires disclosure of confidential information about an individual (i.e., to protect the individual's welfare or the interest of others), the professional has the responsibility to inform the individual served of the circumstances.

Principle 9: Competence

Recreational Therapy personnel have the responsibility to maintain and improve their knowledge related to the profession and demonstrate current, competent practice to persons served. In addition, personnel have an obligation to maintain their credential.

Principle 10: Compliance With Laws and Regulations

Recreational Therapy personnel are responsible for complying with local, state, and federal laws, regulations, and ATRA policies governing the profession of Recreational Therapy.

Revised November 2009
American Therapeutic Recreation Association
629 North Main St
Hattiesburg, MS 39401
Tel: 601-450-ATRA (2872) Fax: 601-582-3354
http://www.atra-online.com
Reprinted, by permission, from ATRA.

NTRS Standards of Practice

National Therapeutic Recreation Society
Standards of Practice for Therapeutic Recreation
Services

Introduction

The National Therapeutic Recreation Society
(NTRS) Board of Directors approved the revised
Standards of Practice for Therapeutic Recreation
Services in September, 1994. What follows are the
basic Standards of Practice, without criteria for each
standard.

Standard I – Scope of Service

A. Treatment services are available which are
goal-oriented and directed toward rehabilitation, amelioration, and modification of specific physical, emotional, cognitive, and social
functional behaviors. Therapeutic recreation
intervention targeting these functional behaviors is warranted when the behaviors impede
or otherwise inhibit participation in reasonable
and customary leisure participation. (Note: This
may not apply to all therapeutic recreation settings for all clients.)

B. Leisure education services are available which
are goal-oriented and directed toward the
development of knowledge, attitudes, values,
behaviors, skills, and resources related to socialization and leisure involvement. (Note: This
may not apply for all clients.)

C. Recreation services are available that provide
a variety of activities designed to meet client
needs, competencies, aptitudes, capabilities,
and interest. These services are directed toward
optimizing client leisure involvement and are
designed to promote health and well being, and
improve the quality of life.

Standard II – Mission and Purpose, Goals, and Objectives

Mission, purpose, goals, and specific objectives are
formulated and stated for each type of therapeutic
recreation service based upon the philosophy and
goals of each agency. These are then translated into
operational procedures and serve as a blueprint for
program evaluation.

Standard III – Individual Treatment/Program Plan

The therapeutic recreation specialist develops an
individualized treatment/program plan for each
client referred to the agency for therapeutic recreation services.

Standard IV – Documentation

The therapeutic recreation specialist records specific
information based on client assessment, involvement, and progress. Information pertaining to the
client is recorded on a regular basis as determined
by the agency policy and procedures, and accrediting body standards.

Standard V – Plan of Operation

Therapeutic recreation services are considered a
viable aspect of treatment, rehabilitation, normalization, and development. Appropriate and fair scheduling of services, facilities, personnel, and resources
is vital to client progress and the operation of therapeutic recreation services. (See the NTRS Guidelines
for the Administration of Therapeutic Recreation
Services for additional reference information.)

Standard VI – Personnel Qualifications

Therapeutic recreation services are conducted by therapeutic recreation specialists whose training and experience have prepared them to be effective at the functions they perform. Therapeutic recreation specialists have opportunities for involvement in professional development and lifelong learning.

Standard VII – Ethical Responsibilities

Professionals are committed to advancing the use of therapeutic recreation services in order to ensure quality, protection, and to promote the rights of persons receiving services.

Standard VIII – Evaluation and Research

Therapeutic recreation specialists implement client and service-related evaluation and research functions to maintain and improve the quality, effectiveness, and integrity of therapeutic recreation services.

A copy of the NTRS Standards of Practice is available from the National Recreation and Park Association / National Therapeutic Recreation Society, 22377 Belmont Ridge Road Ashburn, Va 20148-4501, 800.626.NRPA (6772) www.nrpa.org

Reprinted, by permission, from NRPA.

ATRA Standards for the Practice of Therapeutic Recreation

The Standards for the Practice of Therapeutic Recreation, developed by the American Therapeutic Recreation Association, reflect standards for the quality of therapeutic recreation practice by therapeutic recreation professionals and paraprofessionals in a variety of settings. The standards are divided into two distinct areas: Direct Practice of Therapeutic Recreation; and Management of Therapeutic Recreation Practice. The standards, originally released in 1991, revised in 1994, and again in 2000, reflect state of the art practice in therapeutic recreation. This represents a brief overview.

The standards as listed in this appendix do not stand alone and should not be used without the measurement criteria of structure, process, and outcome provided in the manual. For instance, the following examples illustrate the use of the measurement criteria to aid in interpretation and evaluation of each standard.

The Self Assessment Guide includes useful worksheets on standards scoring, documentation audit, management audit, outcome assessment, competency assessment, and clinical performance appraisals.

■ Standard 1: Assessment

The therapeutic recreation specialist conducts an individualized assessment to collect systematic, comprehensive, and accurate data necessary to determine a course of action and subsequent individualized treatment plan. Under the clinical supervision of the therapeutic recreation specialist, the therapeutic recreation assistant aids in collect-ing systematic, comprehensive, and accurate data necessary to determine a course of action and subsequent individualized treatment plan.

● Example: Structure Criteria. 1.1.2. The assessment process generates culturally appropriate baseline data that identifies the patient's/client's strengths and limitations in the following functional areas: physical, cognitive, social, behavioral, emotional, and leisure/play.

● Example: Process Criteria. The therapeutic recreation specialist: 1.2.3. Provides a summary of the assessment process that contains information relative to the patient's/client's strengths, patient's/client's limitations, analysis of assessment data, and summary of functional status. The therapeutic recreation assistant: 1.2.3.1. Provides a summary of assessment information relative to the patient's/client's strengths and weaknesses to the therapeutic recreation specialist.

● Example: Outcome Criteria. The patient/client, family, and/or significant other(s): 1.3.3. Benefits from the assessment process and does not incur adverse consequences due to participation in the assessment.

■ Standards for the Practice of Therapeutic Recreation*

Direct Practice of Therapeutic Recreation

Standard 1. Assessment

Standard 2. Treatment Planning

Standard 3. Plan Implementation

Standard 4. Re-Assessment and Evaluation

Standard 5. Discharge and Transition Planning

Standard 6. Recreation Services

Standard 7. Ethical Conduct

Management of Therapeutic Recreation Practice

Standard 8. Written Plan of Operation

Standard 9. Staff Qualifications and Competency Assessment

Standard 10. Quality Management

Standard 11. Resource Management

Standard 12. Program Evaluation and Research

*Please note: The standards as listed in this appendix do not stand alone and should not be used without the measurement criteria of structure, process, and outcome provided in the manual.

A complete copy of the ATRA Standards of Practice and Self Assessment Guide is available from

American Therapeutic Recreation Association

629 North Main St

Hattiesburg, MS 39401

Tel: 601-450-ATRA (2872) Fax: 601-582-3354

http://www.atra-online.com

NRPA Position Statement on Inclusion

Diversity is a cornerstone of our society and culture and thus should be celebrated. Including people with disabilities in the fabric of society strengthens the community and its individual members. The value of inclusive leisure experiences in enhancing the quality of life for all people, with and without disabilities, cannot be overstated. As we broaden our understanding and acceptance of differences among people through shared leisure experiences, we empower future generations to build a better place for all to live and thrive.

Inclusive leisure experiences encourage and enhance opportunities for people of varying abilities to participate and interact in life's activities together with dignity. It also provides an environment that promotes and fosters physical, social, and psychological inclusion of people with diverse experiences and skill levels. Inclusion enhances individuals' potential for full and active participation in leisure activities and experiences. Additionally, the benefits of this participation may include:

- providing positive recreational experiences which contribute to the physical, mental, social, emotional, and spiritual growth and development of every individual;

- fostering peer and intergenerational relationships that allow one to share affection, support, companionship, and assistance; and

- developing community support and encouraging attitudinal changes to reflect dignity, self-respect, and involvement within the community.

■ Purpose

The purpose of the National Recreation and Park Association (NRPA) Position Statement on Inclusion is to encourage all providers of park, recreation, and leisure services to provide opportunities in settings where people of all abilities can recreate and interact together.

This document articulates a commitment to the leisure process and the desired outcomes. Accordingly, the NRPA Position Statement on Inclusion encompasses these broad concepts and beliefs:

Right to Leisure

- The pursuit of leisure is a condition necessary for human dignity and well-being.

- Leisure is a part of a healthy lifestyle and a productive life.

- Every individual is entitled to the opportunity to express unique interests and pursue, develop, and improve talents and abilities.

- People are entitled to opportunities and services in the most inclusive setting.

- The right to choose from the full array of recreation opportunities offered in diverse settings and environments and requiring different levels of competency should be provided.

Quality of Life

- People grow and develop throughout the life span.

- Through leisure an individual gains an enhanced sense of competence and self-direction.
- A healthy leisure lifestyle can prevent illness and promote wellness.
- The social connection with one's peers plays a major role in his or her life satisfaction.
- The opportunity to choose is an important component in one's quality of life; individual choices will be respected.

Support, Assistance, and Accommodations

- Inclusion is most effective when support, assistance, and accommodations are provided.
- Support, assistance, and accommodations can and should be responsive to people's needs and preferences.
- Support, assistance, and accommodations should create a safe and fun environment, remove real and artificial barriers to participation, and maximize not only the independence but also the interdependence of the individual. People want to be self-sufficient.
- Support, assistance, and accommodations may often vary and are typically individualized. Types of support, assistance, and accommodations include, but are not limited to: qualified staff, adaptive equipment, alternative formats for printed or audio materials, trained volunteers, or flexibility in policies and program rules.

Barrier Removal

- Environments should be designed to encourage social interaction, "risk-taking," fun, choices, and acceptance that allow for personal accomplishment in a cooperative context.
- Physical barriers should be eliminated to facilitate full participation by individuals with disabilities.
- Attitudinal barriers in all existing and future recreation services should be removed or minimized through education and training of personnel (staff, volunteers, students, and community at-large).

The National Recreation and Park Association is dedicated to the four inclusion concepts of:

- *Right to Leisure* (for all individuals)
- *Quality of Life* (enhancements through leisure experiences)
- *Support, Assistance, and Accommodations*
- *Barrier Removal* in all park, recreation, and leisure services. Properly fostered, inclusion will happen naturally. Over time, inclusion will occur with little effort and with the priceless reward of an enlightened community. Encouraged in the right way, inclusion is the right thing to plan for, implement, and celebrate.

GLOSSARY

action research—Research conducted by practitioners in a systematic and organized manner to improve the quality of their own practice.

active treatment—Services that are considered medically necessary for the treatment or rehabilitation of an individual and are instrumental in achieving efficient and effective outcomes.

activity analysis—A systematic procedure for identifying the specific behaviors required to participate in a given activity. These behaviors can be categorized according to the four behavioral domains: physical, cognitive, affective or emotional, and social.

adaptations—Changes or modifications in the activity process, rules, equipment, setting, or leadership style to facilitate the participation of an individual in a given recreation activity.

adapted aquatics—Learn-to-swim programs for individuals with disabilities.

addiction—A compulsion to do something over which the individual has little control.

administrative leadership—Leadership provided by those who have risen to the top of their department or organizational structure; may include responsibilities for management, operations, strategic planning, and policy development; budgeting, fund-raising, and grantsmanship; recruiting, hiring, training, and evaluating personnel; marketing; ensuring compliance with regulations; and functioning as a member of the administrative team.

adventitious—Acquired after birth.

adventure therapy—Recreation in novel physical and social settings emphasizing the development of new skills and behaviors to master the challenges inherent in the situation. While most adventure therapy takes places outdoors, there are indoor therapies with ropes courses, climbing walls, and initiative games that use the elements of adventure.

affective content—Unspoken or verbal expression of feelings.

affective or **emotional domain**—Behaviors that indicate one's capacities for enjoying life; successfully managing life's stressful situations; and experiencing healthy self-esteem, motivation, and control over one's actions.

agility—The ability to change body position, which depends on balance, coordination, and speed.

aging in place—An arrangement in which people who are growing older can continue to reside in their own homes and can obtain the support services they may need as their health declines.

alphapoem—A 26-line free verse poem on a given topic, in which each line is a word or phrase beginning with a letter of the alphabet.

American Therapeutic Recreation Association (ATRA)—A professional organization with full membership restricted to Certified Therapeutic Recreation Specialists.

animal-assisted therapy—The introduction of an animal into an individual's or group's immediate surroundings, with therapeutic intent.

APIE—An acronym for the four steps in the TR process: assessment, planning, implementation, and evaluation.

aquatic fitness—Aquatic exercise to increase physical or mental health or both.

aquatics—Activities that take place in the water.

aquatic therapy—The application of therapeutic exercises to improve functioning.

art—Creation of an artwork as a form of aesthetic expression.

arts and crafts—Activities in which people make, by hand, objects that typically have a useful purpose but are also decorative.

assertiveness—The ability to directly express one's feelings, needs, and desires to the appropriate person in an appropriate manner.

assertiveness training—A program that uses instruction, role playing, modeling, feedback, and homework assignments to help people develop the social skills needed for interpersonal interaction in a variety of situations, including recreation, and learn how to communicate their feelings, desires, and needs in an honest and straightforward manner.

assessment—A systematic process of gathering and synthesizing information about a client and his environment using a variety of methods, including interviews, observation, standardized tests, and input from other disciplines and significant others, in order to devise an individualized treatment or service plan.

assessment protocol—A compilation of the types of assessment methods to be used, such as standardized tests, questionnaires, and interview questions; areas for observation; and general guidelines for carrying out the assessment procedures.

assessment toolkit—A collection of simple, everyday objects with which the client can interact during the assessment interview; used by the TRS in order to obtain an accurate understanding of the client's capabilities and functional limitations.

assisted living—A form of congregate housing for older adults, offering health-related services, recreation and social activities, transportation, personal services such as laundry and housekeeping, and assistance with activities of daily living.

attention-deficit disorders—A group of conditions characterized by patterns of inattention or hyperactivity.

attention span—The amount of time and effort a person can focus on a single activity.

authoritarian or **autocratic leadership style**—A style of leadership in which the leader reserves the right to make all the decisions and choices about the activity and the individuals' participation.

autonomy—The right to govern oneself, to make one's own decisions and choices, and to be self-determining.

backward chaining—A procedure used to teach a task starting with the final step; once the step is mastered, the remaining steps are taught in reverse order, one at a time.

balanced programming—Programming that varies the components of each aspect of the total program in accordance with the availability of facilities and resources and the needs of the clients. Components include the behavioral domains, levels of social interaction, program formats, group size, time frames, and leadership styles.

bariatrics—The field of medicine that offers treatment for a person who is overweight using a comprehensive program that can include diet and nutrition, exercise, behavior modification, lifestyle changes, and medical treatment.

behavioral objective—Specific indicator of goal achievement, characterized by identification of an expected behavior, a condition under which the behavior will occur, and a criterion or standard of performance for determining whether the expected behavior has been demonstrated.

beneficence—The aim and actions of doing good, promoting the well-being of others, and acting in their best interests.

benefits—The enhancements and enrichments experienced from participation in a recreation program.

benefits-based programming (BBP)—An approach to program planning based on identifying the benefits and outcomes of recreation experiences, as well as linking the outcomes of participation in a given activity to the outcomes the client is trying to attain.

bibliotherapy—A therapeutic program that involves guiding a person's reading in order to foster self-understanding, help resolve therapeutic issues, provide solutions to personal problems, develop life skills, and enhance self-image.

bioethics—The area of ethics related to the provision of health care and services.

body composition—The total body mass index and body fat distribution.

body mass index (BMI)—The measure of how body weight is distributed, which is affected by the relationship between the amount of activity a person participates in and the type and amount of food consumed on a daily basis.

boredom—A lack of interest in or difficulty concentrating on the current activity.

boundary—The invisible line that defines the limits between professional and personal behavior.

boundary intelligence—The ability to apply interpersonal skills in a professional manner and to establish a therapeutic relationship.

cardiovascular endurance—The ability to sustain moderate whole-body activity for a prolonged period of time.

casual observations—The things we happen to notice about people and their actions.

Centers for Medicare and Medicaid Services (CMS)—The U.S. federal agency that oversees Medicare, Medicaid, and the Health Insurance Portability and Accountability Act (HIPAA), among other programs.

certification—A process by which practitioners are evaluated and are judged as possessing required qualifications in order to be granted a credential.

Certified Therapeutic Recreation Specialist (CTRS)—A professional credential awarded by the National Council for Therapeutic Recreation Certification to college graduates who meet predetermined criteria for academic preparation and experience in the area of TR.

chronic pain—Pain that persists longer than the expected time frame, or pain associated with disease that cannot be eradicated or cured in most cases.

cinematherapy or **videotherapy**—A program in which a therapist selects films for clients to view for therapeutic purposes.

clinical supervision—An ongoing relationship between a clinical supervisor and a practitioner, focused on helping the practitioner develop his knowledge and skills in order to provide the highest-quality services.

coaching—A person-centered approach in which a coach assists a client to take on a leadership role in the change process in order to practice lifelong skills and reach goals, drawing on her own resources and potential; not considered therapy but the next step after therapy.

code of ethics—A written document that represents a public declaration of a profession's values, duties, and intentions to protect clients. Codes contain the standards of behavior of the profession, which describe how professionals ought to act, their responsibilities and commitments to society, and what is considered right or wrong to do in practice.

coercive power—Power based on the ability to take away benefits or privileges from an individual or group.

cognition—The ability to learn and process information in order to engage optimally with one's environment.

cognitive content—Concrete, tangible events, people, and activities.

cognitive or intellectual domain—Category including behaviors that indicate a person's abilities to think clearly and reason, including attention span and concentration, memory, following instructions, comprehension, and executive functioning.

cohesion—The mutual attraction that holds a group together.

collaboration—Process in which two or more people share information and work together to achieve a goal or outcome.

Commission on Accreditation of Rehabilitation Facilities (CARF)—An independent nonprofit accreditor of over 5,000 health and human services providers in the United States, Canada, South America, and Western Europe.

common concerns—Issues and factors that are common to a group of clients regardless of their particular diagnosis, disability, health condition, or circumstances.

communication—The expression of ideas and thoughts verbally through words and nonverbally through body language, as well as receiving what others are expressing both verbally and nonverbally.

community gardening—An activity in which a group of community members grow flowers and foodstuffs on plots of land for personal or collective benefits.

community reintegration—The process of returning to community living, which means being part of the mainstream of family and community life, discharging normal roles and responsibilities, and being an active and contributing member of one's social groups and of society as a whole.

comparative justice—Balancing the needs of the individual with the needs of others when there is competition for scarce resources.

comprehension—The capacity to fully understand an idea, concept, or information. Literal comprehension involves identifying the facts, whereas inferential comprehension is "reading between the lines."

confidentiality—Limiting access to personal information about clients to only those who have a right to this information as part of their work with the client.

congenital—Referring to conditions that are present at birth.

contextualized approach—An approach to planning that takes into consideration the circumstances of a person's life as well as the important role of the physical and social environment in contributing to health and quality of life.

continuity of lifestyle—Maintaining consistency in one's life as personal circumstances change.

continuum—Comprehensive and integrated network of services that guides and tracks patients or clients over time and provides the most appropriate level of care, ranging in intensity and leading to minimal distinction between different types of services.

countertransference—A condition that can occur when a therapist begins to treat the client as if the client were a person from her past.

creative or **expressive writing**—Writing that expresses thoughts and feelings in an imaginative way and is guided more by the writer's need to express feelings and ideas than by restrictive demands for factual and logical progression.

credential—A document certifying that an individual has met a defined set of requirements set forth by the credentialing body. Requirements typically include knowledge and skills validated by assessment, demonstration of competency, work or practical or field experience, and sometimes professional activities or contributions.

cross-cultural competence—Understanding and respecting the individual differences of each client and consistently demonstrating this in one's behaviors, attitudes, and beliefs.

culture change—The movement, primarily in long-term care facilities, away from institutional provider-driven models to more humane consumer-driven models that embrace flexibility and self-determination.

dance—A form of personal expression through movement, usually in rhythm with sound or music.

debriefing—Discussion and skillful questioning of clients or a group after an activity in order to enhance understanding, learning, or insight.

decisional autonomy—The individual's right to have preferences and make decisions.

democratic or **shared leadership style**—A leadership style in which the leader shares control and decision making with the group members.

diagnostic protocol—A standardized set of steps identifying the approaches used to address the needs of clients with a particular diagnosis (such as dementia, schizophrenia, depression).

digital storytelling—The process of combining the spoken word, images, sound, and motion to tell a story in a short (2-4 minute) video format.

direct leadership or **the leadership of everyday practice**—The day-to-day contact with clients in one-to-one or group TR programs.

discharge planning—A process to help the client prepare for discharge from an institutional setting or from the services of an agency, resulting in a formal plan.

discrepancy evaluation—Evaluation method based on analyzing the discrepancy, or gap, between what was intended or planned and what was actually carried out in the delivery of a program.

distributive justice—Ensuring that persons are not excluded from an equitable share of society's benefits and obligations and have equal access to programs and services.

diversity—The variety of people and groups that exist within any society.

documentation—The written (or electronic) record of the client's experience in the agency that is part of the official and legal record of client services.

downshifting—Movement of the group back and forth among the stages of group development in order to resolve problems that have not been fully addressed at each stage; it is an action taken by the leader.

dramatics activities—Activities involving acting or performing, which can be classified as informal or creative or formal, with a director, a written script, staging, and costuming, resulting in a performance to an audience for their entertainment and reactions.

duration—A period of time for which a program is offered.

ecological perspective—The view that people are interconnected with all the systems in their environment and that individuals' growth and change occur as a result of their interactions with these systems. Environment includes the community, neighborhood, social institutions, family, friends, and other people that individuals come into contact with.

Eden Alternative—Creation of a homelike environment in long-term care facilities that integrates people, plants, and animals to encourage continued growth and achievement among residents.

effectiveness research—Research that evaluates interventions as they are actually practiced with clients.

efficacy research—An experimental study that is methodologically rigorous in its effort to determine whether a cause-and-effect relationship exists between the TR intervention and client outcomes.

emotional intelligence (EI)—The ability to understand and handle emotions critical to success in life and to feeling empathy for others.

empathy—Acknowledgement of and respect for the client's experience from his own perspective.

enjoyment—A considerable degree of psychological involvement in an intrinsically motivated activity that engenders concentration, effort, and a sense of control and competence.

environment—The community, neighborhood, social institutions, family, friends, and other people that individuals come into contact with.

environmental assessment—Assessment of the equipment, supplies, space, furnishings, and resources available to the client in her home or living situation; the other people and support networks that are or can be part of her life; and the resources of the neighborhood and surrounding community.

environmental press—The concept that environments can influence a person's ability to accomplish tasks.

ethical dilemma—A situation that may not present clear-cut or desirable choices of the ethical course of action to take.

ethical practice—Professional practice that conforms to established professional standards.

ethic of care—A set of principles according to which the professional approaches the client as a growing person and not as a diagnostic label, with the interaction between the two relational rather than clinical.

ethics—"Moral rules" about what one should or "ought" to do, not what one "has" to do in order to comply with laws and regulations.

ethnocentrism—The belief that one's culture is superior to others.

evaluation—A systematic process of collecting and analyzing data for the purposes of making decisions about programs and services.

evidence-based practice (EBP)—Treatment and services based on selecting the intervention that can most successfully address a given health care condition or disease according to the findings of well-designed and -executed research studies.

executional autonomy—Ability to carry out one's decisions.

executive functioning—The higher-level cognitive skills required to perform daily activities involving planning, organizing, making connections, self-monitoring, judgment, and decision making; the ability to plan, organize, initiate, sustain, and complete actions or a course of behavior.

exercise—Planned, structured, and repetitive bodily movement with the objective of improving one's physical fitness.

existential outcomes—Outcomes that center on achieving meaning in one's life and developing and reinforcing one's identity or both.

expert power—The ability to influence others due to one's professional knowledge and expertise.

explicit norms—Norms that are either written or stated.

extrinsic motivation—Motivation through use of factors or incentives that are external to the individual.

facilitation techniques—The methods the TRS uses to help clients attain outcomes, including motivation processes, reinforcement strategies, leadership styles, and teaching methods that are best suited to the client's particular needs and characteristics.

feedback—Information given to individuals in response to their actions or behaviors with the intention of reinforcing an existing behavior or promoting a change in behavior.

fine or **visual arts**—Visual arts expressions in painting, sculpting, and photography that are intended to be viewed.

flexibility—The range of motion at a joint or a series of joints.

flow—An optimal psychological experience that may occur when the challenges of an activity are matched to the skill level of the individual. Flow can be compared to experiencing a "natural high," being "in the moment" or in "the zone," or having a "peak" experience.

formal observation—Systematically and deliberately observing, at regular intervals, a specific behavior that has been identified as a target of TR intervention.

formative evaluation—Evaluation that is ongoing, occurs during the actual activity, and leads to immediate changes in an activity as needed.

forward chaining—Teaching a person specific skills in a logical sequence from the first to the last step, moving from one step to the next as each step is mastered.

frontloading or **framing**—Explaining the purpose of the activity before the client begins participating.

functional assessment—Assessment of the client's physical, cognitive, social, and emotional abilities and behaviors in order to develop a fuller understanding of the client's skills and needs.

functional intervention—Activities designed to overcome physical, social, cognitive, and emotional deficits in order to improve performance of skills, such as gross motor skills, social skills, attention span, and concentration, needed for everyday functioning, including recreation participation.

functional outcomes—Outcomes centered on improving aspects of health and functional abilities needed for everyday living.

functional skills—Skills such as vision, hearing, speaking ability, fine and gross motor skills, mobility, social interaction, and ability to follow directions, as well as comprehension, emotional expression, and control, that have an impact on the client's daily activities.

gardening—The growing and caring for plants as an enjoyable leisure activity to produce food or to create beautiful landscapes.

goal—A broad, general statement of intent or direction of services.

Great Man Theory—Theory stating that a successful leader is a person who was born with inherent traits or abilities; as the theory evolved, it was reinterpreted to support the belief that potential leaders could be developed through appropriate training, education, and mentoring.

group—Two or more people who acknowledge that they share a common purpose and interact with each other to achieve it.

group morale—The mood or feeling of a group that reflects how the group members feel about the group as a whole.

groupthink—Phenomenon that occurs when groups develop a faulty decision-making process and seek unanimity on all decisions to prevent disagreements among members or resolve a situation quickly.

health—According to the World Health Organization, "a state of complete physical, social, and mental well-being, and not merely the absence of disease or infirmity" (Fazio, 2008, p. 113). Also can be seen as "a dynamic level of psychophysical well-functioning, suitable for adapting to one's circumstances and effective for choosing and acting on the private and public values that constitute one's plan for life" (Sylvester, 1987, p. 79).

Health Insurance Portability and Accountability Act (HIPAA) privacy rule—This federal law set standards for the use and disclosure of "individually identifiable" information related to a person's physical or mental condition or the provision of health care to an individual.

Health Protection/Health Promotion Model—A practice model that describes three components of TR service—prescriptive activities, recreation, and leisure—in which the purpose of TR is to help the client to recover from a threat to health and to achieve optimal health.

Healthy People 2010—A national health agenda aimed at preventing threats to and promoting health, including increasing the number of people with disabilities who engage in physical activity and improving their access to community health and wellness programs.

hippotherapy—A specific form of animal-assisted therapy in which physical, occupational, and speech therapists use equine movement as a treatment to meet goals. It does not include teaching horseback riding; rather the movement of the horse is a form of therapeutic intervention.

horticultural therapy—Use of plant life and gardening activities to bring about therapeutic outcomes and improve physical and mental health.

hospice—A range of services offered in the last few months of life in one's home, a hospital, or a long-term care facility, with the focus on comfort, not treatment.

humanistic or **growth psychology**—A school of psychology based on the assumption that people are autonomous, are capable of self-direction, and are motivated to become more self-aware in order to better themselves. The trusting relationship between the therapist and the client is seen as essential to client growth and change.

humanistic perspective—The view that individuals are capable of growth and change and desire to fulfill themselves as well as demonstrate concern for others.

implicit norms—Norms that are understood without being stated or heard.

inclusion—Empowering people who have disabilities to be valued and active members of their communities by making choices, being supported in daily life, and having opportunities to grow and develop to their fullest potential.

inclusion approach—A process of minimizing barriers to full participation with the goal of full inclusion.

Individuals with Disabilities Education Act (IDEA)—The 1990 reauthorization of the 1975 landmark federal legislation that requires a free and appropriate education for all children regardless of disability, which was the first federal education law to include recreation as a related service; specified development of an individual education plan (IEP).

inputs—The components of program structure, including scheduling, facility, space, equipment, supplies, and staffing.

intensity—Length of time of a single session of a program.

interdependence—Reciprocal interaction among people.

interpersonal skills—Skills used in face-to-face contact with clients and coworkers, including the ability to read and manage the emotions, motivations, and behaviors of oneself and others during social interactions.

intrinsic motivation—Motivation that comes from within the individual and is derived from the satisfaction or positive feelings associated with doing an activity or task, with more satisfying and longer-lasting results.

Joint Commission (JC)—A private, not-for-profit organization that accredits over 19,000 health care programs in the United States.

judgment-based practice of care or **clinical judgment**—The practitioner's use of his or her experiences, creativity, empathy, and knowledge in providing services.

justice—Treating everyone fairly and ensuring that resources and services are allocated in a fair and equitable manner.

lability—The sudden and uncontrollable expressions of emotions, such as excessive laughing or crying, as well as emotional expressions that are the opposite of what one is really feeling (e.g., laughing when one is angry).

laissez-faire leadership style—A more lenient or relaxed style of leadership in which people act without interference from the leader.

learned helplessness—A condition in which a person has developed feelings of being helpless due to a perceived lack of control over events and therefore doesn't make an effort.

learning—A relatively permanent change in behavior or knowledge that is the result of experience.

learning style—The process by which people gain and retain knowledge, analyze information, and demonstrate what they have learned.

legacy building—Process by which the TRS helps a client create something that expresses his feelings and wishes to his family and loved ones; can be in the form of a letter, poem, picture, plant, CD, or any other item.

legitimate power—Influence that derives from an appointed position and the authority placed in that position according to the organizational structure of the agency or department.

Leisure Ability Model—Practice model that describes three components of TR services, functional intervention, leisure education, and recreation participation, provided along a continuum, with the purpose of helping clients develop an appropriate leisure lifestyle.

leisure counseling—An intervention based on a counseling relationship between the counselor (TRS) and the client to address leisure-related attitudes and behaviors that are detrimental to the client's health and well-being.

leisure education—A process that helps people develop awareness of the value of leisure, identify potential leisure interests, learn new leisure skills, and acquire knowledge of leisure resources and how to use them in order to achieve positive leisure functioning.

leisure lack—The chronic or temporary absence of the experience of leisure resulting from personal or societal factors or their interaction.

leisure lifestyle—The day-to-day behavioral expression of one's leisure-related attitudes, awareness, and activities revealed within the context and composite of the total life experience

leisure "state of mind"—A state of mind characterized by feelings of competence and mastery, accomplishment, self-satisfaction, freedom, and the meaning leisure holds for the individual.

life review—A structured program in which participants review their entire life span with the goals of resolving issues, conflicts, regrets, and disappointments.

limited mobility—A diminished capacity to move the body independently.

listening—The process by which the brain absorbs the meaning of what is being said in order for the person to understand the facts and ideas expressed.

logic model—A chart or visual representation that displays a plan for a program or organization; connects specific actions with the outcomes they are designed to achieve; used to plan services and the organization's activities programs.

measurable goal—A goal that is modified by a specific performance measure or measurable outcome.

medical play—Use of toys and dolls with children to enable them to work out (or "play" out) their feelings or anxieties regarding medical treatments and procedures.

memory—The ability to store, retain, and retrieve information. Short-term memory refers to the ability to learn new information, and long-term memory is the ability to recall information that was learned in the past.

mindset—A mental attitude that reflects one's values and beliefs and influences how one interprets and responds to situations.

Minimum Data Set (MDS)—The comprehensive federal assessment used in long-term care facilities.

minute vacation—Stopping what you are doing, sitting still with your eyes closed, and letting your mind relax or drift for a very short period of time.

motivation—The cause or stimulus of action; the driving force that initiates and directs behavior.

muscular strength and endurance—The ability to exert force and the ability to sustain force over a period of time as needed to complete activities of daily living, carry or lift objects, and climb stairs without relying on one's arms.

National Council for Therapeutic Recreation Certification—An independent organization that issues the CTRS credential to certify therapeutic recreation specialists.

National Therapeutic Recreation Society—A branch of the National Recreation and Park Association whose membership is open to any interested person wishing to promote the provision of TR services.

new arts—Arts that use technology, such as digital photography, computer art, and so on.

nonmaleficence—Not doing harm; not providing ineffective services or acting with malice toward clients (also known as nonmalfeasance).

normalization—The principle that people with disabilities are entitled to patterns and conditions of everyday life that are the same as, or as similar as possible to, those of their community and should exercise self-determination to attain their optimal living conditions.

norms—The rules by which a group operates, representing a standard of behavior for the members of the group.

obesity—A weight disorder that occurs when excessive body fat is accumulated beyond what is considered typical based on age, sex, and body type.

observation—A systematic and structured method of assessment in which the TRS views the client and gathers relevant information.

one-to-one program—The provision of a TR program to a single person.

outcome-oriented programming—Designing one-to-one or small-group programs to produce measurable, relevant, and meaningful client outcomes.

outcomes—Measurable short- or long-term change in clients' health status or well-being after they have received TR services.

outdoor recreation—Activities that require a meaningful and intentional relationship with the natural environment.

overweight—Weighing too much in proportion to one's height.

parentalism—A principle acknowledging that some clients may truly be in a state of diminished capacity that affects their decision-making ability; therefore professionals can act as caring, nurturing parents who at times need to intervene to protect their well-being and safety.

paternalism—Thinking one always knows what is best for clients and acting accordingly.

paternalistic leadership style—A style of leadership in which the leader protects and guides the client, based on paternalism.

patience—The ability to postpone gratification or wait for something rather than expecting something to happen immediately.

performance improvement—A total management process that should be integrated into the overall operations of the agency daily and emphasizes the *outcomes* produced by the agency's programs and services.

performing arts—Arts such as music, dance, and drama in which the participant is a performer and the mode of artistic expression.

person-centered planning—An ongoing problem-solving process used to help people with disabilities plan for their future; planning emphasizes collaboration among a network of supporters.

physical activity—Bodily movement produced by skeletal muscles that results in an increased expenditure of energy.

physical domain—The physical behaviors used in the performance of daily activities and in maintenance of a healthy body.

physical fitness—The ability to carry out daily tasks with alertness and vigor, without undue fatigue, and with enough energy reserve to meet emergencies and to enjoy leisure time.

pleasure—A positive, desired, joyful experience, the opposite of pain.

Positive Behavior Support Plan—A plan designed to prevent a behavior from happening or decrease the frequency of the behavior; provides detailed directions to staff on how to address targeted behaviors.

positive psychology—A branch of psychology that focuses on using strengths and virtues to enable people to develop constructive and life-enhancing feelings and behaviors and to thrive in their lives and their communities.

power—The degree of influence one has over people's behaviors and the environment, or the ability to control the environment and the behaviors of others in a given situation.

practice model—A visual representation of the relationships among philosophy, theories, and the real world that serves as a guide for professional practice.

principles—Fundamental beliefs that guide professional practice.

privacy—The right to control access to one's person and to information about oneself.

private spaces—Spaces with restricted access.

processing—A therapeutic technique primarily involving verbal discussion of client behaviors, thoughts, feelings, and external factors that relate to the behavior.

process orientation—A group's focus on developing and promoting interpersonal relationships.

profession—An occupation that meets the criteria for a profession: distinct body of knowledge, standards of practice, code of ethics, practitioner qualifications, professional organization, and having value in the eyes of the public.

program formats—The organizational structures used to present activities.

program protocol—A standardized set of procedures to be used in carrying out a specific program or intervention in order to attain predetermined client outcomes.

progress notes—The periodic written or electronic recording of a client's progress, or lack thereof, at designated intervals.

prosocial behaviors—Behaviors that foster social relationships including helping others, offering compliments and encouragement, sharing, cooperating, and resolving conflicts.

proxemics—The study of how human beings use space in their personal relationships and physical environments and in urban planning and design.

public spaces—Spaces that have open access to any person who can freely enter the area.

qualitative measures—Rich descriptions of people's experiences within a program or as a result of an intervention, in order to gain a deeper understanding of the impacts the programming has on a person. The descriptions themselves are the qualitative measures.

quality assurance—An inspection procedure to ensure that health care facilities meet minimal standards set by government regulatory agencies, focusing on identifying and correcting errors that come to light during medical chart reviews or audits.

quality of life—A person's perception of her position in life, based on her physical and psychological health, family and social relationships, level of independence, work, financial status, and living situation, in the context of her environment and values. Quality of life involves both subjective measures, such as one's sense of well-being and availability of opportunities, and objective measures, including functional status and access to resources.

quantitative measures—Data that can be counted, or quantified, in numbers. Minutes or percentage of time are examples of quantitative measures.

readiness—An individual's state of mind and level of preparedness to take action.

readiness assessment—An assessment of how ready for or receptive to treatment a client is.

recreation—An activity one chooses to do for fun or to share an experience with others, or for some specific benefit that is personally meaningful.

recreation participation—Engaging in recreation activities in the optimal environment and with the desired supports in order to maximize a meaningful and satisfying experience.

referent power—Power based in group members' high degree of identification with, and admiration and respect for, the leader.

reinforcer—Event that occurs following a desired response, which increases the likelihood that the behavior will occur again.

relaxation—A process by which people retreat mentally from their surroundings by quieting their thoughts and relaxing their muscles and maintaining this state long enough to decrease anxiety and tension.

relaxation room—A soothing environment designed for individuals who are particularly susceptible to overstimulation.

relaxation techniques—Methods used to deal with excess tension brought about by stress, to achieve a state of relaxation, or both.

reminiscence—The structured verbal interaction process or act of recalling long-term memories, generally with a focus more on positive memories than on negative ones.

replacement behavior training (RBT)—Teaching participants to replace an inappropriate behavior with an appropriate one that meets the same need.

reward power—Power based on the ability to control a person or a group receiving a reward or benefit.

risk management—Anticipating what might go wrong in a program, planning ways to avoid problems, and developing procedures to respond appropriately when something does go wrong.

roles—Consistent behaviors based on a specific task or relationship function.

scheduling—Specifying the time at which a program is offered, the length of each session, the number of sessions offered, and the locations and spaces in which programs are held.

secondary conditions—Problems that may be triggered by an initial medical condition; often a target of TR intervention.

self-awareness—Knowledge and understanding of one's own feelings, attitudes, and values and how they influence one's behaviors.

self-determination—People's rights to make their own choices and to determine the course of their lives.

self-disclosure—The careful and thoughtful sharing of personal information by the TRS in the context of the therapeutic relationship for the purpose of increasing the client's self-understanding.

self-efficacy—One's perception of being able to meet one's goals and satisfy personal needs in a positive way, or the judgment of one's own capability to accomplish a task or a particular level of performance.

self-esteem—A person's overall evaluation or appraisal of his own worth.

sensory stimulation—Interventions designed to stimulate one or more of the senses to try to provoke responses, which may reduce the severity and duration of a coma, or to reactivate senses that have become dulled from illness or lack of use.

sexual assessment—An assessment to determine residents' sexual needs and interests.

soap opera therapy—Watching soap operas with a therapist who guides clients to develop insights about their own issues and learn how to apply problem-solving skills to their personal situation.

social domain—Behaviors that are used in social interactions and most often displayed during group experiences.

social health—Possessing the social abilities necessary to live in society interdependently and engage in reciprocal relationships.

social intelligence or **social competence**—Making judgments about how to enter a new group of people, what to say and when to say it, and how to react in a range of social situations on a daily basis in order to establish and maintain relationships in all the environments of a person's life.

social interaction patterns—The classification of interaction patterns found in recreation activities according the level and degree of interpersonal interaction required.

social recreation—Familiar, casual, and enjoyable experiences conducted by a leader to promote relaxed and appropriate social behavior within groups.

special events—Out-of-the-ordinary activities that are offered infrequently, based on the length of stay or duration of service provided by the department, and that generate interest, excitement, enthusiasm, and participation by creating a "buzz."

sports—Activities characterized by physical exertion, competition involving physical skills, and rules.

stage theory of group development—The theory that groups develop in five stages: forming, storming, norming, performing, and adjourning.

stages of change—Various stages of readiness of a person to make changes in her life; include precontemplation, contemplation, preparation for change, action, and maintenance.

standardized assessment tools or instruments—Assessment tools that have been developed to deliver reliable and valid information and have been tested repeatedly; results can be accepted as accurate and as a true representation of what is being measured.

standards of (or **for**) **practice**—A set of standards that specifies the minimum acceptable level for delivery of the services and specific procedures of the profession; includes the scope of services, professional qualifications, and commitment to ethical practice.

stigma—The labeling of a particular group of people as less worthy of respect, based on their health condition or disability; labeling is due to fear and ignorance and leads to prejudice and discrimination.

strengths-based approach—A planning approach that represents a shift in service provision from focusing on the problems, deficits, or disorders of clients to emphasizing the strengths, resources, and capabilities of the clients, their families, and communities.

substituted judgment—Professional decision making based on what clients would decide they want for themselves, if they were competent to do so, and not what the professional would decide.

summative evaluation—Evaluation that occurs at the end of the program to determine if the program was a success, if any changes are needed to improve the program, and if the program should be offered again.

supervisory leadership—Overseeing the actions of other staff, volunteers, and interns; keeping an eye on the big picture of equipment, supplies, facility use, and safety; conducting in-service training; scheduling programs; and providing input to agency committees and other groups.

support groups—Groups offered for emotional support, coping, information, building interpersonal skills, and socialization to clients and their families; centered on living with a common issue or concern related to their health condition, disability, or challenges in daily life.

sympathy—Compassion for another person's thoughts, feelings, or experiences.

synergy—The working together of two or more components to lead to a result greater than the sum of their individual results.

task analysis—A procedure for identifying the steps or behaviors needed to complete a task or activity in the sequence in which the steps should occur.

task orientation—Focus of a group primarily on completing a task or producing a product.

team—A group of professionals who work together with a common purpose.

team leadership—The TRS's active fulfillment of the professional responsibility to make clear to the team the purpose and value of TR, the client's recreational needs and goals, the TR plan for the client, and the aims of the plan, as well as her provision of a report of the client's functioning and behaviors as observed in TR programs.

themed programming—A group of programs of varying durations connected by a common focus.

therapeutic communication—A goal-directed, focused dialogue between the TRS and a client specifically fitted to the needs of the client.

therapeutic horseback riding—A broad term that includes equine-assisted activities (E-AA) and equine-assisted therapy (E-AT). E-AA involves learning horse-related skills, such as riding and grooming, to improve one's quality of life; in E-AT, a therapist uses the horse as an intervention in goal-directed treatment.

therapeutic outdoor programming—An umbrella term for adventure therapy and wilderness therapy, which use direct experience of the outdoors as a treatment intervention as well as structured interventions in the outdoor setting for treatment purposes.

therapeutic recreation—Engaging individuals in planned recreation and related experiences in order to improve functioning, health and well-being, and quality of life, while also focusing on the whole person and needed changes in the optimal living environment and recognizing the potential of leisure for contributing to the quality of life.

therapeutic recreation environment—The distinctive atmosphere that exists in a TR room or space, surrounds a TR program, or is present in the structured or unstructured contact between a TRS and a client or group of clients. The TR environment promotes interaction; offers opportunities for self-expression, feelings of control, making choices, taking chances, creativity, and enjoyment; and demonstrates respect for the autonomy of the individual.

therapeutic recreation intervention—The combination of recreation activities with the TRS's interactions and communication skills, which become the TR programs or experiences that help the clients achieve functional and existential outcomes.

therapeutic recreation leadership—The unique blending of the therapist's purposeful application of therapeutic strategies and facilitation techniques with the recreation specialist's abilities to create and facilitate leisure experiences in order to deliver TR services according to the highest ethical standards.

Therapeutic Recreation Outcome Model—A practice model that focuses on increasing functional capacity and health status to improve quality of life.

therapeutic recreation process—The series of steps carried out by the TRS to fulfill the purposes of TR; steps include assessment, planning, implementation, and evaluation.

Therapeutic Recreation Service Model—A practice model that describes four areas of TR service—diagnosis/needs assessment, treatment/rehabilitation, education, and prevention/health promotion; the purpose of TR in this model is to improve functioning, health status, and quality of life through participation in recreation activities.

therapeutic recreation toolkit—A collection of information, resources, and activities that the TRS uses in his work.

total task instruction (TTI) or **whole task instruction**—The process of teaching all the steps of a task at once so the learner is observing the entire sequence.

transference—A condition that occurs when clients project or redirect issues and feelings that are an outgrowth of prior experiences and relationships onto the TRS.

transformational leadership—The concept that leaders achieve success by inspiring others to believe that they can achieve great things.

Transtheoretical Model—A model that identifies the key stages in the change process.

triangulation—Use of multiple methods of measurement.

Type I programs—Also known as cafeteria programs; typically, large groups in which all clients receive the same program without a focus on individual goals.

Type II programs—Also known as outcome-oriented programs; typically one-to-one or small-group programs designed to produce measurable outcomes.

unit-wide programming—The group of TR programs offered to a single setting and for which a single schedule is developed; such as a psychiatric ward of a general hospital or one floor in a long-term care setting, or a day care program.

universal precautions—A set of precautions used to avoid contact with patients' bodily fluids to prevent the transmission of HIV, hepatitis B virus, and other bloodborne pathogens.

value-based behavior—Behavior based on reflection on one's beliefs, attitudes, and values and on making a conscious effort to act with thought and insight.

values—The established ideals of a profession that are reflected in professional ethics; they identify what the profession considers of worth and usefulness and may arouse an emotional response due to their significance and meaning.

values clarification—A process using activities and exercises through which clients examine their values, explore how these values influence their behaviors, and make decisions to act in accordance with their values.

verbal persuasion—The use of words to convince a client that he is capable of a certain action and can reach a goal.

well-being—One's judgment of his existence as good and satisfactory based on having access to and being able to successfully use psychological, social, cognitive, physical, and environmental resources.

wellness—An active process of becoming aware and making choices to create a healthier lifestyle that will enhance well-being while decreasing the risk of disease.

wilderness therapy—Program involving adapting to and coping with the wilderness environment; similar to adventure therapy except that adventure therapy does not necessarily take place in what is considered a wilderness area.

workaholism— "Addiction" to work; people spend long hours and large amounts of energy on their jobs, perhaps because of internal or external pressures to produce and perform, and also use work as an excuse not to go home and face other issues in their life.

REFERENCES

Adams, J. (2005). *Boundary issues: Using boundary intelligence to get the intimacy you want and the independence you need in life, love, and work.* New York: Wiley.

Agazarian, Y. (1999). Phases of development in the system-centered psychotherapy group. *Small Group Research*, 30(1), 82-106.

American College of Sports Medicine. Certification. Retrieved August 15, 2008, from www.acsm.org/AM/Template.cfm?Section=Get_Certified&Template=/CM/HTMLDisplay.cfm&ContentID=10927.

American Council on Exercise. Accredited fitness certifications. Retrieved August 15, 2008, from www.acefitness.org/get-certified/default.aspx.

American Institute of Stress. (2008). America's no. 1 health problem. www.stress.org.

American Psychiatric Association. (2000). *Diagnostic and statistical manual of mental disorders DSM-IV-TR* (4th ed.). Washington, DC: Author.

American Therapeutic Recreation Association (1993). *Standards for the practice of therapeutic recreation.* Hattiesburg, MS: Author.

American Therapeutic Recreation Association. (2009). *ATRA code of ethics.* Hattiesburg, MS: Author.

American Therapeutic Recreation Association (1991). *ATRA standards for practice.* Hattiesburg, MS: Author.

Anderson, L. & Heyne, L. (2007). Assessing strengths: Tools for positive change. Paper presented at the meeting of the New York State Therapeutic Recreation Association, Saratoga Springs, NY.

Anspaugh, D. & Ezell, G. (2007). *Teaching today's health* (8th ed.). New York: Pearson Benjamin Cummings.

Arts Council of Wales. (2007). *Arts in health and well-being.* Cardiff, Wales. www.arstwales.org.uk.

Associated Press. (2008, February 9). Doctors use Wii games for rehab therapy.

Atkinson, D., Kim, A., Ruelas, S. & Tzu-Min Lin, A. (1999). Ethnicity and attitudes toward facilitated reminiscence. *Journal of Mental Health Counseling*, 21(1), 66-82.

Austin, D. (2001). The therapeutic recreation process. In D. Austin & M. Crawford (Eds.), *Therapeutic recreation: An introduction* (3rd ed., pp. 45-56). Needham Heights, MA: Allyn & Bacon.

Austin, D. (2002a). A call for training in physical activity. In D. Austin, J. Dattilo & B. McCormick (Eds.), *Conceptual foundations for therapeutic recreation* (pp. 225-234). State College, PA: Venture Publishing.

Austin, D. (2002b). The therapeutic relationship. In D. Austin, J. Dattilo & B. McCormick (Eds.), *Conceptual foundations for therapeutic recreation* (pp. 115-132). State College, PA: Venture.

Austin, D. (2004). *Therapeutic recreation: Processes and techniques* (5th ed.). Champaign, IL: Sagamore.

Austin, D. (2009). *Therapeutic recreation: Processes and techniques* (6th ed.). Champaign, IL: Sagamore.

Austin, E., Johnston, Y. & Morgan, L. (2006). Community gardening in a senior center: A therapeutic intervention to improve the health of older adults. *Therapeutic Recreation Journal*, 40(1), 48-56.

Avedon, E. (1974). *Therapeutic recreation service: An applied behavioral science approach.* Englewood Cliffs, NJ: Prentice Hall.

Baglin, C., Lewis, M. & Williams, B. (2004). *Recreation and leisure for persons with emotional problems and challenging behaviors.* Champaign, IL: Sagamore.

Ball, E. (1971). The meaning of therapeutic recreation. *Therapeutic Recreation Journal*, 4(1), 17-18.

Balzer-Riley, J.W. (1996). *Communications in nursing* (3rd ed.). St. Louis: Mosby.

Bandura, A. (1997). *Self efficacy: The exercise of control.* New York: Freeman Press.

Barksdale, A. (2003). *Music therapy and leisure for persons with disabilities.* Champaign, IL: Sagamore.

Bartalos, M. (1993). Work, health and recreation: Aspects of the total person. *Loss, Grief and Care*, 6(4), 7-14.

Batavia, A. & Batavia, M. (2003). Karaoke for quads: A new application of an old recreation with potential therapeutic benefits for people with disabilities. *Disability and Rehabilitation*, 25(6), 297-300.

Beagan, B. & Chapman, G. (2004). Family influences on food choice: Context of surviving breast cancer. *Journal of Nutrition Education and Behavior*, 36(6), 320-326.

Beard, M. & Ragheb, M. (1983). Measuring leisure motivation. *Journal of Leisure Research*, 15(3), 219-228.

Beebe, S. & Masterson, J. (2000). *Small group development* (6th ed.). New York: Longman Press.

Beland, R. (2004). Using children's books in bibliotherapy for older adults. In M. Devine (Ed.), *Trends in therapeutic recreation* (pp. 89-109). Ashburn, VA: National Recreation and Park Association.

Benda, W. (2005). The therapeutic nature of the human-animal bond. *International Journal of Therapy and Rehabilitation*, 12(7), 284.

Benda, W., McGibbon, N. & Grant, K. (2003). Improvements in muscle symmetry in children with cerebral palsy after equine-assisted therapy (hippotherapy). *Journal of Alternative and Complementary Medicine*, 9(16), 817-825.

Bergland, A. & Narum, I. (2007). Quality of life demands comprehension and further exploration. *Journal of Aging and Health*, 19(1), 39-61.

Bizub, A., Joy, A. & Davidson, L. (2003). "It's like being in another world": Demonstrating the benefits of therapeutic horseback riding for individuals with psychiatric disability. *Psychiatric Rehabilitation Journal*, 26(4), 377-385.

Blackwell, J. (2003). Use of great books in the development of assertiveness training. *Education*, 123(3), 462-465.

Bliss, B. (1997). Alternative: Complementary therapies. Therapeutic horseback riding? *RN*, 60(10), 69-70.

Bonadies, V. (2004). A yoga therapy program for AIDS-related pain and anxiety: Implications for therapeutic recreation. *Therapeutic Recreation Journal*, 38(2), 148-166.

Botner-Marigold, E. & Miller, W. (2007). A qualitative evaluation of the Idyll Arbor leisure battery for individuals with spinal cord injury. *Therapeutic Recreation Journal*, 41(3), 244-258.

Brady, E. & Sky, H. (2003). Journal writing among older learners. *Educational Gerontology*, 29(2), 151-163.

Breen, L. (2007). Therapeutic use of soap operas in autistic-spectrum disorders. *Psychiatric Bulletin*, 31, 67-69.

Broach, E. & Dattilo, J. (2000). Aquatic therapy. In J. Dattilo (Ed.), *Facilitation techniques in therapeutic recreation* (pp. 65-98). State College, PA: Venture.

Broach, E., Dattilo, J. & Loy, D. (2000). Therapeutic use of exercise. In J. Dattilo (Ed.), *Facilitation techniques in therapeutic recreation* (pp. 355-383). State College, PA: Venture.

Broach, E., Dattilo, J. & McKenney, A. (2007). Effects of aquatic therapy on perceived fun or enjoyment experiences of participants with multiple sclerosis. *Therapeutic Recreation Journal*, 41(3), 179-200.

Brocklebank, S. & Mauer, R. (1990). *The group development guidebook*. Washington, DC: Mid-Atlantic Training Association.

Brodie, S. & Biley, I. (1999). An exploration of the potential benefits of pet-facilitated therapy. *Journal of Clinical Nursing*, 8(4), 329-337.

Bruck, L. (1999). What's cooking at Sarah Neuman? *Nursing Homes: Long Term Care Management*, 48(11), 37-38.

Buettner, L. & Martin, S. (1995). *Therapeutic recreation in the nursing home*. State College, PA: Venture.

Bullock, C. & Johnson, D. (1998). Recreational therapy in special education. In F. Brasile, T. Skalko & J. Burlingame, *Perspectives in recreational therapy: Issues of a dynamic profession* (pp. 106-124). Ravensdale, WA: Idyll Arbor.

Bullock, C. & Mahon, M. (2000). *Introduction to recreation services for people with disabilities: A person-centered approach* (2nd ed.). Champaign, IL: Sagamore.

Burlingame, J. & Blaschko, T.M. (2002). *Assessment tools for recreational therapy and related fields* (3rd ed.). Ravensdale, WA: Idyll Arbor.

Burlingame, J. & Singley, J. (1998). Adult learning: Andragogy and adults with learning disabilities. In F. Brasile, T. Skalko & J. Burlingame, *Perspectives in recreational therapy: Issues of a dynamic profession* (pp. 345-366). Ravensdale, WA: Idyll Arbor.

Cantor, J. (2008). *Delivering instruction to adult learners* (3rd ed.). Toronto, CA: Walt & Emerson.

Caplan, A. (1990). The morality of the mundane: Ethical issues arising in the daily life of nursing home residents. In R. Kane & A. Caplan (Eds.), *Everyday ethics: Resolving dilemmas in nursing home life* (pp. 37-50). New York: Springer.

Carpenter, G. (2006). Arts and culture. In Human Kinetics, *Introduction to recreation and leisure* (pp. 333-352). Champaign, IL: Author.

Carruthers, C. (2003). Objectives-based approach in evaluating effectiveness. In N. Stumbo (Ed.), *Client outcomes in therapeutic recreation services* (pp. 185-200). State College, PA: Venture.

Carruthers, C. & Hood, C. (2002). Coping skills theory as an underlying framework for therapeutic recreation services. *Therapeutic Recreation Journal*, 36(2), 137-153.

Carruthers, C. & Hood, C. (2004). The power of the positive: Leisure and well-being. *Therapeutic Recreation Journal*, 38(2), 225-245.

Carruthers, C. & Hood, C. (2007). Building a life of meaning through therapeutic recreation: The leisure and well-being model, part I. *Therapeutic Recreation Journal*, 41(4), 276-297.

Carter, M., McCown, K., Forest, S., Martin, J., Wacker, R., Gaede, D. & Fernandez, T. (2004). Exercise and fitness for adults with developmental disabilities: Case report of a group intervention. *Therapeutic Recreation Journal*, 38(1), 72-84.

Carter, M. & O'Morrow, G. (2006). *Effective management in therapeutic recreation service* (2nd ed.). State College, PA: Venture.

Carter, M., Van Andel, G. & Robb, G. (1996). *Therapeutic recreation: A practical approach*. Prospect Heights, IL: Waveland Press.

Carter, M., Van Andel, G. & Robb, G. (2003). *Therapeutic recreation: A practical approach* (3rd ed.). Prospect Heights, IL: Waveland Press.

Cave, J., LaMaster, C. & White, S. (1987). *Plan instruction for adults, Module N-4*. The National Center for Research in Vocational Education, Columbus, OH: Ohio State University.

Centers for Medicare and Medicaid Services. (2008). MDS 2.0 for nursing homes. www.cms.hhs.gov/nursinghomequalityinits.

Chadsey, J. (2007). Adult social relationships. In S. Odum, R. Horner, M. Snell & J. Blacher, *Handbook of developmental disabilities* (pp. 449-466). New York: Guilford Press.

Chow, Y. (2002). The case of an in-home recreation program for an older adult in a naturally occurring retirement community (NORC). *Therapeutic Recreation Journal*, 36(2), 203-212.

Coelho, E. (1998). *Teaching and learning in a multicultural classroom: An integrated approach*. Clevedon, UK: Multicultural Matters/Channel View.

Coffman, J. (1999). *Learning from logic models: An example of a family/school partnership*. Cambridge, MA: Harvard Family Research Project.

Collopy, B. (1988). Autonomy in long term care: Some crucial distinctions. *Gerontologist*, 28 (Suppl.), 10-17.

Collopy, B. (1996). Bioethics in therapeutic recreation: Expanding the dialogue. In C. Sylvester (Ed.), *Philosophy of therapeutic recreation: Ideas and issues, Volume II* (pp. 10-19). Ashburn, VA: National Therapeutic Recreation Society.

Commission on Accreditation of Rehabilitation Facilities. (2008). Sampling a CARF standard. www.carf.org/consumer.

Cordes, K. & Ibrahim, H. (2002). *Applications in recreation and leisure: For today and the future* (3rd ed.). New York: McGraw-Hill.

Corey, G., Schneider Corey, M. & Haynes, R. (2000). *Evolution of a group: Student video & workbook*. Belmont, CA: Wadsworth.

Covey, S. (2004). *Seven habits of highly effective people: Powerful lessons in personal change* (2nd ed.). New York: Free Press.

Coyle, C. & Shank, J. (2004). Guest editors' introduction to the special issue on health and health promotion: Do we care? *Therapeutic Recreation Journal*, 38(2), 112-115.

Crawford, M. (2001). Issues and trends. In D. Austin & M. Crawford (Eds.), *Therapeutic recreation: An introduction* (3rd ed., pp. 333-359). Needham Heights, MA: Allyn & Bacon.

Csikszentmihalyi, M. (1990). *Flow: The psychology of optimal experience*. New York: Harper Collins.

Cullen, L., Titler, M. & Drahozal, P. (2003). Family and pet visitation on the critical care unit: Protocols for practice. *Critical Care Nurse*, 23(5), 62-68.

Curtright, A. & Turner, G. (2002). The influence of a stuffed and live animal on communication in a female with Alzheimer's dementia. *Journal of Medical Speech-Language Pathology*, 10(1), 61-72.

DaGama, G. & Hironaka-Juteau, J. (2002). Action research: A new tool in program evaluation. *California Parks and Recreation Magazine*, 58(3), p. 38.

Dattilo, J., Born, E. & Cory, L. (2000). Therapeutic use of animals. In J. Dattilo (Ed.), *Facilitation techniques in therapeutic recreation* (pp. 327-354). State College, PA: Venture.

Dattilo, J. & Guerin, N. (2001). Mental retardation. In D. Austin & M. Crawford (Eds.), *Therapeutic recreation: An introduction* (3rd ed., pp. 130-156). Needham Heights, MA: Allyn & Bacon.

Dattilo, J. & Kleiber, D. (2002). Self-determination and enjoyment in therapeutic recreation. In D. Austin, J. Dattilo & B. McCormick (Eds.), *Conceptual foundations for therapeutic recreation* (pp. 73-92). State College, PA: Venture.

Dattilo, J., Kleiber, D. & Williams, R. (1998). Self-determination and enjoyment enhancement: A psychologically-based service delivery model for therapeutic recreation. *Therapeutic Recreation Journal*, 32(4), 258-271.

Davies, A. (2000). The practical management of claudication: As a marker for cardiovascular disease it needs active treatment. *British Medical Journal*, 321(7266), 911-912.

Davies, J., McCrae, B., Frank, J., Dochnahl, A., Pickering, T., Harrison, B., Zakrzewski, M. & Wilson, K. (2000). Identifying male college students' perceived health needs, barriers to seeking health, and recommendations to help men adopt healthier lifestyles. *Journal of American College Health*, 46(6), 259-268.

Davis, C. (2006). *Patient practitioner interaction: An experiential manual for developing the art of health care,* (4th ed.). Thorofare, NJ: Slack.

DeGeest, G. (2007). *The living dementia case-study approach.* Victoria, BC: Trafford.

Delta Society (1992). Does pet ownership reduce your risk for heart disease? InterActions, 10(3), 12-13.

Delta Society. (2008). Health benefits of animals. www.delta-society.org.

DeMarco-Sinatra, J. (2000). Relaxation training as a holistic nursing intervention. *Holistic Nursing Practice*, 14(3), 30-45.

DeMars, N. (1998). *You want me to do what? When, where and how to draw the line at work.* New York, NY: Fireside Press.

Devine, M. & O'Brien, M. (2004). Inclusion: Beyond simple sharing of the same space. In M. Devine (Ed.), *Trends in therapeutic recreation: Ideas, concepts, applications* (pp. 201-232). Ashburn, VA: National Recreation and Park Association.

Devine, M. & O'Brien, M. (2007). The mixed bag of inclusion: An examination of an inclusive camp using contact theory. *Therapeutic Recreation Journal*, 41(3), 201-222.

DeVries, D. & Lake, J. (2002). *Innovations: A recreation therapy approach to restorative programs.* State College, PA: Venture.

Dickason, J. & London, P. (2001). Pediatric play. In D. Austin & M. Crawford (Eds.), *Therapeutic recreation: An introduction* (3rd ed., pp. 255-268). Boston: Allyn & Bacon.

Dieser, R. (2002). A cross-cultural critique of newer therapeutic recreation practice models: The self-determination and enjoyment enhancement, Aristotelian good life model, and the optimizing lifelong health through therapeutic recreation. *Therapeutic Recreation Journal*, 36(4), 352-368.

Dieser, R. (2004). Leisure education: Breaking free from individualistic notions. In M. Devine (Ed.), *Trends in therapeutic recreation: Ideas, concepts, applications* (pp. 1-25). Ashburn, VA: National Recreation and Park Association.

Dieser, R. (2008). History of therapeutic recreation. In T. Robertson & T. Long (Eds.), *Foundations of therapeutic recreation* (pp. 13-30). Champaign, IL: Human Kinetics.

Dieser, R., Magnuson, D. & Scholl, K. (2005). Critically rethinking the benefits based approach from a cross-cultural perspective. In C. Sylvester (Ed.), *Philosophy of therapeutic recreation: Ideas and issues, Volume III* (pp. 59-72). Ashburn, VA: National Therapeutic Recreation Society.

Dixon, J. (2008). Paradoxes in leisure services and therapeutic recreation. In T. Robertson & T. Long (Eds.), *Foundations of therapeutic recreation* (pp. 251-265). Champaign, IL: Human Kinetics.

Dole, S. & McMahan, J. (2005). Using videotherapy to help adolescents cope with social and emotional problems. *Intervention in School and Clinic*, 40(3), 151-155.

Donatelle, R. (2004). *Health: The basics* (6th ed.). San Francisco: Pearson Benjamin Cummings.

Donatelle, R., Snow, C. & Wilcox, A. (1999). *Wellness: Choices for health and fitness* (2nd ed.). Florence, KY: Cengage Learning.

Dower, C., O'Neil, E. & Hough, H. (2001). *Profiling the professions: A model for evaluating emerging health professions.* San Francisco: University of California San Francisco, Center for the Health Professions.

Drake, R. (2005). The principles of evidence-based mental health treatment. In R. Drake, M. Merrens & D. Lynde (Eds.), *Evidence-based mental health practice* (pp. 15-32). New York: Norton.

Drench, M., Noonan, A., Sharby, N. & Ventura, S. (2007). *Psychosocial aspects of health care* (2nd ed.). Upper Saddle River, NJ: Pearson/Prentice Hall.

Dresser, N. (2005). *Multicultural manners: Essential rules of etiquette for the 21st century.* Hoboken, NJ: Wiley.

Dunlop, J. (1990). Peer groups support seniors fighting alcohol and drugs. *Aging*, 3, 28-33.

Durstine, J., Painter, P., Franklin, B., Morgan, D., Pitetti, K. & O'Roberts, S. (2000). Physical activity for the chronically ill and disabled. *Sports Medicine*, 30(3), 207-219.

Edginton, C., DeGraaf, D., Dieser, R. & Edginton, S. (2006). *Leisure and life satisfaction: Foundational perspectives* (4th ed.). New York, NY: McGraw-Hill.

Edginton, C., Hudson, S., Dieser, R. & Edginton, S. (2004). *Leisure programming: A service-centered and benefits approach* (4th ed.). New York, NY: McGraw-Hill.

Edwards, N. & Beck, A. (2002). Animal-assisted therapy and nutrition in Alzheimer's disease. *Western Journal of Nursing Research*, 24(6), 697-712.

Ell, K. & Reardon, K. (1990). Psychosocial care for the chronically ill adolescent. *Health and Social Work*, 15(4), 272-282.

Engleberg, I. & Wynn, D. (2000). *Working in groups: Communication principles and strategies.* New York: Houghton Mifflin.

Ewert, A., Voight, A. & Harnishfeger, B. (2002). An overview of therapeutic outdoor programming. In D. Austin, J. Dattilo & B. McCormick (Eds.), *Conceptual foundations for therapeutic recreation* (pp. 133-150). State College, PA: Venture.

Fabry, B. (2002). Building strengths to build health. *FSWP News*, 2(2), 1-2.

Fast, B. & Chapin, R. (2000). *Strengths-based care management for older adults*. Baltimore: Health Professions Press.

Fazio, L. (2008). *Developing occupation-centered programs for the community* (2nd ed.). Upper Saddle River, NJ: Pearson Education.

Fiatarone, M., O'Neill, E., Ryan, N., Clements, K., Solares, G., & Nelson, M. et al., (1994). Exercise training and nutritional supplementation for physical frailty in very elderly people. *New England Journal of Medicine*, 330(25), 1769-1725.

Fiedler, F. (1967). *A theory of leadership effectiveness*. New York: McGraw-Hill.

Fisher, C. (1993). Boredom at work: A neglected concept. *Human Relations* (46)3, 395-417.

Floyd, P., Mimms, P. & Yelding, C. (2008). *Personal health: Perspectives and lifestyles* (4th ed.). Boston: Thomson/Wadsworth.

Foose, A. & Ardovino, P. (2008). Therapeutic recreation and developmental disabilities. In T. Robertson & T. Long (Eds.), *Foundations of therapeutic recreation* (pp. 127-144). Champaign, IL: Human Kinetics.

Ford-Martin, P. (2005). Relaxation. *Gale encyclopedia of alternative medicine*. Detroit: Gale Group.

Freeman, E. (2006). The art of therapeutic recreation. *Parks and Recreation*, 41(12), 44-47.

Frye, V. & Peters, M. (1972). *Therapeutic recreation: Its theory, philosophy and practice*. Harrisburg, PA: Stackpole Books.

Gardner, J. & Chapman, M. (1993). *Developing staff competencies for supporting people with developmental disabilities: An orientation handbook* (2nd ed.). Baltimore: Brookes.

Garner, H. & Dietz, L. (1996). Person-centered planning: Maps and paths to the future. *Four Runner*, 11(2), 1-2.

Getz, D. (2002). Increasing cultural competence in therapeutic recreation. In D. Austin, J. Dattilo & B. McCormick (Eds.), *Conceptual foundations for therapeutic recreation* (pp. 151-164). State College, PA: Venture.

Gillespie, C. (2003). A case report illustrating the use of creative writing as a therapeutic recreation intervention in a dual-diagnosis residential treatment center. *Therapeutic Recreation Journal*, 37(4), 339-348.

Glasser, W. (1998). *A new psychology of personal freedom*. New York: Harper Collins.

Glazer, H., Clark, M. & Stein, D. (2004). The impact of hippotherapy on grieving children. *Journal of Hospice and Palliative Nursing*, 6(3), 171-175.

Glover, T., Parry, D. & Shinew, K. (2005). Building relationships, accessing resources: Mobilizing social capital in community garden contexts. *Journal of Leisure Research*, 37(4), 450-475.

Glover-Graf, N. & Miller, E. (2006). The use of phototherapy in group treatment for persons who are chemically dependent. *Rehabilitation Counseling Bulletin*, 49(3), 166-181.

Goldstein, J., Cajko, L., Oosterbroeck, M., Michielsen, M., Van Houten, O. & Salverda, F. (1997). Video games and the elderly. *Social Behavior and Personality*, 25(4), 345-352.

Goleman, D. (1995). *Emotional intelligence*. New York: Bantam Books.

Gollnick, D. & Chinn, P. (2008). *Multicultural education in a pluralistic society* (8th ed.). Englewood Cliffs, NJ: Prentice Hall.

Goodwin, D., Krohn, J. & Kuhnle, A. (2004). Beyond the wheelchair: The experience of dance. *Adapted Physical Activity Quarterly*, 21(3), 229-243.

Gordon, J., Staples, J., Blyta, A., Bytyqi, M. & Wilson, A. (2009, January 17). Treatment of posttraumatic stress disorder in postwar Kosovar adolescents using mind-body skills group: A randomized controlled trial. *Journal of Clinical Psychiatry*. www.psychiatrist.com.

Gregory, K. & Vessey, J. (2004). Bibliotherapy: A strategy to help students with bullying. *Journal of School Nursing*, 20(3), 127-133.

Groff, D., Lawrence, E. & Grivna, S. (2006). Effects of a therapeutic recreation intervention using exercise: A case study with a child with cerebral palsy. *Therapeutic Recreation Journal*, 40(4), 269-283.

Grossman, A. & Caroleo, O. (2001). HIV disease. In D. Austin & M. Crawford (Eds.), *Therapeutic recreation: An introduction* (3rd ed., pp. 297-317). Boston: Allyn & Bacon.

Grote, K., Hasl, M., Krider, R. & Mortensen, D. (1995). *Behavioral health protocols for recreational therapy*. Ravensdale, WA: Idyll Arbor.

Gunn, S. & Peterson, C. (1978). *Therapeutic recreation program design: Principles and practices*. Englewood Cliffs, NJ: Prentice Hall.

Haasen, B., Hornibrook, T. & Pedlar, A. (1998). Researcher and practitioner perspectives on a research partnership. *Journal of Leisurability*, 25(3).

Hall, E. (1966). *The hidden dimension*. New York: Anchor Books.

Harlan, J. (1993). The therapeutic value of art for persons with Alzheimer's disease and related disorders. *Loss, Grief and Care*, 6(4), 99-106.

Harris, J. (1998). *Does gestalt need a theory of group development?* Manchester Gestalt Center. www.mgc.org.uk.

Hart, M., Primm, K. & Cranisky, K. (2003). *Beyond baskets and beads: Activities for older adults with functional impairments*. State College, PA: Venture.

Haun, P. (1965). *Recreation: A medical viewpoint*. New York: Teacher's College Press.

Hebblethwaite, S. & Pedlar, A. (2005). Community integration for older adults with mental health issues: Implications for therapeutic recreation. *Therapeutic Recreation Journal*, 39(4), 264-276.

Hebert, P. (1997). Treatment. In R. Kane (Ed.), *Understanding health care outcomes research* (pp. 93-124). Gaithersburg, MD: Aspen.

Hemingway, J. (1987). Building a philosophical defense of therapeutic recreation: The case of distributive justice. In C. Sylvester (Ed.), *Philosophy of therapeutic recreation: Ideas and issues, Volume I* (pp. 1-16). Ashburn, VA: National Therapeutic Recreation Society.

Henderson, K., Bialeschki, M., Hemingway, J., Hodges, J., Kivel, B. & Sessoms, H. (2001). *Introduction to recreation and leisure services* (8th ed.). State College, PA: Venture.

Higgins, M., McKevitt, C. & Wolfe, C. (2005). Reading to stroke unit patients: Perceived impact and potential of an innovative arts-based therapy. *Disability and Rehabilitation*, 27(2), 1391-1398.

Ho, A., Sen, S., Kuperus, J. & Kohlsa, M. (n.d.). *Culinary therapy*. University of Alberta: Rehabilitation Medicine.

Hodges, J., Luken, K. & Hubbard, A. (2004). Supporting the transition of one man with autism from work to retirement. *Therapeutic Recreation Journal*, 38(3), 301-311.

Homes, L. & MacNeil, R. (1995). Case histories focusing on older adults: Practice issues. *Therapeutic Recreation Journal*, 29(4), 260-267.

Hood, C. (2001). Clinical practice guidelines—a decision making tool for best practice? In N. Stumbo (Ed.), *Professional issues in therapeutic recreation: On competence and outcomes* (pp. 189-213). Champaign, IL: Sagamore.

Hood, C. (2003). Standardizing practice and outcomes through clinical practice guidelines: Recommendations for therapeutic recreation. In N. Stumbo (Ed.), *Clinical outcomes in therapeutic recreation services* (pp. 149-164). State College, PA: Venture.

Howard, D., Russoniello, C. & Rodgers, D. (2004). Healthy People 2010 and therapeutic recreation: Professional opportunities to promote public health. *Therapeutic Recreation Journal*, 38(2), 116-132.

Howe-Murphy, R. & Charboneau, B. (1987). *Therapeutic recreation intervention: An ecological perspective.* Englewood Cliffs, NJ: Prentice Hall.

Howe-Murphy, R. & Murphy, J. (1987). An exploration of the new age consciousness paradigm in therapeutic recreation. In C. Sylvester (Ed.), *Philosophy of therapeutic recreation: Ideas and issues, Volume I* (pp. 41-54). Arlington, VA: National Therapeutic Recreation Society.

Hoysniemi, J. (2006). International survey on the Dance Dance Revolution game. *Computers in Entertainment*, 4(2).

Hudson-Barr, D. (2004). How to read a research article. *Journal for Specialists in Pediatric Nursing*, 9(2), 70-72.

Humphries, T. (2003). Effectiveness of dolphin-assisted therapy as a behavioral intervention for young children with disabilities. *Bridges*, 1(6).

Hutchinson, P. & Lord, M. (1979). *Recreation integration.* Ottawa, ON: Leisurability.

Hutchinson, S. & Dattilo, J. (2001). Processing: Possibilities for therapeutic recreation. *Therapeutic Recreation Journal*, 35(1), 43-56.

Hutchinson, S., LeBlanc, A. & Booth, R. (2006). More than "just having fun": Reconsidering the role of enjoyment in therapeutic recreation practice. *Therapeutic Recreation Journal*, 40(4), 220-240.

Hutchinson, S., Loy, D., Kleiber, D. & Dattilo, J. (2003). Leisure as a coping resource: Variations in coping with traumatic injury. *Leisure Sciences*, 25, 143-161.

Idyll Arbor. (2001). *Idyll Arbor's therapy dictionary* (2nd ed.). Ravensdale, WA: Author.

Indiana Family and Social Services Administration. (n.d.) *Guidelines.* http://www.in.gov/fssa/ddrs/3575.htm.

Institute of Medicine. (2001). *Crossing the quality chasm: A new health system for the 21st century.* Washington, DC: National Academy Press.

Jacobson, J. & James, A. (2001). Ethics: Doing right. In N. Stumbo (Ed.), *Professional issues in therapeutic recreation: On competence and outcomes* (pp. 237-248). Champaign, IL: Sagamore.

Jalongo, M. (2005). "What are all those dogs doing at school?" Using therapy dogs to promote children's reading practice. *Childhood Education*, 81(3), 152-159.

Jalongo, M., Astorino, T. & Bomboy, N. (2004). Canine visitors: The influence of therapy dogs on young children's learning and well-being in classrooms and hospitals. *Early Childhood Education Journal*, 32(1), 9-16.

Janis, I. (1982). Group think: Psychological studies of policy decisions and fiascos (2nd ed.). Boston: Houghton Mifflin.

Jeffrey, J. & Morof Lubkin, I. (2002). Chronic pain. In I. Morof Lubkin & P. Larsen (Eds.), *Chronic illness: Impact and interventions* (5th ed., pp. 77-118). Sudbury, MA: Jones and Bartlett.

Jelalian, E., Mehlenback, R., Lloyd-Richardson, E., Birnaker, V. & Wiley, R. (2006). "Adventure therapy" combined with cognitive-behavioral treatment for overweight adolescents. *International Journal of Obesity*, 30, 31-39.

Jones, E., Herrick, C. & York, R. (2004). An intergenerational group benefits both emotionally disturbed youth and older adults. *Issues in Mental Health Nursing*, 25(8), 753-767.

Jonsdottir, H., Jonsdottir, G., Steingrimsdottir, E. & Tryggradottir, B. (2001). Group reminiscence among people with end-stage chronic lung disease. *Journal of Advanced Nursing*, 35(1), 79-87.

Jordan, D. (2007). *Leadership in leisure services: Making a difference* (3rd ed.). State College, PA: Venture.

Journal of Physical Education, Recreation and Dance. (2004). Outdoor activities improve mental and physical health. *Journal of Physical Education, Recreation and Dance*, 75(7), 7-8.

Kassing, G. & Jay, D. (2003). *Dance teaching methods and curriculum design.* Champaign, IL: Human Kinetics.

Keller, J. (1996). Care ethics as a health care ethic. *Contexts: A forum for the medical humanities.* Stony Brook, NY: Institute for Medicine in Contemporary Society.

Kelley, T. (2007, November 4). Theater workshop embraces those with autism. *New York Times*, p. NJ6.

Kelly, P. (2008). *Nursing leadership and management* (2nd ed.). Clifton Park, NY: Delmar Learning.

Kinney, J. & Kinney, W.B. (2001). Psychiatry and mental health. In D. Austin & M. Crawford (Eds.), *Therapeutic recreation: An introduction* (3rd ed., 57-76). Needham Heights, MA: Allyn & Bacon.

Klitzing, S. (2004). Women who are homeless: Leisure and affiliation. *Therapeutic Recreation Journal*, 38(4), 348-365.

Kloseck, M. & Crilly, R. (1997). *Leisure competence measure: Adult version professional manual and user's guide.* London, ON: Leisure Competence Measurement Data Systems.

Kornblau, B. & Starling, S. (2000). *Ethics in rehabilitation: A clinical perspective.* Thorofare, NJ: Slack.

Kouzes, J. & Posner, B. (2008). *The leadership challenge* (4th ed.). San Francisco: Jossey-Bass.

Kraus, R. (1997). *Recreation programming: A benefits-driven approach.* Boston: Allyn & Bacon.

Kraus, R. & Shank, J. (1992). *Therapeutic recreation service: Principles and practices* (4th ed.). Dubuque, IA: Brown.

Kunstler, R. (1999). Private means, public good: Therapeutic recreation entrepreneurs. *Journal of Leisurability*, 26(4), 27-32.

Kunstler, R. (2000). Project FRESH: Fitness, recreation and education for senior health. *Journal of Park and Recreation Administration*, 18(4), 104-112.

Kunstler, R. (2001). Substance abuse. In D. Austin & M. Crawford (Eds.), *Therapeutic recreation: An introduction* (3rd. ed., pp. 94-112). Needham Heights, MA: Allyn & Bacon.

Kunstler, R. (2004a). Therapeutic recreation's contribution to living with chronic, stigmatized illness: Health promotion for HIV, HCV, and substance abuse. In M. Devine (Ed.), *Trends in therapeutic recreation: Ideas, concepts and applications* (pp. 111-125). Ashburn, VA: National Recreation and Park Association.

Kunstler, R. (2004b). The naturally occurring retirement community: Therapeutic recreation supports aging in place. In M. Devine (Ed.), *Trends in therapeutic recreation* (pp. 27-45). Ashburn, VA: National Recreation and Park Association.

Kunstler, R., Greenblatt, F. & Moreno, N. (2004). Aromatherapy and hand massage: Therapeutic recreation interventions for pain management. *Therapeutic Recreation Journal*, 38(2), 133-147.

Kunstler, R. & Sokoloff, S. (1993). Clinical effectiveness of intensive therapeutic recreation: A multiple case study of private practice intervention. *Loss, Grief and Care*, 6(4), 23-30.

LaBarre, L. & Magnino-Rabig, M. (2008). Your first job. In P. Kelly (Ed.), *Nursing leadership and management* (2nd ed., pp. 614-635). Clifton Park, NY: Delmar Learning.

Lahey, M. (1987). The ethics of intervention in therapeutic recreation. In C. Sylvester (Ed.), *Philosophy of therapeutic recreation: Ideas and issues, Volume I* (pp. 17-26). Arlington, VA: National Therapeutic Recreation Society.

Lahey, M. (1996). The commercial model and the future of therapeutic recreation. In C. Sylvester (Ed.), *Philosophy of therapeutic recreation: Ideas and issues, Volume II* (pp. 20-29). Ashburn, VA: National Therapeutic Recreation Society.

Lahey, M. (1998). Impacts of global trends. In F. Brasile, T. Skalko & J. Burlingame (Eds.), *Perspectives in recreational therapy: Issues of a dynamic profession*. Ravensdale, WA: Idyll Arbor.

Lahey, M. (2001). Cognitive rehabilitation. In D. Austin & M. Crawford (Eds.), *Therapeutic recreation: An introduction* (3rd ed., pp. 220-232). Boston: Allyn & Bacon.

Larson, C. (2006). The fine art of healing the sick. *U.S. News and World Report*, 140(21), 54-56.

Lawton, M.P. & Nahemow, L. (1973). Ecology and the aging process. In C. Eisdorfer & M.P. Lawton (Eds.), *Psychology of adult development and aging* (pp. 657-668). Washington, DC: American Psychological Association.

Lee, Y. & McCormick, B. (2002). Toward evidence based therapeutic practice. In D. Austin, J. Dattilo & B. McCormack (Eds.), *Conceptual foundations in therapeutic recreation* (pp. 165-189). State College, PA: Venture.

Leedy, P.D. (1981). *How to read research and understand it*. New York: Macmillan.

Lehman, A. (1995). Measuring quality of life in a reformed health system. *Health Affairs*, 14(3), 90-101.

Leith, K., Phillips, P. & Sample, P. (2004). Exploring the service needs and experiences of persons with traumatic brain injury and their families: The South Carolina experience. *Brain Injury*, 18(12), 1191-1208.

Leitner, M. & Leitner, S. & Associates. (2004). *Leisure enhancement* (3rd ed.). New York: Haworth Press.

Lesser, J. & Pope, D. (2007). *Human behavior and the social environment: Theory and practice*. Boston: Allyn & Bacon/Pearson Education.

Leung, C., Lee, G., Cheung, B., Kwong, E., Wing, Y., Kan, C. & Lau, J. (1998). Karaoke therapy in the rehabilitation of mental patients. *Singapore Medical Journal*, 39(4), 166-168.

Levine, G. (2001). Neuromuscular disorders. In D. Austin & M. Crawford (Eds.), *Therapeutic recreation: An introduction* (3rd ed., pp. 190-219). Boston: Allyn & Bacon.

Listokin, J. (2003). Complementary comfort on request. *Nursing Homes: Long Term Care Management*, 52(11), 47-48.

Long, L., Huntley, A. & Ernst, E. (2001). Which complementary and alternative therapies benefit which conditions? A survey of the opinions of 223 professional organizations. *Complementary Therapies in Medicine*, 9(3), 178-185.

Long, T. (2008a). Therapeutic recreation and mental health. In T. Long & T. Robertson (Eds.), *Foundations of therapeutic recreation* (pp. 145-164). Champaign, IL: Human Kinetics.

Long, T. (2008b). The therapeutic recreation process. In T. Long & T. Robertson (Eds.), *Foundations of therapeutic recreation* (pp. 79-100). Champaign, IL: Human Kinetics.

Long, T. & Robertson, T. (2008). Orthopedic and neurologic impairment. In T. Robertson & T. Long (Eds.), *Foundations of therapeutic recreation* (pp. 115-125). Champaign, IL: Human Kinetics.

Longmuir, P. (2003). Creating inclusive activity opportunities. In R. Steadwind, G. Wheeler & E. Watkins (Eds.), *Adapted physical activity* (pp. 363-382). Edmonton, AL: University of Alberta Press.

Luskin Biordi, S. (2002). Social isolation. In I. Morof Lubkin & P. Larsen (Eds.), *Chronic illness: Impact and interventions* (5th ed., pp. 119-146). Sudbury, MA: Jones & Barlett.

Maag, J. (2005). Social skills training for youth with emotional and behavioral disorders and learning disabilities: Problems, conclusions and suggestions. *Exceptionality*, 13(3), 155-172.

Maciejewski, M., Kawiecki, J. & Rockwood, T. (1997). Satisfaction. In R. Kane (Ed.), *Understanding health care outcomes research* (pp. 67-90). Gaithersburg, MD: Aspen.

Malkin, M., Coyle, C. & Carruthers, C. (1998). Efficacy research in recreational therapy. In F. Brasile, T. Skalko & J. Burlingame (Eds.), *Perspectives in recreational therapy* (pp. 141-164). Ravensdale, WA: Idyll Arbor.

Malley, S. & Dattilo, J. (2000). Stress management. In J. Dattilo (Ed.), *Facilitation techniques in therapeutic recreation* (pp. 215-244). State College, PA: Venture.

Martin, A. (2007). The changing nature of leadership. Center for Creative Leadership. www.ccl.org.

Martin, F. & Farnum, J. (2002). Animal-assisted therapy for children with pervasive developmental disorders. *Western Journal of Nursing Research*, 24(6), 657-670.

Maslow, A. (1971). *Toward a psychology of being*. New York: Van Nostrand Reinhold.

Mayer, J. (1999). Emotional intelligence: Popular or scientific psychology. *APA Monitor* 30, 50, Washington, D.C.: American Psychological Association.

McArdle, S. & Byrt, R. (2001). Fiction, poetry and mental health: Expressive and therapeutic uses of literature. *Journal of Psychiatric and Mental Health Nursing*, 8(6), 517-524.

McCauley, B. (2006). Animal-assisted therapy for persons with aphasia: A pilot study. *Journal of Rehabilitation Research and Development*, 43(3), 357-366.

McCauley, B. & Gutierrez, K. (2004). The effects of hippotherapy for children with language-learning disabilities. *Communication Disorders Quarterly*, 25(4), 205-217.

McClannahan, L. & Krantz, P. (1999). *Activity schedules for children with autism: Teaching independent behavior*. Bethesda, MD: Woodbine Press.

McCormick, B. (2002). Social support in therapeutic recreation. In D. Austin, J. Dattilo & B. McCormick (Eds.), *Conceptual foundations for therapeutic recreation* (pp. 49-72). State College, PA: Venture.

McCormick, B. (2003). Outcomes measurement as a tool for performance improvement. In N. Stumbo (Ed.), *Client outcomes in therapeutic recreation services* (pp. 221-232). State College, PA: Venture.

McDongall, T. & Jones, C. (2007). Dialectical behaviour therapy for young offenders: Lessons from the U.S.A., part 2. *Mental Health Practice*, 11(2), 20-21.

McGraw-Hunter, M., Faw, G. & Davis, P. (2006). The use of video self-modelling and feedback to teach cooking skills to individuals with traumatic brain injury: A pilot study. *Brain Injury*, 20(10), 1061-1068.

McGuire, F., Boyd, R. & Tedrick, R. (2009). *Leisure and aging: Ulyssean living in later life*, (4th ed). Champaign, IL: Sagamore Publishing.

McKenney, A. (2004). Using a sport context to promote prosocial behavior in adolescents with disruptive behavior disorders. In M. Devine (Ed.), *Trends in therapeutic recreation* (pp. 47-70). Ashburn, VA: National Recreation and Park Association.

McLean, D., Hurd, A. & Brattain Rogers, N. (2005). *Recreation and leisure in modern society* (7th ed.). Sudbury, MA: Jones and Bartlett.

McLean, D. & Yoder, D. (2005). *Issues in recreation and leisure: Ethical decision making.* Champaign, IL: Human Kinetics.

McNeil-Haber, F. (2004). Ethical considerations in the use of nonerotic touch in psychotherapy with children. *Ethics & Behavior*, 14(2), 123-140.

McNicholas, J. & Collis, G. (1995). Relationship between young people with autism and their pets. Paper presented at the meeting of the 7th International Conference on Human-Animal Interactions, Geneva.

Melillo, K. & Houde, S. (2005). *Geropsychiatric and mental health nursing.* Sudbury, MA: Jones and Bartlett.

Meriwether, R., Lee, J., Lafleur, A. & Wiseman, P. (2008). Physical activity counseling. *American Family Physician*, 77(8), 1129-1136.

Meyerstein, I. & Ruskin, G. (2007). Spiritual tools for enhancing the pastoral visit to hospitalized patients. *Journal of Religion and Health*, 46(1), 109-122.

Miller, G. & Happell, B. (2006). Talking about hope: The use of participant photography. *Issues in Mental Health Nursing*, 10, 1051-1065.

Mitchell, R. (2006). Shooting into the past. *Nursing Older People*, 18(10), 12-14.

Mobily, K. (2000). An interview with Professor Seppo Iso-Ahola. *Therapeutic Recreation Journal*, 34(4), 300-305.

Mobily, K. & MacNeil, R. (2002). *Therapeutic recreation and the nature of disabilities.* State College, PA: Venture.

Mobily, K. & Ostiguy, L. (2004). *Introduction to recreation: U.S. and Canadian perspectives.* State College, PA: Venture.

Mosby's dental dictionary. (2008). 2nd ed. Philadelphia: Elsevier.

Mosconi, J. & Emmett, J. (2003). The effects of a values clarification curriculum on high school students' definitions of success. *Professional School Counseling*, 7(2), 68-78.

Mundy, J. (1998). *Leisure education: Theory and practice* (2nd ed.). Champaign, IL: Sagamore.

Murray, S. (2003). Conveying the possible with client-directed outcomes and social marketing. In N. Stumbo (Ed.), *Client outcomes in therapeutic recreation services* (pp. 233-254). State College, PA: Venture.

Musgrove, M. (2007, May 27). Games as therapy for Walter Reed's wounded. *Washington Post*, p. F1.

Music for your health. (2004). *Activities, adaptation & aging*, 28(4), 83.

Nagourney, E. (2008, February 12). The tango may help Parkinson's patients. *New York Times*, p. F5.

National Academy of Sports Medicine. Certification. Retrieved August 15, 2008, from www.nasm.org/certification/default.aspx?id=96.

National Center for Learning Disabilities. (2008). Executive function fact sheet. www.ncld.org.

National Council on Strength and Fitness. Retrieved August 15, 2008, from www.ncsf.org/.

National Federation of Professional Trainers. Retrieved August 15, 2008, from www.nfpt.com/.

National Recreation and Park Association. (1999). *Position statement on inclusion.* Ashburn, VA: Author.

National Therapeutic Recreation Society. (2000). *Definition statement.* Ashburn, VA: Author.

National Therapeutic Recreation Society. (1994). *Interpretive guidelines.* Ashburn, VA: Author.

National Therapeutic Recreation Society. (1990). *NTRS code of ethics.* Ashburn, VA: Author.

Neulinger, J. (1978). *Leisure counseling: Process or content?* Paper presented at the Dane County Recreation Coordinating Council Conference on Leisure Counseling, Madison, WI

Nicholson, J. & Pearson, Q. (2003). Helping children cope with fears. *Professional School Counseling*, 7(1), 15-19.

Niepoth, E. (1983). *Leisure leadership.* Englewood Cliffs, NJ: Prentice Hall.

Noble, A., Best, D., Sidwell, C. & Strang, J. (2000). Is an arcade-style computer game an effective medium for promoting drug education to schoolchildren? *Education for Health*, 13(3), 404-406.

Norton-Meier, L. (2005). Joining the video-game literacy club: A reluctant mother tries to join the "flow." *Journal of Adolescent and Adult Literacy*, 48(5), 428-432.

Nowicka, P. (2005). Dietitians and exercise professionals in a childhood obesity treatment team. *Acta Paediatrica*, 94 (Suppl. 448), 23-28.

Nowicka, P. & Flodmark, C-E. (2007). Physical activity—key issues in the treatment of childhood obesity. *Acta Paediatrica*, 96, 39-45.

O'Keefe, C. (2005). Grounding the therapeutic recreation process in an ethic of care. In C. Sylvester (Ed.), *Philosophy of therapeutic recreation: Ideas and issues, Volume III* (pp. 73-84). Ashburn, VA: National Recreation and Park Association.

Okun, B. (2007). *Effective helping* (7th ed.). Pacific Grove, CA: Brooks/Cole.

O'Morrow, G. (1976). *Therapeutic recreation: A helping profession.* Reston, VA: Reston.

Palo-Bengtssen, L., Winblad, B. & Ekman, S-L. (1998). Social dancing: A way to support intellectual, emotional and motor functions in persons with dementia. *Journal of Psychiatric and Mental Health Nursing*, 5, 545-554.

Patrick, G. (2001). Perspective: Clinical research: Methods and mandates. In N. Stumbo (Ed.), *Professional issues in therapeutic recreation: On competence and outcomes* (pp. 401-418). Champaign, IL: Sagamore.

Pederson, D. (2008). *Psych notes: Clinical pocket guide* (2nd ed.). Philadelphia: Davis.

Pedlar, A., Hornibrook, T. & Haasen, B. (2001). Patient focused care: Theory and practice. *Therapeutic Recreation Journal*, 35(1), 15-30.

Pedlar, A., Yuen, F. & Fortune, D. (2008). Incarcerated women and leisure: Making good girls out of bad? *Therapeutic Recreation Journal*, 42(1), 24-36.

Peniston, L. (1998). *Developing recreation skills in persons with learning disabilities.* Champaign, IL: Sagamore.

Perese, E. & Wolf, M. (2005). Combating loneliness among persons with severe mental illness: Social networks and interventions' characteristics, effectiveness and applicability. *Issues in Mental Health Nursing*, 26, 591-609.

Perham, A. & Accordino, M. (2007). Exercise and functioning levels of individuals with severe mental illness: A comparison of two groups. *Journal of Mental Health Counseling*, 29(4), 350-362.

Peterson, M. & James, L. (2008). Principles of leadership for the 21st century. www.extension.org/pages/Principles_of_Leadership_for_the_21st_Century/print/.

Phillips, K. (1993). The effectiveness of cueing on anagram solving by cognitively impaired nursing home elderly. *Loss, Grief and Care*, 6(4), 107-116.

Pies, R. (2007, January 2). Cookie conundrum in the doctor-patient drama. *New York Times*, p. C5.

Polkinghorne, D. (2004). *Practice and the human sciences: The case for a judgment-based practice of care*. Albany, NY: State University of New York Press.

Preboth, M. (2001). Aquatic programs for infants and toddlers. *American Family Physician*, 63(1), 155-156.

Prochaska, J. & DiClemente, C. (1982). Transtheoretical therapy: Toward a more integrative model of change. *Psychotherapy: Theory, Research and Practice*, 19, 276-288.

Prochaska, J. & DiClemente, C. (1983). Stages and processes of self-change of smoking: Toward an integrative model of change. *Journal of Consulting and Clinical Psychology*, 51(3), 390-395.

Purnell, L. & Paulanka, B. (2003). *Transcultural health care: A culturally competent approach*. Philadelphia: Davis.

Purtilo, R. & Haddad, A. (2002). *Health professional and patient interaction* (6th ed.). Philadelphia: Saunders.

Quam, J. & Abramson, N. (1991). The use of time lines and life lines in work with chronically mentally ill people. *Health and Social Work*, 16(1), 27-33.

Quinn, E. (2008). Body composition and body fat. http://sportsmedicine.about.com/od/fitnessevalandassessment/a/Body_Fat_Comp.

Rancourt, A. (1989). Older adults with developmental disabilities/mental retardation: Implications for professional services. *Therapeutic Recreation Journal*, 23(1), 47-57.

Ravelin, T., Kylma, J. & Korhonen, T. (2006). Dance in mental health nursing: A hybrid concept analysis. *Issues in Mental Health Nursing*, 27, 307-317.

"Reflective listening" (n.d.)

Relf, P. (2005). The therapeutic value of plants. *Pediatric Rehabilitation*, 8(3), 235-237.

Rhodes, M. (1991). The use of patient satisfaction data as an outcome monitor in therapeutic recreation quality assurance. In B. Riley (Ed.), *Quality management: Applications for therapeutic recreation* (pp. 83-105). State College, PA: Venture.

Richeson, N. (2004). Therapeutic recreation music intervention to decrease mealtime agitation and increase food intake in older adults with dementia. *American Journal of Recreation Therapy*, 3(1), 37-41.

Richeson, N., Croteau, K., Jones, D. & Farmer, B. (2006). Effects of a pedometer-based intervention on the physical performance and mobility-related efficacy of community-dwelling older adults: An interdisciplinary health care intervention. *Therapeutic Recreation Journal*, 40(1): 18-32.

Richter, K. & Kaschalk, S. (1996). The future of therapeutic recreation: An existential outcome. In C. Sylvester (Ed.), *Philosophy of therapeutic recreation: Ideas and issues, Volume II* (pp. 86-91). Ashburn, VA: National Therapeutic Recreation Society.

Ridgeway, C. (1983). *The dynamics of small groups*. New York: St. Martin's Press.

Riley, B. (1991). Quality assessment: The use of outcome indicators, In B. Riley (Ed.), *Quality management: Applications for therapeutic recreation* (pp. 54-67). State College, PA: Venture.

Rimmer, J. (1998). Aging, mental retardation and physical fitness. Arlington, TX: The Arc of the United States. (ERIC Document Reproduction Service No. ED417517).

Rimmer, J., Wolf, L., Armour, B. & Sinclair, L. (2007, October 5). Physical activity among adults with a disability—United States, 2005. *Morbidity and Mortality Weekly Report*, 56(39), 1021-1024.

Robertson, T. & Long, T. (2008). Considering therapeutic recreation as your profession. In T. Robertson & T. Long (Eds.), *Foundations of therapeutic recreation* (pp. 3-12). Champaign, IL: Human Kinetics.

Rollnick, S., Mason, P. & Butler, C. (1999). *Health behavior change: A guide for practitioners*. London, England: Churchill Livingstone.

Ross, J. & Ashton-Shaeffer, C. (2001). Therapeutic recreation practice models. In N. Stumbo (Ed.), *Professional issues in therapeutic recreation: On competence and outcomes* (pp. 160-187). Champaign, IL: Sagamore.

Ross, J. & Ashton-Shaeffer, C. (2003). Selecting and designing intervention programs for outcomes. In N. Stumbo (Ed.), *Client outcomes in therapeutic recreation services* (pp. 127-148). State College, PA: Venture.

Rossman, J. & Schlatter, B. (2000). *Recreation programming: Designing leisure experiences* (3rd ed.). Champaign, IL: Sagamore

Rossman, J. & Schlatter, B. (2003). *Recreation programming: Designing leisure experiences* (4th ed.). Champaign, IL: Sagamore.

Ruderman, M., Hannum, K., Brittain, L. & Steed, J. (2001). Making connections: Leadership skills and emotional intelligence. *Leadership In Action*, 21(5), 3-7.

Russell, R. (2004). *Leadership in recreation* (3rd ed.). New York: McGraw-Hill.

Russell, R. (2005). *Pastimes: The context of contemporary culture*, (3rd ed.). Chicago, IL: Sagamore.

Russell, R. & Jamieson, L. (2008). *Leisure program planning and delivery*. Champaign, IL: Human Kinetics.

Sable, J. & Bocarro, J. (2004). Transitioning back to health: Participants' perspectives of project path. *Therapeutic Recreation Journal*, 23(2), 206-224.

Salzman, A. (2007). www.aquaticnet.com.

Santelmann, L. (2001). Reading primary literature. Retrieved September 29, 2006, from www.web.pdx.edu/~dbls/Readingresearch.htm.

Santiago, M. & Coyle, C. (2004). Leisure-time physical activity and secondary conditions in women with physical disabilities. *Disability & Rehabilitation*, 26(8), 485-494.

Sausser, C. & Dattilo, J. (2000). Therapeutic horseback riding. In J. Dattilo (Ed.), *Facilitation techniques in therapeutic recreation* (pp. 273-302). State College, PA: Venture.

Schiesel, S. (2007, April 30). P.E. classes turn to video game that works legs. *New York Times*, pp. A1, A15.

Schlein, S., Fahnestock, M. & Miller, K. (2001). Severe multiple disabilities. In D. Austin & M. Crawford (Eds.), *Therapeutic recreation: An introduction* (pp. 157-189). Boston: Allyn & Bacon.

Schlein, S., Meyer, L., Heyne, L. & Biel Brandt, B. (1995). *Lifelong leisure skills and lifestyles for persons with developmental disabilities.* Baltimore: Brookes.

Scholl, K., Dieser, R. & Davison, A. (2005). Together we play: An ecological approach to inclusive recreation. *Therapeutic Recreation Journal*, 39(4), 299-311.

Schreur, G. (2006). Using bibliotherapy with suspended students. *Reclaiming Children and Youth*, 15(2), 106-111.

Shank, P. (1996). Doing ethics: Toward the resolution of ethical dilemmas. In C. Sylvester (Ed.), *Philosophy of therapeutic recreation: Ideas and issues, Volume II* (pp. 30-56). Ashburn, VA: National Therapeutic Recreation Society.

Shank, J. & Coyle, C. (2002). *Therapeutic recreation in health promotion and rehabilitation.* State College, PA: Venture.

Shank, J., Kinney, W. & Coyle, C. (1993). Efficacy studies in therapeutic recreation research. In M. Malkin & C. Howe (Eds.), *Research in therapeutic recreation: Concepts and methods* (pp. 301-335). State College, PA: Venture.

Simeonsson, R.J. & McDevitt, L. (1999). *Disability & health: The role of secondary conditions and quality of life.* Chapel Hill, NC: University of North Carolina.

Simpson, E. (2005). What teachers need to know about the video game generation. *Tech Trends*, 49(5), 17-22.

Sklar, S., Anderson, S. & Autry, C. (2007). Positive youth development: A wilderness intervention. *Therapeutic Recreation Journal*, 41(3), 223-243.

Sklar, S. & Autry, C. (2008). Youth development and therapeutic recreation. In T. Robertson & T. Long (Eds.), *Foundations of therapeutic recreation* (pp. 165-183). Champaign, IL: Human Kinetics.

Smith, R. & Watkins, N. (2008). Therapeutic environments. www.wbdg.org/resources/therapeutic.php.

Smyth, J.M. & Helm, R. (2003). Focused expressive writing as self-help for stress and trauma. *Journal of Clinical Psychology*, 59(2), 227-235.

Sourby, C. (1998). The relationship between therapeutic recreation and palliation in the treatment of the advanced cancer patient. www.recreationtherapy.com/cancer.htm.

Spangler, K. & O'Sullivan, E. (2006). Health, fitness, wellness and livability. In Human Kinetics, *Introduction to recreation and leisure* (pp. 289-306). Champaign, IL: Author.

Stavola Daly, F. (2002). A study of the relationship between a home-based TR program and the reduction of excess disability in persons with early to mid-stage Alzheimer's disease. Unpublished dissertation, Temple University, Philadelphia.

Stavola Daly, F. & Kunstler, R. (2006). Therapeutic recreation. In Human Kinetics, *An introduction to recreation and leisure* (pp. 177-196). Champaign. IL: Author.

Stein, J. (2002). Adapted aquatics or just aquatics. *Parks and Recreation*, 37(2), 46-48.

Stewart, D. (2006). Fine art, indeed. *Nursing Homes: Long Term Care Management*, 55(6), 43-44.

Stone, B. (2010, January 10). Old fogies by their 20's. *The New York Times*, p. WK5.

Streitfeld, E. (1993). Recreation in the nursing home. *Loss, Grief and Care*, 6(4), 117-126.

Stumbo, N. (1996). A proposed accountability model for therapeutic recreation services. *Therapeutic Recreation Journal*, 30(4), 246-259.

Stumbo, N. (2002a). *Client assessment in therapeutic recreation services.* State College, PA: Venture

Stumbo, N. (2002b). *Leisure education II: More activities and resources* (2nd ed.). State College, PA: Venture.

Stumbo, N. (Ed.). (2003). *Client outcomes in therapeutic recreation services.* State College, PA: Venture.

Stumbo, N. & Peterson, C. (2004). *Therapeutic recreation program design: Principles and procedures* (4th ed.). San Francisco: Benjamin Cummings.

Stumbo, N. & Peterson, C. (2009). *Therapeutic recreation program design: Principles and procedures* (5th ed.). San Francisco: Benjamin Cummings.

Sulcas, R. (2007, August 25). Getting their groove back, with help from the magic of dance. *New York Times*, p. B9.

Sutin, K. (2005). Getting better in the kitchen: Cooking can be part of rehabilitation after brain injuries. *Sauce*, 12/18.

Swade, T., Bayne, R. & Horton, I. (2006). Touch me never? *Therapy Today*, 17(9), 41-42.

Swann-Guerrero, S. & Mackey, C. (2008). Wellness through physical activity. In T. Robertson & T. Long (Eds.), *Foundations of therapeutic recreation* (pp. 199-216). Champaign, IL: Human Kinetics.

Sylvester, C. (1987). Therapeutic recreation and the end of leisure. In C. Sylvester (Ed.), *Philosophy of therapeutic recreation: Ideas and issues, Volume I* (pp. 76-89). Arlington, VA: National Therapeutic Recreation Society.

Sylvester, C. (2002). Ethics and quest for professionalization. *Therapeutic Recreation Journal*, 36(4), 314-334.

Sylvester, C. (2005). Personal autonomy and therapeutic recreation. In C. Sylvester (Ed.), *Philosophy of therapeutic recreation: Ideas and issues, Volume III* (pp. 1-31). Ashburn, VA: National Therapeutic Recreation Society.

Sylvester, C., Voelkl, J. & Ellis, G. (2001). *Therapeutic recreation: Theory and practice.* State College, PA: Venture.

Tam, C., Schwellnus, H., Eaton, C., Hamdani, Y., Lamont, A. & Chan, T. (2007). Movement-to-music computer technology: A developmental play experience for children with severe physical disabilities. *Occupational Therapy International*, 14(2), 99-112.

Teague, M., Mackenzie, S. & Rosenthal, D. (2006). *Your health today: Choices in a changing society.* New York: McGraw-Hill.

United States Department of Health and Human Services. (2000). *Healthy people 2010: Understanding and improving health.* Washington, DC: Author.

United States Navy. (n.d.). *Complete navy nursing manual: Hospital corpsman revised edition.* http://www.tpub.com/content/medical/14295

Valentine, J. (2006). *Planning and organizing group activities in social recreation.* State College, PA: Venture.

Van Andel, G. (1998). TR service delivery and TR outcome models. *Therapeutic Recreation Journal*, 32(3), 180-193.

Vance, C. (2003). Practice builders: Enhance patient compliance by targeting different learning styles. *Podiatry Today*, 16(8), 28-29.

Vander Molen, N. (2007). Therapeutic recreation evaluation. Paper presented at the meeting of the New York State Therapeutic Recreation Association, Saratoga Springs, NY.

Van Puyenbroeck, J. & Maes, B. (2006). Program development of reminiscence group work for ageing people with intellectual disabilities. *Journal of intellectual and developmental disability,* 31(3), 139-147.

Vare, J. & Norton, T. (2004). Bibliotherapy for gay and lesbian youth: Overcoming the structure of silence. *Clearing House,* 77(5), 190-194.

Velde, B., Cipriani, J. & Fisher, G. (2005). Resident and therapist views of animal-assisted therapy: Implications for OT practice. *Australian Journal of Occupational Therapy,* 52, 43-50.

Vismara, LL. & Lyons, G. (2007). Understanding perseverative interests to elicit joint attention behavior in young children with autism: Theoretical and clinical implications for understanding motivation. *Journal of Positive Behavior Interventions,* 9(4), 214-228.

Voelkl, J. & Aybar-Damali, B. (2008). Aging and the life span. In T. Robertson & T. Long (Eds.), *Foundations of therapeutic recreation* (pp. 185-196). Champaign, IL: Human Kinetics.

Voelkl, J., Carruthers, C. & Hawkins, B. (1997). Special series on therapeutic recreation practice models: Guest editors' introductory comments. *Therapeutic Recreation Journal,* 31, 210-212.

Wachter, C.J. & McGowan, A.L. (2002). Inclusion practices of special recreation agencies in Illinois. *Therapeutic Recreation Journal,* 36, 172-185.

Wallace, M. (2008). Assessment of sexual health in older adults. *American Journal of Nursing,* 108(7), 52-60.

Wedding, D. & Niemiec, R. (2003). The clinical use of films in psychotherapy. *Journal of Clinical Psychology,* 59(2), 207-215.

Weston, R., Tinsley, H. & O'Dell, I. (1999). Wilderness adventure therapy for at-risk youth. *Parks and Recreation,* 34(7), 30-38.

West Virginia Department of Education. (2008). *21st century classroom assessment for learning.* Charleston, WV: Author.

Wholihan, D. (2004). The value of reminiscence in hospice care. San Diego: San Diego Hospice and Palliative Care Center. www.cpsonline.info/content/education/volunteers.

Widmer, M., Zabriskie, R. & Wells, M. (2003). Program evaluation: Collecting data to measure outcomes. In N. Stumbo (Ed.), *Client outcomes in therapeutic recreation services* (pp. 201-219). State College, PA: Venture.

Wilhite, B., Hodges, J. & Peebles, M. (2003). Other voices, other rooms: Consumers' and healthcare professionals' perspectives on valued client outcomes in therapeutic recreation. In N. Stumbo (Ed.), *Client outcomes in therapeutic recreation services* (pp. 87-109). State College, PA: Venture.

Wilhite, B., Keller, M.J. & Caldwell, L. (1999). Optimizing lifelong health and well-being: A health enhancing model of therapeutic recreation. *Therapeutic Recreation Journal,* 33(2), 98-108.

Williams, R. (2008). Places, models, and modalities of practice. In T. Robertson & T. Long (Eds.), *Foundations of therapeutic recreation* (pp. 63-76). Champaign, IL: Human Kinetics.

Williams, R. & Dattilo, J. (2000). Therapeutic use of humor. In J. Dattilo (Ed.), *Facilitation techniques in therapeutic recreation* (pp. 385-407). State College, PA: Venture.

Winkelman, M. (2003). Complementary therapy for addiction: "Drumming not drugs." *American Journal of Public Health,* 93(4), 647-651.

Witt, P. & Ellis, G. (1989). *The leisure diagnostic battery: Users manual and sample forms.* State College, PA: Venture.

Worden, E., Frohne, T. & Sullivan, J. (2004). *Horticultural therapy.* Gainesville, FL: University of Florida IFAS Extension.

Yalom, I. (1995). *The theory and practice of group psychotherapy* (4th ed.). New York: Basic Books/Harper Collins.

Young, L. (2007). Sowing the seeds of health: Plants and clients thrive with horticultural therapy. *CrossCurrents: The Journal of Addiction and Mental Health,* 10(4).

Zabriskie, R. (2003). Measurement basics: A must for TR professionals today. *Therapeutic Recreation Journal,* 37(4), 330-338.

Zamir, T. (2006). The moral basis of animal-assisted therapy. *Society and Animals,* 14(2), 179-199.

INDEX

Note: Page numbers followed by an italicized *f* or *t* refer to the figure or table on that page, respectively.

ABOUT THE AUTHORS

Photo courtesy of City of New York University. Photographer Lenore Schultz.

Robin Kunstler, ReD, CTRS, is a professor in the department of health sciences and the director of the recreation education and therapeutic recreation programs at Lehman College in New York. She has over 35 years of experience in the field of therapeutic recreation as both a practitioner and a professor. She has presented at many state and national conferences and has authored numerous articles and book chapters on therapeutic recreation.

Kunstler has been coeditor and reviewer for *Therapeutic Recreation Journal, Schole,* and the American Therapeutic Recreation Association's *Annual in Therapeutic Recreation.* She has served as a board member and committee chair for several national and state organizations, including National Therapeutic Recreation Society, Society of Park and Recreation Educators, New York State Therapeutic Recreation Association (NYSTRA), and New York State Recreation and Park Society (NYSRPS). She was awarded the Lifetime Achievement Award from NYSTRA and the NYSRPS Literary Research Award.

In her free time, Kunstler enjoys creating and viewing artwork, reading, and hiking.

Frances Stavola Daly, EdD, CTRS, CPRP, is an associate professor and program coordinator in the department of recreation administration at Kean University in New Jersey. She has 35 years of experience in the recreation field as both a practitioner and a professor. Stavola Daly also has extensive experience in presenting on all aspects of therapeutic recreation.

Stavola Davy has been extensively involved in professional organizations at both the national and state levels. She has served as the president of the National Therapeutic Recreation Society (NTRS) as well as a Board of Trustees member. She was a founding member of the New York State Therapeutic Recreation Association and served as chair of the Mid-east Therapeutic Recreation Symposium and the New Jersey Recreation and Park Association's Therapeutic Recreation Public Policy Group. Stavola Daly has received several honors, including the Presidential Citation from the NTRS in 2007 and the Distinguished Service Award in 2004 from the New York State Therapeutic Recreation Association.

In her free time, Stavola Daly enjoys reading, fitness walking, and traveling.

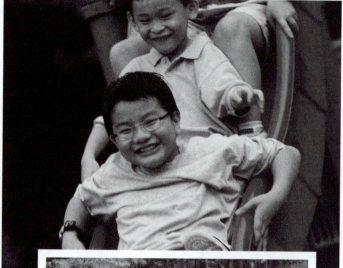

You'll find other outstanding
recreation resources at
www.HumanKinetics.com